ATLANTIC CANADA HANDBOOK

NEW BRUNSWICK, NOVA SCOTIA, PRINCE EDWARD ISLAND, NEWFOUNDLAND AND LABRADOR

ATLANTIC CANADA HANDBOOK

NEW BRUNSWICK, NOVA SCOTIA, PRINCE EDWARD ISLAND, NEWFOUNDLAND AND LABRADOR

FIRST EDITION

NAN DROSDICK & MARK MORRIS

MOON
PUBLICATIONS INC.

ATLANTIC CANADA HANDBOOK
FIRST EDITION

Published by
Moon Publications, Inc.
P.O. Box 3040
Chico, California 95927-3040, USA

Printed by
Colorcraft Ltd., Hong Kong

© Text copyright Mark Morris, 1995. All rights reserved.
© Illustrations copyright Moon Publications, Inc., 1995.
  All rights reserved.
© Maps and photographs copyright Moon Publications, Inc., 1995.
  All rights reserved.
  Some photos and illustrations are used by permission
  and are the property of the original copyright owners.

ISBN: 1-56691-007-2
ISSN: 1082-5150

Editors: Don Root, Emily Kendrick
Copy Editors: Deana Corbitt Shields, Sharon Brown
Production & Design: David Dohn Hurst
Cartographers: Bob Race, Brian Bardwell
Index: Valerie Sellers Blanton

Front cover photo: Peggy's Cove, Nova Scotia, by Bob Krist/Leo DeWys, Inc.
All photos by Nan Drosdick unless otherwise noted.

Please send all comments,
corrections, additions,
amendments, and critiques to:

**ATLANTIC CANADA HANDBOOK
MOON PUBLICATIONS, INC.
P.O. BOX 3040
CHICO, CA 95927-3040, USA**
e-mail: **travel@moon.com**

Printing History
1st edition—November 1995

Distributed in the United States by Publishers Group West

Printed in Hong Kong

CONTENTS

MAPS

CHARTS

SPECIAL TOPICS

MAP SYMBOLS

🌊	WATER	—————	INTERNATIONAL BORDER		TOWN, VILLAGE	○
▲	MOUNTAIN	—·—·—·—	PROVINCE BORDER		CITY	⊙
	GOLF COURSE	—··—··—	COUNTY BORDER		CHURCH	▪
⚲		——————	FERRY		CATHEDRAL	⛪
⛺	CAMPING	═════	BRIDGE		AIRPORT	✈
🍁	TRANSCANADA HIGHWAY	— — —	UNPAVED ROAD		PROVINCIAL PARK	P.P.
○	PROVINCE HIGHWAY	—————	SECONDARY ROAD		POINT OF INTEREST	▪
		—————	MAIN ROAD		HOTEL / ACCOMMODATION	●
		—·—·—·—	PATH / TRAIL			

ABBREVIATIONS

B&B—bed-and-breakfast inn
C—Celsius
d—double occupancy
F—Fahrenheit
GST—Goods and Services Tax
Hwy.—highway
km—kilometers
kph—kilometers per hour
OW—one-way
PEI—Prince Edward Island

pop.—population
pp—per person
RCMP—Royal Canadian Mounted Police
RT—round-trip
RV—recreational vehicle
s—single occupancy
tel.—telephone
WW I—World War I
WW II—World War II

ACKNOWLEDGMENTS

Nan Drosdick

A travel guide is written in solitude yet is immeasurably enriched by other people. I would like to acknowledge a few among many: Steve Pisni of Air Canada, whose steadfast friendship and enthusiasm inspired me for the dozen years that I roamed Atlantic Canada; Mary Keith of Air Nova, for her kindness and encouragement during the manuscript's progress; and Lois Gerber of the Canadian Consulate General in New York City for her ready help and invaluable provincial contacts. For their nurturing care and gracious Canadian demeanor, special thanks to provincial tourism officials: Helen-Jean Newman and Debbie Thorne, New Brunswick; Kay Coxworth, Newfoundland; Randy Brooks and Don Blackwood, Nova Scotia; and Lynda Hanscome and Carol Horne, who took Lynda's place on Prince Edward Island. I am also particularly grateful for the Canadian concept of journalism, which allows freedom of expression as long as the text is accurate, a keen task as travel information changes rapidly. The manuscript in respective parts was read and corrected for accuracy but was unaltered by the above officials plus: Yvonne Huntington, Saint John; Sheila McParland and Nancy Lockerbie, Fredericton; Audrey Williston, Moncton; Patricia Pye, Corner Brook; Kathy Crotty, Labrador; Doug Sanders, Happy Valley/Goose Bay; and Bernadette Walsh of St. John's, who thoughtfully bound the city's coverage in loose-leaf before returning it to me. I am especially appreciative of my family: my sons, Joseph, who helped with research; Robert, the computer expert; and David, who supplied me with a computer, fixed its maladies, and handled the technical functions for this lengthy project; and my dearest husband and friend, Joseph, whose enduring patience, kindness, and wisdom have been the rock of my life's work as a writer. The best of you all made this book possible. Any shortcomings are mine.

Mark Morris

Many thanks are due to many people for help with this book. Thanks first must go to Nan Drosdick, who is such a professional and easy writer to work with. Thanks to editors Don Root and Emily Kendrick, for conscientious work above and beyond the normal course of duty; to Bob Race and Brian Bardwell for their careful labors on illustrations and maps; to Bill Newlin for his long patience; and to everyone else at Moon who works so hard to make these books so good. Thanks to Mark Fraser and friends for showing me another side of Halifax. And thanks, finally, to Elizabeth Rhudy, for her support and kind assistance.

IS THIS BOOK OUT OF DATE?

Travel information changes constantly and even the most diligent travel writer has a hard time keeping up with everything. We look to our readers to help keep us apprised of up-to-the-minute developments. Found a restaurant with the world's greatest goulash? The bed-and-breakfast of your dreams? That perfect deserted beach? Let us know. And if you spot information that is no longer valid, we want to hear from you, too, so we can incorporate the changes in the next edition. Address your letters to:

ATLANTIC CANADA HANDBOOK
c/o Moon Publications
P.O. Box 3040
Chico, CA 95927-3040 USA

e-mail: travel@moon.com

BOB RACE

INTRODUCTION

They that go down to the sea in ships,
That do business in great waters,
These see the works of the Lord,
And his wonders in the deep.

—Psalm 107

Atlantic Canada is a picture-book painting, a broad canvas splashed with brightly colored seaports, red-clay roads, boulder-bound coasts, shadowy forests, and undulating fields of barley and potatoes, all framed by the variegated blues of the sky and surrounding seas.

This seacoast realm is an extraordinarily captivating place. Life in its hundreds of seaports has bred an insular culture. For centuries, the folk of Atlantic Canada have gone down to the sea in ships to ply their trade on the great waters. The hard seafaring life has given them what so much of the modern world has thoughtlessly let slip through its fingers: nearness to nature's honest rhythms, replete with the old values of kindness and thriftiness. In a world crowded with too many people and too much

development, Atlantic Canada is a refuge of sorts. This is not to imply that old-time values are bereft of sophistication. Rather, the people here embody the good life in a modern world too often prepackaged and bland.

Atlantic Canada makes a harmony out of contending elements, a fortuitous combination of place and people far from the maddening crowd and peaceful now after centuries of strife. In 1992, the United Nations published the *Human Development Report* and named Canada the best country on the planet to live in. Visualize Atlantic Canada as a seacoast component of the world's most exemplary place.

The region is imbued with a sense of majesty. Great original slabs of the world, as the land was first formed eons ago, lie along Newfoundland's western seacoast. The Atlantic Ocean, funneled between New Brunswick and Nova Scotia, sweeps into the Bay of Fundy and creates the world's highest tides. Millions of seabirds nest on the coastal rims of New Brunswick and Newfoundland. Whales summer in the seas off New Brunswick, Nova Scotia, and Newfoundland. Seals laze on the rocky outcrops in

ATLANTIC CANADA

LABRADOR SEA

HEBRON

NAIN

DAVIS INLET

LABRADOR

HAPPY VALLEY-GOOSE BAY

LABRADOR CITY

QUEBEC

FORTEAU

ST. ANTHONY

PORT AU CHOIX

ST. LAWRENCE RIVER

ANTICOSTI ISLAND (QUEBEC)

CORNER BROOK

GANDER

GASPÉ PENINSULA

QUEBEC

GULF OF ST. LAWRENCE

NEWFOUNDLAND

EDMUNDSTON

BATHURST

ILES-DE-LA-MADELEINE (MAGDALEN ISLANDS) (QUEBEC)

PORT AUX BASQUES

ST. PIERRE & MIQUELON

ST. JOHN'S

NEW BRUNSWICK

PRINCE EDWARD ISLAND

CHARLOTTETOWN

CAPE BRETON ISLAND

MAINE (U.S.A.)

FREDERICTON

MONCTON

NORTHUMBERLAND STRAIT

SIDNEY

ST. STEPHEN

SAINT JOHN

PICTOU

NOVA SCOTIA

ATLANTIC OCEAN

BAY OF FUNDY

DIGBY

HALIFAX

YARMOUTH

0   100 mi

0   100 km

© MOON PUBLICATIONS, INC.

Prince Edward Island's harbors. Icebergs, as imperial as glistening blue fortresses, drift down from the far north and follow Newfoundland's eastern coastline to melt in the warm waters of the Grand Banks.

THE LAND

Even among Canadians, there is sometimes confusion about the definition of the eastern Canada region. The Maritime Provinces include New Brunswick, Nova Scotia, and Prince Edward Island. Together with Newfoundland, they form the Atlantic Provinces, or, as defined by this book, Atlantic Canada. Newfoundland is a source of further confusion. It is the name of both the large island *and* of the entire province, which includes the huge mainland section of Labrador.

Atlantic Canada as a whole forms one-twentieth of the country's total area. The provinces, and the distances separating them, are far larger than they may seem at first glance. Nova Scotia, for example, is Canada's second-smallest province, yet it is a full day's drive from Yarmouth at the southwestern tip to Cape Breton Highlands National Park at the other end of the province. And from Cape Breton, it's a six-hour ferry ride to the next landfall, the island of Newfoundland, which itself is nearer to Liverpool, England, than to Toronto.

More than any other region of Canada, the Atlantic Provinces are defined by water. Mighty tides surge through the Bay of Fundy between New Brunswick and Nova Scotia. The Cabot Strait lies between Nova Scotia's Cape Breton and the island of Newfoundland's southern coastline. The unexpectedly warm Northumberland Strait, heated by the Gulf Stream, is a broad blue parenthesis dividing Prince Edward Island from Nova Scotia and New Brunswick. On the island's north side is the Gulf of St. Lawrence. The Baie des Chaleurs, its warmth owing to its shallow depth, lies between northeastern New Brunswick and Québec's Gaspé Peninsula.

Along Labrador's coast, the Labrador Sea moves south with chillier waters and forks into a channel known as the Strait of Belle Isle, which separates the island of Newfoundland from the mainland, while other currents wash along Newfoundland's eastern coast.

The sea's pervasive presence is felt throughout the region, but the ties to the ocean are strongest in Nova Scotia and Newfoundland, whose outer coasts face the open Atlantic. Prince Edward Island is surrounded by water, of course, so fishing is a major industry. But agriculture is also an important component of the economy, the benevolent result of the last ice age, which blessed the land with a fertile loam. New Brunswick faces the sea on two sides and joins the mainland with a massive sweep of land rich in forests and ores, hence an economy comprised of fishing, forestry, and mining.

The ribs of the Appalachian Mountains extend throughout the region; 820-meter-high Mt. Carleton in northwestern New Brunswick is the Maritimes' highest point, while other pitched extensions spread across Cape Breton and as far as Newfoundland. The highest point in Atlantic Canada rises 1,729 meters at soaring Mt. Caubvick, overlooking the Labrador Sea in northern Labrador. Otherwise, the region's terrain is mostly low and undulating, dipping and swelling in innumerable variations.

Hundreds of streams and rivers streak the region's landscapes, pouring into copious bays and wide-mouthed estuaries at the seas. Uncounted thousands of lakes, another ice-age legacy, speckle the provinces' interiors.

THE PROVINCES

New Brunswick

New Brunswick is the largest (73,437 square km, pop. 724,000) of the Maritime provinces. Québec and Maine share its thick Appalachian woods, which cover almost 90% of the province. But New Brunswick is not just one giant forest; it has a 2,200-km-long coastline along the Bay of Fundy, Northumberland Strait, Gulf of St. Lawrence, and Baie des Chaleurs.

Maine lies immediately to the west, and Prince Edward Island is a quick ferry ride across the

Northumberland Strait from Cape Tormentine. The province's coastal edges and the fertile Saint John River valley, which cuts a mammoth swath across the western woodlands, attract the most tourists.

Nova Scotia

Nova Scotia (54,490 square km, pop. 890,000) typifies Atlantic Canada, with a dramatic, 7,459-km coastline notched with innumerable coves and bays holding scores of working seaports. The province is shaped something like a mammoth lobster, with Cape Breton Island at the northeastern tip forming the crustacean's claws, and the curving southwestern end around Yarmouth forming its tail.

Almost an island, Nova Scotia is tagged onto the mainland by the narrow Chignecto Isthmus at the New Brunswick border. Some 4,000 islands lie offshore; the largest of them is Cape Breton, which is nearly a quarter the size of the province's mainland.

Much of the terrain is level or rolling hills, remnants of the ancient Appalachian Mountains. The land rises gradually from sea level at Yarmouth in the southwest to finally peak at the rugged mountaintops of Cape Breton Highlands National Park in the northeast. The population is concentrated along the coasts, while much of the interior is thickly forested and sparsely inhabited.

Prince Edward Island

Prince Edward Island ranks as Canada's smallest province (5,656 square km, pop. 130,000), as well as its most densely populated, most cultivated, most ribboned with roads, and most bereft of original wilderness. The province also has the country's smallest provincial capital—Charlottetown, with just 16,000 inhabitants.

The land is gentle, with no point reaching over 152 meters in elevation. And it's fertile, thanks to mineral-rich soil deposited during the last ice age. Half the world's supply of potatoes originates from the island, and fields of grain and pasturelands support a large dairy industry. Some 10 million oysters (Canada's largest share) are harvested from the island's sheltered bays and estuaries each year.

The sea is visible most everywhere: from atop every knoll and around every curve. No point on the island, in fact, is farther than 16 km from the shore.

Newfoundland and Labrador

New Brunswick, Nova Scotia, and Prince Edward Island comprise the Maritimes, the triumvirate of provinces that lie at the region's south and southwestern rim. The inclusion of the province of Newfoundland, three times the size of all the Maritimes put together, redefines the region as Atlantic Canada. The province is *large* (total area 405,720 square km, pop. 568,474), larger in fact than the United Kingdom and Ireland. And for those who don't know the province, the name leads to some confusion. The province of Newfoundland includes the island of Newfoundland as well as Labrador on the mainland, which is three times the size of the island.

The Maritime Provinces share a kindred climate, history, and lineage, but Newfoundland is different. About half of the mountainous island is boreal forest, while much of the rest is rocky, barren, or boggy. Labrador is more heavily wooded, with a northern tundra. The province is sparsely populated, and the people are generally more Irish or English than culturally blended or archetypically Canadian.

The world at its most ancient is revealed at Gros Morne National Park, where, according to the plate-tectonics theory, the northwestern seacoast was formed of the earth's mantle and crust. Tossed asunder during primordial internal upheavals, the coastline today is an odd jumble of verdant meadows, volcanic formations, landlocked fjords, and moonlike canyons.

CLIMATE

Maritime weather varies from province to province, and from region to region within the provinces. Extremes are generally moderated by proximity to the sea. June through September are the most pleasant and popular months for visiting. The regions' landscapes and seascapes are recast by the changing seasons. In springtime, occasional banks of thick fog blanket the coast from Yarmouth to St. John's. In summer, a pervasive balminess ripens the blueberry fields from Cumberland County in Nova Scotia to

SUMMER TEMPERATURES
(in degrees Celsius)

	JULY		AUGUST	
	LOW	HIGH	LOW	HIGH
Fredericton, NB	10	23	12	25
Moncton, NB	10	25	12	24
Saint John, NB	12	22	11	22
Halifax, NS	14	23	14	23
Sydney, NS	12	23	13	23
Yarmouth, NS	12	20	12	21
Charlottetown, PEI	14	23	14	23
St. John's, NF	11	21	12	20
Corner Brook, NF	12	22	12	21
Happy Valley–Goose Bay, NF	10	21	9	19

Newfoundland's Codroy Valley. Autumn brings the last burst of Indian summer, then colors the forests until winter's sea winds swirl in and send the leaves tumbling down to finish another year.

Below are overviews of the climate of each province; additional details are given in the Introduction to each chapter.

New Brunswick
New Brunswick's continental climate contrasts hot summers with cold winters. Extremes are moderated by the surrounding seas, more so near the coast than in the interior. Summer means warm days and cool nights, with an average daytime high temperature of 23° C in June, 26° C in July, and 25° C in August. July is the sunniest month. September and October are pleasantly warm, with increasingly cool days toward November. Winter is cold.

Precipitation throughout the province averages 115.2 cm annually. The Bay of Fundy coast is steeped in dense fog about 70 days a year.

Nova Scotia
The province has a pleasant, modified continental climate, moderated by air and water currents from the Gulf Stream and the arctic. Summers are warm and winters are mild. Cape Breton is subject to more extreme weather than

the mainland. Precipitation provincewide averages 130 cm, falling mainly as rain during autumn and as snow in winter.

Spring high temperatures range from -2.5 to 9° C, though the days begin to warm up toward the end of March. Summer weather has a reputation for changing from day to day; daytime highs range up to 30° C, while nights are cool, averaging 12° C. Inland areas are generally 5° C warmer during the day. The coasts often bask in morning fog. Caribbean hurricanes, having spent their force farther south, limp through the region, bringing to the northwestern Atlantic short spells of rain and wind.

In autumn, the evenings start to cool, but pleasant days continue through September at up to 18° C. The days are cool to frosty October through mid-November. Winter lasts from late November through early March, with temperatures averaging -10 to 4° C.

Prince Edward Island
The island basks in a typical maritime climate with one major exception: its growing season of 110-160 days is Atlantic Canada's longest. The island also gets more than its share of year-round breezes, pleasant and warm in summer but fiercer come fall. Spring is short, lasting from early to mid-May until mid-June. Summer temperatures peak in July and August, when temperatures range from 18 to 23° C; an unusually warm day can reach 35° C, while the other extreme can be quite cool at just 5° C. Autumn brings with it Atlantic Canada's brightest and most dramatic fall foliage. Winter temperatures can dip below 0° C in December and January.

Annual precipitation amounts to 106 cm, with half of that falling from May to October.

Newfoundland
The climate is harsher and more extreme here than in the Maritimes. A sultry summer day can

be interspersed with chilly breezes, brilliant sun, dark clouds, and showers from light to drenching. The island's eastern and southern sea-coasts are often foggy due to the offshore melding of the warm Gulf Stream and cold Labrador current.

Overall, the island has cool, moist, maritime weather. Summer days average 16-21° C, dropping to 9-12° C at night, but hot spells are common, and the swimming season starts by late June. The island's low-lying interior and coastal areas are warmest and sunniest. Annual rainfall averages 105 cm. Frost begins by early October on the southern coast, earlier farther north. Snowfall averages 300 cm a year.

Winter high temperatures average -4 to 0° C, warm enough to turn snow to rain, while nighttime lows can tumble to -15° C. Expect year-round blustery winds along Marine Drive and nearby Cape Spear.

Conditions are severe in the Long Range Mountains' upper elevations; the peaks are snow-covered year-round, while winds can blow to gale force.

Labrador

Labrador's climate is continental, and subject to great extremes. Summers are short, cool to sometimes hot, and brilliantly sunny with periodic showers. A July day averages 21° C, but temperatures have been known to rise to 38° C at Happy Valley–Goose Bay. Temperatures drop rapidly after mid-August. By November, daytime highs at Goose Bay fall to 0° C.

Winter is very cold and dry. Daytime high temperatures average -20° C in the subarctic, -18 to -21° C in the interior, and -51° C in the western area.

FLORA

Trees

Canada's provincial forests abound with ash, balsam fir, birch, beech, cedar, hemlock, maple, oak, pine, and spruce. Thick woodlands now blanket over 81% of Nova Scotia, and 93% of New Brunswick. Prince Edward Island, by contrast, is the country's least-forested province, with its land area about equally divided between farmlands and woodlands.

Newfoundland's forests are mainly black spruce and balsam fir with occasional stands of larch, pin cherry, pine, paper and white birch, aspen, red and mountain maple, and alder. In Newfoundland's alpine and coastal areas, you may encounter the formidable "tuckamore," a thicket composed of stunted, hopelessly entangled fir and spruce. Labrador's southern forests are cloaked with spruce, tamarack, juniper, and birch. Thirty-meter-high white spruce dominates the central area, while stunted black spruce, a mere meter high, speckles the timberline area. Farther north on the arctic tundra, dwarf birch and willow are common.

With so many provincial tree varieties, visitors may easily be confused. For a helpful general introduction, visit Odell Park Arboretum in Fredericton, New Brunswick, where a 2.8-km trail winds through woods made up of every tree native to the area.

Wildflowers and Other Plants

The Maritimes host magnificent wildflower shows. Common wildflowers throughout New Brunswick and Nova Scotia—seen especially along roadsides in summertime—include lupine, Queen Anne's lace, yarrow, pearly everlasting, and a variety of daisies. The showy spikes of purple loosestrife, a pretty but aggressive and unwelcome pest, can be seen everywhere.

The bayberry bush and wild rose bloom on the Chignecto Isthmus during June. The yellow beach heather colors the Northumberland Strait dunes and sandy plains, and the rhodora (miniature rhododendron) brightens coastal marshes. Nutrient-rich bogs in northeastern New Brunswick nurture plant exotica, especially at Lamèque and Miscou islands, where the wild cranberry and insectivorous pitcher plant and sundew grow among peat moss beds.

Prince Edward Island is like one large cultivated garden when late spring and summer's warm temperatures urge columbines, bachelor buttons, pansies, lilacs, wild roses, pink clover, and the delicate lady's slipper (the provincial flower) into blossom.

Across Newfoundland's marshes and bogs, you'll see white and yellow water lilies, rare orchid species, purple iris and goodwithy, and insectivorous plants (such as the pitcher plant, the provincial flower). Daisies, blue harebells,

the lady's slipper, Prince Edward Island's provincial flower

BOB RACE

yellow goldenrod, pink wild roses, and deep pink fireweed thrive in the woodlands. Marsh marigolds, as brightly yellow as daffodils, are native to the western coast's Port au Port Peninsula.

Yellow poppies, heather buttercups, miniature purple rhododendrons, violets, and deep blue gentian, mixed among the white cotton grass, brighten Labrador's arctic tundra; farther south, the daisy-like arnica and purple saxifrage grow in plateau rock niches.

No poison ivy, poison oak, or ragweed grows anywhere in the province. Mushrooms are everywhere; know the species before sampling—the chanterelles are culinary prizes, but the amanitas are deadly poisonous.

FAUNA

Birds

If you're an avid birder, the variety and abundance of Atlantic Canada's birdlife will leave you breathless. In addition to hundreds of year-round resident species, the Atlantic migratory route stretches across part of the region, bringing in millions of seasonal visitors.

Among the richest areas is the Bay of Fundy. In July, seabirds descend on the Mary's Point mudflats at Shepody National Wildlife Area; across Shepody Bay, 100,000 sandpipers en route to South America stop at the Dorchester Peninsula. With over 300 species, Grand Manan Island is a prime birdwatching site. The show is thickest during September, when migratory seabirds arrive in force. Ornithologist-artist John James Audubon visited the island in 1833 and painted the arctic tern, gannet, black guillemot, and razorbill specimens he found there.

Even greater numbers of seabirds—the region's greatest concentrations—gather on the coastlines of Newfoundland's Avalon Peninsula. Species found there include common and arctic terns, kittiwakes, great and double-crested cormorants, Leach's storm petrels, razorbills, guillemots, murres, gannets, and 95% of North America's breeding Atlantic puffins. In Labrador, ruffled and spruce grouse, owl, woodpecker, ravens, gyrfalcon, jay, chickadee, nuthatch, grouse, and ptarmigan are a few of the birds you may spot.

In New Brunswick's interior, crossbill, varied woodpecker species, boreal chickadee, and gray jay nest in the spruce and fir forests. Ibis, heron, and snowy egret wade among lagoons and marshes. Among Nova Scotia's 300 or so bird species, the best known is the bald eagle. About 250 pairs nest in the province, concentrated on Cape Breton—the second-largest population on North America's east coast after Florida. The season for eagle watching is July and August.

The noisy blue jay, Prince Edward Island's official provincial bird, is at home throughout the province, but the island's showiest species is the enormous, stately great blue heron, which summers there from May to early August. The rare piping plover may be seen (but not disturbed) on the island's national park beaches, and arctic terns nest along the coast near Murray Harbour.

Land Mammals

Black bears, bobcats, red fox, coyotes, white-tailed deer, porcupines, squirrels, and lynx are widespread throughout all of Atlantic Canada's provinces except diminutive Prince Edward Island. Kouchibouguac National Park, in northeastern New Brunswick, is also home to timber wolves and moose. Recently, verified sightings prove that eastern cougars have returned to New Brunswick after more than 50 years.

Newfoundland's wildlife also includes hares, beavers, otters, muskrats, martens, and mink. Labrador has populations of red wolf, wolverines, and, on the northern tundra coastline, polar bears.

Sea Life
Some 20 whale species cruise offshore, lured by foodstocks of plankton and schools of smeltlike capelin. Prime whalewatching areas are in the Bay of Fundy—especially around Grand Manan Island and Brier Island—and off the shores of Cape Breton. Minke, pilot, finback, orca, and humpback whales are the most populous species. The whales that frequent Nova Scotia arrive from the Caribbean between June and mid-July and remain through October; the sea-

son peaks during August and September. On Newfoundland's western coast, fin, minke, humpback, and pilot whales are sighted off Gros Morne National Park.

Newfoundland and Labrador's seal industry ended in 1981, finally succumbing to pressures by animal activists. But 30,000 seals are still legally culled by Native people each spring.

In 1977, the federal government sought to curb the Grand Banks fisheries' depletion by establishing a 320-kilometer offshore fishing zone. The codfish landings remained sparse, however, and in 1992 the government announced a two-year moratorium on codfishing in Newfoundland and Labrador waters—a ban that put 30,000 fishermen and fish processors out of work. The moratorium on codfishing was extended in 1994. Abundant quantities of flounder, tuna, haddock, salmon, and other fish still swim the waters of the Atlantic Canada coast.

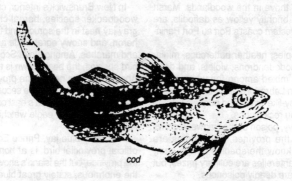

cod

NOVA SCOTIA MUSEUM COMPLEX

HISTORY

BEGINNINGS

Atlantic Canada's earliest inhabitants arrived in Labrador nearly 10,000 years ago. Archaeological research documents that these Maritime Archaic Indians hunted seals and whales along the Strait of Belle Isle around 7500 B.C.; they eventually crossed the strait to the island of Newfoundland's northern portion and established encampments such as Port au Choix, where their burial grounds and artifacts date to 2300 B.C.

Brendan the Navigator, a fifth-century Irish monk, may have been the first European to explore the area; he sought Hy-Brazil, the "wonderful island of the saints," and later accounts of his voyage describe an island with coastal topography similar to Newfoundland's.

Atlantic Canada's link to the Vikings is more certain. The Norsemen sailed the Labrador coastline and established a temporary settlement at L'Anse aux Meadows on Newfoundland's Northern Peninsula in A.D. 1000. "Newfoundland" as a place-name originated with the explorer John Cabot, who sighted the "New Founde Lande" in 1497 and claimed the island for England.

The Fabulous Fisheries

Although undocumented, European fishermen are believed to have preceded Cabot. Legends in Newfoundland describe the Basques as whale hunters in the Strait of Belle Isle as early as the 1470s. France's fishing exploits are better known. In the early 1500s, French fleets roamed the seas from the Grand Banks—where they caught cod and dried them on Newfoundland's beaches—to inland rivers such as the salmon-rich Miramichi in what is now New Brunswick. England's fishing fleets were equally active, leading an American diplomat to describe Newfoundland as "a great ship moored near the Grand Banks for the convenience of English fishermen."

England also dabbled in other commercial interests in Newfoundland. A group of merchants from England's West Country settled Trinity in the mid-1500s. Cupids, England's first chartered colony on the island, began in 1610. In contrast, St. John's evolved independently and belonged to no nation; the port served as a haven and trading center for all of Europe's fishing fleets, and Signal Hill, the lofty promontory beside the harbor, dates as a lookout and signal peak from the early 1500s.

French Interests

Ultimately, France was more interested in trading posts and settlements than in fishing. The French Crown granted Sieur de Monts a monopoly to develop the fur trade, and in 1604, the nobleman-merchant, with explorer Samuel de Champlain, led an exploratory party to the mouth of the Bay of Fundy. The expedition established a camp on an island in the St. Croix River (the river that now separates New Brunswick from Maine). The group barely survived the bitter first winter and relocated across the Bay of Fundy, establishing Port Royal as a fur-trading post in the Annapolis Basin the following spring.

The grant was canceled, and while most of the expedition returned to France in 1607, a group of French settlers took their place at Port Royal in 1610. The French dubbed the area "Acadia," or "Peaceful Land."

The French settlement and others like it ignited the fuse between England and France. John Cabot had claimed the region for England, but explorer Jacques Cartier also claimed many of the same coastlines for France several decades later. For France, the region was a choice piece of property, a potential New France in the New World. On the other hand, England's colonial aspirations centered farther south, where colonization had begun at Virginia and Massachusetts. England didn't *need* what is now Atlantic Canada, though the region offered much with its rich fisheries, and was a place to confront the expansion of the French, England's most contentious enemy in Europe.

an early European
settlement, Port Royal
Habitation

NAN DROSDICK

In terms of military strength, the British had the upper hand. An ocean separated France from its dream of settlement, while England's military forces and volunteer militias were located along the eastern seaboard. In 1613, a militia from Virginia plundered and burned the buildings at Port Royal. The French relocated the site to a more protected site farther up the Annapolis River, built another fort named Port Royal, and designated the setting as Acadia's colonial capital in 1635.

France's Sphere Develops

The French Acadian settlements quickly spread beyond the Port Royal area to the Fundy and Minas Basin coastlines. The merchant Nicholas Denys, whose name is entwined with France's early exploration, established a fortified settlement on Cape Breton at St. Peters, and also at Guysborough in 1653. So many Acadians settled at Grand-Pré that it became the largest settlement and hub of villages in the area. Other settlements were established across Acadia on Cape Breton, the Cobequid Bay and Cape Chignecto coastlines, and from the Restigouche Uplands to the Baie des Chaleurs in what's now northern New Brunswick.

France needed a military center and created it in the mid-1600s at Plaisance, one of the earliest and most important fishing ports on the Avalon Peninsula in Newfoundland. Here, they erected another tribute to the French Crown and named the new fortification Fort Royal.

British reprisals against the French increased. The British hammered Port Royal again and again, and in 1654, a militia from New England destroyed some of the Acadian settlements. In Newfoundland, France's presence at Plaisance prompted the British to counter by building forts around St. John's in 1675.

The Treaty of Utrecht

Hostilities between England and France in the New World mirrored political events in Europe. Fighting ebbed and flowed across Atlantic Canada as the powers jockeyed for control on the European continent. Queen Anne's War (1701-13), the War of Austrian Secession (1745-48), and the Seven Years' War (1756-63) were all fought in Europe, but corresponding battles between the English and French took place in North America as well (where they were known collectively as the French and Indian Wars).

The Treaty of Utrecht in 1713 settled the Queen Anne's War in Europe. Under the terms of the treaty, England fell heir to all of French Acadia (though the borders were vague). In Newfoundland, Plaisance came into British hands and was renamed Castle Hill. The treaty awarded France the token settlements of the offshore Île Saint-Jean (Prince Edward Island) and Île Royale (Cape Breton). Acadia became an English colony. Nova Scotia (New Scotland) rose on the ashes of New France and the fallen Port Royal; the British took the fort in 1710, renamed it Fort Anne and renamed the settlement Annapolis Royal. The town was designated the colony's first capital until Halifax was established and became the capital in 1749.

The French military regrouped. They fled from the peninsula and began to build (and never finish) the Fortress of Louisbourg on Île Royale's Atlantic seacoast in 1719. Once again, the French envisioned the fortification as a New Paris and France's major naval base, port city, and trading center in North America. Simultaneously, they sent 300 fishermen and farmers across the Northumberland Strait to create a new settlement at Port la Joye; the enclave, at what is now Charlottetown's southwestern, outer edge, was intended to serve as the breadbasket for the Fortress of Louisbourg.

The British quickly responded. A fort at Grassy Island on Chedabucto Bay was their first effort, a site close enough to the Fortress of Louisbourg to watch the arrivals and departures of the French fleets. By 1745, Louisbourg represented a formidable threat to England, so the Brits seized the fortress and deported the inhabitants. But no sooner had they changed the flag than the French were moving back in again. The War of Austrian Succession in Europe ended with the Treaty of Aix-la-Chapelle in 1748, which, among other things, returned Louisbourg to France.

Full-fledged War

Peace was short-lived. Eight years later, in 1756, the Seven Years' War broke out in Europe, and once more both powers geared for confrontation in Atlantic Canada. Britain's Grassy Island fort was strategically located but too small a military base. In 1749, a British convoy sailed into Halifax Harbour, established England's military hub in the North Atlantic in the capacious harbor, and named Halifax the capital of Nova Scotia. Fort Edward near the Fundy seacoast went up in the midst of an Acadian area and guarded the overland route from Halifax. Fort Lawrence on the Chignecto Isthmus, between Nova Scotia and New Brunswick, was built to defend the route to the mainland. The fort defiantly faced two of France's most formidable forts: Fort Beauséjour and Fort Gaspéreau.

The stage was set for war, and the region's civilian inhabitants, the Acadian farmers, were trapped in the middle. Decades before, England had demanded but not enforced an oath of allegiance from the Acadians who lived under their jurisdiction. By the 1750s, however, the British decided to demand loyalty and also readied a plan to evict the Acadians from their land and replace noncompliant French inhabitants with Anglo settlers. In 1755, the British swept through the region and enforced the oath. In a show of force, more than 2,000 troops from Boston captured Fort Beauséjour and renamed it Fort Cumberland.

THE ACADIAN DEPORTATION

England's actions unleashed chaos on the Acadians. Those who refused to sign the oath of allegiance were rounded up and deported, and their villages and farmlands were burned. By October, 1,100 Acadians had been deported, while others fought the British in guerrilla warfare or fled to the hinterlands of Cape Breton, New Brunswick, and Québec.

The Acadians being deported were herded onto ships bound for the English colonies on the eastern seaboard or anyplace that would accept them. Some ships docked in England, others in France, and others in France's colonies in the Caribbean. As the ports wearied of the human cargo, many of them refused the vessels entry, and the ships returned to the high seas to search for other ports willing to accept the Acadians. In one of the period's few favorable events, the Spanish government offered the refugees free land in Louisiana, and they settled there in 1784, where the Acadians became known as the "Cajuns."

Refugee camps, rife with disease and malnutrition, sprang up across the Maritimes. Beaubears Island on New Brunswick's Miramichi River began as a refugee center. About 3,500 Acadians fled from Nova Scotia to Île du Saint-Jean (Prince Edward Island); 700 lost their lives on two boats that sank on the journey. Many deported Acadians returned, only to be deported again, some as many as seven or eight times.

Exact Deportation numbers are unknown. Historians speculate that 10,000 French inhabitants lived in Acadia in 1755; by the time the Deportation had run its course in 1816, only 25% of them remained.

England's Final Blow

In 1758, the British moved in for the kill. They seized the Fortress of Louisbourg and toppled Port la Joye, renaming it Fort Amherst. The French stronghold at Québec fell the next year. In the ultimate act of revenge, the British troops returned to Louisbourg in 1760 and demolished the fortress stone by stone so it would never rise again against England. New France was almost finished; bereft of a foothold in Atlantic Canada, the French launched a convoy from France and captured St. John's in 1762. The British quickly swooped in and regained the port at the Battle of Signal Hill, the final land battle of the Seven Years' War. Finally, the bitter French and Indian Wars were finished.

Postwar Developments

Atlantic Canada, as you see it now, then began to take shape. After the British had swept the Acadians from their land, prosperous "planters," gentlemen-farmers from New England, were lured to the lush Annapolis Valley with free land grants. Merchants settled Yarmouth in the 1760s, and other Anglo settlers went to Prince Edward Island. The island, formerly part of Nova Scotia, became an English colony in 1769.

Some of the Acadians had evaded capture, and settlements such as the Pubnico communities south of Yarmouth date to the pre-Deportation period. But most of the region's surviving Acadian areas began after the refugees returned and settled marginal lands no one else wanted, such as the rocky seacoast of La Côte Acadienne (the Acadian Coast) in western Nova Scotia.

England lucked out. Even the inglorious defeat in the American Revolution benefitted the British. Loyalists (Americans loyal to England) by the thousands poured into Nova Scotia and New Brunswick. The influx was so great in Saint John and Fredericton that New Brunswick, originally part of Nova Scotia, became an English colony, and Saint John became the first incorporated city in Canada.

An Uneasy Peace

Even as peace settled across Atlantic Canada, the specter of war loomed again in Europe. Ever wary of their contentious enemy, the British feared a French invasion by Napoleon's navies in Atlantic Canada. In Halifax, the British built up the harbor's defenses at the Halifax Citadel and other sites. At St. John's, the British fortified Signal Hill with the Queen's Battery.

As if Britain didn't have enough problems with the Napoleonic Wars, at the same time the War of 1812 ensued as England and the U.S. wrangled over shipping rights on the high seas. More British fortifications went up, this time across the Bay of Fundy in New Brunswick with harbor defenses such as the Carleton Martello Tower at Saint John, the blockhouse at St. Andrews, and other strongholds at more than a dozen strategic places.

TOWARD CONFEDERATION

The Napoleonic Wars ended in June 1815 with Napoleon's defeat at Waterloo. Atlantic Canada emerged unscathed. The war years had fostered shipping, and Halifax earned a questionable reputation as the home port of privateers who raided ships on the high seas and returned to port to auction the booty at the harborfront. In Newfoundland, many ships had been lost on the treacherous shoals outside St. John's Harbour, prompting the British to build the lofty Cape Spear Lighthouse in 1836.

In 1864, a landmark event in Canadian history took place in Atlantic Canada. The **"Fathers of the Confederation,"** from New Brunswick, Nova Scotia, Prince Edward Island, Ontario, and Québec, met at Province House in Charlottetown. The small city owes its fame as the birthplace of Canada to the discussions of a potential joint dominion that followed. In 1867, England gave the union its blessing and signed the British North America Act of Confederation; Canada, as a fledgling nation, was born on 1 July. (Prince Edward Island initially bowed out as a confederation member, but joined the dominion several years later.)

World Wars and the Depression

Atlantic Canada became a hotbed of controversy during WW I, when the sensitive issue of Francophone rights was raised. The federal government had decided to initiate a military conscription, and French Canadians were afraid that the draft would decrease their already minority population. All told, 60,000 Canadians died in battle. After the war, Atlantic Canada had a brief brush with prosperity as mining and manufacturing were expanded.

But the Maritimes were not immune to the Great Depression of the 1930s, and businesses collapsed under the financial crisis. When WW II came along, Atlantic Canada took part in shipping much of the munitions and food supplies for the Allies, which served to revive the economy.

Newfoundland voted to become Canada's 10th province on 31 March 1949.

A Constitution

Since 1867, the British North America Act required British Parliament approval for any Canadian constitutional change. On 5 November 1981, Canada's federal government and the premiers of every province except Québec agreed on a Canadian Constitution and Charter of Rights and Freedoms. The Canada Act formally went into effect on 17 April 1982, removing the British Parliament's remaining control. Canada remains a member of the Commonwealth.

GOVERNMENT AND ECONOMY

GOVERNMENT

Canada is the world's largest democratic country by land area. The federation of 10 provinces and two territories operates under a parliamentary system in which power is shared between the federal government (based in Ottawa) and provincial governments.

The Federal Government

Under Canada's constitutional monarchy, the head of state is the queen of England, who appoints a governor general to represent her for a five-year term. The governor general stays out of party politics, and performs largely ceremonial duties, such as opening and closing parliamentary sessions, signing and approving state documents on the queen's behalf, and appointing a temporary replacement in the event the prime ministership is vacated without warning. Head of government is the prime minister, who is the leader of the majority party or party coalition in the House of Commons.

The country's legislative branch, the Parliament, is comprised of two houses. The House of Commons, with 295 members, is apportioned by provincial population and elected by plurality from the country's districts. The Senate has 104 members appointed by the governor general for life (though retirement is mandatory at age 75) on the advice of the prime minister. Laws must be passed by both houses and be signed by the governor general.

National elections are held every five years, or whenever the majority party is voted down in the House of Commons.

Provincial Governments

Each of the nation's provincial Legislative Assemblies (in Newfoundland, it's called the House of Assembly) consists of a one-house legislative body with members elected every four years. The nominal head of the provincial government is the lieutenant governor, appointed by the federal government. Executive power, however, rests with the cabinet, headed by a premier, the leader of the majority party.

The Judicial System

Canada's judicial system consists of county courts, provincial supreme courts, and the Supreme Court in Ottawa, highest in the land.

ECONOMY

The Fur Trade

The initial impetus for investment in the Maritimes was not gold or land or timber or oil, but fur. Its hostile terrain precluded the others, and Atlantic Canada's plentiful wildlife provided warmth as well as wealth. By the 1700s, France and England had both built empires on the fur trade. The Hudson's Bay Company, financed by British entrepreneurs, ran one of North America's most powerful corporations, spanning Canada's Arctic to what would later become Oregon.

Commercial fox farming began on Prince Edward Island back in 1894, and soon grew into big business, accounting within a couple of decades for nearly one-fifth of the provincial economy.

Fishing

Canada was once the world's largest fish-exporting country, but overfishing has destroyed its once-bounteous supplies. Fisheries and fish processing still remain the third-biggest contributor to Nova Scotia's gross domestic product (GDP), and cod, haddock, herring, and lobster are caught inshore and off the Atlantic's Scotian Shelf. The province is Canada's largest lobster exporter.

New Brunswick's fisheries produce groundfish, lobster, crab, scallops, and herring. The newest aquaculture developments are Atlantic salmon farms and blue mussel beds. Black Harbour–area canneries rank first in Canada's sardine production.

Labrador fisheries, a chronic boom-or-bust industry, contribute some $230 million yearly to

tools of the fishing trade

the economy with catches of mackerel, flounder, capelin, herring, squid, eel, fish roe, sole, salmon, perch, turbot, halibut, lobster, and farmed mussels and rainbow trout. Labrador also produces half of Canada's commercial char.

Natural Resources

Atlantic Canada's fisheries have declined as a consequence of the local industry's own modern fishing methods as well as foreign competition. As a result, the area has turned to its other resources: timber, coal, and other minerals. New Brunswick harbors Canada's largest silver, lead, and zinc reserves, and also mines potash, coal, and oil shale. Peat moss is collected in northeastern New Brunswick, especially from Lamèque and Miscou islands—enough to make the province the world's second-largest exporter of this fuel.

Mining contributes $886 million to New Brunswick's economy and is the second-largest segment of Nova Scotia's. Over 30 mines and quarries in Nova Scotia are worked for their coal, limestone, and tin.

Nova Scotia's extensive forests supply a substantial lumber and paper industry; among the largest operators are Bowater Mersey Paper (half owned by the *Washington Post*) on the South Shore, and the Kraft pulp mills at Abercrombie Point, Point Tupper, Brooklyn, Hantsport, and East River.

Western Labrador's mines contribute about 80% of Canada's iron ore share. Other Newfoundland metals and minerals include: copper, lead, zinc, gold, silver, chromium, limestone, gypsum, aluminum silicate, and asbestos. Newfoundland also holds Canada's sole commercial deposit of pyrophyllite, which is used in the production of ceramics. Newfoundland is economically on the bottom rung of Canada's per-capita income, yet the province may find itself among the world's richest places when the offshore oil fields start producing in the late 1990s.

Agriculture

Agriculture contributes $275 million to New Brunswick's GDP; Victoria and Carleton counties' seed potatoes make up 20% of Canada's total potato crop, and are exported to Mexico, Portugal, and the United States. The benevolent spring floods wash the Saint John River valley with rich silt, helping to sustain a healthy mixed farming economy. The farms at Maugerville yield two crops each season. Other agricultural products include livestock (exported to France, England, Denmark, and the U.S.), dairy products, and berries.

Though just eight percent of Nova Scotia's land is arable, agriculture contributes heavily to the economy. The province produces fruits (including Annapolis Valley apples), dairy products, poultry, hogs, and Canada's largest share of blueberries.

Diminutive PEI ranks first in Canada's potato production, contributing half of the world's supply. Half of the crop is grown in Prince County, and the remainder is produced by farms scattered across the province. Local farmers travel abroad to 32 nations to advise their foreign counterparts on varieties and farming methods. The province harvests 10 million oysters annually and most are exported.

The island's beauty may be attributed to its investments in agriculture, which contributed 9.5% to the gross domestic product (GDP). The sector yields $120 million a year and employs 5,000 islanders on 2,800 farms, each of which averages 96 hectares. Grains, fruits, beef, pigs, sheep, and dairy products are other components of mixed farming production.

Agriculture in Labrador earns $28 million a year in hay, root crops, vegetables, berries, and mink farms.

Power

Water is ubiquitous in the Atlantic Provinces (one-third of all the world's fresh water is found in Canada), and hydroelectricity generation is a cheap, clean export. Québec Hydro alone, for example, sells over $1 billion a year to New England. The Mactaquac Generating Station, on the Saint John River near Fredericton, New Brunswick, is the Maritimes' largest hydroelectric station.

New Brunswick also built Atlantic Canada's first nuclear power–generating plant, at Point Lepreau.

The high ocean tides in the Bay of Fundy have been studied to ascertain the feasibility of harnessing that incredible power as well.

Trade and Industry

Almost three-fourths of Atlantic Canada's export and import business is with the United States. With the latest Free Trade Agreement (1994), Canada has been made increasingly aware of this interdependence. The economies of the U.S. and Canada are so inextricably linked that America's car industry, for example, would quickly grind to a halt if it were not for the auto parts manufactured just across the border. Canadians are also major investors in the American economy, primarily as financial backers for urban development.

But trade continues to grease the Maritimes' economic wheels. Eleven of Nova Scotia's 267 harbors are major shipping ports, and Halifax, Sydney, and Point Tupper on the Strait of Canso rank as the busiest ports. A 36-hectare auto port, which handles 100,000 vehicles a year, is based at Dartmouth.

Saint John's merchant-shipping fleet ranks as Canada's largest, as does the city's sugar-refinery plant. Other industries include pulp mills, oil-refining plants, food-processing plants, and two breweries.

New Brunswick's annual gross domestic product (GDP) is $15.4 billion. Manufacturing and shipping contribute two-thirds of this, which includes food products, beverages, fabricated metal products, plastics, chemicals, and forestry products.

In 1991, Nova Scotia's GDP was $19.375 billion. Manufacturing topped the list as the highest earner. Among the largest companies are Michelin Tire Canada, Volvo Canada, Crossley Karastan Carpet, and Pratt and Whitney. The province is also the region's federal civil service and military center. Halifax has served as a naval center since its founding in 1749 as headquarters for the Royal Navy. The city is now Maritime Command headquarters for the Canadian Armed Forces. Other military installations are at Shearwater, Cornwallis, and Greenwood; training stations are located at Barrington, Mill Cove, Shelburne, and Sydney.

Farming and fishing remain crucial to Prince Edward Island's economy, but it is slowly changing. In the late 1960s, after the request for a mainland fixed link collapsed, economic efforts were rechanneled to the **Comprehensive Development Plan,** aimed at education and industry. Optics and medical-component light industry formed the gist of new industrial parks. Unemployment measures 10-15%, due to the seasonal nature of fishing and farming. Today the bridge to New Brunswick is under construction, and it holds the potential to dramatically alter PEI's economy and, indeed, the island's society in general.

Tourism

Tourism ranks as Atlantic Canada's fourth-largest industry. The majority of visitors arrive by car, RV, or on motorcoach tours, while only 20% fly in. Air arrivals are increasing, however, as long-distance air links improve beyond Atlantic Canada. Most visitors (41%) are from the neighboring provinces, while central Canada contributes 29%, and the U.S. adds almost 25%. Of the 1.2 million people who arrive annually, more than three-fourths of that number are returning visitors. About 80% of the 1.5 million tourists who visit the Maritimes annually enter the region through New Brunswick, Atlantic Canada's land gateway. In PEI, tourism earns $95 million annually and employs 2,500 islanders year-round and another 6,500 on a seasonal basis.

PEOPLE

Centuries of sometimes turbulent history bind the Atlantic Canadians together: the mutual grief of the early wars, the Acadian Deportation, the immigration upheavals, and, in more recent times, resettlement schemes in Newfoundland. In the same sense, the early events have given each resident ethnic population an indisputable identity.

The region's ethnic fabric is far richer than one might at first suspect—over 60 ethnic groups have been stirred into the melting pot. In spite of the cultural diversity, the region shares an identity as a place apart from the rest of Canada. Unlike the rest of the country, the provinces of Atlantic Canada share provincial economies that rise and fall on the vicissitudes of the fisheries. The region is separated from the body of Canada by the equally insular bastion of Québec Province, and the U.S., a foreign nation, borders the southwest.

Atlantic Canada's cultural diversity has had its effect on religion, too. The new and vast Maritime territories offered all foreign denominations the opportunity to start anew, especially oppressed minority groups, such as Mennonites, Ukrainians, Doukhobors, and Russian Jews. Christian faiths predominate today, but generally Canadians tend to be tolerant of different belief systems.

Prior to colonization and proselytizing, the Indian and Inuit populations practiced a kind of spiritual animism, deeply tied to the land. The trees, animals, and landforms were respected and blessed. Before food could be consumed or a tree felled, for example, it was appreciated for its life-sustaining sacrifice. Mythology also played an important part of spiritual life, along with rituals, shamanism, and potlatch ceremonies. Unfortunately, when the French and British arrived, they set about converting the natives. Today, native peoples struggle to maintain pieces of their old way of life and religion.

New Brunswick

The province is, in a sense, a miniature Canada, a provincial composite of Anglophones and Acadian Francophones who harmoniously coexist —the exception rather than the rule in a nation whose two dominant cultures are so often at odds. One suspects the harsh history that divided New Brunswick at its inception has run its course and mellowed. As Canada's only bilingual province, it steps to an agreeable duple beat.

The duality repeats itself in numerous ways. New Brunswick has an Anglophone region and another equally distinctive Acadian Francophone counterpart. The distinctions were set in stone centuries ago when the British evicted the Acadians from their original settlements and resettled the Loyalists. The Anglophone cities, towns, and settlements lie along the Fundy seacoast and throughout most of the Saint John River valley. The French-speaking Acadian region lies beyond there, on the province's outer rim in the northwestern woodlands along the Saint John River and on the coastlines of the Baie des Chaleurs, the open gulf, and the sheltered strait.

Historically, the Acadians have clung to a lean subsistence, while Anglos have prospered. The Acadians have traditionally been fishermen and loggers. Caraquet, on the Baie des Chaleurs, is Acadia's cultural heart, and the center for seafaring families along the shores of the bay. Moncton is another Acadian stronghold, which has emerged today with nouveau-riche status and wealth as a light-industry, distribution, and educational center. Acadian loggers ended up in northwestern New Brunswick. Known as Brayons, their domain is the Madawaska Republic, centered at Edmundston on the upper Saint John River near the Maine border.

The Anglophones, meanwhile, steer the provincial ship of state from Saint John, New Brunswick's largest city, major port, and industrial center. The Anglo aristocracy, many with roots traceable to Loyalist times, is entrenched at Fredericton, the provincial capital and home campus of the University of New Brunswick.

Roman Catholics, the majority of whom are Acadians, make up 52% of the population. Protestants are spread among the Baptist, United Church of Canada, Anglican, Pentecostal, and Presbyterian sects. An evangelical "Bible Belt" runs strong through Carleton and Victoria counties in the upper Saint John River valley and north of Moncton in Westmoreland County. Saint John has a small Jewish population.

Nova Scotia

Nova Scotia cut its teeth as a host in Halifax's early years when Her Majesty's Royal Navy sailed into the harbor. The duke of Kent and his French mistress led the social scene during the late 1700s, and modern-day royalty still comes calling.

But the "commoners" created the backbone of the province. German, Swiss, and French "foreign Protestants" arrived in 1753. In 1760, England resettled the prime Fundy seacoast with 12 shiploads of farmers (New England "planters") from its colonies farther south. For many visitors, the Scots of Nova Scotia typify the province: the first shipload of Scots docked at Pictou in 1773, and by 1830, there were 50,000 Scots in Pictou and Antigonish counties.

After the American Revolution, 25,000 United Empire Loyalists poured into Nova Scotia. Several thousand African Americans arrived during the War of 1812, followed by Irish immigrants from 1815 to 1850. Recent worldwide immigration has added more than 50 other ethnic groups to the province's cultural milieu.

Roman Catholics predominate at 37% of the mainland population and 62% on Cape Breton. Anglicans account for almost 16% on the mainland and 10% on Cape Breton. Other Protestant denominations present include the United Church of Canada, and the Baptist and Presbyterian churches. There is a small Jewish population in Halifax.

Prince Edward Island

PEI's 125,646 people are said to be Canada's most homogeneous population, and also the most densely concentrated, with 22.4 people per square km. The province's ancestry is 80% Anglo—a third Irish and the remainder Scottish. Acadians represent 17% of the population, of whom five percent speak French. The Micmacs form four percent of the population. PEI still lures immigrants, mainly from Ontario, Nova Scotia, New Brunswick, and Alberta.

Religious affiliations are important to islanders, who are overwhelmingly Christian. More than half are Roman Catholic, and the remainder belong to the Protestant sects, mainly Presbyterian and Anglican.

Newfoundland

In Labrador, Inuits, Innu, and Anglo-Labradorians inhabit the sparsely settled eastern coastline and remote central interior. The island of Newfoundland is an Anglo and Celtic cultural mix, whose psyche is linked to the sea and the Grand Banks's fisheries. Though a full-fledged province since 1949, Newfoundland was a colony of England's for centuries, hence you'll hear a clipped King's English accent in St. John's, a West Country dialect in some of the small, remote fishing villages (called outports), and a softly brushed Irish brogue on the Avalon Peninsula.

A merry penchant for a good time notwithstanding, Newfoundlanders are also a realistic people. The weather is always in the news and is reported as though life depended on it (as it often does for a fisherman at sea).

Newfoundland's Irish and French are Roman Catholics, and the English belong to the Anglican or United churches. Protestant evangelical denominations have strong followings and include the Pentecostals and Seventh-day Adventists. Labrador has a similar distribution, plus Moravians, members of the Church of the Nazarene, Plymouth Brethren, Baptists, and Methodists. There's also a small Jewish population in St. John's.

LANGUAGE

English is the language of choice for most Atlantic Canadians. But many do speak French in New Brunswick (which is officially bilingual), Prince Edward Island, and Nova Scotia. The French spoken here is not a patois; it's closely tied to the language that was brought to the continent by the original settlers from France. Some Dutch is spoken on Prince Edward Island, and, with the arrival of Asian immigrants starting around the 1960s, Chinese, Vietnamese, Punjabi, Hindi, and Urdu can be overheard in urban areas.

Canadian English is subtly different from American English, not only in pronunciation but also in lexicon ("Eh?"). For instance, Canadians say "serviettes" and "depot" while Americans would say "napkins" and "station." Spelling is a bit skewed as well, as Canadians have kept many of the British spellings; e.g., colour, centre. Nevertheless, these language variations pose no serious threat to communicating in the provinces.

ON THE ROAD
SIGHTSEEING HIGHLIGHTS

New Brunswick

Best Known For: The Bay of Fundy, with the world's most dramatic tides; picturesque covered bridges; the bizarre eroded formations at Rocks Provincial Park; Roosevelt Campobello International Park on Campobello Island; birdwatching and whalewatching expeditions around Grand Manan Island; the warm beaches of the Northumberland Strait; world-class salmon fishing on the Miramichi River; Acadian Historical Village and Kings Landing historical parks; the contrasting cultural legacies of Irish immigrants, United Empire Loyalists, and Acadians; vibrant weaving, quilting, pottery, and other craft industries.

Most Interesting City Sights: In Fredericton, Officers' Square and the Beaverbrook Art Gallery; Moncton's Magnetic Hill amusement park, and the Galerie d'Art et Musée Acadien at Université de Moncton; Saint John's historic Trinity Royal area, Old City Market, Partridge Island's poignant immigration landmarks, and Reversing Falls Rapids.

Outstanding Lodgings: Fredericton's Lord Beaverbrook and the nearby Kingsclear Hotel and Resort upriver at the Mactaquac Dam; Moncton's Hotel Beauséjour and Bonaccord House Bed and Breakfast; the Saint John Hilton, Delta Brunswick Hotel, and Parkerhouse Inn in Saint John; the Algonquin Resort in St. Andrews.

Outdoor Highlights: Hiking and backpacking in Mount Carleton Provincial Park; bicycle touring in the Saint John River Valley; houseboating on Grand Lake; canoeing on the Tobique and other rivers; swimming and boardsailing on the warm Northumberland Strait; sea-kayaking on the Baie des Chaleurs and Bay of Fundy; whalewatching off Grand Manan; birdwatching in the Tintamarre Marshes; fishing for Atlantic salmon, brook trout, shad, perch, bass, and other game fish.

Nova Scotia

Best Known For: Centuries of seafaring tradition; Cape Breton's indelible Scottish heritage;

the gorgeous rocky coastlines; the quintessential Atlantic fishing port of Peggy's Cove; photogenic lighthouses; the unforgettable roller coaster of the Cabot Trail scenic drive; Lunenburg's shipbuilding heritage and European-inspired architecture; the meticulously re-created Fortress of Louisbourg.

Most Interesting City Sights: Halifax's Citadel and the harborfront Historic Properties, the Art Gallery of Nova Scotia, the Nova Scotia Centre for Craft and Design, the Public Gardens; Cumberland County Museum at Amherst; Victoria Park at Truro; the Fisheries Museum of the Atlantic and the historic inns of Lunenburg; the Historic District at Shelburne; the Yarmouth County Museum in Yarmouth; the Acadia University Art Gallery at Wolfville; the waterfront Heritage Quay at Pictou; the Cossit House in Sydney; the fascinating Alexander Graham Bell National Historic Site.

Outstanding Lodgings: Halifax's Sheraton Halifax; the Best Western Glengarry at Truro; the Bluenose Lodge and Compass Rose Inn in Lunenburg; Cooper's Inn at Shelburne; the Pines Resort Hotel in Digby; the Tattingstone Inn in Wolfville; the Consulate Inn, Braeside Inn, and Pictou Lodge in Pictou; the high-rise Delta Mariner Hotel, Cambridge Suites Hotel, and the Holiday Inn Sydney in Sydney; the Keltic Lodge near Ingonish.

Outdoor Highlights: Sailing the sheltered waters of Halifax Harbour, Mahone Bay, and Bras d'Or Lake; hiking the varied trails of Cape Breton Highlands National Park; rafting the Fundy tidal bore on the Shubenacadie River; canoeing the extensive waterways of Kejimkujik National Park; fishing for trophy bluefins in St. George's Bay; golfing the world-class Cape Breton Highland Links at Ingonish Beach.

Prince Edward Island

Best Known For: *Anne of Green Gables* and the Lucy Maud Montgomery landmarks; succulent Malpeque oysters and all-you-can-eat lobster suppers; family holidays and the touristy summer scene at Cavendish; the Prince Edward Island National Park coastal wilderness.

Most Interesting City Sights: In Charlottetown, the rejuvenated interior of Province House, the Confederation Centre of the Arts exhibits, the murals at the All Souls' Chapel, the bookshop and archives at Beaconsfield, the Farmers' Market, Victoria Park, and the Royalty Oaks Woodlot; the Green Gables House in Cavendish.

Outstanding Lodgings: Charlottetown's Great George Inn, the main house at the Dundee Arms Inn, the Elmwood Heritage Inn, Charlottetown Hotel, and Prince Edward Hotel overlooking the harbor; the Silver Fox Inn and Loyalist Country Inn at Summerside; Dalvay by the Sea Hotel in Grand Tracadie.

Outdoor Highlights: Hot-air ballooning over northern Queens County; bicycling the easygoing roads everywhere; seal-watching excursions in Murray Harbour; horseback riding at Brudenell River Provincial Park; camping and hiking in Prince Edward Island National Park; deep-sea fishing charters from Rustico Harbour.

Newfoundland and Labrador

Best Known For: The otherworldly fjords and mountains of Gros Morne National Park; naturalist excursions for whale, seabird, and iceberg watching; outstanding fishing and hunting; knitted crafts; the Viking settlement at L'Anse aux Meadows; summer festivals or any excuse for music; and an abundance of moose.

Most Interesting City Sights: In St. John's, the Newfoundland Museum, Signal Hill National Historic Park, Quidi Vidi Battery, Bowring Park, and the Newfoundland Freshwater Resource Centre (fluvarium) at C.A. Pippy Park, the folk art at the Sticks and Stones House, and the Historic Train at Corner Brook; and the Labrador Heritage Museum at Happy Valley–Goose Bay.

Outstanding Lodgings: St. John's Prescott Inn Bed and Breakfast, Radisson Plaza Hotel, and Hotel Newfoundland; the Glynmill Inn and Best Western Mamateek Inn in Corner Brook; and the Aurora Hotel at Happy Valley–Goose Bay.

Outdoor Highlights: Iceberg-watching excursions around Twillingate; boat tours in the fjords of Gros Morne National Park; hiking in the Long Range Mountains; the seabird spectacles at Witless Bay and Cape St. Mary; the amazing light show of the aurora borealis; berry-picking outings in summertime; whalewatching off the east coast; salmon and arctic char fishing and big-game hunting in remote Labrador; whitewater canoeing and kayaking on the Upper Humber, Main, and Gander rivers; scuba diving off the Avalon Peninsula; caribou and polar bear–spotting flights in Labrador.

RECREATION AND ENTERTAINMENT

OUTDOOR ACTIVITIES

In Atlantic Canada's great outdoors, just about every form of recreation is feasible and first-rate: bicycling and hiking, mountaineering, scuba diving, houseboating, river rafting and canoeing, ocean and river kayaking, sailing, windsurfing, rockhounding, birdwatching, hunting, fishing, hockey, tennis, golf—you name it. No matter what the temperature is—35° C in summer or -15° C in winter—people can be found throughout the year enjoying some form of recreation.

The region's several national parks and scores of provincial parks come in a wide range of personalities, and offer an equally eclectic array of activities and facilities, from wilderness backpacking at New Brunswick's Mt. Carleton, say, to lounging in luxury at Cape Breton Highlands' Keltic Lodge resort.

Spectator sports popular in the Atlantic provinces include minor-league professional ice hockey, harness racing, and rugby.

Fishing and Hunting

For rural Maritimers, nature is the biggest playing field around. Hunting and fishing are year-round activities. Game selection depends on season, but hunters will find game birds and bigger game such as deer, moose, and bear.

Sportfishing here is legendary, especially for Atlantic salmon in New Brunswick and Cape Breton, and for tuna and other deep-sea species off Prince Edward Island and elsewhere. Ice-fishing is popular in the winter. See the travel chapters for specific suggestions.

Licenses are required for hunting or fishing. Visitors must purchase a nonresident license. Regulations vary from province to province; for more information, contact:

New Brunswick: Fish and Wildlife Branch, P.O. Box 6000, Maritime Forestry Complex, Fredericton, NB E3B 5H1, tel. (506) 453-2440.

Nova Scotia: Information Officer, Department of Lands and Forests, 1701 Hollis St., P.O. Box 698, Halifax, NS B3J 2T9, tel. (902) 424-6608.

Prince Edward Island: Environmental Resource, Fish and Wildlife Division, P.O. Box 2000, Charlottetown, PE C1A 7N8, tel. (902) 368-4683.

Newfoundland and Labrador: Department of Tourism and Culture, P.O. Box 8700, St. John's, NF A1B 4J6, tel. (800) 563-6353.

Camping and Hiking

The hiking season in the Maritime provinces spans spring to autumn; hiking and camping in Newfoundland and Labrador is relegated for the most part to the height of summer, except for the hardiest outdoorspersons. Coastal areas

beachcombing near St. Andrews

are generally free of pesky insects, but insect repellent is wise inland from May through September. Pets must be kept on a leash at all times in the national and provincial parks.

For specific information on backpacking, hiking, and recreational facilities, see the provincial travel chapters. Or call the respective tourism bureaus: in New Brunswick, tel. (800) 561-0123; in Nova Scotia, tel. (902) 424-6608; in Prince Edward Island, tel. (800) 463-4PEI; in Newfoundland and Labrador, tel. (800) 563-6353.

Cycling

Reasonably good roads and gorgeous scenery make the Maritimes excellent bicycling territory. Except on main arteries, particularly the Trans-Canada Hwy., car traffic is generally light and roads are safe for cyclists.

In New Brunswick, following the Saint John River valley and the complex of lakes north of Saint John makes for pleasant touring. The narrow roads that slice through Prince Edward Island's gentle countryside are sublime avenues for biking. Touring opportunities, through a variety of terrains, are numerous in Nova Scotia; probably the ultimate trip is the five- to six-day trek around Cape Breton's Cabot Trail.

Many shops rent decent- to good-quality road and mountain bikes. But if you plan to do some serious riding, you'll probably want to bring your own; most airlines will let you bring a bike for little or no extra charge. Bike shops are also excellent resources for tips on local riding conditions and for information on cycling club rides you can join. For more details, see the specific travel chapters.

Water Sports

With so much water surrounding and flowing through the provinces, **boating** opportunities are nearly infinite. Sailing is popular in the Bay of Fundy, around Passamaquoddy Bay, and in spacious Halifax and Sydney harbors, as well as in protected inland areas such as Bras d'Or Lake and the extensive inland waterways of New Brunswick's Saint John River and Mactaquac Lake. Canoeing is extremely popular on the region's hundreds of lakes and streams. Coastal kayaking is another adventure, especially along Cape Breton's turbulent Atlantic or inland on the more placid Bras d'Or.

Windsurfing in the Maritimes has a growing legion of fans. Windsurfers exploit breezy waters everywhere, and flock in particular to the beaches on the Gulf Stream–warmed Northumberland Strait. New Brunswick's Chaleur Provincial Park east of Dalhousie is situated at a prime coastal windsurfing area and has a windsurfing school with board rentals. On Prince Edward Island, the winds are best in northern Queens County on the Gulf of St. Lawrence.

This seabound region has no shortage of beaches, and most waterside provincial parks have a supervised **swimming** area. Warmest beaches are found along the Baie des Chaleurs ("Bay of Warmth") and the Northumberland Strait. The Bay of Fundy and Atlantic shores tend to be somewhat cooler, though conditions vary considerably throughout the region.

Winter Sports

Few visitors come to the Atlantic provinces outside of the prime travel season—late spring to early autumn. But you'll still find plenty to do should you arrive in winter. The national parks and many of the provincial parks stay open year-round. In winter, hiking routes are transformed by snow into excellent **cross-country ski** trails, and **snowmobilers** take to the woods and trails with a vengeance. Many city and regional parks, such as Halifax's Point Pleasant and Moncton's Centennial Park, also offer cross-country trails, along with frozen lakes for **ice skating** and **hockey.** Downhill skiers head to Marble Mountain in Newfoundland, or Sugarloaf Provincial Park and Mont-Farlagne, both in northwestern New Brunswick.

ENTERTAINMENT AND EVENTS

The Canada Council gives grants to theaters, dance troupes, orchestras, and arts councils to promote and keep the arts alive. Provincial tourism offices can tell you what's going on, or you can check out the local paper. See each travel chapter for specific listings detailing nightlife, theater, dance, and music options.

Museums

With an ethnic heritage as varied as Atlantic

Canada's, it's no wonder that museums are plentiful. Nova Scotia's 147 museums are among the region's best. Some museums are grand-scale provincial heritage sites, such as New Brunswick's King's Landing Historical Settlement—which recreates early Anglo years with authentic buildings and demonstrations—and Nova Scotia's magnificently rebuilt Fortress of Louisbourg National Historic Site.

On a smaller scale, county and town museums document regional historic, cultural, and economic subjects. Municipal or privately operated museums in towns and villages put the emphasis on local history or specialties.

NATIONAL HOLIDAYS	
New Year's Day	1 January
Good Friday	late March to mid-April
Easter Monday	early to mid-April
Victoria Day	third or fourth Monday in May
Canada Day	1 July
Labour Day	first Monday in September
Thanksgiving Day	second Monday in October
Remembrance Day	11 November
Christmas Day	25 December
Boxing Day	26 December

Festivals

It's said that Nova Scotia is the land of 100,000 summer festivals; one might say the same about the whole of Atlantic Canada. Each province seems to have one sort of festival or event taking place somewhere just about every day of summer's peak travel season. But special events and performances are held throughout the year. The events listed in the accompanying chart are just a small sampling; others are described in each travel chapter. Or you can stop by one of the tourism information offices found in just about every town to get more complete listings.

SHOPPING

Quilts, sweaters, hooked rugs, porcelains, and wooden carvings are deftly mixed among the watercolors, oils, and sculptures in many arts and crafts venues. The handwoven tartans of Loomcrofters (the weavers who designed the New Brunswick provincial and Royal Canadian Air Force tartans) at Gagetown, New Brunswick, and the work of the Madawaska Weavers, in New Brunswick's Acadian northwest, are well known on the provincial fashion scene.

New Brunswick's craftspeople specialize in yarn portraits, glass-blowing, pottery, wood sculptures, and pewter goods. The tourism department publishes the *Crafts Directory,* available at any tourism office. Antique buyers should head to Nova Scotia, where many historic sites

and homes have been converted into antique shops. The Nova Scotia tourism department produces a buyer's guide, available at tourism offices. Newfoundland is known for a wide selection of labradorite jewelry as well as down jackets. The basketry work of the Micmacs of Lennox Island (Prince Edward Island) has received much attention. PEI shops also carry beadwork, leather goods, silver jewelry, pottery, and woodcarvings.

Export Details

Americans can bring $400 worth of duty-free goods back into the U.S. after a 48-hour stay in Canada; $25 is the duty-free limit following stays of less than 48 hours. Gifts sent by mail and worth a total of $50 or less are duty-free also.

If you are interested in shopping for exotic wares, such as whalebone carvings or bearskin rugs, beware of customs regulations prohibiting the export of these goods; hundreds of animals and their by-products are listed on the International Trade in Endangered Species (CITES) list. For a list of imports banned in your home country, contact your nearest customs office before departure.

Likewise, the export from Canada of certain items considered to be cultural property is restricted. Such items include fossils, archaeological artifacts, archival material, some fine and decorative art, and some old or rare books. For details or an export permit, contact the **Canadian Cultural Property Export Review Board,**

SUMMERTIME EVENTS

JUNE

Charlottetown Festival	Charlottetown, PEI	late June-Sept.
Int'l Gathering of Clans	throughout NS	late June-Aug. (odd-numbered years)
Nova Scotia Int'l Tattoo	Halifax, NS	14 days, late June-early July

JULY

Highland Games	Antigonish, NS	three days, mid-July
Lobster Carnival	Summerside, PEI	seven days, mid-July
Loyalist Days Festival	Saint John, NB	seven days, mid-July
Exploits Valley Salmon Festival Grand Falls	Windsor, NF	five days, mid-July
Int'l Festival of Baroque Music	Île Lamèque, NB	two weekends, mid-July
Festival of Tartans	New Glasgow, NS	five days, mid-July
Hangashore Folk Festival	Corner Brook, NF	three days, mid-July
New World Island Fish, Fun, and Folk Festival	Twillingate, NF	four days, late July
Southern Shore Folk Festival	Ferryland, NF	two days, late July
Foire Brayonne	Edmundston, NB	five days, late July

AUGUST

Oyster Festival	Tyne Valley, PEI	five days, early Aug.
Labrador Canoe Regatta	Happy Valley, NF	two days, early Aug.
Acadian Festival	Caraquet, NB	12 days, early Aug.
Miramichi Folksong Festival	Newcastle, NB	six days, early Aug.
Newfoundland and Labrador Folk Festival	St. John's, NF	three days, early Aug.
Festival by the Sea	Saint John, NB	10 days, early Aug.
Gaelic Mod	St. Ann's, NS	seven days, early Aug.
Bakeapple Folk Festival	southern Labrador, NF	four days, mid-Aug.
Old Home Week	Charlottetown, PEI	nine days, mid-Aug.
Players Ltd. Grand Prix	Summerside, PEI	two days, mid-Aug.

SEPTEMBER

Acadian Festival	Mont-Carmel, PEI	three days, early Sept.

tel. (613) 990-4161, or write to them at Communications Canada, Ottawa, ON K1A 0C8.

Business Hours
Shopping hours are generally Mon.-Sat. 9 a.m.-5:30 p.m. Late shopping in most areas is available until 9 p.m. on Thursday and Friday. Generally, banks are open Mon.-Wed. 10 a.m.-4 p.m., Thurs.-Fri. 10 a.m.-5 p.m. A few banks may be open on Saturday, but all are closed on Sunday.

ACCOMMODATIONS AND FOOD

Reservations
The large local, national, and international hotel, resort, and motel groups listed in the "Hotel, Motel, and Resort Groups" chart have properties in Atlantic Canada; if you want to make advance reservations at any of their lodgings, simply phone the toll-free reservation center.

Reservations at many bed-and-breakfast and country inns can be made through a provincial reservations center. In Nova Scotia, most of the properties belong to Check In—the reservation service operated by the province—which has a toll-free phone line in North America. In New Brunswick, Dial-A-Night takes reservations at any of the provincial tourist offices at the border crossings. (For details, see the special topic, "Provincial Lodging Reservations and Information.")

Selected places to stay are detailed in the following chapters; the rates quoted are for a double room unless noted otherwise. Many motels and hotels promote discounted weekend, off-season, and senior rates. Call individual lodgings directly to find out what discounts might be available at any given time.

CAMPING
Whenever possible, reservations for campsites—especially at the national parks and most popular provincial parks—should be made at least six weeks in advance. Most provincial parks, however, do not accept reservations, but instead assign sites on a first-come, first-served basis. At those parks, it's best to arrive before noon to assure yourself a spot. Most provincial parks are open mid-May to mid-October. Most privately owned campsites accept reservations, which are more likely to be held if you send a small deposit.

FARMSTAYS AND HOSTELS

Farm Vacations
Farm vacations—a stay at a working farm with a room in the family homestead—are another option. In Nova Scotia, for example, more than 80 farms welcome guests; you will find rewarding opportunities to dabble in rural life, eat at the family's table, and meet other local folks. Nova Scotia's farm-vacation opportunities are listed in the *Farm and Country Bed and Breakfast Guide;* for a copy, contact the **Nova Scotia Farm and Country Bed and Breakfast Association** at Site 5, P.O. Box 16, RR 1, Elmsdale, NS B0N 1M0, tel. (902) 883-8496. For the farm-vacation locations in the other provinces, contact the provincial tourist offices in New Brunswick, Newfoundland, and Prince Edward Island.

Hostelling International
Formerly known as the Canadian Hostelling Association, this hostel operation maintains a network of budget-price hostels across Atlantic Canada. Their list of participating hostels tends to change as new ones are added and others are deleted from year to year. For details, call (902) 425-5450 or write to them at P.O. Box 3010 South, Halifax, NS B3J 3G6.

As this book went to press, HI hostels were located in New Brunswick at Fredericton, Campbellton, Alma (Fundy National Park), and Nelson; in Nova Scotia at Halifax, Kingston, Lake Ainslie (Cape Breton), Darling Lake, LaHave, Lunenburg, St. Peter's, South Milford, and Wentworth; in PEI at Charlottetown; in Newfoundland at Woody Point (Gros Morne National Park).

Details on some (but not all) hostels are included in the following chapters; for a reservation, call the hostel directly. For hostels not detailed in the chapters, call Hostelling Interna-

PROVINCIAL LODGING RESERVATIONS AND INFORMATION

New Brunswick

The province sponsors a free **Dial-A-Night** reservations system for all lodgings and privately operated campgrounds. Visitors may also make a reservation at any of the provincial tourist information centers situated at the entry points to New Brunswick. The provincial *Getaway and Stay in New Brunswick* is a collection of lodgings' advertisements with special-interest packages.

Nova Scotia

More than 90% of the province's lodgings and campgrounds (they're all listed with details in the provincial *Travel Guide*) are affiliated with **Check In**, the province-sponsored, free reservation system. To make a reservation, call (902) 425-5781 in Halifax, (800) 565-0000 from the rest of Canada, or (800) 341-6096 from the U.S.; you can also write to Check In at 1800 Argyle St., Halifax, NS B3J 3N8, Canada. The tourist office publishes *Nova Scotia Inside*, a booklet that advertises special packages offered by the lodgings.

Prince Edward Island

Hundreds of lodgings are listed and described in the provincial *Visitors Guide*. If you have questions about where to stay, call **Dial The Island**, the provincial information service at (902) 368-5555, (800) 565-7421 in Atlantic Canada, or (800) 565-0267 from elsewhere in North America. **Murphy Tour Service Central Reservations**, tel. (902) 892-0606, is another source; write to them at 64 Great George St., Charlottetown, PE C1A 4K3.

Another extremely useful reservations service is offered by **Paradise Island Reservations**, tel. (800) 265-6161, which can book all sorts of accommodations islandwide at no charge. Its hours are daily 8 a.m.-midnight, Atlantic standard time. The **Bed and Breakfast and Country Inns Association of Prince Edward Island**, P.O. Box 2551, Charlottetown, PE C1A 8C2, produces a handy booklet, available at tourist information centers, which details some 80 or so member lodgings.

Newfoundland

The province has no central reservation system. The properties are listed with details in the provincial *Travel Guide;* for reservations, contact the lodgings directly.

---

tional's main office in Halifax, tel. (902) 425-5450, and they'll supply the phone numbers.

CANADA SELECT

Lodgings in Atlantic Canada are graded by a standard established by Canada Select, a nationwide grading system. The lodgings are grouped in four categories: hotels/motels; inns and bed and breakfasts; resorts (with recreational facilities); and sports lodges and cottages (fishing/hunting lodges, cottages, and cabins).

The gradings range from one to five stars. At a one-star property, expect basic, clean, and comfortable accommodations with no frills; a two-star lodging has the same basics with some amenities. The three- to five-star lodgings have better-to-deluxe accommodations with an increasing range of facilities and services. The provincial lodgings inspectors are *very* stringent in awarding star gradings; comparable properties (especially in the three- and four-star categories) in other parts of the world would rate higher grades.

The system is voluntary and is still too new to include the majority of the lodgings, so an absence of a star grading carries no weight. The provincial tourist offices emphasize the Canada Select program, and the provincial tourist guides include the star grades with the properties' details; the following chapters do not.

Rates more or less correspond with the star grades; the lowest grades are the cheapest places to stay, and the hotels and resorts at the scale's higher end cost considerably more. Some of Atlantic Canada's top-grade hotels and resorts have not been rated as highly by Canada Select as their reputations would seem to justify. But the owners of these establishments know what their lodgings are worth according to world standards, and guests pay top dollar, regardless of Canada Select's rating.

HOTEL, MOTEL, AND RESORT GROUPS

ATLANTIC INNS OF NEWFOUNDLAND

The Tudor-style Glynmill Inn in Corner Brook, one of Newfoundland's prettiest hotels, is this Newfoundland-owned company's grande dame. For reservations at the Glynmill, call (800) 563-4400 or (709) 634-5181. The company's other Newfoundland properties are motels situated on or near the Trans-Canada Hwy., including: Mount Peyton Hotel, Grand Falls–Windsor, tel. (800) 563-4894 or (709) 489-2251; Albatross Motel, Gander, tel. (800) 563-4900 or (709) 256-3956; and Sinbad's, Gander, tel. (800) 563-4900 or (709) 651-2678. The toll-free phone numbers are valid only within Atlantic Canada.

AUBERGE WANDLYN INNS

This New Brunswick-owned company started in its home province and now has motels throughout the Maritimes. The chain emphasizes reasonable rates —ask about special weekend rates, supersavers, and senior discounts.

Locations include: Edmundston, Fredericton, Moncton, Newcastle, St. Stephen, and Woodstock, New Brunswick; Amherst, Antigonish, Annapolis Royal, Bridgewater, Dartmouth, Halifax (outskirts), Kentville, Port Hawkesbury, and Sydney, Nova Scotia; and Charlottetown, Prince Edward Island.

For reservations, call (800) 561-0000 from central and eastern Canada; (506) 452-0000 from Fredericton, New Brunswick; (800) 561-0006 from the United States.

BEST WESTERN

Some of Best Western's properties are landmarks, such as the Shiretown Inn at St. Andrews—the resort town's first hotel and now a splendidly restored historic inn. Others are strictly highway motels. But regardless, all the lodgings are better than average.

Locations include Bathurst, Dalhousie, Grand Falls (Grand Falls/Grand-Sault), Dieppe, and Saint Andrews, New Brunswick; Antigonish, Dartmouth, Kingston, Sydney, Truro, and Yarmouth, Nova Scotia; Charlottetown, Prince Edward Island; and Corner Brook and St. John's, Newfoundland.

For reservations, call (800) 528-1234 from Canada and the U.S.; Australia, tel. (02) 212-6444 or 008-222-166; France, tel. (331) 4487-4040; Germany, tel. 49 6196 4710, 0130 44 55; Great Britain, tel. (4481) 541-0050, (081) 541-0033; Ireland, tel.

353 1 762366, 1-800-709-101; Japan, tel. (81-3) 3572-7003, 0120-42 1234; and New Zealand, tel. (649) 520 5418, (09) 520-5418.

CANADIAN PACIFIC HOTELS AND RESORTS

Canada's top-notch hotel group is well represented across Atlantic Canada with high-quality, stunning hotels in the major cities and the bonus of the Algonquin, a gorgeous, Tudor-style resort spread across manicured grounds with gardens at St. Andrews, New Brunswick.

Besides the Algonquin, the group has hotels in Moncton, New Brunswick; Halifax, Nova Scotia; Charlottetown, Prince Edward Island; and St. John's, Newfoundland.

For reservations, call (800) 268-9411 in Canada, (800) 828-7447 in the United States. Reservations from overseas may be made through any Canadian Airlines International reservations office.

CHOICE HOTELS INTERNATIONAL

This company is composed of a number of different groups: the Journey's End and Sleep Inn motels are clean, comfortable, and inexpensive, while the Quality Inn properties are a notch up with fancier surroundings and facilities. The values are hard to beat, and the rooms are always in demand; make reservations beforehand.

The Journey's End motels are located in New Brunswick at Bathurst, Campbellton, Edmundston, Fredericton, Moncton (two), Newcastle, and Saint John; in Nova Scotia at Amherst, Bridgewater, Dartmouth, New Glasgow, Sydney, Truro, and Yarmouth; in Newfoundland at Corner Brook and St. John's. There's a Sleep Inn at New Minas, Nova Scotia, and a Quality Inn at Summerside on Prince Edward Island.

For reservations, call (800) 221-2222 from Canada and the U.S.; France, tel. (05) 908536; Germany, tel. (0130) 85-5522; Ireland, tel. (800) 500-600; United Kingdom, tel. 0 (800) 44-44-44; Australia, tel. (008) 090-600; Japan, tel. (0120) 123-999 (Tokyo, tel. 03-3354-2400); and New Zealand, tel. 0 (800) 808-228 (Auckland, tel. 09-309-4420). Reservations for the Journey's End lodgings may also be made by calling (800) 668-4200 in Canada and the United States.

(continues)

CLAYTON INNS

Another Newfoundland-owned company, Clayton Inns has stylish, above-average motor hotels situated on or near the TransCanada Hwy. from St. John's to Corner Brook, including Hotel Gander, tel. (800) 563-2988 or (709) 256-3931, and Fox Moth Motel, tel. (709) 256-3535, in Gander; Best Western Mamateek Inn, tel. (800) 563-8600 or (709) 639-8901, in Corner Brook; and the Best Western Travellers Inn, tel. (800) 528-1234 or (709) 722-5540, in St. John's. The toll-free phone numbers are valid only in Atlantic Canada.

COUNTRY INNS AND SUITES

These well-designed motor hotels with reasonably priced, junior- and full-size suites are always in demand, especially for families. Reservations are wise. The properties are located in Bathurst, Moncton, and Saint John, New Brunswick; and in New Glasgow and Dartmouth, Nova Scotia. For reservations, call (800) 456-4000 from Canada and the United States.

DAYS INNS

This chain offers clean, pleasant rooms at very reasonable prices. You'll find them in Nova Scotia on the outskirts of Halifax and in Antigonish.

For reservations, call (800) 633-1414 from Canada and the United States.

DELTA HOTELS

This Canadian-owned company is a class operation; expect fine hotels with splendid facilities in notable settings. Locations include Saint John, New Brunswick; and Halifax and Sydney, Nova Scotia. For reservations, call (800) 268-1133 in Canada (Toronto, tel. 416-927-1133); from the U.S., call (800) 877-1133.

The Delta Hotels properties may also be booked through the Supranational Hotels' reservations centers: from Canada and the U.S., call (800) 843-3311; France, tel. 0505 0011 (Paris, tel. 4071-2121); Germany, tel. 0130-6969 (Cologne, tel. 0221-219-672); London, England, tel. (071) 937 8033; Dublin, Ireland, tel. (01) 605-000; and Tokyo, Japan, tel. (03) 3545 9571.

HILTON HOTELS CORPORATION

Luxurious trappings and superior facilities are the hallmarks of the Hilton Hotels. In Atlantic Canada,

you'll find them in Saint John and Halifax. For reservations, call (800) 268-9275 in Canada (Toronto, tel. 416-362-3771); U.S., tel. (800) HILTONS; Australia, tel. 008-22-22-55 (Sydney, tel. 267-6000); France, tel. 05-31 80 40 (Paris, tel. 01-46 87-34-80); Germany, tel. (0130) 2345 (Frankfurt, tel. 069-25 01 02); Japan, tel. 0120-489852 (Tokyo, tel. 03-213-4053); Auckland, New Zealand, tel. (9) 775-874; and the United Kingdom, tel. 0800-289-303 (London, tel. 01-631-1767).

HOLIDAY INNS

These properties are motor hotels rather than generic motels and often serve as hubs of the local social scene. Expect spacious rooms, exemplary dining, nighttime entertainment, and an array of facilities.

Locations include Dartmouth, Halifax, and Sydney, Nova Scotia; Clarenville, Corner Brook, Gander, and St. John's, Newfoundland.

For reservations, call (800) HOLIDAY in Canada (Toronto, tel. 416-486-6400) and the U.S.; Australia, tel. 008-221-066 (Sydney, tel. 02-2614922); Paris, tel. 1-43553903; Germany, tel. 0130-5678; Dublin, Ireland, tel. 01-725499; Japan, tel. 0120-381489 (Tokyo, tel. 03-54850311); New Zealand, tel. 0800-44-2222. From the United Kingdom: London, tel. (071) 722-7755; Birmingham, tel. (021) 643-4480; Glasgow, tel. (041) 221 9510; Leeds, tel. (0532) 461-280; and Manchester, tel. (061) 834-3464.

HOWARD JOHNSON HOTELS AND LODGES

These moderately priced motor hotels feature spacious rooms, facilities such as health centers and, in many locations, a pool. Ask about the special prices for seniors and families. The properties are located in Campbellton, Edmundston, Fredericton, Moncton, and Saint John, New Brunswick. For reservations, call (800) 446-4656 in Canada and the U.S.; Sydney, Australia, tel. (612) 319-6624; Tokyo, tel. (81) 3 3276-8121/8118; Paris, tel. (33) 1 4293 0012; Germany, tel. 6102-25002; and Croydon, England, tel. (44) 81 688-1418.

ITT SHERATON CORPORATION

These stunningly designed waterfront hotels are noted for top-quality accommodations, luxurious amenities, and comfortable ambience. You'll find them in Fredericton and Halifax. For reservations, call (800) 325-3535 in Canada and the U.S.; Australia, tel. 008-073535; France, tel. 05-907635; Germany, tel. 0130-853535; Ireland, tel. (800) 535353; Japan, tel. 0120-003535; New Zealand, tel. 0800-44-3535; and the United Kingdom, tel. 0800-353535.

KEDDY'S HOTELS AND INNS

Atlantic Canadian–owned, the Keddy properties range from landmark hotels like the high-rise Lord Beaverbrook Hotel in Fredericton to the newer, sprawling Bathurst Hotel, both in New Brunswick. The hotels feature comfortably appointed rooms, health centers with free facilities for guests, and dining rooms that serve some of the best food in town. Locations include Saint John, Fredericton (two), Moncton (two), and Bathurst, New Brunswick; Halifax (outskirts), Dartmouth, Truro, Port Hastings, and Sydney, Nova Scotia; and Summerside, Prince Edward Island. For reservations, call (800) 561-7666 in Canada and the United States.

PROVINCE OF NOVA SCOTIA

Nova Scotia's provincial resorts appeal to the carriage trade, the type of traveler who likes the understated ambience of a resort lodge with a tony rustic setting and furnishings, gourmet dining, a remote location with manicured grounds, and the genteel sports of golf or fly-fishing.

Provincial resorts in Nova Scotia are the Pines Resort Hotel at Digby and the Keltic Lodge at Ingonish Beach, Cape Breton, and the Liscombe Lodge at Liscomb Mills.

For reservations, contact Check In, the provincial reservations center, in Halifax at tel. (902) 425-5781; in the rest of Canada at (800) 565-0000; and the U.S. at (800) 341-6096. Ask for the resorts' phone numbers if you want to contact the lodgings directly.

RADISSON HOTELS INTERNATIONAL

Radisson's fine hotel in St. John's, Newfoundland, is splendidly designed, comfortably outfitted, replete with facilities, and boasts incredible harbor views. It is, unfortunately, Radisson's only hotel in Atlantic Canada. For reservations, call (800) 333-3333 in Canada and the U.S.; Australia, tel. (008) 333-333; France, tel. (05) 90-06-78; Germany, tel. (0130) 81-44-42; Ireland, tel. (800) 55-7474; Japan, tel. (0031) 12-3531; New Zealand, tel. (088) 44-3333; and the United Kingdom, tel. (0800) 89-1999.

RAMADA RENAISSANCE HOTELS

Ramada's choicest hotels are the Renaissance properties, and its luxuriously appointed hotel in Dartmouth, Nova Scotia, is one of the finest. For reservations, call (800) 854-7854 in Canada; U.S., tel. (800) 228-9898; United Kingdom, tel. 0800-181-737; Germany, tel. (0130) 2340; France, tel. 0590 4093; Sydney, Australia, tel. (612) 251-8888; and Japan, tel. (0120) 222-332.

RODD HOTELS AND RESORTS

This locally owned hotel company is Prince Edward Island's lodgings standard bearer. The handsome Loyalist Country Inn at Summerside is the newest hotel, the Charlottetown Hotel in the capital is the oldest. Two full-facility resorts are situated within provincial-park settings at either end of the island; near Cardigan (Roseneath, Brudenell River Provincial Park), and O'Leary (Woodstock, Mill River Provincial Park).

Other Rodd locations include two more properties in Charlottetown; one in Moncton, New Brunswick; and two in Yarmouth, Nova Scotia. For reservations, call (800) 565-RODD in Canada and the United States.

FOOD AND DRINK

Maritime cuisine reflects its English and Acadian heritages, with some local specialties that reflect the character of the region and its available ingredients. The down-home dining is irresistible: a bountiful lobster feed in one of the community halls on Prince Edward Island; pickled Solomon Gundy herring sold from a roadside peddler's cart or planked Atlantic salmon cooked over an open fire at a resort in Nova Scotia; and seal-flipper pie, moose burgers, and roasted wild game—partridge, rabbit, and caribou— in Newfoundland.

Coastal dwellers nibble on dulse—a dried, purple, iodine-rich Fundy seaweed; in the spring they eat a cream soup made from ostrich fern fronds. Smelts are fried or baked. Vegetables and potatoes are stewed. Typical desserts include walnut toffee, trifle, homemade ice cream, or Ganong chocolates from St. Stephen.

While Anglo cuisine features red meats, Acadian fare is based on seafood. Common Acadian-style dishes include seafood chowder, shellfish (shrimp and queen crab), and fish (especially mackerel, herring, and cod). For variety, Acadian menus might offer chicken *fricot* (chicken stew), *poutine râpé* (boiled or deep-fried pork and grated raw potatoes, rolled into a ball and dipped in corn or maple syrup or molasses), and desserts such as sugar pie, apple dumplings, or cinnamon buns. Acadian cooking may be terribly hard on the waistline, but it's delicious.

Save room for an Acadian culinary variation in Edmundston or another of the Madawaska area towns. Brayon cooking, as it's known, creates *les ployes*—buckwheat pancakes that are splashed with butter, molasses, or maple syrup or used as a wrapper for spicy pâté or seafood.

The Danes immigrated to Nova Scotia and New Brunswick in the late 19th century and still cling to Scandinavian ways at New Denmark in New Brunswick's upper Saint John River valley. A typical Danish meal may consist of homemade sausage, roast beef and red cabbage, ground beef patties, and apple cake.

Alcohol

French imports and local wines from the Jost and Grand-Pré wineries are available at many fine restaurants. Regional and locally brewed

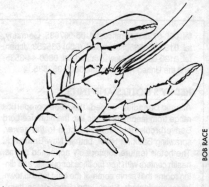

BOB RACE

beers are also popular; favorites include Schooner and Keith's. The Granite Brewery in Halifax produces a variety of brews, including stouts and seasonal specialties, but these beers may be scarce outside Nova Scotia.

As elsewhere in Canada, strict regulations govern alcohol consumption. Licensed restaurants, dining rooms, and cocktail lounges serve liquor daily 11 a.m.-2 a.m. Beverage rooms with beer, wine, and draft beer are open Mon.-Wed. 10 a.m.-11 p.m., Thurs.-Sat. to midnight; lounge hours are Mon.-Sat. 11 a.m.-2 a.m.; and cabarets are open nightly 7 p.m.-3 a.m. Alcohol is sold at the government liquor stores, open Mon.-Thurs. 10 a.m.-6 p.m., Fri. to 10 p.m., Sat. to 5 p.m. The minimum drinking age is 19.

GETTING THERE

BY CAR

Most visitors drive to Atlantic Canada. From the U.S., Hwy. 9 heads east from Bangor, Maine, and enters New Brunswick—Atlantic Canada's main land gateway—at St. Stephen near the coast. The TransCanada Highway from central Canada (another main entry route) is more roundabout and follows the St. Lawrence River through Québec Province to enter northwestern New Brunswick at Saint-Jacques near Edmundston. Once in New Brunswick, you can take a car ferry to Prince Edward Island or continue driving east into Nova Scotia. From Nova Scotia, you can get a car ferry to Newfoundland, from where you can take another to Labrador.

Labrador can also be reached from Québec Province on Hwy. 389, a 581-km drive that takes 10 hours; the two-lane road starts at Baie-Comeau on the St. Lawrence River's northern bank and wends through the province's wilderness to enter western Labrador at Labrador City.

The TransCanada

The TransCanada Highway is a godsend within Atlantic Canada. The high-speed highway skirts across New Brunswick past Fredericton and Moncton, crosses the Chignecto Isthmus into Nova Scotia near Amherst, and speeds east to Cape Breton. The major highway on Prince Edward Island is also designated as the TransCanada, as is the major thoroughfare on the island of Newfoundland.

Scenic vistas are not, however, among the highway's greatest attributes, and long hours on the route can be incredibly boring. Nonetheless, the benefits of direct routes and expressway speed outweigh the tedium in some cases.

Ferries

Depending on where you're going, getting around the region generally includes one or more sea crossings. The TransCanada crosses Nova Scotia's Cape Breton, ending at North Sydney, where two ferry routes leave for the island of Newfoundland: one to Port aux Basques at the island's southwestern corner, the other to Argentia on the southeastern Avalon Peninsula near St. John's. The most popular (and usually crowded) ferry crossing to Prince Edward Island is from Caribou (near Pictou), Nova Scotia. It crosses to Wood Islands, PEI, southeast of Charlottetown.

Vehicle Insurance

Vehicle insurance ($200,000 minimum liability) is mandatory, and if there's an accident, the RCMP will ask the drivers for proof of financial responsibility. Nonresident drivers can obtain such proof in the form of a **Canadian Non-Resident Inter-Provincial Motor Vehicle Liability Insurance Card,** available from insurance companies outside Canada.

Car Rental

All the major car-rental companies—Budget, Thrifty, Hertz, Avis, and Tilden—have offices at the airports and usually in the adjacent cities. Some have branches in other towns. A few outfits like Budget run periodic local or regional price specials; call at the city (not airport) locations to inquire. Renting a car from a local company is another way to trim costs.

BY RAIL

VIA Rail Canada, the federal passenger-rail service, is best known for the transcontinental rail route, the spectacular journey from Vancouver to Toronto through the Rockies and central Canada's farmlands. But VIA Rail has replicated the transcontinental route's deluxe trappings and service in Atlantic Canada with its "Easter-

ly Service." The service, begun in spring 1993, is featured on the **Montréal-to-Halifax** routes aboard a vintage fleet of stainless-steel trains, similar to the transcontinental route on the "Canadian" run from Vancouver to Toronto.

The trains to Halifax take two different routes. The **Ocean** departs Montréal, follows the St. Lawrence River's southern shore to northern New Brunswick, cuts across the province to Moncton, speeds into Nova Scotia via Amherst and Truro, and finishes at Halifax. The **Atlantic** heads through Québec's eastern townships, crosses Maine, U.S.A., and enters New Brunswick at Saint John before traveling to Moncton, from where it follows the same route as the Ocean to Halifax. Both trains make stops at towns along the way.

Each of the revamped trains includes a domed car with three small salons (one of which is a replica of the transcontinental's mural lounge), a dining car with art-deco trappings, and another more informal car designed for lighter dining. Interiors on all the cars have been refurbished. VIA Rail promises home cooking, and the dining-car meals are served all day, rather than at sittings. A free continental breakfast is served in the dome car, and beverages are complimentary as well. Overnight accommodations (from $209 pp, OW) include one-passenger roomettes or two-passenger bedroom compartments with a private toilet in the room or nearby. Each sleeping car also has a shower room.

A less-expensive coach fare (from $134 pp, OW) is available also. To further trim a fare price, you may want to check out a VIA Canrailpass, similar to Europe's rail passes. The pass provides a discounted coach-class fare and allows 12 days of rail travel within a 30-day period. Senior citizens (60 years or older) and students (the ticket agent will ask to see a student identification card) get 10% off the price of the pass. Further, the "Discount Days" promotion in Atlantic Canada shaves 40% off all fares during the off-season; restrictions apply, and the ticket has to be purchased at least five days before departure. All fares are highest during the peak tourist season, early June-Sept., and holidays; lower during spring and autumn; and lowest in winter, aside from holidays.

If you are heading for Atlantic Canada from Vancouver, you may also want to consider a **transcontinental connection.** From Vancouver, the trip on the Canadian takes three and a half days to Toronto. After changing trains there, it's four more hours on an express train to Montréal. A Vancouver-Toronto ticket is $266-443 pp, OW, in coach; $425-708 pp, OW, for an upper berth or $483-708 pp, OW, for a lower berth; or $555-924 pp, OW, for a roomette (two passengers minimum for a larger roomette). A Toronto-Montréal ticket is $45-75 pp, OW in coach, or $105 in first class (a meal and liquor are included).

For reservations or information, contact the nearest VIA Rail Canada office or your travel agent. Also see the accompanying "VIA Rail Canada Contacts" chart. You can write to VIA Rail directly c/o Marketing Department, P.O. Box 8116, Station A, Montréal, PQ H3C 3N3.

BY AIR

Most long-haul international and domestic flights set down at Toronto, Ottawa, or Montréal with connecting or ongoing flights to Halifax and Atlantic Canada's other major gateways. Halifax, the region's air gateway, also gets nonstop international flights from Bermuda, Glasgow, London, Boston, and Newark on Air Canada; Boston on Canadian Airlines International. A few nonstop transatlantic flights arrive at St. John's and Gander.

Air Canada and Canadian Airlines International

compete for national dominance. Among the best airfare deals is Air Canada's "Seat Saver," a discounted fare of as much as 60% off the price of a regular economy ticket. Restrictions apply, and seats are limited—it's wise to make a reservation as far ahead as possible. Both of the airlines offer a 10% discount to senior citizens. Air Canada also has a service agreement with Continental Airlines in the U.S., making for easy connections from America cities. From any city served by Continental, you first fly to Newark International Airport, one of the airline's

---

VIA RAIL CANADA CONTACTS

ATLANTIC CANADA

New Brunswick: Moncton, tel. (506) 857-9830; Saint John, tel. (506) 642-2916; from other areas, call (800) 561-3952.

Nova Scotia: Halifax, tel. (902) 429-8421; from other areas, call (800) 561-3952.

Prince Edward Island: Call (800) 561-3952.

Newfoundland: CN Rail handles the rail ticketing in St. John's, Gander, Grand Falls–Windsor, Corner Brook, Stephenville, and Channel–Port-aux-Basques; for more information call VIA Rail at (800) 561-9181.

ONTARIO AND QUÉBEC

Ontario: Hamilton, tel. (416) 522-7533; Kingston, tel. (613) 544-5600; London, tel. (519) 672-5722; Ottawa, tel. (613) 244-8289; Toronto, tel. (416) 366-8411; Windsor, tel. (519) 256-5511; from area codes 416, 519, 613, or 705, call (800) 361-1235; from area code 807, call (800) 561-8630.

Québec Province: Montréal, tel. (514) 871-1331; Québec City, tel. (418) 692-3940; from other areas, call (800) 361-5390.

From other provinces and territories: Call (800) 561-8630.

INTERNATIONAL CONTACTS

U.S.: Call (800) 561-9181 or contact a travel agent.

Australia: Walshes World, 92 Pitt St., G.P.O. Box 51, Sydney, New South Wales 2000; tel. (02) 232-7499.

Germany: Canada Reise Dienst, Rathausplatz 2, D-2070 Ahrensburg/Hamburg; tel. 04102 51167.

Japan: Japan Travel Bureau, 1-6-4 Marunouchi, Chiyoda-ku, Tokyo 100; tel. (03) 3284-7376.

New Zealand: Walshes World, Second Floor, Dingwall Building, 87 Queen St., Private Bag 92136, Auckland 1; tel. (09) 3793708.

United Kingdom: Long-Haul Leisurail, P.O. Box 113, Peterborough, England, PE1 1LE; tel. (0733) 51780.

major hubs. From there you'll board Air Nova and be in Halifax in less than two hours. Another very workable connection is Continental's service from Houston to Toronto, connecting to Air Canada for the flight to Halifax or any of the other major cities in Atlantic Canada.

GETTING AROUND

BY AIR

Halifax International Airport, 40 minutes from Halifax, serves as Atlantic Canada's regional air hub. Air Nova/Air Canada and Air Atlantic/Canadian Airlines International saturate the region with frequent flights to other provincial gateways. Reservations and information are handled by Air Nova/Air Canada in Atlantic Canada and through Air Canada worldwide; for details from the U.S., call (800) 776-3000.

Air travel is the transportation of choice throughout the provinces. While the airlines haven't put bus or ferry travel out of business, the airports are usually crowded, and the flights are often filled. Be sure to confirm your flights beforehand, and be at the airport 30 minutes before departure. Passengers not checked in 10 minutes before the flight may forfeit their seats to any stand-by passengers waiting to board.

BY FERRY

The region is webbed with an efficient ferry service. **Marine Atlantic** handles most of the interprovincial links in the Atlantic Provinces. Routes include: Cape Tormentine, New Brunswick, to Borden, Prince Edward Island; Saint John, New Brunswick, to Digby, Nova Scotia; North Sydney, Nova Scotia, to Port aux Basques and Argentia, Newfoundland, plus several coastal routes in Newfoundland; and Bar Harbor, Maine, to Yarmouth, Nova Scotia. For ferry reservations and information, call Marine Atlantic at (902) 794-5700 in the Maritimes, (800) 341-7981 in the United States.

The **Prince of Fundy Cruises'** *Scotia Prince* links Portland, Maine, to Yarmouth, Nova Scotia. For more information, write P.O. Box 4216, Station A, Portland, ME 04101, in the U.S.; or P.O. Box 609, Yarmouth, NS B5A 4B6, in Canada. Or call (800) 565-7900 in the Maritime provinces,

(800) 482-0955 in Maine only, (800) 341-7540 in the rest of the United States.

Northumberland Ferries operates between Caribou, Nova Scotia, and Wood Islands, in eastern Prince Edward Island. For additional details, call (800) 565-0201 from Nova Scotia or PEI, (902) 566-3838 from other locations.

BY BUS

The provinces are obliged by the government to provide relatively cheap, long-haul transportation. Government-funded or privately operated buses chug along on all the major highways and pull off to stop and pick up passengers at designated places in main towns.

A few cities, such as St. John's, also have commuter bus links with the outlying, smaller ports. If you have a day on your hands and no other plans, consider an early-morning bus to an unexplored area, and a late-afternoon or early-evening return to the city. Few outsiders do it, but mixing among the locals on a bus circuit is a terrific way to explore a province. Public transit in the cities is spottier: there's none in places like Charlottetown or Amherst where you might expect it, but more than enough in the larger communities like Halifax, Sydney, and St. John's.

TRAVEL PACKAGES

Hotel–Rental Car Packages

Air Canada Vacations, Air Canada's travel division, markets a car-rental/hotel package for Halifax. The package gives you a room at the Airport Hotel ($45 pp) or the Delta Barrington ($68 pp) and a rental car for either three or five days in a choice of vehicle categories ranging from a small economy car ($118 for three days or $237 for five days) to a minivan ($200 or $400, respectively). The first 200 km (on a three-

(continues on page 36)

BUS TOURS

The following Canadian travel companies market bus tours within Atlantic Canada's provinces.

ATLANTIC TOURS LTD.

Atlantic Tours Ltd. markets two coach tours from Halifax: an eight-day "Atlantic Maritimes" trip ($1019 pp) through the Maritime provinces, offered early June to early Oct.; and a nine-day "Newfoundland" tour ($1119 pp), offered mid-June to mid-September. The price includes some meals with taxes and tips.

Expect to cover a lot of ground punctuated with many of Atlantic Canada's sightseeing highlights. The Maritimes trip heads out of Halifax, stops at Peggy's Cove on the Atlantic, crosses the peninsula to Grand-Pré and Port Royal on the Fundy coastline, and travels by ferry across the Fundy to New Brunswick's Saint John, Fundy National Park and Rocks Provincial Park. From there, another ferry takes the tour across the Northumberland Strait to Prince Edward Island's Charlottetown for sightseeing and the *Anne* musical and then heads for the national park and the Green Gables house. A third ferry crossing takes the tour back to Nova Scotia and a Cabot Trail drive with stops on Cape Breton at Baddeck and the Fortress of Louisbourg before returning to Halifax.

The Newfoundland trip also departs from Halifax and starts with a drive to North Sydney on Cape Breton for the ferry to Port aux Basques. From there, the drive follows the TransCanada Highway with side trips to Gros Morne and Terra Nova national parks and the museums at Twillingate and Gander. The trip finishes at St. John's with a city tour and a sightseeing boat trip to the seabird sanctuaries at Witless Bay. The return ferry departs from Argentia near St. John's and docks at North Sydney for the ride back to Halifax.

The company also has "Mini Tours in the Maritimes" from Halifax; the short trips are segments of the foregoing "Maritimes" tour. For example, the "Annapolis Valley–New Brunswick–Prince Edward Island" tour ($597 pp) is a five-day sampler. The "Prince Edward Island–Cape Breton" tour ($640 pp) includes both islands in five days, while the "Cape Breton Tour" ($419 pp) visits a single location for three days.

For details, call (902) 423-6242 in Halifax, tel. (506) 849-3331 in Rothesay, NB, or (800) 565-7173 elsewhere in Canada and the United States. Or write to Atlantic Tours, Ltd. at P.O. Box 3596, Halifax, NS B3J 3J2, or at 40 Neck Rd., Rothesay, NB E2G 1J5.

AQUILA TOURS

Aquila Tours, a New Brunswick–based outfit, offers a short two-night plan for the Tattoo in Halifax and a 14-day swing through Labrador and Newfoundland. For details, write to them at 107 Germain St., P.O. Box 6895, Station "A," Saint John, NB E2L 4S3, or call (506) 633-1224 or (800) 561-9091 in Atlantic Canada.

HANOVER HOLIDAYS

Hanover Holidays, a tour company based in Hanover, Ontario, offers a joint Maritimes-and-Newfoundland tour, and a Newfoundland-only tour. Tours depart from the Ottawa area and from Toronto.

The 16-day "Best of the Maritimes and Newfoundland" ($2685 pp) leaves from the Ottawa area, crosses Québec Province, stops at Québec City, enters New Brunswick at Edmundston, and follows the Saint John River to Fredericton and Moncton. Ferry crossings take the passengers to and from PEI, with time on Cape Breton's Cabot Trail before heading for Halifax and the flight to Corner Brook in Newfoundland. From there, the tour travels to Gros Morne National Park, Grand Falls–Windsor, Twillingate, Gander, Terra Nova National Park, Trinity, and several outports on Conception Bay. The tour finishes at St. John's, with a return flight to Toronto.

The company's "McCarthy's Party of Newfoundland" tour is an eight-day, Newfoundland-only package ($1895 pp) with an itinerary similar to the above trip's second half. Four departures are scheduled from mid-July to early September.

If you have more time (and money), consider the "McCarthy's Party Deluxe Newfoundland and Labrador Tour," a gem of a sightseeing trip across Newfoundland island and southwestern Labrador. The 14-day trip costs $3085 pp; two departures are scheduled between mid-July and mid-August.

While all Hanover Holiday tours feature worthy sightseeing, this "Deluxe" tour is among Newfoundland's best. The visit to Gros Morne National Park includes a stop at the interpretation center to see a film on the park's geology, plus another stop at a fjord for a boat tour. Other sightseeing on the Northern Peninsula includes Port aux Choix, L'Anse aux Meadows, and the Grenfell landmarks at St. Anthony. The tour's ferry excursion to communities on the Strait of Belle Isle is an interesting side trip rarely included on bus tours.

The tour stops at museums, crafts shops, and lighthouses across the island and budgets time for whale- and iceberg-watching on the route from Grand Falls–Windsor to Lewisporte, Twillingate, Gander, Salvage, Terra Nova National Park, Bonavista, and Trinity. The three days in St. John's include tours of the city and Cape Spear, and an optional trip to Witless Bay to see the seabird sanctuary.

Hanover Holidays tour prices include lodgings, some meals, sightseeing admission fees, and coach, ferry, and air travel (but not the airport departure taxes). For details, call the company at (519) 364-4911 in Hanover or (800) 265-5530 in Canada; or write to them at 286A 10th St., Hanover, ON N4N 1P2.

TRENTWAY TOURS

Trentway Tours, another tour operator from Ontario, also includes rarely seen parts of Atlantic Canada in its itineraries. The "Labrador and Quebec" trip ($1100 pp) includes western Labrador with Québec Province on a 10-day tour. Three departures are scheduled between early July and early August. The Labrador aspects are unusually interesting, including a train ride aboard the Québec North Shore & Labrador Railroad, an iron-ore train with passenger quarters that enters the area from Sept-Îles; a two-day tour of the iron-ore mines in the Labrador City area; and sightseeing at Grande Hermine Park and Caribou Gardens.

The "Atlantic Canada" tour ($1325 pp) melds New England, the Maritimes, and Québec Province; 19 departures are offered late May to early October. The Maritimes segment includes a stop at St. Andrews, rarely included on bus tours, and also city sightseeing at Halifax, Charlottetown, and Fredericton. A 19-day "Newfoundland" tour ($1895 pp) combines Québec Province, Atlantic Canada (for 14 days), and New England; 13 departures are scheduled between early June and late August.

The cost includes some meals, most entrance fees, and tour insurance. For details, call (705) 748-6411 in Peterborough, (416) 961-9666 in Toronto, or (800) 461-7661 in Canada and the U.S.; or write to Trentway at 791 Webber Ave., P.O. Box 1987, Peterborough, ON K9J 7X7.

TRIUM TOURS

Trium Tours hails from New Brunswick, and its trips depart from Fredericton. Each of the short tours focuses on one specific destination, and just one departure per tour is offered each season. For example, the company has programs for the International Tattoo in Halifax (three days, $249 pp); the apple-blossom season in Nova Scotia's Annapolis Valley (three days, $229 pp); and Grand Manan Island in the Fundy Isles (three days, $239 pp).

Other trips include: Prince Edward Island in early Sept. (three days, $289 pp) and Cape Breton's Cabot Trail later in the month (four days, $379 pp). Prices include guided motorcoach touring and ferry fares, lodgings, entrance fees, baggage handling, the GST, and some meals. For details, call (506) 459-2047 in Fredericton or (800) 561-0024 in the Maritimes; or write to them at P.O. Box 1385, Fredericton, NB E3B 5E3, Canada.

KILOMÈTRE VOYAGES

Kilomètre Voyages, a French Canadian outfit, markets a **"Maritimes"** package ($869-899) with departures from Montréal, Longueuil, St.-Hyacinthe, Drummondville, and Ste.-Foy. Three departures are offered late June to late July. The nine-day tour includes sightseeing at Port-Royal, Moncton, Bathurst, Peggy's Cove, Baddeck, and Charlottetown.

BRIAN MOORE INTERNATIONAL TOURS

This tour company, with offices in the U.S. and worldwide, offers an outstanding variety of trips. For a trips catalog, write the company at 116 Main St., Medway, Massachusetts 02053.

PRINCE OF FUNDY CRUISES

Prince of Fundy Cruises can whisk you by ship from Maine to Yarmouth and can also make arrangements for land packages, mainly in Nova Scotia. For details, contact them at P.O. Box 4216, 468 Commercial St., Portland, Maine 04101, or call them at (800) 482-0955 in Maine, or (800) 341-7540 elsewhere in the U.S. and in Canada.

day rental) or 1,500 km (on a five-day rental) are free; each additional kilometer costs 14-21 cents, depending on the vehicle. For reservations, contact the tour desk at Air Canada's reservations offices worldwide, or let a travel agent handle the reservations.

Cycling Trips

Freewheeling Adventures, a Nova Scotia–based company, leads "pampered pedaling" cycling trips: an agreeable arrangement of guided trips in small groups, each accompanied by a support van to carry the luggage and, if necessary, the weary biker. Owners Cathy and Philip Guest plan everything: snacks, picnics, and meals at restaurants en route, and overnights at country inns. If a bike malfunctions, they can fix it promptly.

Expect to pay $850 to $1200 pp, all inclusive, for a five- to seven-day trip during the late May to early or mid-October season. You can bring your own wheels (ask what's best for the terrain) or rent one of theirs; a mountain or touring bike is $16 a day, $90 for a week. The trips start from each area's central gateway such as Halifax, Baddeck, Saint John, Charlottetown, Deer Lake, or Corner Brook, and head out into some of Atlantic Canada's prettiest, off-the-beaten-track countryside. If you need transportation beyond Halifax, the company can make arrangements for inexpensive travel for you at an extra charge.

The company has a program for each province. For example, the **New Brunswick** trip centers on the Bay of Fundy's Fundy Isles near the Maine coast and includes trips across Grand Manan, Deer, and Campobello islands as well as the ferry rides between islands. The tour is geared to an average cycling ability, and the distances are short.

The **Newfoundland** trip demands more cycling skills plus endurance as some of the route heads into the strong coastal winds on the Northern Peninsula. The route is magnificent: north on the peninsula through Gros Morne National Park (with a sightseeing boat trip on one of the fjords and a day's mountain climbing on Gros Morne Mountain), past remote coastal outports to Port au Choix and L'Anse aux Meadows.

Three trips are designed for **Nova Scotia,** and each calls for a different level of cycling ability. The **South Shore** trip works nicely for a recreational biker: the easygoing tour travels mainly level terrain along the Atlantic from Peggy's Cove to Lunenburg and Lower LaHave to Liverpool with time for beach exploration, shopping, and leisurely dining. The **Evangeline Adventure** asks more of a biker, and though the Annapolis Valley's floor is flat, the roads up the surrounding mountains can be steep. The itinerary covers the valley from Annapolis Royal to Grand-Pré with the bonuses of a rafting trip on the Gaspéreau River and also a coastal hike.

The **Cabot Trail** around Cape Breton's tip is every cyclist's ultimate challenge as the scenic route takes in mountainous ascents and descents. A top-notch bike equipped with excellent brakes is mandatory. The itinerary's well-timed pauses take in hikes into the national park and opportunities for whalewatching. Golfing on the Highlands Links is another option.

The terrain on **Prince Edward Island** is a cyclist's dream: flat or undulating with gently rising grades; the tour is pure pleasure for a cyclist of any level. The itinerary features a circuit through the coastal farmlands, the national park's coastline in northern Queens County, and northern Kings County to East Point at the island's northeastern tip.

A 40% deposit is required with the reservation (80% refundable up to 30 days before the trip); for details or reservations, call them at (902) 857-3600 or write to them at RR 1, Hubbards, NS B0J 1T0.

Educational Stays

Several universities and colleges in the region offer short-term summer classes, most commonly in the arts and crafts fields (you're on your own to arrange for lodgings and meals).

Elderhostel Canada has classes for older adults in a variety of subjects in conjunction with universities across Atlantic Canada. The subjects are often linked with the setting. For example, at Corner Brook, a class in geology explains the formation of nearby Gros Morne National Park, and day trips to the park form part of the program. At Fredericton, a class is oriented to tracing family roots, a subject of popular interest to many visitors who come to New Brunswick to research ancestral records.

Elderhostel's five- or six-day programs operate year-round; classes are held at the University of New Brunswick in Fredericton, Memorial University of Newfoundland in St. John's and Corner Brook, Dalhousie University in Halifax, and Acadia University at Wolfville in Nova Scotia, and the University of Prince Edward Island at Charlottetown. Expect to pay under $350 pp, all-inclu-

sive. You must be at least 60 years old to participate.

The nonprofit organization publishes a free, quarterly *Elderhostel Canada Catalog* with program details and a registration form. There's no charge to be added to their mailing list. For details, call (613) 530-2222, or write to 308 Wellington St., Kingston, ON K7K 7A7.

INFORMATION AND SERVICES

VISAS AND OFFICIALDOM

Canadian Consulate General
Offices of the Canadian Consulate General in the U.S. and overseas are geared to answer questions about documents, immigration, and other subjects related to foreigners traveling within Canada. For general travel information, ask for a copy of *Canada Travel Information*. The offices are open Mon.-Fri. 9 a.m.-5 p.m. and are closed on the Canadian public holidays and the national holidays of the host country. The best sources of information on a particular province are the tourist offices in that province.

Travel Documents
Foreigners entering Canada are allowed to stay for 180 days. For an extension, contact the immigration office for an appointment. Citizens and most permanent residents of the U.S. may enter Canada with a birth, baptismal, or voter-registration certificate. Naturalized citizens should carry a naturalization certificate, U.S. passport, or other citizenship evidence. Proof of residence may also be required; check with the nearest Canadian Consulate General office (see the chart for the locations). A passport is the easiest such proof and will speed re-entry into the United States.

Visitors from the U.S. with other citizenship status require special documents. Non-U.S. citizens who are permanent residents need a resident alien card, and U.S. residents with a temporary resident card or employment authorization card are required to carry a passport and in some cases a visitor's visa; for a visitor's visa, contact a Consulate General office *outside* Canada. For an update on required

documents, or for other questions, contact the U.S. Immigration and Naturalization Service before departure.

For entry documents from other nations, contact the nearest Canadian Embassy, High Commission, or Consulate before departure.

Finally, any visitor under age 18 and unaccompanied by a parent needs a letter from a parent or guardian giving permission for the visit.

Clearing Customs
Visitors are allowed to bring in personal items that will be used during a visit such as cameras, fishing tackle, and equipment for camping, golf, tennis, and scuba diving. The duty-free limits are: 1.1 liters of liquor or wine (19 years minimum age); 50 cigars, 200 cigarettes, and

---

TOURISM OFFICES

Tourism New Brunswick: P.O. Box 12345, Fredericton, NB E3B 5C3; tel. (800) 561-0123 in North America.

Nova Scotia Department of Tourism and Culture: P.O. Box 456, Halifax, NS B3J 2R5; tel. (902) 424-4247 in Halifax, (800) 565-0000 in Canada, or (800) 341-6096 in the United States.

Prince Edward Island Visitor Services: P.O. Box 940, Charlottetown, PE C1A 7M5; tel. (902) 368-5555 or (800) 463-4734 in North America.

Newfoundland Department of Tourism and Culture: P.O. Box 8730, St. John's, NF A1B 4K2; tel. (709) 729-2830 in St. John's or (800) 563-6353 in North America (except the Yukon and Alaska).

400 grams of manufactured tobacco, plus 400 tobacco sticks (18 years minimum age); and gifts (not tobacco or alcohol) with a total value of $40 or less.

Firearms are strictly regulated. To bring a hunting rifle or shotgun into the country you must be at least 16 years old. Customs inspectors will not allow handguns, most pellet guns, or any firearm with no legitimate sporting or recreational use. A long gun (hunting rifle or shotgun) is permitted and must be declared at entry.

If you are driving into Atlantic Canada, be sure you have the vehicle's registration. If the vehicle is rented or is registered by someone else, you'll need a rental contract or a letter from the owner that authorizes the vehicle's use. A valid driver's license from your home country is acceptable for driving in Canada. Wearing seat belts is mandatory in Canada, and studded tires are illegal except during winter.

If you're coming in by boat, you must contact Canada Customs or a regional customs of-

OFFICES OF THE CANADIAN CONSULATE GENERAL

UNITED STATES

Atlanta: 400 South Tower, One CNN Center, Atlanta, GA 30303-2705; tel. (404) 577-6810.

Boston: Three Copley Place, Suite 400, Boston, MA 02116; tel. (617) 536-1731.

Buffalo: 3000 Marine Midland Center, Buffalo, NY 14203-2884; tel. (716) 852-1247.

Chicago: Two Prudential Plaza, 180 N. Stetson Ave., Suite 2400, Chicago, IL 60601; tel. (312) 616-1860.

Dallas: 750 N. Saint Paul St., Suite 1700, Dallas, TX 75201; tel. (214) 922-9806.

Detroit: 600 Renaissance Center, Suite 1100, Detroit, MI 48243-1704; tel. (313) 567-2086.

Los Angeles: 300 S. Grand Ave., Suite 1000, Los Angeles, CA 90071; tel. (213) 687-7432.

Minneapolis: 701 Fourth Ave. S, Suite 900, Minneapolis, MN 55415-1899; tel. (612) 333-4641.

New York: 1251 Avenue of the Americas, 16th Floor, New York, NY 10020-1175; tel. (212) 596-1600.

San Francisco: 50 Fremont St., Suite 2100, San Francisco, CA 94105; tel. (415) 495-6021.

Seattle: 412 Plaza Building 600, Sixth St. and Stewart St., Seattle, WA 98101-1286; tel. (206) 443-1777.

AUSTRALIA

Fifth Level, Quay West, 111 Harrington St., Sydney, New South Wales 2000, Australia; tel. (61-2) 364-3000.

FRANCE

37 Avenue Montaigne, 75008 Paris, France; tel. (33-1) 44 43 32 00.

GERMANY

Immermannstrasse 65D, 4000 Dusseldorf 1, Germany; tel. (49-211) 353471; ask to be transferred to the consulate general office or the tourism section.

JAPAN

Canadian Embassy, 3-38 Akasaka 7-Chome, Minato-ku, Tokyo 107, Japan; tel. (81-3) 3479-5851.

UNITED KINGDOM AND IRELAND

MacDonald House, One Grosvenor Square, London W1X 0AB, United Kingdom; tel. (44-71) 629-9492.

fice immediately after reaching port; if they're unavailable, get in touch with the RCMP.

Working in Canada

Employment authorizations are not issued to foreigners if qualified Canadians or permanent Canadian residents are available for the job. To start the employment or study authorization process, contact the immigration officer at the nearest Canadian Embassy or Consulate General office. They'll charge a processing fee and require a medical examination and, for a job, an employment validation.

HEALTH AND SAFETY

Medical Care

No special health inoculations are needed before entering the country. Intraprovincial agreements cover the medical costs of Canadians traveling across the nation. For foreigners, however, medical care can be very expensive; a hospital's basic rate (without the physician's charge) can be up to $3000 a day.

Insurance

As a rule, the usual health-insurance plans do not include medical-care costs incurred while traveling; ask your insurance company or agent if supplemental health coverage is available, and if it is not, arrange for coverage with an independent carrier before departure.

Outdoor Precautions

• Protect yourself from the sun. Pack plenty of sunscreen year-round, as the sun's reflection on the snow can be even more dangerous to your skin than direct sunlight.

• If you are visiting during the summer or spring months (mosquito season), bring insect repellent.

• Frostbite can occur in a matter of seconds if the temperature falls below freezing and if the wind is blowing. Layer your clothing for the best insulation against the cold, and don't forget a hat and gloves.

Crime

The Atlantic provinces enjoy some of the country's lowest crime rates. Violent crimes are in-

frequent; the most common crime is petty theft. If you must leave valuable items in your car unattended, keep them out of sight, preferably locked in the vehicle's trunk. Women have few difficulties traveling alone throughout the region.

Halifax, St. John's, and Saint John are international ports with seamy (albeit interesting) bars and taverns at or near the waterfronts; keep your wits about you in these areas, especially late at night. Better yet, leave the night scenes to the sailors who frequent the areas.

Both possession and sale of illicit drugs are considered serious crimes and are punishable with jail time or severe fines. Furthermore, Canadians consider drinking while driving equally serious; the penalty upon the first conviction is jail and/or a heavy fine, and a subsequent conviction can be grounds for exclusion from Canada.

MONEY

Unless noted otherwise, **prices quoted in this book are in Canadian currency.** Canada's money is issued in notes ($2, $5, $10, and $20 are the most common) and coins (1, 5, 10, and 25 cents, and the "loonie," worth a dollar). Exchange rates vary from day to day, and the most favorable exchange rates are given at banks, rather than commercial places like shops and restaurants. Many banks charge an extra fee (usually $2-2.50) to convert a traveler's check to cash. It helps to arrive with a small amount of Canadian funds to pay for tips and the airport-to-hotel taxi fare. Banks are open Mon.-Fri. 9 a.m. to 3 p.m. or 5 p.m.; a few banks are open Saturday morning.

U.S. and English currencies are accepted in the larger cities, but the exchange rates are often less than favorable. All the major credit cards are accepted, Visa most widely. But many of the smaller, privately operated lodgings and dining places want cash.

Service charges and tips are *not* usually added to the dining tab; a 15% tip is customary, 20% if the service is extraordinarily good.

The Goods and Services Tax (GST)

The Goods and Services Tax, better known as the GST, is a seven percent tax on most goods and services in Canada. All Canadians must pay the tax. Foreigners with sufficient amounts of patience and a minimum of $100 in purchase receipts are eligible for refunds.

Items not eligible for refunds are: meals and beverages, alcohol, tobacco, transportation (including a cruise trip, train, or a vehicle's fuel), services like auto repair or entertainment, goods consumed in Canada, some goods worth $2000 or more (such as paintings, jewelry, and rare books), and accommodations such as a rented campsite, houseboat, tent, recreational vehicle, or trailer.

A Visitor Rebate Program refunds the tax on accommodations for less than one month's stay and also for goods taken home. Further, the tax on a tour package's accommodations is refundable if it had originally been paid in full; an applicant has a choice of claiming $5 a night up to $75 or requesting a refund for one-half of the tour package's full GST.

The program provides two methods for a refund. An applicant may apply for an on-the-spot tax refund of up to $500 when departing the country, by submitting the application form and original receipts to a participating duty-free store. The federal government suggests that you process the refund at the duty-free shops at New Brunswick's border. These shops are open daily and include: Cammex Inc., tel. (506) 992-2664, at 7 Bridge St. in Claire, open mid-May to mid-Oct. 8:30 a.m.-8 p.m., the rest of the year Mon. 8:30 a.m.-8 p.m. and Tues.-Sun. 10 a.m.-8 p.m.; Cammex Inc., tel. (506) 423-7646, at 7 Bridge St. in Saint-Léonard, open mid-May to mid-Oct. 8 a.m.-10 p.m., the rest of the year Sun. 10 a.m.-9 p.m., Mon. 8:30 a.m.-9 p.m., and Tues.-Sat. 8:30 a.m.-9 p.m.; and the Woodstock Duty Free Shop on Hwy. 95 at the Houlton Border Crossing, tel. (506) 328-8888, open mid-May to mid-Oct. 7 a.m.-11 p.m., the rest of the year 8 a.m.-8 p.m.

Or, you can return home and mail a completed application with the original receipts (keep photocopies) within 12 months of purchase to **Revenue Canada, Customs and Excise,** Visitor Rebate Program, Ottawa, ON K1A 1J5, Canada. For details or an application and instructions, call them at (613) 991-3346 in Ot-

tawa or (800) 66-VISIT in Canada. It takes six to eight weeks to process a refund, and the original receipts and other documents are returned after that in an unspecified number of weeks.

The *Goods and Services Tax Refund* instruction brochure includes an application form and an explanation of the process. Copies of the brochure are available from any Canadian Consulate office outside Canada or at any provincial tourist office in the region.

Provincial Taxes

Provincial-tax refund applications are available at provincial tourist offices. Follow the directions carefully. Most provinces allow 90 days after you've left the province to submit the application for a refund and will accept photocopied duplicates of the receipts. **Note:** Save the original receipts if you expect to apply for a GST refund.

In **New Brunswick,** the provincial tax of 11% is nonrefundable; footwear, campground fees, and most articles of clothing are exempt from the tax.

The 10% tax in **Nova Scotia** applies to most purchases, dining, and lodgings. The tax is rebated on goods taken out of the province within 30 days and also on amounts paid on accommodations *after* 30 days at the same lodging. Ask for a refund application at any provincial tourist center. (The minimum claimable refund amount is $15 in tax paid.)

Prince Edward Island has a 10% tax, which is nonrefundable except on goods shipped from a vendor to a visitor's address.

In **Newfoundland,** a 12% tax is levied on accommodations, meals, gasoline, and vehicle rentals. Some items are exempt, such as crafts made in the province, children's clothing and shoes, groceries, books without advertising, prescriptions, and purchased items shipped out of the province within 30 days. For a refund ($100 minimum in purchases), ask for a tax refund application at any provincial visitor information center. After you've left the province, send the completed application and copies of your receipts to the Tax Administration Branch, Office of the Comptroller General, Department of Finance, P.O. Box 8720, St. John's, NF A1B 4K1, Canada.

MEDIA AND MAPS

Atlantic Canada is too massive in size to have one newspaper, but plenty of regional and big-city papers are available. The *Toronto Globe and Mail* is distributed throughout the Atlantic provinces, and Halifax's *Chronicle Herald, Mail-Star,* and *Daily News* are found throughout Nova Scotia. Publications for the other provinces are listed under each specific province.

Canada's best news magazine is *Maclean's; L'Actualité* is the French counterpart. *Newsweek, Time,* and other big American publications are available at drugstores, bookstores and corner groceries.

Maps

Map offices and some bookstores and other shops stock general, topographic, and hydrographic maps; for details, see the "Information" sections in the travel chapters.

To obtain a general or topographic map through the mail, call the federal **Canada Map Office** at (613) 952-7000, or write to the office at the Energy, Mines and Resources Canada, 130 Bentley Ave., Ottawa, ON K1A 0E9. Maps cost $8-9.50 plus $3 handling charge.

Nautical maps are handled by the **Hydrographic Chart Distribution Office,** Fisheries and Oceans Canada, 1675 Russell Rd., P.O. Box 8080, Ottawa, ON K1G 3H6, Canada, tel. (613) 998-4931. They distribute *Sailing Directions,* a composite of general navigational information, port facilities' descriptions, and sailing conditions (in English or French) for Nova Scotia ($29.25 including shipping and handling), the Gulf of St. Lawrence ($19.95), and Newfoundland ($23.75). Also, a *Small Craft Guide* ($7) is available for the Saint John River in New Brunswick, plus the *Tides, Currents and Water Level Information* ($6.50 each, English only) for the Atlantic Coast and Bay of Fundy (Vol. 1) and the Gulf of St. Lawrence (Vol. 2).

Another source for maps of the region is the federal **Canada Communication Group,** tel. (819) 956-4802.

POST, TELEPHONE, AND TIME

POSTAL ABBREVIATIONS

New Brunswick: NB

Newfoundland: NF

Nova Scotia: NS

Prince Edward Island: PE

To address a letter to Canada, use a five-line format: (1) name of addressee; (2) street address; (3) city and province; (4) postal code; (5) Canada. Ontario and Québec provinces are mentioned in the text also; their postal abbreviations are ON and PQ, respectively.

TELEPHONE AREA CODES

New Brunswick: (506)

Nova Scotia: (902)

Prince Edward Island: (902)

Newfoundland: (709)

TIME ZONES

New Brunswick: AST

Newfoundland: AST and NST

Nova Scotia: AST

Prince Edward Island: AST

Atlantic standard time (AST) is one hour ahead of eastern standard time (EST).

Newfoundland standard time (NST), one and a half hours ahead of EST, is used on the island of Newfoundland and southeastern Labrador's communities on the Strait of Belle Isle; the rest of Labrador is on AST.

Daylight saving time starts throughout the Atlantic provinces the first Sunday in April, when the clocks are pushed ahead one hour; it ends on the last Sunday in October, when time reverts to standard time and the clocks go back one hour.

WHAT TO TAKE

If the Atlantic provinces are your first stop in Canada, it helps to arrive with some Canadian currency for taxi rides and incidental expenses. For the best exchange rates, convert foreign currency at the local banks, rather than at the airport.

No special inoculations or other health precautions are required. But if you plan on camping or other outdoor activities out in the countryside, you'll be wanting insect repellent; the mosquitoes and biting black flies can be merciless.

Clothing

The season and itinerary determine clothing. Late spring to autumn visitors should pack comfortable, informal clothing, including a lightweight to heavy sweater or jacket depending on the month, dressier garb for dinnertime, and comfortable walking shoes. Shorts and T-shirts and other cool clothing are called for during the hottest summer days and evenings. For winter travel, you'll want a rainproof jacket, down wear, gloves, hat, warm boots, and thermals. For breezy coastal sightseeing, a sweater or windbreaker, hat, sunscreen, and comfortable shoes with rubber soles will come in handy.

For inland trekking, bring hiking shoes or boots and heavy cotton or woolen socks, and be prepared to dress like an onion with several layers to peel to accommodate changing temperatures. Even in summer, an umbrella or some kind of rainwear is good insurance against sudden showers.

Don't fret too much about clothing you've forgotten to pack—consider it an opportunity to shop for some of Atlantic Canada's most attractive and skillfully made apparel at local crafts shops. See the Introductions to the following travel chapters for additional suggestions.

Photographic Supplies

The weather is variable, with days of both blinding sun and lead-gray overcast. Bring film of various light speeds, and bring enough of it—film is expensive in Canada. Include a telephoto lens for catching distant whales, icebergs, and seabirds. A water-resistant camera cover can also come in handy. And pack your film in a zinc-lined film bag that protects the rolls during the airport X-ray process. If photography is an important part of your visit, bring two cameras; the cities have the best-equipped camera shops, but if your camera malfunctions and can't be fixed on the spot, the only other recourse is to send it out of the province.

WEIGHTS AND MEASURES

Canadians use the metric system, with temperature measured in degrees Celsius, liquid measurements in liters, solid weights in kilograms and metric tons, land areas by the hectare, and distances in kilometers, meters, and centimeters. Many Atlantic Canadians, nevertheless, still think in terms of the imperial system; expect to hear a lobster described in pounds, distance measured in miles, and the temperature measured in Fahrenheit degrees. The electrical voltage is 120 volts.

NEW BRUNSWICK

BOB RACE

INTRODUCTION

Canada meets the Atlantic at New Brunswick, the largest (73,437 square km, pop. 724,000) and most accessible of the Maritime provinces. Dense Appalachian forests spill across the borders of Québec and Maine and blanket almost 90% of the province. Beyond the forests, a coastline over 2,200 km long lies along the Bay of Fundy, Northumberland Strait, Gulf of St. Lawrence, and Baie des Chaleurs.

The adjacent provinces of Nova Scotia and Québec are accessible by land, as is the state of Maine, U.S.A., immediately to the west. The province of Prince Edward Island is a quick ferry ride across the Northumberland Strait from Cape Tormentine. A web of regional air service via Halifax, Nova Scotia, also connects New Brunswick with its neighbors.

The tourist's New Brunswick lies mainly around the province's coastal edges and along the fertile Saint John River valley, which cuts a mammoth swath across the western woodlands. The sparsely populated interior is immensely rich in minerals and forestry products, the source of New Brunswick's dominant industrial status within Atlantic Canada.

SIGHTSEEING HIGHLIGHTS

Canada's only bilingual province, New Brunswick combines Anglos (two-thirds) and French Acadians (one-third) in a generally harmonious cultural blend. Cultural differences flare occasionally, and new political parties from time to time spring forth spouting old notions of ancestral "superiority." But on the whole, the two vastly different cultures interact amicably. In fact, Canada's popular *Chatelaine* magazine cited Moncton as "one of the best" Canadian cities for its "enviable secret" of harmony between the Anglophones and Francophones.

Historic and natural sites are recognized nationally and internationally. The St. Croix River's Douchet's Island, eight km from St. Andrews on Hwy. 127, is an international historic site marking the location of explorer Samuel de Champlain's first New World settlement in 1604. On Campobello Island, one of the Bay of Fundy islands, Franklin Delano Roosevelt's former summer compound is now an international park.

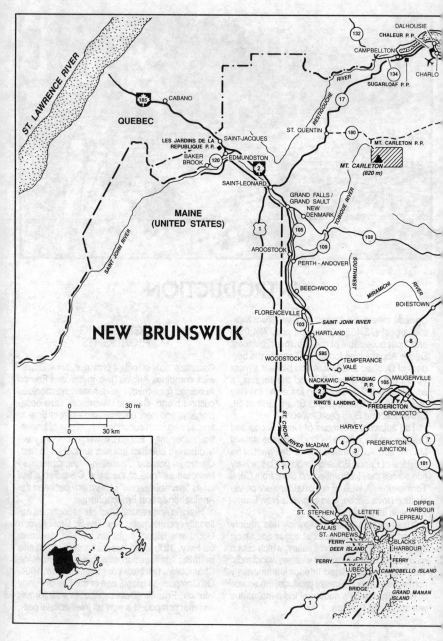

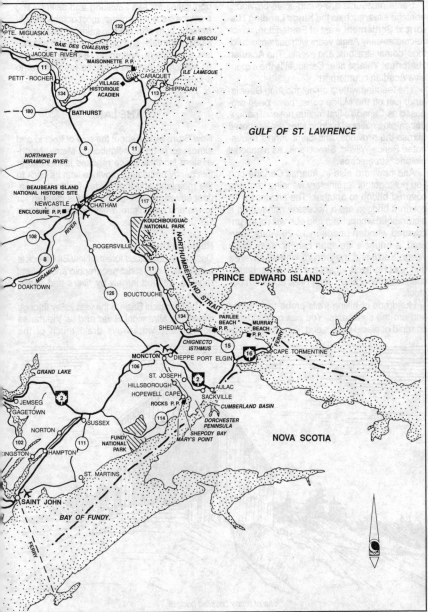

PTE. MIGUASKA

132

BAIE DES CHALEURS

JACQUET RIVER

11

PETIT-ROCHER

134

180

BATHURST

8

NORTHWEST
MIRAMICHI RIVER

BEAUBEARS ISLAND
NATIONAL HISTORIC SITE

NEWCASTLE
ENCLOSURE P. P.

108

8

DOAKTOWN

MAISONNETTE P. P.

ILE MISCOU

CARAQUET

ILE LAMEQUE

SHIPPAGAN

113

VILLAGE
HISTORIQUE
ACADIEN

11

GULF OF ST. LAWRENCE

11

CHATHAM

117

RIVER

NEWCASTLE

KOUCHIBOUGUAC
NATIONAL PARK

ROGERSVILLE

NORTHUMBERLAND STRAIT

PRINCE EDWARD ISLAND

11

126

BOUCTOUCHE

134

SHEDIAC

PARLEE
BEACH
P. P.

MURRAY
BEACH
P. P.

FERRY

CHIGNECTO
ISTHMUS

15

MONCTON   DIEPPE PORT ELGIN

106

ST. JOSEPH

HILLSBOROUGH

HOPEWELL CAPE

ROCKS P. P.

114

16

1

CAPE TORMENTINE

2

AULAC

SACKVILLE

CUMBERLAND BASIN

GRAND LAKE

2

JEMSEG

GAGETOWN

NORTON

102

KINGSTON   HAMPTON

SUSSEX

111

FUNDY
NATIONAL
PARK

DORCHESTER
PENINSULA

MARY'S POINT   SHEPODY BAY

NOVA SCOTIA

SAINT JOHN

ST. MARTINS

BAY OF FUNDY

FERRY

N

© MOON PUBLICATIONS, INC.

Some museums are grand-scale provincial heritage sites, such as the **Kings Landing Historical Settlement** west of Fredericton, which re-creates early Anglo years with authentic buildings, demonstrations, and events. The **Acadian Historical Village** near Caraquet is the expansive Acadian counterpart.

The teeming waters off neighboring Deer Island, just off the Maine coast, have been proposed as Canada's first marine national park. A dozen-plus national historic sites are scattered across the province, and Saint John's rejuvenated Prince William Street ranks as a national historic "streetscape."

And nowhere else in Atlantic Canada can you put together an itinerary wending from one covered bridge to another. The province's 73 covered bridges are a necessity rather than a picturesque whim. Rain and sun will rot an uncovered wooden bridge in 10-20 years; covered, a bridge's life span can increase to 80 years. You'll find the world's longest covered bridge at Hartland, where the 391-meter bridge spans the upper Saint John River above Woodstock.

Hundreds of hiking trails probe the interior and rim the seacoasts. You can go canoeing on rapid or placid waters and find abundant opportunities for sea kayaking and sailing. The province's scores of rivers, most notably the Miramichi, brim with Atlantic salmon. Bear, deer, small mammals, and birds attract both naturalists and hunters. And prime 18-hole golf courses stretch across the province from border to shore.

THE LAND

New Brunswick is about the size of Ireland and almost as large as neighboring Maine. Northeastern North America reaches land's end in this gently undulating province with its back to the mainland and three sides facing the sea. Just seven percent of the land is cleared for towns and agriculture, while nearly all the rest lies under woodlands.

Regional Disinctions
Despite its ubiquitous forests, New Brunswick is a collection of distinct geographic and cultural regions, defined largely by rivers and coastlines.

The Miramichi Basin is the vast valley through which the Miramichi River and its tributaries flow. These waterways drain much of the

one of many covered bridges

BOB RACE

province's interior and empty into the Gulf of St. Lawrence at Chatham. North and east of the basin, the Acadian Coast, notched with French-speaking communities and seaports, rims the Northumberland Strait and the Baie des Chaleurs. The Restigouche Uplands, named for the Restigouche River, lies northwest of the basin and forms the province's northwestern corner, rising in the interior to peak at 820-meter-high Mt. Carleton, highest point in the Maritimes.

While the Miramichi Basin is New Brunswick's geographic center, the Saint John River valley forms the province's spiritual heart. New Brunswickers have dubbed the river the "Rhine of North America"; it originates in Maine, winds 724 km across the province, and empties into the Bay of Fundy at the city of Saint John.

The Fundy tidal coast, a naturalist's dream, encompasses almost all of the southern coastline. The world's highest tides surge in twice daily—flooding the land's edge and floating fishing fleets off the mud—and then retreat six hours later, leaving gifts of seashells and marine flora. The Fundy tides rise and fall an average of eight meters (26 feet), and have been measured at 16 meters (52 feet) at Chignecto Bay, off southeastern New Brunswick.

The province's eastern corner fronts the upper Fundy on one seacoast and the Northumberland Strait on the other. New Brunswick's summertime beach scene is focused along the Strait, where the waters are as warm and tranquil as the Fundy's are chilly and turbulent.

Green Spaces

The province distinguishes between "super parks" and smaller multiuse parks. Among the super parks is **Mactaquac Provincial Park,** a 567-hectare spread with a lodge, hiking trails, campgrounds, and an 18-hole golf course alongside the Saint John River near Fredericton. The other super parks are: **Les Jardins de la Republique,** with a theater and tennis and canoeing facilities at Edmundston; **Sugarloaf,** with a lodge, hiking trails, tennis, and a chair lift near Campbellton; and **Mt. Carleton,** the wilderness domain southeast of Saint-Quentin.

The multiuse parks are a diverse group. **Chaleur Provincial Park,** east of Dalhousie, is situated at a prime coastal windsurfing area and has a windsurfing school with board rentals.

The lure of **Enclosure Provincial Park** is its historical setting of French, Acadian, and English settlements near Newcastle. This newest provincial park features ongoing archaeological digs.

Parlee Beach near Shediac reigns as everybody's favorite shoreline, with a long warmwater beach and summertime sports tournaments. Birdwatching is a provincial passion, and **Murray Beach** near Cape Tormentine and **Anchorage Provincial Park** on Grand Manan are two of the prime places.

The national parks include 206-square-km **Fundy National Park** and 238-square-km **Kouchibouguac National Park;** both preserves have coastal campgrounds.

CLIMATE

New Brunswick has hot summers and cold winters, both moderated somewhat by the surrounding seas. For **weather conditions** and forecasts anywhere in the province, call (506) 446-6240 (English), or 451-6004 (French).

Summer high temperatures average 23° C in June, 26° C in July, and 25° C in August; nights are cool. July is the sunniest month. September and October are pleasantly warm, with increasingly cool days. Winter is cold, with temperatures frequently dipping well below freezing.

The province's growing season—about 125 days—spans May to September. Precipitation throughout the province averages 115.2 cm annually. Rainfall is greatest on the Fundy coast, with 120-140 cm typical at Grand Manan and Sackville; Saint John gets an average of 115 cm a year.

Fredericton has a moderate climate, with hot summers and moderate to very cold winters. The capital's average summer temperature is 27° C, with 8.5 centimeters of rain a month. In spring and summer, Saint John and the Fundy coast are periodically steeped in fog, with visibility under a kilometer about 70 days a year. Fog occasionally closes the airport, so travelers flying in or out of the city may find themselves rerouted.

The seas are chilly most of the summer, but in places they warm to bathtub temperatures by August. The warmest waters are at Maisonnete

Provincial Park, on a two-km-long sandy beach at Caraquet. The Baie des Chaleurs here heats to 30° C. Kouchibouguac National Park is another warmish gem and has a 17-km beach on a sheltered lagoon. Other noteworthy places for pleasant saltwater swims are the supervised beaches at Shediac's Parlee Beach Provincial Park (19-24° C) and Charlo's Eel River Bar (15-24° C). The water along the Fundy coast tends to be colder, though it's nonetheless inviting and very refreshing on a hot summer day.

FLORA AND FAUNA

Flowers

The province hosts magnificent wildflower shows. Early spring's purple violet (the provincial flower) is one of some 200 wildflower species in New Brunswick. Many of these wildflowers are rare, endangered varieties, such as the Furbish's lousewort, a native of the upper Saint John River valley.

The tall-stalked lupine blooms with a profusion of blue, pink, white, or cream flowers during late June to mid-July, from Saint John to Blacks Harbour and Fundy Isles. The red cardinal flower thrives along southwestern riverbanks and lakes.

The bayberry bush and wild rose bloom on the Chignecto Isthmus during June. The yellow beach heather colors the strait and gulf dunes and sandy plains, and the rhodora (miniature rhododendron) brightens eastern coastal marshes. Farther northeast, nutrient-rich bogs nurture plant exotica; at Lamèque and Miscou islands at the extreme northeastern tip, wild cranberries and insect-eating pitcher plants and sundews grow among the peat moss beds.

Other common wildflowers, seen especially along roadsides in summertime, are Queen Anne's lace, yarrow, pearly everlasting, and a variety of daisies.

Woodlands

The significance of New Brunswick's timber resources was recognized in 1991, when the Canadian Forestry Association named Nackawic, west of Fredericton, as Forestry Capital of Canada. Provincial forests abound with balsam fir (the provincial tree), spruce, and pine (without rival for strong, white paper products), as well as black spruce, birch, beech, cedar, hemlock, ash, and oak.

With so many provincial tree varieties, visitors to the province may see the forests, rather than the trees. For a manageable introduction, visit Fredericton's Odell Park Aboretum, where a 2.8-km trail winds through woods made up of every tree native to the province.

The provincial Clean Environment Act regulates New Brunswick's natural resources and development, especially the dominant forestry industry. Critics warn that the forest is vanishing, and debate continues on how best to maintain the forests while supplying demand. Environmentalists advocate selective forest cutting. The paper-and-pulp industry counters that taking only the biggest and best trees is both difficult and costly. The industry favors cheaper "clearcut" methods, leveling forests wholesale and replanting seedlings.

Animals

The highlands, deep valleys, and swampy lowlands of Fundy National Park are protected habitat for bobcats, snowshoe hares, porcupines, and large white-tailed deer. Farther north, at Kouchibouguac National Park, local fauna includes the timber wolf, coyote, red fox, black bear, lynx, bobcat, deer, moose, and many small mammals.

Over the decades there had been occasional unconfirmed sightings of cougars (*Felix concolor*) in New Brunswick, but the last verified sighting had been recorded 50 years ago. The big cats are apparently making a comeback, however. Recent official sightings prove that the cougar has returned to the province.

New Brunswick's prime whalewatching region lies off Grand Manan Island. Minke, pilot, finback, and humpback whales are the most numerous species; the season peaks during August and September.

Birds

New Brunswick's varied ecosystems and climatic differences make it a haven for all sorts of birds. Over 350 resident and migrant species find some corner of the province to their liking. The chickadee is the provincial bird.

New Brunswickers are active birdwatchers, and many birders belong to **New Brunswick**

Federation of Naturalists, a private group based at New Brunswick Museum. The museum publishes a free provincial bird list that describes range areas and population densities of the many indigenous species; for details, write to the Natural Sciences Division, 277 Douglas Ave., Saint John, NB E2K 1E5, or call (506) 658-1842.

The crossbill, various woodpecker species, the boreal chickadee, and gray jay nest in New Brunswick's interior spruce and fir forests. The crossbill likes the Appalachian uplands and Mt. Carleton's spruce forests. The ibis, heron, and snowy egret wade among lagoons and marshes. The Baie des Chaleurs coastline lures the gannet, and the northeastern tip's Île Miscou is the piping plover's nesting ground.

In March, many songbirds fly south—their numbers peak in late May. In late July, seabirds descend on the Mary's Point mudflats at Shepody National Wildlife Area. On Shepody Bay's opposite side, 100,000 sandpipers, en route to South America, stop at the Dorchester Peninsula during July's last two weeks.

An awesome birdwatching show takes place in spring and early autumn at Grand Manan Island in the Bay of Fundy. This was the haunt of John James Audubon, the ornithologist and artist, who visited in 1833 and painted the arctic tern, gannet, black guillemot, and razorbill. Birding is still the island's claim to fame, and over 300 species have been sighted on wet heath, woods, ponds, and sedge reserves. The bird show is thickest during September, when migratory seabirds—including auks, puffins, razorbills, murres, guillemots, phalaropes, gannets, storm-petrels, and kittiwakes—can be spotted. Grand Manan is also the gateway for boat tours to the Atlantic puffin rookery at Machias Seal Island, a rocky outcrop in the Fundy.

HISTORY

The Malecite (or Maliseet, as New Brunswickers spell the word) and Micmac Indian settlements date back to 2000 B.C. on the interior's Miramichi River, and to 1000 B.C. at the Fundy's Passamaquoddy Bay.

In 1534, the explorer Jacques Cartier claimed the northeastern seacoast for France and named the waters off the northern coast the Baie des Chaleurs ("Bay of Warmth").

In 1604, Samuel de Chaplain and Sieur de Monts attempted to reinforce France's claim by establishing the first settlement in the New World north of Florida on a St. Croix River island. A harsh winter devastated the population and sent the survivors fleeing across the Fundy to establish Port Royal in Nova Scotia as Acadia's hub in 1605.

The French influence in the New World radiated from Port Royal. The French Crown sold land grants to competitive developers, who established fortified trading posts. Eventually, a French presence returned to New Brunswick. French settlers arrived and carved out farmlands spreading from the Chignecto Isthmus marshes to the Restigouche Uplands.

War erupted between France and Britain in 1689, and eastern regions of Canada were pulled into the conflict. The 1713 Treaty of Utrecht (see "The Treaty of Utrecht," under "History" in the Introduction chapter) favored the English, granting them what is now New Brunswick. But the vagueness of boundaries north of the Bay of Fundy left much of the area in controversy, and fighting continued sporadically for another five years. Acadians fleeing Nova Scotia settled Saint-Anne's Point (Fredericton) in 1732. To counter the expanding British presence in Nova Scotia, France bolstered its position in New Brunswick with fortifications at the mouth of the Saint John River, plus the forts Gaspéreau and Beauséjour, which guarded the route across narrow Chignecto Isthmus into northern Acadia.

England Triumphs
Territorial disputes flared again into war in 1755. Acadians deported from British territories poured into New Brunswick and settled the northern and gulf coasts. Over the ensuing years, the French military sustained several defeats. Decades of war wound down to a military whimper at Baie des Chaleurs near Campbellton. There England vanquished the French at the Battle of Restigouche—the final naval battle of the Seven Years' War—in 1763.

The Peace of Paris awarded the plums of victory to England, and Anglo migration increased. The New England planters (the influential and rich "farmers" from England's original 13 colonies farther south) arrived in waves from 1760 to 1775 and were followed by the immigrant Scottish Highlanders through 1815.

Loyalists fleeing the American Revolution made the most significant impact. Though historians still argue about the exact numbers, it's estimated that 40,000 Loyalists fled to eastern Canada. The first influx of 3,000 refugees to New Brunswick (then part of Nova Scotia) arrived in Saint John from New York in 1783. Before the great refugee wave finished that year, 14,000 Loyalists had settled that port, as well as other parts of the Fundy coastline. They also sailed up the Saint John River and settled Saint-Anne's Point, naming the town Fredericton for George III's son.

Almost overnight, Saint John was transformed from village to city, and was incorporated as Canada's first city in 1785. Flexing its population strength, the colony petitioned England for separate colonial status and cut the tie with Nova Scotia the same year. New Brunswick took its name from Germany's duchy of Brunswick (Braunschweig), ruled also by England's King George III.

Fighting between England and France erupted again during the Napoleonic Wars and the hostilities spilled over to North America in the war of 1812. The British fortified St. Andrews with a blockhouse and added the Carleton Martello Tower at Saint John to defend against U.S. invasion. Timber prices shot up, and New Brunswick rode to riches with shipbuilding and trade. Saint John was dubbed North America's Liverpool and ranked fifth in registered tonnage worldwide.

The Thriving Colony

The good years continued. King's College, now the University of New Brunswick, opened at Fredericton in 1785, and the Collège de Saint-Joseph at Saint-Joseph-de-Memramcook started in 1864 as the colony's first Acadian college. The colony's population soared from 25,000 in 1809 to 200,000 in the 1850s. Irish immigrants, fleeing religious and political persecution as well as the potato famine, settled at Saint John and transformed the port into Canada's most Irish city.

Shipbuilding made New Brunswick rich. The *Marco Polo* was launched at Saint John in

1851. The ship flew like the wind on a route from Liverpool, England, to Melbourne, Australia, in 76 days and made history as the first vessel to circumnavigate the globe in less than six months.

Confederation: A Mixed Blessing

New Brunswick fared poorly initially with Confederation. High tariffs favored internal trade but discouraged international shipping. Provincial trade declined, and the population took a tumble as out-of-work New Brunswickers immigrated to the "Boston States" (Massachusetts and neighboring states in America).

One of the promises of Confederation, however, was a railroad, and when it was built the economy rebounded quickly. It funneled the Dominion's manufactured wares to Saint John for shipping, and brought with it vacationers. The entrepreneurial spirit thrived. On the Fundy coast, St. Andrews emerged as a resort town with the opening of the first Algonquin Hotel in 1880. At Saint John, Susanna Oland started the brewery that became Moosehead Beer, and A.D. Ganong developed the first chocolate bar in 1906, founding the Ganong Chocolatier factory at St. Stephen.

The economy faltered in the early 1900s. The Bank of Nova Scotia took over the Bank of New Brunswick in 1913. The province prospered briefly during WW I, but the economy took another tumble during the 1920s, and the Great Depression worsened the bleak conditions. By the 1940s, New Brunswick's illiteracy and infant-mortality rates were Canada's highest.

The federal government sent assistance. Loomcrofters, the famed crafts center at Gagetown, began as a federally sponsored youth-training program. Canadian Forces Base Gagetown opened north of Oromocto in the 1950s and went on to become the British Commonwealth's largest military training base. Hinterland New Brunswickers began to migrate to the cities. The province's population, predominantly rural in 1941, was predominantly urban just 30 years later.

The Contemporary Province

The 1960s inaugurated a decade of self-appraisal. The cumbersome provincial government was redesigned in 1963. The official Languages Act put Anglos and Acadians on equal linguistic footing, and New Brunswick became Canada's first (and only) bilingual province. Education received top priority. The Université de Moncton opened and is the only French-speaking university east of Québec City. The University of New Brunswick added a Saint John campus. The province now has four universities, nine community colleges, and 38 research centers.

In the 1970s and '80s, Saint John was revitalized with high-speed highways and a harbor bridge. The port's historic harborfront warehouses were transformed into Market Square, with shops, restaurants, and an adjacent convention center and hotel.

GOVERNMENT

New Brunswick is governed by a lieutenant governor, an executive council dominated by the ruling party, and a 58-member legislative assembly with a five-year mandate. The province sends 10 senators and 10 House of Commons members to Ottawa.

A two-party system dominated provincial politics until 1987, when Liberals won all assembly seats. Liberal dominance decreased to 46 seats in 1991 as minority parties wooed voters. The Confederation of Regions Party, a strong political newcomer that opposes bilingualism, is comprised of dissatisfied Tories, disenchanted Liberals, and discouraged New Democrats. Other minority parties include the Parti Acadien, New Democrats, and the once-powerful Progressive Conservatives.

ECONOMY

New Brunswick harbors Canada's largest share of silver, lead, and zinc reserves. Zinc deposits near Bathurst are among the world's largest supply. The province built Atlantic Canada's first nuclear–power–generating plant, at Point Lepreau between Saint John and Blacks Harbour. The Mactaquac Generating Station, on the Saint John River near Fredericton, is the Maritimes' largest hydroelectric station.

Saint John's claim to fame is industry and shipping. The city's merchant shipping fleet ranks as Canada's largest, as does the city's sugar refinery. Other industries include pulp mills, oil refineries, food-processing plants, and two breweries.

The province's annual gross domestic product (GDP) is $15.4 billion. Manufacturing—of food products, beverages, fabricated metal products, plastics, chemicals, and forestry products—and shipping contribute two-thirds of this. Saint John's Forest Products Terminal, Canada's largest forestry port facility, annually ships 800,000 metric tons of paper, lumber, and other forest products, as well as another 1.5 million metric tons in potash and salt. Moncton, located at the Maritimes' geographic center, serves as a distribution center for ports up and down the coast.

Mining contributes $886 million to the economy. In addition to the large silver, lead, and zinc deposits south of Bathurst, other mineral resources include potash in Sussex, coal in the Grand Lake area, oil shales in Westmoreland County; and gold in veins along parts of the Fundy's coastline. Peat moss collected in the northeast, especially from Lamèque and Miscou islands, makes the province the world's second-largest exporter of the fuel.

Agriculture contributes $275 million to the GDP. Victoria and Carleton counties' seed potatoes make up 20% of Canada's total production, and are exported to Mexico, Portugal, and the United States. The benevolent spring floods, with their ensuing silt, enrich the Saint John River valley's mixed farming picture, and the farms at Maugerville yield two crops each season. Other agricultural products include livestock (exported to France, England, Denmark, and the U.S.), dairy products, and berries.

New Brunswick's fisheries produce $99.5 million annually in ground fish, lobster, crab, scallops, and herring. The newest aquaculture developments are Atlantic salmon farms and blue mussel beds. Black Harbour–area canneries rank first in Canada's sardine production.

About 80% of the 1.5 million tourists who visit the Maritimes annually enter the region through New Brunswick, Atlantic Canada's land gateway. Tourism brings in about $600 million in revenues annually.

THE PEOPLE

The province's 724,000 New Brunswickers are now divided almost evenly between urban and rural populations. Anglos, comprising about two-thirds of the population, live along the lower Saint John River valley and Fundy coast. About a quarter-million Acadians form the other third of the population and are concentrated in the northwest and along the northern and eastern coastlines; Caraquet is considered Acadia's cultural heart, while Moncton is its educational and commercial center.

The Micmac and Malecite Indians, both eastern Algonquin tribes, are spread among 13 reserves. Other minority groups include Germans, Dutch, Scandinavians, Asians, Italians, and Eastern Europeans.

"There is a New Brunswick character," wrote Michael Collie in his reflective *New Brunswick*, "a personality, which is at first difficult to fathom: proud yet hospitable, somewhat dour yet essentially warm-hearted, independent in spirit yet with the virtues of neighbourliness . . . This distinctiveness that is the New Brunswick character derives in large measure from the ruggedness of the life and the ruggedness of the stock."

Some say the friendly, affable New Brunswickers have Atlantic Canada's best sense of humor. A strong sense of tolerance prevails above propriety, and no one raises an eyebrow if a visitor uses the wrong fork at dinner. (But *never* make the the mistake of shortening the name of Newfoundland's provincial capital of Saint John to St. John, or worst yet, St. John's—*that* is simply going too far.)

The crime level here is Atlantic Canada's lowest. Commonest infractions are petty theft and burglary. Women can generally travel alone without problems. As general tourist precautions, roll up car windows and lock car doors, take cameras and other valuables with you, and keep luggage in the trunk or otherwise out of sight.

FAMOUS NEW BRUNSWICKERS

New Brunswickers, who are less than modest about their famous, native-born compatriots, say the legend of **Paul Bunyan** originated with 19th-century Acadians who worked as lumbermen in northwestern New Brunswick's Edmundston area.

Joseph Cunard, the brother of Samuel Cunard (of the famed Cunard shipping empire that began in Halifax), carried on the family's tradition at his own shipyards on the Miramichi River. **Andrew Bonar Law,** Great Britain's only prime minister to be born outside the British Isles, came from New Brunswick.

Dr. Abraham Gesner, kerosene's inventor, was born in Saint John, as were Hollywood movie mogul **Louis B. Mayer** and actors **Walter Pidgeon** and **Donald Sutherland.** Hollywood makeup artist **Anthony Clavet** came from Edmundston, and **Antonine Maillet,** the well-known author, was born in Bouctouche on the Acadian Coast.

From Bouctouche also came the entrepreneurial industrialist **Kenneth Colin Irving,** born there in 1899. Before he died in 1992, he left an indelible mark on New Brunswick's economy.

Irving began with a pre–WW I gas station and by 1924 had formed the Irving Oil Company, whose holdings now include shipbuilding concerns, oil tankers and cargo vessels, forestry-product plants, four provincial newspapers, TV stations in Saint John and Moncton, bus lines, and numerous small companies, including the ubiquitous Irving service stations, all now managed by family members. *Forbes* magazine has ranked the elder Irving among the world's 10 richest men.

The Ontario-born **William Maxwell Aitken,** better known as Lord Beaverbrook, grew up in Newcastle as the son of a Presbyterian minister and became Great Britain's minister of aircraft production under Winston Churchill during WW II. This millionaire financier, politician, and publisher lavished gifts worth millions of dollars on his beloved adopted province. The provincial capital at Fredericton was among the major recipients: Lord Beaverbrook funded the Theatre New Brunswick's start, and gave the Beaverbrook Art Gallery to the city.

Language and Religion

The province is equally tuned to English and French. Some Acadians in remote Acadian towns and seaports speak only French, and la République du Madawaska has its own dialect. Grand Falls/Grand Sault is an official bilingual town.

In religious followings, Roman Catholics dominate at 52%, of whom the majority are Acadians. Protestants are spread among Baptist, United Church of Canada, Anglican, Pentecostal, and Presbyterian sects. The evangelical "Bible Belt" runs strong through Carleton and Victoria counties in the upper Saint John River valley and north of Moncton in Westmoreland County. Saint John has a small Jewish population.

Tracing Family History

Genealogical searches start at the **Provincial Archives of New Brunswick,** University of New Brunswick, the province's most complete heritage records. To begin, you'll need to know your ancestor's name and village, town, or county. The archives also publishes 15 county genealogy guides to help family researchers; for details, contact the archives at P.O. Box 6000, Fredericton, NB E3B 5H1.

Acadian lineage records are kept at the **Centre d'Études Acadiennes** at the University of Moncton and the **Société Historique Nicholas Denys** at the Centre Universitaire de Shippagan. Family records detailing early Irish Miramichi settlers are held at **St. Michael's Museum** in Chatham near Newcastle.

RECREATION

The *New Brunswick Outdoor Adventure Guide* covers the sports spectrum from hiking and cycling to whalewatching, sailing, houseboating, canoeing, kayaking, scuba diving, and birding. The booklet includes workshop listings, plus hiking-trail specifics, addresses of guides and outfitters, etc.; it's available by calling (800) 561-0123. Larger provincial parks levy a beach-entrance fee, but the national park beaches and most municipal beaches are free.

Hiking and backpacking are popular pastimes, and a number of trails splice through the provincial and national parks. Mount Carleton Provincial Park is a favorite destination for wilderness hiking. Tourism New Brunswick provides detailed trail information and small locator maps for some areas. Another excellent resource, describing over 100 trails, is the *Hiking Guide to New Brunswick,* published by Gooselane Editions, 469 King St., Fredericton, NB E3B 1E5; tel. (506) 450-4251.

Bicyclists should have a look at another Gooselane publication, *Biking to Blissville,* which outlines a number of provincial cycling routes. Except on main arteries, particularly the Trans-Canada Hwy., car traffic is generally light and the roads safe for cyclists. Following the Saint John River valley past the complex of lakes north of Saint John makes for pleasant touring; along the Fundy and Northumberland Strait coasts, scores of local highways loop off the main routes to take cyclists even closer to the sea.

Twenty-five 18-hole **golf courses** dot the province; you'll find seven of the best spread across the pastoral lower Saint John River valley.

New Brunswickers enjoy a variety of **water sports.** Houseboats, with space enough for six to 10 passengers, roam the lower Saint John River and Grand Lake and rent for $800-1700 a week. Inland canoeing is extremely popular on numerous rivers, such as the 137-km Tobique River, which feeds into the upper Saint John River. Windsurfers exploit breezy waters everywhere, from Shediac on the strait to the interior's Saint John and Kennebecasis rivers.

Kayakers like the contrasting Baie des Chaleurs and the Bay of Fundy. The two seas also lure scuba divers. The Baie des Chaleurs, from Caraquet to Bathurst, offers good visibility and fascinating shipwrecks, while the western Bay of Fundy is especially rich in marine life and has excellent visibility before July's plankton blooms. **Whalewatching** off Grand Manan makes for a popular day-trip offered by a number of tour-boat companies. More than 20 whale species frequent the Bay of Fundy; most commonly seen are finbacks, minkes, humpbacks, and North Atlantic right whales, in addition to Atlantic white-sided dolphins and harbor porpoises.

Outdoor Workshops and Classes

Eastern Outdoors near Blacks Harbour is one of

Grand Falls

several outfits with year-round introductory and advanced **sea kayaking and whitewater canoeing** classes; they charge $195 for a weekend trip, more for three- to five-day trips. Call (506) 659-2769 for details or write to them at Dipper Harbour, NB E0G 2H0.

Broadleaf Tourist Farm on Hwy. 114 near Hopewell Cape, tel. (506) 882-2349, has **horseback-riding** classes ($13 an hour) taught by Canadian Equestrian Federation–qualified instructors, May-October. One of the best **photography** seminars ($600 for a week's classes, lodgings, and meals) is led by the province's own Freeman Patterson and Doris Mowry, whose professional skills are known far beyond New Brunswick. The seminar sites are in photogenic places, like the Hampton Peninsula or Grand Manan; for details, call them at 763-2271.

Hunting and Fishing

The woodlands and fields teem with white-tailed deer, black bear, moose, rabbit, ruffled grouse, geese, woodcock, partridge, and other game. Hunting licenses are required, and hunters must also obtain a Federal Migratory Game Bird Permit for ducks, geese, woodcock, and snipe.

Bass fishing, in the fast-running streams and rivers in the northwestern hinterlands and in the lakes in southwestern New Brunswick, is among Atlantic Canada's best. The season runs from mid-April through September. Other inland game fish include brook trout, shad, perch, and pickerel. And New Brunswick, of course, is famous worldwide for its Atlantic salmon fishing, particularly on the revered Miramichi—considered by many to be the premier salmon-fishing river anywhere. Fly-fishing is the only allowed method for taking salmon; nonresidents are also required to hire a guide. Inland fishing requires a license, and fishing in the national parks requires a federal angling license, available at the parks.

Details on hunting and fishing seasons and regulations are available from the Department of Natural Resources and Energy, **Fish and Wildlife Branch,** P.O. Box 6000, Fredericton, NB E3B 5H1, tel. (506) 453-2440. Ask for their booklets, *Hunting Summary, Sport Fishing Summary,* and *Atlantic Salmon Angling.* The province is thick with **outfitters and guides,** the majority of whom can arrange both fishing and hunting expeditions. They're detailed in Tourism New Brunswick's *Aim and Angle* booklet.

ENTERTAINMENT AND EVENTS

Holidays and Festivals

Everything shuts down on national holidays and on **New Brunswick Day,** the province's natal celebration on August's first Monday.

Summer in New Brunswick brings sheaves of annual festivals, many of them conceived as celebrations of ethnic or historical heritage. These are listed in the travel chapters; a few of the biggest are described here.

The **Loyalist Days** festival in Saint John recalls the Loyalists who settled New Brunswick. The event gives Anglos (and everyone else) reason to celebrate with costumed parades, street casinos, and general merriment for seven days in mid-July. Caraquet's **Acadian Festival**, the French Acadian version, reportedly ranks as Canada's largest Acadian event, with theater, concerts, food, and cabaret entertainment for 12 days in mid-August. Edmundston's **Foire Brayonne** celebrates the heritage of the Madawaska Republic—an Acadian cultural offshoot—and showcases arts, crafts, sports, and culinary delights in late July.

The province is at its unquestionable best in concert festivals. The 11-day **International Festival of Baroque Music** has had astonishing success as a setting for international musicians who perform in the acoustically perfect Ste-Cécile-de-Petite-Rivière sanctuary on remote Île Lamèque during mid-July. Farther south down the gulf coast, Newcastle's **Irish Festival on the Miramichi** (mid-July) and the **Miramichi Folksong Festival** (July/August) are outstanding showcases for traditional music expressing the Miramichi Basin's Celtic musical soul. Saint John's **Festival by the Sea** is another top winner and includes 10 days of performing arts and concerts in early to mid-August.

Love of good food drives the **Shediac Lobster Festival** for six days in mid-July. The **Chocolate Fest** at St. Stephen, where Ganong's chocolate factory reigns, celebrates its raison d'etre for five days in early August.

Nightlife

The provincial night scene is low-key. New Brunswickers like intimate small bars, lounges, and watering holes. Bars are open Mon.-Sat. to 2 a.m.; beverage rooms serve alcohol Mon.-Sat. 9 a.m.-1 a.m. *Nothing* happens on Sunday.

ARTS AND CRAFTS

Crafts here are carefully handmade, and are varied and abundant. The province boasts 800 artisans who work in 125 studios and crafts shops. The **New Brunswick College of Craft and Design** in Fredericton deserves much credit for the quality and profusion. The school is Canada's sole postsecondary school that grants degrees to artisans, and many of New Brunswick's best craftspeople are alumni.

Certain places are known for specific crafts. Kings County's Sussex, Norton, and Hampton, for example, excel in handwoven tweeds. Sussex also has a reputation for fine silver jewelry, and Hampton shops stock some of the best provincial quilts and woodworking wares. Grand Manan knitters embellish apparel with seagull and whale motifs. Fredericton is the provincial pewter center.

Loomcrofters in Gagetown designs the official tartans for New Brunswick Province and the Royal Canadian Air Force. **Madawaska Weavers** in Saint-Léonard shines in chic apparel; **Briggs and Little,** Harvey Station near Fredericton, spins soft, lush blankets and 50 shades of wool yarn in seven weights.

The *New Brunswick Craft Directory,* published by Tourism New Brunswick, is free and lists craftspeople and their locations and telephone numbers; it's available from the provincial tourism office and also at tourist centers and some shops. Crafts studios have varying hours, and it's wise to call ahead. Stores are open Mon.-Sat. 9 a.m.-5:30 p.m., Thurs.-Fri. to 9 p.m.; the shopping centers are open Mon.-Sat. 10 a.m.-10 p.m.

Crafts Shows

The **Annual Quilt Fair** at Doaktown's Miramichi Salmon Museum is a showpiece of provincial quilting expertise and runs seven days in mid-June. On June's third weekend, the two-day **Village of Gagetown Craft Festival** showcases the finest-quality crafts and is generally acknowledged as one of Atlantic Canada's premier crafts fairs. The **Albert County Historic Quilt Sale** in Hillsborough spans three days in mid-July. The **Mactaquac Craft Festival** in Mactaquac Provincial Park reigns as the top crafts show and finishes August with a two-day fair.

Check out farmers' markets for arts and crafts, too; most are open on Saturday mornings May-October. You'll find them in Fredericton, Saint John, Moncton and nearby Dieppe, Chatham, Sackville, Kingston, St. Stephen, St. Andrews, Temperance Vale, Florenceville, Jemseg, Newcastle, Bathurst, Sussex, Campbellton, and Edmundston. Expect a range of wares from handwoven apparel to dried herbs and flowers, decoys, carvings, furniture, raku and other pottery, pewter, and stained glass.

The Arts Scene
Provincial fine arts are superb. John Hammond, Miller Brittain, Alex Colville, Jack Humphrey, and photographer Freeman Patterson are among New Brunswick's premier artists. Isaac Erb's moody, mystical, early-20th-century photography is legendary.

Simply put, New Brunswickers enjoy art—their own and everyone else's. Salvador Dali's *Santiago el Grande* greets visitors in the foyer at the **Beaverbrook Art Gallery** in Fredericton, and up the street, the **New Brunswick Legislative Library** holds John James Audubon's *Birds of America,* with 435 original paintings. At Sackville, the **Owens Art Gallery** at Mount Allison University boasts an extensive collection of graphics and Alex Colville's paintings. **Galerie d'Art et Musée Acadien,** Université de Moncton, showcases Acadian fine arts.

ACCOMMODATIONS

The province's wide gamut of lodgings includes hotels and motels, inns, resorts, bed-and-breakfasts, farmhouses, sport lodges, and cottages. Some accommodations are awarded one to five stars in a voluntary lodging evaluation system; an absence of grading stars carries no weight, however.

Lodgings and campgrounds are exhaustively listed by towns and cities in Tourism New Brunswick's *New Brunswick Travel Guide.* **Dial-A-Night** is a free reservations phone located at the provincial tourist information centers at New Brunswick's entry points. To make a reservation, you'll need the date, day, number of people, and arrival time; reservations are held until 6 p.m. unless guaranteed. Lodgings can also be phoned directly.

Note: The prices included in the following lodgings coverage are for a double room (least expensive with a double bed and at a higher cost for two twin beds)—that's for two people, *not* per person. Rates given do not include 11% provincial sales tax and seven percent GST, which are added to most accommodations.

For a memorable splurge, consider staying at one of the province's historic inns, many of which were once grandiose private residences. A select number are members of **New Brunswick's Heritage Inns,** a private group of innkeepers whose lodgings meet special standards and were built before the 1930s. The group publishes a folder depicting and describing the member inns; provincial and municipal tourist offices have copies.

The $8.3 million **Kingsclear Hotel and Resort** near Fredericton is the newest deluxe lodging in the province. The resort is owned by the Malecite Indians, the first native Canadian people to amend traditional fishing rights in return for resort ownership. Tribal members work as sports guides and craftspeople.

Hostelling International, tel. (902) 425-5606, has hostels in Campbellton, Edmundston, Fredericton, Sackville, Saint John, and Fundy National Park. Rates range $10-16.

Camping
The season at the majority of parks spans mid-June to early Sept., though some operate May-Oct., and a few stay open year-round. Camping fees average around $11 per site, with a discount for stays of seven or more days. Many of the larger provincial parks charge a day-use fee of $2-4. At the national parks, camping fees range from $7 for a barebones backpacker site to up to $16 with full amenities. Day use is $5, $10 for a four-day pass. The maximum stay for campers is 14 days.

Reservations are not accepted by either provincial or national parks. Additional details on specific parks are given in the following travel chapters. For a complete listing, see the New Brunswick tourism department's *Outdoor Adventure Guide* or *Activity Guide,* available free, tel. (800) 561-0123.

In addition to provincial and national parks, New Brunswick has some 125 or so private campgrounds; the majority are concentrated along the coasts and along the Saint John River. The campgrounds can be anything from simply a grassy field with the barest essentials to cushy resorts with all the amenities. Unserviced tent sites generally run $8-12, while sites with two- and three-way hookups cost $12-17.

FOOD AND DRINK

New Brunswick cuisine reflects its English and Acadian heritages, with some local specialties. New Brunswickers nibble year-round on salty, chewy dulse, a purple, iodine-rich Fundy seaweed that's dried in the sun and sold in little bags. Spring is celebrated with "fiddleheads," an ostrich fern's unopened fronds that are served boiled as a vegetable or in cream soup. Smelts are fried or baked. Vegetables and potatoes are often melded as hodgepodge, a nutritious stew served by the steaming bowlful. Dessert favorites include walnut toffee, trifle, homemade ice cream, or Ganong chocolates from St. Stephen.

Acadian cooking may be terribly hard on the waistline, but it's delicious. *Poutine râpé* combines boiled or deep-fried pork and grated raw potatoes, and it's customary to dip the ball in corn or maple syrup or molasses. A well-rounded Acadian meal includes seafood chowder, shellfish (shrimp and crab), fish (especially mackerel, herring, and cod), poultry (usually in the form of chicken stew), and, for dessert, sugar pie, apple dumplings, or cinnamon buns.

Save room for an Acadian culinary variation in Edmundston or another of the Madawaska area towns. Brayon cooking, as it's known, creates buckwheat pancakes, *les ployes,* splashed with butter, molasses, or maple syrup. Another pancake use is as a wrapper for spicy pâté or seafood.

The Danes immigrated to the province in the late 19th century and still cling to Scandinavian ways at New Denmark in the upper Saint John valley. If you're interested in Danish cuisine, try the town's Valhalla Restaurant for homemade sausage, roast beef and red cabbage, ground beef patties, and Danish apple cake.

Drink

New Brunswickers are wine drinkers, and you'll find an ample assortment of national and imported brands. For a decent martini or a mixed-drink variation, any place in Saint John, Fredericton, Moncton, or Sackville will do. In the hinterlands, ask for the local specialty or limit your imbibing to whiskey and water. Moosehead and Labatt's beer are the brewed hops of choice.

Provincial liquor stores are open 9 a.m.-9 p.m. or 10 a.m.-10 p.m., Sat. 9:30 a.m.-6 p.m. The legal drinking age is 19.

INFORMATION AND SERVICES

Tourist Information

Extremely helpful **Tourism New Brunswick** answers questions and distributes piles of provincial literature, including the 100-page *Activity Guide,* which describes attractions, travel routes, accommodations, and events. They also offer maps and more specific booklets on fishing and hunting, outdoor recreation, crafts producers, and other topics. Call them at (800) 561-0123 from throughout Canada and the continental U.S., or write to P.O. Box 12345, Fredericton, NB E3B 5C3.

If you're looking for tourist info during your stay in the province, check out any of the local provincial and municipal tourist offices; most places stock the same general provincial literature, with additional local and regional information. **Provincial tourist information centers** are located at the border crossings at Aulac (tel. 364-4090), Saint-Jacques (tel. 735-2747), Woodstock (tel. 325-4427), St. Stephen (tel. 466-7390), Campobello (tel. 752-2997), Saint-Léonard (tel. 423-3000), and Campbellton (tel. 789-2367); all open mid-May to mid-October. Fredericton, Saint John, Moncton, Edmundston, Sackville, and another 50 towns operate **municipal tourist information offices** with varying seasons.

The free **tourist magazines** are another good information source. One example is the thick tabloid *Holiday New Brunswick,* which is replete with travel features, coverage and information, plus advertisements for dining, accommodations, and sightseeing.

Communications and Media

New Brunswick's telephone area code is **506.**

Canada Post offices are open Mon.-Fri. 8:15 a.m.-5 p.m. **Retail post offices** augment the postal system; mall locations are open Mon.-Sat. 10 a.m.-10 p.m. Tourist information centers also sell stamps.

Newspapers flourish with dailies like Saint John's *Telegraph-Journal* and *Times-Globe* and

Fredericton's *Daily Gleaner.* Twenty-seven weeklies cover towns and counties from Campbellton, Dalhousie, Caraquet, and Bathurst to Victoria and Kings counties.

Immigration

Steps toward immigration must be made at consulate offices outside Canada. Federal offices in the province can also explain the process; for details, call the Fredericton office, (506) 452-3707. Other offices are at St. Stephen, Woodstock, Saint-Léonard, Edmundston, Bathurst, Fredericton, Moncton, and Saint John's airport and port; hours vary.

Health and Safety

In an emergency, call 0 or 911. Cities, towns, and smaller municipalities have police departments; the RCMP patrols highways. Thirty-four hospitals serve cities and towns; **Saint John Regional Hospital** in Saint John is equipped for kidney dialysis. A basic one-day hospital stay for nonresidents of the country, excluding treatment or physician costs, averages $558 ($402 for the hospital fee and an additional $156 nonresident fee). The province has no special health problems, and no inoculations are required. Ragweed, the weed that triggers summer allergies, is rare in New Brunswick, and nonexistent on the seacoasts.

MONEY, MEASUREMENTS, AND TIME

The most favorable currency-exchange rates are found at banks, open Mon.-Fri. 9 a.m.-5 p.m.; some mall banks are open Thurs.-Fri. to 7-8 p.m., Sat. 9 a.m.-noon. Some provincial tourist information centers at border crossings exchange currency, at a reasonable rate; shops with the service display a symbol rate card on the window. Major credit cards are widely accepted; Visa is most common.

Visitors can obtain a refund of the seven percent federal GST by submitting a signed application with original receipts attached at provincial tourist centers at Aulac, Edmundston, Saint-Léonard, St. Stephen, Woodstock, and the airports at Saint John and Fredericton. Or they may apply by mail; for details, write or call Reve-

nue Canada Customs and Excise Visitors Rebate Program, Ottawa, ON K1A 1J5, tel. (800) 66-VISIT in Canada, (613) 991-3346 outside Canada. The minimum refund is $7, maximum $500. The provincial sales tax is 11%, but does not apply to footwear, campground fees, and most clothing.

Measurements are metric throughout the province. Atlantic standard time is an hour ahead of eastern standard time; daylight saving time starts on April's first Sunday and finishes on October's last Sunday.

WHAT TO BRING

The clothing you bring should be selected based on your travel season and itinerary. During the peak travel season, from late spring to autumn, visitors should pack comfortable informal clothing, including a sweater or jacket, dressier garb for dinnertime, and comfortable walking shoes. Bring a raincoat and umbrella—showers are brief but drenching. Seacoasts are breezy. For outdoor activities, pack comfortable, warm clothing. In summer, you'll want shorts and T-shirts and other cool clothing. Between November and April, a heavy jacket, sweaters, and boots are in order.

Don't fret too much about clothing you've forgotten to pack—consider it an opportunity to shop for some of Atlantic Canada's most attractive and skillfully made apparel at local crafts shops. New Brunswickers dress modestly; revealing, outrageous, or sloppy attire is inappropriate.

GETTING THERE

By Air

Saint John, Moncton, Fredericton, and Charlo have airports served by **Air Canada/Air Nova** and **Canadian Airlines International/Air Atlantic.** Air Canada flies nonstop to Saint John from Montreal and also connects Fredericton with Toronto via Saint John. **Northwest Airlink,** an affiliate of Northwest Airlines, started service in April 1992 and flies daily to Saint John, Moncton, and Fredericton from Boston.

Advance reservations pay off. **Air Canada/Air Nova**'s restricted "Seat Saver" fares are steeply discounted. Newark-Halifax-Saint John costs US$273 RT with a discounted fare or US$739 RT for an unrestricted excursion fare. Similarly, Halifax-Saint John is C$179 restricted versus C$357 unrestricted, and Halifax-Fredericton costs C$192 at the cheap rate compared to C$382 normally.

By Land
Main U.S. border crossings are at Edmundston, Woodstock, Campobello, Saint-Léonard, and St. Stephen. From Québec, the TransCanada Highway enters at Saint-Jacques near Edmundston, and Hwy. 132 enters at Campbellton. Aulac, in southeastern New Brunswick, is where the TransCanada Hwy. crosses into and out of Nova Scotia.

VIA Rail enters the province with two routes: the northern line arrives from Québec at Campbellton and runs to Moncton; the other enters southwestern New Brunswick en route from Sherbrooke, Québec, and links Fredericton Junction and Saint John before arriving in Moncton and continuing on to Halifax. Call (800) 561-3952 in the Maritimes, (800) 561-3952 from the United States. See "Getting Around," below, for more details.

SMT buses connect with Nova Scotia's Acadian Line, Québec's Voyageur, and the U.S.'s Greyhound. See "Getting Around," below, for more details.

By Sea
Marine Atlantic, tel. (902) 794-5700, (800) 341-7981 in the U.S., links Borden, PEI, to southeastern New Brunswick's Cape Tormentine with a 45-minute ferry service. Another route connects Saint John with Digby, Nova Scotia. Both routes operate year-round, daily.

Car ferry service crosses the Baie des Chaleurs' western end from Miguasha, Québec, to Dalhousie ($3 pp, $11 vehicle); it operates mid-June to mid-September, daily 8:30 a.m.-8:30 p.m.

Cruise ships to Saint John are gaining popularity every year. Among ship lines calling there are: Crown Cruise Line, Cunard Line, Seabourn Cruise Line, and Clipper Cruise Line. The latter stops at Saint John and also docks at St. Andrews and Campobello Island. If you're arriving on your own yacht, you can clear customs at provincial **ports of entry** at Campobello, St. Andrews, St. Stephen, Grand Manan, and Saint John.

GETTING AROUND

By Car
Speed limits are 80 kph (50 mph) on highways and 50 kph (30 mph) in cities and towns, unless posted otherwise. In urban areas, vehicles yield to pedestrians at crosswalks, and cars are permitted to turn right on a red light after a full stop unless otherwise posted. Seat belts are required for driver and passengers; children under five years old or under 18 kg (40 pounds) must be in an infant carrier or approved child restraint. Helmets are required for motorcyclists and their passengers.

Minimum vehicle insurance coverage is $200,000, and if there's an accident involving damage over $1000 or injury or death, it must be reported immediately to the local police or RCMP. Drinking while driving and "impaired driving" carry severe penalties.

Be particularly careful driving the provincial roads at early morning and dusk, when deer and moose roam woodlands and cross roads. Annually, about l,000 deer and 100 moose are hit by cars. Watch out too for slow-moving porcupines, especially at night.

Highways are classified by numbers; for example, high-speed, principal highways are distinguished with single-digit numbers. Secondary highways, either paved or unpaved, have low-number triple digits, and local highways are marked with high-number triple digits. Local roads are unnumbered. The **Maritime Automobile Association,** tel. 652-3300, provides daily 24-hour emergency road service for members.

Public Transportation
In cities, **taxis** cruise downtown areas and wait outside hotels. They're also found at airports during flight arrivals. Fredericton, Moncton, and Saint John have public **city bus** service; exact fare is a loonie (Canada's coin version of a dollar).

The **SMT (Eastern Ltd.)** bus service, tel. 458-6000, serves the province with terminals in Saint John, Fredericton, Moncton, Bathurst, Campbellton, Edmundston, Newcastle, St. Stephen, Sussex, and Woodstock. Fredericton to Edmundston costs $34 OW, and Fredericton to St. Stephen is $28 OW.

VIA Rail fares can be good buys. For example, Saint John to Sackville costs $17 OW with a five-day advance purchase or $27 OW at departure. Moncton to Newcastle costs $12 OW advance, or $20 OW at departure.

Major **car rental** companies have locations in the larger cities and airports. Weekly rates are less expensive per day than daily rates. At the Saint John airport, for example, an Avis subcompact rents for $199 a week with 1,400 free kilometers, compared to $36 per day with 100 free kilometers. Collision insurance costs $13 per day, and personal insurance costs $3.50. All

rental charges are subject to 18% taxes. A U.S. driver's license is valid.

Two rail routes cross the province and both operate thrice weekly. One route services Sackville, Moncton, Sussex, Saint John, Fredericton Junction, and McAdam; the other Sackville, Moncton, Rogersville, Newcastle, Bathurst, Petit-Rocher, Jacquet River, and Charlo.

Ferries are a fun way to get around. Free cable ferries connect many riverbanks in the lower Saint John River valley and along the Kennebecasis River. Other toll ferries run from the mainland to Deer Island, from Blacks Harbour to Grand Manan, and from Deer Island to Campobello Island, all in the southern corner of the province.

THE SAINT JOHN RIVER VALLEY

The Saint John River's original name was the Woolastook, an Indian word that translates aptly as the goodly (or godly) river. The French explorer Samuel de Champlain christened it the Saint John to mark his arrival at the river's mouth on Saint John's feast day in 1604. Other French explorers followed and tracked the river's circuitous route 724 km north from the Bay of Fundy to the forested interior. This watery highway, dubbed the "Rhine of North America," was mapped before any other part of New Brunswick.

The great river originates in remote northern Maine near the Québec border and enters New Brunswick's northwestern corner alongside Hwy. 205, a backcountry road used more by loggers than sightseers. The young river tumbles along, over riverbed boulders and through glistening pools frequented by moose and white-tailed deer. It flows through Edmundston and then curves southeast through the French-flavored towns and villages of Madawaska until it's squeezed into a spuming torrent at the stony gorge at Grand Falls.

The rest of the river's journey grows increasingly placid. It's tamed by hydro dams at Beechwood and Mactaquac, spanned by the world's longest covered bridge at Hartland, and flows gently through the capital city of Fredericton and finally on to Saint John—a pretty stretch houseboaters love to explore. The following coverage starts in Fredericton, then moves upriver.

Mount Carleton Provincial Park, though deep in the northern interior and far from the Saint John River, is accessible by two routes off the TransCanada Hwy., and so is included in this chapter.

FREDERICTON

Fredericton (pop. 47,000) in the southwestern heart of the province is New Brunswick's legislative, cultural, and educational center. The city is the exception to the usual rule of thumb that a province's busiest and largest city is the logical choice for the capital. Fredericton (Fred-RIK-ton) is hardly a metropolis. Rather, it's small, elegant, picture-book pretty, and very Anglo in tone and shape. "There is something subtle and elusive about it," Michael Collie wrote of Fred-

ericton, "like a person who has had long sessions of psychoanalysis and has become more sophisticated and charming in the course of them."

Visitors flying in to New Brunswick will find Fredericton makes a good introduction to the province and a good sightseeing base. Roads lead from here to every part of the province. St. Andrews and Saint John on the Fundy are each about a two-hour drive south, and Moncton is

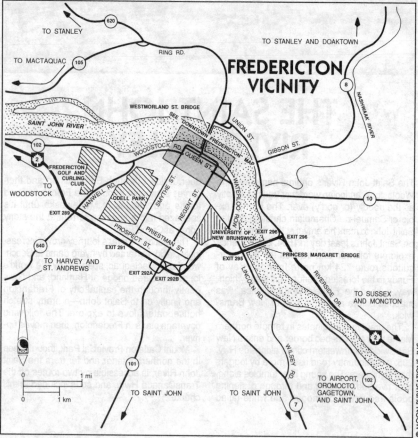

FREDERICTON VICINITY

TO STANLEY

TO MACTAQUAC

RING RD.

TO STANLEY AND DOAKTOWN

WESTMORLAND ST. BRIDGE

SAINT JOHN RIVER

SEE "DOWNTOWN FREDERICTON" MAP

UNION ST.

NASHWAAK RIVER

GIBSON ST.

WOODSTOCK RD.

QUEEN ST.

WATERLOO ROW

FREDERICTON GOLF AND CURLING CLUB.

TO WOODSTOCK

HANWELL RD.

ODELL PARK

SMYTHE ST.

REGENT ST.

PRIESTMAN ST.

EXIT 289

EXIT 291

PROSPECT ST.

UNIVERSITY OF NEW BRUNSWICK

EXIT 296

EXIT 296

PRINCESS MARGARET BRIDGE

EXIT 295

EXIT 292A

EXIT 292B

TO HARVEY AND ST. ANDREWS

LINCOLN RD.

RIVERSIDE DR.

TO SUSSEX AND MONCTON

MOON

0   1 mi

0   1 km

WILSEY RD.

TO SAINT JOHN

TO SAINT JOHN

TO AIRPORT, OROMOCTO, GAGETOWN, AND SAINT JOHN

© MOON PUBLICATIONS, INC.

another hour to the east. And it's always nice to return to Fredericton, the province's quintessential hometown.

Also Known As . . .

New Brunswickers have dubbed Fredericton "North America's Last Surviving Hometown"—a disputable claim, perhaps, but one that nonetheless sums up local priorities.

Also called the "Cathedral City," Fredericton and Christ Church Cathedral had a tightly woven beginning. The town was barely three generations old when Queen Victoria got wind of an Anglican sanctuary project in the capital. But with fewer than 10,000 inhabitants, the settlement was hardly the proper setting for the foundation of the first Anglican cathedral to be built on British soil since the Reformation. Royalty, of course, can do anything it wants, and Queen Victoria remedied the hitch. She elevated little Fredericton to an official "city," the status required for an Anglican cathedral's setting. Begun in 1845, Christ Church Cathedral opened in 1853, was rebuilt after a fire in 1911, and is still the place where the city's nabobs go to pay their respects to the benevolent powers that be.

Or perhaps you'll enjoy more another Fredericton nickname, "City of Stately Elms," a testament to Fredericton's leafy ambience. The quiet streets are lined mainly with elms, a choice that goes back to founding Loyalist times. They've survived centuries, even beating Dutch elm disease, which the city quelled in the 1960s and '70s.

Fredericton's reputation as "Canada's Poets' Corner" is a tribute to native sons Bliss Carmen, Sir Charles G.D. Roberts, and Francis Joseph Sherman. And, finally, the nickname "Canada's Pewtersmith Capital" singles out the city's preeminent craft, developed here first by pewtersmith Ivan Crowell in the 18th century.

HISTORY

Fredericton is one of North America's oldest cities, though early attempts at settlement were short-lived. The French tried settlements in the late 1600s. Joseph Robineau de Villebon, Acadia's governor, built a fur-trading fort on the northern bank of the Saint John River, at the mouth of the Nashwaak River. Heavy winter ice wrecked the fortification, and the inhabitants fled to Port Royal across the Bay of Fundy. In 1713, the Treaty of Utrecht awarded mainland Nova Scotia to the British, and Acadians fled back across the Fundy and founded Saint-Anne's Point (now site of Fredericton's historic area). The British demolished the village after the Acadian Deportation. Malecite Indians camped along what is now Woodstock Road, but moved upriver to the Kingsclear area before the Loyalists arrived in the late 18th century.

The Capital's Fortuitous Beginning

The situation that created Fredericton as provincial capital was an interesting one. After the American Revolution, Loyalists by the thousands poured into New Brunswick at Saint John. England directed the mass exodus from New York, but military forces at Saint John were unprepared for the onslaught.

Arriving Loyalists and families, finding limited food and no housing, rioted. Stung by the backlash, the British directed subsequent migrants 103 km upriver to Saint-Anne's Point. The Loyalists arrived in the wilderness, founded a new settlement as a "haven for the King's friends," and named it Frederick's Town in honor of King George III's second son. Two years later, in 1785, provincial governor Thomas Carleton designated the little river town as colonial capital, and the people of Saint John were permanently miffed.

England had great plans for Fredericton. Surveyor Charles Morris drew up the first street grid between University Avenue and Wilsey Road. By 1786, the population center had shifted, and central Fredericton as you will see it now was redrawn by another surveyor and extended from riverfront to George Street, bounded by University Avenue and Smythe Street.

Priorities were established. Space was set aside for the Church of England sanctuary and King's College, now the University of New Brunswick. Public commons were marked off between riverfront and Queen Street, except for two blocks earmarked for the British Army garrison.

The first winters were brutal, and Loyalists buried their dead at Salamanca on Waterloo Row. Wooden boardwalks were laid as sidewalks along muddy streets, and sewage was funneled into the river. The colonial government began at Government House in 1787, and New Brunswick's first assembly met at a coffeehouse the next year.

Expansion

The infamous Benedict Arnold lived awhile in Fredericton—and was burned in effigy at Saint John. Jonathan Odell, an influential Loyalist politician whose former estate land is now Odell Park, acted as negotiator between Arnold and England. American artist and naturalist John James Audubon visited Fredericton in 1830 and painted the *Pine Finch,* one of his best-known works, during his stay at Government House.

By 1800, wharves from Waterloo Row to Smthye Street lined the riverfront, and sloops, schooners, and brigantines sped between the capital and Saint John. Shipping lumber was a profitable early business, and Fredericton added foundry products, processed leather, carriages, and wagons to its economy in the 1800s. The city was incorporated in 1848, and in 1873 the city limits were extended to nearby towns, doubling the population. The city hall opened three years later.

Fires and Floods

Fredericton had its share of scourges. In the 1800s, locals ruefully joked that the city had a fire every Saturday night and dubbed it the "City of Fires." Flames consumed even the sturdiest stone buildings, from Government House to the Military Compound's Guard House. Great conflagrations leveled 300 downtown buildings in 1849, 46 houses and stores in 1854, and took the first Christ Church Cathedral's steeple in 1911. Even the Westmorland Street Bridge was vulnerable, and the first bridge, built in 1885, burned in 1905.

River floods were equally devastating: Queen Street was frequently under water during spring's ice melt. Floods in 1887 and 1923 swamped the capital. The upriver Mactaquac Dam was built to divert the river's impact, but floods again threatened the capital during 1973-74.

The Town Evolves

England's plan for Fredericton as a miniature London was never fulfilled. Shipping and manufacturing diminished in the early 1900s, and Fredericton settled in as a prosperous, genteel government town, university center, and haunt of the Anglo establishment. The **New Brunswick College of Craft and Design** started up in the 1940s and relocated to the renovated Military Compound in the 1980s. The **University of New Brunswick,** with 7,500 engineering, arts, education, business, and science students, overlooks the city from a steep hilltop and shares the campus with **St. Thomas University,** a Roman Catholic institution with 1,200 liberal-arts students.

William Maxwell Aitken, better known as Lord Beaverbrook, paved the way for Fredericton's cultural accomplishments. The **Beaverbrook Art Gallery** was a gift to the city in 1959, and **Lord Beaverbrook Playhouse** across the street followed in 1964 and evolved as the home of Theatre New Brunswick, Atlantic Canada's only provincial repertory touring company.

City planners wisely avoided commercial saturation and set most of the city's dozen shopping malls and its motel row beyond the residential area on the outskirts of Prospect St., which parallels the TransCanada.

SIGHTS

The tourist's Fredericton is easy to understand and very manageable. The town started at the riverfront with Queen, King, Brunswick, George, and Charlotte streets, and everything important lies adjacent or nearby. For most sightseeing, follow Queen Street, a block inland from the river. At riverfront, walking paths weave through **The Green,** the slender, five-km-long promenade that encompasses the whole curving riverbank from Princess Margaret Bridge to the Sheraton. Queen Street also forms the shopping area's edge, and the city's notable crafts shops lie along Regent and other cross streets. From there, tree-lined streets feed back to shady, quiet residential areas of historic oversize houses with open porches, bay windows, and gardens of pearl-colored peonies and scarlet poppies.

Metered parking is plentiful in parking lots behind sites and curbside on Queen, King, upper York, Carleton, Regent, and Saint John

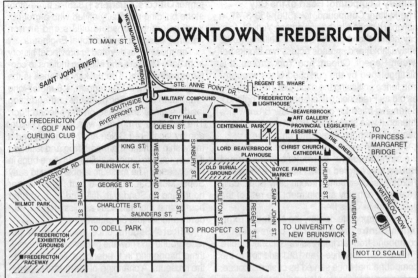

DOWNTOWN FREDERICTON

streets. The city provides free parking for out-of-province visitors in the lot behind city hall; parking passes are available at city hall and the Legislative Assembly building, both on Queen Street. Sites listed below start at city hall and proceed southeast on Queen Street.

Photogenic Vistas

If you're interested in capturing a scene of the river rimming the town, start with the red-and-white-striped Fredericton Lighthouse near the Regent Street Wharf. A trudge up the lighthouse's interior steps to the top opens up sweeping views of the Saint John River as it curves around the historic area. Another encompassing view a few blocks inland is from the University of New Brunswick; the campus edge on a steep hilltop peers across the city and river.

The most memorable angle, though, is from the Princess Margaret Bridge, at Hwy. 102 at the town's southeastern outskirts. The Saint John flows alongside Fredericton like a long looking glass, and scenes of stately old houses set back on green lawns reflect across the water's surface.

City Hall

The brick city hall, as pretty as a gingerbread house, anchors one end of the downtown sightseeing district. The elegant building, at the corner of Queen and York streets, began in 1876 as city offices, jail, farmers' market, and opera house. Its high tower houses the city's copper clock, and the decorative fountain in front—crowned by the figurine Frederictonians have dubbed "Freddie, the little nude dude"—was added in 1885.

The building was used as an opera house into the 1940s. Today it's mainly city offices. The Council Chamber, once an opera house, is adorned with a series of 27 locally produced tapestries depicting the city's history. The tapestries were woven for Fredericton's bicentennial. The Fredericton Visitors Bureau, tel. (506) 452-9500, in the building's front vestibule, conducts chamber tours mid-May to early Sept., daily 8 a.m.-7:30 p.m., weekdays until 4:30 the rest of the year. Free guided walking tours, led by the informative, entertaining, and period-dressed members of the Calithumpians—the city's theatrical troupe—start from here too, in July and August. For details, ask at the bureau desk.

Military Compound: Heart of the City

The Military Compound, tel. (506) 453-3747, a national historic site, begins across York St. from city hall at the imposing Justice Building (tours unavailable) and spreads across two blocks between Regent, Queen, and York streets. It is distinguished by the curlicued black wrought-iron fence enclosing the expanse. The complex, as old as Fredericton itself, began as England's defensive base for guarding New Brunswick's interior. It was staffed with British Army and subsequent Canadian regiments until 1914.

At the corner of Queen and Carleton streets, the stone **Soldiers' Barracks** and the **Guard House** are restored rooms harking back to the 1820s-60s; open June through early Sept., daily 10 a.m.-6 p.m., by appointment the rest of the year. Admission is free.

On the opposite corner, the **National Exhibition Centre,** tel. 453-3747, peers over the compound from an impressive Second Empire French Revival edifice—an 1881 addition to the compound that once served as customs house, post office, and library. National art, history, science, and technology exhibits are on the first floor; upstairs is the **New Brunswick Sports Hall of Fame,** with exhibits on provincial sports history. The Centre is open May to early Sept., daily 10 a.m.-6 p.m.; all other months Tues.-Sun. noon-5 p.m.

Facing the greensward of the old Parade Square, the **York-Sunbury Historical Society Museum,** tel. 455-6041, is housed within the former **Officers' Quarters** (1825), a three-story stone building unusually styled with a ground-level colonnade of white pillars and an iron handrail, designed by the Royal Engineers.

The museum is devoted to provincial history from early Malecite and Micmac Indians to contemporary events. The unlikely surprise is the **Coleman Frog,** a 17-kilogram, 1.6-meter-long amphibian stuffed for posterity and squatting inside a glass showcase on the second floor. The believe-it-or-not frog was found a century ago by local Fred Coleman, who developed a friendship with the mammoth frog and fattened it up by feeding it rum pudding and June bugs in honey sauce. The museum is open May to early Sept., Mon.-Sat. 10 a.m.-6 p.m.; open longer hours and on Sunday in July and Aug., shorter hours other months. Adult admission is $1, students and seniors 50 cents.

Officers' Square, once the regimental parade ground and now the grassy center of everything happening in Fredericton, lies alongside the museum. A changing-of-the-guard ceremony takes place hourly, July-Aug., Tues.-Sat. 11 a.m.-7 p.m. The 1832 **Militia Arms Store,** the only surviving wooden building in the complex, is now used for offices and is closed to visitors.

New Brunswick Power Electricity Museum

Originally located upriver at the Mactaquac Generating Station, the museum was recently moved across from the Military Compound to 514 Queen St., tel. (506) 458-6805. Exhibits detail

the military compound

NAN DROSDICK

generating and distribution developments by NB Power, the provincial electricity utility. It's open July-Aug., Mon.-Fri. 9 a.m.-9 p.m. and other months 9 a.m.-4:30 p.m. Admission is free.

Historic Cemeteries

The **Old Burial Ground,** bounded by Regent, Brunswick, George, and Sunbury streets, is a two-block walk inland from the NB Power Museum. The site—spliced with walkways beneath tall trees—is one of two historic burial grounds in town. This spread of greenery was the final resting place for Loyalist notables. The **Loyalist Cemetery** (formerly the Salamanca graveyard), on an unmarked gravel road off Waterloo Row at riverfront, is simpler and marks the final resting place of the founding Loyalists who died in that first winter of 1783-84.

Fredericton Lighthouse

Walking back up Regent St. to The Green at riverfront will bring you to this privately operated lighthouse, tel. (506) 459-2515, which still guides river traffic. The tower's interior consists of 13 separate landings exhibiting shipping and river-sailing artifacts The top level commands a magnificent riverfront view. At ground level, you'll find a gift shop and summertime outdoor cafe serving light lunches. The lighthouse is open July-Aug., daily 10 a.m.-9 p.m.; June and Sept., Mon.-Fri. 9 a.m.-4 p.m., Sat. noon-4 p.m. and shorter hours other months. Adult admission is $2, children $1.

Beaverbrook Art Gallery

Take any of the short streets back into town to the Beaverbrook Art Gallery, 703 Queen St., tel. (506) 458-8545, which was given to the city in 1959 by New Brunswick art maven Lord Beaverbrook, also known as William Maxwell Aitken. The gallery boasts an impressive 2,000-piece collection—the most extensive British fine-arts collection in Atlantic Canada, if not the nation. Among the British painters represented are Thomas Gainsborough, Sir Joshua Reynolds, John Constable, and Walter Richard Sickert. You'll find Graham Sutherland's sketches of Winston Churchill—drawn in preparation for Churchill's official portrait—and works by Atlantic Canada's Miller Brittain, Alex Colville, and

Jack Humphrey. Also central to the collection are the oils of Cornelius Krieghoff, depicting social and domestic scenes of early life in Acadia. Nor could Lord Beaverbrook resist the European masters—Salvador Dali's large-scale *Santiago El Grande* and Botticelli's *Resurrection* are prominently displayed.

The gallery and gift shop are open year-round. Summer hours are Sun.-Mon. noon-5 p.m., Tues.-Sat. 10 a.m.-5 p.m., longer hours July and August. Admission is $3 for adults, $2 for seniors over 65, and $1 for children 5-16.

Legislative Assembly Building

The splendidly regal legislative building lies kitty-corner from the gallery on Queen St., tel. (506) 453-2527. The sandstone French Revival building spreads across a manicured lawn, its massive wings pierced with high, arched windows, and the upper floor and tower rotunda washed in glistening white.

The building was completed in 1882 at a cost of $120,000, including construction and furnishings. The front portico entrance opens into an interior decorated in high Victorian style—the apex of expensive taste at the time. Glinting Waterford prisms are set in brass chandeliers, and the spacious rooms are wallpapered in an oriental design. The interior's pièce de résistance is the **Assembly Chamber,** centered around an ornate throne set on a dais and sheltered with a canopy.

John James Audubon's *Birds of America* is kept in the **Legislative Library.** One of four volumes is on display in a climate-controlled exhibit, and pages are periodically turned to show the meticulous paintings. Each of the building's nooks and corners has a story, which tour guides are eager to relate. Half-hour tours operate early June to late August, daily 9 a.m.-8 p.m.; otherwise the building is open year-round, Mon.-Fri. 9 a.m.-4 p.m. Legislative sessions (Feb.-May, October) are open to the public.

Christ Church Cathedral

Gothic-styled cathedrals were designed to soar grandiosely toward heaven, and this storied stone cathedral is no exception. With a lofty, copper-clad central spire and elegant linear stone tracery, the cathedral rises from a grassy city block at Church and Brunswick streets.

Begun in 1845 and consecrated in 1853, this was the first entirely new cathedral founded on British soil since the Norman Conquest of 1066. It's open year-round, and free guided tours of the cathedral are given mid-June to Labour Day; tel. (506) 450-8500.

City Parks

Of the 355 hectares of lush parkland throughout the city, **Odell Park** alongside Smythe St., tel. (506) 454-3550, is the choice spread. The park is Fredericton's largest, covering 175 hectares (388 acres), and is best known for an arboretum holding every tree species in the province. A 2.8-km walking trail divided in three loops wanders through the shady expanse, past a duck pond, deer pen, cooking pits, and picnic tables. The park is open dawn to dusk.

Christ Church

ACCOMMODATIONS

Budget and Camping

The **Fredericton Youth Hostel** is centrally located in an 1890s four-story brick schoolhouse building at 193 York St., tel. (506) 454-1233. It's one of Hostelling International's hostels, and has 30 beds ($9-16 pp), laundry, and kitchen facilities; open June-August. The **UNB-Tourist Hotel** at the University of New Brunswick on Bailey Dr., tel. 453-4891, is the campus's official name for eight dormitory buildings with 1,382 rooms. The school rents the dorm rooms out after students go home for the summer. They're open July to mid-August; $11.50 pp student, $20 pp for everybody else, and bring your own towels.

The closest camping to Fredericton is at **Hartt Island Campground,** about seven km west of town on the TransCanada Hwy., tel. 450-6057. Its 125 sites cost $15-20 per night. Self-contained motor homes and trailers can park free overnight in the lot behind the Justice Building.

Inns and B&Bs

The Queen Anne Revival **Carriage House Inn** at 230 University Ave., tel. (506) 452-9924 or (800) 267-6068, has 10 rooms furnished with antiques ($50-75 with full breakfast). Facilities include a solarium and laundry facilities. Basic **Elm's Tourist Home,** 263-269 Saunders St., tel. 454-3410, charges $35 s, $45 d.

Motels

Lodgings are concentrated along Prospect St., which parallels the TransCanada (Hwy. 2) about three km southwest of the town center. The **Auberge Wandlyn Inn** at 58 Prospect St. West, tel. (506) 452-8937 or (800) 561-0000 in eastern Canada, (800) 561-0006 in the U.S., has 116 rooms and suites ($55-85), a restaurant, swimming pools, a hot tub, sauna, and exercise room. The **Fredericton Inn,** 1315 Regent St., tel. 455-1430, is a good-looking lodging near Prospect St. between the Regent and Fredericton shopping malls and has 200 rooms ($57-129), a dining room and lounge, and whirlpool. The **Comfort Inn** at 255 Prospect St., tel. 453-0800, has 60 basic, clean rooms ($56-77) with no frills.

The **Keddy's Inn Fredericton,** 368 Forest Hill Rd., tel. 454-4461, overlooks the river near the Princess Margaret Bridge near Lincoln Rd. and has 120 rooms ($40-69), a dining room, pub, and sauna. And the **Howard Johnson's Motor Lodge** on the TransCanada Hwy., tel. 472-0480, is just across the bridge with 120 rooms ($64-110), a dining room, exercise room, and sauna.

Hotels

The four-star **Sheraton Inn Fredericton** at 225 Woodstock Rd., tel. 457-7000, (800) 325-3535, fax 457-4000, reigns as the city's newest property. It hugs the Saint John River several blocks west of downtown in a splendid architectural statement, and has 223 rooms ($65-112), a restaurant, lounge, exercise room, and sauna. Also first-rate is **Keddy's Lord Beaverbrook Hotel,** 659 Queen St., tel. 455-3371, which puts you within quick striking distance of downtown sightseeing and has 165 spacious rooms ($79-119; ask for a riverfront room for terrific views), a dining room, sauna, and exercise room.

BOB RACE

FOOD

Fredericton has a reputation for so-so dining. Don't believe it. True, you won't find tony dining rooms by the dozens, and aside from at a few fine restaurants, the cooking is less than fancy. Nonetheless, you can sample virtually all the capital's fare without a qualm, and your dining dollar will go a long way, too.

Light Fare and Food Stores

Plenty of fast food is clustered along Regent St. and across the river on Main Street. If you're planning a picnic, the **J M & T Deli** at 66 Regent St., tel. (506) 458-9068, has a tempting assortment of cold cuts, breads, muffins, bagels, and carrot cake. The **Boyce Farmers' Market,** facing George St. between Regent and Saint John streets, lures *everybody* with stalls heaped with baked goods, homemade German sausage, other local delicacies, and crafts. It's open year-round, Sat. 6 a.m.-1 p.m. **Sobey's** on Prospect St. is the largest supermarket, open Mon.-Sat. 24 hours a day.

The provincial **liquor stores** are at the Fredericton Mall on Prospect St.; at 225 King Street; at the Devon Shopping Plaza on Union St.; and at the Brookside Mall on Brookside Drive.

Dinner

The **Hilltop Pub & Steak House,** 152 Prospect St., tel. (506) 458-9057, specializes in aged charbroiled beef. The **Lobster Hut,** 1216 Regent St., tel. 455-4413, is City Motel–Sequoia's claim to fame. They'll boil, broil, stuff, fry, or serve cold the best lobsters in town starting at $16— and the largest-available (more expensive) lobsters can be requested with an advance phone call. Other entrees range $5-25.

The **Lunar Rogue** at 625 King St., tel. 450-2065, reigns as Fredericton's definitive pub, with dining indoors or alfresco on the patio. The Rogue serves worthy light dinners ($6-12) like Cornish pasties, stir-fry chicken, and sirloin strip, as well as pub-grub specials such as barbecued chicken wings. The beer selection is excellent. Across the street and a block down, **Mexicali Rosa's,** 546 King St., tel. 451-0686, is a popular spot for reasonably priced fajitas, enchiladas, and daily lunch specials.

The **La Vie en Rose** at 570 Queen St., tel. 455-1319, is a honey of a place with a menu of Canadian dishes to match. For a modest $7-16, you can savor pasta Alfredo with vegetables, stuffed rack of lamb, or beef Wellington with mushroom pâté; Sunday brunch costs $9. Desserts are New Brunswick's best—try the homemade cheesecake ($4).

The **Acadian Room** at the Auberge Wandlyn Inn at 58 Prospect St. West, tel. 452-8937, has been a local dining favorite for years. Dishes are basic seafood, red meats, and poultry ($7-19), but they're thoughtfully conceived and quickly served. The sauced salmon steak (cooked any way you'd like) served with fiddleheads ($15) deserves special praise.

The **Terrace Room** at the Keddy's Lord Beaverbrook Hotel at 659 Queen St., tel. 455-3371 (reservations required), meets all culinary demands with weekday noon buffet ($10); Sunday noon buffet ($13); basic dinners ($7-19).

Bruno's Cafe, in the Sheraton Inn Fredericton, tel. 457-7000, lures crowds for fare new to Fredericton like chicken saltimbocca—a sautéed stuffed chicken breast basted with white wine and served on linguine. Dinner entrees range $10-20; Sunday brunch costs $16; and weekday noon Corner Deli buffet is a terrific buy at $7.

ENTERTAINMENT AND EVENTS

Theater and Cinema

Fredericton specializes in entertaining summertime visitors. Festivities center around the Military Compound's Officers' Square, where the **Calithumpians,** the city's theatrical troupe, take to the boards July to early September. Their humorous and historical productions take place weekdays at 12:15 p.m. and weekends at 2 p.m. Local pipe bands and folk, country, and bluegrass groups also entertain at the same location, July-Aug., Tues. and Thurs. at 7:30 p.m. For more information call (506) 452-9500.

The **Theatre New Brunswick,** the province's only professional English-speaking theater company, operates full-tilt during the autumn-to-spring theater season at the Lord Beaverbrook Playhouse, Queen Street. Past presentations have included *A Streetcar Named Desire* and

Shirley Valentine. The playhouse presents several shows in summer; for details, call 458-8344.

The **Plaza Cinemas** at the Kmart Plaza on Smythe St. near Prospect St. has a multiplex offering four first-run film choices every night, as well as weekend matinees. For the schedule, call 458-0898. The **Nashwaaksis Twin Cinemas** has two screens at the Nashwaaksis Plaza, on Ferry Avenue, tel. 457-0286.

Nightlife
With seven individual bars, the private **Club Cosmopolitan** at 546 King St., tel. (506) 458-8165, has a cozy corner for most moods ($2 admission for nonmembers). It's liveliest around the main dance floor, where music is orchestrated by a disc jockey Mon.-Sat. 9 p.m.-2 p.m. Touring rock groups and big bands head for **Sweetwaters** at 339 King St., tel. 459-5565, where admission costs $8-20. The nightclub presents pulsating, high-energy rock to 2 a.m., Thurs.-Sat. ($3 cover charge).

Otherwise, the locals like dimly lit pubs. The **Lunar Rogue** at 625 King St., tel. 450-2065, heads the list with English pub ambience, Canadian and British draft beer, and live music—usually with a Celtic flavor—several nights a week. The **Hilltop Pub,** 152 Prospect St., is another choice pub and spreads out with nooks and corners on several levels.

Tamer tunes and country-and-western are the specialty of the **River Room** at the Keddy's Lord Beaverbrook Hotel. It's open until 1 or 2 a.m. If a balmy summer riverside evening with a guitar player sounds appealing, check out the hotel's outdoor **Top Deck,** open July-Aug. to midnight. The Sheraton Inn Fredericton devotes a spacious corner without music to **D.J. Purdy's** (named for an old-time, local riverboat), where it serves deftly mixed drinks in pleasant riverside surroundings.

Events
The summer season opens with the four-day **Cathedral Festival of the Arts,** an arts-and-crafts showcase during May's third weekend at Christ Church Cathedral; call (506) 450-8500 for details. The **Festival Francophone** follows for three days late in the month, celebrating Acadian language and culture with concerts, dancing, and children's activities. It all takes place at Le Centre Communautaire Sainte-Anne, on Priestman St. near Regent St., tel. 458-5689.

Late June–early July's stellar event is the **Fredericton River Jubilee,** with the Maritimes' step-dancing championships, outdoor concerts, a parade, art exhibits, and other hoopla for four days; call 452-1954 for details. The **Highland Games,** a local three-day Celtic tribute featuring pipe bands, Highland dancing, Gaelic singing, clan booths, and more, takes over the city during late July.

New Brunswick Day, the first Monday in August, brings parades, street-food vendors, and fireworks. Fredericton had its first fall fair in 1825, and the tradition continues at the **Fredericton Exhibition,** with six days of country-fair trappings, including harness racing and stage shows, at the Fredericton Exhibition Grounds during early Sept.; tel. 458-8819. The season finishes in a clamor of music, as the outdoor **Harvest Jazz and Blues Festival** takes over the downtown streets in mid-September; tel. 454-2583.

RECREATION

The **Fredericton Small Craft Aquatic Center,** located at riverfront off Woodstock Rd., tel. 458-5513, rents recreational rowing shells, canoes, and kayaks. It's open July-Aug., daily 9 a.m.-1 p.m. and 4-9:30 p.m., Sat.-Sun. 10 a.m.-4 p.m., and shorter hours until early October closing. The center also gives two-evening lessons ($45).

The **Fredericton Golf and Curling Club,** tel. (506) 458-0003 (reservations are wise), has user-friendly links (aside from the 18th hole—known as "Cardiac Hill"). The course lies beyond the Sheraton Inn Fredericton on Woodstock Rd.'s inland side, and is open May-September. Greens fee is $29, and rental carts and clubs are available.

The **Fredericton Raceway,** Fredericton Exhibition Grounds, Smythe St., tel. 458-8819, has harness racing ($2 admission) from mid-May to mid-Oct., Wed. 7:30 p.m., Sat. 1:30 p.m.

Physical Fitness
The **Lady Beaverbrook Gymnasium,** at the University of New Brunswick on University Ave.,

admits visitors to its pool, weight room, and squash court facilities with a day-use pass ($2.50). For hours, call (506) 453-4793. **Keddy's Inn Fredericton** does the same with pool and sauna ($2.50); open daily, 7 a.m.-midnight. The **Keddy's Lord Beaverbrook Hotel** admits nonguests to fitness facilities ($3) on Monday, noon-midnight.

SHOPPING

Shopping areas are concentrated downtown, mainly along Regent, Queen, York, King, and the adjacent side streets, plus on Woodstock Rd. and at the malls. The Regent Mall is on upper Regent St., on the south side of the Trans-Canada Hwy.; the Fredericton Mall is on Prospect St. near Regent, just north of the Trans-Canada. Kings Place shopping center is in the heart of downtown. The downtown shops are open Mon.-Wed. and Sat. 9 a.m.-5 p.m., Thurs.-Fri. to 9 p.m., while the mall stores are open Mon.-Sat. 10 a.m.-10 p.m. A few small shops and craft studios are open weekdays only.

Craft Shops
Several shops are known for craft specialties. **Aitkens Pewter** at 81 Regent St., tel. 450-8188, stocks handcrafted pewter holloware, jewelry, and decorative ware. **Carriage House Studio** at 136 Aberdeen St. is the place for enamel jewelry. For porcelain and stoneware, check out **Garden Creek Pottery** at 1538 Woodstock Rd., tel. (506) 455-7631.

The **Shades of Light,** 288 Regent St., tel. 455-1318, sells stained glass, pewter, pottery and Maritime crafts, while the **Craft Corner,** tel. 458-8097, at the Fredericton Mall on Prospect St., stocks a wealth of provincial crafts.

Art Galleries and Artists
The **Gallery Connexion,** prominently placed within the Military Compound near York St., tel. (506) 454-1433, is a nonprofit artists' outlet with an eminent reputation for provincial arts, open Tues.-Fri. noon-4 p.m., Sun. 2-4 p.m. For local artists' works, check out **Capital Art Gallery** at the Fredericton Mall, tel. 458-8192. **Print Gallery** at the King's Place Mall, tel. 459-7493, has a nice selection of Fredericton sketches. **Gallery**

78 at 796 Queen St. at the corner of Church St., tel. 454-5192, stocks a national collection.

Several **local artists** are well known. Cathy Ross has established a fine reputation for prints, as has David Mackay, who works in egg tempera. Bruno Bobak is known for provincial scenic paintings, and no one does wildflower renderings like Molly Lamb.

Sundries
Across the river are **Gem Star Pawnbrokers,** 37 Main St., tel. (506) 450-6383; and **Pawnbrokers and Estate Jewellery,** 409 Union St., tel. 452-7949.

The city has a half dozen camera shops, mainly at the malls. **Harvey Studios,** 372 Queen St., tel. 459-1155, is a downtown source for Pentax, Canon, Minolta, and Olympus and stocks film and equipment. A malfunctioning camera has no quick solution; repair jobs are sent to Toronto. To spare yourself heartbreak, have a questionable camera checked out at home, or bring along an extra.

Coles The Book People at the Regent Mall shopping center stocks the city's most extensive book assortment, and there are a dozen other bookstores in town. **Libart Ltd.,** at 247 Main St. across the river, tel. 459-0885, handles the bilingual book market. It's open Mon.-Sat. 10 a.m.-5:30 p.m. The **Reading Corner,** at 132 Main St., is nearby and has a trove of used books and paperbacks.

INFORMATION AND SERVICES

Visitor Information
The friendly staff at the **Fredericton Visitors Bureau** stocks literature about the city; the office is located in the front vestibule of city hall at Queen and York streets. It's open mid-May to early Sept., daily 8 a.m.-8 p.m.; early Sept. to early Oct., daily to 4:30 p.m.; and early Oct. to mid-May, Mon.-Fri. 8:15 a.m.-4:30 p.m. For more information, call (506) 452-9500 (ask for the tourist bureau) or write P.O. Box 130, Fredericton, NB E3B 4Y7. A **tourist bureau** branch is at TransCanada's exit 292A, tel. 458-8331; open mid-May to Sept., daily 8 a.m.-8 p.m.

The **New Brunswick Geographic Information Corp.,** tel. 453-3390, stocks provincial topographical maps for 120 areas ($8), as well as a Saint John River canoe map ($10), and other detailed, local renditions. The office is part of the Land Information Centre in Fredericton Square at Queen and Westmorland streets. It's on the second floor, open weekdays 8:30 a.m.-5 p.m.

The Department of Forests, Mines and Resources at the Forestry Complex on Regent St., tel. 453-2440, has a public information center stocked with appropriate **fishing and hunting** regulations and license information. The center is open weekdays 8:15 a.m.-5 p.m. A branch office is located at 498 York Street.

Library and Archives

The **Fredericton Public Library** is at 12 Carleton St. alongside the Military Compound, tel. (506) 458-8154. It's open July-Aug., Mon.-Tues. and Thurs. 10 a.m.-5 p.m., Wed. and Fri. to 9 p.m.; the rest of the year it has longer weekday hours and is open on Saturdays.

The **New Brunswick Public Archives,** tel. 453-2122, stocks provincial ancestral records.

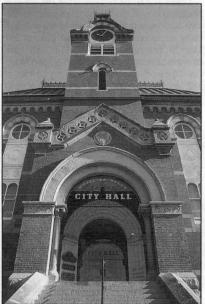

NAN DROSDICK

historic City Hall

To get there, take University Ave. to the end and turn right to Dineen Drive. The archives are in the Bonar Law Bennett Building, and are open year-round, Mon.-Fri. 10 a.m.-5 p.m., Sat. 8:30 a.m.-5 p.m. The archives publish *Tracing Your Ancestors,* a how-to guide ($20); for details, call the archives or write to them at P.O. Box 6000, Fredericton, NB E3B 5H1.

Classes

In summer, **New Brunswick College of Craft and Design** offers two-week photography, drawing, and painting classes. Courses cost $495 pp; lodgings, meals, and materials are extra. For registration, call the college at (506) 453-2305, or write to Advanced Education and Labour, P.O. Box 6000, Fredericton, NB E3B 5H1.

The **University of New Brunswick** hosts one-week Elderhostel classes in family heritage and roots searching. For details and registration, contact Elderhostel, 33 Prince Arthur, Suite 300, Toronto, ON M5R 1B2, tel. (416) 964-2260.

Environmental Organization

Lacking heavy industry, Fredericton boasts clear air and few problems. The Saint John River is clean within city limits, but conditions vary up- and downriver. The privately operated **Conservation Council of New Brunswick,** 180 Saint John St., tel. (506) 458-8747, keeps abreast of ecological issues throughout New Brunswick. Their efforts publicizing underground oil spills from storage tanks in Fredericton brought about city intervention. Currently the group is actively opposing plans for construction of a second nuclear plant at Point Lepreau near Saint John, as well as the forestry industry's clearcut timber harvesting, particularly along the Fundy between St. Martins and Fundy National Park.

Services

In an emergency, call 911. The **RCMP** is at 1445 Regent St., tel. (506) 452-3400. The **Dr. Everett Chalmers Hospital** is on Priestman St., tel. 452-5400, and the **Fredericton Medical Clinic** is at 1015 Regent St., tel. 458-0200.

Bank hours among the city's eight major banks and numerous branches are Mon.-Wed. 10 a.m.-4 p.m., Thurs.-Fri. to 5 p.m. A few banks, such as the **Bank of Montreal** at 575 Prospect

St. and the **Toronto Dominion** at the Regent Mall, are open Sat. 9:30 a.m.-3:30 p.m.

Hours at the **Canada Post** at 527 Queen St., tel. 452-3345, are Mon.-Fri. 8 a.m.-5 p.m.; the retail outlets at Kings Place and Fredericton Mall shopping centers have longer hours and are open Saturday.

The **Immigration Centre** at Kings Place, tel. 452-3090, is the provincial head office for foreign immigration. It's open Mon.-Fri. 8:30 a.m.-4:30 p.m. If you're thinking of extending your visit, it pays to call ahead; the office has a two-week request backlog and schedules Mon. and Fri. appointments.

Launderettes are plentiful; the **Regent Street Laundromat,** 403 Regent St., tel. 459-5146, is open Mon.-Fri. 7:30 a.m.-9 p.m., Sat. from 8 a.m., Sun. from 9 a.m. **Spin & Grin** is at 518 Smythe St., open daily to 9:30 p.m.

If you arrive with luggage to stash, you can leave it at the bus terminal at **SMT** at 101 Regent St.; a storage locker costs $1 per day.

TRANSPORTATION

Getting There
The Fredericton Airport is a 15-minute drive from downtown Fredericton and lies off Hwy. 102 alongside the Saint John River; taxis ($18 to downtown) wait outside during arrivals. **Avis, Hertz,** and **Tilden** car-rental counters are near the baggage carousels.

The airport is served by **Air Canada,** tel. (506) 452-0166, and its inter-Maritimes affiliate, **Air Nova,** tel. 458-8561. Other airlines serving Fredericton include **Canadian Airlines International,** tel. 466-6034; **Air Atlantic** tel. 446-6034; and Northwest Airlink, tel. 446-3005.

SMT at 101 Regent St., tel. 458-6009, offers frequent bus service to all parts of the province at low prices (Fredericton-Edmundston, for example, costs $33 OW). The terminal is open 8 a.m.-8:30 p.m.; storage lockers are available for $1 per day.

The **Regent Street Wharf,** Regent St. at riverfront, tel. 455-1445, is where you'll tie up if you arrive under your own sails. It's open daily from late June to Aug., and weekends only from Sept. to mid-October. Overnight mooring (first-come, first-served) costs $5-10.

Getting Around
Fredericton Transit, tel. (506) 458-9522, has a web of bus routes connecting downtown with outlying areas. Fare is a loonie (Canadian one-dollar coin), and drivers prefer exact change. The buses run daily except Sunday.

The city is saturated with **taxis** that cruise downtown city streets, wait at hotels, and are on-call. Rates are based on city zones, and tips—50 cents to $1 for a basic fare—are expected, although optional. **Trius Taxi** at 185 Handwell Rd., tel. 459-3366, is among the largest outfits and charges $2-12 within the city.

Car rental firms are plentiful. Renting a car from a local firm can be a good deal. For example, **Wood Motors,** 170 Prospect St., tel. 452-6611, rents a Ford Tempo for about $29 per day with free personal insurance coverage, 100 km free, and 12 cents each additional km; optional collision coverage costs $10 a day. For $10 extra, they'll have the car at the airport when you arrive and will drive you back to the airport free at departure.

Avis at the airport charges about $46 per day for an economy car with 100 km free and 17 cents for each additional kilometer, or $195 per week with 1,050 km free; optional collision insurance costs $10, personal injury insurance $2.50. Others companies include: **Budget,** 407 Regent St., tel. 452-1107; **Delta,** 304 King St., tel. 458-8899; **Hertz,** at the airport, tel. 446-5130; **Tilden,** 240 Prospect St., tel. 453-1700; and **Sears,** 407 Regent St., tel. 458-8550.

The Savage Mountain Bikes sold worldwide originate at **Savage's,** 449 King St., tel. 458-8985. The company rents its celebrity bikes, plus a host of other styles and makes, at $2-3 per hour, $10-15 per day. It's open Mon.-Wed. and Sat. 8:30 a.m.-5:30 p.m., Thurs.-Fri. to 9 p.m.

VICINITY OF FREDERICTON

The Saint John River below Fredericton is dotted with islands, around which a skein of twisting channels is braided. In the beautiful countryside between Upper Gagetown and Saint John, a series of free car ferries link the two sides of the river, making it easy to get around the scenic tangle of waterways.

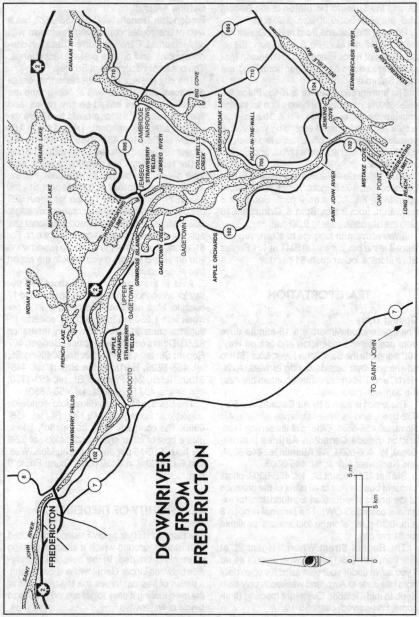

DOWNRIVER FROM FREDERICTON

TO SAINT JOHN

© MOON PUBLICATIONS, INC.

5 mi

5 km

Oromocto

This riverfront town's raison d'etre is the Canadian Forces Base Gagetown, the military training installation located near town center off Broad Road. The **CFB Gagetown Military Museum,** tel. (506) 422-2630, has exhibits on the past and present of the Canadian armed forces since the late 18th century—weapons, uniforms, and other memorabilia. The museum is open July-Aug., Mon.-Fri. 9 a.m.-5 p.m., Sat.-Sun. from noon; Sept.-June to 4 p.m. Admission is free.

Gagetown

Highway 102 follows the river to the pretty riverfront town of Gagetown, an hour from Fredericton. The handful of lanes here are lined with craft shops, small restaurants, and inns. Quite a bit goes on in this little town of 600 over the course of the season. The Summer Theatre Festival is staged June-Sept.; call (506) 454-8930 for details. Other events include the late-May Apple Blossom Festival, the Village of Gagetown Craft Festival at the fairgrounds in late June, and the four-day Queens County Fair in mid-September.

On Front St., the **Steamers Stop Inn,** tel. 488-2903, is a heritage inn with seven guest rooms ($49) and a well-known dining room that caters to guests of the inn, as well as to boaters who tie up at the Gagetown Creek pier out back. It's open May to September.

The **Queens County Museum** is also on Front St., tel. 488-2966. A national historic site, the handsome white wooden house was the birthplace of Sir Leonard Tilley, one of the "Fathers of Confederation." The first floor is dutifully furnished with Loyalist antiques, and upstairs there are vintage county exhibits. It's open June to mid-Sept., daily 10 a.m.-5 p.m. Admission is $1.

Gagetown's **Loomcrofters,** tel. 488-2400, located at the south end of the village in a 1761 fur-trading post known as the Blockhouse, demonstrates weaving techniques and produces renowned tartans, draperies, scarves, and upholstery fabrics.

UP THE SAINT JOHN RIVER

MACTAQUAC AND VICINITY

Once navigable from end to end, the Saint John River's course was first stemmed by the dam at Grand Falls/Grand-Sault. The hydroelectric dam at Beechwood near Bath came next. The **Mactaquac Hydro Dam,** some 20 km west of Fredericton, was completed in 1968. The dam rerouted the river and raised the water level 60 meters, flooding the valley and creating Mactaquac Lake Basin. Historic buildings from the flooded area found a new home at the Kings Landing Historical Settlement, a provincial heritage park that opened in 1974.

Not all New Brunswickers were pleased with this massive river alteration (it's the Maritimes' largest hydroelectric scheme), the abundant and cheap electrical power notwithstanding. The province sweetened the project with benefits, including an Atlantic salmon hatchery near the dam (visitors can tour the hatchery grounds), and 567-hectare Mactaquac Provincial Park— now the province's prime super-park—which opened in 1969.

The **Mactaquac Generating Station,** on the river's southern bank and just off the Trans-Canada, offers guided tours mid-May to early Sept., daily 9 a.m.-4:30 p.m.; call 363-3071 for details. Nearby, the **Mactaquac Fish Culture Station,** tel. (506) 363-3021, has Atlantic salmon of all sizes in the tanks. It's open year-round; guided tours depart the visitor center May-early Sept., daily 9 a.m.-4 p.m.

Mactaquac Provincial Park

This provincial park showpiece, 24 km upriver from Fredericton on Hwy. 105, tel. 363-3011, was created from prime forest and farmland. The wooded campground has 305 sites ($12 unserviced, $14 with electrical hookups) with kitchen shelters, hot showers, a launderette, and a campers' store fronting the Mactaquac Lake Basin. There's also a restaurant, supervised beaches, hiking trails, picnic areas, fishing streams, and a pond stocked with smallmouth

DOWNRIVER ON A HOUSEBOAT

Boating on the Saint John River's historic waters is an idyllic and popular pastime, and houseboating is a pleasant and memorable way to do it. As you glide down the Saint John, you'll pass fields of strawberries and apple orchards along the banks, and small islands in midstream—inhabited only by occasional cows and horses barged over by riverfront farmers to graze.

Renting a Houseboat

Tidy, compact houseboats have all the trappings and comforts of home in a scaled-down package. In general, the main deck has a forecabin equipped with one or more foldaway beds. Heading aft, you'll typically find a galley with a fridge, stove, oven, small sink, and cupboards stocked with cooking and dining utensils. Next comes the head with a hot shower, sink, and flush toilet. The sitting room brings up the rear with couches that convert to foldaway beds. Upstairs, a railed sundeck with chairs and space to sunbathe extends the houseboat's full length.

If your party consists of six or fewer passengers, contact **Houseboat Vacations,** tel. (506) 433-4801 or 433-1609. Bob and Judy Hutton have five houseboats for rent a week, partial week, or weekend. Season determines the rates: a week—from Saturday at 10 a.m. to Friday at 4 p.m.—costs $1000 during June's first three weeks, $1100 between late June and late August, and $900 through mid-October.

Advance reservations are wise, especially during peak summer season. The Huttons require a $250 deposit with the reservation and the balance when you pick up the boat at the village of Codys on Washademoak Lake, one of the Saint John River's offshoots. Insurance is optional but wise at $15 a day; a $200 damage deposit is refunded when you return the boat. For details, contact the company at P.O. Box 2088, Sussex, NB E0E 1P0.

Groups larger than six can get in touch with Tom Colpitts's **River Buoys Houseboat Vacations** at Gagetown. The 14-meter-long houseboat has ample room for up to 10 passengers and features extras such as a swim platform and waterslide from the stern. The houseboat rents for a week or day, mid-May to mid-October. The rates on a rental for a week range from $1400 during mid-June to mid-September to $1200 during the off-season. A day's rental, regardless of the season, costs $250; if you want a

captain along, it's $50 more. Colpitts advises reservations by the previous January; the reservation requires 50% down (or the full amount on one-day rentals), and you pay the balance when boarding the boat. The damage deposit is $500; buying the $15 per day damage insurance is wise.

Renting a houseboat is like renting a car. You'll get a full tank of gasoline to start and refill along the way. Marinas with **fuel stops** are at Fredericton, Oromocto, Jemseg, Cambridge-Narrows, Codys, and Gagetown.

What to Bring

Bring jeans, shorts, a few shirts, rubber-soled shoes, sunglasses, a jacket, a sweatshirt or sweater, and rain gear for the occasional summer showers. Unless you've made arrangements to the contrary with the rental company, you'll need to bring bedding and towels for everyone in your group. And before boarding the houseboat, stop at a local grocery store for enough food to stock the shelves until the next houseboat stop. Once on the water, everything you'll need lies along the lower Saint John River downriver from Fredericton. And by all means, bring fishing gear. Trout, smallmouth bass, sturgeon, pickerel, and striped bass lurk in the river.

Where to Boat

Check with the houseboat operators for the idyllically best or the dangerously worst places to ply the waterways. The operators know what's safest for you (and their valuable houseboat). Two areas are off-limits. Stay clear of windy **Grand Lake,** the largest lake east of the Great Lakes, where sudden, strong storms and high waves can engulf a boat. The river stretch below **Oak Point** is another treacherous area for houseboats, marking the northern end of the equally windy waters of Long Reach above the city of Saint John.

Otherwise, lope along anywhere for 300 km between Fredericton and Oak Point. Secluded coves and offshoot waterways abound. The aroma of apple blossoms drifts over the river late May and early June. During June, Fredericton celebrates the **River Jubilee,** and Gagetown has a **Craft Festival** late in the month. Barbecues and food vendors are part of Oak Point's **Fun Days** in mid-August. At Gagetown during mid-September, country-fair fixings are the highlights of the **Queens County Fair.** Gagetown Creek ambles off the main river; you can tie up at the public marina or at the backyard pier of Steamers Stop Inn.

At **Middle Island** near Fredericton, the beach on a peninsula is lapped by shallow, warm water, and ospreys, bald eagles, and blue herons soar overhead. **Grimross Island,** above Gagetown, is populated by goats; you'll hear them bleating as your houseboat glides past.

For More Information
The **Lower Saint John River Promotion Association** publishes a map with details on events, sightseeing, lodgings, and crafts shops; for a copy, write to them at P.O. Box 105, Gagetown, NB E0G 1V0.

A 48-minute video on the Lower Saint John River, entitled "A Gift of River" ($29.95 plus tax), and *A Cruising Guide to the Bay of Fundy and the Saint John River* are available from **Gooselane Editions;** call (506) 450-4251, fax (506) 459-4991, or write to the publisher at 469 King St., Fredericton, NB E3B 1E5.

---

bass, trout, pickerel, and Atlantic salmon. A marina rents paddleboats ($5 per half hour), and you can also rent bikes, kayaks, and windsurfing boards. The park is open mid-May to mid-October. There's a $3.50-per-vehicle dayuse fee to enter the park.

The setting's pièce de résistance is the challenging 18-hole **Mactaquac Provincial Park Golf Course.** Ranked seventh among Canada's prime, public courses, the links were the setting of the Atlantic Classic tournament in 1992. The greens fee is $28 on the weekend, $24 for a weekday, and $12 at twilight. For reservations call (506) 363-4139.

Kingsclear Hotel and Resort
The province gained another prime resort when the Kingsclear Hotel and Resort opened as the final addition to the dam project in 1991. In a historic first among Canada's native peoples, the Kingsclear Malecite Indians, who had lived in the area for centuries, had relinquished their traditional fishing rights in exchange for resort ownership in 1989. It was a sweet deal. As resort owners, the tribe reaps the resort's profits, and the tribal members apply their historic fishing and hunting skills as guides for the guests (only the Malecite guides have access to the river's Chapel Bar pool, famed for Atlantic salmon and bass). Atlific Hotels and Resorts, a Canadian management company, operates the resort.

A half-hour drive from the capital, the resort is within a stone's throw of exit 274 off the Trans-Canada. In the main lodge are 75 rooms and suites ($99-150, some nonsmoking), a dining room with lounge, and a health center with a heated indoor pool, jacuzzi, and exercise deck.

Six two-bedroom chalets ($100-150) are situated on the manicured grounds. The resort caters to a mix of tourists, anglers, and hunters. For reservations and package details, call (506) 363-5111 or (800) 561-5111.

KINGS LANDING HISTORICAL SETTLEMENT

A marvelous counterpoint to Caraquet's Acadian Historical Village, this grand-scale provincial heritage site meticulously re-creates a typical 19th-century Anglo settlement with authentic buildings, demonstrations, and events. Bring comfortable walking shoes, as the site spreads across 121 hectares (299 acres) with 60 vin-

an old sawmill at Kings Landing

tage houses and buildings in a beautiful setting alongside the Saint John River.

At each of the authentically detailed buildings—among them a sawmill, farmhouses, a school, forge, and printing office—informative costumed "residents" depict rural New Brunswick life as it was lived from 1784 to 1900. Demonstrations include horse shoeing, metal forging, cloth spinning and weaving, and farm-

ing. Special events include an Agricultural Fair in late August, the Provincial Town Criers' Competition in early September, and a Harvest Festival in early October to close out the season.

The Kings Head Inn restaurant here serves hearty, 19th-century fare. Fast food is available at a cafeteria at the Visitor Reception Centre. The Kings Theatre has changing entertainment shows and nature programs. The mood is easy

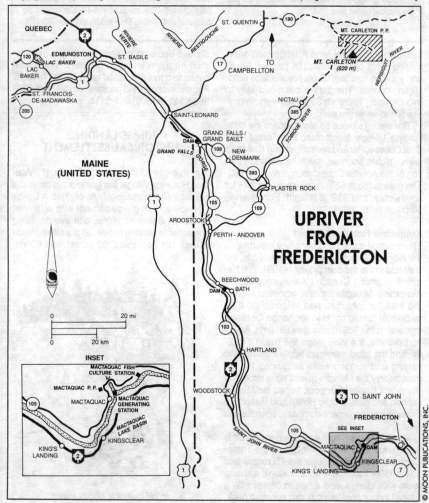

UPRIVER
FROM
FREDERICTON

MAINE
(UNITED STATES)

QUEBEC

INSET

© MOON PUBLICATIONS, INC.

and down-home, and if you'd like to dress the part, the staff can provide costumes; ask at the main gate or call the costume department at (506) 363-5090.

To get to the site, take exit 259 off the Trans-Canada Hwy. (Hwy. 2), 37 km west of Fredericton. Kings Landing is open early June to mid-Oct., daily 10 a.m.-5 p.m.; it's also open some dates off-season for special events, such as Christmas in the Valley in early December and Victoria Day weekend in late May. Admission is $7.50 adults, $6 for ages 6-18, $17.50 for a family. For more information, call 363-5805.

TO GRAND FALLS/GRAND-SAULT

West from Kings Landing, the TransCanada Hwy. and Hwy. 105 follow the river along one of its loveliest stretches. The Saint John is wide and blue, bounded by green fields and forests of maple and hemlock. Handsome, elm-shaded **Woodstock** is an agricultural service center for this rich potato-producing region. North of Woodstock at **Hartland**, Hwy. 103 crosses the Saint John River on the **world's longest covered bridge.** Built in 1899, the bridge measures 391 meters (1,283 feet).

Grand Falls

The otherwise placid Saint John River becomes a frothing white torrent when it plunges 23 meters over the stony cataract which gave Grand Falls, or Grand-Sault, its name. Below the falls, which have been harnessed to produce hydroelectric power, the tremendous force of the river has worn a two-km-long, horseshoe-shaped gorge through 70-meter-high rock walls. Here, the river is at its narrowest, and the gorge's bottleneck impedes the water's force. The river pushes through the narrows in tumultuous rapids, like pent-up champagne bursting from the bottle. The erosive power of flowing water and gravel have also combined to scoop out the "Wells-in-Rocks," circular potholes up to nine meters deep.

In town, **Malabeam Reception Centre,** off Front St., makes a convenient starting point. From the center's rear windows, you'll see the thundering cataracts tumbling through the gorge.

The bridge that extends east from Broadway and crosses the gorge is another good vantage point from which to view the falls; paths lead down to the river from there. If you're lucky, you'll also see a rainbow hovering over the falls.

From there, follow a series of two-km-long footpaths alongside the gorge to **La Rochelle,** the second visitor center at riverfront Centennial Park on Chapel Street. Here, a rock staircase leads down to the cataract edge, where the agitated river swirls in the rocky wells. Locals say the scene was far more impressive in the 1920s, before the province diverted the river's force for a hydroelectric plant and dam. Regardless, don't expect impressive, year-round waterfall shows; the river level is lowest during late summer and highest between March and early June.

The gorge's footpaths and staircases are walkable year-round (be careful when it's wet); the visitor centers are open daily 9 a.m.-9 p.m. from early June to early Sept., then to 5 p.m. until early October.

In late June or early July, Grand Falls celebrates the area's economic mainstay with the **Potato Festival.** Several well-priced B&Bs in Grand Falls make the town all the more appealing for overnighting. **Coté Bed and Breakfast** is centrally located at 575 Broadway, tel. 473-1415; $30 s, $35 d, with a full breakfast. **Maple Tourist Home Bed and Breakfast,** 142 Main St., tel. 473-1763, charges $45 d.

THE RÉPUBLIQUE DU MADAWASKA

War is hell, and often it spawns subsequent conflicts, like red hot coals that tumble from a central conflagration and flare up anew. The République du Madawaska, the independent Acadian republic based in Edmundston alongside the Maine border, had such an origin.

The republic owes its creation (in a roundabout way, you might say) to the American Revolution. The rebellious Americans won the war, and England lost the Eastern Seaboard colonies. But a few loose ends remained. A few international boundaries between Canada and the U.S. remained hazy, one of which was the border between New Brunswick and Maine.

No Border, No Peace

Border delineation was a slow process that took a toll among settlers. Pity the Acadians. First they had been forced to resettle by the Acadian Deportation. Some fled to New Brunswick's remote forested northwestern corner where they worked as lumberjacks and hoped to find peace. But by 1839, disputes over contested lumber rights pitted the Acadian lumberjacks against Maine loggers, and once again the Acadians found themselves in confrontations with the Anglos. Fistfights ensued. As the dispute picked up steam, it became known as the **Pork and Beans War,** named ironically for the lumbermen's ubiquitous main meal. Neither Canada nor the U.S. officially recognized the dispute. At least, not until an Anglo lumberman named John Baker, from Baker Brook near Edmundston, set the boundaries of the jutting thumb of land that pokes oddly into Maine and proclaimed the area the "American Republic of Madawaska." High treason, cried the British, who jailed him for several months.

England Takes a Hand

Treason or not, Baker's outrageous deed riveted England's interest on the area—not particularly in the remote western hinterlands, but rather on the upper Saint John River valley from Grand Falls/Grand-Sault to Woodstock. Loyalists had settled the richly fertile riverbanks, and believed they resided in Canada. But rumors assigned the area to Maine.

England's honor was at stake. Years before, the British had lost face at Castine, Maine, south of Bangor. Fleeing Loyalists had settled there as the Revolutionary War wound down, but were soon forced to relocate to St. Andrews—some 200 kilometers farther up the coast—when the international border between New Brunswick and Maine was officially set at the St. Croix River.

The Pork and Beans War dragged on unmercifully, and by 1842 it had turned into the larger international Aroostook War, named for the Aroostook River (which originates in Maine and empties into the Saint John River near Perth-Andover).

Both nations were ready for war. Troops for both sides were mounted at Aroostook. England's Sir John Harvey and American Gen. Winfield Scott drew up a hasty truce, and the **Webster-Ashburton Treaty** settled the boundary issue. The U.S. gained more than half of the contested land, but New Brunswick won the Saint John River valley with a few kilometers to spare on the western bank. Baker's American Republic of Madawaska dropped out of sight and reemerged as the Acadians' République du Madawaska, named for New Brunswick's major players in the issue. Regardless, the oddly shaped wedge of land between Québec Province and the Saint John River remained part of New Brunswick.

The République Lives On

Madawaska as a mythical republic and political oddity still thrives. The republic flies its own flag (an eagle on a white background, overhung by six red stars representing the republic's six founding ethnic groups), and the titular governor, who doubles as Edmundston's mayor, rules the area. The regional culture evolved as an amalgamation of several Acadian groups (collectively known as the Brayons) with a distinct dialect and lifestyle. Summertime's Foire Brayonne festival at Edmundston sums up the area's heritage flavor; the event has been so successful that the tourists arriving from throughout North America and even Europe outnumber by a wide margin the illustrious Brayons.

Saint-Basile

There's a paucity of canoeing on the Saint John these days, but **Le Canotier,** 1480 Principale/TransCanada in Saint-Basile, tel. (506) 735-3685 or 735-6184, rents canoes ($25 per day) and knows the other waterways, such as the remote Rivière Verte ("Green River") and Restigouche River in the interior. They're open May-August. Saint-Basile is about 16 kilometers southeast of Edmundston on the TransCanada Highway.

Edmundston

The "capital" of Madawaska, Edmundston is by far the largest town hereabouts, with some 12,000 people. Originally settled by Acadian refugees on the site of a Malecite Indian Village, it was first called Petit Sault for the rapids here at the confluence of the Saint John and Madawaska rivers. The town was renamed after a visit in 1850 by Sir Edmund Head, the provincial governor.

For an insight into the area's checkered history, stop in at the **Madawaska Regional Museum,** at the junction of the TransCanada and Hebert Blvd., tel. (506) 737-5064. Admission is $1. But to experience Madawaska's Acadian-flavored culture, come for the **Foire Brayonne,** at the end of July. Over 100,000 people show up for the celebration of Brayon foods, music, dance, and other entertainment. Call 739-6608 for more information.

In summer, golf is popular at the 18-hole **Edmundston Golf Club,** accessed via Hwy. 2, exits 15A or 18, tel. 735-3086. **Petit Témis Linear Park** follows the bank of the Madawaska River and connects Edmundston, Saint-Jacques, the New Brunswick Botanical Garden (see below), and Cabano (Québec) with a 62-km bicycle trail. You can rent bicycles from **Jessome's La Source du Sport,** 12 D'Amours St., tel. 735-6292, and **Studio Cardio Forme,** 258 Victoria St., tel. 739-5995.

Snowmobiling and **cross-country skiing** are popular winter pastimes in the area. **Joe Loue Tout Rent All,** 535 Victoria St., tel. 735-7122, rents snowmobiles. Nearby Mont-Farlagne, with 17 runs, offers the province's longest **downhill skiing** season. To get there, take exits 15 or 15A off the TransCanada, tel. 735-8401.

Two fairly central budget accommodation choices lie close together on rue du Pouvoir. **Beaulieu Tourist Rooms** is at 255 rue du Pouvoir, tel. 735-5781. It's basic, but only $20 s, $22 d, with breakfast. With similar rates and amenities is **City View Tourist Home,** at 226 rue du Pouvoir, tel. 739-9058. **Le Fief Bed and Breakfast,** 87 Church St., tel. 735-0400, charges $45-60 for its four comfortably furnished rooms.

For a taste of the local French cuisine and a good selection of seafood, try **La Chaumiere,** at 100 Rice St., tel. 739-7321, in the Howard Johnson Plaza. Dinner entrees run $11-20.

Saint-Jacques

North of Edmundston, about halfway to the Québec border, is Saint-Jacques, home of **Les Jardins de la République Provincial Park** complex. To get there, take Hwy. 2 for eight km north of Edmundston, exit 8. The park offers an eclectic mix of sights, including the **New Bruns-**

wick Botanical Garden, tel. (506) 739-6335. If you've admired the flower-filled setting at the Montreal Botanical Garden in Montreal, you will see a resemblance here. The formal garden complex on 17 hectares was designed by the same skilled Michel Marceau. The garden brims with 60,000 plants of 1,500 species. Roses, perennials, and rhododendrons bloom among the prolific posies in nine gardens, all orchestrated with classical music in a romantic vein. Admission is $5. It's open May-Sept., daily 9 a.m.-dusk.

Also at the park is the **Antique Automobile Museum,** tel. 735-8769, a fascinating collection of vintage and rare cars including a primitive 1905 Russell, a 1933 Rolls-Royce Phantom, and one of the only 2,880 Bricklins that were manufactured during New Brunswick's brief experiment with auto production. Admission is adults $2.50, ages 6-18 $1.50; open year-round.

The park's **campground,** tel. 735-4871, has 100 serviced and 13 unserviced camping spaces and an abundance of amenities, including a boat ramp, tennis courts, a swimming pool, and playgrounds. It's open June-September.

Nearby, **Camping Panoramic,** tel. 739-6544, has 150 sites at $12-14, open May-October. The **provincial tourism information center,** tel. 735-2747, is located on the TransCanada.

Lac-Baker

Lac-Baker is in New Brunswick's remote northwestern corner, near where the Saint John River flows into the province from the northern reaches of Maine. Here you'll find all the quiet woodlands you could ever want, as well as the rustic **M & G Camping & Cabins,** off Highway 120, tel. (506) 992-2136 or 992-3427. The lakeshore complex lies several kilometers north of the river and has eight cabins ($165-190 per week) and a dining room.

MOUNT CARLETON PROVINCIAL PARK

From Perth-Andover on the Saint John River, Hwy. 109 branches off northeast into the interior to Plaster Rock. From there, Hwy. 385 continues another 84 km northeast to remote Mount

Carleton Provincial Park. The park can also be reached off of Hwy. 17, which runs between the TransCanada at Saint-Léonard and Campbellton on the Baie des Chaleurs (take Hwy. 180 east from St.-Quentin).

This provincial park, surrounding the Maritimes' highest mountain, is strictly wilderness, and it takes some determination to get there. Count on a two- to three-hour drive to reach the park entrance from either the TransCanada or Campbellton.

If you're interested in climbing the mountain (elev. 820 meters), wear sturdy shoes, and bring a jacket to combat the winds. The easiest, marked ascent goes up a 4.4-km trail through a spruce, fir, and yellow birch forest. The mountain's peak rises above the tree line and the view is marvelous, overlooking the adjacent mountains and blue Nepisiguit and Nictua lakes

from a summit strewn with mountain cranberries and wild blueberries. Other trails in the network include an 0.8-km wheelchair-accessible path.

Incidentally, Mt. Carleton's peak divides the provincial watershed. The waters on the summit's western side drain into the Saint John and Tobique rivers and eventually reach the Bay of Fundy; on the peak's east side, the waters drain to the Nepisiguit River and the Baie des Chaleurs.

The park's 88 campsites at four campgrounds are pretty rustic, though there is a dump station for RVs. Other facilities include dry toilets, kitchen shelters, unsupervised lake beaches, a boat launch, and nine hiking trails. The park is open year-round; winter activities include snowmobiling and cross-country skiing. For more information, call the ranger office at (506) 235-2025.

THE FUNDY COAST
INTRODUCTION

The natural beauty of New Brunswick's Fundy coast is sublime. Sea breezes bathe the shore in crisp, salt air, and the sun illuminates the seascape colors with a clarity that defies a painter's palette. Wildflowers bloom with abandon, nourished by the moist coastal air. And fog, thick as cotton, sometimes envelopes the region during the summer. Yet despite the luxuriant growth, there's a notable absence of ragweed. Visitors who suffer from hay fever are among the coast's most frequent vacationers. (Anything below 1.00 on the ragweed index translates as easy breathing; here, the index registers just 0.23.)

The Fundy Tides
Imagine the scene. An unearthly stillness pervades. Seabirds wheel and dart across the horizon. Suddenly, the birds cry out in a chorus as the incoming tide approaches. The tidal surge, which began halfway around the world in the southern Indian Ocean, quietly and relentlessly pours into the Fundy's mouth, creating the high-

est tides on the planet. Fishing boats are lifted from the muddy sea floor, and whales in pursuit of silvery herring hurry along the summertime currents, their mammoth hulks buoyed by the 100 billion tons of seawater that gush into the long bay between New Brunswick and Nova Scotia.

The cycle from low to high tide takes a mere six hours. The tide peaks, in places high enough to swamp a four-story building, and then begins to retreat. As the sea level drops, coastal peninsulas and rocky islets emerge from the froth, veiled in seaweed. The sea floor reappears, shiny as shellac and littered with sea urchins, periwinkles, and shells. Where no one walked just hours ago, local children run and skip on the beaches, pausing to retrieve tidal treasures. New Brunswickers take the Fundy tides for granted. For visitors, it's an astounding show.

The incoming sea first smacks against the Fundy Isles at the entrance to the bay, creating riptides, big waves, and swirling currents. At peak tide, the world's second-largest whirlpool,

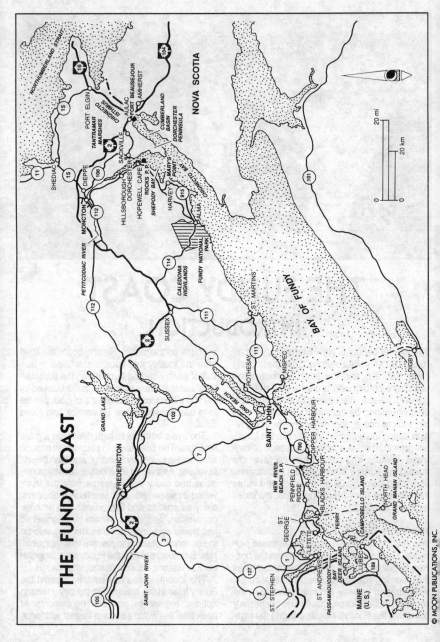

THE FUNDY COAST

© MOON PUBLICATIONS, INC.

dubbed the "Old Sow," swirls here just off Deer Island. The high tide lashes at the mainland, foaming against granite headlands and low-lying peninsulas from St. Stephen up to Saint John. Beyond Saint John, the bay narrows, and the high tide's relentless pounding of the coastline has carved caves at St. Martins. At Alma, near Fundy National Park, the tide floods the beach, rising a vertical distance of 14 meters. At Hopewell Cape's Rocks Provincial Park, the sea rises 16 meters and has sculpted massive, bizarrely shaped pillars crowned with miniature forests.

Warning: High tide arrives every 12.5 hours, and the quickly rising sea is *always* treacherous. Tidal times are posted everywhere and warn sightseers away from the seacoast at peak times. Incoming tides are especially formidable during new- and full-moon phases, when the Fundy peaks 20% higher than normal. So be aware of tidal schedules and pay careful attention along the seashore to avoid unpleasant surprises.

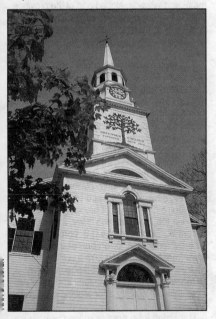

historic Greenock Church, St. Andrews

Sightseeing Highlights

Many visitors come to New Brunswick's 250-km-long tidal coast to take advantage of the diverse outdoor-recreation possibilities it provides. Kayakers enjoy the complex fringe of bays and inlets. Scuba divers explore the sea depths, which are enriched by the sea's turbulence. Hikers follow the coastline for some of the province's most challenging trekking. Birdwatchers come to the region for its abundance of migratory birds, which soar through the province's Atlantic flyway from Mary's Point to Grand Manan.

Saint John has the Fundy coast's best supply of lodgings, shopping, and nightlife. **St. Andrews** and **Sackville** anchor opposite ends of the coastline and add a rural aristocratic flavor with quality accommodations, meals, and historical ambience. The Fundy Isles settlements offer smaller shares of creature comforts; advance reservations are a must, especially on **Grand Manan,** the province's foremost naturalist destination. In between are small coastal towns, seaports, and **Fundy National Park.**

HISTORY

Early French Settlement

In 1604, a French exploration party led by Samuel de Champlain sailed into the Bay of Fundy and named the Saint John River. After rejecting the site of the present city of Saint John as a proper spot for a settlement, the group spent the bitterly cold winter of 1604-05 on Douchet's Island in the St. Croix River. Champlain complained in his diary: "Winter in this country lasts six months." The encampment barely survived; hunger and scurvy claimed 35 lives. (Douchet's Island can be seen from the highway about nine km northwest of St. Andrews.) The following spring, they packed up and headed for Nova Scotia's more agreeable side of the Fundy. There they established Port Royal, the early hub of "Acadia," the name they gave this part of eastern Canada.

From the Port Royal base, Champlain explored the bay and named Grand Manan and Campobello islands. Acadia's development followed. The merchant Charles de la Tour set up a trading post at Saint John Harbour's northern end. French settlers, who knew the Bay of

Fundy as the Baie Française, founded settlements along the coast from the Sackville area to Campobello Island. In the upper Fundy, sea marshes were reclaimed as fertile farmland with *aboideaux,* a system of dikes that opened at low tide, allowing river water to drain, and closed at high tide, shutting the sea out.

Strategic Chignecto Isthmus

Acadian settlements were densest on the Chignecto Isthmus. A hundred French families (ancestors of today's Maritime Acadian population) reclaimed 207 square km of land across the Tantramar Marshes. Tantramar is a corruption of *tintamarre* (hubbub), the early settlers' description of the ceaseless racket raised by the local wildfowl. More Acadians fled into the area after the Treaty of Utrecht awarded most of the Nova Scotia peninsula to England in 1713. The British dominated Nova Scotia, and the Acadians found life safer across the Fundy.

The French tried to prevent the British from crossing the Chignecto Isthmus corridor with Forts Gaspéreau and Beauséjour, which faced England's Fort Lawrence on the isthmus. France's defense might have worked had it not been for Thomas Pichon, the secretary to the Abbé le Loutre at Fort Beauséjour, who passed military strategies on to the British. In 1755, the British sailed into Chignecto Bay with 2,000 troops. The French forts quickly fell; Fort Beauséjour was renamed Fort Cumberland, and Fort Gaspéreau was demolished (its ruins still lie at the end of Fort Street in the town of Port Elgin).

Resettling the Anglos

The British quickly reinforced the mouth of the Saint John River on the Fundy with Fort Frederick, situated near an earlier French trading post. Advertisements for pro-Crown settlers were posted in the colonies farther south, and New England planters immigrated north to Campobello Island, St. Andrews, and Sackville. Other immigrant convoys landed at St. Stephen, Grand Manan Island, and Dorchester. A Loyalist infusion to St. Andrews arrived from Castine, Maine, after international conflicts forced their resettlement farther up the Fundy coast.

Simultaneously, insurrection stirred in England's colonies on the eastern seaboard. In a flare of pre-Revolutionary defiance, patriot privateers from the rebellious New England colonies attacked Saint John and destroyed Fort Frederick. Fort Howe replaced the demolished fort three years later.

At Sackville, the New England planters and Yorkshire immigrants took the place of the expelled Acadians. The town's Mount Allison University, begun as an academy in 1843, grew to a full-fledged university by 1886. The New Englanders also settled the shipbuilding communities of Alma and St. Martins.

At St. Andrews, shipbuilding and trade with the West Indies greased the economic wheels until 1850. When the era of wooden ships ended, the town made an easy transition into a resort center. The Shiretown Inn opened in 1881; the first Algonquin Hotel burned and was rebuilt in 1915.

GETTING AROUND

The Fundy coast is a paradox: it's at once the most- and least-developed part of the province. Saint John—the province's largest city and major port—sits at the midpoint. To either side, the coastline is remotely settled and wonderfully wild.

The region is best considered as two distinct areas, with Saint John interposed between them. The **Lower Fundy,** situated at the bay's southwestern end, includes St. Andrews—the province's definitive resort town on the sheltered Passamaquoddy Bay—and the Fundy Isles, the archipelago (made up of Grand Manan, Deer, and Campobello islands) that dangles into the sea alongside Maine's northernmost coast. The **Upper Fundy** area, situated at the coast's northeastern end, takes in Fundy National Park, Sackville, and several coastal bird sanctuaries.

If you're driving, you'll probably enter Saint John via the TransCanada (Hwy. 2), then Hwy. 1; from St. Stephen at the U.S. border; on Hwy. 7 from Fredericton; or on one of the expressways from Moncton. If you're traveling the 125 km from Fredericton to St. Stephen via Hwy. 3, be forewarned that gas stations and other services thin out quickly after leaving the TransCanada.

The Saint John area is spliced with an excellent road system; beyond city limits, traffic moves on narrower, two-lane roads. If time is a consideration, use the TransCanada whenever possible, especially as a high-speed access route to the bird sanctuaries on the Chignecto Isthmus.

If you have the time, by all means leave the main highway and amble down the scenic local roads that loop along the shoreline. Note that between St. Martins and Fundy National Park, no roads access the coast. Transportation is forced far inland, with the most expedient route being along Hwy. 1 and the TransCanada (Hwy. 2).

THE LOWER FUNDY COAST AND THE FUNDY ISLES

ST. ANDREWS

An immensely attractive seaside town, St. Andrews, the province's first—and now definitive—resort town, sits at the end of a peninsula dangling into tranquil Passamaquoddy Bay, sheltered from the tumultuous Fundy by Deer Island and Letang Peninsula. The resort crowd revels in St. Andrews's version of old-time, velvet-glove Canadiana, especially visible at the Algonquin Hotel.

The seaport rivals Grand Manan Island as the area's major destination. Naturalists come for ecological programs sponsored by the Sunbury Shores, a private environmental group, and tourists like the picturesque lodgings and the plethora of crafts shops and small dining places.

History

The town has a special, almost sacred historic status among New Brunswickers. It was founded by Loyalists who sailed into the Fundy and followed the coastal curve to the peninsula's tip in 1783. The courageous journey was a technical wonder. The settlers, originally from England's former colonies farther south, had moved to what they believed was Canada at Castine, Maine. But a subsequent international boundary decision forced them to relocate once again. The pro-Crown settlers reloaded convoys with all their possessions, disassembled houses and reloaded the structures on barges, and set sail for a safe homeland.

St. Andrews was their creation. Most every street is named for George III or one of his kin. A few Loyalist houses remain and sit cheek-to-jowl with similar New England-style houses fronting narrow residential streets.

Historic Buildings

St. Andrews is a historic gem. Nearly half the buildings in the town core date back 100 years or more, and most have been maintained or restored to mint condition. Water Street is the main avenue, following the bayshore through the five-block commercial district. Pick up a free copy of *A Guide to Historic St. Andrews* at one of the tourist information offices. The guide details a walking tour with over 30 buildings of historical or architectural significance.

The **St. Andrews Blockhouse National Historic Site,** tel. (506) 529-4270, lies along Joe's Point Rd., a western extension of Water Street. The fortification, the last survivor of 12 similar structures, was intended to protect the town from attack in the War of 1812, but nary a shot was fired in battle at this site. The interior depicts the War of 1812 era with re-created soldiers' quarters. The site is open June to mid-Sept., daily 9 a.m.-8 p.m. The adjacent **Centennial Park** is a pleasant spot for a picnic.

In the town's center, the **Sheriff Andrews 1820 House and Garden,** 63 King St., tel. 529-5080, offers an attractive visual insight into the early Loyalist era. Costumed guides will show you around the county sheriff's Georgian-style house, which is simply but elegantly furnished in local period style. The house is open July-Sept., Mon.-Sat. 9:30 a.m.-4:30 p.m., Sun. from 1 p.m. Admission is free.

Another national historic site, the white-painted **Charlotte County Court House** on Frederick St., dates to 1840 and is thought to be the country's oldest courthouse in continuous use. It's open July-Aug., Mon.-Sat. 9:30 a.m.-noon and 1-4:30 p.m. The adjacent gaol (jail), built in 1832, houses the Charlotte County Archives.

The **Ross Memorial Museum,** 188 Montague St., tel. 529-3906, in an early 19th-century neoclassical brick home, preserves the furniture, porcelains, rugs, mirrors, paintings, and other items of Henry and Sarah Ross, discerning collectors of antiques and objets d'art. It's open late May to early October. Free guided tours are offered.

Two-hour tours of **Covenhaven,** the modest 50-room summer home of Canadian Pacific Railway magnate William Van Horne, are offered June to mid-October. The massive house, built of locally quarried sandstone and completed in 1903, stands on Minister's Island, a privately owned island just east of St. Andrews and accessible by a sandbar that's driveable at low tide. Call 529-5081 to arrange a tour.

Tide Watching and Whalewatching

St. Andrews not only offers a splendid historical setting, but is also the area's naturalist hub. The town is a prime place for Fundy watching; for the best times, check out the high-tide schedules posted in the shop windows. Then take a seat at

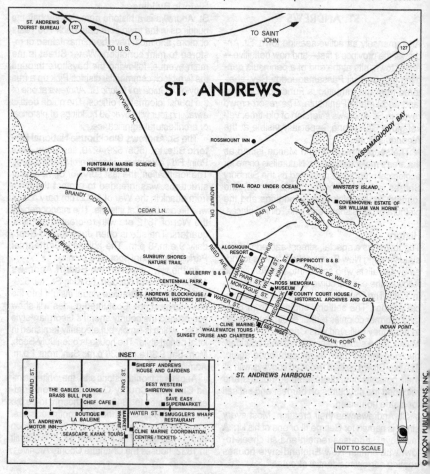

the end of the pier off Water Street and wait for the show. The tide plows into Passamaquoddy Bay like water filling a bathtub. On a quiet evening, you may even *hear* it, gurgling over rocks and filling in small depressions. And then the tidal rise ceases, idles for a time, and flows back out to start all over again.

For an impressive low-tide scene, check out the beachfront at the St. Andrews Blockhouse, where the retreating tide bares the sea floor to reveal a rocky peninsula and pools that had been fully submerged during high tide. Beachcombers strolling the shores around St. Andrews may come across bits of coral and pebbles of polished flint, neither of which occurs naturally here. Both were carried as ballast by 18th- and 19th-century merchant ships, which loaded themselves with flint from Dover, England, and coral from the Caribbean, and then jettisoned these loads here when they arrived to collect their cargoes of fish and timber.

For whalewatching, contact **Cline Marine Inc.,** tel. (506) 529-4188 or (800) 567-5880. The company offers six-hour cruises (adults $50, children $25) departing from the Water St. pier, July-Sept.; the outfit also picks up passengers at Campobello and Deer islands. Scheduled passenger tours run July to Labour Day; in June and Sept. additional tours are organized when enough passengers are interested.

Activities and Classes
At the **Sunbury Shores Art and Nature Centre** on Water St., tel. 529-3386, an art gallery displays watercolors and sculptures for sale. The center also hosts films, lectures, workshops, concerts, and other activities focused on arts, crafts, and natural history. Painting classes ($160-200 per week), special programs for kids, and free, guided nature walks are popular. The center is open daily 9 a.m.-5 p.m., May-September.

The **Huntsman Marine Science Centre and Aquarium,** three km northwest of town center on Brandy Cove Rd., tel. 529-1202, is a nonprofit marine-biology study center that draws researchers from far and wide. The aquarium is stocked with hundreds of local fish, crustaceans, mollusks, and marine plant species. A "touch-me tank" lets children get personal with intertidal animals, as well as seals that cavort in the out-

door pools. The facility is open mid-May to mid-Oct., daily 10 a.m.-6 p.m.; admission is $4 adults, $2.75 for ages 5-18. The center also sponsors environmental classes with guest lecturers and field/lab work ($470-650 per week), and scuba sessions in July ($700-900 per week). For details, write to the center's Public Education Department, Brandy Cove, St. Andrews, NB E0G 2X0.

Water Sports
The **Beaton Aqua Dive and Charter** on Mowatt Drive, tel. (506) 529-3443, runs charter trips for scuba divers, but they'll also accept walk-on divers on weekends, year-round. Expect to pay $65 for a day's dives, including two tanks of air and other equipment (or use your own equipment and pay less); call for details, or write to them at 37 Oak Court., St. Andrews, NB E0G 2X0.

Seascape Kayak Tours, based at the Market Wharf at the foot of King St., tel. 529-4866, offers a variety of sea-kayak classes and guided expeditions around Passamaquoddy Bay. A one-day introductory skills course, for example, costs $85. Tour packages include a sunset paddle ($30); a half-day tour ($50); a four-day, three-night expedition ($370, with meals); and the six-day Environmental Discovery Program ($600).

Katy's Cove is a privately operated saltwater swimming area with a good sandy beach at the end of Acadia Drive, close to the Algonquin. There's a day-use fee. Swimming is free at Indian Point, east of downtown, and nearby on the sandy tidal bar leading out to Minister's Island.

The Algonquin Resort Hotel
In a class by itself among the town's lodgings is the Canadian Pacific hotel group's elegant Tudor-style Algonquin, 184 Adolphus St., tel. (506) 529-8823, (800) 268-9411 in Canada, (800) 828-7447 in the U.S., whose expansive, manicured grounds dominate the hill above St. Andrews.

Here are visions of old-time, velvet-glove Canadiana: golfers ambling across the fairways, the tinkling of crystal in the hotel's dining room, and young couples in tennis whites leisurely sipping cool drinks on the veranda. The tony Algonquin and everything about it bespeak gentility and class. Verdant lawns are everywhere, and the hotel is fronted by deftly designed flower beds. Within, the public and guest rooms are arrayed with overstuffed furniture, oriental carpets, and gleaming dark furniture. The resort's image is very proper, and so are the members of the staff, who are snappily attired in Scottish ceremonial-style garb, replete with kilts.

The older, main hotel has 184 spacious rooms with large, old-time windows and comfortable period furnishings. Another 54 units (with kitchenettes—perfect for families) are situated in a similarly styled recent addition and are connected by a second-floor walkway to the main hotel. Room rates run $108-176 s, $123-181 d, with optional meal plans available. The resort is open May-October.

The facilities include dining rooms and lounges, an outdoor pool, tennis courts, a health spa, and squash/racquetball courts. The baronial estate overlooks the bay and offers a choice of two manicured golf courses. Greens fee is $30; for reservations, call 529-3062.

To get to the Algonquin, turn onto Harriet St. from Reed Ave. (the continuation of Hwy. 127/Bayview Dr.) and watch for Adolphus Street. The hotel's Saint John Airport shuttle costs $29 OW per person, far cheaper than a taxi; reservations are required.

Other Accommodations

In addition to the Algonquin, the town has a splendid assortment of comfortable lodgings, many of them just a short stroll from the historical town center.

The white, wooden **Best Western Shiretown Inn,** 218 Water St., tel. (506) 529-8877, is a commendable choice in the heart of the town overlooking Passamaquoddy Bay. Wide wooden steps lead up to the open front veranda set with comfortable chairs. The rambling, historic inn, built in 1881, was one of Canada's first summer hotels. It has 54 rooms ($45-95) and a dining room; open year-round.

The downtown core has a full complement of bed-and-breakfasts. Quietly elegant **Pippincott Bed and Breakfast,** 208 Prince of Wales St., tel. 529-3445, two blocks from the waterfront, charges $60-80. **Heritage Guest House,** 100 Queen St., tel. 529-3875, has three homey rooms at $40-45, with a private entrance. A block away, the **Mulberry Bed and Breakfast,**

96 Water St., tel. 529-4948, is a cheery and comfortable place with three rooms; $35-65 with a delicious full breakfast.

Across the street and right on the edge of the bay, **St. Andrews Motor Inn,** 111 Water St., tel. 529-4571, charges $65-100, $20 more for housekeeping units.

The **Rossmount Inn,** a provincial heritage inn six km northeast of St. Andrews on Hwy. 127, tel. 529-3351, reflects historic St. Andrews at the town's sumptuous best. Within the three-story mansion are a dining room, lounge, and 17 nonsmoking guest rooms ($65-95) furnished with Victorian antiques. Outdoors, guests congregate on the patio or use the walking trails to explore the expansive, 87-acre grounds.

Camping is available close in at **Passamaquoddy Park,** on Indian Point Rd. east of town center, tel. 529-3439. The 31 unserviced tent sites are $11, while the 104 serviced sites are $15-17. The campground is just a short walk to the beach.

Food

The Gables Lounge/Brass Bull Pub, 143 Water St., tel. (506) 529-3440, occupies a choice spot right on the bay. The seafood specials get high marks, and the wooden deck out back couldn't be more romantic—a great spot for sipping an after-dinner cognac and watching the lights shimmer across the water. **Smuggler's Wharf Restaurant,** two blocks away at 225 Water St., tel. 529-3536, is also popular for its steaks and seafood.

The **Chef Cafe,** 180 Water St., tel. 529-8888, caters to families for breakfast, lunch, and dinner, serving burgers, pizza, fish and chips, chowder, and sandwiches. It's nothing fancy, but prices are reasonable. Open daily 6:30 a.m.-9 p.m. For a quick bite or take-out, **Passamaquoddy Fish and Chips** at the wharf is handy.

The **Algonquin Hotel,** tel. 529-8828 (reservations recommended), serves a fixed-price lunch Mon.-Sat. noon-2 p.m., and a Sunday brunch ($18.50 per person) based on a different culinary theme each week, mid-May to mid-Oct., 11 a.m.-2 p.m.

If you'd rather do it yourself, you can pick up groceries at the **Save Easy Supermarket** in the center of town at the corner of Water and Frederick.

Shopping and Services

Craft and gift shops abound. Whether you're looking for sweaters, souvenir T-shirts, locally produced pottery, or what-have-you, one of the de rigueur activities in St. Andrews is strolling along Water St. and drifting in and out of the shops. One of the nicest is **Boutique la Baleine,** 173 Water St., tel. (506) 529-3926. **Cockburn's Corner Drug Store,** across the street, carries magazines and the local newspapers.

Three tourist information offices are in the vicinity. The **St. Andrews Tourist Bureau** is at the junction of Hwy. 1 and Hwy. 127, the turnoff for St. Andrews. The **Welcome Centre** is on Reed Ave., near the Algonquin Resort. And there's a small tourist office in the town center on Water St. near King.

GRAND MANAN ISLAND

As the Fundy Isles' largest and most southerly island, Grand Manan gets the brunt of the mighty Fundy high tide. Pity the centuries of ships that have been caught in the currents during malevolent storms; near the island, shipwrecks litter the sea floor and pay homage to the tide's merciless power. Four lighthouses atop the island's lofty headland ceaselessly illuminate the sealanes and warn ships off the island's shoals.

Apart from the surging tide, Grand Manan is blissfully peaceful. White, pink, and purple lupines and dusty pink wild roses nod with the summer breezes. Windswept spruce, fir, and birch shade the woodland pockets. Amethyst and agate are mixed with pebbles on the beaches at **Whale Cove, Red Point,** and **White Head Island** offshore. Dulse, a nutritious purple seaweed rich in iodine and iron, washes in at **Dark Harbour** on the western coast, and islanders dry and package the briny snack for worldwide consumption.

Offshore, every species of marinelife known to the Bay of Fundy congregates in the bay's nutrient-rich mouth. Whales in pursuit of herring schools swim in on incoming currents—the right, finback, humpback, and minke whales cavort in the tempestuous seas. They're at their most numerous when the plankton blooms, mid-July through September.

Outings

Space is limited (and is always in demand) on the scheduled land and boat tours; always make reservations beforehand.

One of the finest, most well-established sightseeing outfits in town is **Ocean Search;** they're based at the Marathon Inn at North Head, tel. (506) 662-8488, and operate guided whalewatching tours ($69 with lunch) from July to mid-September. **Sea Watch Tours** in North Head, tel. 662-8552, is equally commendable and has sightseeing boat tours ($45 for a sixhour trip) to Machias Seal Island, mid-June to early August. Their whalewatching tours are scheduled Aug.-September. **Whales-R-Us,** in North Head, tel. 662-8130, schedules two daily cruises, departing from the North Head pier; adults $35, ages 6-16 $20.

For sea-kayaking, talk to the folks at **Adventure High Seas Kayaking,** in North Head, tel. 662-3563. They organize a variety of trips.

Birdwatching, diving, and kayaking outfits come and go. The provincial *Outdoor Adventure Guide* is the best source for an update on the current outfitters; another source is the **Grand Manan Tourist Association,** tel. 662-3216, P.O. Box 193, North Head, Grand Manan, NB E0G 2M0.

Birdwatching

Birds of almost 350 species flutter everywhere in season, and each species has a place on this rock in the sea. Seabirds and waterfowl nest at the **Castalia Marsh** on the island's eastern side. Ducks and geese by the thousands inhabit **Anchorage Provincial Park,** part of which is a wet-heath bird sanctuary, speckled with ponds. Expect to see bald eagles and other raptors on the southern cliffs from mid-August through November. The eider, storm petrel, and Atlantic puffin prefer offshore islets.

Bird populations are thickest early April through June and late summer to autumn. A great way to see the birds is by hiking one of the 18 trails totaling 70 km that crisscross the headland. Many wind through bird sanctuaries. Another incredible place for birdwatching is **Machias Seal Island** (Ma-CHI-as), the outermost bird-sanctuary island. Boat tours, restricted to a limited number of passengers, depart Grand Manan to see the archipelago's highest concentration of exotic bird species, including the razorbill, arctic tern, and 900 pairs of nesting Atlantic puffins.

Accommodations

Though lodgings have blossomed across the island during recent years, it's smart to book ahead. Among the island's best is the **Compass Rose,** tel. (506) 662-8570, a provincial heritage inn atop a lofty, headland edge in North Head with nine guest rooms ($45-55); open May-October. Other commendable properties in North Head are **Aristotles Lantern,** tel. 662-3788, another small lodging with two nonsmoking rooms ($50-60 with a full breakfast), open June-Sept.; the year-round **Surfside Motel,** tel. 662-8156 or 662-8452, with 26 rooms ($48-55); and the **Marathon Inn,** tel. 662-8488, a historic inn built in 1812, with 28 rooms ($44-89) and a dining room, heated outdoor pool, and tennis court.

The **Shorecrest Lodge** at North Head, tel. 662-3216, accommodates birdwatchers for the late Aug. through Sept. migratory pelagic-bird season. They charge $55 and up with breakfast for an overnight; the services of a birding guide are extra.

At **Anchorage Provincial Park** at Seal Cove, tel. 662-3215, facilities include 80 campsites ($12 unserviced, $14 with electricity) with toilets, hot showers, and kitchen shelters; open June-September. Reservations are not accepted, so it's wise to call ahead to check on availability.

Food

For a quick pizza or burger, try the **Fundy House Takeout** in Seal Cove; open seven days a week till 11 p.m. In North Head, the **Griff-Inn Restaurant,** tel. (506) 662-8360, specializes in seafood and sea views.

For groceries, the **Newton Store** in Grand Harbour is open daily; **High Tide Groceries** in Seal Cove and **Grand Manan IGA** in Woodward's Cove are both closed Sundays.

Getting There

The 27-km ferry crossing between Blacks Harbour and Grand Manan's North Head takes about 90 minutes. The car/passenger ferries sail daily year-round. Up to 12 daily departures

are scheduled late June to early Sept., as few as three in the off-season. Toll rates are: adults $8.20, children 5-12 $4.10, under 5 free; cars $24.60, motorcycles $8.20, bicycles $2.80; motor homes and cars with trailer $6.10 per meter. Expect at least a half-hour wait in line at both ends. If the car ferry fills up quickly, you'll have to keep your place in line for the next one. For arrival and departure details call (506) 662-3606; for other inquiries call 662-3724.

CAMPOBELLO AND DEER ISLANDS

The sea swirls mightily around Grand Manan but diminishes in intensity as the currents spin off around the coast of Maine to Campobello Island and Deer Island. These two islands hug the neighboring U.S. so closely that their sovereignty was disputed for decades after the American Revolution; a treaty gave the islands to New Brunswick in the 1840s.

Campobello Island

Campobello, cloaked in granite, slate, and sandstone, was a favorite isle of former U.S. President Franklin Delano Roosevelt. The shingle-sided, green and bell-pepper-red family vacation home is now the main attraction at the **Roosevelt Campobello International Park,** on Hwy. 774 at Welshpool. The 34-room interior is furnished with authentic family trappings, made somehow all the more poignant as FDR was stricken with polio while on vacation here. The house is open late May to mid-Oct., daily 10 a.m.-6 p.m. Admission to the house and grounds is free.

Herring Cove Provincial Park, tel. (506) 752-2396, near the island's south end, has hiking trails, a two-km-long beach, and a golf course. It's open June-Sept., with 40 serviced and 51 unserviced sites. The seaside **Lupine Lodge,** in Welshpool on the island's west side, tel. 752-2555, has 10 cozy rooms and great views; $40-65 with breakfast. The dining room also serves meals daily noon-9 p.m., plus Sunday brunch 11 a.m.-2 p.m.

Cline Marine Inc., tel. 529-4188, schedules two two-hour whalewatching tours daily from July to Labour Day, departing from Head Harbour; adults $30, children $15.

A **tourist information center,** tel. 752-2997, is close to the bridge from Maine.

Deer Island

The more low-profile and wilder Deer Island is devoted to fishing and is encircled with herring weirs (stabilized seine nets); other nets create the "world's largest lobster pounds" in the inlets. The **Old Sow,** the largest tidal whirlpool in the Western Hemisphere, can be viewed three hours before high tide from Deer Island Point Park, at the island's south end.

The **Gardner House,** in Lambert's Cove, tel. (506) 747-2462, combines bed-and-breakfast accommodations with a steak-and-seafood dining room. In Fairhaven, on the island's west side, **Clam Cove Bed and Breakfast,** tel. 747-2025, charges $50 for smaller suites, $60 for larger suites.

Getting to the Islands

Ferry systems connect Letete, New Brunswick, with Deer Island (year-round, free). East Coast Ferries, tel. (506) 747-2159, schedules a half-dozen daily crossings June-Sept. linking Eastport, Maine, with Deer Island and Campobello Island. Between Eastport and Deer Island, departures are hourly from midmorning to early evening, with an extra evening crossing in July and August. Rate for car and driver is $8, passenger $2.

Between Deer Island and Campobello Island, departures are roughly hourly, from midmorning to late afternoon, with an additional early-evening run in July and August. Fare for car and driver is $11, $2 per passenger (up to a maximum of $16 per car).

Campobello is also accessible by a bridge from Lubec, Maine.

EAST TO SAINT JOHN

In addition to the intrinsic beauty of the coast—with thick forests growing right down to the rocky shoreline—several detours spice up the drive eastward to Saint John.

The specialty at **Oven Head Salmon Smokers** is Atlantic salmon, smoked to perfection over hickory and oak chips.

The smokehouse wholesales to culinary notables such as the Algonquin Hotel. If you're interested in picnic ingredients, stop at the retail outlet on Hwy. 1 at St. George, open Mon.-Sat. 8 a.m.-5 p.m. An impressive site in **St. George** is the thundering granite gorge of Magaguadavic Falls. Visitors can park and walk down a staircase beside the falls to watch salmon swimming upstream past a viewing window.

St. George is also the place to turn off Hwy. 1 for the short drive to the Deer Island ferry terminus at Letete. Highways 772 and 776 lead to Black Bay, picturesque **Blacks Harbour** (terminus for the Grand Manan Island ferry), and a welter of other islets. If you find yourself in Blacks Harbour in early September, don't miss the North American Sardine Packing Championship. Only in the Maritimes!

At **Pennfield Ridge,** a few kilometers northeast of Blacks Harbour, blueberry farms offer roadside stands or fields for do-it-yourself picking. A few kilometers beyond, **New River Beach Provincial Park** lies alongside the highway and has picnic tables, a long, curving sandy beach, hiking trails through bogs and spruce woodlands, and boat-launching facilities. The 100 campsites are open June-Sept.; there's a day-use fee for access to the beach.

A few kilometers east, **Point Lepreau Nuclear Generating Station** is off Hwy. 790 at the end of a broad peninsula jutting into the Fundy. Canada's first nuclear-power station is open for tours Sun.-Fri. June-Aug., by appointment other months. Call the public affairs office

Roosevelt Cottage

BOB RACE

at (506) 659-2220, ext. 6433, for details. A three-km, wheelchair-accessible nature trail starts at the information center. On the east side of the peninsula, deep-sea fishing charters operate out of Dipper Harbour. **Deep Sea Fishing**

Tours, tel. 659-3222, offers charters in July and August. **Eastern Outdoors/Fundy Yachts,** tel. 634-1530, organizes coastal kayaking, canoeing, and yachting, and rents vessels.

SAINT JOHN AND VICINITY

Saint John (pop. 75,000) ranks as New Brunswick's largest city, its major port, and its principal industrial center. It is also Canada's largest city in terms of area, sprawling across 321 square km. The city perches on steep hills, laid out southwest to northeast across two peninsulas that almost mesh, like two hands about to meet in a handshake. The setting is among Atlantic Canada's most unusual—Saint John looks east across the spacious Saint John Harbour to the Bay of Fundy, and is backed on the west by the confluence of the Saint John River and Kennebecasis Bay. You may recognize parts of Saint John and neighboring communities from the movie *Children of a Lesser God,* which was filmed here in the summer and fall of 1985.

Saint John began as a collection of small Loyalist settlements, which today maintain their identities in the form of neighborhoods within greater Saint John. This accounts for numerous street-name duplications, a confusing fact of life you will have to deal with as you sightsee across the oddly laid-out city. For example, one Charlotte Street runs through the city's historic part, while another Charlotte Street may be found in western Saint John. It helps to keep a map handy, or just ask: the locals are sympathetic to the visitor's confusion. (See "Getting Oriented" and "Getting Around," below.)

HISTORY

On 24 June 1604, the feast day of St. John the Baptist, French explorer Samuel de Champlain sailed into the harbor area and named the river in the saint's honor. He dismissed the site, however, as unsuitable for settlement, and continued on to a disastrous winter farther west on the St. Croix River near St. Andrews.

Saint John as an Anglo settlement began with 14,000 Loyalists, who arrived by ship in 1783. The refugees quickly settled the fledgling town and spread out to create Carleton west of the harbor and Parrtown to the east. The city was incorporated in 1785, making it Canada's oldest. The port was an immediate economic success, and the **Carleton Martello Tower** was built to guard the harbor's shipping approaches during the War of 1812.

The city's next great wave of immigrants brought the Irish, who were fleeing poverty and persecution at home. Saint John's reputation as Canada's most Irish city began with a trickle of Irish in 1815; before the wave subsided in 1850, the city's 150,000 Irish outnumbered the Loyalists, and Saint John's religious complexion changed from Protestant to Roman Catholic. The clash between religious factions led to the York Point Riot in 1849, which left 12 dead.

Many of the Irish immigrants arrived sick with cholera, typhus, and smallpox. The city earmarked **Partridge Island** in the harbor for a quarantine station with 13 hospitals (and six graveyards).

The "Liverpool of America"
Despite its early social woes, Saint John strode ahead economically and became known as the "Liverpool of America." The *Marco Polo,* the world's fastest ship in its heyday, was launched in 1852 during an era when the port ranked third worldwide as a wooden ship builder. After steel-hulled steam vessels began to replace the great sailing ships in the 1860s, the city plunged into a decline, which was deepened by the Great Fire of 1877. The fire at harborfront's Market Square area raged for nine hours and left 18 people dead and another 13,000 residents homeless.

The blaze cost the city $28 million but, undaunted, Saint John replaced the damage with more elaborate, sturdier, brick and stone buildings designed in the ornate Victorian style. The economic surge continued after New Brunswick

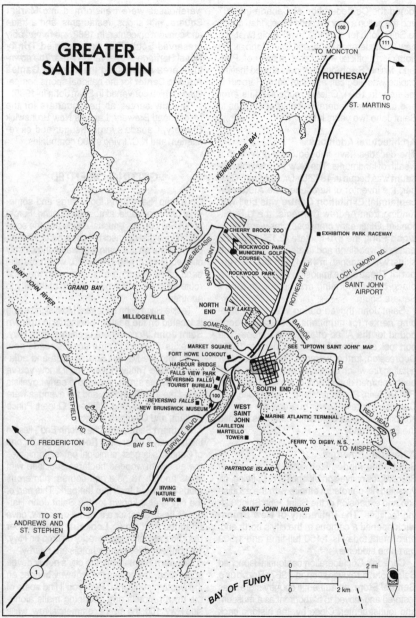

GREATER
SAINT JOHN

© MOON PUBLICATIONS, INC.

joined the Confederation of Canada in 1867 and the nation's new railroads transported goods to Saint John for shipping. In an ironic twist, the new Confederation bypassed Saint John as the dominion's official winter port, in favor of Portland, Maine. Saint John's officials argued that the choice was illogical, as Saint John Harbour is ice-free. In 1894, Ottawa recognized its error and transferred federal shipping operations to Saint John two years later.

Architectural Additions

The decades have imbued Saint John with a wealth of landmarks. The **New Brunswick Museum** was begun in 1842 by Dr. Abraham Gesner, the inventor of kerosene. The **Aitken Bicentennial Exhibition Centre** was built with funding from Andrew Carnegie, the U.S. billionaire. Other early grandiose sites were **Rockwood Park,** the 870-hectare (2,150-acre) expanse of woodland and lakes on the city's outskirts, which opened in 1894; and the 1913 **Imperial Theatre,** the imposing vaudeville showplace-cum-performing arts center on King's Square South.

Saint John thrived during WW I as a shipping center for munitions, food, and troops bound for the Allied offensive in Europe. The port took an economic plunge during the 1930s Depression, further worsened by another devastating fire which destroyed port facilities. Prosperity returned during WW II; the fortifications at Fort Dufferin, Partridge Island, Fort Mispec, and Carleton Martello Tower guarded the nation's shipping lifeline as German submarines roamed the Bay of Fundy.

A New City Emerges

Saint John modernized after the war. New Brunswick's native-son billionaire, K.C. Irving, diversified his petroleum empire with the acquisition and expansion of the Saint John Shipbuilding facilities. The **University of New Brunswick** opened a campus at the city's north end; enrollment today is 1,150 full-time and 1,500 part-time students.

Canada's Confederation centennial launched Saint John's rejuvenation in 1967. **Barbour's General Store,** an authentic country store, was restored and moved to harborfront as a museum and tourist center. Close by, the historic brick warehouses were transformed into **Market Square,** with shops, restaurants, and a trade and convention center. In 1982, the remarkably preserved South End was renamed **Trinity Royal Heritage Preservation Area.** The downtown area also gained the **Canada Games Aquatic Center** for the national sports competitions which convened in Saint John in 1985.

The city serves as headquarters for the Moosehead Brewery, Labatt's New Brunswick Brewery, Canada's largest sugar and oil refineries, and K.C. Irving's 300 companies.

GETTING ORIENTED

On a map, Saint John looks large and somewhat unmanageable, almost intimidating. Forget about Saint John's unusual shape and the soaring bridges that connect the city's parts. Rather, concentrate on the main highways: the closely aligned Hwy. 1 and Hwy. 100, which parallel each other in most parts, are often the best route for getting from one section of the city to another.

Tackle Saint John by areas. Most sightseeing is located on the eastern peninsula in **uptown Saint John.** Access here is easiest from Hwy. 1's exits 112 or 111; the access roads peel down into the Market Square area and adjacent historic Trinity Royal. You'll know you've arrived by the street names: the early Loyalists called the area Parrtown, and the avenues were royally named as King, Princess, Queen, Prince William, and Charlotte streets.

Northern Saint John (the "North End") lies on the highways' other side. **Rockwood Park,** one of Canada's largest municipal parks, dominates the area with wooded hectares speckled with lakes and an 18-hole golf course; numerous roads off Hwy. 1 feed into the park. This part of the city is also known for the Saint John Harbour's best views; for a sublime overview, drive up to the **Fort Howe Lookout,** where timber blockhouses perch atop a rocky outcrop on Hwy. 1's northern side. Worthy hotels are nearby.

Western Saint John, the city's newly developing area, lies across the highway bridges on the western peninsula. Here you'll find some of the newer motels and shopping malls alongside Hwy. 100, the area's commercial row, while

Hwy. 1 widens as the Saint John Thruway on its way west to St. Stephen. The residential area, with several interesting bed-and-breakfasts, spreads out closer to the water, while the Marine Atlantic ferry terminal (with service to Digby, Nova Scotia) is at the harbor's edge.

BOB RACE

Barbour's General Store

Tours

Taking a guided tour can be a good way to become familiar with the city in a short time. The **Saint John Transit Commission,** tel. (506) 658-4700, covers the whole city with three-hour bus tours ($13.50). The tours depart from Barbour's General Store at the Market Slip, mid-June to early Oct., daily at 12:30 p.m. The **Saint John Visitor and Convention Bureau** operates free guided walking tours of the historic areas departing from Barbour's General Store, July-Aug. twice daily. For do-it-yourself walking tours through the city's historic areas, ask at the bureau office at Market Square (opposite city hall) for the three free informative maps with descriptive texts. **Saint John Department of Recreation and Parks** sponsors free **Walks 'n' Talks,** insightful walking tours designed for locals (but visitors are welcome, too). The tours are given year-round, but the schedule varies. For details, call 658-2893. Their office is open Mon.-Fri. 8:30 a.m.-4:30 p.m.

SIGHTS-UPTOWN

The sights below start at harborfront's Market Square and proceed inland, then fan out to outlying areas.

Barbour's General Store/
Little Red Schoolhouse

At the foot of steep King St., opposite Market Square, the essence of old-time New Brunswick is re-created at this restored country store-cum-museum, formerly upriver at Sheffield. In-

side are 2,000 artifacts typical of the period from 1840 to 1940, as well as a restored turn-of-the-century barbershop in the back room. It's open mid-May to mid-Oct., daily 9 a.m.-6 p.m., mid-June to Sept. to 7 p.m.; tel. (506) 658-2939. Free, guided walking tours of the historical town center depart from here daily in July and August. The adjacent Little Red Schoolhouse houses a **tourist information center,** also tel. 658-2939.

Prince William and Germain Streets

A block up from Market Square, these two parallel streets delineate the commercial heart of old Saint John. Following the devastating fire of June 1877, the city hurried to rebuild itself in even grander style. The stone and brick edifices along Prince William Street are a splendid farrago of architectural styles, incorporating Italianate facades, Corinthian columns, Queen Anne Revival elements, scowling gargoyles, and other decorative details. One of the country's finest surviving examples of 19th-century streetscape, this was the first "national historic street" in Canada. Some good art galleries and craft shops are ensconced here among the other businesses. Two blocks east, Germain Street is the more residential counterpoint, with a number of opulent townhouses.

For a brief history and description of each of the magnificent buildings, pick up a copy of *Prince William's Walk* at any tourist information office.

New Brunswick Telephone Pioneers Museum

Exhibits explaining NBTel's past and present developments—from a model of Alexander Graham Bell's first phone to contemporary fiber-optic technology—are on display in One Brunswick Square's lobby on Germain St., tel. (506) 694-6388. The museum's open year-round, Mon.-Fri. 10 a.m.-4 p.m.; free admission. If you're planning to travel to Cape Breton, however, to the immensely interesting Alexander Graham Bell National Historic Site, you might want to pass on this.

Loyalist House National Historic Site

This simple, white clapboard Georgian-style house was built between 1810 and 1817 by pioneer David Merrit, and remained in his family for five generations. Having survived the 1877 fire and now meticulously restored, it's the oldest unaltered building in the city.

The original front door with brass knocker opens into an authentic evocation of the early Loyalist years, furnished with Sheraton, Empire, and Duncan Phyfe antiques. The house is at 120 Union St. at the corner of Germain, tel. (506) 652-3590. Open June to Labour Day, Mon.-Sat. 10 a.m.-5 p.m.; also open Sun. 1-5 p.m. July-Aug., by appointment the rest of the year. Admission is $2 adults, 25 cents for ages 4-18.

Saint John Jewish Historical Museum

Half a block away, this modest museum at 29 Wellington Row off Union St., tel. (506) 633-1833, has a functioning Hebrew school, chapel, *mikvah,* sacred and secular artifacts, and exhibits about the city's small Jewish community, which dates its arrival to 1858. The museum is open June-Sept., Mon.-Fri. noon-4 p.m., plus Sun. 1-4 p.m. during July and August. A free guided tour is offered.

Aitken Bicentennial Exhibition Centre (ABEC)

The grandiose former Carnegie Library (known locally as the ABEC), tel. (506) 633-4870, fronts 20 Hazen Ave., two blocks west of Wellington Row. Fine arts, photography, and science exhibits fill five galleries, and exhibits change frequently. ScienceScape is a permanent interactive science gallery for children. ABEC is open year-round, Tues.-Sun. 11:30 a.m.-4:30 p.m.; June to early Sept., daily 10 a.m.-5 p.m. Admission is free.

Saint John City Market

For a visual and culinary treat, spend some time at Saint John's Old City Market, which spans a whole city block between Charlotte and Germain streets. The national and provincial historic site is open year-round, Mon.-Thurs. 7:30 a.m.-6 p.m., Fri. to 7 p.m., Sat. to 5 p.m.

Everyone shops at City Market. It's a great venue for people-watching, and for sampling freshly baked goods, cheeses, seafood, meat, and produce. If you haven't yet tried dulse, a leather-tough purple seaweed that's harvested from the Bay of Fundy, dried, and sold in little packages for a dollar or two, here's your chance. Antiques and splendid, reasonably priced crafts have a sizable niche here, too.

The setting is impressive. The original ornate iron gates stand at each entrance, and there's usually a busker or two working the crowd. Inside the airy stone building, local shipbuilders framed the expansive ceiling in the form of an inverted ship's hull. "Market Street," the market's central, widest aisle, divides the space in half; alongside the adjacent aisles, the bustling stalls stand cheek-to-jowl, their tables groaning with wares. Notice the building's pitched floor, a convenient arrangement on the slanted hillside that makes hosing the floor (a tradition since 1876, when the building opened) easier after the market closes each day.

The founding Loyalists started the first farmers' market at Market Square in 1785, a tradition (though transplanted to the present city market) that makes Saint John's market Canada's oldest Common Law Market (it was chartered by George III). The first market outgrew the original site and relocated to the present site a year before the Great Fire destroyed the harborfront; Saint John was rebuilt around it.

King's Square and the Loyalist Burial Ground

Across Charlotte St. from the City Market are two maple-shaded, vest-pocket green spaces situated on separate, kitty-corner blocks. At King's Square, the walkways are laid out like

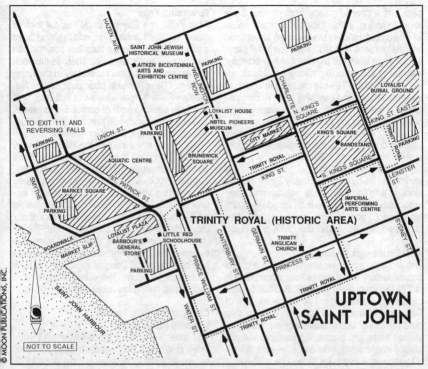

the stripes on the British Union Jack, radiating from the 1908 bandstand, the site of summertime concerts.

Across Sydney St. is the Loyalist Burial Ground, a surprisingly cheerful place with benches and flower gardens, scattered with old-style headstones dating back to 1784.

As busy as the square and burial ground are —alive with schoolchildren on field trips, bantering pensioners, and mums with strollers— **Queen's Square,** three blocks south, is virtually deserted.

Trinity Anglican Church

A victim of the city's historic fires, this handsome Loyalist church at 115 Charlotte St., tel. (506) 693-8558, was built in 1791, rebuilt in 1856, and rebuilt again in 1880 after the Great Fire. The sanctuary's famed treasure is the House of Hanover Royal Coat of Arms from the reign of George I, which had been rescued by fleeing Loyalists from the Boston Council Chamber in 1783 and rescued again from the 1877 runaway fire. Guided tours are available Mon.-Fri. 9 a.m.-3 p.m.

SIGHTS FARTHER AFIELD

Fort Howe National Historic Site

The blockhouse of 1777 did double duty as harbor defense and city jail. The structure itself is now closed, but the rocky promontory site on Magazine St. nonetheless offers an excellent panoramic view of the city and harbor. It's about a five-minute drive from the historic area. Get there by following St. Patrick St. north, then turn left (west) on Main.

Rockwood Park

This huge woodland park, speckled with lakes and laced with foot and horse trails, is a real gem just a short distance from central Saint John. In spring, yellow lady's slipper and colorful wild orchid varieties bloom on the forest floor, and the gardens and arboretum are in full glory. Activities in summer include fishing, boating, swimming, birdwatching, hiking, horseback riding, golfing at the 18-hole course, picnicking at lakeside tables, and camping (see "Accommodations," below). In winter, the ice-skaters come out and the trails are taken over by cross-country skiers. The park is open year-round, daily dawn to dusk. Entry to the park is free. For general information, call (506) 658-2883.

The **Cherry Brook Zoo,** tel. 634-1440, at the park's northern end off Sandy Point Rd., is stocked with lions, leopards, zebras, and other exotic animals. Admission is $3.25 adults, $2.25 for students and seniors, children under two free. It's open year-round, daily 10 a.m. to dusk.

New Brunswick Museum

The province's prime resource for fine arts and natural-history lore is this hulking stone building at 277 Douglas Ave., tel. (506) 643-2300, west of uptown Saint John. The museum, one of Canada's oldest, is packed with elegant ship models, shipbuilding tools, war memorabilia, stuffed birds and beasts, agricultural and domestic implements, you name it—and there's a Discovery Centre for kids. The museum's bookstore stocks books about the province, and its archives keep records about the city's businesses and people. The museum is open year-round, daily 10 a.m.-5 p.m.; adults $2, ages 7-19 $1.

Reversing Falls

At low tide, the Bay of Fundy lies 4.4 meters below the Saint John River, and the river flows easily out to sea. During the slack tide, the sea and the river levels are equal. Then, as the slack tide grows to high tide, the waters of the rising sea enter Saint John Harbour, pour into the Reversing Falls gorge, where the sea and river collide in a roiling froth of contending currents. The powerful Fundy tide reverses the river's direction, muscling it inland for 100 km.

For the best views, use the railed walkway located alongside the city's **Reversing Falls Tourist Bureau,** on Bridge Road West (Hwy. 100), tel. (506) 658-2937. If you're interested in a capsule version of the sea and river encounter, check out the movie ($1.25 admission) inside the bureau; open mid-June to Labour Day, daily 8 a.m.-9 p.m., then 8 a.m.-7 p.m. until mid-October. **Falls View Park** overlooks the spectacle from another angle, from the east side of the river, off Douglas Ave. near the New Brunswick Museum. The scene is at its most impressive during low, slack, and high tides.

Carleton Martello Tower
National Historic Site

The massive circular stone tower on Fundy Drive at Whipple St. in western Saint John has served as a harbor defense outpost since 1812, and the superstructure above it was a military intelligence center during World War II. Within, stone staircases connect the restored quarters and powder magazine. The observation decks provide splendid views of the harbor. The site is

the longest covered bridge in the world

open June to mid-Oct., daily 9 a.m.-5 p.m.; free admission.

Partridge Island

This island near the mouth of Saint John Harbour, a national and provincial historic site and now a coast guard light station, was formerly a quarantine station for almost a million arriving immigrants during the 19th and 20th centuries. Some 2,000 newcomers who never made it any farther are buried here in six graveyards. A Celtic cross was erected for the Irish refugees, and a memorial stone commemorates Jewish immigrants. From the early 1800s up to 1947, the island was used as a military fortification. The site serves as a memorial to the new settlers' courage, and has a museum devoted to them and to the island's history.

The **Partridge Island and Harbour Heritage** group operates a 2.5-hour guided tour ($10), departing from Market Slip, May-Nov.; for reservations, call (506) 635-0782.

ACCOMMODATIONS

Ideally, you'll want to be within walking distance of historic old Saint John and the harborfront. The area's growing number of bed-and-breakfasts often provide sumptuous accommodations for lower cost than many hotels. Lodgings beyond walking distance include the Fort Howe–area hotels, with great harbor vistas at reasonable prices; and the many budget choices on Rothesay Avenue northeast of uptown Saint John, and along motel row—Fairville/Manawagonish/Ocean West Way—in western Saint John.

The city could use more lodgings. Nonetheless, the available accommodations provide generally good value and enough variety of facilities and prices.

Camping

Rockwood Park, tel. (506) 652-4050, has 250 campsites ($12-15) at Lily Lake, most with electricity and water; the facilities include toilets, kitchen shelters, fireplaces, hot showers, and a campers' canteen. Available recreation includes golfing at the nearby golf course, swimming, boating at the lake, and hiking on trails around the lake. The park is just a five-minute drive from city center. The easiest way to get there is to take Hwy. 1 exit 111 or 113 and follow the signs north. The campground is open May-October on a first-come, first-served basis; no reservations are taken.

Uptown and Near Harborfront

The **Saint John YM/YWCA**, 19-25 Hazen Ave., tel. (506) 634-7720, a Hostelling International member, is mainly a resident lodging but is equipped with 16 single rooms for men and another five single rooms for women. Rooms cost $24, and the $10 key charge is refundable. Facilities include a pool, saunas, steam rooms, and a racquet court.

Pretty bed-and-breakfast lodgings cluster near King's Square. The **Earle of Leinster Inn** at 96 Leinster St., tel. 652-3275, is an excellent choice with congenial hosts and a very central location just a couple blocks from King's Square. This gracious brick Victorian townhouse has nine rooms ($35-50 with full breakfast), most with private bath. One of the rooms is a family suite. Amenities include laundry facilities, a game room with pool table, a courtyard, and a fax machine and photocopier for use by business guests.

Nearby, **Cranberry's Bed and Breakfast** has three nonsmoking guest rooms ($50-65) tucked within a three-story Victorian brownstone mansion at 168 King St. E, tel. 657-5173.

The **Parkerhouse Inn** at 71 Sydney St., tel. 652-5054 (reservations required), reigns as the city's top-notch inn and is styled as an oversize Victorian townhouse with all the elements of grand style. Within the three-story mansion are stained-glass windows, a curved staircase, fireplaces, a solarium, and a terrace. The nine guest rooms ($65-95), some nonsmoking, are furnished with antiques.

Hotels with great views peer over the harbor. The avant-garde high-rise **Delta Brunswick Hotel,** 39 King St., tel. 648-1981 or (800) 268-1133, forms part of the Brunswick Square mall almost at harborfront and has 112 rooms ($79-135), a restaurant and lounge, and an indoor pool and saunas. The hotel is connected by a pedestrian walkway to the nearby Aquatic Center and Market Square complex.

The **Saint John Hilton International,** One Market Square, tel. 693-8484 or (800) 561-8282, commands great views of the harbor and is also linked by the pedway to the adjacent malls. It offers 197 rooms and suites ($115-160), a restaurant and lounge, and a health center with an indoor pool, saunas, a whirlpool, and an exercise room.

Farther Afield

Not far from the historic area, the hotels near Fort Howe overlook the harbor from the city's North End. The eight-floor **Keddy's Fort Howe Hotel,** 10 Portland St. (at Main St.), tel. (506) 657-7320 or (800) 561-7666, shares the same view as the fort and has 107 rooms and suites ($64-79; ask for a room with a view), rooftop dining, lounges, and a health center with an indoor heated pool, saunas, and a whirlpool.

The **Howard Johnson Hotel,** 400 Main St. (at Chesley Drive/Hwy. 100), tel. 642-2622, has 100 rooms ($69-102) and a health center with an indoor heated pool, whirlpool, sauna, and exercise room.

A few motels are strung along Rothesay Ave. (Hwy. 100) east of central Saint John, which is convenient if you're flying into town at night. The **Fundy Line Motel,** 532 Rothesay Ave., tel. 633-7733, is clean, comfortable, and generic, with 90 rooms at $47-51. The **Glen Falls Motel,** 650 Rothesay Ave., tel. 633-9214, is a low-budget choice just adequate for one night; $30-32, with cable TV and creaking old bedsprings.

Western Saint John

In western Saint John, the **Five Chimneys Bed and Breakfast,** 238 Charlotte St. W, tel. (506) 635-1888, has two nonsmoking guest rooms ($50-55) in historic quarters. Nearby, the **Dufferin Inn and San Martello Dining Room,** 357 Dufferin Row, tel. 635-5968, was the former provincial premier's residence and has been re-created as a pleasant lodging with nine nonsmoking guest rooms ($45-75) and a creative restaurant.

Motel row—which is handy if you're arriving on the night ferry from Nova Scotia—lies north of the residential area along Hwy. 100 (Fairville Blvd., Manawagonish Ave., and Ocean West Way). The **Comfort Inn by Journey's End Motel,** 1155 Fairville Blvd., tel. 674-1873, has 60 basic rooms ($52-70). The **Country Inn and Suites,** 1011 Fairville Blvd., tel. 635-0400, boasts fancier trappings with larger rooms and suites and space enough for families ($56-74 with a light breakfast).

The **Hillcrest Motel,** 1315 Manawagonish Ave., tel. 672-5310, is new and spacious, with views of the Fundy; rooms with cable TV run $40-46. Farther west is the **Regent Motel,** 2121 Ocean Way West, tel. 672-8273, which charges $38 s or d.

FOOD

Saint John has limited dining choices for a high-style dinner out—a tribute to the locals' culinary skills at home but an inconvenience, nonetheless, for visitors looking for formal dining. What's available represents the city's *very* special places, fine enough to lure the locals out of the kitchen. Most everyone eats out at noontime, and there's a spectrum of choices.

Dinners

Shucker's at 39 King St., the Delta Brunswick Hotel's seafood dining room, offers tempting selections such as grilled Fundy Bay salmon fillet splashed with lemon butter or served with capers and cream ($17); entrees range $10-17. An alternative "Heart Smart" menu features low-fat poultry, seafood, and fruit-salad dishes. Reservations are wise, tel. (506) 648-1981.

Grannan's Seafood Restaurant and Oyster Bar has an enviable harborside location with easy access from Market Square's main level. Servings are lavish with salmon, halibut, oysters, scallops, shrimp, clams, and the ubiquitous lobster prepared in numerous variations. The entree prices range from $10 for breaded calamari to $30 for a heaping platter of the province's choicest fish fillets and shellfish; reservations are wise, tel. 634-1555.

The **Top of the Town,** 10 Portland St., tel. 657-7320 (reservations required), overlooks the whole harbor from the top floor of Keddy's Fort Howe Hotel and matches exquisite views with sumptuous steak and seafood selections ($15-20). The emphasis is on beef with porterhouse, strip, and sirloin steaks prepared at tableside. Seafood choices include scallops, lobster, shrimp, halibut, and salmon.

At **Leo's Supper Club** in western Saint John, 2171 Ocean West Way, tel. 672-6090, the chef's culinary flair is evident in the selection of entrees ($17-25) including veal stew or Cordon Bleu, and grilled or deep-fried seafood.

The Hilton Hotel's **Turn of the Tide,** One Market Square, is right on the waterfront, with awesome views and a seafood and beef menu ($20-24) to match. Try the pan-fried Atlantic salmon served with stewed tomatoes and fiddleheads ($20) or one of the tenderloin steak variations ($20-30). Reservations are required, tel. 693-8484.

Light Meals
City Market offers an array of places to get a good lunch or between-meal snack. **Jeremiah's Delicatessen** is one of several delis in the market with smoked meats, cheeses, salads, and creamy coleslaw.

Near the market, **Reggie's** at 26 Germain St., tel. (506) 657-6270, is a great old-fashioned diner in a historic building. It serves commendable homemade chowders, lobster rolls, corned beef hash, and a huge menu of breakfast specials, sandwiches, and burgers, all at good prices.

For soup, sandwich or quiche, and a rich dessert, check out the **Incredible Edibles** at 42 Princess St., tel. 633-7554. The **Historic Cafe** at 179 Prince William St., tel. 634-7999, lures locals with hearty, homemade meat pies (under $5) and salads; open Mon.-Friday. **Wild Willie's,** 112 Prince William St., tel. 652-3009, serves a variety of vegetarian dishes (such as lasagna) and large salads. **Mexicali Rosa's,** a few doors up at 88 Prince William St., tel. 652-5252, is a popular hangout that serves Mexican food, margaritas, and imported beers.

E.J.'s at 94 Germain St. serves the fast-food crowd with sandwiches and homemade tea biscuits, muffins, and pies. **Mother Nature's Pita Bakery and Restaurant** has soups, sandwiches, stuffed pita pockets, and salads at 20 Charlotte St., tel. 642-2808, and another outlet at Brunswick Square, tel. 634-0955. The **Winning Ways** at Brunswick Square, tel. 658-0818, is the place for nondairy hard and soft ice cream and yogurt cones. The shop also carries food supplements, organic foods, and other health wares. It's open Mon.-Wed. and Sat. 10 a.m.-5:30 p.m., Thurs.-Fri. to 9 p.m.

If hunger strikes while you're out shopping, you'll find food courts with virtually infinite meal choices at Brunswick Square's **Courtyard** and at **Market Square.** Out at Reversing Falls, you may want to combine sightseeing with a sandwich or daily meal special ($6-17) at **Riviera Reversing Falls Restaurant,** 200 Bridge St.; open May-September.

Groceries
For a picnic or snack fixings, make **City Market** your first stop. Beyond the historic area, **Sobey's** supermarkets has six locations in the city, all with extensive delicatessens, bakeries, and produce sections; open Mon.-Sat. 9 a.m.-10 p.m. The store at 149 Landsdowne Ave. near Fort Howe is closest to the historic district. Otherwise, the city is peppered with small Green Gables and other convenience and corner grocery stores.

Provincial **liquor stores** are at 75 King St., open 9 a.m.-10 p.m., and at Prince Edward Square, open 10 a.m.-10 p.m.

ENTERTAINMENT AND EVENTS

Movies
The **Empire Theatre** group, tel. (506) 633-8814, handles the phone information line for the city's cinemas: the **King Square Cinema** at 95 Charlotte St., the multiplex screens at the **Parkway Cinema** at the Parkway Mall, and **Place 400** at 400 Chesley Place.

Nightlife
Saint John's nightlife is concentrated around the harborfront's boardwalk. Most places stay open till 2 a.m. **Grannan's Seafood Restaurant,** in Market Square, tel. (506) 634-1555, forms a hub for the many nearby bars of many moods (none with cover charges).

The restaurant's own **Grannan's Bar** has an inviting pub ambience, while **Spirit's** has the upscale action with bands on Mon. and Tues., karaoke on Wed., and something special Thursday. **Chevy's** caters to retro folks with a jukebox and tunes from the '60s and '70s. The T-shirt crowd goes to the **Beaches Pub** for informal atmosphere.

The Historic Trinity Royal area, bounded by Prince William, Princess, King, and Germain streets, is another nightlife center with a trove of nightclubs, pubs, lounges, and sports bars. Locals and tourists like **O'Leary's** at 46 Princess St., tel. 634-7135, which has two bars with draft beer and Irish and Cape Breton music, Thurs.-Saturday.

Club 74 at 74 Prince William St., tel. 642-7474, is a variation on Grannan's. It's pub, dance floor, bar, and pool room are spread out on several floors within a grandiose former post-office building. For sports events, locals get together to bend elbows at **Callahan's Sports Bar,** 122 Prince William St., tel. 634-0366.

Performing Arts

When major rock concerts and other large shows come to town, the venue is the **Saint John Trade and Convention Center** at Market Square, tel. (506) 635-1530. Smaller performing-arts events are staged at **Saint John High School,** tel. 693-8888. For a current schedule of events, contact one of the city tourist offices.

The **Saint John Department of Recreation and Parks** sponsors varied concerts; for details, call 658-2893, Mon.-Fri. 8:30 a.m.-4:30 p.m. They also handle the rock, blues, piping bands, and country concerts that take place at King's Square, mid-June to the start of July's Loyalist Days, at noon and 7 p.m. Another offshoot is the classical-music concert series at the Centenary Square United Church at Wentworth and Princess streets, late May to Aug., Tues. 8 p.m.

Events

The annual **New Brunswick Competitive Festival of Music** features performers from across the province in late April. Locations and times vary; call (506) 672-3082 or check at the tourist information offices for details.

Summer opens with the six-day **Saint John YM/YWCA Quilt Fair** at the Aitken Bicentennial Exhibition Centre, 20 Hazen Ave., late May to early June. June features the **Fête de la Francophonie,** a six-day Acadian festival. In early July, the **Saint John Festival of Light** has fireworks, a midway, and family entertainment in various locations throughout the city; tel. 658-5100.

The weeklong mid-July **Loyalist Days Festival** is one of the summer's biggest hoedowns, emphasizing the contributions of the province's Loyalist, Acadian, Celtic, and Aboriginal communities. Highlights include parades, street vendors, music and dance events, arts and crafts exhibits, and costumed New Brunswickers. Events take place in various venues; call 634-8123 for details.

The **Buskers** arrive early in August and stage impromptu performances at Market Square's boardwalk. Canadian and international performers join forces at the **Festival by the Sea** for 10 days in August. Activities include free daily stage shows, evening concerts, a children's festival, and more. Call 632-0086 for details.

The seven-day **Atlantic National Exhibition** finishes the summer with a supersize county fair geared to families. It runs from late August to early September at the Exhibition Grounds on McAllister Dr., tel. 633-2020.

RECREATION

Water Sports

The **Dive Shack,** 70 Saint James St. off Charlotte St., tel. (506) 634-8265, is the city's prime source for dive trips ($25 for a place on a charter) to the Bay of Fundy. The shop also rents dive outfits ($45 per weekday, $65 per weekend) and can provide a dive guide ($60 per day). Hours are Mon.-Wed. 9 a.m.-5:30 p.m., Thurs.-Fri. to 9 p.m., Sat. to 5 p.m.

R.W. Ring Marine Services, 1019 Millidge Ave., tel. 633-0044, has a fleet of yachts and sailboats available for private charters at $100 per hour.

For canoes and sea kayaks, check out the **Fundy Yachts Sales and Charters** at Brunswick Square, tel. 634-1530. They're open Mon.-Thurs. 9:30 a.m.-5:30 p.m., Fri. to 9:30 p.m., Sat. 11 a.m.-5 p.m. The company also leads two- and three-day sea kayaking and whale-watching tours ($300 and up) departing Saint John for Grand Manan, June to early October.

A to Z Rentals at 535 Rothesay Ave., tel. 633-1919, also rents canoes equipped with life jackets and paddles at $25 per day (credit-card deposit required). They're experts on local canoeing and can recommend appropriate begin-

SAINT JOHN'S BEST BIRDING

Irving Nature Park has an improbable setting. The remote reserve encompasses an entire peninsula dangling into Saint John Harbour, the province's busiest port. At the harbor's northeastern corner rises the skyline of New Brunswick's largest city. Across the harbor's center, oceangoing vessels enter and leave the port. Yet at the harbor's northwestern corner, this speck of natural terrain remains blissfully remote and as undeveloped as it was when the city's founding Loyalists arrived centuries ago.

To get there, take Hwy. 1 out of the city to western Saint John and watch for the Sand Cove Road turnoff. The narrow road angles south off the highway, takes a jog to the west and lopes across the undeveloped harborfront to the 225-hectare reserve. A sandy beach backed by the Saints Rest Marsh heralds the park's entrance. Beyond here, the road divides and follows the peninsula's edges, while three trails probe the park's interior and also wander off to parallel the water.

The reserve's mixed ecosystem offers interesting trekking terrain and draws songbirds, waterfowl, and migratory seabirds. More than 240 bird species are seen regularly; 365 species have been sighted over the past 20 years. Rare red crossbills and peregrine falcons are occasionally spotted in the marsh. Eastern North America's largest cormorant colony lies offshore on Manawagonish Island. Semipalmated plovers like the reserve's quiet beaches and tidal flats. You can count on sandpiper varieties on the beach in July, greater shearwaters and Wilson's stormy petrels gliding across the water during summer, and a spectacular show of loons, grebes, and scoters during the autumn migration along the Atlantic flyway.

Bring binoculars; the birding season goes on and on. Songbirds nest during April and May; great blue herons, common flickers, and tree swallows appear during summer. The black-capped chickadee, the provincial bird, makes its home here throughout winter.

Birds are the most noticeable, but by no means the only, wildlife to be found here. Deer, porcupines, red squirrels, and snowshoe hares inhabit the reserve. And starfish and sea urchins laze in the tidal pools.

Arrive prepared. The dirt hiking trails may be dry or muddy. Wear sturdy, rubber-soled shoes or hiking boots for the mudflat and marsh trails. The beach is pleasant to walk barefoot, but be aware that the expanse is unsupervised and can be dangerous during high tide or windy storms. Mosquitoes and biting insects thrive in the woodlands during summer; bring insect repellent. The boulders may be slippery, so watch your step.

---

ner-to-expert inland routes. Hours are Mon.-Fri. 7:30 a.m.-5:30 p.m., Sat. 8 a.m.-4 p.m.

The top-notch facilities at the **Canada Games Aquatic Centre,** 50 Union St. near Market Square, tel. 658-4715, include a 50-meter pool with five diving boards, two shallower pools (one with a water slide), whirlpools, saunas, a weight room, and a cafeteria. The center is open Mon.-Thurs. 6:30 a.m.-8:30 p.m., Fri. to 8 p.m., Sat.-Sun. 1-4 p.m. A day-use pass is $6.

Public beaches are another option for a hot summer day. You'll find city-operated supervised beaches at Lily and Fisher lakes in **Rockwood Park;** at **Dominion Park** in western Saint John; and at **Little River Reservoir** off Loch Lomond Rd. in the city's eastern area. The parks are open dawn to dusk.

Mispec Beach at Saint John Harbour's eastern edge is unsupervised and the water is cold, but it's a nice spot on a warm day and provides close-up views of ships from around the world entering and leaving the harbor. To get there, take Union St. to the causeway to eastern Saint John; there, take the sharp right turn to Bayside Drive, which turns into Red Head Road.

Golf

The 18-hole **Rockwood Park Municipal Golf Course,** tel. (506) 658-2933, is a challenging, narrow terrain bordered with pastoral woodlands ($20 for the weekday greens fee or $22 on the weekends). It's open mid-May to mid-Oct.; rental clubs and pull carts are available. If lobbing a few long drives over the water sounds interesting, try the park's **Aquatic Driving Range** at Crescent Lake; the buoyant golf balls cost $5-8 a bucket.

Other Activities
The **Saint John YM/YWCA** on Hazen Ave., tel. (506) 634-7720, admits guests ($7 for a day-use pass) to the facility's pool, sauna, steam room, and racquet courts.

Harness-racing addicts go to the **Exhibition Park Raceway** on McAllister Drive, tel. 633-2020, for year-round races on Wed. evening and Sat. afternoon ($1 admission); during late August's Atlantic National Exhibition, the racing schedule accelerates with provincial and other cup competitions.

SHOPPING

Arts and Crafts
The province boasts an excellent reputation for crafts, profusely available at many shops around the city. The local penchant for high-quality weaving and handmade apparel is particularly evident. In addition, woodworking and furniture are outstanding, thanks in part to New Brunswick's plentiful native oak, pine, and birch, as well as the skill of local craftspeople. A preeminent selection of fine-arts galleries gets rave reviews by visitors, due mainly to the wide array of multimedia works displayed by well-known provincial artists like Jack Humphrey, Miller Brittain, Fred Ross, Herzl Kashetsky, and Robert Percival.

The **Rocking Chair** at 104 Prince William St. is awash in fine-quality furniture, pottery, and the Madawaska Weavers' domestic linens and clothing, while the **Country Treasures** shop at 91 Prince William St. carries an equally laudable stock of folk art, furniture, and handwoven domestic linens.

The specialty of the **Croft House** at Market Square is women's apparel (especially attractive in woolen and mohair styles) and tartans, while varied household crafts are found at the **Waterside Shoppe** at 114 Prince William Street. Both the **Craft Emporium,** 12 Church Ave., and **Sir Edward's Smorgasbord,** 525 Rothesay Ave. in eastern Saint John, have good selections of provincial crafts.

Saint John is Canada's most Irish city, and Celtic wares are abundant. The **House of Tara** at 72 Prince William St. is stuffed with Irish imports, including plentiful jewelry and clothing (the tweeds are particularly attractive).

Paul Ferris Arts Studio and Gallery, 177 Prince William St., boasts an exquisite selection of original provincial and Saint John landscapes in acrylic, oil, watercolor, and photography. **Impressions Gallery,** 12 King St., and **Ring Gallery,** 97 Prince William St., specialize in limited-edition prints, original paintings, and other works of art.

Sundries
If you're looking for an unusual child's gift, browse at the **Bunkin's** at 80 King St., where the shelves brim with toys and designer-style clothing. Shoppers who like labels will enjoy the **Moosehead Country Store,** the beer company's outlet at 49 Main St. W, where the brand name is embellished on sportswear and accessories. It's open Mon.-Wed. 9 a.m.-6 p.m., Thurs.-Fri. 9 a.m.-9 p.m.

The city's main shopping district lies along Charlotte, Union, Princess, Germain, and Prince William streets. Business hours are typically Mon.-Wed. and Sat. 9:30 a.m.-5:30 p.m., Thurs.-Fri. to 9 p.m. Some **Market Square** shops nearby are also open Sunday noon-6 p.m.

If your camera malfunctions, head to **Appleby's** at 30 Germain St., tel. 634-2918, one of several city shops that handle minor repairs and stock film and equipment. Appleby's is open Mon.-Thurs. and Sat. 8:30 a.m.-6 p.m., Fri. to 9 p.m.

Books
Two shops are best bets for books about the province: **New Brunswick Museum** at 277 Douglas Ave., tel. (506) 658-1842, and **Canterbury Tales** at 18 King Street. The latter also stocks children's books in French. Other worthy book sources are **Coles The Book People** at the Brunswick Square, Lancaster Mall, and McAllister Place shopping centers, and **Book Mart** at the Parkway Mall, Place 400, Loch Lomond Mall, and Prince Edward Square shopping centers.

Used books (with some collector's editions mixed among the stock) are sold at the **Book**

Broker at 196 Union St., and at **United Book Stores,** 25 Charlotte Street.

INFORMATION AND SERVICES

Tourist Information

City Centre Tourist Information, located in the Little Red Schoolhouse at Market Slip (at the foot of King St.), tel. (506) 658-2588, is the most convenient for visitors. It's open mid-May to mid-Oct., daily 9 a.m.-6 p.m. (to 7 p.m. mid-June to Sept.).

The **Saint John Visitor and Convention Bureau,** on the 11th floor of city hall on King St., tel. 658-2990, is a bit of a hassle to get to. The office does, however, produce a number of very useful booklets and pamphlets (*Saint John Visitor Guide, A Victorian Stroll,* and others). It's open weekdays, so you could drop in, but it's probably more useful to contact them by mail (P.O. Box 1971, Saint John, NB E2L 4L1) or phone before your arrival.

The **Reversing Falls Tourist Bureau,** on Hwy. 100 at Reversing Falls, tel. 658-2937, is open mid-May to mid-Oct., as is the **Highway 1 Tourist Information Centre,** west of the city at Island View Heights, tel. 658-2949.

Health and Safety

Saint John Regional Hospital is at Tucker Park Rd. near Rockwood Park, tel. 648-6000 (or for quick help, tel. 506-648-6900). The hospital has a kidney-dialysis unit. **St. Joseph's Hospital** is at 130 Bayard Dr., tel. 632-5555. For the police or other emergencies, call 911.

Banks

You can change foreign currency everywhere, but the city's nine major banks with many branch outlets have the most favorable exchange rates. Most are open Mon.-Wed. 10 a.m.-4 p.m., Thurs.-Fri. to 5 p.m. The **Bank of Nova Scotia,** the city's largest bank operation, does not charge to convert foreign currency to Canadian dollars, but you'll pay $2 extra to cash a traveler's check.

Banks are concentrated in uptown Saint John. Opposite King's Square are a Bank of Nova Scotia and a Royal Bank. Along King St. are another Bank of Nova Scotia, a Bank of Montreal, Toronto Dominion Bank, and others.

Other Services

Canada Post is at 125 Rothesay Ave., tel. (506) 636-4781; open Mon.-Fri. 8 a.m.-5:15 p.m. For philatelic services, go to **Postal Station B** at 41 Church St. in western Saint John, tel. 672-6704; open 8 a.m.-3 p.m. and to 5 p.m. for other postal services. **Lawton's Drugs** at Brunswick Square serves as one of the city's numerous retail postal outlets and has longer hours.

For immigration information, contact the **Immigration Centre** at 189 Prince William St., tel. 636-4587. The office is open Mon.-Fri. 8:30 a.m.-4:30 p.m.; it helps to have an appointment beforehand.

If you arrive in town with gear to stow, you can stash the smaller items at the **SMT Eastern Ltd.** bus terminal at 300 Union Street. The **VIA Rail** station at 125 Station St. also has storage space in the baggage area and charges $1.50 for each piece.

GETTING THERE

By Air

The **Saint John Airport** is open daily 6:30 a.m.-11:30 p.m. Taxis wait outside during flight arrivals; the 15-minute cab ride to Market Square costs about $22. Car rentals from **Thrifty, National, Tilden, Hertz, Avis, Delta,** and **Budget** are available at the airport.

The airport is served by **Air Canada** from Ottawa, Toronto, and Montreal; **Air Nova** from Halifax, Montreal, and Québec City; **Air Atlantic** from Halifax and Montreal; and the **Northwest Airlink** from Boston. To reach **Air Canada/Air Nova,** call (506) 632-1500 for reservations or 632-1517 for information.

By Sea

The ferry from Digby, Nova Scotia, arrives at the **Marine Atlantic Ferry Terminal** off Lancaster St. in western Saint John, tel. (506) 636-4048.

The **Royal Kennebecasis Yacht Club,** tel. 652-9430, welcomes sail-in visitors at the club's marina on Kennebecasis Bay, open May to mid-October. An overnight berth at the marina costs 75 cents for each foot under 50 feet, $1 foot for a boat 50 feet or longer. **Note:** Passage from the Bay of Fundy through the Reversing Falls gorge can *only* be accomplished during slack tide, a twice-daily occurrence; check tidal charts.

By Land
SMT Eastern Ltd., 300 Union St., tel. (506) 648-3500, has frequent bus service throughout the province. The terminal is open 7:30 a.m.-9 p.m. A ticket from Saint John to Sackville, for example, costs $26 OW, to St. Andrews $15 OW.

The **VIA Rail** terminal at 125 Station St. off Rothesay Ave. has rail service from Montreal and Halifax; for details, call 642-2916.

GETTING AROUND

Saint John is a walking town in the historic area, but beyond there you'll need wheels. Highway 1 serves as the city's high-speed expressway and routes east-west traffic through Saint John from St. Stephen and Moncton. Highway 100 is the city's local traffic route, and it serves as a feeder route for Hwy. 7 to and from Fredericton. Driving is slow going most everywhere in Saint John, and is worst during the 7-9 a.m. and 4:30-6 p.m. rush hours.

Public Transportation
The **Saint John Transit Commission,** tel. (506) 658-4700, operates public buses ($1 a ride) throughout the city; buses operate Mon.-Fri. 6 a.m.-midnight, with limited service on weekends.

Taxi cabs wait at the hotels and also cruise the Market Square and Brunswick Square areas. The fares are based on 14 city zones; expect to pay under $5 from Market Square to Fort Howe

(most passengers tip the driver 50 cents and up). **Vet's Taxi,** tel. 658-2020, has 24-hour service and charges $22 OW to the airport, $80 OW to St. Andrews, $120 OW to Moncton, and $175 OW to Sackville.

Car Rentals
The **Thrifty** car rental at Saint John Airport, tel. (506) 634-6070, rents a compact car for $189 per week with 1,400 kilometers free, plus 14 cents per each additional kilometer. Optional collision-damage coverage is $10 per day, and personal-injury insurance is $2.50 per day.

Local independent car-rental companies are another option. Perhaps the best value is **Delta Rent-A-Car** at 378 Rothesay Ave., tel. 634-1125. Delta rents a compact car for $149 per week with 1,000 free km, 12 cents for each additional kilometer, and optional collision insurance at $8 per day.

Downtown Parking
Parking garages and lots in the historic area are plentiful and inexpensive at 75 cents an hour, $6 a day, overnight $2 extra. The most central are located behind Market Square off Smythe St.; behind the Barbour General Store on Water St.; off Chipman Hill at Brunswick Square; beside the Trinity Church on Charlotte St.; and opposite the Loyalist Burial Ground on Sydney Street. Summertime **RV parking** is free at the lot at the south end of Water Street.

Meters cost a quarter per hour. Free one-hour parking vouchers are available at city tourist offices (see "Tourist Information" under "Services and Information," above).

THE UPPER FUNDY COAST

The impact of high tide is extraordinarily dramatic on the Upper Fundy's coastline. The sea floods into the bay and piles up on itself, ravaging the shore at Mispec—where it has clawed into the land's edge to reveal gold veins—and pocking the coastline with spectacular caves at St. Martins. St. Martins also marks the starting point for the region's most challenging trek—to Fundy National Park. The backpacking trip involves just 40 km, but expect to spend three to five days. In places the high tide washes out all beach access and forces hikers back inland.

Beyond the national park, the tide's strength increases as the bay forks into the narrow Chignecto Bay and Cumberland Basin. *No* place is safe at high tide, especially the remote seacoast from Saint John to Hopewell Cape. At Alma, the village at the park's eastern edge, the sea rises waist-high in a half hour and continues rising to a height of 14 meters.

The Fundy orchestrates its final swan song at Hopewell Cape. Beyond the cape, its tidal impact is exhausted; some of the sea moves inland as a tidal bore and flows up the Petitcodiac River to Moncton, and the remainder washes Dorchester Peninsula's coastal marsh edges.

Birdwatching

Here where the Fundy peaks and dissipates, the setting belongs to a few remote villages and one of North America's most spectacular shows of migratory birds. The American bittern, Virginia rail, short-eared owl, marsh wren, and hundreds of other species soar across the wide stage (see "Flora and Fauna" in this chapter's "Introduction").

Several bird sanctuaries are found in the sizable area extending from upper Chignecto Bay's western coast across Shepody Bay to the Dorchester Peninsula and the Chignecto Isthmus. The birdwatching season varies according to the species, but is generally late March to late May and Aug.-September.

Most of the sanctuaries are owned and managed by the **Canadian Wildlife Service** (CWS) and the province. **Ducks Unlimited (Canada),** a private environmental group, owns additional protected hectares; they've endeared themselves to hikers with sanctuaries threaded with trails and dikes—making for far easier birdwatching terrain than the usual muddy lanes.

The sanctuaries are easily bypassed. Signs are often obscure, and numbered roads may be the only landmarks. The reserves are often known locally by other than the official names, a situation that may further confuse the visitor. If you need help, contact the CWS, tel. (506) 536-3025. Their office is next to the post office on Main St. in Sackville. For birding literature and a map, you can write to them at P.O. Box 1590, Sackville, NB E0A 3C0.

St. Martins

St. Martins, founded in 1783 as Quaco, became one of the busiest shipbuilding centers in the Maritimes in the 1800s, turning out more than 500 ships over the course of the 19th century. The handsome little village today is a fishing port, as evidenced by the stacks of lobster traps on the quay. At the harbor, two covered wooden bridges stand within a stone's throw of one another. The local tourist information office is housed in the lighthouse close by.

Some of the great attractions in the vicinity are the seaside caves scooped out of the red sandstone cliffs by the Fundy tides. The caves can be explored at low tide.

Fundy Hiking Holidays, tel. (506) 833-2534, operates hiking and birdwatching tours, June to early October. Expect to pay $255 pp for an all-inclusive weekend hike for three days and two nights in the St. Martins area. They also arrange trips to Mary's Point combined with St. Martins ($598-661 for five days) or Saint John to Sackville ($900-1000 for seven days). **East Coast Expeditions,** tel. 833-4689, has similar hiking arrangements June to mid-Oct.; for details, write to them at P.O. Box 15, St. Martins, NB E0G 2Z0.

The historic **Quaco Inn** on Beach St., tel. 833-4772, has comfortable beachhouse quarters with seven nonsmoking rooms ($55-60), a dining room, a hot tub housed outdoors in a gazebo, and bicycles for rent.

Overlooking the Fundy, the Victorian Gothic **Saint Martins Country Inn,** tel. 833-4534 or (800) 565-5257, former home of one of the seaport's most prosperous shipbuilding families, has aptly been dubbed "the castle" by locals. The 12 antique-furnished rooms, each with private bath, run $57-80. The inn is open year-round and has a dining room on the premises.

FUNDY NATIONAL PARK

This magnificent park is a bit out of the way but well worth the effort to get to. The 206-square-km park encompasses a cross section of Fundy environments and landforms: highlands, deeply cut valleys, swampy lowlands, dense forests of red and sugar maple, yellow birch, beech, red spruce, and balsam fir, and a shoreline of dizzying seacliffs and sand and shingle beaches.

From Saint John, Hwy. 1 feeds into the Trans-Canada expressway, and the backcountry Hwy. 114 branches off east of Sussex, peels over the Caledonia Highlands, and plummets through woodlands to sea level. Thick woods rise on one side and conceal the park's deep valleys sewn with rivers and waterfalls. Glimpses of the sea, cradled by beaches, appear on the road's other side; most of the 13-km shoreline is wrapped with formidably steep sandstone cliffs.

For all its wilderness, though, Fundy National Park has a surprising number of civilized comforts, including rustic housekeeping chalets, a motel, a restaurant, and a golf course.

The park is open year-round, though most services operate May-September. Admission to the park is $5 a day per vehicle, $10 for four days. For more information, contact the park administration at P.O. Box 40, Alma, NB E0A 1B0, tel. (506) 887-2000.

Recreation

The **golf** course's nine-hole links tumble down the hillside near the administration building and slice through the coastal forest, like a green velvet glove whose fingers reach into the woodlands. Greens fee is $9.50 a round; call the pro shop at 887-2970 to reserve a tee time. The course is open mid-May to mid-October.

A path nearby leads across the highway to the seaside **pool** filled with heated seawater piped

in from the Fundy. Admission is $2.50 adults, $1.50 children. It's open 11 a.m.-7 p.m.

Two dozen **hiking trails** wander the coastline or reach up into the highlands. The highlands hikes are easy-to-moderate treks, while the toughest trails lie along the coast, impeded with cliffs, ridges, fern glades, and thick forests.

Shorter, easy trails include the **Caribou Plain,** a 3.4-km loop on flat terrain through forest and bog; and **Dickson Falls,** a 1.5-km loop that offers views above and below the waterfall via a system of boardwalks and stairs. The moderately difficult **Goose River Trail** is 7.9 km each way, along an old cart track to a wilderness campground at the mouth of Goose River, in the park's southwestern corner. The 10-km **Coastal Trail** is graded as difficult, but the rewards include lush fern glades and forest and great ridgetop views over the bay and coastal seastacks. Get more detailed information at Park Headquarters or Wolfe Lake information center, both of which sell the useful *Fundy National Park Trail Guide.*

Mountain biking is permitted only on the Goose River, Marven Lake, Black Hole, Bennett Brook, and East Branch trails.

The park's lakes are open to nonmotorized **boats.** Sailboats, canoes, and rowboats can be rented at Bennett Lake for $3-5 per hour. There are **tennis** courts and **lawn bowling** courts in the Headquarters area; rental equipment is available at the Pro Shop.

Fishing is good for the plentiful trout found in the lakes and rivers; a national park fishing license, available at the vistor center, is required ($4 per day, $6 per week).

Accommodations and Food

Four **campgrounds** in the park offer a total of 600 sites: Wolfe Lake, near the northwest park entrance; Point Wolfe, near the beach; and Chignecto and Headquarters, close to the southeast entrance near Alma. Unserviced sites range $6-10, serviced sites $14-16.

Hike-in **wilderness camping** is available at Goose River, Marven Lake, Tracey Lake, Foster Brook, and Upper Salmon River campsites. To use these, you must register in advance at the visitor center, Pointe Wolfe Campground, or Wolfe Lake Information Centre. Sites cost $2 per person per night. Micmac Campground, on

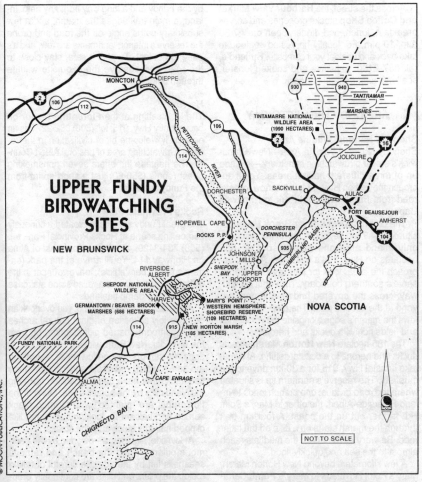

UPPER FUNDY
BIRDWATCHING
SITES

NEW BRUNSWICK

MONCTON DIEPPE

PETITCODIAC RIVER

DORCHESTER

HOPEWELL CAPE

ROCKS P. P.

JOHNSON MILLS

RIVERSIDE-ALBERT

SHEPODY NATIONAL WILDLIFE AREA

HARVEY

GERMANTOWN / BEAVER BROOK MARSHES (686 HECTARES)

FUNDY NATIONAL PARK

ALMA

CAPE ENRAGE

CHIGNECTO BAY

TINTAMARRE NATIONAL WILDLIFE AREA (1990 HECTARES)

TANTRAMAR MARSHES

JOLICURE

SACKVILLE AULAC

FORT BEAUSEJOUR

AMHERST

DORCHESTER PENINSULA

SHEPODY BAY UPPER ROCKPORT

CUMBERLAND BASIN

MARY'S POINT WESTERN HEMISPHERE SHOREBIRD RESERVE (109 HECTARES)

NEW HORTON MARSH (185 HECTARES)

NOVA SCOTIA

NOT TO SCALE

Pointe Wolfe Rd., is a **group camping site.** No reservations are taken at any sites; call (506) 887-6000 to check availability.

For roughing it in style, the **Fundy Park Chalets,** tel. 887-2808, has 29 housekeeping units at $47-62; open May-October. **Caledonia Highlands Inn and Chalets,** tel. 887-2930, also has housekeeping units, $60. **Fundy National Park C.H.A. Hostel** is open to members and non-members, on Devil's Half Acre Rd., west of the visitor center, tel. 887-2216; open June to Labour Day. The **Seawinds Restaurant and Takeout** in the park overlooks the golf course.

In the village of **Alma,** just outside the park's southeastern entrance, you'll find nearly a dozen motels, inns, and B&Bs. The seaside **Alpine Motor Inn,** tel. 887-2052, has 40 rooms and housekeeping units at $40-50, a swimming pool, and a dairy bar. Also overlooking the bay, the **Parkland Village Inn,** tel. 887-2313, has rooms at $42-60, and a dining room and lounge on the premises.

Across the street, the **Harbour View Market and Coffee Shop** stocks groceries and serves breakfast, lunch, and dinner; open daily 7:30 a.m.-10 p.m. For locally harvested seafood to take back and cook at your campsite, **Butland's,** tel. 887-2190, sells live and cooked lobster, scallops, salmon, and haddock.

AROUND CHIGNECTO BAY

Shepody National Wildlife Area

Shepody National Wildlife Area—New Brunswick's stellar birdwatching sanctuary—is made up of three different habitat areas. You'll approach the first on Hwy. 114, the narrow, coastal road from Fundy National Park to Hopewell Cape.

The **Germantown/Beaver Brook Marshes,** situated 14.7 km beyond Alma, is the reserve's only inland area and spreads out on 686 hectares on Hwy. 114's east side. As you approach the area, look for Midway Rd., the reserve's southern boundary. Turn right on Midway, cross the covered bridge, and park beyond at the second path. The nine-km trail follows the marsh's edge alongside the woodlands and fields rich with ducks and heron.

The 185-hectare **New Horton Marsh** attracts ducks and herons to a coastal setting. At Alma, take coastal Hwy. 915 for a 30-km drive to the mudflats. The reserve's northern tip is situated where the road divides; one branch leads to inland Riverside-Albert, the other to Mary's Point Rd. farther out on the coast. A four-km trek through the marsh starts on a dike off the latter road. **Be wary of the tides:** the mudflats reach almost to the sea and quickly flood.

A few kilometers beyond New Horton Marsh, Mary's Point Rd. leads to **Mary's Point,** Canada's only shorebird reserve. Shorebirds by the hundreds of thousands set down on the 109-hectare coastal reserve, their numbers peaking mid-July through mid-August. Among the onslaught are about 9,000 blue herons and an uncountable number of cormorants, all of which swarm over the intertidal zone.

Be very aware of high tide at Mary's Point. The road ends at a remote loop on the reserve's edge, where you'll be surrounded on three sides by the Fundy and a long way from any help. Inland, a main trail edges the marsh, and a few subsidiary paths angle off the road and probe the reserve's interior; landmarks are few, and it's easy to get lost. To play it safe, stay close to the road and observe the exquisite wildlife through binoculars.

Harvey

The lush setting at the **Florentine Manor** on backcountry Hwy. 915, tel. (506) 882-2271, is an especially welcome bit of civilization in the remote birdwatching area of pastoral Albert County. The heritage inn offers seven nonsmoking guest rooms ($50-60) just a short sprint from the Fundy seacoast.

Rocks Provincial Park

The great Fundy tides have created a curiously compelling scene at Rocks Provincial Park, tel. (506) 734-3429, 45 minutes northeast of Alma on Highway 114. You'll arrive at the park (entrance fee $4 per vehicle), leave your car in the clifftop lot, and descend a railed stone staircase leading to the damp tidelands.

At the staircase's first landing, you overlook an otherworldly collection of giant natural arches and mushroom-shaped pillars jutting up from the sea floor. New Brunswickers call the formations "flowerpots," a poetic way of describing the sea-sculpted red shale and conglomerate seastacks that have been separated from the mainland cliffs by the abrasive tide. Many of the flowerpots are "planted" with stunted black spruce and balsam fir, looking somewhat like clipped haircuts stuck atop the stacks.

At low tide, sightseers—dwarfed by the enormous pillars—roam the beach and retrieve seashells left by the tide. Be careful of falling rocks; the pillars and cliffs are continually eroding, and there's always a chance that rocks will loosen and tumble. Also, pay special attention to the time-to-go clock at the stairwell's top. **The seabed is safe only from three hours before low tide to two hours after.**

Catch the scene again at high tide and you'll understand why. The tide rises 16 meters here, fully flooding the area. All you'll see are the pillars' tree-covered crowns.

SACKVILLE

The 17th-century French settlers who founded Sackville originally called the town Tintamarre, from the French word for a noisy commotion. They were referring to the din produced by the geese and other birds which inhabit the surrounding wetlands. The name was later anglicized to Tantramar, a name which today refers to the entire marsh system of the area.

These first settlers had emigrated from around the estuaries of western France, so they were experienced in wresting tidelands from the sea. By creating an extensive system of dikes, called *aboideaux*, they reclaimed thousands of acres of Chignecto Isthmus marsh and brought the extremely fertile alluvial lands into agricultural production. Their raised dikes can be seen around Sackville and into Nova Scotia, and are occasionally signposted along the highway, with a date given to indicate their antiquity.

Mount Allison Academy (later University) was founded here in 1843; 11 years later, a "Female Branch" was opened. In 1875, the university gained the distinction of being the first in the British Empire to grant a college degree to a woman.

The beautiful campus is still at the heart of this town, surrounded by stately houses and tree-shaded streets. A number of artists have chosen Sackville as their home, and one of the best places to see their work is at Mount Allison University's **Owens Art Gallery** on York St. (at the campus's edge near downtown), tel. (506) 364-2574. The Owens ranks as one of the major galleries in the province and emphasizes avant-garde work by local, regional, and national artists. It's open Mon.-Wed. and Fri. 10 a.m.-5 p.m., Thurs. 7-10 p.m., Sat.-Sun. 2-5 p.m.

Reid's Bookstore, 8 Bridge St., tel. 536-3777, stocks an unusually fine collection of provincial waterfowl, environmental, and naturalist books. It's open Mon.-Wed. 8:30 a.m.-5:30 p.m., Thurs.-Fri. to 9 p.m., Sat. 10 a.m.-5 p.m.

For a place to stay, the **Marshlands Inn,** 59 Bridge St., tel. 536-0170, is among the town's finest lodgings. The inn, built in the 1850s, got its name from an early owner, who named the mansion in honor of the adjacent Tantramar Marshes. The resplendent, white, wooden heritage inn sits back from the road under shady trees and offers 21 guest rooms ($50-89, meal plans available) furnished with antiques, and a dining room of local renown.

In mid-August, the three-day Atlantic Waterfowl Celebration acknowledges the wealth of wildlife and the rich wetlands habitat of the surrounding area. The event features arts and crafts and tours of the Waterfowl Park (see below). For information, call 364-8080.

Sackville Waterfowl Park
If you're short on time and can stop at only one of the area's several wildlife sanctuaries, make it the Sackville Waterfowl Park—it's an idyllic, vest-pocket tribute to the Tantramar Marshes. The site, a few blocks from downtown and owned mainly by Mount Allison University, was restored as a marsh with flooding in 1988; a trail and boardwalks were added the following year to maximize access.

It's easy to find. The sanctuary lies at the campus's edge opposite the town's tourist center on E. Main Street. Drive in the parking lot beside the university service building; the trailhead starts on the other side of the bushes.

The 22-hectare sanctuary spreads out with trails routed through bushes, and bleached wooden walkways crossing wet areas. The university town's bustle lies just outside the reserve, yet the stillness here is penetrating. Ring-tailed ducks paddle through the waters. Pie-billed grebes surface and dive. Coots dabble here and there. Bitterns chase frogs. Summer breezes rustle among cattails and bulrushes. Is this heaven or what?

THE DORCHESTER PENINSULA AND TANTRAMAR MARSHES

Another prime birding site is not far from Sackville. From Dorchester, 14 km west of Sackville on Hwy. 106, turn off on Hwy. 935. The back-country gravel road loops south around the Dorchester Peninsula—the digit of land separating Shepody Bay from the Cumberland Basin.

Some 50,000 semipalmated sandpipers nest from mid-July to mid-September between Johnson Mills and Upper Rockport, as the road loops back towards Sackville. Roosting sites lie along pebble beaches and mudflats, and the birds are most lively at feeding time at low tide. Smaller flocks of dunlins, white-rumped sandpipers, and sanderlings inhabit the area late September to October.

Continuing on Hwy. 935, the road follows the peninsula's coast alongside the Cumberland Basin and ends at Hwy. 106, a few kilometers from the TransCanada (Hwy. 2). Be prepared to deal with the fast-moving, TransCanada traffic, more intent on speeding to Aulac, the province's land gateway to Nova Scotia, than on the slow-moving, idyllic pastime of birdwatching.

Speeding cars notwithstanding, this area across the Chignecto Isthmus forms an entree into the Tantramar Marshes, an incredibly fertile habitat so rich in waterfowl and birds that the early Acadian settlers described the area as a *tintamarre* ("ceaseless din"). A few roads haphazardly thread through the marshes, and there's no official approach to birdwatching here. Head off the TransCanada anywhere and wander; you can't go wrong on any of the backcountry roads from the Sackville area to the province's border crossing.

Fort Beauséjour

A signpost marks the turnoff from the Trans-Canada, eight km east of Sackville, to the Fort Beauséjour National Historic Site, located on the Cumberland Basin just west of the Nova Scotia border. Continue on the road to the fort ruins, which mark France's last-ditch military struggle against the British, who threatened Acadia centuries ago. France lost the fort in 1755 after a two-week siege. The Brits renamed it Fort Cumberland, and used it in 1776 to repel an attack by American revolutionaries. The fort stood ready for action in the War of 1812, though

no enemy appeared. Fort Cumberland was abandoned in the 1830s, and nature soon reclaimed the site.

Some of the ruins have since been restored. Facilities include a picnic area and a museum/visitor center, tel. (506) 536-0720, with exhibits on what life was like in the old days. The fort is open June to mid-Oct., daily 9 a.m.-5 p.m. Admission is free.

The setting is also prime birdwatching terrain. Keep an eye out and you'll be rewarded with sightings of the sharp-tailed sparrow or one of the other species that nest in the tall grasses rimming the ruins.

The Tintamarre Sanctuary

The Tintamarre National Wildlife Area fans out beyond the fort ruins. To get there, get back on the TransCanada for a short drive toward the Nova Scotia border and turn off at Hwy. 16, the highway's spur that turns northeast at Aulac to Cape Tormentine. Continue on Hwy. 16 for about 10 km to Jolicure, a village at the reserve's edge. No trails penetrate the 1,990-hectare mix of marshes, uplands, old fields, forests, and lakes. A few dikes provide steady ground through some of the terrain, but you are asked to stay on the roads encircling the area to do your birdwatching.

Amid the cattails, sedges, and bulrushes, sightings include migratory mallards, grebes, red-winged blackbirds, yellow warblers, swamp swallows, common snipes, black ducks, Virginia rails, and bitterns; short-eared owls take wing at dusk.

Bring binoculars—and insect repellent. The area is thick with mosquitoes. For more information on the area, call (506) 364-5044.

THE ACADIAN COASTS
INTRODUCTION

Along the eastern edge of New Brunswick are the Acadian Coasts—a French-flavored realm of seaports, barrier beaches, sand dunes, salt marshes, sandy pine-clad shores, and rocky coastlines shaped by three seas.

The Northumberland Strait is the shallow, narrow sea strip between New Brunswick's southeastern coast and Prince Edward Island. Here the coastline attracts summertime sunbathers, swimmers, and windsurfers to welcoming beaches on Gulf Stream–warmed waters.

Farther north, the warm sea mixes with the cooler Gulf of St. Lawrence. Here the Labrador Current swirls in the open gulf, and the swift currents arrive ashore with low rolls of surf. Offshore, barrier islands hold sheltered seaports.

Farthest north, the Baie des Chaleurs ("Bay of Warmth") is the shallow sea pocket between northern New Brunswick and Québec's Gaspé Peninsula. It was named by early French explorer Jacques Cartier, who sailed into the bay in 1534 and was impressed by the surprisingly tepid waters.

The essence of French-speaking Acadia is entwined in its dining and festivals. To understand the region's cultural roots, visit the Acadian Historical Village at Caraquet, where early Acadian life has been re-created with authentic buildings and costumed animators. In the south, Moncton, Acadia's trendy urban commercial and educational center, is Caraquet's bustling modern counterpoint—a very successful Acadia of the 1990s.

Acadian pride runs high, and everywhere in the region the Acadian flag—the red, white, and blue French tricolor with a single gold star—is displayed prominently. But other ethnic groups are represented here as well. Canada's Irish Festival has been held every July since 1984 at Newcastle/Chatham. And throughout the year you can find the local Irish community celebrating its cultural roots with dancers, pipe bands, food, films, workshops, lectures, and, of course, a St. Patrick's Day parade.

Stretched-out distances notwithstanding, getting around is easy and very manageable. High-

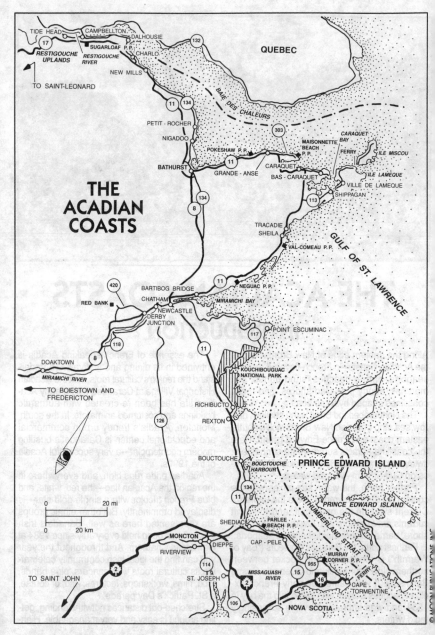

way 11 lopes along most of the three coasts from seaport to seaport, with the sea almost always within view. End to end, it's an easygoing, 10-hour drive one way between Campbellton and Shediac, if you take your time. But by all means, take the side roads branching off the main route and amble even closer to the seas to explore the seaports and scenery. For example, Hwy. 11 diverges from the coast and cuts an uninteresting bee line between Chatham and Bouctouche. Coastal Hwy. 117 is far more scenic, running through Kouchibouguac National Park and curling out to remote Point Escuminac—a lofty shale plateau at Miramichi Bay's southeastern tip, frequented, in season, by thousands of migratory seabirds.

HISTORY

From earliest times, the Micmac Indians camped on the seacoasts during their journeys from the Saint John River valley to summertime hunting and fishing grounds on Prince Edward Island. In the 1500s, French and Basque fishermen ventured into the area to catch salmon offshore and on the Miramichi River.

Cartier claimed the land for France in 1534, and a century later the explorer-merchant Nicolas Denys built a fort on Île Miscou, started a settlement in the Bathurst area, and scouted the Miramichi River.

Early French settlements spread up the coast all the way to the Restigouche area at Baie des Chaleurs' western end. By 1739, the region's population reached 8,000, swelled by Acadians who fled mainland Nova Scotia as the British established military dominance there.

The Acadian Deportation

In the mid-1700s, decades of war between England and France were winding down in England's favor. The British demanded unqualified oaths of allegiance from the Acadians, who refused and claimed neutrality. Instead, they fled Nova Scotia for Acadia's more peaceful north. The British followed, burning villages and crops as they went. The Acadian Deportation began in 1755, when about 1,100 Acadians were deported to England's other colonies in South Carolina, Georgia, and Pennsylvania. Guerrilla warfare raged as the Acadians fought for their lives and then fled to the hinterlands.

Refugee camps sprang up, the most famous of which were Beaubears Island, now a national historic site on the Miramichi River, and the nearby swatch of land now set aside as Enclosure Provincial Park (at Derby Junction, five km west of Newcastle), one of the province's most important archaeological sites. Many Acadians died of scurvy and starvation.

The Peace of Paris in 1763 ushered in an uneasy truce. France surrendered its mainland possessions, but during the ensuing decades about 3,800 Acadians returned to the region. The Deportation officially finished in 1816.

Early Post-Deportation Settlements

England swept the lower Saint John River valley as far north as Saint-Anne's Point (now Fredericton) and evicted the Acadians. The French settlers' intense love of the land prevailed, however, and they fled north to the remote Baie des Chaleurs: Caraquet began in 1758, Campbellton in 1773, Cap-Pelé in 1780, and Tracadie in 1785.

The British resettled Anglo immigrants and others who were more amenable to the English Crown on the vacated land. Moncton began as Monckton, named for the British officer who had led the Acadian Deportation north of the Missaguash River; Germans from Pennsylvania, lured with free land grants, founded the settlement in 1766. Scots, Loyalists, and Irish poured into the region and carved settlements in the Miramichi River forests. Their descendants moved on to the Restigouche Uplands and the Baie des Chaleurs' western end. The sea shaped the early economy. Bathurst and Monckton shipyards began operations in the early 1800s, and in the Newcastle and

Chatham area, Joseph Cunard (the brother of Samuel Cunard, who launched the Cunard shipping empire at Halifax) started his own shipyard in 1825.

Moncton Emerges as an Economic Kingpin

As shipbuilding petered out in the 1870s, Moncton tumbled into bankruptcy. But the town revived quickly when the Intercolonial Railway chugged into New Brunswick and designated the town as the railroad's Atlantic hub. (Note Moncton's new spelling; the provincial legislature misspelled its official name in 1855.) By 1885, the city was an industrial center with a tannery, soap factory, cotton mill, brass works, sugar refinery, foundries, lumber yards, and riverside wharves.

In the hinterlands, the Great Miramichi Fire charred 15,500 square km of forests and almost destroyed Newcastle in 1825. And while the name of Max Aitken (Lord Beaverbrook) is traditionally linked to Fredericton, the philanthropic industrialist's earliest years began at Newcastle when his father, a Presbyterian minister, moved the family from Ontario to the town on the Miramichi River in 1880. Max, youngest of six children, arrived as an infant and grew up in the stately house with the black mansard roof on

Mary Street, a provincial heritage site that now serves as the town's public library.

The Contemporary Region

The region dozed through the first half of the 20th century. In the early 1950s, Bathurst developed as an industrial center when zinc, lead, silver, and copper were discovered 35 km south of the city. Since 1964, Brunswick Mining and Smelting has mined the ore body, which is 975 meters deep and said to be among the world's largest. Moncton has maintained its economic edge through the decades. The city has thrived as the geographic center of the Maritimes, an enormous shipping and distribution advantage. The Université de Moncton, which began with a single building, now spreads across a large campus with an enrollment of 4,000 students. It is Atlantic Canada's sole French-speaking university and grants degrees in business, fine arts, science, education, nursing, and law.

Though development in the rest of the region is more low-key, the towns on the Baie des Chaleurs have added lodgings and restaurants as visitor demand has increased. On the gulf, Kouchibouguac National Park is so popular it's run out of campground space, and there's talk of expansion.

MONCTON AND VICINITY

Moncton (population 57,000) is a bustling small city involved in a renaissance of arts, commerce, and physical expansion. The economy hums, fueled by the city's advantageous position as the Maritimes' geographic center and distribution hub. Lodgings and shops are plentiful. Local restaurants offer some of New Brunswick's best cooking. The city also works nicely as a sightseeing base for drives to the strait.

You can't help but sense the city's vitality and energy. The *Commercial News,* Atlantic Canada's business and economic monthly magazine, summed up its essence in calling Moncton "the Renaissance City"; and a 1994 *New York Times* article described it as one of the most attractive cities in North America for business.

Moncton has maintained its economic edge through the decades, and the wealth has spilled

over into the suburbs of Dieppe and Riverview. Riverview keeps a low profile. Dieppe is another story. After WW II, returning soldiers renamed the town, formerly Leger Corner, to honor their fallen comrades who died on the beaches at Dieppe, France. The suburb now rivals Moncton in economic importance and is the site of the Moncton Airport; the Palais Crystal, Atlantic Canada's largest shopping/amusement center; and Champlain Place, another large shopping mall. The Magic Mountain Water Park, a large theme park close to Magnetic Hill on Moncton's northwestern outskirts, opened in the late 1980s and attracts 120,000 visitors a year.

One-third Acadian and two-thirds Anglo, the city is officially bilingual; while most everyone speaks English, a knowledge of French will help the visitor here.

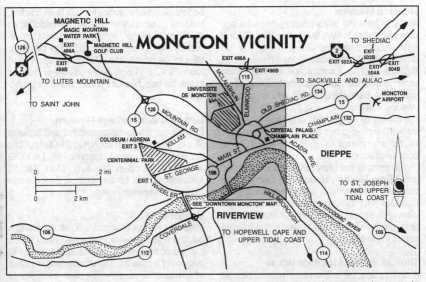

SIGHTS

Getting Oriented

Moncton started at "The Bend," a sharp turn in the Petitcodiac River, and developed outward. Rejuvenated, historic **Main Street,** a block in from the river, has new brick sidewalks, old-time lampposts, and park benches beneath fledgling trees. This is the place for people-watching; Acadia at its most chic passes this way.

The rest of the city spreads out in the shape of a fan. The adjacent suburb of Dieppe lies on Moncton's eastern side; **Hwy. 15,** a fast-moving expressway, rims the western side; and the **TransCanada** wraps around the city's north side and has well-marked exits.

Mountain Road, the city's commercial and fast-food stretch, starts four blocks inland from Main St. and works its way northwest across town to the northwestern corner and the Magnetic Hill theme-park area. The **Université de Moncton** lies north of the city center off Wheeler Boulevard.

Moncton's interior is a confusing maze of mainly residential streets; it helps to keep a map handy. Wheeler Blvd. makes a big loop around

the town, connecting at its west and east ends with Main St., so if you can find Wheeler it'll eventually take you back into the town center.

The following sights are located at the riverfront and outward. There's no parking on Main Street. Instead, use one of the adjacent side streets and plug a loonie ($1 coin) for an hour into a metered parking slot, or park in one of the nearby lots.

Bore Park

The Fundy's tidal bore, a lead wave up to 60 centimeters high, pulses up the Petitcodiac River twice daily as the tide rises on the Bay of Fundy. Within an hour or so, the muddy bed of the Petitcodiac—locally dubbed the "Chocolate River"—will be drowned under some 7.5 meters of water. The tourist information center, nearby on Main St., can provide a tidal schedule.

The best place to witness the tidal phenomenon is off Main St. at the riverside Bore Park, which is dotted with shade trees and park benches. Founding settlers landed here, too, and the site is marked with a cairn. On weekdays in July and August, free outdoor concerts are offered at the park; times vary, so check at the tourist information center for a schedule.

Moncton Museum

Artifacts from the city's history—from the age of the Micmacs to WW II— and touring national exhibits are displayed at the former city hall building. When the building was modernized, the city architect concocted an interesting arrangement that combined the building's original native-sandstone facade with an updated interior. The museum is at 20 Mountain Rd. at the corner of King Street. It's open July-Aug., daily 10 a.m.-5 p.m.; Sept.-June, Tues.-Sun. with shorter hours; tel. (506) 856-4383. Donations requested.

Adjacent to the Moncton Museum, the tidy, small **Free Meeting House** (Moncton's oldest building) dates to 1821 and served as a sanctuary for religious groups as diverse as Anglicans, Adventists, Jews, and Christian Scientists. If you're interested in seeing the interior, ask at the museum.

Thomas Williams Heritage House

A century ago, the Intercolonial Railroad brought the movers and shakers to town. Among them was Thomas Williams, the railroad's former treasurer. His 12-room Victorian Gothic mansion, elegantly furnished with period pieces, is now the city's showpiece of the good old days at 103 Park St., tel. (506) 857-0590. It's open June-Aug., Mon.-Sat. 10 a.m.-6 p.m., Sun. from 1 p.m.; Sept.-May, shorter hours. Formal tea is served on the veranda, July-Aug., Tues.-Sat. 11 a.m.-4 p.m., Sun. 1-4 p.m. Donations requested.

Galerie d'Art et Musée Acadien

The Acadian region is as creatively avant-garde as it is historic. At the Université de Moncton, in the Clément Cormier Building, this gallery and museum touch upon numerous aspects of Acadian culture in the combined exhibits—a foretaste of the excellent Acadian Historical Village near Caraquet. The gallery and museum are open June-Aug., Mon.-Fri. 10 a.m.-5 p.m., Sat.-Sun. 1-5 p.m.; Sept.-May, shorter hours; tel. (506) 858-4088. Admission is free.

Centennial Park

At the western side of town, the 121-hectare spread of greenery off St. George Blvd. makes a pleasant place to picnic and relax amid woodlands with hiking trails and a lake with a sandy beach. Summer activities include lawn bowling, swimming, tennis, and canoeing or paddling on the lake. In winter, lighted trails invite cross-country skiers, ice-skaters, and hockey players to take to the frozen lake. The park is open year-round, 9 a.m.-11 p.m. A day-use fee is charged to use the beach: adults $3, discounts for youngsters.

Lutz Mountain Heritage Museum

Exhibits on the founding settlers and artifacts fill this former Baptist church at 3143 Mountain Rd. (Hwy. 126 beyond Magnetic Hill), tel. (506) 384-7719. It's open July-Aug., Mon.-Sat. 10 a.m.-6 p.m. Call for admittance during other months. Admission is free.

Magnetic Hill

Magnetic Hill on Moncton's outskirts is just a hill, but if you believe your eyes, you'll agree it's one of the world's oddest. Is Magnetic Hill magnetic? It must be. The unassuming dirt road, which seems to defy the rule of logic, is Canada's third most popular natural tourist attraction, behind Niagara Falls and the Rockies.

The hill's slope plays tricks on anything with wheels. Set your car at the hill's "bottom," shift into neutral, and release the brake. The car appears to coast backward *up* the hill. Cars aren't the only things that defy gravity here. A stream alongside the road seems to flow uphill, too.

The illusion baffled Monctonians for decades. Before the 1900s, the local farmers fought the incline when they tried to haul wagons "down" the hill. Several decades later, reporters from Saint John discovered Magnetic Hill. Their newspaper coverage of the "natural phenomenon" brought a slew of spectators, and the stream of nonbelievers hasn't stopped since.

So many tourists arrived to observe the illogical hill that local Muriel Lutes (whose ancestors named nearby Lutes Mountain) opened a gift shop and restaurant for visitors. In 1974, Stan Steeves, another Monctonian, bought the operation and began serving as the hill's unofficial host. His favorite story involves a Japanese film crew that plied the hill with a plastic hose, beach ball, and a bicycle built for two. As expected, the hose's water current, the ball, and the bike riders coasted backward up the hill.

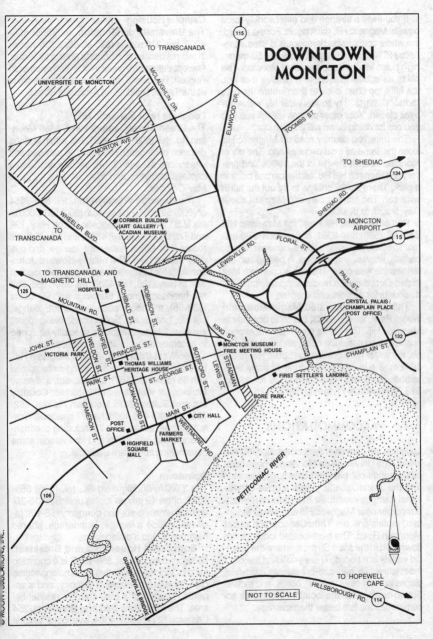

DOWNTOWN MONCTON

UNIVERSITE DE MONCTON

TO TRANSCANADA

TO TRANSCANADA

TO TRANSCANADA AND MAGNETIC HILL

TO SHEDIAC

TO MONCTON AIRPORT

MCLAUGHLIN DR.

ELMWOOD DR.

TOOMBS ST.

MORTON AVE.

WHEELER BLVD.

SHEDIAC RD.

FLORAL ST.

LEWISVILLE RD.

PAUL ST.

CORMIER BUILDING (ART GALLERY / ACADIAN MUSEUM)

HOSPITAL

MOUNTAIN RD.

ARCHIBALD ST.

ROBINSON ST.

KING ST.

CHAMPLAIN ST.

CRYSTAL PALAIS / CHAMPLAIN PLACE (POST OFFICE)

JOHN ST.

VICTORIA PARK

HIGHFIELD ST.

WELDON ST.

PRINCESS ST.

PARK ST.

BONACCORD ST.

ST. GEORGE ST.

BOTSFORD ST.

LEWIS ST.

STEADMAN ST.

THOMAS WILLIAMS HERITAGE HOUSE

MONCTON MUSEUM / FREE MEETING HOUSE

FIRST SETTLER'S LANDING

BORE PARK

CAMERON ST.

MAIN ST.

POST OFFICE

FARMERS MARKET

CITY HALL

WESTMORELAND ST.

HIGHFIELD SQUARE MALL

PETITCODIAC RIVER

GUNNINGSVILLE BRIDGE

HILLSBOROUGH RD.

TO HOPEWELL CAPE

NOT TO SCALE

N

© MOON PUBLICATIONS, INC.

If you think a strange and otherworldly force powers Magnetic Hill, think again. For the record, the whole countryside hereabouts is tilted. Magnetic Hill forms the southern flank of 150-meter-high Lutes Mountain northwest of Moncton. The hill is an optical illusion, and believe it or not, the hill's top crest is lower than where the hill's "bottom" starts. Try to walk the hill with your eyes closed. Your other senses will tell you that you are traveling down rather than up.

The unpaved country road on Magnetic Hill looks the same as it did decades ago. The city of Moncton bought the hill in the 1980s and preserved Magnetic Hill Rd. as the central point in a park. There's a $2 charge to try out the hill in your car. The site is open mid-May to Labour Day, 9 a.m. to dusk.

Part of Magnetic Hill Park, the **Magnetic Hill Zoo,** tel. (506) 384-9381, houses some 80 animal species, including zebras, reindeer, tigers, camels, wolves, and gibbons. A petting zoo entertains the wee ones. The zoo is open late May to mid-Oct., daily 9 a.m.-dusk. Admission is $5, discounts for seniors and children.

The privately operated **Magic Mountain Water Park,** tel. 857-9283, sits off to one side of Magnetic Hill. The theme park has a wave pool, numerous chutes, tube rides, and minigolf. And no, the water here doesn't run uphill. Hours are 10 a.m.-8 p.m. daily, mid-June to early September. Admission is a stiff $17.25 for adults, $12.75 for kids 4-11, family rate $53.25.

ACCOMMODATIONS

Lodgings are conveniently concentrated in three areas. The Université de Moncton, whose campus spreads out between downtown Moncton and the TransCanada, offers a trove of seasonal campus rooms. At the city's northwestern corner near Magnetic Hill and Magic Mountain, motels line the TransCanada and upper Mountain Road. The best-located lodgings are downtown in the Main St. area, where the splendid variety is a bonus. There you'll find the city's most attractive bed-and-breakfasts (convivial places to meet other visitors), hotels, and motels. But no matter what the location, Moncton's accommodations are better than average.

Campus Housing
The **Université de Moncton,** tel. (506) 858-4008, has 310 rooms ($25 student, $30 visitor) in two residences and accepts guests May-Aug. (except during one week in July and another in August). For details, ask at the registration office at the Taillon Building on Archibald Street.

Lodgings Near Magnetic Hill
The **Green Acres Campground,** 1380 Mountain Rd., tel. (506) 384-0191, lies within walking distance of Magnetic Hill, with 100 serviced and unserviced sites ($12-14), kitchen shelters, a canteen, showers, and a launderette. It's open May-October.

The **Auberge Wandlyn Inn,** tel. 384-3554 or (800) 561-0000 in Canada, (800) 561-0006 in the U.S., is close to Magnetic Hill off Hwy. 126 and TransCanada's exit 488B, and has 76 basic rooms ($57-80), a restaurant, lounge, and outdoor heated pool. The nearby **Howard Johnson's Motor Lodge** spreads out on the northern side of Hwy. 126, exit 488B, tel. 384-1050, and has handsome motel trappings with 99 rooms ($59-95), an indoor pool, restaurant, lounge, hot tub, and sauna. Some nonsmoking rooms are available, as are rooms specially equipped to accommodate guests with disabilities.

Nor-West Court Ltd. at 1325 Mountain Rd., tel. 384-1222, is another low-slung motel spread with 33 rooms ($52-67), a restaurant, and some facilities for visitors with disabilities. **Country Inn and Suites,** 2475 Mountain Rd., tel. 852-7000 or (800) 456-4000, has 77 spacious, nicely appointed suites ($60-78 including continental breakfast) with VCRs and free videos; some nonsmoking suites are available.

Downtown
The **YWCA,** 35 Highfield St., tel. (506) 855-4349, offers 12 private rooms upstairs ($15-20) and a downstairs six-bed dormitory ($6-10); facilities include a lounge, launderette, shared bathrooms, and a dining room.

Bonaccord House Bed and Breakfast, 250 Bonaccord St., tel. 388-1535, is a charming meld of Victoriana with five nonsmoking rooms ($35-53 with breakfast), a balcony, and a veranda, located in a tree-shaded residential area. The **Park View Bed and Breakfast,** 254 Cameron St., tel. 382-4504, overlooks Victoria

Park nearby and is an art-deco charmer with three nonsmoking rooms; $35-45 with full breakfast.

Keddy's Brunswick Hotel, 1005 Main St., tel. 854-6340 or (800) 561-7666, peers over bustling downtown with 191 high-rise rooms and suites ($60-85; some nonsmoking rooms), restaurants, an indoor heated pool, sauna, whirlpool, and exercise room. The **Rodd Park House Inn,** 434 Main St., tel. 382-1664 or (800) 565-7633, overlooks Bore Park with 97 rooms ($59-82; highest rate gets you a room with views), a restaurant, lounge, and indoor pool. Some nonsmoking and some barrier-free rooms are available.

Canadian Pacific Hotel Beauséjour, 750 Main St., tel. 854-4344 or (800) 441-1414 in Canada and the U.S., is *the* best in Moncton. One side of the hotel overlooks the river. It has 314 well-appointed, large rooms and suites ($89-129), three restaurants, a piano bar, and an outdoor pool. Some nonsmoking and some barrier-free rooms are available.

FOOD AND DRINK

You might stumble on a few Acadian dishes, but the city's most sophisticated chefs tilt toward continental cooking, with an emphasis on nouvelle cuisine ingredients and presentation. California culinary variations are new and encompass a trove of healthy foods such as fruit

sauces, mixed-grain breads, salad sprouts, and legume variations. Otherwise, Moncton is a steak-and-seafood town—expect unadorned, hearty basics and a side dish or two of salad and fries.

Fast food is ubiquitous in Moncton, with the usual pizza, burger, and fried-chicken suspects —and no fewer than 15 Tim Horton's doughnut shops—clustered along Mountain Rd., Main St., and Main's extension into Dieppe, Champlain Street.

Dinners
The **Wharf Village Restaurant,** at Magnetic Hill Park, tel. (506) 858-8841, does a fine job feeding the theme-park visitors with seafood family fare at good value for the dollar ($6-12). It's open May-Oct., daily to 8 p.m.

The **Park Bench** at the Rodd Park House Inn, tel. 382-1664, overlooks the river. The mixed menu ($9-19) is strong in beef, especially filet mignon. Sunday brunch ($6) is an excellent buy. It's open 9 a.m.-2 p.m.

Boomerang's at Westmoreland and Main streets, tel. 857-8325 (reservations are wise), also caters to a beef-eating clientele and opens at 4 p.m. daily with entrees of the best western Canadian beef ($10-15) prepared any way you'd like it. Boomerang's is proud of the chef's seafood and features the freshest catches, especially shrimp and the scallops from Cape Enrage served *en brochette* ($14). The setting is among Moncton's prettiest and features old-time architectural elegance throughout its three dining rooms.

The **Riverboat Restaurant,** Magic Mountain Water Park, tel. 857-9282, serves basic seafood ($13-16) with daily specials. It's open mid-July to early Sept., daily 5-8 p.m.

The **Top Deck** atop Keddy's Brunswick Hotel rooftop, tel. 854-6340 (reservations required), offers incredible views and fine dining to match. The menu ($13-22) is mixed with beef (especially prime rib, $16-19 depending on weight) and seafood with lobster-stuffed shrimp or shellfish in pastry.

Gaston's, 644 Main St., tel. 858-8998, is the people-watching place, with windows overlooking downtown's Blue Cross Centre. The ambitious menu ($14-25) is at its flavorful best with Gaston's pepper steak smothered in peppercorns and brandy ($19), Cajun blackened redfish ($14), and sauced salmon baked in pastry ($17). Reservations are wise at this popular eatery.

The **Chez Jean-Pierre** at 21 Toombs St., tel. 382-0332 (reservations required), has been a culinary legend for decades. Locals relish the dimly lit, intimate setting and creative menu ($15-20). The chef likes to explore such culinary exotica as cod cheeks, quail, and guinea hen, and is equally skilled in less complicated local favorites such as Atlantic salmon sautéed in lightly spiced butter.

Cy's Seafood Restaurant, 170 Main St., tel. 857-0032, has garnered decades of plaudits for seafood and serves every conceivable variation (under $20). Lobster is the specialty (any way you like it), especially the Newburg dish, thick with lobster chunks ($17).

The **Windjammer,** at Canadian Pacific Hotel Beauséjour, tel. 854-4344 (reservations required), has all the creative trappings of dining excellence in a plush, intimate setting. The hallmark is the inventive chef, who introduced California-style dining to Moncton in a splendid array of presentations such as Atlantic salmon sautéed in pecan butter ($18) and lobster awash in mango sauce served over pasta ($23).

Light Meals and Groceries
Sub-sandwich shops, Chinese takeouts, and pizza places are everywhere. If you'd like something quick but more substantial, check out the **Fancy Pocket** at 589 Main St., which features stuffed pita sandwiches, quiches, and salads; or **Good For You,** which serves soups, sandwiches, meat pies, and homemade desserts at Highfield Square shopping center, Main and Highfield streets.

For picnic ingredients, stop at **Sobey's,** which has a deli corner and bakery. The supermarkets are located at the downtown Highfield Square shopping center, at the Moncton Mall at 1380 Mountain Rd. near Magnetic Hill, and at Champlain Place shopping center, 477 Paul St. in Dieppe. All are open Mon.-Fri. 9 a.m.-9 p.m., Sat. to 6 p.m. Numerous smaller **Green Gables** corner groceries are scattered throughout the city. **Back to Eden,** a health-food store that stocks packaged and fresh wholesome foods, is at the Moncton Mall.

Provincial **liquor stores** are open Mon.-Sat. 10 a.m. to 9:30 or 10 p.m. They're located at 936 Mountain Rd., 409 Elmwood Dr., and St. George Blvd. at Mount Royal Boulevard.

ENTERTAINMENT AND EVENTS

Nightlife
For Moncton's steamy night scene, check out the quartet of clubs at Main Street's other end for imbibing and people-watching. The karaoke at **Fat Tuesdays,** 740 Main St., lures crowds with a stage version and audience participants who lustily sing lyrics, backed by laser-disc words on a screen. On other nights, the club presents jam sessions and jazz groups. **Ziggy's,** 730 Main St., features bands and stand-up comedy. **Stages,** at 679 Main St., puts on jazz and rock, jam sessions, and often has a guitarist on the patio. The **Club Cosmopolitan,** 700 Main St., better known as The Cos, has a dance floor and excels in jazz. Both Stages and The Cos are open nightly to 2 a.m., charge $1-10, and fill in with disc jockeys between the live shows.

Chevy's Rock 'n Roll, 939 Mountain Rd., features retro rhythms and rock with a disc jockey to 2 a.m.; $3 cover. The **Press Box,** 834 Mountain Rd., pours draft beer and has big-screen sports television. For dim lights and mixed drinks, slink into the **Smuggler's Jug Lounge** at the Rodd Park House Inn, or **Top Side Lounge** at Keddy's Brunswick Hotel.

Movies and Shows
The **Paramount Theatre,** 84 Main St., has two flicks nightly year-round, plus weekend matinees in summer. For show times, call (506) 382-3092.

The **Capitol Theatre** at 811 Main St. reopened in 1993. This lovely old grande dame, ornately decorated with frescoes and murals, began as a vaudeville venue in the 1920s and glitters again since a $1.5 million rejuvenation. Concerts, ballets, shows, and film festivals come to the theater on a regular basis. For what's on, call 856-4379. The **Coliseum-Agrena,** Killam Dr. off Wheeler Blvd., gets the big shows such as Tina Turner or Anne Murray concerts; for details, call 857-4100.

Festivals

In late June and early July, the **Moncton Jazz Festival** features summer concerts, beer gardens, and fireworks for nine days downtown. Mid-August features the **Craft and Folk Festival** at Victoria Park and also an **Acadien Festival.** Early October's two-day **Octoberfest,** sponsored by the New Brunswick Arts and Crafts Association, brings reminiscences of the German founding settlers, appropriate German fare, beer gardens, and an arts and crafts fair.

RECREATION

Locals like golf, and they have eight courses in Greater Moncton to serve them. The **Magnetic Hill Golf Club,** a public course, is known for having the most challenging terrain—18 holes among rough hills, with one of the holes across a pond. The greens fee is $22, and you can rent carts and clubs. For reservations, call (506) 858-1611. The **Lakeside Golf and Country Club** on the old Shediac Rd. is more user-friendly ($20 greens fee). It's semiprivate, and members play first. For reservations, call 859-4202.

The city's **Centennial Park** has a sandy beach and a pool ($2.50 admission); open daily 10 a.m.-8 p.m. Keddy's Brunswick Hotel allows nonguests use of the hotel's fitness facilities (pool, jacuzzi, sauna, and weight machine) with a $5 day-use pass; open daily 7 a.m.-midnight.

SHOPPING

The local flair for arts and crafts surfaces at a trove of local shops. Craft shop and studio hours vary, and it's wise to call ahead for an appointment. Artisans market wares at the **Farmers' Market** on Robinson St.; open year-round, Sat. 7 a.m.-1 p.m. Check out **Say It With Grace,** 210 McSweeney Ave., tel. (506) 854-3689, for custom tablecloths and quilts; **Margaret Sawyer,** 62 Williams St., tel. 388-3013, for quilts; and **Fiddlehead Fleece,** Hwy. 115 off the TransCanada, tel. 856-6881, for knitted wares also sold at the Craft Gallery in Sackville.

It helps to speak French at some shops, such as **Top Notch Enterprises,** 49 Saint George St., tel. 857-2898, with local folk art, and **Galerie Sans Nom,** 140 Botsford St., Suite 11, tel. 854-5381, the local arts and crafts cooperative.

Apparel and other stores are found along Main St., most open Mon.-Wed. and Sat. 10 a.m.-6 p.m., Thurs.-Fri. to 9 p.m. Hours are Mon.-Sat. 9:30 a.m.-9:30 p.m. at both **Highfield Square Mall** (with a well-stocked Eaton's department store) at Main and Highfield streets, and **Moncton Mall** at 1380 Mountain Rd. (at Wheeler Blvd.).

Sundries

Ivan's Camera stocks basic film and equipment at 181 Saint George, as does **Black's Photography** in Moncton Mall. **United Book Store,** 347 Mountain Rd., stocks secondhand and rare books. Old comic books are big at **Wilkies,** 987 Main St., and **Million Comix,** 345 Mountain Road.

INFORMATION AND SERVICES

Visitor Information

Moncton Visitor Services, tel. (506) 853-3596, fax 856-4352, is based at City Hall, 774 Main St., Moncton, NB E1C 1E8; open year-round, Mon.-Fri. 8:30 a.m.-4:30 p.m. A seasonal tourism service, **Information Moncton,** has branches at 575 Main St., tel. 853-3590, and Lutes Mountain (TransCanada at Magnetic Hill), tel. 853-3540; both open mid-May to early Sept., daily 8:30 a.m.-6:30 p.m.

The **Greater Moncton Chamber of Commerce,** tel. 857-2883, is another source for information and has maps and literature at 910 Main St., Suite 100; open weekdays 8:30 a.m.-4:30 p.m.

For recorded **weather updates** for the Moncton area, call 851-6610.

Media, Books, and Maps

The *Times-Transcript* is the local six-day daily newspaper, and *L'Acadie Nouvelle* covers Acadian facets. **Reid's Newsstand,** 985 Main St., has a good selection of local newspapers and magazines and Canadian, British, and U.S. dailies. **Coles The Book People** stocks new books and an assortment of New Brunswick literature at Highfield Square and Moncton Mall. And if you're looking for French-language reading material, **Librairie Acadienne** has it at the Université de Moncton's Taillon Building on Archibald St.; open Mon.-Fri. 8:30 a.m.-4:30 p.m.

The **Public Library,** tel. (506) 857-8731, is at Blue Cross Centre, 644 Main St.; open Mon. and Fri. 9 a.m.-5 p.m., Tues.-Thurs. 9 a.m.-8:30 p.m. **N.B. Geological Information Centre/Land Information Centre** stocks the best assortment of topographical and nautical maps in town. They're at Assumption Place, 774 Main St., 8th floor, tel. 856-2322; open Mon.-Fri. 8:30 a.m.-4:15 p.m.

Environmental Organization

ECO Action, a citizens' environmental group, works in the forefront of local ecological concerns. Major issues include preserving the Wheeler Blvd. marshlands—where potential development threatens the environmentally sensitive terrain—and the Petitcodiac River's tidal bore, whose height has been diminished by a causeway on the city outskirts. For details, contact the group at P.O. Box 66, Moncton, NB E1C 8R9, tel. (506) 859-0618.

Services

Moncton City Hospital is at 135 MacBeath Ave. near Mountain Rd., tel. (506) 857-5111; **Hôpital Dr. Georges L. Dumont,** the French hospital, is at 330 Archibald St., tel. 858-3232. For the RCMP, call 851-6155; police, tel. 857-2400. In emergencies, dial 911.

The **Bank of Nova Scotia,** 780 Main St., changes U.S. and British currency to Canadian dollars without an extra fee but adds $1 for each traveler's check; open Mon.-Fri. 10 a.m.-5 p.m.

Canada Post has branches at 281 St. George St. (at the corner of Highfield St.), open Mon.-Fri. 7:30 a.m.-5:30 p.m.; and at 19 Katherine Ave., off Mountain Road. The St. George St. branch has a philatelic counter. A retail post office in Moncton Mall is open longer hours. The **Employment and Immigration Office,** 1600 Main St., tel. (506) 851-6666, handles immigration questions; open Mon.-Fri. 9 a.m.-5 p.m.

The VIA Rail terminal behind Highfield Square, Main St., has **storage lockers,** as does the SMT bus terminal, 961 Main Street. **St. George Laundromat** at 66 St. George Blvd. is open daily 8:30 a.m.-9 p.m.

TRANSPORTATION

By Air

The **Moncton airport** is 10 minutes from downtown on Champlain St./Hwy. 132 (a continuation of Main St. in Moncton) in adjacent Dieppe. The airport has a basic layout with no frills, and it's easy-in, easy-out. Air passengers from Saint John occasionally jam the facility when fog closes Saint John Airport. A taxi ride to Main St. in Moncton costs $12 OW.

The airport is served by **Air Canada** and affiliated **Air Nova,** as well as Canadian International's **Air Atlantic** commuter service from Atlantic Canada gateways. Other service includes **Air Alliance** from Quebec City, **Air Ontario** from Ontario, **NWT Air** from Northwest Territories, and **Air BC** from British Columbia. **Northwest Airlink** flies in from Boston.

For **flight information,** call Air Canada/Air Nova at (506) 857-1021; Air Atlantic, tel. 857-9929.

Avis, Hertz, Thrifty, and **Tilden** car rentals are at or near the airport. **Delta Rent-A-Car,** Mountain Rd. and High St., tel. (506) 853-1113, will pick you up at the airport and deliver you back there at departure; a compact car rental costs $170 a week and 12 cents a kilometer, and $60 for a week's collision insurance.

By Land

Moncton is served by **VIA Rail,** tel. (506) 857-9830; the terminal is behind Highfield Square on Main Street. Trains depart to Saint John on Mon., Thurs., Sat. ($22 OW or $13 OW if you buy the ticket five days in advance); to Newcastle and points northwest, service operates Wed., Fri., and Sun. ($20 OW or $12 OW in advance).

Buses from throughout the province arrive at the **SMT terminal** at 961 Main St. (open 7:30 a.m.-8:30 p.m.), tel. 859-5060; a ticket to Saint John costs $20 OW, and to Sackville it's $8 OW.

Getting Around

Codiac Transit, tel. (506) 857-2008, operates local bus service ($1), Mon.-Sat. 6:20 a.m.-7 p.m., Thurs.-Fri. to 10:15 p.m. Taxis are metered. **Air Cab,** tel. 857-2000, charges $2 to start and about $1 per kilometer.

Hitching is another way to get around, and if you're on the way to Saint John, try upper Mountain Rd. near its intersection with the Trans-Canada Highway. For Shediac and the strait coast, connect with a ride along Hwy. 15 in Dieppe, beyond the rotary (traffic circle).

VICINITY OF MONCTON

Dieppe
A short, narrow river tributary separates Moncton from adjacent Dieppe, and **Palais Crystal** (Crystal Palace) lies aside the Hwy. 15 rotary. The complex is an architectural wonder, a geodesic dome of angled glass walls with an amusement park ($13 for 20 tickets) and science center within. **Champlain Place,** Atlantic Canada's largest

one-level shopping mall, is next door.

The **Crystal Palace Hotel,** tel. (506) 858-8584, takes up most of the complex's space with 119 rooms and suites ($85-140), a dozen of which are gussied-up fantasies, such as a sultan's tent or a rock 'n' roll theme where the bed's a pink Cadillac. Facilities include an indoor pool, whirlpool, and sauna. Some rooms are non-smoking and some are adapted for guests with disabilities.

Saint-Joseph-de-Memramcook
A half hour southeast of Moncton off Hwy. 106, **Acadian Odyssey,** on the Memramcook Institute campus, explains Acadian survival with a series of exhibits and displays in Canada's only national historic site theme park; open daily 9 a.m.-5 p.m., June to mid-October.

THE STRAIT COAST

CAPE TORMENTINE TO KOUCHIBOUGUAC

Cape Tormentine, easternmost extremity of New Brunswick, is the jumping-off point for the ferry to Prince Edward Island. PEI is clearly visible from here, just 14 km away across the Northumberland Strait. On Main St., overlooking the strait and close to the beach, **Hilltop Bed and Breakfast,** tel. (506) 538-7747, is a comfortable and convenient place to overnight if you're arriving late or planning to catch an early ferry. Its three rooms cost $30-40, and there's a hot tub.

To the west, on coastal Hwy. 955, is beachside **Murray Corner Provincial Park,** tel. 538-2628, with 111 campsites ($11-15); open June-September.

Cap-Pelé, farther west on Hwy. 15, is close to a pair of good sandy beaches. At Gagnon Beach, **Gagnon Beach Camping,** tel. 577-2519, has 200 sites with full hookups plus a separate wooded tenting area. The **Ocean Retreat Bed and Breakfast,** tel. 577-6070, close to the beach, has rooms and housekeeping units at $30-55.

Shediac
The self-proclaimed "lobster capital of the world,"

20 km east of Moncton, Shediac backs up its claim with the "world's largest lobster"—an 11-meter-long, cast-iron crustacean sitting aside the road into town. For the real stuff, head for the town's restaurants, which have a reputation for some of the province's best lobster dinners.

The little town can be crowded on weekends, and it's packed during the early July Lobster Festival. Another big event is the weeklong Festival Baie Jazz and Blues in mid-July; call (506) 382-6464 for details. **Parlee Beach Provincial Park,** tel. 532-1500, at Shediac's eastern edge, is one of the main attractions here. Its placid, three-km-long beach is popular for the warmth of the water, which reaches 24° C in summer; day-use fee for the beach is $3. The park's 165 camping spaces fill up fast, and reservations are not accepted, so plan accordingly. Basic **Park Chedik Camping,** toward town center on E. Main St., tel. 532-6713, absorbs some of the overflow; it has 68 sites at $15-17.

The beautiful white **Auberge Belcourt Inn,** tel. 532-6098, boasts special provincial status as a heritage inn. The inn sits back at 112 Main St. beneath stately trees, with seven rooms ($60-85) and a dining room. It's near the western edge of town, just a quick stroll from the beach.

Another historic lodging is the 1853 **Hotel Shediac,** on Main St. in the town center, tel.

Lobster is big in Shediac.

NAN DROSDICK

532-4405. It's well priced at $39-59, and offers indoor and patio dining, a swimming pool, and volleyball courts.

Bouctouche

North of Shediac, Hwy. 11 zips through a wooded corridor, sacrificing scenery for efficiency. For a taste of the slower pace of rural, coastal Acadia, strike out on any of the local highways (such as 530, 475, or 505) to the east, which hug the coast and lead to quiet beaches at Saint-Thomas, Saint-Edouard-de-Kent, and Cap-Lumière.

The literary world learned about the often lean Acadian life during the Depression from the novels of Antonine Maillet, the famed writer who grew up in this small seaport north of Shediac. Maillet's fictional settings have been recreated at the **Pays de la Sagouine,** tel. (506) 743-1400, situated on a peninsula and islet with a hamlet of houses and other buildings, a reception center, an outdoor theater with changing entertainment, and a crafts shop. Admission is $8 adults.

The complex's spacious restaurant serves authentic Acadian fare, and on Wed.-Thurs. ($30) and Sat. ($35) evenings, dinner theater is performed (in French). Reservations are wise. The theme park is open June-Aug., daily 10 a.m.-8 p.m., Sept. to 6 p.m. To get there, take Hwy. 134 off Hwy. 11 and follow the signs to the waterfront site.

Rexton

This anglophone enclave near the mouth of the Richibucto River prospered as a shipyard in the 19th century. The town was the birthplace of Bonar Law, the only British prime minister in history who was born outside the British Isles. He was elected in 1922. **Bonar Law Historic Park,** aside Hwy. 116, tel. (506) 523-7615, preserves Law's ancestral homestead and farm. Costumed guides take you around the house and outbuildings. The park is open daily 9 a.m.-5 p.m., July-September.

KOUCHIBOUGUAC NATIONAL PARK

The Northumberland Strait coast finishes at Kouchibouguac National Park, a 238-square-km gem of a park that takes its name from the Micmac Indian word for "River of the Long Tides"—a reference to the waterway that meanders through the midsection of the low-lying park. It's pronounced "KOOSH-buh-gwack," more or less, but you'll hear many variations.

Slender barrier islands and white beaches and dunes, laced with marram grass and false heather, face the gulf along a 25-km front. A gray-seal colony occupies one of the offshore islands. In the park's interior, boardwalks ribbon the mudflats, freshwater marshes, and bogs, and nature trails probe the woodlands and old fields.

Make your first stop the **visitor information center,** one km inside the main entrance off Hwy. 134; open daily 9 a.m.-5 p.m. mid-May to mid-Oct., until 8 p.m. mid-June to early September. The park is open year-round; some campgrounds are seasonal (see below). For a memorable introduction, be sure to see the 20-minute slide presentation, *Kouchibouguac,* which takes the viewer on a seasonal trip through the park's sublime beauty and changing moods. Campsite registration is handled at the center, and information on activities, outdoor presentations, and evening programs is posted here, too.

Licenses are required for all vehicles traveling in the park and stopping to use facilities. It's $5 per day, $10 for four days. Fishing in the national park also requires a license: $4 daily, $6 weekly, $13 for the season, plus a special $13 license for taking salmon. Hunting is not permitted in Canada's national parks.

Camping

The national park, tel. (506) 876-2443 or 876-4205, offers the **South Kouchibouguac Campground,** with 219 serviced sites ($12, $8 in late spring and fall). The campground's civilized comforts include showers, flush toilets, kitchen shelters, launderettes, and a campers' store near the beach. It's open May-October. In summer, campers outnumber sites available, and people line up in droves. Site occupancies change most frequently on Sunday and Monday, so put your name on the waiting list, take a number, be patient, and wait for the week's exodus.

La Côte-à-Fabien Campground has 34 unserviced wilderness sites ($9) with toilets, trails, and a supervised beach; open mid-June to early September. The Côte-à-Fabien Group Campground has five sites for up to 25 people per site (at $1.25 per person); open late May to early October. Primitive campgrounds at **Petit-Large** (accessible by foot or bicycle, open year-round), **Sipu** (accessible on foot or by canoe), and **Pointe-à-Maxime** (accessible by canoe only) charge $3.50 per day.

Recreation

The land and coast are environmentally sensitive; park officials prefer that you stay on the trails and boardwalks or use a bike to get around on the 30 km of bike trails. Naturalist-led programs and outings are organized throughout summer. Check at the visitor information center for schedules.

Trails that explore the park's varied ecosystems include the short **Kelly's Beach Boardwalk,** the **Pines** and **Salt Marsh** trails, and the 1.8-km **Bog** trail. You can take longer hikes on the **Clair-Fontaine** (3.4 km), **Osprey** (5.1 km), and **Kouchibouguac** (14 km, allow five hours) trails.

The Black, St. Louis, Kouchibouguac, and other rivers that weave through the park are wonderful to explore by canoe, kayak, rowboat, or paddleboat. Those watercrafts, as well as fishing equipment and bicycles, are available at **Ryan's Rental Center,** tel. (506) 876-3733; open daily 8 a.m.-9 p.m., mid-June to early September. **Kouchibouguac National Park Rental Centre,** tel. 523-4242, also rents bikes. In winter, cross-country skiers take over the 30-km bicycle trails. Tobogganing and snowshoeing are also popular.

Swimming is supervised at Kelly's Beach in summer; swimming at Callander's and other beaches is unsupervised.

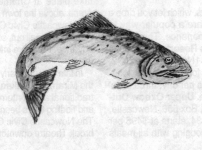

THE MIRAMICHI RIVER

The gorgeous Miramichi (pronounced "meer-ma-SHEE") River and its myriad tributaries drain much of the interior of eastern New Brunswick. The river enjoys a wide reputation as one of the best (if not *the* best) Atlantic salmon waters in the world. In the early 17th century, Nicolas Denys, visiting the Miramichi estuary, wrote of the salmon, saying: "So large a quantity of them enters into this river that at night one is unable to sleep, so great is the noise they make in falling upon the water after having thrown or darted themselves into the air."

Leaving the conurbation of Chatham/Newcastle near the river's mouth, Hwy. 8 follows the river valley southwest for most of its length. Most of the valley is lightly populated.

SALMON FISHING ON THE MIRAMICHI

Fly-fishing is the only method allowed for taking Atlantic salmon. Fish in the 13- to 18-kilogram range are not unusual; occasionally, anglers land specimens weighing up to 22 kg. For nonresidents, licenses cost $25 for three days, $50 for seven days, $100 for the season. The salmon season runs from 8 June to 15 October.

Nonresidents are required to hire guides, who are plentiful hereabouts. Many are based in Boiestown, Doaktown, and Blackville; contact the tourist information centers in Boiestown (tel. 506-369-7214), Blackville (tel. 843-2288), or the Miramichi Region Tourism Association, P.O. Box 264, Chatham, NB E1N 3A7, tel. 778-8444, for listings.

Riverside fishing resorts, which let you drop a line in rustic elegance, are a popular way to enjoy the piscatorial experience. They're not cheap, however. **Pond's Resort,** Porter Cove Rd., Ludlow, NB E0C 1N0, tel. 369-2612, charges $985 pp and up for three nights' lodging, including three meals per day, three days' fishing, and guide service. **Upper Oxbow Outdoor Adventures,** RR 2, Box 556, Newcastle, NB E1V 3L9, tel. 622-8834, starts at $495 per person for three nights' lodging with all meals

and two days of fishing. For a listing of outfitters, contact Tourism New Brunswick at (800) 561-0123 and ask for its *Aim and Angle* booklet.

CHATHAM AND NEWCASTLE

Old French maps of this area show the Miramichi River as the Rivière des Barques, the "River of Ships." From as early as the last quarter of the 18th century, the locally abundant timber and the deep-water estuary has made this an excellent location for the shipbuilding industry. The Cunard brothers began their lucrative shipbuilding empire at Chatham in 1826 and built some of the finest vessels of their day. The industry thrived for half a century and then faltered and faded, leaving no physical evidence—outside of museums—that it ever existed. Near Newcastle's Ritchie Wharf, the new **Shipbuilding Centre** features audiovisual displays, interpretive exhibits, and artifacts from this era.

Events

In the mid-19th century, Middle Island, a river island just east of Chatham, was the destination of thousands of Irish emigrants, many of them fleeing the catastrophic potato famine of the 1840s. Their descendants are still here, and since 1984 the area has celebrated its Irish heritage with the **Irish Festival on the Miramichi.** The four-day event in mid-July includes concerts, dances, a parade, lectures and music workshops, booths selling Irish mementos and books, and the consumption of a good deal of beer. Main events take place at Chatham's Lord Beaverbrook Arena, above the town on University Ave., and at the Newcastle Civic Centre. The evening concerts tend to sell out, so it's wise to buy tickets in advance. For more information, call (506) 778-8810.

In late July and early August, Newcastle hosts the **Miramichi Folksong Festival,** a shindig of traditional and contemporary singing, dancing, and fiddling that's been going strong since 1958. The Newcastle Civic Centre and Lord Beaverbrook Theatre downtown are the main venues.

For information and reservations, call the Information Center of the Miramichi, tel. 627-1495.

In late August, it's the Scots' turn; the **Miramichi Highland Gathering,** held over three days, features Highland dance competitions, pipe and drum bands, a *ceilidh,* and other events; call 622-2036 for details.

Accommodations and Food

During festival weekends, lodging can be scarce, so book ahead if you plan to be here during those times. **Enclosure Provincial Park,** Hwy. 8 and Hwy. 420 at Derby Junction five km west of Newcastle, tel. (506) 627-4071, has 81 campsites ($11), boat-launching facilities, hiking trails, a beach, and playground. It's open year-round; reservations are accepted. See below for more information on the park.

In Newcastle, the **Wharf Inn,** 1 Jane St., tel. 622-0302, is a motel spread out at riverfront with 126 spacious rooms ($60-85), a restaurant, and a pool. In central Newcastle, the **Castle Lodge Tourist Home,** 152 Castle St., tel. 622-2442, charges $30-36.

Elda's Motel, about two km southeast of Chatham on Hwy. 11, tel. 773-3326, is inexpensive and basic (except for the inexplicable four-meter-tall concrete Tyrannosaurus rex standing out front); $30-40. The **Sunny Side Inn,** 65 Henderson St., tel. 773-4232, is in the same price range and centrally located in Chatham.

The **Cunard Restaurant,** 32 Cunard St., tel. 773-7107, in Chatham, serves Canadian and Chinese food. For groceries and sundries, the biggest stores around are the **Sobey's** markets—you'll find one on Chapel Rd. in Chatham and another at Northumberland Square, on Hwy. 8 just over the bridge in Douglastown.

UP THE RIVER

Enclosure Provincial Park

Ongoing digs at this site have yielded post-Deportation Acadian artifacts, including the remains of the communal firepit from the site's refugee-camp days (1756-61). Acadian house ruins and artifacts from later British settlers have also been found. The site is open late June-Aug., Tues.-Sat. 8 a.m.-4:15 p.m.; archaeologists work amid the visitors.

Red Bank

On Hwy. 420 west of Newcastle, the **Red Bank Indian Band,** one of 15 Indian bands in the province, welcomes visitors and sells handicrafts at the band office; open weekdays 9 a.m.-noon and 1-4 p.m. For details and directions, call (506) 836-2366.

Doaktown

Crossing through the deep interior of the province, Hwy. 8 runs alongside the famed salmon-rich Miramichi River to Doaktown, 86 km southwest of Newcastle. Squire Robert Doak from Scotland founded the town and gave it a boom start with paper and grist mills in the early 1800s.

The squire's white wooden house with some original furnishings and nearby barn aside the road miraculously survived the 1825 Great Fire that leveled vast tracts of the Miramichi Basin. **Doak Historical Park** spreads out in a verdant setting, open mid-June to Sept., daily 9:30 a.m.-4:30 p.m.

The **Miramichi Salmon Museum,** on Hwy. 8, tel. (506) 365-7787, will be especially interesting to kids. Exhibits depict the lifecycle and habitat of this king of game fish, as well as the history of the art of catching it (including a collection of rods, reels, and gaudily attractive flies). Live salmon specimens at various stages of development swim in the aquariums. The museum is open June-Sept., daily 10 a.m.-5 p.m., adults $3, children 6-12 $2.

Boiestown and Vicinity

Another well-conceived museum is **Central New Brunswick Woodmen's Museum,** on Hwy. 8 near Boiestown, tel. (506) 369-7214. The museum's exhibits explain forestry's past and present. Hours are May-Sept., daily 10 a.m.-5:30 p.m.; admission is $4.50. The **New Brunswick Agricultural Museum** on Hwy. 1 in Sussex, tel. 433-6799, is open June to mid-Sept., Mon.-Sat. 10 a.m.-5 p.m., Sun. from noon. Admission is $2.

THE GULF COAST

North of Miramichi Bay, the Acadian peninsula juts northeast into the Gulf of St. Lawrence. One side of the peninsula faces the gulf, while the other side fronts the Baie des Chaleurs. The gulf coast from Newcastle/Chatham to Miscou Island is a wild shore where the sea rolls in with a tumultuous surf.

Bartibog Bridge

It's a 20-minute drive on Hwy. 11 from Newcastle to the bayside town where the **MacDonald Farm Historic Park,** tel. (506) 778-6085, re-creates a Scottish settler's life in 1784. Guides take visitors through the stone manor house, fields, orchards, and outbuildings. It's open late June to late Sept., daily 9:30 a.m.-4:30 p.m.; adults $2.75, ages 6-18 $1.25.

Neguac and Val-Comeau Provincial Parks

These remote provincial parks are backed by lush sphagnum bogs, formed when the last ice sheet melted and pooled without a place to drain on the flat terrain. Seabirds inhabit the nutrient-rich marshes; both parks are known for bird-watching, and Val-Comeau has an observation tower for good views. Val-Comeau also offers a campground, tel. (506) 395-4137, with 55 sites, boat-launching facilities, swimming areas, and a playground.

Shippagan

New Brunswick's largest commercial fishing fleet is based in this sheltered bay at the tip of the Acadian Peninsula. Nearby, the **Aquarium and Marine Centre,** on Hwy. 113, tel. (506) 336-4771, opens up the world of gulf fishing with exhibits and viewing tanks holding 125 native fish species; admission is $5.35 for adults, with discounts for youths and seniors. It's open May to early September, daily 10 a.m.-6 p.m.

Shippagan Provincial Park, tel. 336-8673, has 87 basic campsites in a waterside location three km west of town.

The Remote Islands

Offshore of Shippagan, two islands nose out into the gulf one after the other to form the prow of the peninsula. **Île Lamèque** is best known as a venue for early-music concerts, as unlikely as that may seem out here among the peat bogs and fishing villages. Since 1975, the island has hosted the annual **Lamèque International Baroque Music Festival,** which attracts a stellar roster of musicians and singers in mid-July for performances of Bach, Praetorius, Telemann, Beethoven, and others. The setting is superb, almost divine, within the acoustically perfect Ste-Cécile de Petite-Rivière-de-l'Île in Ville de Lamèque, the island's main village. For details and tickets, contact the festival office at P.O. Box 644, Lamèque, NB E0B 1V0, tel. (506) 344-5846. The audiences have increased yearly since the series began, so make sure you book an area lodging beforehand.

La Ferme Larocque Bed and Breakfast, 169 rue du Pêcheur in Ville de Lamèque, tel.

abandoned boat on Miscou Island

NAN DROSDICK

344-8860, has five rooms at $25-40; open year-round. The island has two private campgrounds, both open June-September. **Camping de la Baie,** near Petite-Rivière de l'Île, tel. 344-8416, has 34 sites with two- or three-way hookups ($13-14), and 73 without hookups ($10). On the eastern side of the island, **Le Cabestan,** on Rte. 305 near Pigeon Hill (no phone), has 10 sites for $7-10.

Connected to Lamèque by a free, year-round car ferry, **Île Miscou** is a blissfully remote gem barely touched by the modern world. The island marks New Brunswick's extreme northeastern tip, where the open gulf pounds the island's eastern side, and the Baie des Chaleurs laps peacefully on the other side. Point Miscou Lighthouse, New Brunswick's oldest, has peered

out to sea from the island's northern tip since 1856, and is one of Canada's few remaining manned lighthouses.

The island changes with the seasons: spring brings a splendid show of wildflowers; summer brings wild blueberries ripening on the barrens; autumn transforms the landscape to a burnished red. The spruce trees here are bent and dwarfed by the relentless sea winds, but oysters, moon snails, blue mussels, and jackknife clams thrive along the beautiful white, sandy beaches.

Miscou Island Camping, tel. 344-8638, has 56 serviced sites at $12-13. **Miscou Island Camping Cabins,** Miscou Centre, also tel. 344-8638, has four housekeeping units at $25-35; open June-September.

THE BAIE DES CHALEURS

In contrast to the wild Gulf of St. Lawrence, the shallower Baie des Chaleurs is warm and calm. Busy seaports dot the eastern coast of the bay—the region's commercial fishing fleets lie anchored at Bas-Caraquet, Caraquet, and Grande-Anse. Interspersed between the picturesque harbors are equally beautiful peninsulas, coves, and beaches. Swimming is especially pleasant along the sheltered beaches, where the shallow sea heats up to bathtub warmth in summer. Across the bay, Québec's Gaspé Peninsula is usually visible, sometimes with startling clarity when conditions are right. From Bathurst west, the fishing villages give way to industrial towns.

CARAQUET AND VICINITY

Highway 11 lopes into town and turns into a boulevard lined with shops, lodgings, and sights. Established in 1758, picturesque Caraquet (pop. 4,314) is northern New Brunswick's oldest French settlement and is known as Acadia's cultural heart. The town lives up to its promise with the **Acadian Museum,** 15 Blvd. Saint-Pierre Est (the main street), tel. (506) 727-1713. Within, exhibits and artifacts depict Acadian history. The museum is open mid-June to early Sept., Mon.-Sat. 1-8 p.m., Sun. 1-5 p.m. Adults $3, under 15 free. But if you can budget only

so much time for Acadiana, you should hold out for the Acadian Historical Village (see below).

The museum is at the **Carrefour de la Mer,** tel. 727-1728, a complex that also includes the tourist information office, a restaurant, playground, the boarding point for day-trips out to nearby Caraquet Island, and the **youth hostel,** tel. 727-1712.

The town is also the place to be for early August's 12-day **Acadian Festival,** one of the province's best-attended events. It includes the blessing of the huge fishing fleet by the local Roman Catholic clergy; jazz, pop, and classical music concerts; live theater; food and drink; and the Tintamarre, a massive street celebration.

Small sailboats and kayaks are available for rent at the Plage Centre-Ville. Swimming in the placid bay is supervised and safe for small children.

Caraquet's fishing fleet is based at **Bas-Caraquet,** a 10-minute drive east on Hwy. 145 toward Île Lamèque. In the other direction on Caraquet's western outskirts, the **Ste.-Anne-du-Bocage Shrine** honors early Acadian settlers with a 200-year-old church set on tree-studded grounds at the waterfront.

Accommodations And Food
Chez Rhea Bed and Breakfast, 236 Blvd. Saint-Pierre Ouest, tel. (506) 727-4275, is cen-

trally located and reasonably priced at $22-28. Close by, the **Hotel Dominion,** 145 Blvd. Saint-Pierre, tel. 727-2876, is another bargain accommodation, charging $20-32. The **Auberge de la Baie,** 139 Blvd. Saint-Pierre, tel. 727-3485, has 54 motel rooms ($60-85) and a restaurant. The **Hotel Paulin,** 143 Blvd. Saint-Pierre Ouest, tel. 727-9981, has nine comfortable rooms for $35-65, as well as a restaurant open to nonguests. It's open May-October.

Acadian Historical Village

Ten km west of Caraquet, the Village Historique Acadien (Acadian Historical Village) provides a sensory journey through early Acadia. To re-create the period from 1780 to 1890, more than 40 rustic houses and other authentic buildings were transported to this 1,133-hectare site and restored. The buildings—including a church, smithy, farmhouses, school, printing shop, carpenter's shop, gristmill, and others—are spread across woods and fields along the North River. You walk the dusty lanes or hop aboard a horse-drawn wagon to get from one building to the next, where informative, costumed "residents" describe their daily lives, their jobs, and surroundings, in French and English. A marvelous experience.

Out in the park, two "post houses" serve sandwiches, snacks, and drinks. At the reception center are a cafeteria and the Table des Ancêtres Restaurant, which serves typical Acadian dishes. Acadian Historical Village, tel. (506) 727-3467, is open daily 10 a.m.-6 p.m., early June to Labour Day, then daily 10 a.m.-5 p.m. till mid-October. Admission prices are adults $7.50, college students and seniors $6, youths ages 6-18 $4.50, family rate $18.

Grande-Anse

Highway 11 continues to the coast, where it takes a turn west to Grand-Anse. For a swim in the warm bay, take Hwy. 320, the narrow road that diverges to the right, to **Maisonnette Beach Provincial Park,** an exquisite spread of beach overlooking Caraquet across Baie Caraquet. The warm-water beach is a favorite, especially when the tide retreats to reveal sand-dune fingers washed by shallow, sun-heated waters. Seabirds are everywhere here: you'll see them in large numbers on nearby, aptly named Bird Island, where the long bluffs at **Pokeshaw Provincial Park** overlook rookeries of squawking cormorants.

In town, the **Musée des Papes** ("Popes' Museum"), 184 Acadie St., tel. (506) 732-3003, commemorates the visit of Pope John Paul II to New Brunswick in 1985. Exhibits include vestments, chalices, and other ecclesiastical paraphernalia, plus a detailed scale replica of St. Peter's Basilica. The museum also has a dining room and picnic area. It's open daily 10 a.m.-6 p.m., June to mid-September. Admission is $4.25, with discounts for seniors and children.

BATHURST TO CAMPBELLTON

Bathurst and Vicinity

The town of Bathurst (pop. 14,400) sits by its own fine natural harbor at the vertex of Nepisiguit Bay, a broad gulf on the Baie des Chaleurs. Behind the town, seemingly limitless forests spread as far as the eye can see.

Daly Point Wildlife Reserve spreads across 100 acres of salt marshes, woodlands, and fields northeast of town; an observation tower provides views of nesting ospreys, as well as various seabirds and songbirds. To get there, take Bridge St. (the Acadian Coastal Drive) east from Bathurst, then turn left on Carron Drive. Bring insect repellent.

Gowan Brae Golf Course, Youghall Dr., tel. (506) 546-2707, enjoys a beautiful location and town views on Bathurst Harbor's northwest side. At the end of the road, at the harbormouth, is **Youghall Beach Park,** with supervised swimming at one of the area's nicest strands.

Keddy's Bathurst Hotel, 80 Main St., tel. 546-6691, has a central location overlooking the harbor, plus an indoor swimming pool and hot tub. The glass-walled Cafe Terrasse is a pleasant spot for Sunday brunch. **Luc's Dining Room,** located at 350 MacDonald St. off St. Peter Ave. (over the bridge from downtown), tel. 546-5322, serves a varied board of seafoods, meats, and poultry (entrees $9-23), complemented with a wide selection of wines. It's open for lunch and dinner Tues.-Sunday. Most of the town's fast-food joints and grocery stores are concentrated nearby along St. Peter Avenue.

The **visitor center,** off Hwy. 11 at Vanier Blvd. west of town, tel. 548-9344, is well stocked with information on Bathurst and the rest of the Baie des Chaleurs area.

West to Campbellton

Highway 11 stays inland for the scenically dull 85-km stretch between Bathurst and Charlo. Far preferable is the coastal Hwy. 134, which runs through the fishing villages of Nigadoo, Petit-Rocher, Pointe-Verte, and Jacquet River. The coast between Bathurst and Dalhousie is famed for sightings of a "phantom ship." Numerous witnesses over the years have described a ship under full sail engulfed in flames on the bay; sometimes the vision includes a crew frantically scurrying across the deck. Some say the vision dates from the Battle of Restigouche (1760)—the last naval engagement between France and England in this part of eastern Canada—when France's fleet was destroyed by the British.

La Fine Grobe Sur-Mer, in Nigadoo, tel. (506) 783-3138, makes a nice overnight and fronts the bay off Hwy. 11 with six rooms ($35) and a dining room. The **New Brunswick Mining and Mineral Interpretation Centre,** Hwy. 134 off Hwy. 11 in Petit-Rocher, tel. 783-8714, has exhibits detailing the industry's past and present with a simulated mine shaft. It's open daily 10 a.m.-6 p.m., May-September. Admission is $4.50 adults, seniors and ages 6-18 $3.50.

Farther northwest, in New Mills, the **Auberge Le Heron Country Inn,** tel. 237-5306, has 10 nonsmoking rooms (from $45) furnished with antiques. Set back from the road in an oversized, former farmhouse opposite Heron Island, it's open May-Oct. in a setting worthy of provincial heritage inn status.

In **Dalhousie,** the vessel *Chaleur Phantom,* named for the burning ship apparition, departs Renfrew St. Wharf on sightseeing cruises ($10) daily at 2 and 7 p.m., May to mid-October. Fishing trips for cod, mackerel, and flounder leave the wharf at 8 a.m. ($15 pp, $20 for a couple). For reservations, call 684-4722. A ferry here crosses the bay to Pte. Miguaska, Québec, saving about 70 km of road travel if you're heading that way.

The Eel River Bar, one of the world's longest sandbars, is a popular spot for windsurfing and swimming, with fresh water on one side and salt water on the other.

Campbellton and Vicinity

At the head of the Baie des Chaleurs, the New Brunswick and Gaspé coastlines meet near Campbellton, the area's largest town. A bridge here spans the broad mouth of the Restigouche River to connect with Québec's Hwy. 132.

Campbellton (pop. 9,100) was originally settled by Scots, who founded the local salmon industry. Later, farming, lumbering, and shipbuilding developed, and in the 1870s, the railroad came. The Scottish legacy remains, in place-names such as Glen Livet, Dundee, and Balmoral. After a devastating fire in 1910, the town began to rebuild itself in brick. "Cambellton is not the ugliest town in Canada," Michael Collie wrote in the 1970s, "but it must be one of the most accidental in appearance, because of the medley of wooden and brick houses."

The **Restigouche Gallery,** 39 Andrew St., tel. (506) 753-5750, displays works by local, national, and international artists, as well as natural history and science exhibits. It's open year-round; free admission.

Sugarloaf Mountain Provincial Park, outside Campbellton off Hwy. 11, tel. 789-2366, overlooks the whole region and has a year-round chairlift with views to the 283-meter-high, gumdrop-shaped peak. The park has 65 campsites open May-Sept., lighted tennis courts, hiking trails, and supervised swimming. In winter, it's popular for snowmobiling, ice-skating, and cross-country skiing.

Canoeing on the Restigouche River is a popular pastime. You can rent boats from **LeBlanc Rental,** 2 Boucher St., tel. 753-6080, and from **Restigouche Adventures,** 192 Roseberry St., tel. 684-2120. The latter company also arranges trips.

The **Aylesford Inn,** 8 McMillan Ave., tel. 759-7672, a provincial heritage inn, sits back from the street with wide steps leading to a wraparound porch. Inside are seven rooms ($50-60) and a dining room. The **Wandlyn/Maritime Inn,** 26 Duke St., tel. 753-7606 or (800) 561-1881, is downtown, and has a pool and dining room. Its 60 rooms run $57-85.

Tide Head, a small town at the river's mouth, is known for fiddleheads—fern fronds served as a springtime culinary delicacy. Here, **Sanfar Cottages,** on Restigouche Dr., tel. 753-4287, has tidy housekeeping units at $34-38 with continental breakfast.

Something Else Creative Cuisine, in the Howard Johnson complex at 157 Water St., tel. 753-2510, serves pasta, steak and seafood, and salads. Open year-round for breakfast, lunch, and dinner daily.

From Campbellton, Hwy. 134 connects with Québec's Hwy. 132 at Matapédia. Highway 17 plunges deep into the virtually unpopulated interior, across the region known as the Restigouche Uplands. It's 92 km to Saint-Quentin, from where one can veer east to Mt. Carleton Provincial Park (see "Up the Saint John River" in the Saint John River Valley chapter), or continue another 80 km to join the Saint John River valley at Saint-Léonard.

NOVA SCOTIA

BOB RACE

INTRODUCTION

Beautiful Nova Scotia is almost an island, encircled completely by water except at its narrow, 15-km-long border with New Brunswick. The province's land and the culture of its people are profoundly defined by the surrounding seas. The 7,459-km-long coastline is etched by the Atlantic Ocean, Bay of Fundy, Northumberland Strait, and Gulf of St. Lawrence, and is speckled with almost 4,000 rocky outcroppings and islands, the best known and largest of which is Cape Breton. The province's interior of farmland and thick boreal forest is only lightly inhabited; most Nova Scotians live close to the sea, in coastal towns and in hundreds of little seaports on the sheltered coves, harbors, and bays notching the shore.

Canada's second-smallest province (55,490 square km), Nova Scotia nevertheless offers visitors some of the region's best museums, as well as abundant opportunities for recreation, including bicycling and hiking, inland canoeing and ocean kayaking, deep-sea diving, river rafting, rockhounding, sailing, hunting, fishing, and golfing.

Events here are another draw. Hundreds of happenings of one kind or another are scheduled annually, most during the summer, which has led some wags to switch the province's nickname from "Land of a Hundred Thousand Welcomes" to "Land of a Hundred Thousand Summer Festivals." Many events are linked to the Maritime's seafaring tradition and feature lobster bakes and sailboat races, while others celebrate agricultural harvests, music, and the arts.

Among the most colorful festivals are those that tap into the ethnic spirit. The province's Scottish heritage ("Nova Scotia" translates from Latin as "New Scotland") is held in such high esteem by its Highland cousins that the annual International Gathering of the Clans festival alternates between Scotland and the province (where it's scheduled for odd-numbered years).

But after centuries of immigration, Nova Scotia's heritage draws together more than 50 diverse ethnic and cultural threads from all corners of the world. Ancestry is important and well documented here; numerous genealogical centers are geared to assist visitors with roots searches.

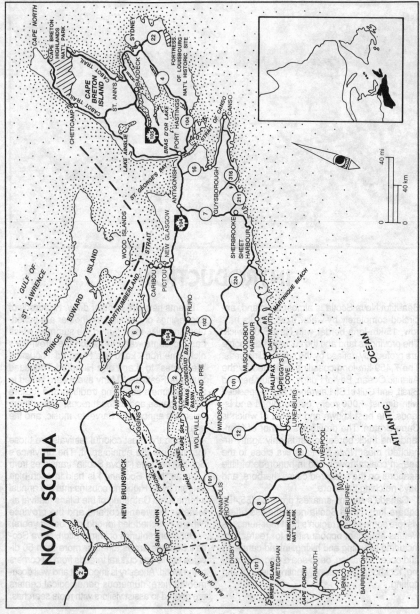

NOVA SCOTIA

© MOON PUBLICATIONS, INC.

THE LAND

The province is predominantly rocky and thinly covered with soil, making it less conducive to farmland than to forests. Consequently, thick woodlands blanket over 80% of the province. The Atlantic coast is rugged, edged with granite, and flanked with sandy beaches, salt marshes, and bogs. The Fundy coast, from Yarmouth to Cape Split, is rimmed by basalt bedrock mixed with tidal flats. Along this coast, Annapolis Valley, famed for its fruit orchards, is a geological oddity; scoured out by glaciers at the end of the Ice Age, the valley is sheltered by mountains north and south, creating a hothouse of warmth and humidity. Along the Northumberland Strait seacoast, rolling terrain with fertile farmlands rises to picturesque high hills and plateaus in Pictou and Antigonish counties.

Cape Breton Island is joined to mainland Nova Scotia by the 1.4-km Canso Causeway. Cape Breton's smaller, eastern portion consists of lowlands and rolling hills, with deeply indented Sydney Harbour on its northern coast. The western part of the island rises gradually from sea level to soaring headlands and highlands culminating at Cape Breton Highlands National Park near the northern tip. Much of the island's center is taken up by the expansive saltwater Bras d'Or Lake.

Another island also falls within the province's domain. Sable Island lies 285 km east from Halifax and is now the site of natural gas and oil exploration. The arc-shaped sandspit is inhabited only by wild horses dropped off by European ships centuries ago. Known as the "Graveyard of the Atlantic," its shores and treacherous shoals are littered with shipwrecks.

In the Beginning

The region was under a shallow sea until 500 million years ago. Then pressurized sand and clay oozed to the surface where it cooled and hardened to create the first landscape of sandstone, quartzite, and slate. Molten granite later emerged the same way, heaved, and broke apart. You can see these primordial extrusions at Peggy's Cove near Halifax, where the coast is strewn with oddly placed mammoth boulders.

The earth's surface heaved and shuddered, and the land contours and seacoasts were formed. Between 405 and 190 million years ago, the turbulent earth devoured its own creations; evidence is visible at Joggins on the upper Fundy's Chignecto Bay, where upright trees were enfolded into cliff edges. Archaeologists date these fossils at 280-345 million years old.

The last ice sheet retreated and took what remained of prehistory with it. The ice had scoured the earth's surface as it raked back and forth, and this too can be seen at Peggy's Cove, where the ancient scratches are etched in the granite boulders.

As the ice sheet moved, it bulldozed glacial debris into drumlins, large islands of fine soil piled up in places on the predominantly rocky land. The best known of these drumlins is the steep hill upon which the Halifax Citadel sits. Many of the province's most fertile farmlands are situated on the pulverized, mineral-rich soil of drumlins.

National Parklands

The Canadian Parks Service oversees two national parks and 14 national historic sites in Nova Scotia. Nova Scotians dote on **Kejimkujik National Park** (kedgie-muh-KOO-jick), which combines interesting ice-age topography and gold-mining history with an interior network of lakes ideal for canoeing. But it is **Cape Breton Highlands** that ranks as the showstopper among Atlantic Canada's national parks. It's more than twice as large as Kejimkujik, and whereas that park can be hot during summer, the Highlands park with its high elevations can range from balmy to downright cool during peak summer months.

At both parks, campsites cost $9 a night for an unserviced site, $14 for a three-way hookup site, all on a first-come, first-served basis. Kejimkujik campgrounds are open year-round. The Highlands's campground season spans mid-May through mid-Oct.; the tent campground near Cheticamp is open during winter. Campground facilities include picnic tables, shelters, stoves, free wood, and potable water. Most national park campgrounds have hiking trails and access to swimming and fishing, while some have hot showers, washrooms, and laundry sinks.

For literature, contact the **Canadian Parks Service,** Atlantic Regional Office, Historic Properties, Upper Water St., Halifax, NS B37 1S9, tel. (902) 426-3436.

Provincial Parks

Of 123 spreads of prime land, 98 provincial park sites are scenic day-use parks with picnic facilities and often hiking trails and beaches for clam digging and swimming; another four day-use sites are wildlife parks with indigenous flora and fauna.

The **day-use parks,** open mid-May to mid-October, daily 9 a.m.-7 p.m., often can boast sensational views; Blomidon Provincial Park, for example, north of Wolfville, provides access to a hiking trail atop steep sandstone cliffs that jut out into the Bay of Fundy and overlook the foaming sea.

In addition, some of Nova Scotia's best beach scenes are found at the day-use parks. While some parks are on the road's inland side, most of them front the sea. Day-use parks and beaches are free; some have lifeguards, but otherwise facilities are limited.

Among the best family beaches are Risser's Beach near Lunenburg; Clam Harbour, northeast of Halifax, which often has sand-sculpture contests; and Sand Hills, near Barrington, where the Atlantic water warms among sandbars. Naturalists go for Martinique Beach near Musquodoboit Harbour because of its dunes, salt marshes, and the nearby bird sanctuary; and Taylors Head near Spry Bay, which has boardwalk-laced dunes, a beach, and peninsula hiking trails.

The younger crowd's haunts are wherever the beach is long enough to kick a football or the surf is heavy enough to ride it to shore on a board. Lawrencetown Beach Provincial Park near Halifax is one of the favorites, and Crystal Crescent Beach at Sambro is another top choice. (Crystal Crescent also makes newspaper headlines every so often, with coverage about illegal nude sunbathers in its remote parts.)

In addition to the day-use parks, 21 other parks are equipped with unserviced, basic **campgrounds** with potable water, cooking shelters and grills, washrooms, pay showers, inexpensive bundled wood, and often hiking trails, playgrounds, and beaches. They're open mid-May to early September. Sites cost $8-9, no reservations. Campground parks are tickets into

some of the province's finest scenery. For example, Five Islands Provincial Park, with hiking trails overlooking the Minas Basin, offers a close-up encounter with the Bay of Fundy's high tides, which wash up against the coastal woodlands.

Wildlife parks include the Shubenacadie park southwest of Truro; Upper Clements near the theme park near Annapolis Royal; Two Rivers park at Marion Bridge, Cape Breton; and the newly developed park at Goshen south of Antigonish. This quartet features indigenous small mammals, birds of prey, and waterfowl in open or enclosed settings, hiking trails outside the animal area, and picnic tables.

Provincial parks are detailed in *Nova Scotia Travel Guide.* The provincial **Division of Parks and Recreation** stocks literature and answers questions; contact them at RR 1, Belmont, Colchester County, NS B0M 1C0, tel. (902) 662-3030 or 424-5935.

CLIMATE

The province's moderate climate is similar to that of Northern Europe. The seasons are distinct, with mild winters and cool summers. Mainland Nova Scotia's climate differs noticeably from Cape Breton's, where more extreme weather patterns occur. Average precipitation amounts to 130 centimeters, falling mainly as rain during autumn and as snow in winter. Frost-free periods range from 120 days on Cape Breton to 145 days in the sheltered Annapolis Valley.

Spring arrives late, with temperatures ranging from -2.5 to 9° C. **Summer** weather varies. Daytime temperatures average up to 30° C. Nights are usually cool at around 12° C, but can dip to 5° C in late summer. Inland areas are generally 5° warmer. The coasts often bask in morning fog, which is later dispersed by sea breezes and the warming sun. Late in the season, Caribbean hurricanes, having spent their force farther south, limp through the region, bringing to the northwestern Atlantic short spells of rain and wind.

In **autumn,** the evenings start to cool, but warm days continue until the end of September at up to 18° C. The days are cool to frosty October through mid-November. **Winter** lasts from late November through early March, with high temperatures averaging -10 to 4° C.

Environment Canada has updated weather forecasts: call (902) 426-9090.

Water Temperatures

Atlantic Canadians know that Nova Scotia is famed for its swimming and surfing. The seas are not bathtub hot, but water temperatures in some areas can be pleasantly warm. Conditions vary on the four seas and in each region. The warmest seas during August are found around Cape Breton's northern tip and along the Northumberland Strait—in both places temperatures reach 18° C. The Atlantic is a cool 10-15° C at Mahone Bay and warms a bit as you head up the coast to the northeast, hence the popularity of surfing at Martinique and Lawrencetown beaches. Generally, Cape Breton's coastal waters range 14-17° C. The Bay of Fundy is always cool to cold, although it becomes bearable at Mavillete Beach above Yarmouth, where low tide leaves shallow pools that warm up.

FLORA AND FAUNA

Flora

In the 1970s, environmentalists were alarmed by the rapid rate of deforestation in the province, as woodlands were felled for their timber and to make room for expanding farmland. In the following decades, however, protective measures were enacted, and today over 80% of Nova Scotia is thickly blanketed by typical Acadian forest of mixed hardwoods and conifers. Common trees include hemlock, spruce, balsam fir, yellow and paper birches, cedar, maple, ash, and oak. In autumn, the brilliant hues of the changing leaves are one of the province's most cherished attractions.

The province has set aside large tracts at Kejimkujik and Cape Breton Highlands national parks, which protect areas of unique plant habitat. In the Cape Breton Highlands, for example, stands of 300-year-old maples (believed to be the oldest in the country) have survived, and unusual wild orchid species thrive there as well. In the Highlands' highest elevations, the stunted taiga and alpine-arctic plant communities have

been included in an international biological preserve. Bogs in the national parks nourish insectivorous pitcher plants, more orchids, and other specially adapted species.

Common wildflowers throughout Nova Scotia—easily seen along roadsides in summertime—include lupine, Queen Anne's lace, yarrow, pearly everlasting, and a variety of daisies. Everywhere, the showy spikes of purple loosestrife, a pretty but aggressive and unwelcome pest, flourishes. Bayberry bushes and wild roses bloom on the Chignecto Isthmus during June. The provincial flower is the trailing arbutus (mayflower), which blooms in early spring in woodlands and barrens.

Fauna

Some 298 bird species inhabit Nova Scotia, but the province is best known for its bald eagles. About 250 pairs nest in the province, the second-largest population on North America's east coast after Florida. The season for eagle watching is July and August. Some of the prime viewing areas are the Lake Ainslie and St. Ann's Bay coastlines; the village of Iona, where Bras d'Or Lake meets St. Andrews Channel on Cape Breton; and the St. George's Bay coastline. Ospreys nest on McNab's Island in Halifax Harbour. Other raptors may be seen at Brier Island on the Bay of Fundy.

As Nova Scotia lies on the Atlantic flyway, many migratory species can be spotted including common and arctic terns, kittiwakes, great and double-crested cormorants, Leach's storm petrels, Atlantic puffins, guillemots, and various gulls, ducks, and geese.

The **whales** that frequent Nova Scotia arrive from the Caribbean between June and mid-July and remain through October. Watching the whales cavort is one of summer's great visitor delights; whalewatching boats leave from Brier Island on the Bay of Fundy and Cape Breton's Chéticamp. The Fundy is especially rich in whales, and the fast incoming tides bring in the mammoth mammals in pursuit of herring schools. Among the 20 species that summer offshore, the most frequently sighted are minke, pilot, fin, orca, humpback, and the rare right.

Other mammals found in the province are black bear, bobcat, lynx, red fox, coyote, white-tailed deer, and moose.

HISTORY

The earliest evidence of human habitation in the region dates from about 8600 B.C. and is found at the present site of Debert, inland from the Minas Basin's northern coast. The Vikings may have visited about A.D. 1000; a boulder inscribed with what may be Nordic runes was found near Cape Forchu, where, some believe, Leif Eriksson and his men put ashore. (The boulder is now on display at the Yarmouth County Museum in Yarmouth.)

Early European Settlement

Nova Scotia's tie to Europe began in 1497, when the explorer John Cabot sighted Cape Breton and claimed it for England. England's claim notwithstanding, France eyed the area for colonization and dispatched explorer Samuel de Champlain to the region in 1604. Champlain's expedition first wintered (and almost perished) at a settlement on the St. Croix River, which now forms the New Brunswick–Maine border. In 1605, the encampment moved across the Bay of Fundy, where the fortified **Port Royal,** one of the earliest European settlements in Canada, was established near what is now Annapolis Royal. The French named the region—encompassing what is now Nova Scotia, New Brunswick, PEI, and part of Maine—Acadia ("Peaceful Land"). Not to be outdone, England's James I named the same region Nova Scotia—New Scotland—and granted it to Sir William Alexander in 1621. The British burned Port Royal in 1613. Scottish settlers arrived in 1629 and staked out the same area, but left within three years.

A 1632 peace treaty forced England to surrender Nova Scotia to the French. Bitter military

sailors in the Royal Navy

confrontations began and flared through the mid-1700s. The two powers had different strategies: France first built settlements, then used its military to defend them. England, boasting a superior military savvy, fought its battles first, then used settlements to stabilize areas. As it turned out, Britain had the edge, and it was upon this advantage that Maritime history frequently turned over the following century and a half.

Expansion

From their Port Royal hub, the French explored the Fundy coast and the Atlantic seacoast as far south as LaHave. By 1632, 45 Acadian villages rimmed the upper Fundy's marshes. The villagers cultivated grains and forage crops on wetlands reclaimed by dikes, and farther southwest planted the region's first orchards. By 1650, merchant-explorer Nicolas Denys had established fortified settlements at Guysborough on Chedabucto Bay and St. Peters on the southern tip of Île Royale. Grand-Pré, just east of Wolfville, was a major Acadian town from 1675 to 1755.

In 1705, France's original Port Royal was relocated to the Annapolis River's other side. Five years later, the British swooped in and took the fort, renaming it Fort Anne in honor of their queen. They also rechristened the town as Annapolis Royal, which served as Nova Scotia's first capital (Halifax took over the role in 1749).

The 1713 Treaty of Utrecht awarded the region to England. The French military fled to Île Royale (Cape Breton Island) where they began construction of the Fortress of Louisbourg and Acadian seacoast settlements. England countered with a fort on Grassy Island in Chedabucto Bay, captured Louisbourg in 1745, again in 1758, and finally demolished the site in 1760.

England had deported 10,000 Acadians from Fort Edward near Windsor in 1755. Some had fled

COURTESY NOVA SCOTIA MUSEUM COMPLEX

to the Île Royale hinterlands—St. Ann's, Chéticamp, Isle Madame—and to other remote areas. But within a few years, the resilient Acadians started to return to the mainland, settling along the Côte Acadienne (Acadian Coast), on the lower Bay of Fundy.

The British began peopling the territory with less fractious, pro-Crown settlers. Lunenburg began with 2,000 German, Swiss, and French "foreign Protestants" in 1753. In 1760, England resettled the prime Fundy seacoast once farmed by the Acadians with 12 shiploads of farmers (New England planters) from its colonies farther south. The Crown officially regained the region, including Île Royale, with the Peace of Paris in 1763. The first shipload of Scots fleeing Scotland's infamous land clearances docked at Pictou in 1773. In 1830, a census counted 50,000 Scots in Pictou and Antigonish counties.

After the American Revolution, 25,000 British Loyalists poured into Nova Scotia. Several thousand American blacks arrived during the War of 1812, followed by Irish immigrants from 1815 to 1850.

Nova Scotia Takes Shape

In the late 18th century, Prince Edward Island and New Brunswick were defined as distinct colonies. Cape Breton, for a while a separate colony, was reannexed to Nova Scotia in 1820. Responsibility for government was granted in 1848.

The province became a founding member of the Dominion of Canada in 1867. Confederation was unpopular, but it offered economic inducements, including the rail connections to eastern Canada that Nova Scotia wanted. By 1876, the Intercolonial Railway had service as far as Ontario, and rail service within the province linked major towns by 1881.

Fortunes were founded on trade. Halifax's Samuel Cunard started a shipping empire based on steamship service to England in 1839. During the Great Age of Sail, shipbuilding seaports thrived. In 1878, Yarmouth ranked as Canada's second-largest port. Coal mining began in 1872 at Springhill, near Amherst, where the 1,220-meter shaft was Canada's deepest.

The luster faded by the 1900s. Shipbuilding's heyday was over. Nova Scotians looking for work migrated to the U.S., and farms were aban-

Bluenose II *under full sail*

BOB RACE

doned. On 15 April 1913, the *Titanic* sank in the chilly waters of the North Atlantic east of Newfoundland. Many nameless victims of the more than 1,500 who drowned were buried in Halifax cemeteries. Four years later, during the height of WW I, two ships collided in Halifax Harbour. The explosion blew out 1,600 buildings, killed 2,000 Haligonians, and injured an estimated 9,000 more. By 1920, the economy collapsed.

Famous Nova Scotians

Prominent personalities emerged with the prosperous times. **Alfred Fuller** was born at Annapolis Royal, lived for a while in Yarmouth, and later moved to the U.S., where he made a fortune with Fuller Brushes. **Alexander Graham Bell,** the Scottish inventor whose business interests were in the U.S., created a retreat at Cape Breton's Baddeck, where he conducted tireless research and, among other achievements, helped launch the first airplane flight in the British Empire in 1909.

Anna Leonowens, later immortalized as the prim governess in Broadway's *The King and I,* joined relatives in Halifax and started an arts school, which evolved into the Nova Scotia College of Art and Design. The 1800s finished as **Joshua Slocum** of Westport sailed around the world and set a record as the first man to do so alone. Among the more famous expatriates are singer Anne Murray and television's Robert MacNeil.

The *Bluenose*

The famous schooner *Bluenose* was launched from Lunenburg in 1921. The schooner won every racing competition it entered and served also as a Grand Banks and Scotian Shelf fishing craft. Sold eventually to foreign investors, the vessel sank off Haiti during World War II. The original *Bluenose,* whose image is on the back of the Canadian dime, was re-created in 1963 as the *Bluenose II* at Lunenburg, where she is now permanently berthed.

GOVERNMENT

The Progressive Conservatives dominate the 52-member provincial Legislative Assembly, while the Liberal, New Democrat, and Cape Breton Labour parties have smaller constituencies. On the federal level, Nova Scotia sends 10 senators to the Upper House and 11 to the House of Commons.

Sixty-six municipalities make up the province, and Halifax is the capital.

ECONOMY

In 1991, Nova Scotia's gross domestic product (GDP) was a little over $19 billion, with manufacturing generating the largest segment. Among the largest manufacturers here are Michelin Tire Canada, Volvo Canada, Crossley Karastan Carpet, and Pratt and Whitney. Mining ranks second, with 30 mines and quarries yielding coal, limestone, and tin. Fisheries and fish processing are third in economic importance—cod, haddock, herring, and lobster are caught inshore and off the Atlantic's Scotian Shelf. (The province is Canada's largest lobster exporter.)

Tourism produces $760 million in gross receipts annually and ranks as the province's fourth-largest industry. Most visitors arrive by car, RV, or on motorcoach tours, while 20% fly in; air arrivals are increasing as long-distance air links improve beyond Atlantic Canada. Most visitors (41%) are from the neighboring provinces, while central Canada contributes 29% and the U.S. adds almost 25%. Of the 1.2 million people who arrive annually, more than three-fourths of that number are returning visitors.

Though just eight percent of Nova Scotia's land is arable, agriculture contributes heavily to the economy, producing fruits (including Annapolis Valley apples), dairy products, poultry, hogs, and Canada's largest share of blueberries. The province's extensive forests support a substantial lumber and paper industries; among the largest are Bowater Mersey Paper (half owned by the *Washington Post*) on the south shore, and the Kraft pulp mills at Abercrombie Point, Point Tupper, Brooklyn, Hantsport, and East River.

The province is also the region's federal civil service and military center. Halifax has served as a naval center since its founding in 1749 as headquarters for the Royal Navy. The city is now Maritime Command headquarters for the Canadian Armed Forces. Other military installations are at Shearwater, Cornwallis, and Greenwood; training stations are located at Barrington, Mill Cove, Shelburne, and Sydney.

And trade still greases the economic wheels here. Eleven of the province's 267 harbors are major shipping ports, and Halifax, Sydney, and Point Tupper on the Strait of Canso rank as the busiest ports. Dartmouth has a 36-hectare auto port that handles 100,000 vehicles a year.

THE PEOPLE

Nova Scotia's population of just under 900,000 is dominated by persons of English ancestry; four of five Nova Scotians trace their lineage to the British Isles. Some 49 original Scottish families, from Archibald to Yuill, are still on the rolls of the Scottish Societies Association of Nova Scotia, which does genealogical surveys. After the American Revolution, Loyalists came here from New York, New Jersey, Connecticut, Rhode Island, and Massachusetts.

The other 20% of the population is a mix of ethnicities. Descendants of the original Acadians now number 35,000, a 4.5% minority. About 25,000 Micmac Indians lived in the region when the Europeans arrived; the Micmacs now number 6,305 on 16 reservations. And the province has more than 50 other minority ethnic groups, including Polish, Ukrainian, German, Swiss, African, and Lebanese.

The province has a youthful population, with 40% of the people under 25 years old. And they're well educated: Nova Scotia has the highest college and university attendance rate of any Canadian province. Population density is about 16.4 people per square kilometer.

Language and Religion

Nova Scotians speak with an eastern Canadian lilt mixed of British and Gaelic, ending each sentence on a high note, as though a question had been asked. English is spoken by 94% of Nova Scotians, while 7.4% are bilingual in English and French. French has gained appeal as a second language, and one in four primary schoolchildren in Halifax is enrolled in French immersion classes.

Roman Catholics predominate at 37% on the mainland and 62% on Cape Breton. Anglicans account for almost 16% on the mainland and 10% on Cape Breton. Other Protestant denominations include the United Church of Canada, Baptist, and Presbyterian. There is a small Jewish population in Halifax.

Tracing Family Roots

If you are interested in tracing family ties, the place to start is the **Public Archives of Nova Scotia,** 6016 University Ave., Halifax B3H 1W4, tel. (902) 424-6060. Its archives, including family and church records, are open year-round Mon.-Fri. 8:30 a.m.-10 p.m., Sat. 9 a.m.-6 p.m., Sun. 1-10 p.m. Ancestries originating on Cape Breton can be traced at the **Beaton Institute,** University College of Cape Breton, Glace Bay Highway outside of Sydney; open year-round Mon.-Fri. 8:30 a.m.-4 p.m. For more information, write to P.O. Box 5300, Sydney, NS B1P 6L2, or call 564-1336.

Other archives are kept at Acadia University, Wolfville; Maritime Museum of the Atlantic, Halifax; and St. Francis Xavier University, Antigonish. Delving for Scottish ancestry can also be done through the **Federation of Scottish Clans in Nova Scotia** at 22 Mt. Pleasant Ave., Dartmouth, plus the **Nova Scotia Highland Village** at the hilltop village of Iona on Cape Breton.

ARTS AND CRAFTS

Arts and crafts shopping opportunities are numerous in Nova Scotia. About 60 major art galleries are scattered across the province. The farmers' markets are a source for local crafts; the major market is in Halifax, while another 16 summer markets are held at major towns and seaports from Annapolis Royal to Tatamagouche.

For a distilled taste of the province's fine arts and crafts, spend several hours at the **Art Gallery of Nova Scotia** in Halifax. Quilts, porcelains, and wooden folk carvings are deftly mixed among the watercolors, oils, and sculptures in the spacious galleries on Hollis St., and the cream of provincial creativity is stocked at the museum's gift shop. The newest crafts developments are nurtured by the **Nova Scotia Centre for Craft and Design** on Barrington Street. The center opened in 1990 in Halifax, and its gallery includes weaving, wood, and jewelry exhibits.

The **Nova Scotia College of Art and Design,** at 1891 Granville, is an accredited college in the avant-garde of the fine art world. The college's Anna Leonowens Gallery provides insight into the artists' direction.

Other homegrown products include the furniture of Bass River Chairs, with its factory and an outlet at Bass River west of Truro; and Grohmann Knives, which sells its cutlery at its factory outlet in Pictou near the Caribou ferry. Nova Scotia is also the place for things Scottish. Tartans in innumerable clan variations are available by the yard in wool or blends; tartan apparel is stocked at shops in Halifax, Yarmouth, and Cape Breton's South Gut St. Ann's.

The *Buyer's Guide to Art and Crafts in Nova Scotia* is a handy shopping guide. The free paperback book divides crafts producers by counties and towns, and an index lists the producers by medium; Nova Scotia Centre for Craft and Design compiles the contents. For a copy, write to the Department of Tourism and Culture, P.O. Box 456, Halifax, NS B3J 2R5, or call (902) 424-4062.

Retail stores are generally open Mon.-Wed. 9 or 9:30 a.m. to 5 or 6 p.m., and Thurs.-Fri. to 9 or 9:30 p.m., Sat. 9:30 a.m.-5 p.m. Independent crafts producers set their own hours.

ENTERTAINMENT AND EVENTS

Halifax attracts concerts and major events to the Halifax Metro Centre near harborfront. Farther up the hillside, the Neptune Theatre hosts year-round repertory theater, as does Dalhousie University's Rebecca Cohn Auditorium, which doubles as the home of the Symphony of Nova Scotia. Dozens of nightclubs and other venues around the capital city showcase some of the many established and up-and-coming local bands—such as jale and Uisce Bheatha—which are earning the province, and especially Halifax, a reputation as an influential breeding ground for pop, rock, and alternative music.

Cape Breton is renowned for its contributions to folk music. Not surprisingly, Scottish and Irish fiddle tunes form much of the source material, but Cape Breton musicians have taken that extremely rich foundation and made something with a uniquely Maritime flavor: frisky jigs and reels for dancing, as well as ballads, often centering on the theme of fishing and the ubiquitous sea. Several annual festivals celebrate this musical tradition.

Events

Nova Scotia bills itself as "Canada's Official Festival Province"—something's almost always going on from spring through fall. Summers are particularly busy; a visitor could easily attend a different festival almost daily from June through August without a spare day.

Early season events provide a warm-up for the busy summer ahead. **Springtime at the Forum** in Halifax in early May provides an indoor market featuring arts, crafts, and antiques. And the **Apple Blossom Festival** is a showstopper when Annapolis Valley's apple trees are drenched in white blossoms during late May and early June.

As the weather heats up, so does the festival schedule. Some events take place over the whole summer. If your ancestral roots are Scottish (and even if they aren't), the **International Gathering of the Clans** will win you to the tartan fold with 80 festivals from Annapolis Royal to Cape Breton spaced over nine summertime weeks. Crustacean-cuisine connoisseurs will appreciate the **Lobster bakes** that take place all summer in the towns of Pictou, River John, and Wallace on the Northumberland Strait.

Befitting its status as Canada's Maritime Command naval center, Halifax hosts the razzle-dazzle **Nova Scotia International Tattoo** over two weeks of festivals in late June or early July. The Tattoo's events unfold in military precision. Crowds cheer as competing national naval-reserve units take apart and reassemble an 1812 cannon in the Naval Gun Run. Bands play. Military units compete in other contests of skill, and 10,000 spectators crowd the Metro Centre each night. Tickets are priced at under $20 and sell out quickly. Ticket sales start the preceding mid-December and are available from Metro Centre, 5284 Duke St., Halifax, NS B3J 3L2, tel. (902) 451-1221.

Celtic merriment comes to Antigonish in mid-July with the three-day **Highland Games,** featuring Highland dancing, pipe bands, piping competitions, concerts, and sports competitions. Also in mid-July the Cumberland County Museum in Amherst holds its **Formal Cream Tea.** In late July, the two-day **Journées Acadienne de Grand-Pré** remembers the Acadian Deportation at Grand-Pré. West Pubnico's early August six-day **Festival Acadien** "Chez Nous a Pomcoup" features a down-home look of an Acadian seaport. And also in early August, the small town of Economy on the north shore of Cobequid Bay holds a three-day **clambake.**

Wrapping up the year, two crafts and antique shows in Halifax provide good Christmas-shopping opportunities; **Christmas at the Forum** is in early November, and the Nova Scotia Designer Crafts Council's **Christmas Market** takes place during November's third week.

Events by the hundreds are listed with dates and sites in the *Nova Scotia Travel Guide*. The province observes federal holidays like the four-day Good Friday to Easter Monday weekend plus Boxing and Christmas days. The province adds its own Natal Day, and shops and public offices close the first Monday in August.

RECREATION

The province boasts a fully developed sports scene, from the pedestrian to the exotic, and you can dabble in tennis or birdwatching, canoeing, deep-sea diving, hiking, and bicycling for starters. Many outfitters around the province rent bicycles, boats, and other equipment, and can equip you for wilderness expeditions and all sorts of other activities.

Bicycling and Hiking

Cycling has two main organizations. The **VELO Halifax Bicycle Club** is a touring organization that schedules trips April through mid-November for all skill levels. For more information, write to P.O. Box 125, Dartmouth B2Y 3Y2, or call (902) 453-5091. The **Bicycle Nova Scotia** group handles cycling information and publishes *Bicycle Tours in Nova Scotia,* a booklet with biking guidelines and 20 detailed routes. The booklet costs $5; for a copy contact the group at P.O. Box 3010 South, Halifax, NS B3J 3G6.

Hiking is well developed. Among the best book guides is *Hiking Trails of Nova Scotia,* available for $10 from the Nova Scotia Government Bookstore in Halifax. The hiking season spans spring to autumn; coastal areas are free of insects, but insect repellent is wise inland from mid-May through August. Eleven provincial parks have marked trails; the **Parks and Recreation Division, Nova Scotia Department of Lands and Forests** has info at RR 1, Belmont, NS B0M 1C0. Cape Breton is laced with trails as well, and the **Cape Breton Development Corp.** has info from P.O. Box 1330, Sydney, NS B1P 6K3.

Water Sports

Canoe Nova Scotia acts as an information source for inland river paddling. Its *Canoe Routes of Nova Scotia* describes 70 routes and costs $5; write to 5516 Spring Garden Rd., P.O. Box 3010 South, Halifax, NS B3J 3G6, or call (902) 425-5450.

Coastal kayaking is another adventure, especially along Cape Breton's turbulent Atlantic or inland on the more placid Bras d'Or. **Kayak Cape Breton** offers weekend clinics ($60 day, or $90 with an overnight) and rents kayaks at $20 day; for details, write to RR 2, West Bay, Roberta B0E 3K0, or call 535-3060).

Nova Scotia Underwater Council handles deep-sea diving, and you will need a valid certification card to buy air. Only advanced divers should attempt the area as ocean currents are swift and conditions change rapidly; divers must assume responsibility for checking out conditions before starting. The council can provide details on the province's dive clubs and dive sites (including 3,000 offshore wrecks). Write the council at P.O. Box 34, Armdale, Halifax, NS B3L 4J7.

Rafts and Zodiacs can be rented to ride the tidal bore as the incoming Fundy high tide pushes inland up the Shubenacadie River. Windsurfing is the fastest growing aquatic sport in Nova Scotia, practiced just about everyplace wind and water meet. Popular spots are Sheet Harbour, Halifax Harbour, Bedford Basin, Inverness, and New Glasgow.

Fishing

Anglers must purchase a fishing license, for which nonresidents pay more than residents. A three-day nonresident license costs $15. If you have salmon in mind, you will need a special license at $20 for three days; the limit is two salmon a day. Vendors, sporting-goods stores, and the Department of Lands and Forests's district offices sell nonresident licenses during the summer (June-Sept.). The salmon-fishing regulatory authority is the **Department of Fisheries and Oceans,** P.O. Box 550, Halifax, NS B37 2S7, tel. (902) 426-5952.

Freshwater and anadromous fish varieties include Atlantic salmon, varied trout, shad, and bass. Salmon fishing with artificial flies or lures is the genteel passion here. Numerous outfitters work with visiting anglers—Cape Breton's **Normaway Inn** (North East Margaree, NS B0E 2C0, tel. 248-2987) is among the best.

Deep-sea fishing's star attraction is the giant bluefin tuna, which runs September-November. In 1979, a bluefin weighing a record 679 kilograms was caught off St. Georges Bay. The bay ranks as the top tuna area, while the Fundy coast off Yarmouth from Cape St. Mary to Wedgeport is another prime fishing area. Expect to pay $100-300 per boat, per day, for a tuna charter. In addition to tuna, other deep-sea catches are pollock, mackerel, striped bass, sea trout, and bottom dwellers like haddock, cod, and halibut.

Other Activities

The province has over 40 golf courses, with nearly a dozen within a short drive of Halifax. Tourism Halifax publishes a brochure listing facilities and phone numbers for each course. The best-known course in the province, considered one of Canada's finest, is the **Cape Breton Highland Links** at Ingonish Beach, within the national park. The 18 challenging holes take a full day to play on a route that winds through woodlands, highlands, and along the seacoast.

After golfing Cape Breton Highlands, you may want to take in a boat tour to the Bird Islands a little farther south down the coast; **Bird Island Boat Tours** takes passengers to the islands to see Atlantic puffins and other seabirds. Tours operate open May-Sept. daily from Mountain View by the Sea, Big Bras d'Or, tel. (902) 674-2384.

Magnam Outfitters leads guided outdoor-photography tours to backcountry areas with photogenic vistas of hills, vales, canyons scooped like gigantic cups, and isolated headlands overlooking precipitous cliffs. For more info, write to them at P.O. Box 1001, Halifax, NS B3J 2X1, or call 685-2967.

The **Nova Scotia Bird Society** can put you onto prime birding sites and answer even the most esoteric questions about the province's 298 species. The group is based at the Nova Scotia Museum, 1747 Summer St., Halifax, NS B3H 3A6.

ACCOMMODATIONS

Nova Scotia has lodgings by the hundreds: historic inns in silk-stockinged towns and salty seaports, sleek hotels in Halifax, and cabins and lodges in the hinterlands.

Hotels and motels range from deluxe high-rise towers and stately buildings to modest properties in the country. Inns and bed-and-breakfasts are often historic lodgings, and at their best are heritage properties furnished with antiques. Resorts are often geared to sports and recreational facilities.

The province set a high standard for resorts with three of its own: the Pines Resort Hotel at Digby; Liscombe Lodge at Liscomb Mills; and Keltic Lodge set on Cape Breton's soaring highlands in the national park.

About 80 properties host visitors with **farm vacations;** for complete details, contact the **Nova Scotia Farm and Country Vacation Association** at Site 5, P.O. Box 16, RR 1, Elmsdale, NS B0N 1M0.

Six hostels affiliated with **Canadian Hostelling Association** are located in the province in Halifax, Lunenburg, Liverpool, Yarmouth, Went-

worth, and South Milford; for details, write to 5516 Spring Garden Rd., P.O. Box 3010 South, Halifax, NS B3J 3G6, or call (902) 425-5450.

Advance reservations (up to a month in advance) at all lodgings are wise during July and August. During June and September to October, reservations a day or two beforehand should be sufficient. Most lodgings accept credit cards, although the smaller places may ask for cash or traveler's checks.

Reservations
About 98% of the lodgings belong to the provincially operated **Check In** reservation system. When phoning with a reservation, be prepared to give your credit card number and its expiration date; tel. (800) 565-0000 in Canada or (800) 341-6096 in the United States.

The reservation system works almost flawlessly. The hitch is late arrivals after 6 p.m., the time when reservations are canceled unless otherwise specified. If you expect to arrive late, ask for a late-arrival guarantee or phone the property yourself. If you change plans, cancel the reservation.

FOOD AND DRINK

Nova Scotian cooking is so distinctive that one of the best souvenirs is a cookbook with some of the culinary secrets. The style varies and is often on the sweet side. Locals shun hot spices and go lightly on other condiments. Dining in Halifax offers sophisticated cuisines from continental to nouvelle cuisine. Country-style cooking embodies the essence of provincial style in the smaller towns and seaports. Some wines are produced locally, and berries and fruits for mouthwatering desserts are harvested in the province.

Seafood, meat, and produce abound here. Local lamb originates in Pictou County. Fruits and vegetables are fresh and are often picked from backyard inn and restaurant gardens. Local delicacies include wild chanterelle mushrooms, smoked mackerel pâté, and seafood from lobster to locally caught Digby scallops and pickled Solomon Gundy herring. Preserves are generally homemade. Soups range from lobster chowder thickened with whipped cream to pea soup brimming with corned beef chunks.

Salmon is often cooked on a board plank before an open fire, as the Micmac Indians historically prepared it. Desserts know no limit and range from trifles rich with raspberry jam and sherry, to cheesecakes concocted of local cheese and cream, to molded flans embellished with fruit toppings.

Acadian cooking is another provincial variation. Acadian chicken *fricot* melds meat, onions, and potatoes in a soup as thick as stew. The *chiard* stew has its base in beef. *Rappie pie,* the best-known regional Acadian dish, mixes clams or chicken with grated potatoes as translucent as pearls.

If you travel on your stomach, look for the Taste of Nova Scotia emblem affixed to restaurant front windows or doors. The emblem is awarded to the dining places judged noteworthy by the province; a booklet of the same name costs $1 and is available from tourist information centers.

Drink

Locals like wine, especially French imports and local wines from the Jost and Grand-Pré wineries. Regional and locally brewed beers are quite popular, too. Nova Scotia favorites include Schooner and Keith's. The Granite Brewery in Halifax produces a variety of local brews, including stouts and seasonal specialties.

As elsewhere in Canada, strict regulations govern alcohol consumption. Licensed restaurants, dining rooms, and cocktail lounges serve liquor daily 11 a.m.-2 a.m. Beverage rooms with beer and wine are open Mon-Wed. 10 a.m.-11 p.m., Thurs.-Sat. to midnight. Lounge hours are Mon.-Sat. 11 a.m.-2 a.m.; and cabarets are open nightly 7 p.m.-3 a.m. Alcohol is sold at the government liquor stores, open Mon.-Thurs. 10 a.m.-6 p.m., Fri. to 10 p.m., Sat. to 5 p.m. The minimum drinking age is 19.

INFORMATION AND SERVICES

Visitor Information

The year-round **provincial tourist information centers** are located at the Halifax waterfront, Halifax International Airport, and Amherst. Sea-

Seafood is not hard to find in Nova Scotia.

NAN DROSDICK

sonal centers are located at Annapolis Royal, Antigonish, Digby, Halifax, Pictou, Port Hastings, Yarmouth, and PEI's Wood Islands.

The **Cape Breton Tourist Association,** 220 Keltic Drive, Sydney River, NS B0A 1M0, tel. (902) 539-9876, (800) 565-9464 in Canada and the U.S., provides information on the island. The office is open year-round, Mon.-Fri. 9 a.m.-5 p.m., July-Aug. to 9 p.m.

The **Nova Scotia League for Equal Opportunities** acts as an information source for the handicapped, and compiles updated lists of lodgings and other places equipped with wheelchair access and special facilities like telephones with amplifying devices. For more info write to P.O. Box 8204, Halifax, NS B3K 5L9, or call 455-6942. The **Canadian Paraplegic Association, Nova Scotia Division** is another source of information at 5599 Fenwick St., Halifax, NS B3H 1R2, tel. 423-1277.

Useful Publications

The **Nova Scotia Department of Tourism and**

Culture publishes the free, information-packed *Nova Scotia Travel Guide,* updated annually. For a copy, write to P.O. Box 456, Halifax, NS B3J 2R5 in Canada, or in the U.S. at 136 Commercial St., Portland, ME 04101. Telephone numbers are (902) 424-4247 (after business hours use 426-1223), (800) 565-0000 in Canada, (800) 492-0643 in Maine, and (800) 341-6096 in the rest of the continental United States.

The free booklet *Nova Scotia Outdoors* details sports from sailing, windsurfing, diving, sea kayaking, fishing, and whalewatching expeditions, to hiking, birdwatching, golf, tennis, biking, horseback riding, and winter skiing. The free *Outdoors Map* shows locations for boat tours, fishing, waterfalls, hiking trails, canoeing, diving, skiing, fossil hunting, and sailing; lists of operators and outfitters are included on the map. Both publications are stocked at the provincial tourist information centers, and Nova Scotia Tourism and Culture has copies also: P.O. Box 130, Halifax, NS B3J 2M7, tel. (800) 565-0000, Canada; (800) 341-6096 in the continental United States.

Communications and Media

The area code for all Nova Scotia phone numbers is **902.**

City and town post offices are open Mon.-Fri. 8:15 a.m.-5:15 p.m., while rural outlets have varying hours and some are open Saturday.

The *Halifax Herald* covers the province with daily editions, while regional weekly and monthly newspapers circulate in various areas.

Immigration

Steps toward immigration must begin outside Canada. Eligibility is based on a point system that includes employment and other factors. **Immigration Centre** decisions are vested in officials, and, for example, a visit's extension is based on an interview that covers proof of funds, return transportation, and possession of a valid passport. The Immigration Centre is on the fourth floor of Park Lane Mall on Spring Garden Rd. in Halifax, tel. (902) 426-2970. It's open Mon.-Fri. 8:30 a.m.-3 p.m.

Health and Safety

No special health problems require inoculations before arrival. The provincial health-care network includes 50 major hospitals like **Victoria General Hospital** in Halifax, and 25 smaller community hospitals. Dialysis centers are at Halifax's Victoria General and **Camp Hill Medical Centre.** The per diem bed rate for non-Canadians ranges from $1,200 at Victoria General to $550 at the smaller hospitals.

The **RCMP** has 51 detachments within the province. Halifax, Dartmouth, and 33 other municipalities have their own police departments. **Search and Rescue** handles problems on the water, tel. (902) 427-8200 or (800) 565-1582 or 565-1742.

Money

Currency exchange rates vary among banks, shops, hotels, and restaurants—it pays to shop around. You can also convert currency at some tourist information centers. Bank hours are generally Mon.-Wed. 9:30 a.m.-5 p.m. and Thurs.-Fri. to 6 or 8 p.m. The Royal Bank and a few other banking institutions are open Sat. 10 a.m.-3 p.m. Usually no fee is levied on U.S. or British currency exchanges; converting traveler's checks can cost $2-2.50 for each transaction or a percentage fee based on the amount, so inquire beforehand.

Federal **goods and services tax** (GST) is seven percent. The provincial **health services tax** is 10% on retail purchases, lodgings, and meals over $2; the tax does not apply to clothing and footwear under $100 or to most groceries. The **Provincial Tax Commission** refunds taxes paid on purchases over $150. Submit copies of your receipts within 30 days; direct inquiries to P.O. Box 755, Halifax, NS B3J 2V4, tel. (902) 424-5946.

MasterCard, Visa (most widely accepted), American Express, En Route, Diners Club, Carte Blanche, and Japan Bank Card credit cards are accepted at most places.

Measurements and Time

Measurements throughout the province are officially metric, but locals still informally compute distance in miles and weight in pounds. Nova Scotia is on Atlantic standard time, one hour ahead of Eastern standard time. Daylight saving time begins on April's first Sunday and continues to October's last Sunday.

WHAT TO BRING

Clothing

Bring lightweight clothing, a sweater or jacket, and a raincoat for a summer visit. Nova Scotians like to wear summer whites, especially in the Chester and Mahone Bay areas. September through mid-October has warm days, though cool spells are likely, so bring a warm jacket or sweater. Mid-November through March is heavy coat and muffler weather. Although the provincial attire is customarily informal, Halifax tends to be a bit dressy, and dinnertime out in the province should elicit your finer duds.

If you plan on camping or other outdoor activities out in the countryside, bring insect repellent; the mosquitoes can be merciless.

Photographic Supplies

Bring what you need in photographic equipment and film, or stock up in Halifax, which has the best-equipped camera shops. If the worst happens and your camera malfunctions, Halifax camera shops are authorized service dealers for Minolta, Pentax, Canon, Nikon, Olympus, and Hasselblad; check the *Yellow Pages.* Out in the province you are at the mercy of less well-equipped shops.

The province has incredible light for photography. The sky turns from a Wedgwood color to sapphire blue—a beautiful background for seacoast photographs. The landscapes can be so spectacular when the weather is favorable—and that's more often than not—that it pays to forget photography on dull or overcast days.

However, don't pass up a morning basking in thick mist, especially in the Yarmouth area, as bright sun illuminates the sky behind the thick clouds. The fog breaks apart gradually, and when it does, the sun radiates like a spotlight, illuminating the sparkling dampness that clings briefly to the landscape.

GETTING THERE

The TransCanada links Nova Scotia and New Brunswick with an easy travel corridor that funnels visitors into and out of the province; in fact, more visitors arrive at Amherst near the border than anyplace else. Frequent air service connects Nova Scotia with neighboring provinces, the States, and Europe. Ferry service links the province with Prince Edward Island, New Brunswick, Newfoundland, and the state of Maine.

By Air

Halifax International Airport, (902) 873-1233, is served by **Air Canada,** tel. 429-7111, and its affiliated airline **Air Nova,** tel. 429-7111. Air Canada offers nonstop flights from Montreal, Ottawa, Toronto, Boston, and Newark, as well as London and Glasgow. Its regional routes on Air Nova connect Halifax with the neighboring provinces. **Canadian Airlines International/Air Atlantic,** tel. 427-5500, also serves the airport with long-haul and regional service. Another regional carrier, **Air St. Pierre,** tel. 873-3566, serves St-Pierre in the gulf.

Smaller airports at Yarmouth and Sydney handle provincial and regional air traffic.

By Land

The TransCanada routes visitors into the province at Amherst near the New Brunswick border. By **bus,** Voyageur from Montreal and Greyhound from New York connect with New Brunswick's SMT, which in turn connects with Nova Scotia's Acadian Lines, tel. (902) 454-9321 or 454-8279.

VIA Rail has frequent service from Montreal via New Brunswick and stops at Amherst, Truro, and Halifax. Call (800) 561-3952 in the Maritimes, (800) 561-3952 from the United States.

By Sea

Two ferry outfits dock at Yarmouth. The *Scotia Prince* links the seaport to Portland, Maine, and operates early May through October, daily. Reservations for the 11-hour crossing are required, and tickets must be picked up two hours before departure. The one-way fare is US$70 per person, $93 for the vehicle, and if you want a cabin, the cost ranges $32-95. For more information write to **Prince of Fundy Cruises,** P.O. Box 4216, Station A, Portland, ME 04101, or in Canada, P.O. Box 609, Yarmouth B5A 4B6. The company's telephone numbers are (800) 565-7900 in the Maritime provinces; (800) 482-0955 in Maine; (800) 341-7540 in the rest of the United States.

Marine Atlantic is the region's largest ferry operator, with ships departing Yarmouth for Bar Harbor, Maine; Digby for Saint John, New Brunswick; and North Sydney for Argentia and Port aux Basques, Newfoundland.

The *Bluenose* sails the Yarmouth to Bar Harbor run year-round (daily mid-June to mid-September). The one-way fare for the six-hour crossing is $43 per adult, $74 per car. The *Princess of Acadia* crosses the Fundy in 2.5 hours from Digby to Saint John, daily year-round (three trips a day during peak months). The one-way fare is $18 per person, $55 per vehicle. The North Sydney to Port aux Basques ferry takes 5-7 hours, depending on the season, with up to 16 crossings per week. One-way fare is $17 adults, $8.50 children 5-12, under 5 years free, seniors $12.75. Cars up to six meters long are $53. Cabins range $42-90. Finally, the North Sydney to Argentia ferry runs mid-June through September only, with two 14-hour crossings per week. One-way fare is $47 adults, $23.50 children 5-12, under 5 years free, seniors $35.25. Cars up to six meters long are $103. Cabins cost $95-125.

Reservations on all three routes are required and must be picked up an hour before sailing (two hours beforehand at North Sydney). For reservations and information contact Marine Atlantic/Reservations, P.O. Box 250, North Sydney, NS B2A 3M3, tel. (902) 794-5700 in Canada, (800) 341-7981 from the United States. Its U.S. contact is Terminal Supervisor, Marine Atlantic, Bar Harbor, ME 04609.

Northumberland Ferries, based in Charlottetown, PEI, operates service between Caribou, Nova Scotia, and Wood Islands, in eastern Prince Edward Island. The crossing takes a little over an hour. Service is May to mid-Dec., up to 12 times daily each way. Round-trip fare is $8.50 per person, $27.25 per car; motor homes and cars with trailers up to nine meters are $40.75, up to 12 meters $54.50. Motorcycles are $13.50, bicycles $4.75. For additional details, call the company at 566-3838 or (800) 565-0201 in Nova Scotia or PEI.

Ports of Entry
If you are planning to arrive in the province on your own yacht, the ports of entry are Halifax, Digby, Liverpool, Lunenburg, New Glasgow, Port Hawkesbury, Shelburne, Yarmouth, and Sydney.

Cruise Ships
Provincial seaports are popular stops for numerous cruise ships touring eastern Canada. Halifax is a prime port-of-call, while Sydney has emerged as a popular cruise port (and provides easy access to the Fortress of Louisbourg). Lunenburg and North Sydney serve as occasional stops.

Among the ship lines calling at Halifax are Crown Cruise Line, Crystal Cruises, Regency Cruises, Cunard Line, Odessamerica Cruise, and Royal Viking Line. Seabourn Cruise Line stops at Lunenburg, and Odessamerica Cruise and Royal Viking Line call at Sydney.

GETTING AROUND

Forget about taking in the whole province on a quick driving circuit. Nova Scotia boasts more sightseeing than a visitor can digest in a lifetime of short visits. Itinerary planning beforehand is essential.

The province consists of the capital at Halifax and three main regions. The **central region** includes the cities of Amherst—where the TransCanada enters the province—and **Truro,** where another expressway (Hwy. 102) heads south to Halifax. The **southwest region** encompasses the mainland peninsula's southwestern end and includes the Atlantic shore southwest of Halifax, Yarmouth and the Acadian Coast, and the Annapolis Valley. The **eastern region** extends northeast beyond Halifax and Truro to Cape Breton's tip; the area includes the Atlantic shore northeast of Halifax, the Northumberland Strait coast, and **Cape Breton Island,** which is treated in this guide as a separate section.

Roads and Driving
Long distances notwithstanding, the province has a superb system of roads, classified by numbers. For example, the TransCanada (Hwy. 104) enters at Amherst, zips east across the mainland, and finishes at North Sydney. The highway is one of the new 100-series roads designed for rapid transit. Similar highways connect major towns in the central region and rim the heavily traveled southwest region's seacoast along the Fundy.

The highways numbered 1-99 often parallel the 100-series expressways and connect major cities and towns. Roads numbered 200-399 are paved, rambling, two-lane routes that take visitors to all the interesting out-of-the-way places. These roads often work as diversionary routes off major sightseeing highways, such as Hwy. 316 which departs the eastern shore's Hwy. 7 and meanders through Canso and Guysborough on its way to the Canso Strait.

The Cabot Trail around western Cape Breton is the exception. It is unnumbered and ranks as a special scenic highway.

The province is strict about driving regulations. Seat belts must be worn. The minimum fine for speeding is $50. Drinking while driving carries a $2000 fine, six months in jail, or both.

Car Rentals

Avis, Budget, Thrifty, Tilden, and **Hertz** rent cars at Halifax International Airport. Avis and Budget also have rentals at the Yarmouth and Sydney airports. Expect to pay about $45 a day for a subcompact car with 100 km free and 12 cents for each additional kilometer. A car rental at Yarmouth is about $5 cheaper; Sydney rentals cost about $13 less. Optional collision insurance costs about $11 a day.

If you are watching travel costs, you may want to look into local car rentals. **Delta Rent-A-Car,** 3550 Kempt St., Halifax, tel. (902) 455-5926, charges $20 a day, 100 km free, and 12 cents for each additional km for a subcompact; collision insurance is $8 a day. The outfit can also have a car at Halifax airport for you, weekdays 9 a.m.-4 p.m.

Combined taxes on rentals amount to 17%; insurance coverage is taxed 10 percent.

Taxis and Buses

Taxis wait at hotels, bus stops and terminals, airports, or are on call. Rates are based on a flat rate per trip or per km at about $2.50 per km for one person and 50 cents for each additional passenger. Tipping is optional, but welcome.

Sydney and its outlying towns, Halifax and Dartmouth, Yarmouth, and Pictou County have local public transit systems. Otherwise, be prepared to hoof it as people in smaller communities rely on private transportation.

The major bus companies are based in Halifax. **Acadian Lines,** the province's largest bus service, has routes throughout the province. **Zinck Bus** serves towns along the Eastern Shore to Sherbrooke. Acadian also works with PEI's Island Motor Transit and meets that province's buses at New Glasgow. For additional details, see the "Transportation" sections in the following chapters.

Biking

Numerous outfits rent bikes and provide guided bike tours. **Freewheeling Bicycle Adventures** designs custom tours emphasizing the secondary roads and wooded trails; you can reach them at RR 1, Boutiliers Point, NS B0J 1G0, tel. (902) 826-2437 or 826-7541. **Down East Tours** meshes bike tours with birding; they're at RR 2, Comp. 41-B, Kingston, NS B0P 1R0, tel. 765-8923.

Cape Breton's **Open Horizons Cycling** also leads biking-birding tours. They rent standard bikes and mountain bikes, and can arrange for overnights at local bed-and-breakfasts. Write to P.O. Box 390, Margaree Valley, NS B0E 2C0, or call 248-2987.

CENTRAL NOVA SCOTIA

Central Nova Scotia was once the realm of Glooscap, the Micmac Indian god who roamed this part of Nova Scotia as a man as large as Gulliver among the Lilliputians. A legend relates that Glooscap slept stretched out over the region's northern portion and used Prince Edward Island as his pillow.

This region is at once the most traveled and least known part of the province. The provincial highway system here is, you might say, too efficient. The TransCanada Hwy. (Hwy. 104 here) enters the province from New Brunswick and breezes past Amherst near the border. From there it slices across the region's northern hinterlands and jogs south to Truro, getting you there in two quick hours. At Truro, the Trans-Canada turns east on the way to Sydney, Cape Breton—a six-hour drive. Truro also marks the place where Hwy. 102 peels off to Halifax, 100 km southwest.

Sightseers on a fast track see central Nova Scotia as a flash of landscape. But why hurry? The region is refreshingly off the beaten tourist track. Lodgings and dining places are plentiful at Amherst, Truro, and innumerable villages. The area's sightseeing is worth several days, more if you have such eclectic interests as geology, archaeology, winetasting, Fundy watching, or river rafting.

The summer climate is pleasant. Beaches on the strait are bathtub-warm. Vineyards flourish in the temperate climate, and the area revels in berries. Strawberries ripen in June, and blueberries are ready in August. Both harvests beget summertime events.

THE COLOSSAL FUNDY TIDES

The world's highest tides rise in the upper Bay of Fundy—up to a 17-meter vertical gain at central Nova Scotia's Burncoat Head, near Truro.

The Fundy and its numerous branches hereabouts have as many place-names as the bay has moods. The upper Fundy is split into two arms by Cape Chignecto, the wedge-shaped point that angles into the bay. On one side, Chignecto Bay with its raw, lonesome coastline penetrates inland and finishes at Cumberland Basin near Amherst. On the cape's other side, the bay compresses itself first into the Minas Channel. Cape Split blocks high tide's route with a hook-shaped peninsula that reaches north almost to the opposite shore. The Fundy surges onward and pours into Minas Basin like a restrained tidal wave. The force finishes in Cobequid Bay, not as a whimper but as an upright tidal bore (lead wave) that rides inland up the area's rivers. The arriving wave can be a dainty, ankle-high ripple or an upright wall of knee-high water, depending on the tide. During the highest tides, rafters ride the advancing bores upstream. At Maitland, for example, at the mouth of the Shubenacadie River, you can take a 28-km raft ride atop the wave's crest as it travels upriver past soaring red cliffs speckled with the nests of bald eagles, doves, swifts, and cliff swallows.

The tides work on a six-hour cycle, and each peak or low arrives 50 minutes later each day. Tide tables are posted in shops and storefronts everywhere. Tides are highest around the full or new moon. The savage high tides rake the northern coasts from Joggins to Parrsboro, churning up a continuous array of agate, amethyst, jasper, bloodstone, hematite, and quartz for beachcombers.

Central Nova Scotia's Fundy can be perilously alluring. The coastal sea floor looks tranquilly bare at low tide. The mud flats glisten like glass. High tide's arrival is subtle and hardly noticeable. The distant tidal stirrings alert sea birds, and they cry out and wheel and turn across the sky.

The sea moves in relentlessly, swelling and pushing forward into the bay at six knots an hour—and up to 13 knots in tidal rips. The incoming sea can wash across the glistening surfaces faster than a person can swiftly walk. Only a foolhardy sightseer walks the mudflats. The high tide stops for nothing.

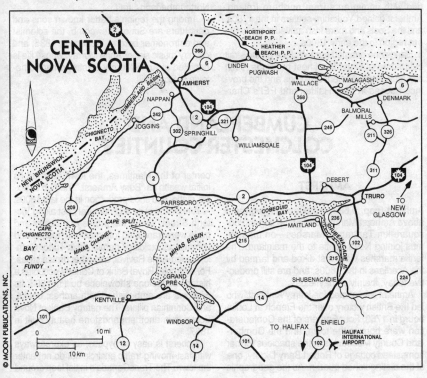

HISTORY

Nova Scotia's first man lived 10,000 years ago in a Stone Age village at Debert northwest of Truro. The site's archaeological dig yielded 4,000 artifacts; arrowhead reproductions are on exhibit at the Debert Development Office near exit 13 on the TransCanada. The first Europeans to find their way here were French. Champlain established Port Royal in 1605 and made an exploratory sweep of the upper Fundy in 1607. French farmers subsequently settled along the coastlines.

England's Acadian Deportation recast the region with an Anglo complexion. The Acadians had settled Les Planches in 1675, but the village became Amherst when New England planters settled it in 1764. The Acadians' village of Cobequid changed to Truro in 1759, when it was settled with immigrants from northern Ireland. Amherst gained Yorkshire settlers in the 1780s, and the Scots and more Irish arrived in the northern region in the early 1800s.

Sandstone quarried from Wallace on the strait built some of Canada's finest buildings, such as Ottawa's Parliament Buildings and the province houses in both Halifax and PEI's Charlottetown. Canada's largest wooden ship was built and launched by Maitland shipbuilding magnate W.D. Lawrence in 1874.

The region's importance as a travel corridor goes back centuries. Dirt roads first traversed the southern area during colonial times. The Shubenacadie Canal project was the next great projected route. The scheme was funded in 1797 and begun in 1826, but the emergence of quicker, cheaper railroad shipping caused its demise in 1870. A century later, the province restored some canal locks in the most picturesque places. Locks 6, 7, and 8 now form the backdrops for picnicking visitors in the Enfield area near Halifax International Airport.

The region has a diverse economy. Manufacturing and light industry are based at Amherst and Truro. Farming, forestry, and quarrying operations lie across the interior, and fishing and fish processing are centered at seaports on Northumberland Strait.

Among the region's better-known sons and daughters are Simon Newcomb, the scientist and astronomer born at Wallace in 1835, and country music singer Anne Murray, whose life is depicted at Anne Murray Centre in her hometown of Springhill.

CUMBERLAND AND COLCHESTER COUNTIES

AMHERST

Amherst (pop. 9,684) is built on high ground above Amherst Marsh—part of the larger, 200-square-km Tantramar Marshes—on the isthmus joining Nova Scotia to the mainland. The fertile marshes were first diked and farmed by the Acadians in the 1600s, and are still productive today, mainly as hayfields.

Amherst was named for Jeffrey Amherst, who led the British victory over the French at Louisbourg in 1758. Four Fathers of the Confederation were born in the town, and the Cumberland County Museum is in the spacious former homestead cottage of Robert Barry Dickey, one of the distinguished quartet. As the geographic center of the Maritimes, the town accrued its initial wealth as "Busy Amherst," the hub of textile, piano, and shoe production in the late 1800s.

Amherst is at its architectural best along Victoria Street, where the profits of industry and trade were translated into gracious houses and commercial buildings garnished in Tudor Gothic, Queen Anne Revival, and other ornate styles. For example, Royal Bank of Canada occupies a historic sandstone showpiece built in 1903. Its windows are embellished with arches, peaks, and Corinthian pillars. The nearby Bank of Nova Scotia is in another sandstone beauty built in 1887.

Amherst is easy to bypass, as expressways with fast-moving traffic encircle but do not enter the town. The TransCanada's initial loop around

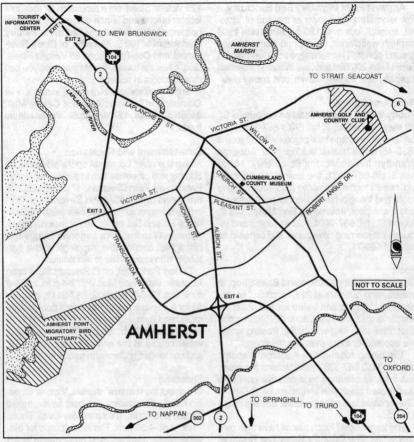

AMHERST

TOURIST INFORMATION CENTER

EXIT 1

EXIT 2

TO NEW BRUNSWICK

LAPLANCHE RIVER

LAPLANCHE ST.

AMHERST MARSH

TO STRAIT SEACOAST

VICTORIA ST.

WILLOW ST.

AMHERST GOLF AND COUNTRY CLUB

CHURCH ST.

CUMBERLAND COUNTY MUSEUM

VICTORIA ST.

PLEASANT ST.

ROBERT ANGUS DR.

EXIT 3

HICKMAN ST.

ALBION ST.

TRANSCANADA HWY.

NOT TO SCALE

EXIT 4

AMHERST POINT MIGRATORY BIRD SANCTUARY

TO OXFORD

TO NAPPAN

TO SPRINGHILL

TO TRURO

© MOON PUBLICATIONS, INC.

Amherst comes up quickly at exit 2, which leads to Laplanche Street. The highway's next exit to Victoria St. is situated on another fast-moving curve, and the following exit is almost beyond town.

None of which helps Amherst, though the town is certainly worth a stop. The historic district is along Victoria Street's eastern end. Laplanche St. is motel row. The town's two shopping malls are on the outskirts on Albion Street. The main streets form routes that lead out of town. Victoria St. turns into Hwy. 6 and heads for the strait seacoast, while Albion St. changes to Hwy. 2 and becomes the scenic backcountry road to Springhill.

Sights

The **Cumberland County Museum,** 150 Church St., tel. (902) 667-2561, is in the 1838 home of early provincial legislator Robert Mc-Gowan Dickey. The museum does an impressive job of tracking the past with exhibits on early Acadian settlements, Amherst's Anglo background, and spicy tidbits relating to Russian revolutionary Leon Trotsky, who was interned in an Amherst POW camp in 1917. The museum is open year-round; between June and early September, hours are Mon.-Sat. 9 a.m.-5 p.m., Sun. 2-5 p.m. Admission is $1.

Amherst Point Migratory Bird Sanctuary, a few kilometers from town at the end of Victoria, spreads out over 190 hectares with trails through woodlands, fields, and marshes, and around ponds. The sediment-rich Cumberland Basin lures 200 bird species, including Eurasian kestrels, bald eagles, hawks, and snowy owls.

Accommodations
Fundy Winds Family Motel on Laplanche St. off Hwy. 104 at exit 2, tel. (902) 667-3881, is a better-than-average basic motel with 32 rooms ($35-45) and a heated outdoor pool. **Auberge Wandlyn Inn** on Victoria St. off Hwy. 104 at exit 3, tel. 667-3331, the town's largest lodging, has 93 rooms and suites ($55-100), a dining room and lounge, heated indoor pool, saunas, and a whirlpool. **Journey's End Motel,** 143 S. Albion St., tel. 667-0404, has 61 rooms and includes the morning newspaper and coffee in its rates of $60-71.

Food
Mother's Country Kitchen and Bake Shop, in unassuming quarters at 21 Church St., serves heaping helpings and value for the dollar on supper dishes like roast pork ($6); the worthy chocolate cake iced with boiled frosting whets the appetite for more than one helping.

The dining room at the Auberge Wandlyn Inn, tel. (902) 667-3331 (reservations are wise), has inspired offerings by a creative chef who likes flamed steak with shrimp sauce ($22) and Caesar salad tossed at the table. Entrees range $11-25.

The town's small lunch places have their own specialties. The **Country Rose Tea Room** at 125 Victoria St. savors a reputation for excellent lobster quiche and lemon chiffon pie. For thick homemade chowders, try **Smithy's Family Restaurant** at 138 S. Albion St., or **Bird's Restaurant and Cecil's Bakery,** 85 Victoria Street. Cecil's has the town's flakiest pies, and you can dine outdoors in summer.

Supermarkets and other food stores are at **Cumberland Mall** and **Amherst Centre Mall. Jacob's Ladder,** 127 Victoria St., stocks natural foods.

Entertainment and Recreation
Amherst is *quiet.* Locals roll up the sidewalks on Sunday and otherwise turn in early other nights. **Paramount Twin Cinemas,** 47 Church St., has two shows nightly. **King Pin Beverage** on Gerard Ave. reigns as the local beer joint; it's liveliest on Fri. and Sat. nights with occasional music. Auberge Wandlyn Inn's **Legends** lounge has dim lights, comfortable trappings, and a bartender who knows how to mix drinks.

Dickey Park pool, on E. Pleasant St., is open for public swimming Mon.-Fri. 2-4 p.m. and 6-8 p.m. The YMCA, tel. (902) 667-9112, charges $4 for a day-use pass to its indoor pool, weight room, and gym. Eighteen-hole **Amherst Golf and Country Club,** tel. 667-8730, is a 5,490-meter course at the end of Robert Angus Dr. and challenges golfers with ravine hazards.

Shopping
Check out the **farmers' market,** Victoria St. behind Bird's Restaurant, for local flavor, baked goods, and crafts. It's open May-Dec., Thurs. 11:30 a.m.-4:30 p.m. The local source for oils, watercolors, graphics, and other media is **Art Collection,** 210 E. Victoria St., open Tues.-Sat. 10 a.m.-4 p.m. **Touch of Country,** 77 Victoria St., stocks crafts, Grohmann Knives from Pictou, and Dominion furniture crafted at Bass River.

You'll find small apparel stores on Victoria St., and Kmart is at Amherst Centre Mall. **Pridham's Studio,** 33 Church St., handles the town's photography needs with film and accessories.

snowy owl

KAREN McKINLEY

Information and Services

The provincial **tourist information center,** tel. (902) 667-8429, is situated out of town on the TransCanada near the New Brunswick border. It's open year-round, daily 8:30 a.m.-4:30 p.m., May-Sept. 8 a.m.-9 p.m. During tourist season, a kilt-clad piper plays solo concerts on the half hour. **Amherst Tourist Bureau** is in a railroad car on Laplanche St., tel. 667-0696; open mid-May to mid-Sept., Mon.-Sat. 10 a.m.-6 p.m., Sun. noon-6 p.m.

Land Registration and Information Services, 16 Station St., tel. 667-7233, stocks local topographic maps and has a map that includes Amherst Point Migratory Bird Sanctuary. The office is open weekdays 8 a.m.-4 p.m.

Canada Post, 38 Havelock St., is open Mon.-Fri. 8:30 a.m.-5 p.m. For questions about **immigration,** a federal officer stops periodically at the Canada Employment office, 98 Victoria St., tel. 667-5163.

Bank of Nova Scotia, 79 Victoria St., is open Mon.-Wed. 10 a.m.-3 p.m., Thurs.-Fri. to 5 p.m. **Royal Bank of Canada,** 103 Victoria St., is open Mon.-Sat. 10 a.m.-5 p.m.

Amherst Highland View Hospital is on Townshend and E. Pleasant streets off Church St. on the town outskirts. Call Amherst **police** at 667-8600, or the **RCMP,** tel. 667-3859.

Transportation

D & J Taxi is one of two local taxi outfits, and charges a flat $3.75 rate anywhere in Amherst. Outside town, ask for a rate estimate. Expect to pay $27 OW to Joggins.

Acadian Lines, 34 Prince Arthur St., tel. (902) 667-8435, has thrice-daily bus service to Truro ($14 OW) and Halifax ($23 OW). **SMT Bus Lines** pulls into the same terminal with service to Moncton, New Bunswick, from where **Greyhound** connects to New York, and **Voyageur** connects to Montreal.

The **VIA Rail** station on Station St., tel. 667-1059, is open when trains stop at Amherst (usually twice a day) on the Montreal–Saint John–Moncton route; Amherst to Truro costs $15 OW. If the station is closed, call VIA Rail at 429-8421 in Halifax.

Bicycle Expert, 81 Victoria St., tel. 667-3949, rents a basic bike at $7 a day or $14-20 for a mountain bike; open Mon.-Sat. 9 a.m.-5 p.m.

SOUTH OF AMHERST

Nappan

Just 10 minutes beyond Amherst on Hwy. 302, the **Canada Department of Agriculture Experimental Farm** provides a look at the latest federal research efforts in cattle feed and fertilizers. Grazing cattle and sheep provide a bucolic backdrop for a picnic; picnic tables are on the grounds. The farm is open year-round, Mon.-Fri. 8:30 a.m.-3:30 p.m. Admission is free.

Joggins

This town on the Chignecto Bay seacoast is 40 km southwest from Amherst. The **Joggins Fossil Centre,** off Hwy. 302 (for directions, call 902-251-2828, or ask around locally), exhibits 300-million-year-old fossils excavated locally. Daily two-hour guided tours are offered ($7) to the fossil-rich Joggins-area cliffs, where ancient trees and other plants were frozen in time eons ago. The site is open June-Sept., daily 9 a.m.-6:30 p.m. Admission is $2.50.

Springhill

The **Anne Murray Centre,** Main at Elgin streets, tel. (902) 597-8614, pays tribute to the beloved local warbler who hit the Top-40 in the 1970s with "Snow Bird" and is still going strong. Exhibits includes photos, clothing, and other memorabilia. It's open year-round, daily 10 a.m.-7 p.m.; admission is $5.

The **Springhill Miners' Museum,** Black River Rd. off Hwy. 2, tel. 597-3449, is all that remains of the former coal industry whose hazards claimed hundreds of miners' lives between 1872, when coal mining began here, and 1958, when the mines shut down. Former miners lead tours of the mine; exhibits document the good and bad times and offer visitors the opportunity to try their hand at digging coal. The museum is open late May to mid-Oct., daily 10 a.m.-5 p.m., and July-Aug. 9 a.m.-8 p.m. Admission is $3.50 adults, seniors and ages 7-14 $3.

Parrsboro

The sea's erosive force has opened a window on the ancient world along the coastlines of Chignecto Bay and Minas Basin. The world's largest discrete fossil find was at Parrsboro on the basin's northern coast. *National Geographic* joined with the province on archaeological digs, which yielded 100,000 fossilized bone fragments of ancient dinosaurs, crocodiles, lizards, sharks, and primitive fishes. Parrsboro's Fundy Geological Museum (see below) exhibits some of the discoveries.

Fossilized bones of the sphenodontid *were uncovered near Parrsboro.*

DAVID KIEFER

The famous digs spanned a decade. By 1980, unrestricted fossil digs by amateur collectors were declared illegal by the province; for permission to dig in restricted areas, you will need a Heritage Research Permit from Nova Scotia Museum, 1747 Summer St., Halifax NS B3H 3A6, tel. (902) 424-7353.

Fundy Geological Museum, in Parrsboro center off Hwy. 2, exhibits fossils, minerals, and gems and sells topographic maps. It's open May to mid-Oct., daily 9 a.m.-5 p.m., July-Aug. to 9 p.m. **Parrsboro Rock and Mineral Shop and Museum,** 39 Whitehall Rd., tel. 254-2981, is local geologist Eldon George's pride. The museum displays dinosaur, reptile, and amphibian footprint fossils. The shop stocks fossil and gem specimens, rockhound supplies, books, and maps. It's open May-Dec., Mon.-Sat. 9 a.m.-9 p.m.

NORTH TO THE STRAIT COAST

Linden
Heather Beach Provincial Park, Hwy. 366, eight km east of East Linden, is the most popular beach in this area of the strait seacoast. If its small parking lot is filled, try **Northport Beach Provincial Park,** on Hwy. 366 three km east of Northport, for warm seas among the sandbars.

Malagash
Jost Vineyards, off Hwy. 6, tel. (902) 257-2636, is the creation of the Jost family from Europe's Rhineland. Their 13-hectare vineyards on the strait provide some of the province's finest white wines. Guided tours are given Mon.-Sat. at 3 p.m. The vineyards are open mid-June to mid-Sept., 10 a.m.-4 p.m.

TRURO

Situated at the convergence of the province's major expressways and served by VIA Rail, Truro (pop. 11,700) is called the "Hub of Nova Scotia." It is the province's third-largest town, with an economy based on shipping, dairy products, and the manufacture of clothing, carpets, plastic products, and wines. Truro's academic side includes a teachers' college in town and an agricultural college on the outskirts.

Due to the expressways, Truro, like Amherst, is easy to bypass. The TransCanada's exit 15 feeds into Hwy. 102, the highway to Halifax, and skirts past Truro Golf Course on the town's western side. Highway 102's exits 14A to 13A peel off in quick succession as the expressway rushes beyond Truro.

The highway's prime access into town is exit 14, which turns into Robie St., which leads shortly into central Truro. Robie ends at Commercial St., which turns into Willow St., the town's motel row, a few blocks farther south.

Sights
Truro makes an excellent base for watching the Fundy tides and **tidal bore.** The town has a prime location on Cobequid Bay at the innermost end of the sea pocket. The twice-daily high tides spill over into the Shubenacadie and other rivers emptying into the Cobequid Bay. At Truro, the lead wave travels up the Salmon River as it flows toward town beneath the Hwy. 102 overpass.

If you want a close-up look at the tidal bore, take Robie St. west out of town toward Hwy. 102 and turn off on one of the roads leading to the river. Tidal-bore arrival times are listed in the *Truro Daily News,* and at the town's tourist office, tel. (902) 893-2922.

Colchester Historical Society Museum, 29 Young St. near Prince St., tel. 895-6284, does a fine job entwining exhibits on the Fundy eccentricities, the area's natural history, and local genealogy. It's open year-round, Tues.-Fri. 10 a.m.-5 p.m., Sat.-Sun. 2-5 p.m. and shorter off-season hours. Admission is 50 cents adults, 25 cents children.

Victoria Park, at Brunswick St. and Park Rd., showcases stands of Norway spruce, hemlock, and white pine. The 400-hectare park has a public swimming pool and is thickly forested and spliced with hiking trails and stone walkways alongside waterfalls. It's open year-round, dawn to dusk.

Accommodations

Lodgings in Truro are plentiful and reasonably priced. **Rainbow Motel,** 341 Prince St., tel. (902) 893-9438, is an unassuming, well-located motel with 42 rooms ($44), a restaurant of local renown,

and an outdoor pool. **Nestle Inn Bed and Breakfast,** 67 Duke St., tel. 893-9413, has a prime midtown location with three nonsmoking rooms ($45 with full breakfast). **Stonehouse Motel,** 165 Willow St., tel. 893-9413, has 41 handsome rooms (under $50) and a restaurant. **Journey's End Motel,** 12 Meadow Drive, tel. 893-0330, has 81 spacious rooms for $62, including morning coffee and newspaper.

Keddy's Motor Inn, 437 Prince St., tel. 895-1651, is on the main drag with 115 better-than-average rooms ($64-80), a restaurant, lounge, indoor pool, sauna, and whirlpool. **Best Western Glengarry,** 150 Willow St., tel. 893-4311, doubles as a convention center. Its 90 spacious rooms ($68-95), are complemented by a restaurant, lounge and piano bar, indoor and outdoor pools, a sauna, and whirlpool.

Food

Keddy's Motor Inn boasts a dining room spe-

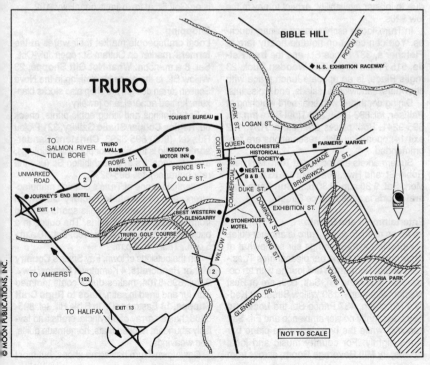

cializing in chicken and ribs or the two combined ($8-11), with other entrees priced $6-20. The **Stonehouse Restaurant** at the Stonehouse Motel is known locally for home-style cooking. Especially tasty are the roast beef, turkey, or pork daily specials ($9). Other entrees range $7-16 and include fried liver smothered with onions and seafood.

The **Best Western Glengarry** restaurant at 150 Willow St. is usually jammed with locals (reservations are wise, call 902-893-4311). The best buy is the weekday evening buffet heaped with casseroles and desserts ($13). On the entree menu, two popular choices are liver heaped with onions, and surf and turf (steak and lobster) for $12-18.

Rainbow Dining Room at the Rainbow Motel, 341 Prince St., features all-you-can-eat buffets early May to early Sept. with unlimited lobster; tasty potato, three-bean, and carrot/pineapple salads; and other fixings. Price varies due to lobster availability; expect to pay in the low $20s.

In Truro, locals eschew fancy culinary touches. You can count on notable hearty fare at **Fletcher's**, 337 Prince St., and the **Iron Kettle**, 515 Prince Street. The **Wooden Duck**, 23 Inglis Place, is an upscale lunch place with chowders, sandwiches, salads, and croissants.

Dining combines with tidal-bore watching at **Palliser**, tel. 893-8951, and **Tidal Bore Inn**, tel. 895-9241. Both places are near at Hwy. 102 exit 14; open May-Oct., reservations are recommended.

Supermarkets are located at Truro Mall near Robie St. and Hwy. 102's exit 14; **IGA** is open Mon.-Sat. 9:30 a.m.-9:30 p.m. **Sun Spun Natural Foods** is at 583 Prince Street.

Entertainment and Events

As far as nightlife goes, Truro is another quiet, low-profile town. Evenings stir somewhat at **Sherlock's** with piano bar pleasantries Tues.-Sat., and at **Scotland Yard** lounge with an occasional rock band Fri.-Sat.; both are at Best Western Glengarry, 150 Willow Street. At Keddy's Motor Inn, 437 Prince St., the **Lock and Key** has slightly noisier ambience and Fri.-Sat. dancing, while the **Ivory's** lounge piano bar hums nightly. For country music and local crowds, try **Mill Beverage Room,** across from Truro Mall, where the joint twangs Wed.-Sat. nights.

Recreation

Nova Scotia Provincial Exhibition Raceway, at Bible Hill Exhibition Grounds, on Rhyland Ave. in Bible Hill, tel. (902) 893-8075, draws harness-racing fans from as far as Halifax. The track is open year-round with races on Thurs. at 7 p.m. and Sun. at 1:30 p.m. Admission is $2. Late July's **Grand Circuit Week** features a busier schedule.

Colchester-Truro YMCA, 752 Prince St., tel. 895-2871, has a weight room with Nautilus equipment. It's open weekdays 6:30 a.m.-9 p.m., Sat. 9 a.m.-4 p.m., Sun. 2-8 p.m. A day-use pass costs $6. The town's **Centennial Pool,** on Kaulback St. behind the teachers' college, charges $3 for a day-use pass; open noontime on weekdays, and Sun. and Thurs. 8:30-10 p.m. The 18-hole **Truro Golf Course,** tel. 893-3673, is on Golf St. at town limits near Hwy. 102.

Shopping

Local craftspeople market their wares at the **farmers' market** on Outram St.; open July-Oct., Sat. 8 a.m.-noon. **What-Not Gift Shoppe,** 23 Willow St., is the place for clothing in the Nova Scotian tartan design; the shop also stocks blankets, knitted apparel, and jewelry.

For paintings and lithographic prints, check out **Regina Coupar Studio Gallery,** 321 Pictou Rd., tel. (902) 895-3293. **Christene Sanderson's** studio is the place for portraits, paintings, and drawings. It's at 57 Exhibition St. (use the rear entrance), tel. 895-3293.

Stanfield is one of Truro's clothing manufacturers, and its **Stanfield Factory Outlet,** on Logan St. off Queen St., sells sports clothing from sweatsuits to golf shirts. The outlet, in a brick factory building is open Wed.-Sat. 10 a.m.-5 p.m., Thurs. to 8 p.m.

On the outskirts of town, Fay Smith's **Country Manor Handcrafts,** 4 Kemptown Estates, Hwy. 2, tel. 895-8104, makes duffel coats trimmed with fur and lined in satin. **Rags to Rugs Craft Shoppe,** 14 Eastmoor Dr. in Bible Hill, tel. 895-5608, has an array of provincial crafts and lavishly abundant hooked mats, homemade quilts, and weavings.

Downtown Truro has some shops, but most

are at Truro Mall on the town outskirts. The mall is open Mon.-Sat. 9:30 a.m.-9:30 p.m. **Carsand-Mosher Photographic Ltd.** handles the town's photography needs and has a mall shop and another store at 56 Esplanade; open Mon.-Sat. 8:30 a.m.-5 p.m., Fri. to 9 p.m.

Information and Services

The **Truro Tourist Bureau,** at Victoria Square alongside Court St., tel. (902) 893-2922, stocks literature about the town and area. It's open year-round; daily 8 a.m.-8 p.m. from late May to mid-Oct., shorter hours the rest of the year.

For a line of books about Truro and the province, check out the **Colchester Historical Society Museum bookstore,** 29 Young St., tel. 895-6284. **Book Nook,** 10 Dominion St., is another source. **Colchester–East Hants Regional Library,** 754 Prince St., is open Tues., Wed., and Sat. 10 a.m.-5 p.m., Thurs.-Fri. to 9 p.m.

Royal Bank of Canada has two locations on Prince St., open Mon.-Fri. 9:30 a.m.-5 p.m. **Bank of Nova Scotia,** on Inglis Place, is open Mon.-Wed. 10 a.m.-3 p.m., Thurs.-Fri. to 5 p.m.

Canada Post is at 664 Prince St., open Mon.-Fri. 8 a.m.-5:15 p.m. **Truro-Colchester County Hospital** is on Willow St., tel. 893-4255. Call the **police** at tel. 895-5351, the **RCMP** at 895-1526.

The town has several launderettes; **Robin Cleaners And Laundramat** is at the mall; open Mon.-Fri. 8 a.m.-9 p.m., Sat. to 5 p.m.

Transportation

Truro has several taxi outfits. **Layton's Taxi,** 42 Outram, tel. (902) 895-4471 or 895-4472, charges $2.90 for each mile (not kilometer). A ride to the Bible Hill track costs about $3.50; Truro to Halifax International Airport costs about $45 OW.

VIA Rail, 104 Esplanade, offers twice-daily service to Halifax ($15 OW); call 895-0189 for a quick taped recording. (If you want a human voice, call 429-8421.) **Acadian Lines,** 280 Willow St., operates seven buses daily to Halifax ($10 OW), and three daily departures to Sydney ($32 OW).

NORTH OF TRURO

North of Truro, the land dips and sweeps in manicured farmlands as far as the Northum-

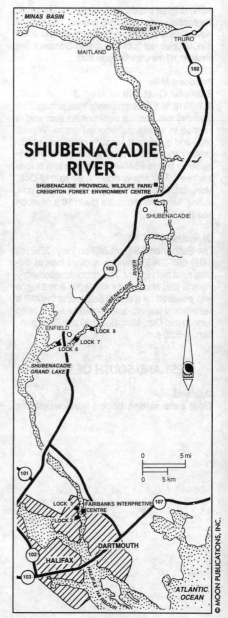

SHUBENACADIE RIVER

SHUBENACADIE PROVINCIAL WILDLIFE PARK/
CREIGHTON FOREST ENVIRONMENT CENTRE

© MOON PUBLICATIONS, INC.

berland Strait coastline. The villages are small; the backcountry roads are scenic. This is rural Nova Scotia at its best. Balmoral Mills is a 40-minute drive north of Truro, and Denmark lies another 10 minutes beyond that.

Balmoral Mills

Balmoral Grist Mill off Hwy. 311, tel. (902) 657-3016, is a photographer's ideal setting. The barn-red mill fronts a fast-running river and is nestled in a verdant, wooded gorge. Wheat, oats, and buckwheat are still ground using 19th-century methods at this historic gristmill-cum-museum built in 1874. A picnic ground is across the river. The site is open June to mid-Oct., Mon.-Sat. 9:30 a.m.-5:30 p.m., Sun. 1-5:30 p.m. Milling demonstrations are given 10 a.m.-noon and 2-4 p.m.

Denmark

The **Sutherland Steam Mill** on Hwy. 326, tel. (902) 657-3365, provides another look at old-time rural technology. The restored woodworking mill that once made carriages and sleighs was powered by a steam boiler, and the mill is periodically put into operation. The site is open June to mid-Oct., Mon.-Sat. 9:30 a.m.-5:30 p.m., Sun. 1-5:30 p.m.

WEST AND SOUTH OF TRURO

Maitland

Tidal bore rafting begins here, where the Fundy's high tide sweeps into the Shubenacadie River. Rafts ride the crest inland for 29 km on half-day expeditions during May-October. Make arrangements through Bill MacKay, tel. (902) 752-0899 or 755-5560, or write him at RR 2, New Glasgow, NS B2H 5C5.

Maitland is also the seacoast village where Canada's largest wooden ship, the three-masted *William D. Lawrence,* was built. Documentaries, ship portraits, and memorabilia are kept at the shipbuilder's former homestead, the **W.D. Lawrence House** on Hwy. 215, tel. 261-2628. It's open June to mid-Oct., Mon.-Sat. 9:30 a.m.-5:30 p.m., Sun. 1-5:30 p.m.

Shubenacadie

Shubenacadie Tidal Bore Park and Upriver Rafting, 10 km off Hwy. 102 (exit 10) on Hwy. 215, tel. (902) 758-4066 or 758-4032, operates two-hour Zodiac raft excursions mid-May to August. Nearby **Green Acres Camping,** tel. 758-2177, promotes rafting as part of its campgrounds attractions. Facilities include 150 campsites ($12 and up), washrooms, showers, a launderette, and campers' store.

Families will enjoy the **Shubenacadie Provincial Wildlife Park,** five km south of Hwy. 102 exit 11, which has indigenous animals on 20 wooded hectares. It's open mid-May to mid-Oct., 9 a.m.-7 p.m.; free admission. The provincial **Creighton Forest Environment Centre,** at the park's entrance, has forestry and wildlife exhibits; open June-Sept., daily 9 a.m.-5 p.m. Admission is free.

HALIFAX AND VICINITY

Halifax (pop. 115,000), the 250-year-old provincial capital, presents Nova Scotia's strikingly modern face, wrapped around a historic heart. It's one of the most vibrant, lively cities in Canada, with an exuberant cultural life and cosmopolitan population. The tourist's Halifax is tidily compact, no bigger than the small, boot-shaped peninsula the city inhabits. Its prettiest parts are clustered between the bustling waterfront and the short, steep hillside that the early British developed two centuries ago. In these areas you'll find handsomely historic old districts meshed with stylishly chic new glass-sheathed buildings.

Halifax's sister city, Dartmouth (pop. 67,000), is a 10-minute ferry ride or quick drive across the harbor. Its harborfront sightseeing-and-dining district fronts what is primarily a bedroom community for Halifax, studded with shipyards and light industry.

HISTORY

Founding

The French learned about the area in the early 1700s, when local Micmac Indians escorted the French governor on a tour of what they called Chebuctook, the "Great Long Harbor," and adjacent waterways. But it was the British who saw the site's potential; in 1749 Col. Edward Cornwallis arrived with about 2,500 settlers on 13 ships, and founded Halifax along what is now Barrington Street. The settlement was named for Lord Halifax, then president of Britain's Board of Trade and Plantations.

Early Halifax was a stockaded settlement backed by the Grand Parade, the town green where the militia drilled. The first of four citadels was built on the hilltop. St. Paul's Church, the garrison church at Grand Parade's edge, opened in 1750, making it Canada's first Anglican sanctuary. It was a gift from King George III. More English settlers arrived in 1750 and founded Dartmouth across the harbor. By 1752, the two towns were linked by a ferry system, the oldest saltwater ferry system in North America. Nova Scotia was granted representative government in 1758.

The Royal Military

The completion of Her Majesty's Royal Dockyard in 1760 was the prelude to Louisbourg's absolute destruction the same year. The harbor's defensibility was ensured by a ring of batteries at McNab's Island, North West Arm, Point Pleasant with its Martello Tower, and the forts at George's Island and York Redoubt. In 1783, the settlement got another massive Anglo infusion with the arrival of thousands of Loyalists from America. Among them was John Wentworth, New Hampshire's former governor. He received a baronet title for his opposition to the revolution in the American colonies, and was appointed Nova Scotia's lieutenant governor. Sir John and Lady Wentworth led the Halifax social scene, hobnobbing with Prince Edward (the Maritimes' military commander-in-chief, who would later sire Queen Victoria) and his French paramour Julie St. Laurent (to the chagrin of propriety-minded local society).

Prosperous Times

The seaport thrived in the 1800s. Halifax became a center of higher education in 1802 with the establishment of Saint Mary's University. By 1807, the city's population topped 60,000 and more schools opened. Dalhousie University, modeled after the University of Edinburgh, began instruction in 1818. A proper government setting—the sandstone Colonial Building (now Province House)—opened in 1819. Other academic institutions followed: University of King's College, Nova Scotia College of Art and Design, Technical University of Nova Scotia, Atlantic School of Theology, and Naropa Institute of Canada.

In 1835, a landmark precedent in British law was established in Halifax when Joseph Howe, a newspaper editor and politician, successfully defended himself against a charge of criminal libel. The decision broadened freedom of the press throughout the British empire.

The harborfront—which during the War of 1812 had served as a black-market trade center for Halifax privateers—acquired commercial legitimacy when native Haligonian Samuel Cunard, rich from lumbering, whaling, and banking, turned his interests to shipping. By 1838, Cunard Steamship Co. handled the British and North American Royal Mail, and by 1840, Cunard's four ships provided the first regular transport between the two continents.

The seaport's incorporation in 1841 ushered in a prosperous mercantile era. Granville Street, with its stylish shops, became in its day Atlantic Canada's Fifth Avenue. Halifax as a fashionable town coexisted, however, with the seaport's military preeminence right up through WW II. Brothels and taverns lined Brunswick, Market, and Barrack streets, and the military police swept through the area often, breaking up drunken fistfights and reestablishing order.

Tragedies Strike

The early 1900s brought tragedies. The *Titanic* sank northeast of Nova Scotia in 1913, and many of its victims were buried at Fairview,

Olivett, and Baron de Hirsch cemeteries, with their graves marked by small black headstones.

On the morning of Thursday, 6 December 1917, the harbor was busy with warships transporting troops, munitions, and other supplies bound for the war in Europe. A French ship, the *Mont Blanc,* stuffed to the gunwales with explosives—including 400,000 pounds of TNT —was heading through the Narrows toward the harbormouth when she was struck by a larger vessel, the *Imo,* which was steaming in the opposite direction. The terrified crew of the *Mont Blanc* took immediately to the lifeboats, as their burning ship drifted close to the Halifax shore.

About 20 minutes later, at 9:05 a.m., the *Mont Blanc* cargo blew, instantly killing an estimated 2,000 people, wounding another 9,000, and obliterating some 130 hectares of northern Halifax. So colossal was the explosion that windows were shattered 80 kilometers away, and the shock wave rocked Sydney, Cape Breton,

HALIFAX HARBOUR

Halifax is more than a city, more than a seaport, and more than a provincial capital. Halifax is a harbor with a city attached, as the Haligonians say.

Events in the harbor have shaped Nova Scotia's history. The savvy British military immediately grasped its potential when they first sailed in centuries ago. In fact, Halifax's founding as a settlement in 1749 was incidental to the harbor's development.

From the first, the British used the 26-km-long harbor as a watery warehouse of almost unlimited ship-holding capacity. The ships that defeated the French at Louisbourg in 1758—and ultimately conquered this part of Atlantic Canada—were launched from Halifax Harbour. A few years later, the Royal Navy sped from the harbor to harass the rebellious colonies on the eastern seaboard during the American Revolution. Ships from Halifax ran the blockades on the South's side during the American Civil War. And during WW I and II, the harbor bulged with troop convoys destined for Europe. From a maritime standpoint, Halifax Harbour is a jewel, the world's second-largest natural harbor (after Sydney, Australia). High rocky bluffs notched

with coves rim the wide entrance where the harbor meets the frothy Atlantic. **McNab's Island** is spread across the harbor's mouth, and is so large that it almost clogs the entrance. Many an unwary ship has foundered on the island's shallow, treacherous Eastern Passage coastline.

On the western side of McNab's Island, the harbor is split in two by Halifax's peninsula. The North West Arm, a fjordlike sliver of sea, cuts off one side and wraps around the city's back side. Along its banks are the long lawns of parks, estates, yacht clubs, and several university campuses. The main channel continues inland, shouldered by uptown Halifax on one side and its sister city of Dartmouth on the other.

The Tourist's Harbor

The harbor puts on its best show where the cities almost face each other. White-hulled cruise ships nose into port and dock alongside Halifax's **Point Pleasant Park** at the peninsula's southern tip. Freighters, tugs, tour boats, and sailboats skim the choppy waters, and ferries cut through the sea traffic, scurrying back and forth between the two cities with their loads of commuters and sightseers.

430 kilometers northeast. The barrel of one of the *Mont Blanc*'s cannons was hurled five and a half kilometers, while her half-ton anchor shank landed over three kilometers away in the opposite direction. It was the largest manmade explosion in history, unrivaled before the Hiroshima bombing.

With a massive international relief effort, the city quickly rebuilt. Near the site of the explosion, Fort Needham, overlooking Halifax's side of the Narrows, serves as a memorial to the tragic events.

The Modern Era

By the 1960s, Halifax looked like a hoary victim of the centuries, somewhat the worse for wear. Massive federal, provincial, and private investment, however, restored the harborfront to its early luster, with its warehouses groomed as the handsome **Historic Properties.** During the late 1960s and '70s, an infusion of upscale ho-

tels added sorely needed lodgings.

The city continued to polish its image, as sandblasting renewed the exterior of architectural treasures like Province House. The Art Gallery of Nova Scotia moved from cramped quarters near the Public Archives and settled within the stunningly renovated former Dominion Building. Municipal guidelines sought to control the city's growth. The unobstructed view on George Street between harborfront and the Citadel was secured with a municipal mandate, and the height of the hillside's high-rise buildings was also restricted to preserve the cityscape.

GETTING ORIENTED

The layout of Halifax is easy to grasp. Lower and Upper Water streets and Barrington Street rim the harbor. A series of short streets rise like ramps from there, past the grassy Grand Pa-

---

The scene has a transfixing quality about it. Tourist season unofficially starts and ends when the harborfront Halifax Sheraton hotel sets tables and chairs for alfresco dining on the waterfront promenade. Stiff summer breezes usually accompany lunch, but the view is worth it. Less hardy diners jostle for tables with a harbor view at **Clipper Clay,** the nearby restaurant with its enviable, wide-windowed dining room overlooking the same scene.

Beyond the tourist's realm and the two cities' harborfronts, the spacious harbor compresses itself into **The Narrows.** Two high-flung steel expressways—the **MacDonald** and **MacKay bridges** (75 cents toll)—cross the Narrows at either end. The MacDonald bridge permits pedestrians, and provides an aerial view of the **Maritime Command** and **Her Majesty's Canadian Dockyard** along the Halifax side.

The slender Narrows then opens into 40-square-km **Bedford Basin,** 16 km long and as capacious as a small inland sea. Sailboats cruise its waters now, but the expanse has seen a parade of ships cross its waters over the years—from the white-sailed British warships of centuries ago to the steel-hulled vessels of the Allies during both World Wars.

The Harbor from Varied Angles

Halifax Harbour reveals itself in different views. Its pulse can be probed from one of the ferries or from

harborfront in either city. The approach from the Atlantic can be seen best from the historic fort at **York Redoubt** on Purcells Cove Road. And you get a good view of North West Arm's ritzy estate and university scene from Fleming Park's **Memorial Tower** on the same road. **Seaview Park** beneath the MacKay Bridge overlooks the Narrows where that slender strait meets Bedford Basin.

Harbor Views

On the Dartmouth side, Windmill Road at waterfront parallels the Narrows, and Hwy. 7 overlooks the basin. Inland, **Brightwood Golf Club** sits atop a rise on the otherwise flat plain and provides yet another harbor view.

For an even more spectacular panorama, **Great Eastern Balloon Adventures,** based in the town of Bedford at the basin's inland tip, takes passengers aloft during the early morning for a look at the harbor, cities, and countryside. For details, call (902) 835-3099.

And for the most adventurous vantage point, head to **Atlantic School of Skydiving,** which offers tandem sky dives—you and a guide in a parachute built for two—above the city. For more information, call 423-9866 or 443-0537.

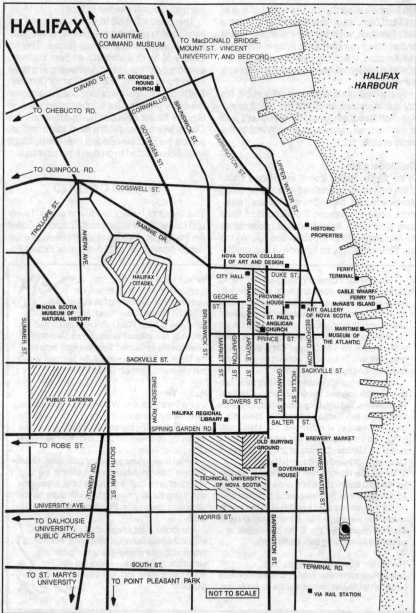

HALIFAX

HALIFAX HARBOUR

TO MARITIME COMMAND MUSEUM

TO MacDONALD BRIDGE, MOUNT ST. VINCENT UNIVERSITY, AND BEDFORD

ST. GEORGE'S ROUND CHURCH

CUNARD ST.

CORNWALLIS

TO CHEBUCTO RD.

BRUNSWICK ST.

GOTTINGEN ST.

BARRINGTON ST.

UPPER WATER ST.

TO QUINPOOL RD.

COGSWELL ST.

TROLLOPE ST.

AHERN AVE.

RAINNIE DR.

HALIFAX CITADEL

HISTORIC PROPERTIES

NOVA SCOTIA COLLEGE OF ART AND DESIGN

CITY HALL

DUKE ST.

FERRY TERMINAL

CABLE WHARF/ FERRY TO McNAB'S ISLAND

NOVA SCOTIA MUSEUM OF NATURAL HISTORY

GRAND PARADE

GEORGE ST.

PROVINCE HOUSE

ART GALLERY OF NOVA SCOTIA

ST. PAUL'S ANGLICAN CHURCH

BEDFORD ROW

MARITIME MUSEUM OF THE ATLANTIC

SUMMER ST.

BRUNSWICK ST.

MARKET ST.

GRAFTON ST.

ARGYLE ST.

PRINCE ST.

GRANVILLE ST.

HOLLIS ST.

SACKVILLE ST.

SACKVILLE ST.

PUBLIC GARDENS

DRESDEN ROW

BLOWERS ST.

HALIFAX REGIONAL LIBRARY

SPRING GARDEN RD.

SALTER ST.

BREWERY MARKET

TO ROBIE ST.

SOUTH PARK ST.

TOWER RD.

OLD BURYING GROUND

GOVERNMENT HOUSE

LOWER WATER ST.

TECHNICAL UNIVERSITY OF NOVA SCOTIA

UNIVERSITY AVE.

TO DALHOUSIE UNIVERSITY, PUBLIC ARCHIVES

ROBIE RD.

MORRIS ST.

BARRINGTON ST.

MOON

SOUTH ST.

TO ST. MARY'S UNIVERSITY

TO POINT PLEASANT PARK

TERMINAL RD.

VIA RAIL STATION

NOT TO SCALE

© MOON PUBLICATIONS, INC.

rade and up Citadel Hill. Around the hill, parks, playgrounds, and gardens cut a great swath of green across the heart of the city. Beyond the hilltop's Citadel, to the south, is the city's academic area, site of Dalhousie University, University of King's College, St. Mary's University, and the Atlantic School of Theology.

From Historic Properties' wharves at the waterfront, sightseeing boats explore the harbor. The splendid Maritime Museum and Art Gallery of Nova Scotia are close by, while the Nova Scotia Museum of Natural History and the Sports Heritage Museum are a few blocks inland. Nova Scotia's finest hotels are set cheek by jowl along the narrow streets. Shopping is more urbane than out in the province; the city's art galleries, bookstores, and crafts shops are especially tempting.

Sightseeing Tours

As of the summer of 1994, the harborfront's former premier attraction, the magnificent schooner *Bluenose II,* no longer offers tours of Halifax Harbour but remains permanently moored in Lunenburg.

Other sightseeing craft, however, have picked up the slack. Murphy's on the Water, Cable Wharf, 1751 Lower Water St., tel. (902) 420-1015, operates several vessels. The sailing season runs from mid- or late May to mid- or late October. The 23-meter sailing ketch *Mar II* makes daily lunch cruises and cocktail cruises from its Nathan Green Square moorage. The *Harbour Queen I* is a 200-passenger paddlewheeler offering a variety of lunch and dinner cruises. The *Haligonian III* takes passengers on narrated, two-hour cruises of the harbor and North West Arm. Murphy's also arranges whalewatching trips, fishing charters, and visits to McNab's Island.

On land, city-sponsored bilingual sightseeing tours are free and depart Grand Parade at City Hall to 30 sites, July-Aug., weekdays at 9:30 a.m. and 2 p.m. The **Pavement Pounders,** all university students, do stints as rickshaw haulers and take sightseers on

guided tours along harborfront streets mid-June through Sept.; a 20-minute ride costs about $6.

Commercial tours with double-decker buses, motorcoaches, and taxis are plentiful.

Double Decker Tours, tel. 420-1155, runs 90-minute tours on red double-decker buses daily, mid-June to mid-October. The tours depart from Historic Properties and from the Halifax Sheraton and take in most of the historic sites of Halifax. Fare is $13 adults, $11 students and seniors, $5.50 ages 5-15.

Scuttlebutt 'N' Bones, Cable Wharf, Boat Tour Centre, tel. 429-9255, rents cassettes ($6, including a Walkman) that guide walkers at their own pace around Halifax. Narration (in English or French), music, sound effects, and great anecdotes make this a fun way to get to know a bit about this historic city. The shop is open May-Oct., daily 9 a.m.-9 p.m.

The **Field Naturalists** is a private nonprofit organization whose thrust, as the name implies, is natural history. The group sponsors periodic local trips tied to local birdwatching, flora and fauna, clam digging, and architecture. Trip capacity is limited, so count yourself among the lucky hikers if you connect with a field outing. For details, check out the trip schedule posted at the Nova Scotia Museum of Natural History, 1747 Summer Street.

SIGHTS

The following sights begin at harborfront, proceed up and over the hilltop, and then spread out from there to include outlying areas. Parking is scarce in Halifax, especially near the waterfront. If you're driving, look for a parking spot a few blocks inland and walk from there.

Historic Properties

Canada's oldest surviving group of waterfront warehouses lies in a three-block expanse on Upper and Lower Water streets known as the Historic Properties. The wooden and stone warehouses, chandleries, and b·ild-

Halifax's historic town clock

BOB RACE

ings once used by shipping interests and privateers have been restored. They now house restaurants, shops, and other sites impressively styled with Victorian and Italianate facades. Sightseeing vessels are based at waterfront.

Maritime Museum of the Atlantic

The seaport's store of nautical memorabilia lies within this sleek, burnished-red museum at 1675 Lower Water St., tel. (902) 424-7490 (for program details, call 424-8793). The museum is one of the crowning achievements of the city's Waterfront Development Project. Exhibits include Queen Victoria's barge, *Titanic* artifacts, Halifax Explosion documentaries, and various historic small craft.

Outside, two historic vessels are tied up at the wharf: the HMCS *Sackville* is the last remaining Canadian WW II convoy escort corvette (open early June to late Sept., Mon.-Sat. 10 a.m.-5 p.m., Sun. 1-5 p.m.); the CSS *Acadia* is Canada's first hydrographic vessel (open June to early Sept., same hours).

The museum is open year-round. From June to mid-Oct., hours are Mon. and Wed.-Sat. 9:30 a.m.-5:30 p.m., Tues. to 8 p.m., Sun. 1-5:30 p.m.; admission $3, ages 5-16 50 cents, family $6.50. The rest of the year, it's open Tues. 9:30 a.m.-8 p.m., Wed.-Sat. 9:30 a.m.-5 p.m. (closed Monday), and admission is free.

Art Gallery of Nova Scotia

Province House

The seat of the provincial government, Province House was completed in 1819. It's the smallest and oldest provincial capitol in the country, and features a fine Georgian exterior and splendid interior. On his visit to modest but dignified Province House in 1842, author Charles Dickens remarked, "It was like looking at Westminster through the wrong end of a telescope . . . a gem of Georgian architecture."

Look closely for interesting details such as the decapitated stone falcons, beheaded by a 19th-century official who said the raptors too closely resembled America's symbolic eagle. The building, at Hollis and Prince streets, tel. (902) 424-8967, is open mid-June to early Sept., Mon.-Fri. 9 a.m.-6 p.m., Sat.-Sun. 9 a.m.-4 p.m.; the rest of the year, Mon.-Fri. 9 a.m.-4:30 p.m. The spring legislative sessions are open to the public.

Art Gallery of Nova Scotia

Atlantic Canada's largest and finest art collection is housed in the refurbished and expanded former Dominion Building at 1741 Hollis St., tel. (902) 424-7542. The building was completed in 1868 of brown sandstone quarried from Pictou and Cumberland counties. Some 2,000 works in oils, watercolors, stone, wood, and other media are exhibited throughout its four floors of spacious galleries. The permanent collections give priority to current and former Nova Scotia residents, and include works by Mary Pratt, Arthur Lismer, Carol Fraser, and Alex Colville. The mezzanine-level regional folk-art collection is a particular delight. The ground-floor Gallery Shop trades in the cream of provincial arts and crafts, and sells books, cards, and gifts.

The museum is open June-Aug., Tues.-Sat. 10 a.m.-5:30 p.m., Thurs. to 9 p.m., Sun. noon-5:30 p.m.; the rest of the year, Tues.-Fri. 10 a.m.-5 p.m., Sat. and Sun. noon-5 p.m. Admission is $2, seniors and children under 12 free.

BOB RACE

Nova Scotia Centre for Craft and Design

Provincial crafts development and innovation are nurtured at this tidy workshop geared to weaving, woodworking, metal, and multimedia production. Its galleries at Barrington and Prince streets, tel. (902) 424-4062, showcase the center's newest creations. The center is open year-round, Tues.-Fri. 9 a.m.-4 p.m., Sat. 10 a.m.-4 p.m.

St. Paul's Anglican Church

This stately, white wooden church was built in 1750, making it the oldest surviving building in

Halifax and the first Anglican church in Canada. The interior is full of memorials to Halifax's early residents. Notice the bit of metal embedded above the door in the north wall; it's a piece of shrapnel hurled from the exploding *Mont Blanc*, two kilometers away. The church is between Barrington and Argyle streets at the edge of the Grand Parade; look for the square belfry topped by an octagonal cupola. It's open year-round.

Old Burying Ground

Designated a national historic site in 1991, this cemetery sits opposite Government House at Barrington St. and Spring Garden Road. Its history goes back to the city's founding. The first customer, so to speak, was interred just one day after the arrival of Cornwallis and the original convoy of English settlers. Also among the thicket of age-darkened, old-fashioned headstones is the 1754 grave of John Connor, the settlement's first ferry captain. The grounds are open June-Sept., daily 9 a.m.-5 p.m.; literature with details on the site and gravestones is available at St. Paul's Anglican Church, Grand Parade.

Halifax Citadel National Historic Site

Halifax's premier landmark is also the most visited national historic site in Canada. The Citadel crowns the hill at the top of George Street, commanding the strategic high ground above the city and harbor, with magnificent views of the entire area. This star-shaped, dressed-granite fortress, the fourth military works built on this site, was completed in 1856. In its heyday, the Citadel represented the pinnacle of defensive military technology, though its design was never tested by an attack.

In summer, students in period uniforms portray soldiers of the 78th Highlanders and the Royal Artillery, demonstrating military drills, powder magazine operation, changing of the sentries, and piping. At the stroke of noon each day, they load and fire a cannon with due military precision and ceremony, a shot heard 'round the city. Most of the fortress is open for exploration; exhibits include a museum, barrack rooms, a powder magazine, and a 50-minute audiovisual presentation on the fort's history.

Guided bilingual tours are available. Friends of the Citadel, a volunteer group, operates a shop and restaurant within the fortress. The Citadel is open mid-June to Labour Day, daily 9 a.m.-6 p.m.; the grounds are open year-round. Admission is $2 adults, $1 ages 5-16, free during the off-season. For more information, call (902) 426-5080.

On the harbor side of Citadel Hill stands the green-domed **Old Town Clock,** itself as much a symbol of Halifax as the Citadel. The four-faced clocktower, which could be seen from every corner of the town, was completed in 1803 by order of the compulsively punctual Prince Edward.

Nova Scotia Museum of Natural History

One of Atlantic Canada's finest natural-history museums, this spacious, modern building holds a trove of dinosaur relics and gem specimens, Micmac artifacts, and plant- and animal-life exhibits. One of the centerpieces is a huge, complete whale skeleton.

A few minutes' walk from the Citadel, the museum is at 1747 Summer St., tel. (902) 424-7353. It's open year-round. From June to mid-Oct., hours are Mon., Tues., and Thurs.-Sat. 9:30 a.m.-5:30 p.m., Wed. to 8 p.m., Sun. 1-5:30 p.m. Admission is $2.25, children 5-16 50 cents. The rest of the year, hours are shorter and admission is free.

St. George's Round Church

Architect William Hughes designed this unusual and charming church, which at once accommodated the overflow of parishioners from the nearby Dutch Church on Brunswick St. and satisfied Prince Edward's penchant for round buildings. The cornerstone was laid in 1800, and the chancel and front porch added later. St. George's is located a few blocks north of the Citadel at Brunswick and Cornwallis streets. The church is normally open year-round by appointment, but damage from a fire in the summer of 1994 may disrupt visits until repairs are made; call (902) 423-4927 to check the status.

Maritime Command Museum

The Georgian-styled Admiralty House, tel. (902) 427-8250, exhibits photos, uniforms, ship models and other artifacts relating to the history of the Canadian Maritime Military Forces. Now a national historic site, the museum is five blocks north of Citadel Hill (a 10-minute walk) at Gottingen at Almon streets. It's open year-round, Mon.-Fri. 9:30 a.m.-8:30 p.m., Sat.-Sun. 1-5 p.m.; Sept. to mid-June, Mon.-Fri. 9:30 a.m.-3:30 p.m. Admission is free.

PARKS

Public Gardens

South across Sackville St. from the Citadel grounds, the Public Gardens are an irresistibly attractive oasis spread over seven hectares in the heart of the city. Bordered by Spring Garden Rd., S. Park St., Summer St., and Sackville St., this is considered one of the loveliest formal gardens in North America and is reminiscent of the handsome parks of Europe, such as Dublin's St. Stephen's Green.

Inside the wrought-iron fence (main entrance at the corner of S. Park St. and Spring Garden Rd.), the setting revels in roses, lilacs, dahlias, and exotic and native trees, as well as lily ponds and fountains, gravel walkways, and benches. The ornate bandstand dates from Queen Victoria's Golden Jubilee, and is the site of free Sunday afternoon concerts in July and August. Also during the summer months, vendors of arts and crafts hawk their wares outside the gardens along Spring Garden Road. The gardens are open May to mid-Oct., 8 a.m.-dusk.

Seaview Park

Halifax's peninsula is bookended by a pair of expansive green spaces. Seaview Park is at the north end, overlooking Bedford Basin from the foot of the A. Murray McKay Bridge. This was the former site of Africville, a community of black Haligonians established in the 1840s but since demolished. George Dixon, holder of three world boxing titles, was born here in 1870.

Point Pleasant Park

This park at the peninsula's southern tip (at the end of Young Ave.) spreads out on 75 hectares of harborfront greenery, with terns, gulls, and ospreys winging overhead. A field of heather (rare hereabouts) was seeded from a Scottish soldier's split mattress in the 1800s. The park's Quarry Point has interesting ice-age striations. Forty km of trails here allow for hiking, jogging, and cross-country skiing in winter. A bit of real-estate trivia: the park is still rented from the British government, on a 999-year lease, for one shilling per year.

Point Pleasant's military significance is evidenced by the Prince of Wales Martello Tower (ordered built by Prince Edward in 1796) and Fort Ogilvie built in 1862, both part of the Halifax's defensive system. The thick-walled round tower, based on those the British were building at the time to repel Napoleon's forces, was the first of its kind to be built in North America. The park is open year-round, 8 a.m.-dusk; the tower is open July to early Sept., daily 10 a.m.-6 p.m.

Sir Sandford Fleming Park

A 38-hectare grassy spread off Purcells Cove Rd., across the North West Arm from Dalhousie University, the park attracts hikers with trails through woodlands and saltwater habitat. It's open year-round, 8 a.m.-dusk. The land was donated by the Scottish-born Fleming, who lived in Halifax from the 1880s until his death in 1915. The square, stone Dingle Tower, erected at Fleming's suggestion in the early 1900s to commemorate the 150th anniversary of Nova Scotia's first legislative assembly, provides a great view; open June-Aug., daily 9 a.m.-5 p.m. The enterprising Sir Sandford, by the way, also gets credit for devising standard time zones, designing Canada's first stamp, and surveying the first trans-Canadian railway.

OUTLYING SIGHTS

York Redoubt National Historic Site

Set on a bluff with impressive views of the harbor entrance, this park is six km south of Halifax off Purcells Cove Road. The setting draws visitors with hiking paths and picnic tables near the strategic fortifications, which were used from 1793 through WW II. The site, tel. (902) 426-5080, is open year-round, 10 a.m.-dusk, and it is staffed mid-June to early Sept., daily 10 a.m.-6 p.m.

McNab's Island

The five-km-long wooded island at Halifax Harbour's entrance was first fortified as part of the early defensive ring created by the British. Toward the southern end of the island, Fort McNab, now a national historic site, dates to 1888. It was Halifax's first battery designed to hold breech-loading guns. The island has been popular with day-visitors since the 1870s, when several "pleasure grounds" were established. Activities today on the bucolic parcel include exploring the fort ruins, hiking, birdwatching (look for ospreys), and swimming.

The park's open to visitors weekends late May to mid-June, then daily to early September. Access to the island is via McNab's Island Ferry, George St. at Cable Wharf, tel. (902) 422-9523 or 425-3602; $8 round-trip.

ACCOMMODATIONS

Halifax has the province's widest lodgings variety, with 1,800 rooms in hotels and guest houses and another 1,200 motel rooms. Location largely determines cost. The choice properties are at harborfront, and prices decrease from there up the hillside. A plentiful supply of low-cost lodgings at local universities offsets the city's otherwise high-priced hotels. The budget-priced hostel, YWCA, YMCA, and university settings are informal—good places for meeting other travelers.

Budget Overnights
The **Halifax Heritage House Hostel,** 1253 Barrington St., tel. (902) 422-3863, has standard hostel lodgings (50 beds total) in dorm rooms at $12.75 for members, $15.75 for nonmembers. Facilities include a kitchen, laundry room, television in the common room, and a storeroom for bikes. Some good restaurants are in the neighborhood, and it's just a 15-minute stroll to the Citadel or historic harborfront.

Next door, the **YWCA,** 1239 Barrington St., tel. 423-6162, has rooms for women ($30 for a shared room or $40 for a private room). Amenities include a kitchen, exercise equipment, and sauna. The **YMCA,** at 1565 S. Park St., tel. 423-9622, charges $28 s, $39 d, and also has exercise equipment available.

For an academic setting and a prime hillside location, check out **Technical University of Nova Scotia,** 5217 Morris St., tel. 420-7780, with double rooms ($19) available mid-April through August.

Other university lodgings, available mid- to late May through mid- to late Aug., include: **Saint Mary's University,** 923 Robie St., tel. 420-5486, $21-40; **Dalhousie University Residences,** tel. 494-8840, with single rooms at Howe and Shirriff halls, $27-40 with a full breakfast and access to other meals, free parking; and **Mount Saint Vincent University,** Bedford Hwy. on the outskirts of Halifax, tel. 443-4450 ext. 364 or 351, $35 for a room with twin beds.

B&Bs and Inns
Two reasonably priced B&Bs are on Robie St. not far from the Public Gardens. **Virginia Kinfolks,** 1722 Robie, tel. (902) 423-6687 or (800) 668-7829, has three rooms ($35-50, with full breakfast) and is open year-round. Small children are discouraged. The **Fountain View Guest House,** 2138 Robie St., tel. 422-4169, has seven rooms with shared bath ($24-35), with a light breakfast on request.

Oscar Wilde and P.T. Barnum both slept (not together) at the 1876 **Waverley Inn,** at 1266 Barrington St., tel. 423-9346. Rates for the 32 rooms ($75-80) include breakfast and an evening snack. There's a sundeck for sunning and a dining room for dining; the latter is open 4-11 p.m.

A block away, the plush **Halliburton House Inn,** 5184 Morris St., tel. 420-0658, is a beautiful heritage property, with 30 rooms ($90-100, suites $100-125) with bath; continental breakfast is complimentary, and there's an outdoor garden courtyard.

North of Citadel Hill, the **King Edward Inn,** 2400 Agricola at West streets, tel. 422-3266, has some nonsmoking rooms among its 44 rooms and suites ($65-89 with breakfast). Some suites are equipped with jacuzzis.

Fresh Start Bed and Breakfast, 2720 Gottingen St., tel. 453-6616, faces the Maritime Command Museum and has five nonsmoking rooms ($45-70 with full breakfast) and laundry service.

In Dartmouth, **Caroline's Bed and Breakfast,** 134 Victoria Rd., tel. 469-4665, has a convenient location close to the town center, Dartmouth Common, and the cross-harbor ferry. The three rooms ($25-35, with continental breakfast) are available April-November.

Hotels

Cambridge Suites at 1583 Brunswick St., tel. (902) 420-0555, fax (902) 420-9379, has 50 suites ($75-105), a morning dining room, whirlpool and sauna, laundry facilities, and guest parking within a handsome brick structure.

The **Delta Barrington** at 1875 Barrington St., tel. 429-7410, shares space with Barrington Place Mall in the historic area and has 201 impressively furnished rooms from $89. Its McNab's Restaurant offers formal dining, and the hotel also has a bistro, health club with pool, and shopping arcade. The first-floor rooms are for nonsmokers.

The **Halifax Hilton** at 1181 Hollis St., tel. 423-7231 or (800) 445-8667, adjacent to the VIA Rail terminal, has been lushly and extensively refurbished from top to bottom. It has 307 rooms ($99-166), a restaurant, fitness center with an indoor pool, tennis court, and shopping arcade. Historic Properties and sightseeing on the hillside are a quick five-minute jaunt away.

Canadian Pacific Chateau Halifax at 1990 Barrington St., tel. 425-6700 or (800) 441-1414, fax 425-6214, was the first of the city's grande dame hotels and is still a lodging kingpin. Its 300 rooms ($120-155) are outfitted with lavish carpeting and comfortable furniture. The Bluenose Room offers Sunday brunch, the Crown Room is for formal dining. The hotel also has a health club with pool, and shops. The highest-priced rooms feature harbor views.

The **Sheraton Halifax,** 1919 Upper Water St., tel. 421-1700, was designed to resemble the garrison that once occupied the waterfront. The impressive stone hotel is graced with a pitched copper-covered roof and dormer windows that peer across Historic Properties and Halifax Harbour. Its 356 rooms ($165-185) mirror each other in space and furnishing. Ask for a room facing the harbor for incredible views.

The hotel's dining room sets the city's pace for hotel dining. Other facilities include cafes, lounges, a health club with indoor pool, and a shopping arcade. The hotel's second-floor bar is the place to see and be seen, especially early Friday evening as the weekend merriment commences—it's a nice place to meet people.

Keddy's Halifax Hotel, 20 St. Margarets Bay Rd. on the edge of Halifax, tel. 477-5611, matches good value with 135 spacious rooms and suites ($52-80), a dining room, lounge, outside decks, an indoor pool, whirlpool, sauna, fitness center, and a small lake for swimming.

FOOD

Haligonians expect and get good cooking, and lots of it. The town is crowded with restaurants, cafes, pubs, and the province's widest selection of ethnic restaurants.

Dinner Houses

McKelvie's, at 1680 Lower Water St., tel. (902) 421-6161, does a commendable job with every kind of seafood. Try the Crunchy Halibut or Haddock—it's rolled in crushed cereal and almonds, fried, and served with creamy barbecue sauce. Entrees range $10-19. The restaurant is in a refurbished historic former firehouse overlooking Historic Properties.

Clipper Cay at Historic Properties' waterfront, tel. 423-6818, mixes seafood with succulent meat dishes ($10-20) in a sublime setting. Its blueberry grunt (cobbler) is among the best desserts in the province.

Five Fishermen, 1740 Argyle St., tel. 422-4421, occupies one of Halifax's oldest buildings —it was built in 1817, and once used by famed governess Anna Leonowens for her Victorian School of Art and Design. The restaurant is popular with seafood-loving Haligonians for its 68-dish menu ($15-20), which includes swordfish, Louisiana shrimp, Malpeque oysters, and Digby scallops, as well as beef and chicken. All entrees come with complimentary all-you-can-eat mussels, steamed clams, and salad from the salad bar.

O'Carroll's at 1860 Upper Water St., tel. 423-4405, features culinary specialties like steak and kidney pie, duck à l'orange, lobster thermidor, and roast beef. Entrees are $16-19 (lobster costs $10 more). It's closed Sunday.

The **Silver Spoon Restaurant,** 1813 Granville St., tel. 429-6617, whose local fame originated with its outrageously rich and gorgeous desserts, outgrew its Historic Properties setting and does a sizable business at its present location. The cuisine is classic continental, melded with provincial additions and finished with some of the city's best flans and flaky pies. Entrees range $16-21.

Upper Deck Dining Room, Historic Properties, tel. 422-1289, is the upstairs dining room at Privateers Warehouse. The setting is soothingly refined, and the continental menu ($17-26) balances seafood and red meats.

Fat Frank's Snaffles at 5170 Duke St., tel. 423-6633 (reservations are required), is Frank Metzger's newest culinary sensation. Despite the middle-brow name, its upscale casual setting is the backdrop to exquisite dining, and Craig Claibourne of the *New York Times* called it "one of the most elegant restaurants in North America." The full dinner ($30) offers a choice of entrees such as tiger shrimp over pasta, braised rabbit, or veal sweetbreads.

Ryan Duffy's, upstairs at Dresden Row, 5640 Spring Garden Rd. tel. 421-1116, has earned an admirable dining reputation with dishes like scallops in Pernod sauce. Its local fame rests on its prime beef—cut, weighed, and charbroiled or sizzled on hot rocks, $2.25 to $3.50 per ounce. Other entrees range $15-24.

Lighter Meals

Alfredo, Weinstein and Ho, 1739 Grafton St. next to the World Trade and Metro Centre, tel. (902) 421-1977, pleases most everyone with lunch specials at $4 ($5 on weekends) and pizza, cheesecakes, and tortes. Where else can you find Italian, Jewish, and Chinese under one roof? **Le Bistro,** 1333 S. Park St., tel. 423-8428, offers informal French cuisine and a weekend guitarist. It has an open-air patio, and live entertainment Thurs.-Sun. evenings.

The **Granite Brewery,** 1222 Barrington St., tel. 423-5660, is in a historic building and has a lively pub ambience. Its own excellent beers are brewed on-site, and complement lunch specials and a Saturday brunch of steak and eggs ($7) or creamed smoked fish ($5).

The **Lower Deck,** tel. 425-1501, and **Middle Deck,** tel. 425-1500, in the Historic Properties' Privateers Warehouse, both take a comfortable approach to casual dining. The Lower Deck's chili is heartily spiced, burgers are oversized, and the fried seafood is ample and tasty—no one goes away hungry. The Middle Deck specializes in pasta dishes and traditional cuisine.

My Apartment at 1740 Argyle St., tel. 422-5453, has great lunch specials like the $7 haddock or sole. Saturday brunch ($7 or less) is served from 11 a.m.-3 p.m.; Sun. brunch is noon to 3 p.m. Both brunches include a cocktail. **Nemo's,** 1865 Hollis St., tel. 425-6783, offers seafood specialties like crab cakes and grilled scallops, plus fresh and continental dishes. It's open Tues.-Sat. for lunch and dinner; early bird specials 4-6 p.m.

Sweet Basil Bistro, in the Historic Properties, 1866 Upper Water St., tel. 425-2133, serves homemade hot and cold pasta, salads, and great desserts. This is a nonsmoking establishment, as is the **Scanway Cafe,** at 1569 Dresden Row off Spring Garden Rd. in the building behind Nemo's, tel. 422-3733. Scanway's features tasty salads, open-faced sandwiches, seafood, pepper steak, and chicken.

Vegetarian and Ethnic

Some of the best vegetarian fare in town is at **Satisfaction Feast,** 1581 Grafton St., where curry enlivens the casseroles, and carrot juice is the favorite beverage. **Mrs. Murphy's Kitchen,** 5670 Spring Garden Rd., gives a choice of dishes like Mom used to make, or strictly vegetarian tofu, veggies, and brown rice dishes at about $6.

Niji Japanese Restaurant, in the Maritime Mall at 1505 Barrington St., tel. (902) 422-1576, offers intimate, traditional Japanese-style dining, as well as a Western-style dining room and a sushi bar. **Café Cap St. Jacques,** just off Barrington at 5190 Blowers St., tel. 422-9131, prepares authentic hot-and-spicy Vietnamese cuisine; open for lunch and dinner daily.

At 5677 Benton Place, off Spring Garden Rd., **Curry Village,** tel. 429-5010, serves chicken tandoor, biryanis, lamb vindaloo, and other Indian dishes, including vegetarian options. It's open Mon.-Sat. for lunch, daily for dinner. **Chicken Tandoor,** 1264 Barrington St., tel. 423-7725, specializes in North Indian cuisine; reservations recommended on weekends.

Try the **Hungry Hungarian,** 5215 Blowers St., tel. 423-4364, for authentic goulashes and other Eastern European fare, as well as seafood and sandwiches.

Supermarkets

IGA is the largest food chain and has nine supermarkets in Metro Halifax, all of them open Mon.-Tues., Sat. 8 a.m.-6 p.m., Wed.-Fri. to 9:30 p.m. Small groceries like the **Green Gables Food Stores** are everywhere.

Cousins' Corner Store, 6516 Chebucto Rd., is among the most interesting smaller places and carries Greek, Italian, and Lebanese foods. Its deli has picnic ingredients. The lower level at the **Spring Garden Place Mall,** Spring Garden Rd., offers more appetizing ingredients for quick meals and picnics at various bakery, butcher, dairy, and dessert shops.

ENTERTAINMENT AND EVENTS

Cinemas

Cosmopolite Haligonians favor avant-garde, foreign, and documentary flicks. **Wormwood's Dog and Monkey Cinema** touches all bases at 2015 Gottingen St., tel. (902) 422-3700; its film lineup is usually an impeccable sampling of new and classic European and art films. Dalhousie University's **Rebecca Cohn Auditorium,** 6101 University Ave., tel. 494-2646, is another venue for similar film fare.

Recently released mainstream movies are shown at numerous multiple-screen theaters: the **Famous Players Cinemas,** in Park Lane Mall, 5657 Spring Garden Rd., tel. 423-5866; **Empire 6 Dartmouth Cinemas,** Superstore Mall, Dartmouth, tel. 422-2022; **Oxford Theatre,** 6408 Quinpool Rd. at Oxford, tel. 423-7488.

Theater and Shows

Haligonians have a sweet and sometimes bittersweet Canadian sense of humor (somewhat like the British), and local theater revels in their brand of fun. A $30 admission will get you into dinner-theater musical productions at **Grafton Street Theatre,** 1741 Grafton St., tel. (902) 425-1961, or **Historic Feast Company,** Simon's Warehouse at Historic Properties, which offers merriment centered on historic times.

At the **Neptune Theatre,** 5216 Sackville St., private companies like Legends of Broadway take to the boards during summer with musicals and Gilbert and Sullivan shows. The regular theater season runs Sept.-May. For schedule and ticket prices, call the theater at 429-7070. The **Metro Centre** at 5284 Duke St. gets the mammoth shows and concerts like LaToya Jackson or the International Gathering of the Clans.

The Night Scene

Walk the hillside on Friday and Saturday evenings to experience Atlantic Canada's best and most concentrated music, entertainment, and drinking scene.

Varied and notable entertainment is staged at the **Flamingo Cafe,** 1505 Barrington at Salter St., tel. (902) 420-1051, where a typical week's bill goes from stand-up comedy on Saturday afternoon to Mon.-Sat. blues, reggae, jazz, and folk music. A $5-8 cover is usually charged.

Your Father's Moustache, 5686 Spring Garden Rd., tel. 423-6766, puts on excellent live, usually local, music most evenings. On Saturday, they host their popular Blues Matinee. A few doors down, the **Thirsty Duck,** 5472 Spring Garden Rd., tel. 422-1548, doesn't usually have entertainment but it's a popular hangout nonetheless. The open, rooftop deck is a great spot for whiling away an afternoon, sipping draft beer and tasty Caesars (a Bloody Mary made with clam juice—better than it sounds).

For a taste of what has got the mavens of pop, rock, and grunge calling Halifax "the new Seattle," check out the buzz at the **Double Deuce Roadhouse,** Hollis St. near Salter, tel. 422-4033. This is the place to catch bands like the Hopping Penguins, Weasel-Faced Judge, and Nine Cats in a Bag before they're doing stadiums and sardonic Carpenters covers on MTV. The music is loud (but not too), the beer is cold, and the dance floor intimate. There's usually a modest cover.

Steamy jazz is the fare at the **Silver Bullet,** 1554 Hollis St.; **La Cave,** 5244 Blowers St., tel. 429-3551; and **Bistro Too,** 1770 Market Street. **Maxwell's Plum Tavern,** 1600 Grafton St., tel. 423-8465, has an excellent selection of imported draft beers (notably, Beamish Irish Stout, John Courage, and Newcastle Brown Ale) and single-malt scotches. That alone may be reason enough to visit there, but it's also a good venue for straight-ahead jazz, including Sunday afternoon jam sessions.

The local hipoisie mix and dance at the shared quarters of popular **My Apartment** and **Lawrence of Oregano,** 1726 Argyle St., where live bands play six nights a week. **Cheers,** 1743 Grafton St., also has live bands. Expect to pay about a $3 cover.

The college crowd and yuppies go to dance and be seen at **Brandy's,** 1712 Market St., tel. 425-5303; and **Scoundrel's,** 1786 Granville St., tel. 425-5249. The spacious **New Palace Cabaret,** 1721 Brunswick St., tel. 429-5959, caters to singles; live, throbbing rock continues until 3 a.m.

Quieter evenings can be had along the harborfront. A drink or two starting at 6 p.m. at Sheraton Halifax's **Harbourfront Bar** starts the Halignonian weekend. **O'Carroll's** restaurant at Water and Duke streets has Saturday afternoon and weekday sing-alongs from 5 p.m., followed by Cape Breton, Newfoundland, and Irish folk music. The **Middle Deck** bills jazz, rock, and blues bands until 1:30 a.m. at Historic Properties's Privateers Warehouse. **Granite Brewery,** 1222 Barrington St., is a favorite stop for its English-style beers, and **Le Bistro,** 1333 S. Park St., has a varied music format Thurs.-Sunday.

Rumours, Halifax's gay and lesbian social club, is at 2112 Gottingen St., tel. 423-6814. It's open till the wee hours, with music leaning to the latest dance mix. There's a cover charge for nonmembers.

Meeting the Haligonians

Haligonians are a sociable bunch, especially after the long winter finally lets go. One of the most popular pastimes seems to be simple, old-fashioned strolling, stopping for ice cream, chatting with friends. On summer evenings along the Grand Parade, and by the waterfront, *everyone* is out and about—couples, friends, families with kids and prams, gray-haired grannies and grandpas.

Locals congregate spring to autumn days and evenings on the steps of—yes, it's true—the **Halifax Regional Library** on Spring Garden Road. There you'll find much earnest conversation and acoustic guitars in abudance. Food vans park alongside to cater to the hungry bohemians.

Service clubs abound in the city. **Rotary** meets Friday at the Sheraton Halifax. Other organizations are the **Lions, Knights of Columbus, Oddfellows,** and varied **Masonic Lodges.** The **YWCA,** 1239 Barrington St., tel. (902) 423-6162, serves as a mixer for local women and also hosts varied short-term clinics like power walking and weight training.

Fédération Acadienne de la Nouvelle-Écosse, 1106 S. Park St., tel. 421-1772, functions as a political lobby for Nova Scotian Acadians. It is tuned also to business and cultural events and can refer a visitor to local contacts; open Mon.-Fri. 9 a.m.-4 p.m.

Sports Bars

Crowds pack the bars and lounges for the big sports events. Check out: Delta Barrington's **Traders Lounge,** 1875 Barrington St.; **Bart Freeman's Little New York,** 6092 Quinpool Rd.; and the **Graduate,** 1565 Argyle St., open Mon.-Sat. 10 a.m.-1 a.m. with food served until 9 or 10 p.m.

Events

Nothing reflects Halifax's long military heritage better than the **Nova Scotia International Tattoo,** which presents a week of performances in late June or early July. A Nova Scotian "tattoo" translates as an outdoor military exercise given by troops as entertainment. Here it involves competitions, military bands, dancers, gymnasts, and choirs. Tickets (under $20) may be ordered by mail as early as December; by April, they're available by telephone from Metro Centre Box Office, 5284 Duke St., Halifax, NS B3J 3L2, tel. (902) 451-1221; open Mon.-Sat. 9 a.m.-5 p.m.

Noon concerts bring crowds to the Grand Parade July-Aug., and to the Public Gardens July-September. During July, the Mayor of Halifax hosts **Weekday Tea** for visitors at City Hall at the Grand Parade's edge, Mon.-Fri. 2-3 p.m. Late July's nine-day **Atlantic Jazz Festival** rivals Montreal's version, but on a smaller scale. The event includes concerts in various locations: the main stage is at the Dalhousie Arts Centre; free concerts take place at the Sackville Landing at the waterfront; and other performances and workshops are held in clubs and restaurants. Call the Atlantic Jazz hotline at 492-2225 or (800) 565-5277 for details.

The city celebrates **Natal Day** for four days in early August, with live music, entertainment, parades, and fireworks. The **Buskers** arrive for 10 days in mid-August, and you'll find street performers everywhere on the hillside, especially throughout Historic Properties. Summer finishes with the five-day **Atlantic Fringe Theatre Festival.**

Numerous other summertime one-day festivals and family clan gatherings are scheduled; *Nova Scotia Travel Guide* lists them all.

RECREATION

For jogging, tennis, baseball, Frisbee, or just about anything else, go to the adjacent Central Common and Halifax Commons—spacious, grassy parks off Cogswell St. just northwest of Citadel Hill.

Workouts

A **YMCA** is centrally located in Halifax at 1565 S. Park St., tel. (902) 423-9622; another is in Dartmouth at Brookdale Court, tel. 469-5021 (call for directions). The Halifax **YWCA** is at 1239 Barrington St., tel. 423-6162.

Saint Mary's University's **Tower Fitness and Recreation Facility,** 920 Tower Rd., tel. 420-5555, is the city's preeminent fitness center, and facilities are augmented with tennis and squash courts. A day-use pass costs $6. It's open weekdays 7 a.m.-10:30 p.m., weekends 8 a.m.-5:30 p.m.

Many of the city's hotels have splendid health-club facilities. **Halifax Sheraton** charges $5 for a day-use pass, while $8 provides access to the facilities at **Canadian Pacific Chateau Halifax.**

Water Sports

Municipal pools are open to visitors ($3) at **Centennial Pool,** 1970 Gottingen St.; **Northcliffe Pool,** 111 Clayton Park Dr.; and **Needham Pool,** 3372 Devonshire Street. The pools are open Mon. and Wed.-Fri. for noontime adult dips, and Tues. and Sat. 4-6 p.m.

The City of Halifax Recreation Department's **Saint Mary's Boat Club,** tel. (902) 421-6557, offers canoe rentals and lessons on the North-

west Arm, the harbor channel behind central Halifax. Dartmouth's **Recreation Department** also sponsors canoeing on Lakes Banook and Micmac at Graham Grove Park, near the town center off Prince Albert Road.

Also on Lake Banook in Dartmouth, the **Freestyle Windsurfing Club,** tel. 465-3800, rents **sailboards** and offers lessons.

The coastal waters off Nova Scotia are well known among divers for numerous shipwrecks, and local dive shops do a brisk business. A dozen shops rent equipment in Metro Halifax, and most run charters. **Northern Shore Diving Centre,** 1549 Lower Water St., tel. 429-TANK, operates April to late September charters ($30 pp) to two wreck sites and rents equipment ($30).

Cycling

Halifax and vicinity, with its many lakes and harborside coves, is a great area for exploring by bike. Be careful where you park, and be sure to use a lock—there's a lively trade in stolen bicycles here. In summer, **Velo Halifax** organizes several rides a week, ranging from short local spins to multiday outings, and they welcome guest riders. Pick up their schedule at any local bike shop or tourism office.

Pedal and Sea, 1253 Barrington St., tel. (902) 492-0116, next door to the youth hostel, rents top-quality mountain bikes at $6 an hour, $13 a half day, $22 a full day, and $35 a day for a tandem. Hostel members get a discount. The shop is open daily 9 a.m.-6 p.m. The bikes get rented out fast, so it's smart to get there early or make arrangements in advance.

Other sources for rentals, repairs, equipment, and advice are **Cyclesmith,** 6112 Quinpool Rd., tel. 425-1756; the **Trail Shop,** 6210 Quinpool Rd., tel. 423-8736; and **Cyclepath,** 5240 Blowers St., tel. 423-0473.

Golf

Half a dozen public **golf courses** lie within just a 15-km radius of Halifax and Dartmouth. For starters, there's the **Briarwood Golf Club** south of Halifax at 647 1/2 Herring Cove Rd., tel. (902) 477-4677. In Bedford, the **Pin-Hi Golf Course,** tel. 835-2307, is on Hammonds Plains Rd., just west of Hwy. 102, the highway to the airport.

Winter Sports

In winter, walking paths become **cross-country ski trails** at Point Pleasant Park, Sir Sandford Fleming Park, and Hemlock Ravine (north of Halifax). For outdoor **ice-skating** conditions in Dartmouth, call (902) 454-2317. Dartmouth maintains groomed surfaces at Lake Charles. In Halifax, several lakes are great for skating; call the Recreation Department at 421-6464 to check conditions.

SHOPPING

Halifax has numerous shopping malls on Spring Garden Rd. and elsewhere on the hillside; open Mon.-Wed. and Sat. 9:30 a.m.-5:30 p.m., Thurs.-Fri. to 9 p.m. **Eaton's,** the largest department store, is in the Halifax Shopping Centre on Mumford Road.

Arts and Crafts

The city's art galleries are superb. At 1674 Hollis St., **Manuge Galleries** is almost as old as the city itself and exhibits the finest in old prints, lithographs, and watercolors. The newest fine arts trends are on exhibit at Nova Scotia College of Art and Design's **Anna Leonowens Gallery,** 1891 Granville St.; open Tues.-Fri. 11 a.m.-5 p.m., Sat. noon-5 p.m. (The college's Granville Street facade may appear familiar—the college uses a line drawing of the historic storefront row in its literature and catalogs.)

Hundreds of clan fabrics and tartans in kilts, skirts, vests, ties, and other apparel are stocked at **Celtic Traditions,** 1533 Barrington St., and **Plaid Place,** 1903 Barrington Street.

If you're in pursuit of handmade crafts in the capital, check out **La Maison Bleue** with knitted apparel, batiks, jewelry, and home furnishings at Park Lane Mall, Spring Garden Road. Upscale (and expensive) quilted apparel by Vicki Lynn Bardon, whose **Suttles and Seawinds** line is sold throughout Atlantic Canada, is sold in a shop at Sheraton Halifax shopping arcade.

The nearby **Harbour Loft,** 1781 Lower Water St., stocks handmade sweaters, while **Stornoway Gifts** on Granville St. has a wide line of crafts enhanced with hooking from Chéticamp and stained glass from Antigonish. The capital's definitive crafts source is **Jennifer's of Nova Scotia,** 5635 Spring Garden Rd., an outlet for 120 provincial producers.

The **Halifax City Market** is another crafts source, and crafts vendors are part of the scene at the refurbished Brewery (once the home of Alexander Keith's historic brewery) on Lower Water St.; open year-round, Sat. 7 a.m.-3 p.m.

Bookstores

The **Nova Scotia Government Bookstore,** 1700 Granville St., tel. (902) 424-7580, has a trove of titles covering everything from provincial heritage to natural history, hiking, food, and other subjects.

The **Book Room,** 1664 Granville St., tel. 423-8271, is the oldest trade bookstore in Canada, founded in 1839. In addition to a broad general selection, this excellent shop specializes in books on Nova Scotia and Canadiana, Native studies, and genealogy. Upstairs in the Spring Garden Place Mall, **Frog Hollow Book,** 5640 Spring Garden Rd., tel. 429-3318, is a comfortable store which occasionally hosts visiting literati.

Used-book shops tend to specialize. **Nautica Books,** 1579 Dresden Row, deals in literature related to seafaring topics; some volumes are rare editions. For used books and rare editions, try **Schooner Books,** 5378 Inglis St.; **Back Pages,** 1526 Queen St., tel. 423-4750; and **Attic Owl Bookshop,** 5802 South St., tel. 422-2433.

Photography

Fast-processing photography shops are plentiful. **Camera Repair Centre** at 2342 Hunter off Cunard streets, tel. (902) 423-6450, handles repairs. It's open Mon.-Fri. 9 a.m.-5 p.m. Reliable equipment and hard-to-find film speeds are stocked at **Atlantic Photo Supply,** 5505 Spring Garden Rd., tel. 423-8820 or 423-6724, and **Carsand-Mosher Photographic,** 1559 Barrington (at Blowers Street).

INFORMATION AND SERVICES

Visitor Information

Tourism Halifax at Duke and Barrington streets, tel. (902) 421-8736, stocks literature and answers questions at their Old City Hall main office.

Mailing address is P.O. Box 1749, Halifax, NS B3J 3A5. They're open year-round, Mon.-Fri. 11 a.m.-4:30 p.m.; during the June-early Sept. tourist season, they're open Mon.-Wed. 8:30 a.m.-6 p.m., Thurs.-Sat. to 8 p.m. A summertime branch is at Bell Rd. and Sackville St., same hours, tel. 421-2772. They also send requested information to visitors in the city via bike messenger.

Nova Scotia Tourist Information Centres promote Halifax as part of provincial coverage. The tourist office in the city is in the Historic Properties at the Old Red Store, tel. 424-4247; open year-round weekdays 8:30 a.m.-4:30 p.m. and daily mid-June to mid-Sept. until 8 p.m. The administrative office at 1601 Water St., tel. 424-5000, also stocks literature; open Mon.-Fri. 8:30 a.m.-4:30 p.m.

The **Dartmouth Tourist Information Centre** is a short walk uphill from the ferry terminal, at 100 Wyse Rd., tel. 466-5352; open seasonally. For information from the Dartmouth Visitor and Convention Bureau, call 466-2875.

Numerous free tourist magazines circulate, such as *Metro Guide, Halifax Visitors' Guide,* and *Where: Halifax/Dartmouth.* Pick them up at the tourist offices.

Maps and Media
Map sources are plentiful. **Land Registration and Information Service,** 1660 Hollis St., sixth floor, tel. (902) 424-2735, sells topographic maps of provincial regions ($8); it's open weekdays 8:30 a.m.-4:15 p.m. **Trail Shop** is another source at 6210 Quinpool Rd., tel. 423-4438, open Mon.-Wed. 9 a.m.-5 p.m., Thurs.-Fri. to 9 p.m. **Binnacle** at 5240 Bloor St., tel. 423-6464, sells nautical maps. Another prime map source is the provincial Novia Scotia Government Bookstore (see "Bookstores," above).

The daily *Halifax Herald* circulates throughout the province. The monthly *'FAX* magazine, distributed free, is a lively, opinionated tabloid with reviews, performance listings, etc. It's a very handy resource for finding out what's happening where.

Libraries
Halifax City Regional Library is at 5382 Spring Garden Rd., tel. (902) 421-6676; open Tues.-Fri. 10 a.m.-9 p.m., Sat. to 6 p.m., Sun. 2-5 p.m. A branch library is at 2285 Gottingen St., same hours.

Environmental Organizations
Haligonians are well informed and ready to pick-et or protest to express their concerns. Among the numerous environmental groups, **Ecology Action Centre,** 3115 Veith St., Halifax, NS B3K 3G9, tel. (902) 454-7828, is a leader in education, advocacy, and action. Current issues of controversy include the siting of a solid-waste incinerator in Metro Halifax and the feasibility of a coal-burning power station on Cape Breton.

Nova Scotia Wildlife Federation, P.O. Box 654, Halifax, NS B3J 2T3, tel. 423-6793, is another private group with major clout; its concerns are wildlife habitat and the environment.

Classes
Nova Scotia College of Art and Design sponsors intensive five-day classes (about $135) in watercolors, sculpture, and photography during July and August; for details, call (902) 422-7381 or write to Continuing Education, 1867 Granville St., Halifax, NS B3J 3J6.

FOREIGN CONSULATES

Austria; 1718 Argyle St., Ste. 710, tel. 429-8200

Belgium; Halterm Container Pier, tel. 423-6323

Germany; 1809 Barrington St., Ste. 708, tel. 420-1599

Great Britain; 1459 Hollis St., tel. 422-0313

Italy; 1574 Argyle St., tel. 492-3934

Japan; 1475 Hollis St., 3rd Fl., tel. 429-6530

The Netherlands; 6080 Young St., Ste. 315, tel. 455-1731

Norway; 11 Morris Dr., Dartmouth, tel. 468-1330

Sweden; Volvo Canada Ltd., 115 Chain Lake Dr., tel. 450-5252

U.S.; Cogswell Tower, 2000 Barrington St., tel. 429-2480

Dalhousie University's **Henson College** has summer mini-immersion classes in French; for information, call (902) 424-6429, fax (902) 494-7048, or write to Continuing Studies, 6100 University Ave., Halifax, NS B3H 3J5.

Health and Safety
Hospitals include **Victoria General Hospital,** 1278 Tower Rd., tel. (902) 428-2110; **Camp Hill Hospital,** 1763 Robie St., tel. 420-2222; and **Izaak Walton Killam Hospital for Children,** 5850 University Ave., tel. 428-8111.

Municipal **police** are assigned to Halifax and Dartmouth; in emergencies, dial 4105 (yes, just four digits), and for nonemergency business call 421-6840. The **RCMP** can be reached by calling 426-3611.

Banks
As Atlantic Canada's banking center, Halifax has banks by the dozens. Shopping around for the best exchange rate is worth it. **Bank of Nova Scotia** has nine city branches and does not charge to convert foreign currency to Canadian dollars. The fee for cashing traveler's checks is $2, so it pays to convert several checks at one time. The bank is open Mon., Tues., Wed., and Sat. 10 a.m.-3 p.m., Thurs. and Fri. to 8 p.m.

Hongkong Bank of Canada likewise charges no transaction fee. Its three branches are open weekdays, 9 a.m.-4:30 p.m. Other banks in the downtown core include **Bank of Montreal, Barclays of Canada, Canadian Imperial Bank of Commerce, National Bank of Canada, Royal Bank,** and **Toronto Dominion Bank.**

Hotel desks also exchange currency, but rates are more favorable at the banks.

Post Offices
The city has three post offices, open Mon.-Fri. 8 a.m.-5 p.m. The General Post Office is at 1713 Bedford Row, tel. 426-2291; branches are at 6179 Almon St. and 7182 Quinpool Road. Retail postal outlets are at the Scotia Square mall and at IGA food stores; weekday hours vary, but the outlets are open Sat. 8 a.m.-6 p.m.

Communications
Save your overseas phone calls for evening. Calls to the U.S. are discounted 60% between 11 p.m. and 8 a.m.; a 35% discount extends Mon.-Sat. from 6 p.m. to 11 p.m., and all day Sunday. Phoning London, England, will cost about $1.30 minute, daily 6 p.m.-9 a.m.; $1.50 1-6 p.m., and $1.85 9 a.m.-1 p.m.

Laundries and Lockers
Coin-operated laundries are located beyond Halifax's hillside. **Agricola Laundromat,** at 2454 Agricola St., is open Mon.-Fri. and Sun. 7 a.m.-9 p.m., Sat. to 7 p.m. **Bluenose Laundromat,** 2198 Windsor St., will wash, dry, and fold your clothes with same-day service. It's open Mon.-Sat. 7:30 a.m.-7:30 p.m.

Lockers for stashing luggage are at the **Acadian Lines** terminal, 6040 Almon Street. **VIA Rail's** CN Station has limited capacity and stores luggage in baggage storage; the charge is $1.50 a day for each piece.

GETTING THERE

By Air
Air Nova offers flights between Halifax and Yarmouth twice daily; the cheapest restricted fares must be booked 14 days in advance and cost about $149 round-trip for Tues.-Thurs. flights with a Saturday overnight. Its flights between Halifax and Sydney ($155 round-trip) operate four to five times daily, same restrictions. Baggage is limited to two suitcases; you can bring extras, such as a bike, at an extra charge. For **Air Canada/Air Nova** reservations, call (902) 429-7111; for flight updates, call 429-7980. Other airlines serving Halifax include **Canadian Airlines International/Air Atlantic,** tel. 427-5500 or 427-5544; **Air St. Pierre,** tel. 873-3566.

Halifax International Airport is open 24 hours daily and is at Elmsdale, 40 minutes north of Halifax. The airport has doubled in size over the years, and expansion is ongoing though unobtrusive. Facilities include a customs and immigration center, restaurant, bar, duty-free shop, bank machine, a currency exchange counter open 7 a.m.-9 p.m., and varied stores including a lobster pound and a Laura Secord chocolate shop. Car rentals are near the baggage area and include **Budget, Tilden, Hertz, Avis,**

and **Thrifty.** (Use a cart to take your luggage from the car rental to the outside lot—it's quite a hike.)

The **Nova Scotia Tourist Information Centre** has a main-floor counter with Halifax and provincial literature; open year-round, daily 7:30 a.m.-11:30 p.m. Another tourist information center is at the nearby **Atlantic Canada Aviation Museum,** Hwy. 102 exit 6; open late May to early Sept., Mon. 1-5 p.m., Tues.-Sun. 9 a.m.-5 p.m.

A shuttle bus runs between the airport and the city ($12 OW), and also stops at Dartmouth hotels; limo service costs $40 OW. **Share-A-Cab** fills a car with passengers who share the cost of the ride from the airport into Halifax, tel. (902) 429-5555 or 429-7777.

By Land

The Halifax bus terminal is at 6040 Almon, tel. (902) 454-9321. **Acadian Lines** operates bus routes throughout the province. Its Halifax-Yarmouth bus departs the terminal daily at 8 a.m. and 6 p.m., $35 OW; the Halifax-Sydney route has thrice-daily departures, $40 OW. **Zinck Bus,** tel. 468-4342, operates along the eastern shore; the four-hour Halifax to Sherbrooke ride costs $14 OW and leaves at 5:30 p.m. **MacKenzie Bus Lines,** tel. 454-9321, leaves the Acadian Lines terminal in Halifax at 9 a.m. and 5:45 p.m. for Bridgewater ($11 OW); the bus travels the South Shore to Yarmouth.

VIA Rail enters the province from New Brunswick, stops at Amherst and Truro, and finishes at Halifax's CN Station, Barrington at Cornwallis streets, tel. 429-8421.

By Yacht

Three yacht clubs welcome visiting yachts and will contact customs officials to clear the vessel after you disembark. **Armdale Yacht Club,** North West Arm, tel. (902) 477-4617, opens its facilities (showers, meal service) to visitors; the overnight mooring fee is charged by the boat's length. For more info contact them at P.O. Box 40, Armdale, Halifax, NS B30 4J7. Similar facilities and rates are offered at the **Royal Nova Scotia Yacht Squadron,** 376 Purcells Cove Rd., tel. 477-5653, and **Bedford Basin Yacht Club,** 73 Shore Dr., Bedford, tel. 835-3729.

GETTING AROUND

Driving Logistics

Haligonians are painstakingly careful and slow drivers—a wise way to go as hillside streets are steep, and many roads are posted for one-way traffic. Pedestrians have the right-of-way on crosswalks. Two **bridges** link Halifax and Dartmouth, the A. Murray MacKay and the Angus L. MacDonald; toll is 75 cents one-way for cars, free for bicyclists and pedestrians.

Parking is scarce. Commuters clog the hillside streets 7:30-9 a.m. and 4-5:30 p.m., and the university areas are crowded weekdays. Some lodgings, such as the Halifax Sheraton, Cambridge Suites, and the Citadel Inn Halifax, have guest parking. Public parking garages and lots are located on Granville, Upper and Lower Water, Barrington, and Duke streets, plus Spring Garden Road. All charge about $1.35 an hour.

Curbside parking is metered weekdays 8 a.m.-6 p.m.; weekends and holidays are free. Meter violations cost $7.50 if paid within seven days; other parking infractions are fined under $20.

For information on parking RVs and other large vehicles, contact Tourism Halifax at (902) 421-8736 or the Dartmouth Visitor and Convention Bureau at 466-2875.

Pedestrian Walkways

Lofty pedestrian walkways ("pedways") connect many stores, hotels, and other buildings in downtown Halifax. Pedways are quicker than weaving through traffic and are especially helpful during summer showers and winter flurries. The pedway system connects the Sheraton Halifax, Canadian Pacific Chateau Halifax, Scotia Square mall, Delta Barrington Hotel, and a few other places in between. An underground tunnel beneath George St. links the World Trade and Convention Centre to Prince George Hotel.

Buses, Taxis, and Bikes

Metro Transit buses saturate city streets, charge $1.10 (exact change) with free transfers, and operate daily 6 a.m. to midnight. Main bus stops are on Water, Barrington, Cornwallis, Cogswell, and Duke streets, Spring Garden Rd., and Gottingen St. with service to Quinpool Rd. and Bayers Street.

Taxis cruise or wait at hotels and bus and rail terminals. Rides are metered (the rate card is on the back of the front seat); fare is $2.45 at the outset, $1 per km, and 50 cents for each additional passenger; tipping is optional. A drive from Historic Properties to the Public Gardens costs about $6. **Ace-Y Taxi** is one of the largest outfits, with 200 cabs; tel. (902) 429-4444 or 422-4433.

Rental Cars

Rates are similar among the major car rentals. At **Budget,** an economy car with automatic transmission costs about $47 a day with 150 km free, 14 cents for each additional km, $10 collision insurance, and $3 personal insurance. Budget has five outlets in Metro Halifax with its hillside office at 1588 Hollis St., tel. (902) 421-1242.

If travel costs are a consideration, you can get a lower rate from a local car rental. For a subcompact car, **Discount Car Rentals** charges $30 a day with 200 km free, 12 cents for each additional km, $8 collision coverage, and $3 personal injury insurance; they're at 6160 Almon St. across from the post office, tel. 453-5335, and at 1240 Hollis St., tel. 423-6446.

Ferries

The **Halifax-Dartmouth ferry** (terminals at the foot of George St. in Halifax and at Alderney Dr. and Ochterloney St. in Dartmouth) carries pedestrians and bikes on the 15-minute crossing, year-round, Mon.-Sat. 6:30 a.m.-midnight, and June-Sept. on Sun., same hours. Fare is 85 cents OW, 50 cents for children 5-12.

The ferry to Woodside (south Dartmouth) departs the same Halifax-side terminal, year-round, Mon.-Fri. peak hours only.

VICINITY OF HALIFAX

Dartmouth

The **Dartmouth Heritage Museum,** 100 Wyse Rd., tel. (902) 464-2300, explains the natural, historic, and cultural heritage of Halifax's sister city with artifacts and exhibits. At the same location, the Dartmouth Art Gallery displays the work of local artists. Both are open year-round, Mon.-Fri. 9 a.m.-7 p.m., Sat. noon-5 p.m.; free admission.

For a look at Canada's latest deep-sea exploration technology, visit the **Bedford Institute of Oceanography** off the Shannon Park exit on Dartmouth's side of the MacKay Bridge, tel. 426-4093. Self-guided tours explain the institute's fisheries science, oceanography, and hydrography programs. It's open year-round, Mon.-Fri. 9 a.m.-4 p.m. Admission is free.

In 1858, navigation began on a canal system that linked Halifax Harbour with the Bay of Fundy, via Dartmouth's lakes and the Shubenacadie River. The canal was abandoned just 12 years later. Today, two sections of the canal have been restored. At the **Shubenacadie Canal Interpretive Centre,** 140 Alderney Dr., tel. 469-8904, exhibits describe the history and operation of the canal. The center is open June to early Sept., Mon.-Fri. 10 a.m.-6 p.m., Sat.-Sun. 1-5 p.m. On Dartmouth's northern outskirts, the **Fairbanks Interpretive Centre,** Hwy. 318 at Shubie Park, tel. 462-1826, has working canal locks, working models, and other displays; open June to early Sept., Mon.-Fri. 9 a.m.-8 p.m., Sat.-Sun. 1-5 p.m. Admission is free at both centers.

Shearwater Aviation Museum, CFB Shearwater, documents Canadian maritime military aviation history. It's open May-Oct., Tues. and Thurs. 9 a.m.-4 p.m.; during July-Aug. it's open Mon.-Fri., same hours.

Westphal

The **Black Cultural Centre for Nova Scotia,** Cherrybrook Rd. at Hwy. 7, tel. (902) 434-6223, on Dartmouth's eastern outskirts, documents local black history from the 1600s and has a library and exhibit rooms. It's open year-round, Mon.-Fri. 9 a.m.-5 p.m., Sat. 10 a.m.-4 p.m. Admission is $1, children under 12 free.

Bedford Basin Area

Hemlock Ravine Park, Kent Ave. off Hwy. 2, showcases the 75-hectare park of hemlocks, once the romantic retreat of Prince Edward and Julie St. Laurent, his French mistress. The park is open year-round, dawn to dusk. At the town of Bedford, at the head of the basin, **Mount Saint Vincent University Art Galley,** Seton Academic Centre on Hwy. 2, concentrates on fine arts and crafts produced mainly by women. It's open year-round, Mon. and Wed.-Fri. 9 a.m.-5 p.m., Tues. to 9 p.m., Sat.-Sun. 1-5 p.m.

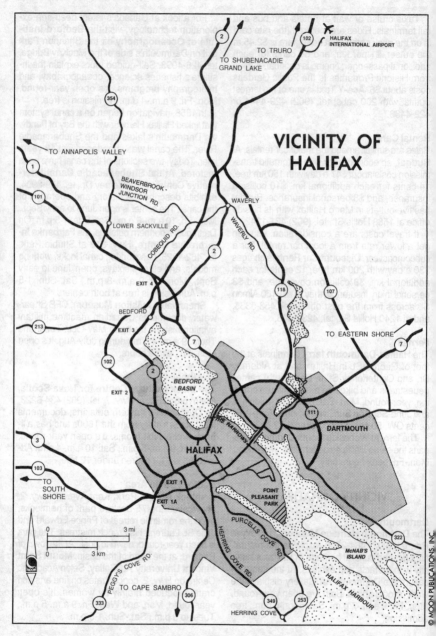

VICINITY OF HALIFAX

TO ANNAPOLIS VALLEY

TO TRURO

TO SHUBENACADIE
GRAND LAKE

HALIFAX
INTERNATIONAL AIRPORT

BEAVERBROOK -
WINDSOR
JUNCTION RD.

WAVERLY

LOWER SACKVILLE

COBEQUID RD.

WAVERLY RD.

EXIT 4

BEDFORD

EXIT 3

TO EASTERN SHORE

BEDFORD
BASIN

EXIT 2

DARTMOUTH

THE NARROWS

HALIFAX

EXIT 1

POINT
PLEASANT
PARK

EXIT 1A

PURCELLS COVE RD.

McNAB'S
ISLAND

HALIFAX HARBOUR

TO
SOUTH
SHORE

PEGGY'S COVE RD.

HERRING COVE RD.

TO CAPE SAMBRO

HERRING COVE

3 mi

3 km

© MOON PUBLICATIONS, INC.

Cape Sambro

Crystal Crescent Beach Provincial Park lies a half hour south of Halifax off Hwy. 349, and is the locals' favorite Atlantic beach. Its sand is fine, and the sea is usually cold, but summer crowds heat up the action. Nature lovers will enjoy the 10-km trail to remote Pennant Point.

Peggy's Cove

Atlantic Canada's most photographed site is a 40-minute drive along Hwy. 333 southwest from Halifax—the place is everything its fans say it is. With the houses of the tiny fishing village clinging like mussels to the weathered granite shelf at the edge of Margaret's Bay, the Atlantic lathering against the boulder-bound coast, the fishing boats moored in the small cove, and the white, octagonal lighthouse overlooking it all, the scene is the quintessence of the Nova Scotia coast. Sightseers clog the site during the daytime, wandering across the rocky expanse around the photogenic lighthouse, which serves as a post office in summer. (Wear rubber-soled shoes on the slippery surfaces.) To miss the crowds, get there before 8:30 a.m. or after 5 p.m.

Also at Peggy's Cove, **William E. deGarthe Memorial Provincial Park** is easily bypassed as the seaport's road curves toward the lighthouse, but it's worth seeking out. DeGarthe sculpted a 30-meter-long frieze on a granite outcropping, depicting 32 of the seaside village's fishermen and families.

Peggy's Cove

SOUTHWESTERN NOVA SCOTIA

Nova Scotians must have had the southwest region in mind when they coined the province's self-descriptive motto, "So Much to Sea." The crashing Atlantic lays itself out in foaming breakers for 300 km along the southern coast, while the formidable Bay of Fundy—site of the world's highest tides—advances and retreats along the northern coast. The seaports and towns along both coastlines follow one another, like a series of glossy, life-size picture postcards.

The region comprises the southwestern half of the Nova Scotian peninsula, and most sightseeing is concentrated around the coastal edges. The highway network consists of a coastline system of efficient expressways and parallel scenic roads. Highway 103 and its continuation as Hwy. 101 speed travel between destinations. But if time allows, route yourself onto the secondary scenic roads meandering through ports and overlooking the Atlantic and Bay of Fundy.

You can skirt the region in a day, driving nonstop. More realistically, plan a day in each place that interests you. As elsewhere in Nova Scotia, dining at its best is superb, and the region's specialty is its abundance of top-notch country inns with public dining rooms. Museums with well-conceived historical exhibits are everywhere. Many lodgings are in historic houses and mansions converted to country inns and in categories best described as better, best, and beautiful.

HISTORY

The history of the southwest region *is* the story of Nova Scotia. France's colonial ambitions began at Port Royal and clashed head-on with England's quest for New World dominance. England prevailed. In 1753, a convoy of 1,453 German, Swiss, and French Huguenot "foreign Protestants" arrived in Lunenburg. New England planters settled Liverpool in 1759, while Shelburne was the destination of 16,000 Loyalists in 1783.

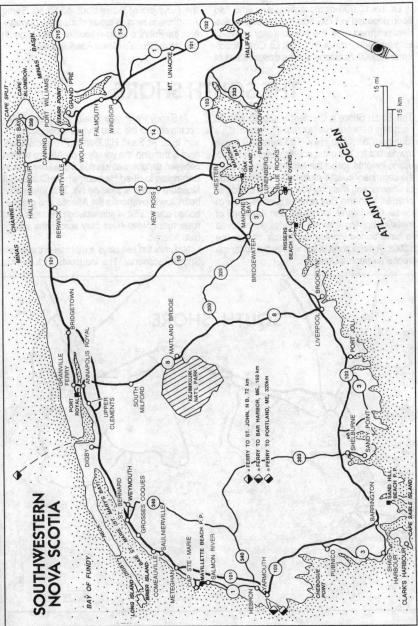

SOUTHWESTERN NOVA SCOTIA

© MOON PUBLICATIONS, INC.

Of the 10,000 or more Acadians who had been deported in 1755, some of the original settlers returned after the peace treaty between England and France in 1763. La Côte Acadienne's 8,000 Acadians are the descendants of the survivors of those troubled times. Some Acadians in remote areas eluded the Deportation; the Pubnico villages southeast of Yarmouth are Nova Scotia's oldest Acadian area.

THE SOUTH SHORE

The South Shore is the deeply scored Atlantic coastline between Halifax and Yarmouth. It's a four-hour drive on Hwy. 103 between these towns, but for the most scenic views and interesting insights, forget the expressway and drive the secondary coastal routes. The wealthy towns of Chester and Mahone Bay overlook crescent-shaped Mahone Bay and its islands. One of these, Oak Island, looms large in the world of treasure-hunting legends—pirates are believed to have buried incalculable booty on it in the 1500s. A deep shaft is still visible, but so far the treasure remains elusive.

At Sandy Point near Shelburne, ground garnet mixed with the sand gives the beach a crimson hue. At Sand Hill Beach Provincial Park near Barrington, the usually chilly Atlantic warms between sandbars at low tide. Take Hwy. 3 from Barrington to Shag Harbour, where Chapel Hill Museum crests a seaside hill. The museum's belfry tower overlooks the Atlantic and granite-bound coast. Visit at sunset when the sky's pink, rose, and golden hues play across the silvery blue Atlantic.

Naturally the sea plays a vital role in the South Shore's economy. The industries include fish

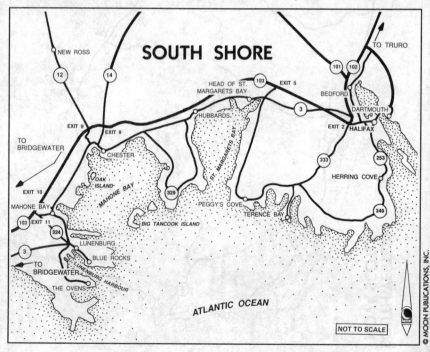

scene from
Mahone Bay

processing, shipbuilding, ship repair, and fishing (the province's richest lobster grounds lie aside the Pubnico seaports). Bridgewater exports Christmas trees and has a Michelin Tires plant. Liverpool deals in paper products, foundries, and machine shops, and nearby Brooklyn has a Bowater Mersey Paper plant, partially owned by the *Washington Post.*

MAHONE BAY AND CHESTER

Mahone Bay

The town of Mahone Bay (pop. 1,100), on the island-speckled bay of the same name, was settled in the mid-1700s by German, French, and Swiss Protestants, who were enticed here by the British government's offer of free land, farm equipment, and a year's "victuals." The little town is known for its distinctive bayside trio of 19th-century churches, gingerbread houses, and its arts and crafts galleries that sell pewter, pottery, quilts, hooked rugs, and other wares made by local artisans.

From 1850 to the early part of this century, shipbuilding thrived in a dozen shipyards along the waterfront. The town's prosperity was mirrored in its architecture, with Gothic Revival, Classic Revival, and Italianate styles in evidence. Many of these buildings have been converted to B&Bs, restaurants, and shops. The visitor information center, 165 Edgewater St., tel. (902) 624-6151, with a very friendly and helpful staff, provides a walking-tour brochure outlining the town's architectural highlights.

Mahone Bay's annual July **Wooden Boat Festival** at Government Wharf celebrates the town's boatbuilding heritage. Activities include coracle- and canoe-building demonstrations, children's workshops and treasure hunts, displays of lovingly handcrafted skiffs and other small boats, races, live entertainment, and refreshments. For more information, contact the visitor information center, or call 624-8443.

The **Settlers Museum,** in a 150-year-old house at 578 Main St., tel. 624-6263, is open year-round with exhibits on topics ranging from boatbuilding to ceramics and furniture dating from the mid-1700s. Its hours are Tues.-Sat. 10 a.m.-5 p.m., Sun. 1-5 p.m. Admission is by donation.

Mahone Bay is well equipped with genteel bed-and-breakfast inns, convivial cafes, and tony shops. Opposite Government Wharf, **Fairmont House B&B,** 654 Main St., tel. 624-6713, is an 1850s Victorian home with three guest rooms furnished with antiques ($35-55, with full breakfast). Half a block south, the **Heart's Desire B&B,** 686 Main St., tel. 624-8766, is another 19th-century house, with a veranda overlooking the bay. It has three rooms with balconies; the $55-68 rate includes full breakfast. Near the highway are the **By-Way Guest House,** off Hwy. 103 at exit 11, tel. 624-9970; and the **Bedspread/Le Couvre-lit,** also off exit 11, tel. 624-8192.

For seafood, head to the Ocean Grill, on Main St. at Government Wharf, tel. 624-1342, or the **Red Buoy Diner,** on Main St. toward the highway, tel. 624-9717. The **Mug and Anchor,** on Main St. at Mader's Wharf, tel. 624-6378, is an

English-style pub serving locally brewed ales, with live music on occasion. At the south end of town, en route to Lunenburg, the **Tingle Bridge Tea House,** tel. 624-9770, brews a savory pot and is locally celebrated for its cheesecake. It's open May-Nov., Wed.-Sun. noon-6 p.m.

Chester

The bayside town of Chester, 12 km northeast of Mahone Bay, was first settled by New Englanders in 1759. Its first hotel was built here in 1827, and the town, with its ideal sailing conditions and many vacation homes, has been a popular summer retreat ever since. Visitors come for the beaches, sailing, golfing, and easy access to Tancook Island as well as the downtown shopping.

The **Chester Theatre Festival** hosts professional talents at the Chester Playhouse, 22 Pleasant St., in July and August. Past seasons have included musicals, Broadway-style revues, comedy improv, puppet shows, and children's programs. For tickets and info, call (902) 275-3933 in the area, or (800) 363-7529. **Race Week,** Atlantic Canada's largest sailing regatta, takes place in mid-August and attracts folks from up and down the coast.

Chester has several noteworthy inns and B&Bs: **Casa Blanca Guesthouse,** 123 Duke St., tel. 275-3385 (open year-round), has eight rooms and a cabin. Rates are $44 (private bath), $36 (shared) including breakfast. **The Captain's House Inn,** 129 Central St., tel. 275-3501, is also open year-round and has nine rooms, with meals available; rates are $60 s, $65 d.

Seafood restaurants abound, serving everything from quiet lunches to huge lobster dinners. **Lobsterworks Restaurant,** 8 Tremont St., tel. 275-2488, specializes in its namesake and other seafood. It's open daily 11 a.m.-10 p.m.

LUNENBURG

Lunenburg (pop. 3,014) lies about equidistant between Halifax and Shelburne off Hwy. 103. Sited on a hilly peninsula between two harbors, this is one of the most attractive towns in Nova Scotia, with a wealth of beautiful homes painted in a crayon box of bold primary colors. In 1991, Lunenburg's Old Town was designated a national historic district.

Protestant German, Swiss, and French immigrants, recruited by the British to help stabilize their new dominion, settled the town in 1753, and their influence is still apparent in the town's architectural details. With its excellent harbor, a protected inner arm of the Atlantic embraced by two long curving peninsulas, Lunenburg became one of the province's premier fishing ports and shipbuilding centers in the 19th century. One of Lunenburg's most famous creations is the schooner *Bluenose,* the proud symbol of Nova Scotia, built here in 1921. The 49-meter fishing vessel won the International Fisherman's Trophy race in 1921, and over the next 18 years remained the undefeated champion of the Atlantic fleets.

In 1942, the era of the sail-powered fishing industry was over, replaced by that of modern, steel-hulled trawlers. The great *Bluenose* was sold to carry freight in the West Indies. Four years later, she foundered and was lost on a Haitian reef. Its image is on the back of the Canadian dime. July of 1963, however, the *Bluenose II* was re-created from the original plans and launched at Lunenburg. Some of the same craftspeople who had built the first *Bluenose* participated in its construction.

Until recently, *Bluenose II* alternated between Lunenburg and Halifax, where she gave harbor tours under sail. Now, however, the schooner is permanently berthed at her home port and open to visitors outside the Fisheries Museum.

Sights

The port's oldest part is set on the hillside overlooking the harborfront. The nine blocks of Old Town rise steeply from the water, and the village green spreads across the center. Bluenose Drive, the narrow lane alongside harborfront, and Montague Street, a block uphill, define the main sightseeing area. A mesh of one-way streets connects Old Town with the newer area built with shipbuilding profits. One of the pleasures of Lunenburg is strolling the residential and commercial streets, admiring the town's many meticulously preserved architectural gems.

The spacious, bright red **Fisheries Museum of the Atlantic,** on Bluenose Dr., tel. (902) 634-4794, boasts a trove of artifacts and exhibits on shipbuilding, seafaring, rum-running, and ma-

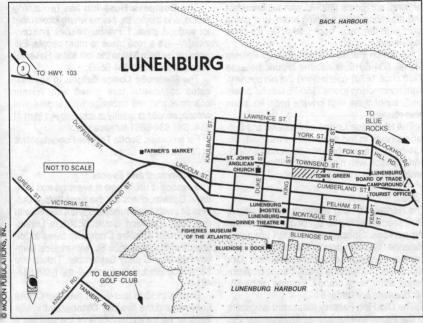

rine biology. The museum engages the visitor with demonstrations on fish filleting, lobster-trap construction, dory building, net mending, and other maritime arts. Inside are aquariums, tanks with touchable marine life, a gallery of ship models, full-size fishing vessels from around Atlantic Canada, a theater, restaurant, and gift shop. Tied up at the wharf outside are the fishing schooner *Theresa E. Connor*, built in Lunenburg in 1938; the steel-hulled trawler *Cape Sable,* an example of the sort of vessel that made the former obsolete; the *Royal Wave,* a Digby scallop dragger; and the *Bluenose II.* All of the vessels may be boarded and explored.

The museum is open June to mid-October, daily 9:30 a.m.-5:30 p.m.; open by appointment on weekdays during the off-season. Admission is $2.50 adults, children 5-16 50 cents.

Gothic **St. John's Anglican Church** at Duke and Cumberland streets, built in 1759, dates nearly to the seaport's founding. The white clapboard church was a gift of the British Crown; it's open July-Aug., Mon.-Sat. 10 a.m.-5 p.m.

Accommodations

The **Lunenburg Board of Trade Campground** at Blockhouse Hill Rd. on Blockhouse Hill, tel. (902) 634-8100, has 28 campsites (from $10) on a hilltop overlooking the harbor. Open mid-May to mid-Oct., the campground has showers and washrooms.

The **Lunenburg Hostel,** 9 King St., tel. 634-9146, has five beds ($13) on the bottom floor of a B&B. Upstairs, the **Snug Harbour B&B,** same address and phone, charges $35-55 with full breakfast for its three rooms. A sundeck overlooks the harbor. It's open May-September. No smoking is permitted. The **Topmast Motel,** Mason's Beach Rd., tel. 634-4661 or 631-4747, overlooks the harbor with outdoor decks adjoining 12 rooms ($50-60); four housekeeping units cost $65-70. It's open year-round.

The ornately detailed **Compass Rose Inn,** 15 King St., tel. 634-8509 or (800) 565-8509, built circa 1825, has four cozy rooms ($55-65 with full breakfast) and a popular dining room. The **Lunenburg Inn,** 26 Dufferin St., tel. 634-3963 or (800) 565-3963, has a front porch for relaxing, six rooms ($60-85 with full breakfast and afternoon tea), a dining room, and sitting room with fireplace, books, and TV. It's open year-round.

Kaulbach House Historic Inn, 75 Pelham St., tel. 634-8818, is another historic treasure (built circa 1880) overlooking the harbor, with eight nonsmoking rooms ($50-75 with full breakfast), six of them with private bath. It's open year-round.

The **Bluenose Lodge,** at Falkland and Dufferin streets in the seaport's newer part, tel. 634-8851, is a refurbished sea captain's Victorian mansion with nine rooms ($65 with a light breakfast) and a dining room.

Food
The **Heritage Dining Room** at 139 Montague St. is short on ambience but long on tasty, heaping portions. Specialties include Lunenburg sausage, German potato salad flavored with apples, onions, and chives, thick fried pork chops, and homemade Black Forest cake enriched with cherry brandy. Entrees range $6-10; desserts are under $4.

The **Old Fish Factory** restaurant is upstairs in the Fisheries Museum at 68 Bluenose Dr., tel. (902) 634-3030. Specialties include Solomon Gundy (pickled herring), creamy seafood chowder, gingerbread cake, and other local favorites. Seafood platters cost $6-14.

Several other Bluenose Dr. restaurants overlook the harbor. The **Rum Runner Inn,** tel. 634-9200, opposite the Fisheries Museum, has upper and lower decks; next door, **Big Red's,** tel. 634-3554, caters to families in its upstairs dining room, which has great views of the *Bluenose II.* **Peg Leg's,** tel. 634-3300, serves fancier fare on its outdoor patio, and the **Dockside Restaurant,** tel. 634-3005, with upper-level decks, specializes in seafood; most dinners $10-18. For a quick bite, baked goods, homemade soup and sandwiches, or a good cup of espresso, **La Bodega Deli and Cafe,** tel. 634-4027, is on the waterfront at the corner of Bluenose and King.

The **Lunenburg Inn** at 26 Dufferin St. creates Mediterranean adaptations of Nova Scotian cuisine in its dining room; entrees run $14-18. It's open June-Oct., and you can dine on a veranda during summer. Reservations are wise; call 634-3963.

The **Compass Rose Inn** has two dining rooms, and they're the places where locals meet for seafood, steak, Lunenburg dishes, and conviviality—it's a nice place to meet people. Entrees range from $10 to the low $20s. Reservations are wise; call 634-8509.

The **Bluenose Lodge** delights in sophisticated continental fare mixed with Wiener schnitzel and red cabbage with apples and onions; service is quietly quick. Entrees start at $14. Call 634-8851 for reservations.

For groceries, **Scotia Trawler Foodmaster** is at 250 Montague Street.

Entertainment and Events
The seaport is usually quiet evenings and Sundays. Uptown, check out the **Knot Pub,** 4 Dufferin St., with "knotwurst" and kraut served with draft beer; open Mon.-Sat. to 12:30 a.m. **Lunenburg Dinner Theatre Company** takes to the boards at 116 Montague St., with musical comedy mid-May to early September. Tickets are $30; for details and reservations, call (902) 634-4814.

Events include mid-July's two-day **Crafts Festival** and the five-day **Oktoberfest** in late Sept. or early October. One of the summer's biggest events is the early Aug. **Lunenburg Folk Harbour Festival,** which attracts a roster of traditional, roots, and contemporary folk musicians over four days. Tickets are available for the entire festival (about $50) or for single days or evenings. Write P.O Box 655, 15 King St., Lunenburg, NS B0J 2C0, or call 634-3180.

Recreation
The nine-hole **Bluenose Golf Club** spreads out across 2,370 meters in a handsome setting overlooking the seaport from the opposite peninsula edge. Hand carts, rental clubs, and lunch are available; for details, call (902) 634-4260.

The **Lunenburg Bicycle Barn,** tel. 634-3426, a kilometer east of town on the road to Blue Rocks, rents, sells, and repairs bikes, and can offer tips on good local routes. Mountain bikes go for $15 per day.

Shopping
The **farmers' market,** Dufferin and Lincoln streets, lures crowds for fresh produce, smoked meats, and crafts at the former railroad depot

grounds; it's open July-Oct., Thurs. 8 a.m.-noon. Wares are high quality and priced accordingly.

Montague Woollens at Montague and King streets stocks exquisite sweaters and apparel. Arts and crafts are for sale at **Montague Gallery,** Montague and King streets, and **Morash Gallery and Gifts,** 55 Pelham Street. The **Houston North Gallery** at 110 Montague St., tel. (902) 634-8869, specializes in folk art, Inuit crafts, and imported sculpture.

Information

The **Lunenburg Tourist Office,** tel. (902) 634-8100, just east of town on Blockhouse Hill, can make lodging reservations. The office also stocks locally written, informative literature about the port's historic architecture. *Understanding Lunenburg's Architecture* ($12) describes the design elements, and *An Inventory of Historic Buildings* ($10) provides details on almost every seaport building, organized street by street. The office is open mid-May to early October, daily 9 a.m.-6 p.m. (July-Aug. to 9 p.m.).

Port Electronics, 144 Montague St., and **Yacht Shop and Marina,** 280 Montague St., sell nautical maps. Genealogical records are kept on the third floor of town hall on Townsend St.; it's open Wed.-Thurs. 2-9 p.m.

Services

Fishermen's Memorial Hospital is on High St. between Dufferin and Green streets, tel. (902) 634-8801. For **police,** call 634-4312; for the **RCMP,** call 634-8674.

The port has several banks. The **Bank of Montreal,** at King and Pelham streets, doesn't charge for currency exchange or cashing traveler's checks. It's open Mon.-Wed. 9:30 a.m.-4 p.m., Thurs.-Fri. to 5:30 p.m.

Canada Post at King and Lincoln streets is open Mon.-Fri. 8:30 a.m.-5 p.m. **Bluenose Mini Mart,** 31-35 Lincoln St., has a retail postal outlet. It's open Mon.-Sat. 7 a.m.-midnight, Sun. from 8 a.m.

The **Soap Bubble Cleanette** at 39 Lincoln St. is the local launderette. It's open Mon.-Sat. 8 a.m.-8 p.m., Sun. from 10 a.m.

Transportation

If you arrive by yacht, the **Lunenburg Yacht Club** has moorings available; for details call

(902) 634-3745. **MacKenzie Bus Line** buses depart for South Shore towns from Bluenose Mini Mart. The bus to Halifax leaves Mon.-Sat. at 9:25 a.m., $10 one-way. For harbor tours check out **Schooner Tours,** based at harborfront near the museum, tel. 634-8966 or 543-9317. Its 90-minute cruises on the schooner *Timberwind* operate mid-June to mid-September ($13 adults, $9 for children 5-12). The motor vessel *Tagashelle* runs seven shorter tours daily; adults pay $10, children under 12 $5.

VICINITY OF LUNENBURG

The Lunenburg area is an upscale place, near enough to the city for well-heeled, commuting Haligonians. An international flavor pervades the area, too, and you'll find Americans among Nova Scotians at Chester and Mahone Bay, and a summer colony of Germans with coastal summer houses on Lunenburg's outskirts. Bridgewater, the area's commercial and industrial center, is 15 minutes west of Lunenburg; New Ross is an hour's drive inland.

Blue Rocks

A short drive east of Lunenburg, toward the end of the peninsula, the coast around the little hamlet of Blue Rocks is wrapped with blue-gray slate and sandstone, and the combination of color and texture will inspire photographers. The scenery rivals Peggy's Cove for beauty, but lacks the crowds.

The Ovens Natural Park

Fifteen minutes west of Lunenburg on Hwy. 232, spectacular sea caves have been scooped out of the coastal cliffs. Early prospectors discovered veins of gold embedded in the slate and white quartz cliffs, sparking a small gold rush in 1861. During the following several decades, the cliffs surrendered 15,500 grams of the precious metal. Visitors can try panning for a bit of color.

The park has a 1.5-km trail leading down to the caves, which you also can visit on boat tours. A campground offers 65 serviced and semiserviced sites ($14 and up), with a pool, campers' store, and restaurant. Ovens Natural Park, tel. (902) 766-4621, is open 15 May to 15 Oct.; the day-use fee is $2.50.

Bridgewater

The **Wile Carding Mill,** Hwy. 325 (Victoria Rd.), tel. (902) 543-4033, was a wool-processing mill to which local farmers hauled their loads of raw wool. The wool was carded for spinning and weaving or made into batts for quilts. The original machinery is still in operation, powered by an overshot waterwheel, and now demonstrates old carding methods. It's open June-Sept., Mon.-Sat. 9:30 a.m.-5:30 p.m., Sun. 1-5:30 p.m.

Rissers Beach Provincial Park

Just one of many parks along this coast, this one boasts a beach of finely ground quartz sand and an area of pristine salt marsh laced with boardwalks.

New Ross

In 1816, Capt. William Ross began clearing 23 hectares of fertile land for a homestead, which would remain in his family for five generations. The **Ross Farm Museum** on Hwy. 12, tel. (902) 689-2210, now an outdoor agricultural museum, commemorates the rural lifestyle of a bygone age. Activities include butter and cheese making, coopering and blacksmithing, and historical farming method demonstrations. It's open June to mid-Oct., daily 9:30 a.m.-5:30 p.m.; open Jan.-March for weekend sleigh rides. Admission is $2.25 adults, children 4-14 50 cents.

SHELBURNE

Like Lunenburg, Shelburne (pop. 2,303) sits at the innermost end of a long harbor shaped by peninsulas. Teardrop-shaped McNutt Island lies across the harbor entrance; the lighthouse on the island was built in 1788. Getting into Shelburne is quick—it's just minutes from Hwy. 103 exit 26 to the town, which sits on the harbor's eastern side.

The seaport was established in 1783 when Loyalists fleeing the newly independent American colonies settled here by the thousands (the word "Loyalist" still appears in the names of numerous local establishments). Rations and free land ran out within a few years, and most would-be settlers moved on to other places. Those who remained started the industries—ship-

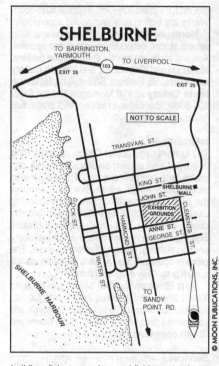

building, fish processing, and fishing—that keep the seaport humming today.

The town is short on lodgings, shorter on restaurants, and long on crowds of tourists who arrive on sightseeing buses. If you intend to stay awhile, advance reservations for lodgings and dining are wise. The historic district lies along harborfront's Dock Street and is backed by Water Street, the main drag. *The Scarlet Letter,* starring Demi Moore, was filmed in 1994-95 in the historic district, which the film crew doctored up a bit to make more "authentic."

Sights

Shelburne Historic District on Dock St. is a hive of historic sites and shops. **Shelburne County Museum,** tel. (902) 875-3219, is the hub, with exhibits on Loyalist heritage and shipbuilding history, and a 250-year-old fire engine believed to be the oldest in Canada. The museum and following sites are open year-round, daily 9:30 a.m.-5:30 p.m. (closed Sun.-Mon. off-season).

Nova Scotians say the dory was reinvented in Shelburne. The **Dory Shop** on Dock St., tel. 875-3219, the last of seven such boat factories in Shelburne, turned out thousands of hand-crafted wooden fishing dories between 1880 and 1970. The shop now houses interpretive displays and gives demonstrations on the dying art. It's open mid-June to mid-September, daily 9:30 a.m.-5:30 p.m.

The **Ross-Thomson House,** on Charlotte Lane, was built in 1784 as a Loyalist store. Today it depicts the period setting with sample wares and an old-fashioned garden. It's open June to mid-October, Mon.-Sat. 9:30 a.m.-5:30 p.m., Sun. 1-5:30 p.m.

Accommodations

Rustic and pretty **Islands Provincial Park,** off Hwy. 3 five km west of Shelburne, tel. (902) 875-4304, faces the town across the upper harbor. It offers 65 unserviced sites ($8) with table shelters and grills, pit toilets, and running water but no showers.

The **Loyalist Inn** at 160 Water St., tel. 875-2343 or 875-3537, a stone's throw from the historic district, has 18 rooms ($44-47) and a dining room. The **Ox Bow Village Motel,** off Hwy. 103 exit 25, tel. 875-3000, combines 47 basic rooms ($40-48) with a dining room, outside pool, and hiking trails.

The **Cooper's Inn,** 36 Dock St., tel. 875-4656, is a two-story colonial beauty overlooking the harbor and next to the tourist bureau and museum. Built in 1783 by a merchant and restored and opened in 1988, the lodging has five rooms ($56-75) and a dining room. It's open May-early October.

Food and Drink

The **Toddle Inn Tearoom** at Water and King streets feeds the noon crowd with lobster sandwiches and entrees such as meatloaf platters ($6-13); it's open 8 a.m.-3 p.m.

The dining room at the **Loyalist Inn** on Water St. (reservations are wise, call 902-875-2343) is usually jammed with bus-tour diners. A table is easiest to get before noon, during midafternoon, or after 8 p.m. The specialty is seafood ($9-15) prepared any way you like it.

Cooper's Restaurant, at the inn of the same name on Dock St., is the place for dinner with gourmet interpretations of lamb, duck, chicken, and seafood entrees ($14 and up). It's open nightly 5:30-9 p.m. in an attractive setting. (Reservations are wise, call 875-4656.)

Grovestine's Grocery at 137 Water St. is an old-fashioned grocery with an ample deli for picnic fixings. It's open Mon.-Sat. 8 a.m.-5:30 p.m. The **Shelburne Mall** on King St. has the supermarkets. Crowds gravitate nightly to **Bruce's Wharf Beverage Room,** downstairs at 1 Dock St., where the glass wall overlooks the harbor. Bruce's offers fish and chips and a pool table; it's open Mon.-Sat. to 11:30 p.m.

Events

Shelburne makes much of 1 July's **Canada Day** celebrations with fireworks, a parade, street vendors, and entertainment. Mid-July's three-day **Founders' Day** festival features yacht races, a crafts sale, music, and food. The **Shelburne County Exhibition** brings country-fair components to the port's exhibition grounds for four days in mid-August.

Information and Services

Shelburne Tourist Bureau, on Dock St., tel. (902) 875-4547, stocks literature and a self-guided tour map. It's open mid-May to mid-Sept., daily 9 a.m.-9 p.m.

Shelburne Roseway Hospital is on Sandy Point Rd., tel. 875-3011. The **RCMP** can be reached by calling 875-2490.

Bank of Nova Scotia at Shelburne Mall at King and Clements streets doesn't charge for currency exchanges or cashing traveler's checks. It's open Mon.-Tues. 10 a.m.-3 p.m., Thurs. to 4 p.m., Fri. to 6 p.m. **Gilligan's Isle,** King St., is one of several launderettes in town; it's open daily 7 a.m.-11 p.m.

Transportation

The **MacKenzie Line** bus stops at Donna's Kitchen restaurant at Shelburne Mall and has Mon.-Sat. departures to Lunenburg ($14 OW), Halifax ($21 OW), and Yarmouth ($11 OW). If you arrive on your own yacht, the **Shelburne Harbour Yacht Club,** tel. (902) 875-2977, can make arrangements for public wharf moorings and clearing customs.

VICINITY OF SHELBURNE

Aside from Shelburne sightseeing, the area tends to be overlooked, and visitors speed on to Yarmouth or Lunenburg and Halifax. Several places are worth a stop, and coastal views especially near Barrington are exquisite.

Kejimkujik National Park Seaside Adjunct

This little-known gem, off Hwy. 3 near Port Joli, is one of the last and largest undisturbed areas of Maritimes coastline. This section of the park, not as popular with visitors as the main, inland park, offers unspoiled beaches and offshore isles. The park is accessible on foot; a two-km walking trail begins at the parking lot on St. Catherine's Rd. and leads to St. Catherine's River beach. Some sections of this beach close from late April to late July to protect piping plover nesting sites. Another access trail into the park starts near Willis Lake at Southwest Port Mouton; the five-km trail ends at undeveloped Black Point beach.

The Seaside Adjunct has no visitor facilities, but camping is allowed at designated areas (permit required from the warden's office in Liverpool).

For more information, contact the Superintendent, Kejimkujik National Park, P.O. Box 236, Maitland Bridge, NS B0T 1N0, tel. (902) 682-2772.

Liverpool

The **Perkins House** at 105 Main St., an hour northeast of Shelburne, is a historic example of a New England planter's adaptation to Nova Scotia. The Connecticut-style white house, built in 1766, is furnished with antiques and open June to mid-October, daily 9:30 a.m.-5:30 p.m.

Barrington

The **Barrington Meeting House** on Hwy. 3, about 35 minutes southwest of Shelburne, is another variation on planter life. The New England-style church is Canada's oldest nonconformist house of worship and was built by 50 Cape Cod families in 1765; it's open mid-June to Sept., Mon.-Sat. 9:30 a.m.-5:30 p.m., Sun. 1-5:30 p.m. The **Barrington Woolen Mill** on coastal Hwy. 3 has wool-spinning demonstrations and exhibits that detail wool processing within the old-time mill; same hours.

Cape Sable Island

Half an hour's drive southwest of Shelburne, Cape Sable Island, connected to the mainland by a causeway, is the southernmost point in Nova Scotia. Feared by early sailors because of its jagged shores, the island was settled by brick-making Acadians during the 17th century. The island also served as a summer base for fishermen from New England, and fishing prevails today as the community's main industry, with tourism a close second.

The island's four main beaches offer surfing, clam digging, swimming, fishing, and bird-watching. At **Hawk Beach,** on the eastern side

Simeon Perkins House, Liverpool

COURTESY NOVA SCOTIA MUSEUM COMPLEX

(turn at Lower Clark's Harbour at Hawk Rd. and go left), you can see the **Cape Lighthouse** on a small nearby sandbar. The original tower, built in 1861, was Canada's first eight-sided structure; the present lighthouse, a protected heritage building, was constructed in 1923. At low tide on Hawk Beach you can also see the remains of a 1,500-year-old forest.

The **Causeway Beach** (turn right at the Corbett Heights subdivision) is a prime sunbathing, unlicensed fishing (for mackerel), and windsurfing spot. **Stoney Island Beach,** as the name implies, is not as popular with sunbathers as it is with seals, which like to sun themselves on the rocks. **South Side Beach** (turn on Daniel's Head Rd. in South Side), too, is popular as a seal-watching and beachcombing locale.

For history buffs, the island's **Archelaus Smith Museum,** on Hwy. 330 at Centreville, features fishing and shipbuilding displays. Summer hours are 9:30 a.m.-5:30 p.m. daily; admission is free.

Services and accommodations are limited. **Geneva's Restaurant,** Lower Clark's Harbour, tel. (902) 745-2659, specializes in seafood; it's open seven days a week 11 a.m.-9 p.m. **Cape Breton B&B,** 2625 Main St., Clark's Harbour, tel. 745-1356, has seven guest rooms for $35 s, $45 d; open year-round. **Penney Estates,** North East Point, tel. 745-1516, has a private beach and rooms for $40 s, $50 d; open year-round.

The **tourism bureau** is at the north end of

Barrington Woolen Mill

Clark's Harbour on Main St. (at Blanchard St.), tel. 745-2586. It's open June-September.

YARMOUTH AND LA CÔTE ACADIENNE

The South Shore ends at Yarmouth, where the Atlantic meets the Bay of Fundy. Locals say the Vikings came ashore a thousand years ago and inscribed the boulder that now sits at the Yarmouth County Museum's front door. Yarmouth's ragged coastline impressed early explorer Samuel de Champlain, who named the seaport's outermost peninsula Cap Forchu ("Forked Cape").

Like the Vikings, Champlain arrived and departed, as do thousands of visitors who arrive on the ferries and quickly disperse on routes to distant provincial destinations. Their loss is the gain of the tourist who stays. Cyclists like to bike the Yarmouth area's backcountry coastal roads. At Chebogue Point south of the seaport, pink, purple, and white lupines bloom in June, and in summertime white-winged willets roam the marshes.

Another bike route goes to Yarmouth Bar across the harbor. The route begins north of the business district with a turn to the left, where a whisper-thin road leads to the lighthouse at Cape Forchu's tip. Locals use the road to watch the ferries come and go through the harbor.

Sailing on "Dry Land"
Low tide on the Fundy tricks your eyes. It almost drains the harbor dry, and the ships sail the main dredged channel, seemingly traveling

a kilted piper greets visitors

across dry land when you see them from the road abutting the channel. You can almost reach out and touch the massive ships as they speed past.

It's a 30-minute drive from Yarmouth to La Côte Acadienne at Salmon River; you'll know you've arrived by the abundance of Acadian flags.

For a look at the dynamic Fundy, check out **Mavillette Beach Provincial Park** at Cap Sainte-Marie. The sign at Cape View Restaurant, Hwy. 1, signals the turn, and the road peels down to the sea and runs alongside high dunes. Boardwalks cross the dunes to the long beach, where sand bars trap low tide into warm pools. On a sunny day, beach trekkers walk the expanse and hunt for unusual seashells.

When fog accompanies the incoming tide, thick mist envelops the trekkers, and shrouded sunshine lights the scene, like cotton encasing a luminous light bulb.

YARMOUTH

Yarmouth (pop. 7,800) was the center of a ship-building empire during Canada's Great Age of Sail, when it ranked as the world's fourth-largest port of registry. Still the region's largest seaport, the town is a prosperous and orderly place supported by shipping—primarily lumber products, Irish moss, and Christmas trees—and fishing. Yarmouth's herring fleet is a major contributor to the local economy. The fleet sails at night and anchors with all its lights blazing farther up the Fundy coast, creating a sight known as "herring city." Tourism also helps the port thrive; two ferry lines bring visitors to town in numbers sufficient to establish Yarmouth as the busiest ferry landing in the province.

Getting Oriented
The town fronts the eastern side of Yarmouth Harbour. Ferries dock at the foot of Forest St., where it meets Water St. at the harborfront. Main St. parallels Water St. and sits astride a hilly ridge with the port's shops, businesses, and banks. Argyle, Forest, and Parade streets and Starrs Rd. spread inland from there. Highway 3 enters Yarmouth on Starrs Rd.; Hwy. 103, the other major access route, zips into town on a parallel road and ends at Hardscratch Rd., which in turn finishes on Starrs Road.

Sights
If **historic architecture** interests you, take a leisurely walk along Main St., where the commercial buildings are styled in late 19th-century Classic Revival, Queen Anne Revival, Georgian, and Italianate. The best of Yarmouth was built with Great Age of Sail profits. At the tourist information center on Forest St., pick up the *Walking Tour of Yarmouth* brochure, which details some two dozen points of architectural and historical interest on a self-guiding four-km walk.

The **Firefighters' Museum of Nova Scotia,** 431 Main St., tel. (902) 742-5525, is Canada's only museum dedicated solely to firefighting equipment. Among the extensive vintage collection is a 1819 Hopwood & Tilley hand pumper and other sparkling equipment. The museum also serves as a national exhibit center with nationwide topics from manufacturing to birding. It's open year-round; during the summer season (June-Sept.), hours are Mon.-Sat. 9 a.m.-5 p.m., with longer hours in July and August, 9 a.m.-9 p.m. and Sun. 10 a.m.-5 p.m. Hours in the off-season (Oct.-May) are Mon.-Fri. 10 a.m.-noon and 2-4 p.m. Admission is $1.

The **Yarmouth County Museum,** 22 Collins St., tel. 742-5539, showcases Canada's largest ship-portrait collection and exhibits a trove of seafaring lore, musical instruments, ship models, furniture, and more. The research library and archives store extensive records and genealogical materials. Open year-round, its summer hours (June to mid-Oct.) are Mon.-Fri. 9 a.m.-5 p.m., Sun. 1-5 p.m.; open Tues.-Sat. 2-5 p.m. the rest of the year. Admission is $1 adults, with discounts for students and children under 14.

Accommodations

The **Yarmouth Ice House Hostel** on Hwy. 1, 22 km northeast of Yarmouth, has four beds ($9) and is open June-Sept.; for directions, call (902) 649-2818. Closest camping to Yarmouth is at **Camper's Haven,** tel. 742-4848 or (800) 565-0000, five km east of Yarmouth in Arcadia. It features canoe rentals and a recreation hall with fireplace.

Just a block from the ferry terminal, the **Murray Manor B&B,** 225 Main St., tel. 742-9625, with three nonsmoking rooms ($45-55 with full breakfast), dates to the 1830s and sits back behind a low stone wall. It's open May to mid-October.

The **Journey's End Motel,** 96 Starrs Rd., tel. 742-1111, is a basic dependable lodging with 80 rooms ($60-72). **Rodd Grand Hotel,** 417 Main St., tel. 742-2446, has high-rise quarters just north of the business area with 138 rooms ($66-110), a dining room, popular lounge, indoor pool, and whirlpool. **Best Western Mermaid Motel,** 545 Main St., tel. 742-7821, has 45 spacious rooms ($80-100), a nearby restaurant, and an outdoor heated pool.

The **Rodd Colony Harbour Inn** on Forest St. overlooking harborfront, tel. 742-9194, is the setting for ferry watching. The inn has 65 pleas-

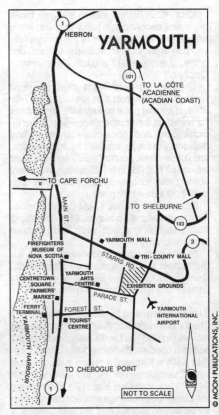

ant rooms with wide windows ($85-92), a restaurant, and lounge; the highest rate gets you a harborfront room.

Food

Harris' Quick 'n' Tasty restaurant on Hwy. 1, three km north of central Yarmouth, tel. (902) 742-3467, is a locally owned landmark. For quick and tasty clam, scallop, lobster, and chicken platters ($7-18), and such desserts as "mile-high" lemon or date meringue pie, this is the place. Locals like **Harris' Seafood Restaurant,** tel. 742-5420, opposite the Quick 'n' Tasty, for its Nova Scotian-styled entrees ($12 and up). Reservations are wise.

The ivy-draped **Manor Inn** on Hwy. 1 about 20 minutes from Yarmouth at Hebron, tel. 742-

2487 or 742-2076 (reservations are wise), basks in gardens surrounding a pond. Sparkling linens and fresh flowers grace the dining room, where you can order lobster, scallops, salmon, and prime rib entrees ($13 and up); it's open May-October.

The **Five Corners Restaurant,** also a bit north of downtown at 624 Main St., tel. 742-6061, is another place popular with Yarmouthers for breakfast, lunch, and dinner. Specialties include beef and homemade chowder and desserts. For soups, sandwiches, light desserts, and coffee drinks, **Joshua's,** 95 Water St., is just a block off Main St. in a 19th-century waterfront building with indoor and outdoor tables. It's open daily 7:30 a.m.-11:30 p.m.

Next door to Joshua's, just up Jenkins St., **Yarmouth Natural Foods,** tel. 742-2336, stocks trail mixes, bulk food, and health foods; it's open Mon.-Saturday.

For stocking up on groceries, the main supermarkets are at the malls on Starrs Road. Centrally located Save-Easy is at the Parade Street Plaza a block from Main Street.

Entertainment and Events

The **Twin Cinemas** at the Kmart Plaza has two movies nightly. The town's lively nighttime pub scene is concentrated along Main Street. **Captain Kelly's Kitchen,** a tavern in a converted white Queen Anne home at 577 Main, tel. (902) 742-9191, is open Mon.-Sat. to 2 a.m. (check out the **Lower Deck Lounge and Sports Pub** here for big-screen sports TV). If live entertainment is in town, it's at the **Clipper Ship Beverage Room** on Main St., Thurs.-Sat. nights. A quieter scene reigns at **Haley's,** at the Rodd Grand Hotel, which has a piano bar.

The **Yarmouth Arts Centre** (known locally as Th'YARC), 76 Parade St., tel. 742-8150, puts on drama and musicals April-September. **Seafest** is another crowd pleaser during seven days in late July, and the **Yarmouth County Exhibition** spans a week with country fair exhibits and entertainment in mid-August. Summer finishes with the three-day **Bluegrass Festival** that runs concurrently with the **Yarmouth Cup International Yacht Race** in early September.

Recreation

The 57-foot wooden schooner *William Moir* sails five times daily on scenic cruises from Killam's Wharf, 90 Water St., tel. (902) 742-8654. Trips last from 40 minutes to two hours, $10-25, with discounts for children under 12.

The welter of lakes and rivers inland from Yarmouth and the maze of inlets to the southeast make the county prime canoeing territory. Pick up the *Canoeing* brochure at the tourist information office, which gives detailed descriptions and directions for 14 paddle trips for boaters of all abilities.

Likewise, the low-lying area makes for wonderful cycling. One easy, rewarding route is the 23-km-round-trip spin out to Yarmouth Lighthouse on Cape Forchu. Follow Main St. north and turn left at Vancouver Street. Just past the hospital complex, turn left on Grove Road. The Faith Memorial Baptist Church marks the site where the famous Yarmouth Runic Stone, believed to have been inscribed by Leif Eriksson's men, was found. Next you come to the lighthouse, perched on a stone promontory. Beyond the parking lot, a trail leads down to Leif Ericson Picnic Park, overlooking the rocky coast. Several other trips are outlined in the *Cycling* brochure, available from the tourist office.

Captain Hubert and Helen Hall, members of the Nova Scotia Bird Society, offer guided **birdwatching** tours around the Yarmouth area ($20 for two hours). Contact them at 742-4467.

The **YMCA,** 348 Main St., has an indoor pool, weight room, and racquetball court, and **Personal Best Fitness,** at Main and Alma streets, offers a weight room and a suntan salon. A day-use pass at either place costs $5.

Shopping

The town's **farmers' market** on Hawthorne St. is the place for fresh-baked goods, marinated or smoked fish, and local crafts. It's open June-Oct., Sat. 9 a.m.-3 p.m.

The **Yarmouth Wool Shoppe** at 352 Main St. is among Nova Scotia's best stocked stores for Hudson Bay coats and blankets and Scottish tartans styled in apparel or by the yard. **R.H. Davis and Company,** 361 Main St., sells locally made crafts along with topographical maps ($8) and nautical charts ($12).

There are several camera shops, but none can repair an ailing camera. **Atlantic Photo Service,** 4 Collins St., tel. (902) 742-4245, and

South West Photo, 614 Main St., tel. 742-4126, stock film and basic equipment.

Information and Services

The provincial **Tourist Information Centre,** 228 Main at Forest St., tel. (902) 742-5033, shares quarters with the **Yarmouth Tourist Bureau** and stocks abundant provincial and seaport literature and information; open May-Oct., daily 9 a.m.-5 p.m. and July-Aug. to 8:30 p.m.

The public library across from Frost Park alongside Main St. is open Mon.-Fri. 9 a.m.-9 p.m., Sat. to 5 p.m. Local newspapers include Tuesday editions of the *Vanguard* and the Acadians' *Le Courrier* in French.

Yarmouth Regional Hospital is at 60 Vancouver St., tel. 742-3124. For the **RCMP,** call 742-9111. The port has seven banks downtown and at the malls, and there's also a currency-exchange counter (exchange rates are better at the banks) at the tourist office, Main and Forest streets. **Canada Post** is at 15 Willow St., open Mon.-Fri. 8 a.m.-5:30 p.m.; the philatelic window is open 8:30 a.m.-noon and 1:30-4:30 p.m. **Pharmasave,** 333 Main St., has a retail postal outlet, open Mon.-Fri. 9 a.m.-9 p.m., Sat. to 5:30 p.m.

Transportation

The **Prince of Fundy Cruises'** *Scotia Prince* links the seaport to Portland, Maine, and operates early May-October. **Marine Atlantic's** car ferry *Bluenose* connects Yarmouth with Bar Harbor, Maine, year-round. For details and schedules, see the "Ferry Schedules" chart in the On the Road chapter.

Air Nova, tel. (800) 776-3000 from the U.S. (various toll-free numbers in Canada, depending on locale; ask the information operator), flies into Yarmouth twice daily on the Halifax-Yarmouth-Boston route. **Yarmouth Airport,** open during flights, is five minutes east of town on Starrs Road. **Avis,** 55 Starrs Rd., tel. (902) 742-3323 or (800) 879-2847, has rentals at the airport and ferry terminal. **Budget,** tel. 742-9500, (800) 527-0700 in the U.S., (800) 268-8900 in Canada, has locations at the airport and at the ferry.

The **MacKenzie Line** bus stops at the Texaco Station on Main Street. **Acadian Lines,** tel. 742-5131, pulls into the former VIA Rail terminal and has daily departures to Halifax ($35 OW)

via its Fundy coastal circuit. Six taxi outfits serve the town; **Yarmouth Town Taxi,** 133 Argyle St., tel. 742-7801, charges a flat $3.50 anywhere in town. **Tri County Cab,** tel. 742-2323, also offers scenic tours of the area.

Bailey's at 339 Main St. rents bikes, as does the bike outlet at **Rodd's Grand Hotel. Designer Tours** designs custom tours of Yarmouth and the area at $30 per hour for up to four visitors; for details, call 742-4849.

LA CÔTE ACADIENNE

North of Yarmouth begins La Côte Acadienne ("Acadian Coast"), a 50-km coastal stretch populated by descendants of the French who resettled here after the Acadian expulsion of 1755. Between Rivière-aux-Saumon ("Salmon River") in the south and Weymouth in the north, the place-names, the soaring Catholic churches, and the proud Acadian flags (a French tricolor with a single yellow star) announce that you're in the largest Francophone enclave in Nova Scotia. The French spoken by the people here retains vestiges of the 17th-century tongue spoken by the original Acadians, spiced with Micmac and English words. (You'll also hear this region called the "District of Clare," a decidedly non-French name given it in 1767 by Nova Scotia's governor Michael Franklin for the area's resemblance to that Irish county.)

The Ice Age left its mark on this rocky seacoast, where 10,000 years ago the ice mass from New Brunswick and the Nova Scotian ice cap met. At the beach at Salmon River, two levels of glacial till show that the Fundy was 15 meters higher during the Ice Age. At Comeauville, between Saulnierville and Grosses Coques, the road to the golf club runs atop an ice-age moraine.

That made the land a challenge for farmers; draft horses are not powerful enough to pull a plow through the boulder-strewn terrain, and you'll see oxen doing the brute-force job. But the early Acadians persevered here and their hard work and thrifty ways paid off. Today the villages are thriving centers of shipbuilding, fishing, and mink ranching.

The villages appear one after another up the sheltered coast of Baie Sainte-Marie ("St. Mary's

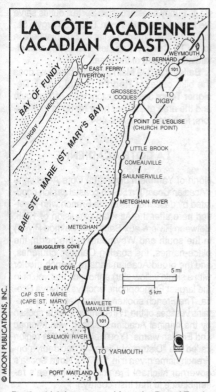

LA CÔTE ACADIENNE
(ACADIAN COAST)

BAY OF FUNDY

DIGBY NECK

BAIE STE-MARIE (ST. MARY'S BAY)

WEYMOUTH
ST. BERNARD
EAST FERRY
TIVERTON
GROSSES COQUES
TO DIGBY
POINT DE L'EGLISE
(CHURCH POINT)
LITTLE BROOK
COMEAUVILLE
SAULNIERVILLE
METEGHAN RIVER
METEGHAN
SMUGGLER'S COVE
BEAR COVE
CAP STE-MARIE
(CAPE ST. MARY)
MAVILETE
(MAVILLETTE)
SALMON RIVER
TO YARMOUTH
PORT MAITLAND

0   5 mi
0   5 km

© MOON PUBLICATIONS, INC.

Bay"), which is separated from the Bay of Fundy by the Digby Neck peninsula. The settlements are small, their austere frame houses speckling the flat coastal plain in colors of white, yellow, blue, or green. The Hwy. 101 expressway from Yarmouth skirts the region on the inland side, while two-lane Hwy. 1 clings to the coast. The latter route, connecting 14 seaports and inland villages that blend from one to the next, has been called the "longest main street in the world."

Mavillette Area
Mavillette Beach Provincial Park on Hwy. 1 lies one-half km from Cap Sainte-Marie. A boardwalk leads over grassy dunes and down to the long sandy beach. From here, a 16-km hiking trail leading north to **Smuggler's Cove Provincial Park** passes coastal cliffs notched with caves, once used by rum-runners during U.S. Prohibition in the 1920s.

Cape View Motel And Cottages on Hwy. l, tel. (902) 645-2258, overlooks beach dunes with 10 basic rooms and five cottages ($40-75); it's open May-October. **Cape View Restaurant,** at the beach's opposite end, has seafood and Acadian dishes ($7-15) and Fundy views; **Cape St. Mary Charters and Tour Fishing,** tel. 645-2519, has its office in the restaurant. The company operates twice-daily deep-sea fishing excursions ($30), sunset plus "herring city" coastal tours ($20), and late summer whalewatching trips ($30).

Meteghan
Settled in 1785, the seaport of Meteghan (from the Micmac word for "Blue Rocks") is the district's commercial hub, with a population of about 984. **Musée La Vielle Maison** ("Old House Museum") on Hwy. 1, tel. (902) 645-2599, is in the Robicheau family's former homestead. The museum features 18th-century furnishings and exhibits explaining the area's history, with help from bilingual guides in traditional Acadian costume. Admission is free, but donations are accepted. It's open July and Aug., daily 10 a.m.-5 p.m.

The museum also houses the **Clare Tourist Bureau,** tel. 645-2389, which stocks bilingual literature and arranges tours to local sites and mink farms. It's open July and Aug., daily 10 a.m.-5 p.m.

The **Festival Acadien de Clare** during early July attracts 30,000 spectators, and a concurrent festival is held at Church Point. For a place to overnight, **Bluefin Motel** on Hwy. 1, tel. 645-2251, has 19 rooms ($60) and a dining room.

A seafood cornucopia is brought in daily by the seaport's scallop draggers, herring seiners, and lobster boats. **Seashore Restaurant** on Hwy. 1 near the museum, tel. 645-3453, and **Countryside Restaurant** on Bonnie Rd., tel. 645-2555, are among the best places for seafood dining. **Maison du Croissant** combines a cafeteria with tea-room trappings and sells homemade delicacies and croissants. **Hometown Market** has a deli counter with picnic ingredients; it's open Mon.-Sat. 8 a.m.-9 p.m., Sun. from 9 a.m.

Royal Bank of Canada handles area bank-

blue whale

ing; it's open Mon.-Tues. 10 a.m.-3 p.m., Wed.-Thurs. to 4 p.m., Fri. to 6 p.m. **Canada Post** is open Mon.-Fri. 8 a.m.-4:30 p.m. **Meteghan Public Library** has genealogical records on its shelves; for hours, call 645-3350. **RCMP** has a Meteghan detachment, tel. 645-2326; call an **ambulance** at 645-2094.

Continuing up the Coast

The town of **Meteghan River** is Nova Scotia's largest wooden-ship-building center. **Comeauville,** a bit farther, is known to golfers for **Terrain de Golf de Clare** off Hwy. 1, tel. (902) 769-2124. It's an 18-hole par-71 course; handcart club and rentals are available. **Golf Course View Bed and Breakfast,** tel. 769-2065, overlooks the course with three rooms ($24 with full breakfast) and hiking trails. In town, **Wayne's IGA** sells groceries and picnic fixings; it's open Mon.-Sat. 7 a.m.-9 p.m., Sun. from 9 a.m.

In **Little Brook,** you can get groceries or a deli sandwich at **Marketeria,** open Mon.-Sat. 8 a.m.-6 p.m. Or stop and bend an elbow with locals at **Le Club Social de Clare,** tel. 769-2128. The bar offers live music and dancing, Mon.-Fri. 8:30 p.m.-midnight.

Pointe de l'Église ("Church Point")

Built between 1903 and 1905, the enormous **Église de Sainte-Marie** (St. Mary's Church), the largest and tallest wooden church in North America, dominates the village of 490 inhabitants. The building is laid out in the shape of a cross, and its soaring 56-meter-high (185-foot) steeple has been ballasted with 40 tons of rock to withstand the winter winds' force. The church is open May to mid-October, daily 9 a.m.-4 p.m.;

a bilingual guide is on hand to answer questions.

The **Université Sainte-Anne,** founded in 1891, is Nova Scotia's only French-language university. **Le Musée Sainte-Marie,** in the library building, exhibits religious artifacts and history. The university's **Restaurant Le Casse-Croûte** welcomes visitors and serves a notable selection of Acadian dishes.

At the university's **Théâtre Marc Lescarbot,** the play *Évangéline,* based on the Longfellow poem of love surviving the Acadian Deportation, is presented in vernacular Acadian French. But it's not just for French speakers. The highly visual performance includes singing and dancing, and an English synopsis is available. Showtime is 8 p.m. Sunday in June and Sept., Sunday and Tuesday in July and Aug.; admission is $12 adults, $10 seniors, $8 children. Call (902) 769-2114 for reservations.

In town, **Marée Haute,** tel. 769-2005, serves heaping portions of Acadian fare and is a place where the locals meet.

The public pool is open for swims, Mon.-Sat. 7:30 a.m.-8 p.m., Sun. 2-4 p.m. **Royal Bank of Canada** handles currency conversion. **La Shoppe à Bois,** tel. 769-2571, sells commendable reproductions of historic furniture.

Grosses Coques

This village of 362 takes its name from the huge bar clams harvested here on the tidal flats, which were an important food source for early settlers. **Art et Mineraux,** tel. (902) 837-7145, is an outlet for local artists and sculptors, and also stocks a selection of fossil, mineral, and crystal specimens.

DIGBY AND VICINITY

DIGBY

The ferry seaport of Digby (pop. 2,558) overlooks the Annapolis Basin's southwestern corner and anchors the Annapolis Valley's western end. As terminus for the ferry from Saint John, New Brunswick, and home port for the world's largest scallop fleet, the modest town serves as the area's commercial hub. Digby derived its name from Admiral Robert Digby, the Loyalist who sailed up the Fundy in 1793 and settled the place with 1,500 Loyalists from New England.

Lying aside the area's main roads, Digby is easily bypassed. High-speed Hwy. 101 lies south of Digby and routes sightseers up the St. Mary's Bay coastline into Annapolis Valley. More scenic Hwy. 1, the pastoral route through the valley, starts beyond Digby to the west. Even the site of Digby's ferry terminal diverts traffic around town, and if you enter the province from New Brunswick, street signs will direct you from Shore Rd. to Hwy. 101 via Victoria St. and Highway 303.

But Digby has its own rewards. The baronial Pines Resort Hotel peers down over the port from the prow of a hill on the town's outskirts. At harborfront, the scallop fleet ties up off Fishermen's Wharf off Water St.; be there at sunset when the pastel-painted draggers lie at anchor in a semicircle, backlit by the intense setting sun. For a double treat, try the view from a table at the Fundy Restaurant overlooking the Annapolis Basin and a platter of deep-fried or broiled scallops. With more scallopy arcana, Digby's newest attraction is the floating museum aboard the 98-foot scallop dragger *Lady Vanessa,* tel. (902) 245-4467, moored next to the Club 99. Onboard are models, a sealife touch tank, and videos relating to the region's key industry.

Digby's place in history is on display at the harborfront **Admiral Digby Museum** at 95 Montague Row, tel. 245-6322, with exhibits of old photographs, maps, and maritime artifacts; it's open late June-Aug., daily 9 a.m.-5 p.m., in September, open Mon.-Sat. 1-5 p.m.

Accommodations

The **Summer's Inn Bed and Breakfast** at 16 Warwick St., tel. (902) 245-2250, has seven rooms ($49-59 with a full breakfast) and a two-bedroom suite, with kitchen and living room ($99 d) within a historic building near waterfront. The **Kingfisher Motel** at the highway end of War-

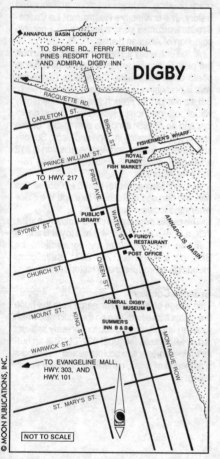

wick St., tel. 245-4747, has 37 rooms ($52), a restaurant, and launderette; it's open mid-May to October.

The **Admiral Digby Inn,** on Shore Rd. between Pines Resort Hotel and the ferry terminal, tel. 245-2531, has better than average motel accommodations with 44 rooms ($67), a restaurant, and launderette; it's open mid-April to mid-October.

The **Pines Resort Hotel,** 103 Shore Rd., tel. 245-2511, appeals to luxury-loving guests. Its niceties include afternoon tea. Open June-Oct., the French Norman manor of stucco and stone was built in 1903 and served as a Canadian Pacific Railway hotel until the province bought it in 1965. The accommodations ($112-250 s, $127-250 d and t) include 83 rooms in the manor and 61 rooms in cottages shaded by spruce, fir, and pine. The hotel offers a dining room of provincial renown, an 18-hole golf course, outdoor pool, fitness center, tennis courts, and hiking trails. Plan your whalewatching excursions at the front desk.

Food
The **Fundy Restaurant** at 34 Water St., tel. (902) 245-4950, overlooks the Annapolis Basin with dining in the main restaurant, in a solarium, or on balconies. Digby scallops are the specialty, prepared any way you'd like them or in combination with other seafood ($9-20); reservations are wise.

The **Pines Resort Hotel** boasts a main dining room whose menu entrees ($35-50) have won plaudits for decades—try the glazed beef tenderloin, chicken basted in white wine, or Digby scallops sautéed in a butter blend of light spices. Reservations are wise; call 245-2511.

In town, locals enjoy meals at the truckers' favorite **Digby Irving Restaurant,** at the intersection of Hwys. 303 North and 101. For picnic ingredients, check out the **Royal Fundy Fish Market** at Fishermen's Wharf. It offers a tempting showcase of seafood chowder, fresh mussels and salmon, cooked lobster, and smoked cod, haddock, mackerel, and Digby chicks (smoked herring). Supermarkets are in town and at the Evangeline Mall, on Warwick St.; the **Foodliner IGA** at Water and Mount streets is open Mon.-Fri. 8:30 a.m.-9 p.m., Sat. to 6 p.m.

Entertainment and Events
Montague Row to Water Street is the place for people-watching, especially at sunset. **Club 98 Lounge** at 28 Water St. in the Fundy Restaurant has a band ($5 cover charge) or disc jockey, Fri.-Saturday. The lounge at **Pines Resort Hotel** is known for tamer pursuits, low lighting, comfortable ambience, and finely tuned mixed drinks; it's open Mon.-Saturday.

The port's famed scallops attract appropriate fanfare during **Digby Scallops Days** with a parade, scallop-shucking competitions, street vendors, the crowning of the Scallop Queen and Princesses, music, fireworks, and crafts sales for eight days in early August.

Recreation
The 18-hole par-71 **Digby Golf Club** overlooks Digby from a hilltop. Cart and club rentals are available. For tee-off time and reservations call (902) 245-4104.

If you're interested in Brier Island whalewatching, contact **Thistle Down Inn** at 98 Montague Row, tel. 245-4490. The inn also rents bikes at $10 per day.

Shopping, Services, and Information
Keeping Room Crafts at 93 Montague Row stocks colonial-style corn-husk dolls, pottery, and ship models. **Marilyn Mullen Crafts,** tel. (902) 245-2831, specializes in handmade quilts at her Shore Rd. shop between the Admiral Digby Inn and the ferry terminal.

Three banks in town have similar hours; the **Bank of Nova Scotia** at 61 Water St. is open Mon.-Thurs. 10 a.m.-3 p.m., Friday to 5 p.m. The nearby **Canada Post** at Water and Church streets is open Mon.-Fri. 8:30 a.m.-5:15 p.m.; **Marshall's Variety Store** at 101 Water St. is the postal retail outlet; it's open Mon.-Sat. 7 a.m.-midnight, Sunday from 9 a.m.

The **public library** at First and Sydney streets is open Tues.-Fri. 3-5 p.m., Saturday 10 a.m.-1 p.m. **Digby General Hospital** is at 67 Warwick St., tel. 245-2501; for the **RCMP** call 245-2579.

The **Digby Tourist Information Bureau,** at waterfront on Water St., tel. 245-5417, is open May-October. The provincial **tourist information centre** on Shore Rd. near the outskirts of Digby, tel. 245-2201, is open mid-May to mid-October, daily 9 a.m.-5 p.m., from mid-June to 9 p.m.

low tide at Bear River

Transportation

Digby is the terminus for Marine Atlantic's MV *Princess of Acadia,* the car ferry to Saint John, New Brunswick. The Marine Atlantic terminal, tel. (902) 245-2116, is five km north of town on Shore Rd. (Hwy. 303). Three crossings (2.5 hours) are made Mon.-Sat., two on Sunday. Reservations are necessary.

The **Acadian Lines** bus pulls into Irving gas station at Hwys. 303 North and 101 on its Fundy loop circuit. Digby to Wolfville is $16 one-way. Anywhere in Digby by taxi costs $4, while a cab to the ferry terminal is $7 from harborfront or $8 from the bus stop. **Basin Taxi,** tel. 245-4408, has a stand on Water Street.

Avis rental cars has an office at Warwick St. and Montague Row, tel. 245-6100.

The Digby Neck

The Digby Neck is a long, spindly peninsula reaching like an antenna from Digby into the Bay of Fundy. Highway 217 runs down its center, through the villages of Centreville, Sandy Cove, and Mink Cove, to East Ferry where a car ferry ($1 round-trip) crosses to Long Island. A second ferry (also $1) connects Long Island to Brier Island, the end of the road. Brier Island, Nova Scotia's westernmost extremity, is known for good whalewatching and birdwatching, as well as swimming, fishing, and rockhounding. Ask about it all at the **visitor information center** in Tiverton, at the north end of Long Island.

For whalewatchers, Brier Island is *the* place.

Brier Island Whale and Seabird Cruises, operating out of Westport, tel. (902) 839-2995 (reservations required), runs daily cruises June-Oct. in search of finbacks, right whales, dolphins, and porpoises.

For island overnighters, the **Westport Inn,** tel. 839-2675, offers home cooking and rooms in a 100-year-old home for $35 s, $45 d. **Brier Island Lodge and Restaurant,** tel. 839-2300, on a bluff overlooking the sea, has 24 rooms and a homestyle restaurant (open 6:30 a.m.-9 p.m.).

KEJIMKUJIK NATIONAL PARK

Deep in the interior of southwestern Nova Scotia, Kejimkujik (pronounced kedgi-muh-KOO-jick, or simply "Keji" or "Kedge" for short) National Park lies off Hwy. 8, about midway between Liverpool and Annapolis Royal. Encompassing 381 square km of drumlins (rounded glacial hills) and island-dotted lakes—legacies of the last ice age—and hardwood and conifer forests, the park and the adjacent Tobeatic Game Sanctuary are an important refuge for native wildlife and town-weary Nova Scotians.

Wildlife enthusiasts visit the park for bird-watching (including barred owls, pileated wood-peckers, scarlet tanagers, great crested fly-catchers, and loons and other waterfowl) and may also spot black bears, white-tailed deer, bobcats, porcupines, and beavers. The many lakes and connecting rivers attract canoeists and swimmers in warm weather, as well as anglers (particularly for perch and brook trout). Hikers can choose from a network of trails, some leading to backcountry campgrounds; some of the campgrounds are also accessible by canoe. In winter, cross-country skiers take over the hiking trails.

The **Beech Grove Trail** on a two-km loop starts at the visitor center and wends along the Mersey River, where it climbs a drumlin hilltop swathed in an almost pure beech grove. The **Farmlands Trail** is another drumlin variation, and the 45-minute hike makes its way up a drumlin to an abandoned farm on the hilltop.

The **McGinty Lake Trail** is the ultimate drumlin trek; the two-hour hike starts on the road inland from the lake. Rewards are quick. The first drumlin appears in less than a kilometer, the second crops up before the lake, and the third hill, with an old farm on its crest, lies halfway through the five-km hike.

You can rent canoes, rowboats, and bicycles at Pabek's Rentals, tel. (902) 682-2817, at Jakes Landing on the northeast side of large Kejimkujik Lake; the adjacent stretch of the Mersey River is placid, suitable for beginning paddlers.

Jeremys Bay Campground, tel. 682-2772, on the north side of Kejimkujik Lake, has 329 unserviced sites for tents and trailers ($11, no reservations), with washrooms and showers, playgrounds, picnic areas, nature programs, and canoe ($13 per day) and bike ($16 per day) rentals. Another 46 wilderness sites (about $12 for the permit and site) are scattered in the woodlands with toilets, tables, grills, and free firewood; reservations are accepted, call 682-2772. The visitor information and administration center, at the park entrance, has literature, a topographical map ($4), and seven-day fishing licenses valid within the park ($6).

The **Sandy Bottom Lake Hostel** off Hwy. 8 in South Milford, about halfway between the park and Annapolis Royal, has 10 beds ($8); for directions, call 532-2497. Swim or cross-country ski nearby.

Kejimkujik is open year-round; be wary of ticks during May-June and poison ivy throughout the summer. For general inquiries, contact the Superintendent, Kejimkujik National Park, P.O. Box 36A, Maitland Bridge, NS B0T 1N0, tel. 682-2772.

THE ANNAPOLIS VALLEY

The Annapolis Valley is a haze of white when its apple orchards bloom in late May to early June. Towns from Digby to Windsor celebrate with the **Annapolis Valley Apple Blossom Festival.** Berwick is so rich in apple blossoms that the town has a concurrent **Blossom Bash.**

The valley supports more than magnificent apple orchards, however; if you look closely you'll also see hectares of strawberries, plums, peaches, pears, and cherries, as well as crops of hay, grains, and tobacco. Strawberries are ready to harvest during July, and Annapolis Royal sets a day aside for its **Strawberry Tea.** At Port Williams, the Anglican parish of Cornwallis marks each harvest, as it has for a century, with the **Strawberry Supper.** The rich New England planters who settled here in the 18th century built resplendent houses, and many of these have been converted to cozy country inns.

The Annapolis Valley has a legion of fans, among them the early Micmac Indians, who first settled this region. According to Micmac legend, Glooscap, a deity taking the form of a giant man, roamed the areas of the upper Fundy. He made his home atop the basalt cliffs of Cape Blomidon —the lofty hook-shaped peninsula that finishes in seastacks at Cape Split—and buried jewels on the Fundy beaches. (Today's tides still claw at the coastline to reveal agate, amethyst, and zeolites from Hall's Harbour to Cape Split's tip.)

Legend also has it that Glooscap chose the area for its magnificent views. For a sweeping overview of the Annapolis Basin, check out **Old St. Edward's Loyalist Church Museum,** on a hilltop at Clementsport near Digby. Farther up the valley, Bridgetown's **Valleyview Provincial Park** sits high on North Mountain and overlooks the valley's western end. At Wolfville, a drive up Highland Ave. on **Wolfville Ridge** opens up another angle of the western valley, and the town's Gaspereau Ave. climbs a similarly steep hill with more views.

ANNAPOLIS ROYAL AND VICINITY

In 1605, Samuel de Champlain and the survivors of the bitter winter in New Brunswick moved across the Bay of Fundy and established the fortified Port Royal Habitation about five km downriver from what is now Annapolis Royal. The first lasting settlement north of Florida, the outpost also boasted other historic firsts: Canada's first play, *Le Théâtre de Neptune*, was written and produced here by the young Parisian lawyer Marc Lescarbot; the continent's first social club, l'Ordre de Bon Temps ("the Order of Good Cheer") was founded here in 1606; and the New World's first grain mill was built here to grind meal from the first cereal crops. Eight years after its founding, the settlement came to an abrupt end as New Englanders attacked and destroyed the Habitation. It has since been reconstructed (see below).

In the 1630s, the French governor Charles de Menou d'Aulnay built a new Port Royal on the south shore of the Annapolis Basin; it included the original earthworks at what is now Fort Anne. The British captured the fort in 1710, renaming it Fort Anne and rechristening the town as Annapolis Royal in honor of their queen. It would serve as Nova Scotia's first capital until 1749, when it was succeeded by the new town of Halifax.

The **Annapolis Royal Tidal Power Project** on Hwy. 1 is the world's only power-generating station to produce electricity from the tides. Its operation is explained inside; it's open May to mid-October, daily 9 a.m.-5 p.m., July-Aug. to 8 p.m. The **tourist office** in the same building, tel. (902) 532-5454, stocks area and provincial sightseeing literature; it's open the same hours.

Fort Anne National Historic Site

This 18th-century fort and grounds, Canada's first national historic site, is on St. George St. in Annapolis Royal and overlooks the confluence of the Annapolis and Allain rivers. The early French fort was designed with a star-shaped layout, and it's impressively banked with sweeping verdant lawns and deep moats. The British added the 1797 officers' garrison, which houses the fort's museum with historical exhibits; tel. (902) 532-2397. It's open year-round, daily 9 a.m.-6 p.m. mid-May to mid-Oct., weekdays 9 a.m.-5 p.m. the rest of the year. Admission is free. The surrounding park grounds are always open.

Annapolis Royal Historic Gardens

The Historic Gardens, off George St. in Annapolis Royal, tel. (902) 532-7018, comprise four hectares of theme gardens, demonstrating gardening techniques of the early Acadians as well as the most modern methods, plus two hectares of reclaimed marshland and a waterfowl refuge. It's open mid-May to mid-Oct., daily 8 a.m. to dusk. Admission is $3.50, with discounts for seniors and students.

Port Royal National Historic Site— The Habitation

The original French settlement of 1605 has been reconstructed at what is believed to be the original site, on the north side of the Annapolis River. Built from Samuel de Champlain's plan, using 17th-century joinery techniques, the rustic build-

showpieces of the Historic Gardens

NAN DROSDICK

ings—governor's house, priest's dwelling, bakery, guard room, and others, furnished with period reproductions—form a rectangle around a courtyard within the palisaded compound.

The site is about 10 km west of Annapolis Royal, off Hwy. 1A. It's open mid-May to mid-Oct., daily 9 a.m.-6 p.m.; tel. (902) 532-2898. Admission is free, but donations help.

Upper Clements

The **Upper Clements Family Vacation Park** off Hwy. 1, tel. (902) 532-7557, is Atlantic Canada's largest theme park. Its style is thoroughly Nova Scotian, featuring a train ride on a historic replica, and a minigolf course designed as the province's map. The park also has a roller coaster, flume ride, carousel, entertainment, dinner theater ($25) Fri.-Sat., a crafts area with demonstrations and a shop, and dining rooms (entrees range $4-10). Admission is free, and a bracelet of tokens ($7-13) buys entrance to the rides and shows. It's open mid-May to mid-Oct., daily 10 a.m.-7 p.m.

Accommodations and Food

Annapolis Royal boasts a brace of lodgings in vintage homes. **Queen Ann Inn,** 494 Upper Saint George St., tel. (902) 532-7850, is a restored mansion, built circa 1865, with 10 rooms ($50-85 with full breakfast) with period furnishings. Across the road, the **Hillsdale House Inn,** 519 Upper Saint George St., tel. 532-2345, set on a 15-acre estate, has 10 antique-furnished bedrooms ($60-80 with full breakfast), a lounge, and patio.

Across the river, spacious **Dunromin Campsite and Trailer Court,** tel. 532-2808, has open and wooded spaces by the riverside, $12-16. It's open mid-April through October.

Leo's Cafe, 222 Saint George St., tel. 532-7424, is open daily throughout the summer for dinner, 5:30-9 p.m., and Sundays noon-4 p.m. Sandwiches, inventive homemade soups and specials, and salads are the bill of fare. A few doors down, the **Old Post Office,** tel. 532-7678, serves hearty country meals—turkey, ham, fresh vegetables, plus seafood—in a gingham-and-oak-furniture atmosphere. It's open July-October daily 5-9 p.m. Around the corner, locals gather for afternoon beer and pub grub on the outdoor patio or for nightcaps in the cozy interior

of English-style **Ye Olde Towne Pub,** 9-11 Church St. (reputed to be the smallest bar in Nova Scotia).

Entertainment

Across the street from Leo's Cafe, the **King's Theatre,** tel. (902) 532-5466 (box office), is the community's main venue for movies and live entertainment—concerts, drama and comedy, revues, and other events. It's open year-round.

WOLFVILLE

The Annapolis Valley's genteel town of Wolfville (pop. 3,235) began with the name Mud Creek, an ignoble tribute from the founding New England planters who wrestled with the Fundy coastal area once farmed by early Acadians. Now the town sits in the lushest part of the Annapolis Valley, and you won't want to miss it. Highway 1 runs through town as Main Street, where large houses with bay windows and ample porches sit comfortably beneath stately trees. Acadia University's ivy-covered buildings and manicured lawns lie along Main and University.

The town, just six blocks deep, has an uncomplicated layout alongside Hwy. 1 and Highway 101. It's a two-hour drive to Digby; Halifax is almost three hours in the other direction.

Sights

The **Randall House Historical Museum,** 171 Main St., tel. (902) 684-3876, is a historic house with period furnishings and local artifacts from the 1760s to the 20th century. It's open mid-June to mid-Sept., Mon.-Sat. 10 a.m.-5 p.m., Sun. 2-5 p.m. Admission is free.

The **Acadia University Art Gallery** in the Beveridge Arts Centre at Highland Ave. and Main St., tel. 542-2202 ext. 1373, has a fine-arts collection of local and regional works, highlighted by Alex Colville's oils and serigraphs. It's open year-round; June to mid-Sept. hours are daily noon-5 p.m. Admission is free.

Accommodations

Victoria's Historic Inn and Motel, 416 Main St., tel. (902) 542-5744, combines a historic house of 10 rooms ($49-89) with an adjacent four-room motel ($59) and a dining room. **Roselawn Lodging,** 32 Main St., tel. 542-3420, is a modest motel with 28 rooms and another 12 in adjacent cottages, open May to early September. Facilities include an outdoor pool, launderette, picnic tables, and a tennis court. Rates range $46-67.

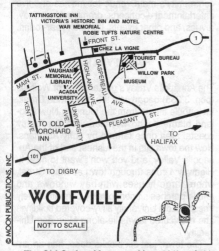

The **Old Orchard Inn,** near Hwy. 101's exit 11 and visible from the highway, tel. 542-5751, is a motel of 110 rooms ($69-88), 30 cabins (from $59 s and d), tennis courts, an indoor pool, saunas, hiking/ski trails, ski rentals, a popular dining room (for breakfast, lunch, and dinner), and a lounge.

The **Tattingstone Inn** at 434 Main St., tel. 542-7696, is casually formal with 10 nonsmoking rooms ($68-125) within the historic main house, as well as a separate carriage house and cottage. The inn also offers a music room, a popular dining room, steam room, heated outdoor pool, and tennis court.

The **Blomidon Inn,** 127 Main St., tel. 542-2291 or (800) 565-2291, is a former sea captain's mansion with expansive grounds. It fronts the main drag with 26 rooms ($69-99), two parlors, a restaurant, and tennis court. Special accommodation/activity packages include Eagle Watching, Winetasting, Honeymoon, and Mystery Dinner.

Food
The dining room at the **Old Orchard Inn,** tel. (902) 542-5751, draws diners with sea views and good food. Specialties are chateaubriand and cherries jubilee. Entrees range $6-27, and reservations are required.

The **Chez la Vigne** at 17 Front St., tel. 542-5077, boasts owner/chef Alex Clavel, who won Canadian Chef of the Year in 1989. His menu is French-inspired and includes pheasant, rabbit, guinea hen, and seafood dishes ($7-19). Terrace dining outside during warm weather augments the pleasant dining room. Reservations are required.

At **Tattingstone Inn,** tel. 542-7696, innkeeper Betsy Harwood creates feasts with pheasant and wild rice spiced with rosemary, raspberry-glazed chicken, and other gourmet fare; a complete meal costs $25, and specialties change daily. Reservations are required.

This university town offers numerous small places for light meals in attractive settings. **Acton's Cafe And Grill** at 268 Main St. features homemade main meal pies ($7). The **Kip Cafe** at 246 Main St. has tasty sandwiches and desserts. **EOS Fine Foods,** 10 Front St., stocks natural foods.

Entertainment and Events
The lounge at **Old Orchard Inn** is quietly crowded, while the **Black Cat,** 17 Front St., opens at 10 p.m. as a bistro with an intellectual buzz and light fare. The **Anvil Beverage Room** at the corner of Front St. and the Gaspereau Ave. extension has live entertainment (no cover charge) Friday and Saturday.

Mud Creek Days celebrates the town's origin as Mud Creek with three days of events, crafts sales, and a parade in late July or early August.

Recreation
The university's **War Memorial Gymnasium,** part of the arena complex across from the main campus on Main St., tel. (902) 542-2201 ext. 197, has a weight room, two indoor pools, a gym, and racquetball courts. The day-use pass costs $3; it's open daily 8 a.m.-10:30 p.m.

Shopping
For local and provincial watercolors, oils, and

pastels, check out the **Carriage House Gallery,** set back from the street at 246 Main Street. The **Weave Shed Crafts Co-operative** at 216 Main St. is an outlet marketing area crafts, especially handmade clothing of natural fibers. The **Sewing Basket** at 324 Main St. is the place for quilts, place mats, sweaters, and the Nova Scotia tartan sold by the yard.

More crafts are hawked at the **farmers' market** on Main St. across from the town hall; it's open June-Oct., Sat. 9 a.m.-1 p.m. For books about Wolfville and the area, check out the **Box of Delights** at 328 Main St. for new volumes, and the **Odd Book** bookstore at 8 Front St. for used paperbacks and hardbacks.

Information

The **Wolfville Tourist Bureau** ensconced at Willow Park on Main St., tel. (902) 542-7000 or 542-7117, is open May to mid-Oct., daily 9 a.m.-5 p.m. The university's **Vaughan Memorial Library** is open Mon.-Thurs. 8 a.m.-10 p.m., Fri. to 4:30 p.m., Sat. 10 a.m.-2 p.m.

The **Blomidon Naturalist Society** is an environmental group. Its interest in local chimney swifts led to the establishment of the **Robie Tufts Nature Centre** at the corner of Front and Elm streets, where the birds nest in the chimney and cavort at sunset. Society members meet at the university once a month. The town hall has updates; call 542-5767.

Acadia University hosts **Elderhostel** summertime sessions ($325 a week); for details call 542-2201 or write to Continuing Education Division, P.O. Box 118, Wolfville, NS B0P 1X0.

Services

Eastern Kings Memorial Hospital is at 23 Earnscliffe Ave., tel. (902) 542-2266. Call the **police** at 542-3817 or the **RCMP** at 679-5555. The **Bank of Montreal** at 282 Main St. is open Mon.-Thurs. 10 a.m.-4 p.m., Fri. to 5:30 p.m. **Canada Post** is open Mon.-Fri. 8:30 a.m.-5 p.m. **Wile's** at 210 Main St. has coin-operated laundry machines; it's open daily 8 a.m.-10 p.m.

Transportation

The **Acadian Lines** bus stops at Nowlan's Canteen at 389 Main St.; a ticket to Halifax costs $11 OW. The town has two taxi companies: **A-1**

Taxi is at Wade's parking lot and charges $3.50 anywhere in town; beyond Wolfville is 65 cents a km or about $65 OW to Halifax. **Valley Cycle Centre,** 234 Main St., rents standard and mountain bikes at $15 a day.

VICINITY OF WOLFVILLE

Starr Point

The **Prescott House** on Hwy. 358, tel. (902) 542-3984, harks back to the valley's orchard beginnings, when horticulturist Charles Ramage Prescott imported species to add to the provincial store of fruit trees; profits built this Georgian-styled homestead. The restored mansion, constructed circa 1814, displays period furnishings and sits amid beautiful gardens. It's open June to mid-Oct., Mon.-Sat. 9:30 a.m.-5:30 p.m., Sun. 1-5:30 p.m.

Grand-Pré

The **Grand-Pré National Historic Site** on Hwy. 1 is all that remains of Acadia's largest settlement, begun in 1680 and put to a premature demise by the 1755 Deportation. That event and the setting of Grand-Pré ("Great Meadow") were the inspiration for Longfellow's poem *Evangeline,* whose fictional heroine—the faithful Acadian girl separated from her lover by the Deportation—is also commemorated with a bronze statue here. The Saint-Charles Church, built by Acadian descendants in 1922, houses an exhibit on the events of the Acadian diaspora. It's open year-round, daily 9 a.m.-6 p.m., with guided tours mid-May to mid-October.

Grand-Pré Vineyards on Hwy. 1 grows wine grapes on 60 hectares of former Acadian farmland. A salesroom with a crafts corner is open year-round, Mon.-Sat. 9 a.m.-4 p.m.; for tour details, call (902) 542-1470.

Falmouth

Sainte Famille Wines, on the corner of Dyke Rd. and Dudley Park Lane, tel. (902) 798-8311, is another vineyard on former Acadian farmland. The winery's premium red and white wines are sold in the retail shop; open year-round, Mon.-Wed. and Sat. 10 a.m.-6 p.m., Thurs.-Fri. to 8 p.m., Sun. noon-6 p.m.

Windsor

Fort Edward National Historic Site, tel. (902) 542-3631, preserves the last 18th-century blockhouse in Nova Scotia. The blockhouse was one of the main assembly points for the deportation of the Acadians from the province in 1755. The site is open year-round; the building is open mid-June to early Sept., daily 10 a.m.-6 p.m. Admission is free.

Haliburton House on Clinton Ave., tel. 798-2915, was owned by 19th-century author, humorist, and historian Judge Thomas Chandler Haliburton, author of the Sam Slick stories. Among the clichés that originated in Haliburton's writings are: "It's raining cats and dogs," "barking up the wrong tree," "facts are stranger than fiction," and "quick as a wink." The Victorian mansion on 10 hectares is open June to mid-October, Mon.-Sat. 9:30 a.m.-5:30 p.m., Sun. 1-5 p.m.

The **Shand House** on Ferry Hill is another vintage beauty and

Thomas Chandler Haliburton

marks the wealthy Shand family's prominence in Windsor. When it was built in the early 1890s, the Queen Anne–style mansion was one of the first residences in the area fitted with electric lights and indoor plumbing. It's open June to mid-Oct., 9:30 a.m.-5:30 p.m., Sun. 1-5:30 p.m.

Mount Uniacke

Uniacke House, tel. (902) 866-2560, is a splendid 1813 colonial-style estate on 2,215 hectares, built by Nova Scotia's attorney general Richard John Uniacke. Uniacke chose this site because the surrounding countryside reminded him of his native Ireland. The home's interior features original furnishings, including four-poster beds and family portraits. The estate hosts woodworking demonstrations and old-time events such as the provincial Historical Equestrian Society riding exhibits. It's open June to mid-Oct., Mon.-Sat. 9:30 a.m.-5:30 p.m., Sun. 1-5:30 p.m. Admission is free.

EASTERN NOVA SCOTIA

Nova Scotia's Scottish heritage originated with the first Highland immigrants who trickled into the area: to Pictou County in the 1770s, New Glasgow in the 1780s, and the Arisaig area in the next decade. Loyalists arrived on Nova Scotia's eastern shore in the 1780s, followed by Irish immigrants at Antigonish in 1784.

It was during the early 1800s, however, that the region's decidedly Scottish complexion was firmly established. England and France were engaged in the Napoleonic War, and the French had blocked British ports. England desperately needed food, and began the Highland Clear-ances—poor tenant farmers in Scotland were turned off their land, their homes were burned, and the farmlands were converted to sheep and cattle pastures. The Clearances continued for almost two decades. Thousands of Scots died of starvation and disease, while thousands more took the Crown up on its offer of free land in Nova Scotia. They left their beloved Highlands forever and re-created their old home in a new land. Intense emotional ties remain to this day, and the Scots' heritage is kept alive with festivals commemorating their history and culture.

THE STRAIT SHORE

The TransCanada promises little besides uninterrupted speed on its route across the northeastern mainland. The best vistas, beaches, camping, and other attractions lie off the expressway, along the strait's coastal roads between Tatamagouche and Cape Breton. Shallow pools of seawater among sandbars turn warm in the sun, making for comfortable wading and swimming at Rushton's Beach Provincial Park, Tatamagouche Bay, and Melmerby Beach Provincial Park, east of Pictou.

PICTOU AND VICINITY

Pictou (pop. 4,413), located on a fine harbor at the confluence of three rivers, was founded by New Englanders in 1767. Six years later, when 33 families and 25 unmarried men arrived from the Scottish Highlands aboard the *Hector,* Pictou became the "birthplace of New Scotland." The Scots platted the town in 1787. Pictou began at Water and Front streets, and harborfront is still the town's focus.

The flamboyant Presbyterian minister and doctor Thomas McCulloch, en route to ministerial duties on Prince Edward Island, arrived here with his family by accident in 1803 when a storm blew his ship into Pictou Harbour. Local immigrants asked him to stay, and McCulloch agreed. In addition to providing medical care to the immigrants, McCulloch tried to reform the province's backward educational system. His efforts helped distance academia from the strictures of the church, and in 1817 he founded the Pictou Academy. He would later become the first president of Dalhousie College in Halifax.

The minister-cum-educator's residence, Sherbrooke Cottage (now McCulloch House), built in 1806 in distinct Scottish vernacular style, is one

of many historic stone houses and buildings designed to reflect local lineage. Small Pictou also has numerous fancier styles; you'll see examples of stone Gothic and Second Empire designs along Water, Front, and Church streets.

Pictou's emergence as a provincial destination is relatively recent. Nothing much happened between the Scots' arrival and the 20th century, and the town dozed through the centuries. The provincial highway system developed and skirted the town. The TransCanada came along and created a fast west-to-east expressway south of Pictou, with Hwy. 106 as the route's spur up to the ferry at Caribou. The somnolence ended with the re-creation of the historic *Hector,* a slow-moving project at harborfront that draws summertime tourists to see the trusty, wide-hulled wooden ship take shape.

The Town Today

Nearly everything in Pictou happens at waterfront, the stretch from Water and Front streets along Pictou Harbour to the ferry terminal at Caribou on the strait. Besides scenery, the varied shore roads boast a ghost. Try the drive along the strait on a misty autumn evening. Locals have seen the image of a burning ship with billowing sails skimming the strait. Nova Scotians aren't the only ones who have seen the ship. Prince Edward Islanders have seen the same sight from the shore directly across the strait.

The centuries have been kind to the town, and Pictou has evaded tacky commercialism. Its industries include the local paper mill, lobster fishing, shipbuilding, and tire production at the Michelin tire plant. The town had a problem with malodorous emissions from Scott Pulp Mill across the harbor. The company initiated a $5 million program with a new steam stripper for processing paper in 1989. While sea winds occasionally bring what remains of the odor across the harbor to Pictou, the smell has been reduced 65%, and efforts are ongoing to eliminate the rest.

Sights

McCulloch House, 100 Haliburton Rd., tel. (902) 485-1150, overlooking the harbor, has period antiques and a small library. The print of a Labrador falcon downstairs was a gift to McCulloch from artist-naturalist John James Audubon. (McCulloch had his own bird collection, and it is now part of Dalhousie University's exhibits in Halifax). The museum is open June to mid-Oct., Mon.-Sat. 9:30 a.m.-5:30 p.m., Sun. from 1:30 p.m.

Hector National Exhibit Centre at 86 Haliburton Rd. near McCulloch House, tel. 485-4563, showcases fine arts as part of the national arts exhibit circuit. The site is also one of the province's best genealogical libraries. It's open year-round, Mon.-Sat. 9 a.m.-5 p.m., Sun. from 1:30 p.m.; it's closed weekends Nov. to mid-May.

The *Hector* is under construction at **Heritage Quay.** Tours operate July and Aug., and the three-floor interpretation center details the Scottish immigrants' arrival and early years. An outside elevated walkway overlooks the ship's construction. It's open July-Aug., daily 9 a.m.-8 p.m.; Sept.-Oct., Mon.-Fri. to 5 p.m. Admission is $3.

Take time to look over the *Hector.* The three-masted, black-and-off-white replica tied up at harborfront is a splendid vessel, wide-hulled and round-ended. From the shape of the ship, though, you'll easily see that the voyage from Scotland was not so splendid. The ship's hull is unusually wide, and indeed the *Hector,* owned by the Dutch and chartered by the Scots for the voyage, was built as a freighter and modified only slightly to carry human cargo. Remarkably, the 200-plus immigrants from the Highlands survived, and Nova Scotia owes its Scottish heritage to those seaworthy voyagers.

The **Northumberland Fisheries Museum** on Front St., tel. 485-1460, has a modest fisheries exhibit within the historic railroad station; it's open July-Aug., daily 9:30 a.m.-5:30 p.m.

Accommodations

The **Consulate Inn,** 115 Water St., tel. (902) 485-4554, dates to 1810. It's a historic building styled in Scottish vernacular and Georgian that was once the American consulate. The restored inn has three guest rooms ($40-60 with a light breakfast) and dining room. The **Walker Inn,** 34 Colraine St., tel. 485-1433, has 10 rooms ($50-65 with a light breakfast) within the restored inn built in 1865.

Braeside Inn, 80 Front St., tel. 485-5046, sits back from the harbor on a hillside and has been restored with oriental touches downstairs and period furnishings upstairs. It has 20 rooms ($55-80), a dining room, summer oil-painting classes, and a bilingual staff. The **Pictou Lodge,** Braeshore Rd., tel. 485-4322, was built in 1926 and belonged to the Canadian National Railway for decades. It's restored with roomy, rustic comforts such as a long outside porch, dining in the high-ceilinged rotunda, and a nearby pond with canoes. The 29 chalets ($75-150) are mainly made of logs and most have a fireplace, kitchen, and living room.

Food
The **Consulate Restaurant,** in the Consulate Inn, has intimate dining June-September. The specialty is seafood with some beef and chicken dishes ($8-20). Reservations are wise; call (902) 485-4554.

Pictou Lodge backs up on the coastline with strait views and serves entrees ($13-23) such as ginger-fried chicken, sauced poached salmon, and smoked trout. Reservations are required; call 485-4322.

Braeside Inn ranks as Pictou's top restaurant and features three-course meals ($16-22), entrees priced from $14, and an emphasis on mixed seafood dishes. Special dishes include

Catch 57 (with haddock, lobster, scallops, and shrimp) and Mariner (with halibut and salmon fillets stuffed with scallops and lobster). Meals are served in the formal inside dining room, in the informal greenhouse overlooking the harbor, or on the outdoor deck. Reservations are required; call 485-4288 or 485-5046.

Light fare is the gist of **Stone House Cafe and Pizzeria,** 12 Water Street. **Your Delight Tea Room,** 20 Water St., serves sandwiches and quiches. **Smith's Restaurant** on Church St. is strong on thick chowders and ample seafood platters.

Sobeys on Haliburton Rd. near Hwy. 106 has a deli counter and bakery in its supermarket; open Mon.-Tues., Sat. 9 a.m.-6 p.m., Wed.-Fri. to 9 p.m. There's an **IGA** grocery on Front Street.

Entertainment and Events
Braeside Inn's **lounge** is inside off the main lobby, and drinks are served on the deck outside after dinner. **Pictou Lodge** features varied weekend entertainment and occasional Sunday jazz sessions. The performing arts scene is based at **deCoste Entertainment Centre** on Water St., tel. (902) 485-8848, with thrice-weekly drama, concerts, and dance.

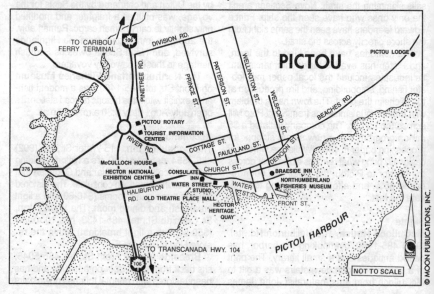

The four-day **Pictou Lobster Festival** attracts 75,000 revelers with parades, entertainment, and food vendors. It's usually held the second weekend of July. **Natal Day,** 3 Aug., commemorates Pictou's founding. *Hector* **Festival** is centered at the shipyard and spans five mid-August days.

Shopping

Shopping for crafts in Pictou brings many rewards. **Water Street Studio** is a crafts outlet with natural-fiber apparel and wares. **Lolly's,** 21A Water St., stocks Chéticamp hooked mats and rugs along with varied provincial crafts mixed among souvenirs. **Wedgwood Art Gallery,** on Hwy. 2 about seven km east of Pictou Rotary, sells oils, folk art, quilts, and carvings.

traditional Scottish dancing

The **Grohmann Knives** line of cutlery and hunting knives is sold throughout Atlantic Canada. The plant's retail outlet, 88 Water St., is open Mon.-Fri. 9 a.m.-3 p.m.; 20-minute plant tours are scheduled May-Sept. at 9 a.m., 11 a.m., and 1 p.m.

Stedmans and other apparel stores line Water Street. **Old Theatre Place** on Water St. serves as the harborfront mall.

Information and Services

The provincial **tourist information center,** at the Pictou Rotary (where Hwy. 106 meets Hwy. 6), tel. (902) 485-6213, is open mid-May to mid-October, daily 9 a.m.-5 p.m., July-Aug. to 10 p.m.

Sutherland-Harris Memorial Hospital is at 1059 Haliburton Rd., tel. 485-4324. For the **RCMP** call 485-5333.

Locals do their banking in style at architecturally resplendent places; the **Bank of Nova Scotia** is in a Second Empire-style building at the corner of Front and Colerain streets. It's open Mon.-Wed. 9 a.m.-3 p.m., Thurs.-Fri. to 5 p.m. **Canada Post,** 49 Front St., is open Mon.-Fri. 8:30 a.m.-5 p.m.

Transportation

It's a 10-minute drive from downtown Pictou to Caribou's **ferry to Prince Edward Island.** Summertime waiting lines—clogged by tourists and commuters—can be horrendous; try to get to the ferry after 9 a.m. and before 3:30 p.m. For fare and schedules, see the "Selected Marine Atlantic Ferry Schedules" chart in the Newfoundland and Labrador chapter. For additional details, call Northumberland Ferries at (902) 566-3838 or (800) 565-0201 in Nova Scotia or PEI.

Pictou County Transit, based in nearby Trenton, tel. 752-4242, operates public bus service throughout the county and stops along Water St. four times daily.

Acadian Lines, tel. 755-5700, operates provincial bus routes from its New Glasgow terminal at East River Plaza at 980 E. River Rd.; fares are $16 OW to Halifax and $26 OW to Sydney. **Island Transit** buses from Charlottetown, PEI (via the ferry) also use the terminal; the Charlottetown–New Glasgow fare costs $38 OW.

Pictou has several taxi companies; **Bob Naylor's Taxi** charges a flat rate—it's $7 to Pictou Lodge and $12 to New Glasgow's bus terminal. **Carefree Cruises,** tel. 485-6960 or 485-6205, is based at Caribou's ferry wharf and offers deep-sea fishing charters (about $60 an hour), as well as daytime and evening sightseeing cruises in the strait and in Pictou Harbour.

Free tours of Pictou and the county for two or more visitors are offered by the Pictou County Tourist Association. Tours are available June-Sept.; make reservations at 755-5180.

Cape George Scenic Drive

The route to fossil hunting at Arisaig and Cape George's ruggedly beautiful eastern coastline lies along Highways 245 and 337 between New Glasgow and Antigonish. Highway 245 passes

Merigomish and Lismore and starts to rise as it approaches coastal **Arisaig Provincial Park,** which has picnic tables and a boardwalk over the dunes to the waterfront. As you walk the beach here, you'll see tiny fossils embedded in mudstone—the ancient remnants of the Arisaig coastline's origin as a shallow, warm sea with a silty bottom. A lane beyond the park turns off the highway and leads to Arisaig Point, where the coastline is wrapped in dark green and orange-red rock, a vestige of the area's volcanic past.

The highway rises steadily and peaks at an elevation of 190 meters at **Cape George.** The setting is a bicyclist's favorite scene and a just reward after the steep coastal climb. The panorama from the lighthouse at the cape's tip takes in the manicured farmlands of the Pictou-Antigonish highlands behind you as well as the misty vision of Prince Edward Island across the strait.

Along Cape George's eastern side, the road becomes Hwy. 337 as it peels down from the peak alongside St. Georges Bay. The scenic 53-km route to Antigonish, dubbed a miniature Cabot Trail for its rugged coastal beauty, passes through the tiny communities of Cape George, Lakevale, Crystal Cliffs, Antigonish Harbour, and finally into Antigonish. Just below Cape George, the turn-of-the-century lighthouse at Ballantynes Cove is perched 300 meters above St. Georges Bay.

ANTIGONISH

First impressions of Antigonish (pop. 5,200) from the west are not promising—Main Street is a thicket of fast fooderies and service stations—but the town is not without its charms. Antigonish (ann-TIGGA-nish—from a Micmac name meaning "place where the branches are torn off by bears gathering beechnuts") is the center of the county and has shopping malls, parks, accommodations, and St. Frances Xavier University. The **Nova Scotia Visitor Information Centre** is at exit 32, tel. (902) 863-4921.

In mid-July, the **Antigonish Highland Festival**—the longest-running in North America, having celebrated its 133rd year in 1994—kicks off with Scottish music, dancing, and sports. Throughout July and August, the **Festival**

Antigonish, Nova Scotia's largest and most successful professional summer theater program, features a varied program of drama, musicals, children's entertainment, and concerts at the university campus. Tickets run $14 for adults, with discounts for children, students, and seniors. Call 867-3954 or (800) 563-PLAY across Canada.

Vicinity of Antigonish

Highway 7 runs due south from Antigonish, following a string of small lakes through pastureland and forest 53 km to Sherbrooke (see "Sherbrooke and Vicinity" under "The Eastern Shore" later in this chapter) and on to the Atlantic coast.

Some of the province's premier saltwater sportfishing happens in **St. George's Bay** east of Antigonish, especially around **Auld Cove,** where the sea meets the Strait of Canso. Late autumn brings bluefin tuna schools close to shore, and a mammoth 679-kg bluefin caught here set the world record in 1979. For information on fishing charters, contact the **Canso Tuna Club,** tel. (902) 727-2660, in Auld Cove.

The bay area, settled by Acadians in the 17th century, also has some fine beaches. Near the village of Pomquet, off exit 35 from the Trans-Canada, is **Pomquet Beach Park,** with supervised swimming and a picnic area. A few kilometers east is another good sandy beach at **Bayfield Provincial Park.**

Accommodations and Food

Auberge Wandlyn Inn, 158 Main St., tel. (902) 863-2672, has 34 units and a dining room. Rates are $58-65 s, $60-75 d. **Best Western Claymore Inn,** Church St., tel. 863-1050, is also open year-round, with 76 units, a pool and sauna for $65-80 s, $70-80 d. **MacIsaac's B&B,** 18 Hillcrest St. (call for directions), tel. 863-3557, is open 1 May-15 October. Rates: $30 s, $38-40 d.

The **Goshen Restaurant,** on Hwy. 104 a few kilometers east of Antigonish, serves chicken and seafood dishes in a Scottish setting. It's open April-Oct. 7 a.m.-11 p.m. daily. **Piper's Pub,** downtown on College St., tel. 863-2590, serves pub food and draft beer in a relaxed atmosphere, and features great music—jazz nights, folk music, and Saturday afternoon *ceilidhs.*

THE EASTERN SHORE

The eastern shore, the fretted, rocky Atlantic coastline stretching east from Dartmouth to the Canso Causeway, is as rugged as the Northumberland Strait shore is tame. Two-lane coastal highways 207, 7, 211, and 316 have been designated as Marine Drive, a twisting, 400-km-long scenic route through tiny fishing ports reminiscent of seafaring life decades ago, and rockbound coves where the forest grows right down to the sea. It's the only major, entirely paved through route to Cape Breton south of the Trans-Canada, but it's not the highway for those in a hurry. The road unfurls itself at a leisurely pace and it's worth slowing down and taking two or three days to travel its length.

DARTMOUTH TO SHERBROOKE

Musquodoboit Harbour and Vicinity
Marine Drive begins on Highway 207, in Dartmouth's eastern suburbs, looping southward to **Lawrencetown Provincial Beach Park,** popular with families and with surfers. The highway swings north from there, connecting with busy Hwy. 107 for a stretch, then becoming smaller Hwy. 7 at Musquodoboit Harbour. With just 900 people, Musquodoboit Harbour is nevertheless the largest community along the western half of this coast. Attractions include the **Musquodoboit Railway Museum,** on Hwy. 7 in the town center, housed in a 1918 railway station and three vintage rail cars. Admission is free. The **tourist information center** is in the same building. Five km south, **Martinique Beach Provincial Park,** site of Nova Scotia's longest beach, spreads out along a coastal curve where ocean currents and shore topography come together just right to produce excellent surfing conditions.

Jeddore Oyster Pond to Liscomb Mills
The **Fisherman's Life Museum,** tel. (902) 889-2053, in the village of Jeddore Oyster Pond just off Hwy. 7, re-creates the early 1900s' inshore fisherman's life in a rustic homestead; it's open June to mid-Oct., Mon.-Sat. 9:30 a.m.-5:30 p.m., Sun. 1-5:30 p.m.

Clam Harbour has an excellent white-sand beach—part of the Eastern Shore Seaside Park system. The beach has a lifeguard, changing rooms, picnic areas, and in mid-August, a sand-sculpting contest.

Marine Drive skirts the granite-bound coastline at **Ship Harbour,** a tiny mussel-fishing burg. The thousands of white buoys on the bay indicate the location of the "collectors," specially designed nets on which the mollusks develop. Suspended just under the water's surface, the mussels grow faster than normal, and are sweet and free of grit and sand.

Back on Marine Drive, a few other fishing towns line the highway: Murphy Cove, Pleasant Harbour, and **Tangier,** site of Atlantic Canada's first gold mine, where gold was discovered in 1858. Mining still goes on here, but these days Tangier is best known for the smokehouse of **J.W. Krauch and Sons Smoked Fish.** The smokehouse's retail shop stocks delicious smoked salmon, mackerel, and eels; it's open year-round, Mon.-Fri. 8 a.m.-6 p.m., Sat.-Sun. from 10 a.m. Tangier is also the place to get outfitted for sea kayaking and canoeing. Call Tangier Adventures, tel. 772-2774, for lessons, equipment, and information on tripping around the coastline.

One-half km east of Spry Bay, **Taylor Head Provincial Park** has a beautiful peninsula-tip location. The park has picnic sections, dunes crossed with boardwalks, and a white sandy beach. For hikers, each parking lot marks trails that probe the coastal woodland, where cormorants nest in windswept spruce, maple, and tamarack.

From Hwy. 7 at Sheet Harbour, Hwy. 374 heads north to the **Liscomb Game Sanctuary,** a vast wilderness area set aside for native wildlife and for hiking, camping, canoeing, fishing, birdwatching, and snowmobiling.

Liscomb Mills and Vicinity
More than 10 small-craft harbors line the coast between Sober Island and Liscomb Mills. The most accessible is Marie Joseph, on the south side of the highway. Another setting for nest-

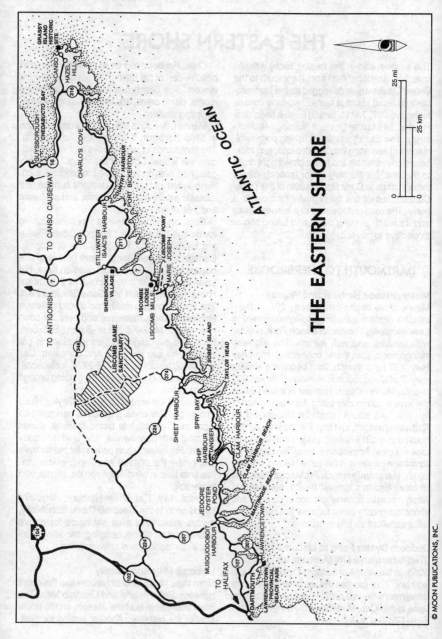

THE EASTERN SHORE

ATLANTIC OCEAN

GRASSY ISLAND HISTORIC SITE

CANSO

HAZEL HILL

GUYSBOROUGH

CHEDABUCTO BAY

316

CHARLO'S COVE

16

TO CANSO CAUSEWAY

TO ANTIGONISH

7

316

STILLWATER

ISAAC'S HARBOUR

211

COUNTRY HARBOUR

PORT BICKERTON

SHERBROOKE VILLAGE

348

LISCOMBE LODGE

7

LISCOMB MILLS

MARIE JOSEPH

LISCOMB POINT

LISCOMB GAME SANCTUARY

374

SOBER ISLAND

TAYLOR HEAD

224

SHEET HARBOUR

SPRY BAY

SHIP HARBOUR

TANGIER

CLAM HARBOUR

CLAM HARBOUR BEACH

7

MARTINIQUE BEACH

JEDDORE OYSTER POND

357

MUSQUODOBOIT HARBOUR

LAWRENCETOWN

LAWRENCETOWN PROVINCIAL BEACH PARK

207

104

102

107

TO HALIFAX

DARTMOUTH

© MOON PUBLICATIONS, INC.

0   25 mi

0   25 km

ing rare species, such as Leach's storm petrel and the black guillemot, is Liscomb Point, a remote peninsula that projects into the ocean an hour beyond Spry Bay.

In Liscomb Mills, the rustic **Liscombe Lodge** off Hwy. 7, tel. (902) 779-2307 or (800) 665-6343, has heritage quilts hanging in the lobby and a comfortable dining room that overlooks a fast-running river. Open June-Oct., the resort has 65 rooms ($90-110) in the new hotel near the main lodge or in outlying chalets and cottages (nice for honeymooners; $83-205 s and d). Facilities include tennis courts, marina with boat and canoe rentals, and fishing rental equipment.

SHERBROOKE AND VICINITY

Highway 7 leaves the coast at Liscomb, turning north to Sherbrooke. Popular among salmon anglers, Sherbrooke is a town of just under 400 people on the St. Mary's River. Most of the town has been restored to its 1800s splendor, and **Sherbrooke Village** on Hwy. 7, tel. (902) 522-2400, fills a sightseeing day with a museum including 25 refurbished buildings that date from the gold-mining years (1860-80). Attractions include an ambrotype photography studio for souvenir pictures on glass, craftspeople demonstrating 19th-century skills, several dining rooms, and a water-powered sawmill. It's open June to mid-October, daily 9:30 a.m.-5:30 p.m. Admission is $2.50 adults, with discounts for seniors and children.

Recreation

For salmon fishing on the St. Mary's River and Sherbrooke Lakes, or the Liscombe River lake system, contact Easter Valley Outfitters, tel. (902) 522-2235. They offer guides and equipment. For deep-sea fishing, contact Liscombe Lodge at 779-2307 or Ecum Secum Bridge, tel. 347-2014. Boat rentals, for Lochiel Lake, are available by calling 783-2309.

Accommodations and Food

For overnight stays, Sherbrooke has a few choices. **St. Mary's River Lodge,** adjacent to Sherbrooke Village, tel. (902) 522-2177, is open year-round and has five rooms for $36 s, $48 d. Dining is available. **Sherbrooke Village Inn**

and Cabins, tel. 522-2235, is open 15 May-31 Oct. (other times by reservation), and has 12 units for $60 s, $65 d. Salmon-fishing guides are available here.

Campers head to the **Riverside Campground,** tel. 522-2913, off Hwy. 7 on Sonora Highway. It's open 15 May-30 Oct., with 12 basic sites (no RVs) from $8. **Try-Your-Tent-In-Place campground,** tel. 522-2581, provides 10 tents with carpet, decks, tables, and chairs near a lake. All you need is a sleeping bag, say the operators. No RVs. It's off the main street on Restoration Dr. and open 1 May-31 October. Rates are $7 s, $13 d, $15 family.

CANSO AND VICINITY

East of Sherbrooke, Marine Drive becomes Hwy. 211 and threads through Stillwater Lake, Jordanville, Indian Harbour Lake, Port Hillford, Port Bickerton, and Isaac's Harbour. The Country Harbour Ferry, seven km northeast from Port Bickerton, is the provincial ferry that runs on the hour from the eastern side of Country Harbour and on the half-hour from the western side.

COURTESY NOVA SCOTIA MUSEUM COMPLEX

Thomas McCulloch's Sherbrooke cottage

Farther east, Hwy. 211 becomes Hwy. 316. When you reach the junction with Hwy. 16, turn right to Hazel Hill, then **Canso.** Canada's oldest fishing village (established in 1605), Canso (from a Micmac word meaning "opposite the lofty cliffs") sits at the opening to the Chedabucto Bay. The town of 1,228 people is minimally equipped for travelers, with banks, a hospital, a museum, grocery, a few accommodations, and a restaurant. Try **Scotia Restaurant** on the main street for good seafood; stay at **Seawind Land,** at Charlos Cove, tel. (800) 563-INNS, with oceanfront dining and lodging.

Whitman House

This museum of county history, tel. (902) 366-2170, in a handsome three-story house, has displays illustrating the history of Guysborough

County and Canso, with period furniture, folk art, and early photos. You can get a panoramic view of the town from the widow's walk on the roof. It's open July-Aug., Mon.-Thurs. 9 a.m.-6 p.m. Admission is free.

Grassy Island National Historic Site

Canada's newest national historic site, a thriving fishing community in the 18th century, is a small island one km off the eastern tip of the mainland. The visitor center, tel. (902) 295-2069, abuts Canso wharf and details the island's history from Louisbourg times to later seafaring years. The free boat service (10 a.m.-2 p.m.) from the visitor center's wharf takes sightseers to the island, where self-guided hiking trails lace the historic reserve. It's open June to mid-September, daily 10 a.m.-6 p.m.

BOB RACE

CAPE BRETON ISLAND

"I have travelled around the globe," wrote Alexander Graham Bell, perhaps Cape Breton Island's most renowned transplant. "I have seen the Canadian and American Rockies, the Andes and the Alps, and the Highlands of Scotland; but for simple beauty, Cape Breton outrivals them all."

Because of its topographical diversity, think of Cape Breton as two separate islands, which it very nearly is. The smaller, eastern part consists of lowlands and rolling hills, with deeply indented Sydney Harbour on its northern coast. The western island is Cape Breton's tourist mecca. Green, steeply pitched highlands begin at the sea in the south and sweep north, cut by salmon-filled rivers. As the elevation increases, the Acadian and boreal forests give way to a taiga tableland of windswept, stunted trees. The western and eastern parts are linked together by a slender isthmus less than a kilometer wide at St. Peters.

In the far northern part of the island, magnificent Cape Breton Highlands National Park stretches from coast to coast, as wild and remote as the Highlands of Scotland. The windswept Cabot Trail, a world-famous, 294-km scenic highway, clings to the park's edges. Nova Scotia's highest point, 532-meter North Barren Mountain, soars within the park near Ingonish.

The Northumberland Strait opens into the Gulf of St. Lawrence on the western coast, while the Atlantic washes the opposite shore. The 1,098-square-km Bras d'Or Lake forms the island's heart. The saltwater "Arm of Gold," though barely influenced by tidal cycles, is an inland arm of the Atlantic consisting of a sapphire blue main lake with numerous peripheral channels, straits, and bays. The two island sections wrap around its edges, connected by bridges, causeways, and ferries.

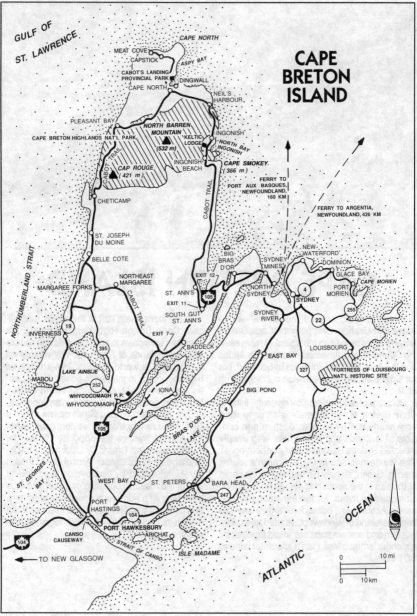

GULF OF ST. LAWRENCE

CAPE BRETON ISLAND

CAPE NORTH

MEAT COVE
CAPSTICK
CABOT'S LANDING
PROVINCIAL PARK
CAPE NORTH

ASPY BAY

DINGWALL

NEIL'S HARBOUR

PLEASANT BAY

NORTH BARREN MOUNTAIN
(532 m)

KELTIC LODGE
INGONISH

CAPE BRETON HIGHLANDS NAT'L PARK

NORTH BAY INGONISH

CAP ROUGE
(421 m)

INGONISH BEACH

CAPE SMOKEY
(366 m)

CABOT TRAIL

CHETICAMP

FERRY TO PORT AUX BASQUES, NEWFOUNDLAND, 160 KM

FERRY TO ARGENTIA, NEWFOUNDLAND, 426 KM

ST. JOSEPH DU MOINE

BELLE COTE

NORTHEAST MARGAREE

BIG BRAS D'OR

NEW WATERFORD

SYDNEY MINES

DOMINION

MARGAREE FORKS

EXIT 12

GLACE BAY

CABOT TRAIL

ST. ANN'S

105

NORTH SYDNEY

CAPE MORIEN

PORT MORIEN

EXIT 11

4

SYDNEY

INVERNESS

19

SOUTH GUT ST. ANN'S

EXIT 7

255

NORTHUMBERLAND STRAIT

395

BADDECK

SYDNEY RIVER

LOUISBOURG

LAKE AINSLIE

EAST BAY

22

MABOU

252

IONA

327

FORTRESS OF LOUISBOURG NAT'L HISTORIC SITE

WHYCOCOMAGH P.P.
WHYCOCOMAGH

BIG POND

105

4

BRAS D'OR LAKE

ST. GEORGES BAY

WEST BAY

ST. PETERS

BARA HEAD

247

OCEAN

PORT HASTINGS

104

PORT HAWKESBURY

CANSO CAUSEWAY

ARICHAT

ISLE MADAME

104

STRAIT OF CANSO

← TO NEW GLASGOW

ATLANTIC

0   10 mi

0   10 km

© MOON PUBLICATIONS, INC.

THE SOUTH

Port Hastings/Port Hawkesbury

Mainland Nova Scotia's roads and highways converge at 1,385-meter-long Canso Causeway, across which all land traffic arrives on Cape Breton at Port Hastings. In addition to linking the island to the mainland, the Canso Causeway—created by dumping millions of tons of rock into the strait—blocks ice from getting into the Strait of Canso.

Highways 104 and 105 (the TransCanada) and Hwy. 19 fan out across the island from here. Highway 19 follows the west coast up to Mabou and Inverness, then links up with the Cabot Trail in the Margaree Valley. The TransCanada lies straight ahead, leading through the center of the island to Baddeck and on to North Sydney. The endless stream of buses packed with tourists makes a beeline along this route, connecting with the Cabot Trail at Baddeck. Highway 104 branches off to the right, joins Hwy. 4, and follows the eastern shore of Bras d'Or Lake, passing Isle Madame en route to Sydney.

There's little in the Port Hastings/Port Hawkesbury area to linger over, but should you need to stay overnight, there's **Keddy's Inn,** tel. (800) 561-7666, at the junction of Highways 104, 105, and Hwy. 19. It's open year-round, with 69 units and a dining room. Rates are $40-80. **MacPuf-**

fin Inn, at the junction of Highways 105 and 4 on Lover's Lane, is open 1 June-30 Oct.; amenities include a/c, full baths, continental breakfast, and pool. Rates are $41-79. For reservations call 625-2283 or write to P.O. Box 558, Port Hawkesbury, NS B0E 2V0. The **Bluefin B&B,** P.O. Box 119, Auld's Cove, tel. (902) 747-2010, is just west of Canso Causeway (on the mainland). Rates are $43 s, $48 d. It's open 15 May-1 November.

The **Nova Scotia Visitor Information Centre** is just off the TransCanada on the Cape Breton side of the causeway.

St. Peters and Vicinity

The name of Nicholas Denys, the prolific French explorer, merchant, scholar, and author, crops up throughout Atlantic Canada's early history. Denys established one of France's first trading posts at St. Peters, the hamlet alongside the narrow isthmus that links Cape Breton's western and eastern parts.

Although Denys is buried in northern New Brunswick, Atlantic Canada's sole museum dedicated to the explorer is the **Nicholas Denys Museum,** a French-style building overlooking St. Peters Canal on Hwy. 4 at St. Peters, about 30 minutes east of Port Hawkesbury. It's open

NAN DROSDICK

Bras d'Or Lake

June-Sept., daily 9 a.m.-5 p.m.; admission is 50 cents.

Photography buffs should check out the **Wallace MacAskill Museum,** also in town on Hwy. 4. MacAskill's memorable black-and-white photography depicted the province's seafaring traditions. The museum exhibits a collection of his original photographs; it's open July-Sept., daily 9 a.m.-5 p.m.

Battery Provincial Park off Hwy. 4, one km east of St. Peters, tel. (902) 535-3094, has hiking trails and ocean views. Rates are $7.50 and up for open and wooded campsites; no reservations.

The **MacDonald Hotel and Dining Room,** 9383 Pepperell St., just off Hwy. 4, tel. 535-2997, is an old-fashioned hotel with small but cozy rooms, most with shared bath ($38-42, with continental breakfast). Rooms over the bar can be noisy until midnight or so. Meals in the dining room—homemade biscuits, seafood, steak, and soup and salad selections, $8-18—are delicious and the service is friendly.

Joyce's Motel and Cottages, tel. 535-2404 or 535-2231, 1.5 km east of St. Peters, has motel rooms and housekeeping units ($35-75), and is also the **youth hostel** ($10). It offers baggage storage, a laundry, and a swimming pool. It's open mid-June to October.

St. Peters RV Campground at the junction of Hwys. 4 and 247, tel. 535-3333, P.O. Box 226, St. Peters, NS B0E 3B0, overlooks Bras d'Or Lake. Open June-Sept., its rates are $8-13.

West of St. Peters at West Bay on the shores of Bras d'Or Lake is **Dundee Resort,** tel. 345-2649, open year-round. Features include cottages, chalets, a jacuzzi, a golf course, tennis, and a marina. Rates are $80-95; suites available. The mailing address is Dundee, RR 2, West Bay, NS B0E 3K0.

North of St. Peters, halfway to Sydney, is five-room **Big Pond B&B,** tel. 828-2476, open May-Oct., where you can swim in Bras d'Or Lake. The rates, $32-42, include breakfast. The Big Pond mailing address is RR 1, East Bay, NS B0A 1H0.

Isle Madame

Lying just off the southern coast of Cape Breton, this 43-square-km island takes its name from one of the honorary titles of the queen of France. Founded by French fishermen in the early 1700s, this was one of the first parts of the province to be settled, and it's one of the oldest fishing ports in North America. Isle Madame, with four main communities—Arichat, West Arichat, Petit Grat, and D'Escousse—lies across the Lennox Passage Bridge, where Hwy. 104 meets 320.

The wooded island is a popular weekend getaway, with two provincial parks (Lennox Passage to the north and Pondville Beach on the east side), and plenty of picnicking, swimming, and vista spots. In Arichat, **LeNoir Forge Museum,** tel. (902) 226-2800, is a restored, working 18th-century forge open to visitors May-Sept.; admission is free. **L'Auberge Acadienne,** on High Rd. in Arichat, tel. 226-2200, is a new lodging designed as a 19th-century Acadian-style inn, with eight rooms in the main building and nine motel units ($60-85 s and d). Other units sleeping up to four, with a hot tub, go for $125. The dining room serves Acadian dishes, and the inn has bicycles for rent. Another option is **D'Escousse B&B** in D'Escousse, with four rooms; full breakfast is included, and ocean swimming and boating are available. Rates are $27-38. It's open mid-May to mid-October; call 226-2936 or write to RR 1, D'Escousse, NS B0E 1K0, for reservations.

Mabou

A 40-minute drive north up Hwy. 19 from the Canso Causeway, the town of Mabou (pop. 425) is the center of Gaelic education in Nova Scotia (the language is taught in the local school) and the location of Our Lady of Seven Sorrows Pioneers Shrine. The Mabou Gaelic and Historical Society Museum, or An Drochaid ("The Bridge"), tel. (902) 945-2311, focuses on crafts, local music and poetry, genealogical research, and Gaelic culture. In nearby West Mabou and other locales, Saturday-night square dances are held in summer, but the big shindig in these parts is the **Mabou Ceilidh,** a celebration of music and dance, held around Canada Day (late June/early July) each year.

Around the estuary, watch for bald eagles. The Mabou Mines area, near the coast, has some excellent hiking trails into a roadless section of the Mabou Highlands.

The Glenora Inn and Distillery, tel. 258-2662, nine km north of Mabou, is the only single-malt whiskey distillery in North America. Better still, it's also a country inn with nine rooms ($68-78), a dining room (featuring traditional Cape cuisine), and lounge.

Glendyer Mills B&B, tel. 945-2455, RR 4, Mabou, NS B0E 1X0, is a municipal registered heritage property. To get there from Hwy. 19 at Mabou, take Hwy. 252 to Smithville-Glendyer Rd. (four km); it's open June-September. Rates are $40-60, including full breakfast.

Camp at **Ceilidh Trailer Park,** tel. 945-2486, on paved West Mabou Rd. It's adjacent to Ceilidh Cottages, four km from Hwy. 19, and is open 15 June to 15 October. Sites cost $12.

Inverness

Known for coal mining, this Scottish settlement is the largest town on the west coast (pop. 2,000). Visitors come for the excellent swimming beaches, windsurfing, and a few shops. The **Inverness Miners Museum,** tel. (902) 258-3283, gives a slide and film show on local mining history, which dates to 1865. It's open May to mid-Oct., weekdays 9 a.m.-5 p.m. Admission is free.

Nearby, at **Broad Cove,** the annual Broad Cove Scottish Concert offers Highland dancing and music in July at the St. Margaret's Parish Grounds.

Inverness Beach Village, P.O. Box 617, Inverness, NS B0E N1O, on Hwy. 9, is open 15 June-15 Oct. with beach swimming, horseback riding, tennis, and dining room. Rates are $11-14. **Inverness Lodge Hotel and Motel,** tel. 258-2193, P.O. Box 69, Inverness, NS N0E 1N0, is also on Hwy. 19. It's open year-round, with a dining room and ocean swimming available. Rates are $49-55. Ten km north of Inverness on Hwy. 19 is **MacLeod's Beach Campsite,** in Dunvegan on the Ceilidh Trail, tel. 258-2433; the campground is open 25 June-25 Sept. with rates starting at $12.

Whycocomagh

Heading north to the Cabot Trail on the Trans-Canada (Hwy. 105), you'll pass through the town of Whycocomagh. Just east of town is **Whycocomagh Provincial Park,** tel. 756-2448. Open 20 May-6 Sept., the park has a boat launch and hiking trails. Sites are $7.50 and up.

THE CABOT TRAIL

Nearly every coastal and inland backcountry road in the western half of the island leads eventually to the Cabot Trail, the scenic highway rimming the unforgettable landscape of northwestern Cape Breton. The 294-km route of steep ascents, descents, and hold-your-breath switchbacks has no official beginning or end, nor, unlike every other highway in the province, is it numbered. Sightseers enter the route from Hwy. 395 through the Margaree Valley; from the coastal road that meets the trail at Belle Cote on the gulf; or from the TransCanada's exit 7 near Baddeck or exits 11 or 12 near Sydney.

BADDECK AND THE MARGAREES

Baddeck (from Abadak, or "Place Near an Island," as the Micmac called it, referring to Kidston Island just offshore) lies on the misty, wooded shore of St. Patrick's Channel, a long inlet of

Bras d'Or Lake. The town marks the traditional beginning and ending point for the Cabot Trail.

Once a major shipbuilding center, Baddeck claims as its most famous resident not a sailor but an inventor—Alexander Graham Bell. The landscape, language, and people all reminded the Scotsman of his native land. He built a grand summer home, Beinn Bhreagh (not open to the public), across the inlet from Baddeck and during the next 37 years carried on countless experiments—with kites, aircraft, hydrofoils, communication devices, genetics, medicine, and more—there and on the lake. In 1904, Bell's *Silver Dart* sped over Bras d'Or Lake for the first airplane flight in the British Empire.

Sights

At the east end of Baddeck is the **Alexander Graham Bell National Historic Site,** tel. (902) 295-2069, a tremendously satisfying museum with displays on Bell's life, family, and seemingly inexhaustible curiosity about science. The multimedia exhibits include working models of Bell's first telephones, a full-size reproduction of his speed-record-setting HD-4 hydrofoil, kite-building workshops in July and August, a children's science program, and evening programs. The museum is open daily year-round, 9 a.m.-5 p.m., July-Sept. to 9 p.m. Admission is $2.50, with discounts for children, students, and seniors.

Alexander Graham Bell National Historic Site

BOB RACE

A free ferry runs from Government Wharf out to **Kidston Island,** which has nature trails for exploring and a supervised beach.

Events
Several events keep Baddeck (pop. 1,100) busy through the summer. The multifaceted **Centre Bras d'Or Festival of the Arts,** running from mid-July to the third week in August, celebrates Maritime, Gaelic, and international culture through dance, music, theater, art, workshops, and children's activities at various venues. Call the festival box office at (902) 295-3044 or (800) 565-0980 for schedules and ticket information. Other July happenings include the **Baddeck Handcraft Festival Ceilidh and Fashion Show** and **Shriners Field of Dreams Folk and Fiddle Festival.** In August, a favorite tradition is the **Baddeck Regatta,** held since 1904.

Accommodations and Food
Built in 1860, **Telegraph House,** in central Baddeck on Chebucto St., tel. (902) 295-9988, has 43 rooms and motel units ($52-75) and a dining room.

The **MacNeil House,** on Shore Rd., tel. 295-2340 or (800) 565-8439, is a country inn with one- and two-bedroom suites (from $125, from $85 off-season), a licensed dining room, outdoor heated pool, bicycle and boat rentals, a lakeside beach, hiking trails on the grounds, and other recreation.

Antique-furnished **Duffus House Inn,** tel. 295-2172, Water St., P.O. Box 427, Baddeck, NS B0E 1B0, is open mid-June to mid-October. Rooms have water views, and breakfast is complimentary. Rates are $50-85. The **Silver Dart Lodge,** tel. 295-2340, P.O. Box 399, Baddeck, NS B0E 1B0, offers Scottish entertainment, a dining room, pool, and flower gardens. Rates are $58-95. To get there, take exit 8 to Shore Rd. The lodge is open May-October.

To get to **The Bay Tourist Home B&B,** tel. 295-2046, P.O. Box 24, Baddeck, NS B0E 1B0, take Hwy. 105's exit 10 to Hwy. 205 and drive 1.5 km. Open 1 May-31 Oct., it serves continental breakfast. Rates are $30-35. **Eagle's Perch B&B,** tel. 295-2640, P.O. Box 425, Baddeck, NS B0E 1B0, is a log home on Baddeck River. To get there, take Hwy. 105 exit 9. At the stop sign turn north and follow Margaree Rd. four km to Baddeck Bridge; cross the bridge and turn left (west). It's one km from the bridge on the left. Open 15 May-15 Oct.; rates are $32-50.

An Seanne Mhanse B&B, South Haven, tel. 295-2538, on Hwy. 105, 12 km east of town, has three large rooms and includes a big breakfast. Rates are $32 s, $40 d.

Baddeck Cabot Trail KOA, on Hwy. 105 eight km west of Baddeck, tel. 295-2288, has lake fishing and camping, cabins, a pool, children's activities, and tours. It's open 15 May-15 October. The rate is $14 a campsite. **Bras d'Or Lakes Campground,** three km west of Baddeck on Hwy. 105, tel. 295-2329, is open 15 May-30 Sept., with sites for $11 a night. You can also arrange tours here. **Silver Spruce Resort,** tel. 295-2417, has all the necessary amenities—showers, laundry, pool, fishing, restaurant, and tours. The rate is $11.

The **Bell Buoy Restaurant,** on Main St. next to the old library, tel. 295-2581, winner of Cape Breton's "Restaurant of the Year," serves seafood, steak, and poultry. Lunch prices range $4.95-9.95; dinner ranges $6.95-24.95. It's open May-November.

For breakfast (7-11 a.m.), sandwiches, pizzas, and light meals, the **Yellow Cello,** on Chebucto St., tel. 295-2303, is centrally located and well priced, with an indoor dining room and veranda in front. It's open daily.

The Margaree River Valley

Eight km west of Baddeck, the Cabot Trail winds northwest through the hills and into the valley of the Margaree River, a renowned salmon-fishing stream and the namesake of seven small communities in the valley. Mid-June to mid-July and September to mid-October are the best months for fishing, and many guides are available locally. Two museums near Northeast Margaree (pop. 164) explore facets of local history and culture. The **Margaree Salmon Museum,** tel. (902) 248-2848, concentrates on the history of angling on the river. It's open mid-June to mid-Oct., 9 a.m.-5 p.m.; admission is 50 cents for adults, 25 cents for children. The **Museum of Cape Breton Heritage** exhibits a collection of household items and demonstrates spinning and weaving techniques. It's also open mid-June to mid-Oct., 9 a.m.-5 p.m.; admission is free.

The **Normaway Inn and Cabins,** in Margaree Valley, tel. 248-2987 or (800) 565-9463, is an elegantly rustic 1920s resort nestled on 250 acres in the hills. The main lodge has nine rooms, and on the grounds are 19 one- or two-bedroom cabins. Rates are $117 s, $159-199 d; discounts apply to stays of two or more nights. The dining room serves dishes of Atlantic salmon, lamb, scallops, and fresh fruits and vegetables.

Activities include nightly films or traditional entertainment, tennis, walking trails, bicycling, weekly barn dances and fiddling contests. The inn can arrange horseback riding, whalewatching, canoeing, and fishing outings for you. The Normaway is about 20 minutes from the junction of the TransCanada Hwy. 105 and Cabot Trail, exit 7, then three km down Egypt Road.

On Lake O'Law in Northeast Margaree, **The Lakes Campsite,** tel. 248-2360, is open mid-

May to mid-Oct., with a restaurant, boat rentals, play area, and camping supplies. Rates: $10.75 minimum. **Margaree Lodge,** tel. 248-2193, P.O. Box 550, Margaree Forks, NS B0E 2A0, is at the junction of Hwy. 19 and Cabot Trail. It's open 15 June-15 October, with a licensed lounge, dining room, and pool. Rates are $50-70. **Duck Cove Inn,** tel. 235-2658, Margaree Harbour, NS B0E 2B0, is at the junction of Cabot and Ceilidh trails. Features include continental breakfast, a dining room, and ocean swimming. Open 1 June-20 October; call for rates.

CHÉTICAMP

Chéticamp is an Acadian fishing village (pop. 980) and tourism center offering accommodations, restaurants, a museum, craft shops, beaches, and golfing. Deep-sea fishing and whalewatching charter boats leave from the central Government Wharf, and the western entrance to the national park is five km northeast of town up the Cabot Trail.

The village was settled by Acadians expelled from the Nova Scotia mainland in the 18th century; today, the weeklong **Festival de l'Escouaette,** held in late July, celebrates aspects of Acadian culture, with a parade, arts and crafts, and music. The **Acadian Museum,** on the highway near the south end of Chéticamp, tel. (902) 224-2170, displays artifacts from early settler days, with an emphasis on the sheepherding past.

Chéticamp's visitor information center, on the highway, has information on accommodations, campgrounds, and other services on the islands.

Arts and Crafts

One of the major cottage industries of this area is the production of hooked rugs, a craft developed by Acadians centuries ago. In the late 1930s, a group of Chéticamp women formed a rug-hooking cooperative that still thrives. The Co-op Artisanale de Chéticamp gives demonstrations and displays its wares at the Acadian Museum. You can also see beautiful hooked rugs and tapestries at **Les Trois Pignons/Elizabeth LeFort Gallery and Museum,** tel. (902) 224-2612, a striking red-roofed building at the northern end of Chéticamp. Admission is $2.50 adults, children under 12 free.

A number of galleries and shops hereabouts also sell locally produced folk arts—brightly colored, whimsical carvings and paintings of fish, seabirds, fishermen, boats, or whatever strikes the artist's fancy. The **Sunset Art Gallery,** tel. 224-1831, is open late May to mid-Oct., daily 9 a.m.-6 p.m.

Magdalen Islands Ferry

Chéticamp is the terminus for a passenger-only ferry to the Magdalen Islands (Îles-de-la-Madeleine), an alternative to the route from Prince Edward Island. The 28-meter *Macassa Bay* makes a daily round-trip (six hours each way), early July to early Sept., leaving Chéticamp at 7:30 a.m., and leaving Havre-Aubert at 2:30 p.m. Round-trip fare is $70 for adults, $35 for ages 5-12.

Accommodations and Food

Fraser Motel and Cottages, on Main St., tel. (902) 224-2411, is central and a good value, with four simple but comfortable motel units ($38-43) and four housekeeping cottages ($32-50). **Germaine Doucet's B&B,** tel. 224-3459, is in Point Cross, six km south of Chéticamp. Rates are $32-42, with full breakfast.

Chéticamp Outfitters B&B, tel. 224-2776, P.O. Box 448, Chéticamp, NS B0E 1H0, offering guide service, is open May-December. Rates, $40-45, include full breakfast.

Plage St-Pierre Camping, tel. 224-2112, is on Île de Chéticamp, which is connected by a causeway to the southern end of the village. It has a good sandy beach, open and wooded sites ($12 and up), showers, minigolf, and volleyball courts. Open May to mid-September. Farther afield, **Chéticamp Campground,** tel. 224-2310, is a few kilometers north of Chéticamp at the entrance to Cape Breton Highlands National Park. It's open year-round, with 24 serviced and 138 unserviced sites. No reservations are taken.

Dine at the **Restaurant Acadien,** 774 Main St., tel. 224-3207, for authentic Acadian food: *fricot*, meat pies, fresh fish, blood pudding, and butterscotch pie. Entrees range $8-15. It's open mid-May to mid-October.

CAPE BRETON HIGHLANDS NATIONAL PARK

Outside Chéticamp, the Cabot Trail begins to climb and enters the national park five km northeast of town. The park is open year-round, though most facilities operate from late May to mid-October. Visitors are charged $5 for a motor vehicle license to use park facilities, including turnouts along the Cabot Trail. A four-day permit is $10; annual permits are $20. Pets are permitted in the park, but only on a leash. The visitor information center at the park entrance has literature and natural-history exhibits; it's open daily 8 a.m.-9 p.m. (Another visitor center is at Ingonish Beach, at the park's southeastern corner.) Contact the park office by writing Cape Breton Highlands National Park, Ingonish Beach, NS B0C 1L0; or tel (902) 285-2535 or 285-2691.

Heath bogs, a dry rocky plateau, and a high taiga 400 meters above sea level mark the interior of the 950-square-km park. Rugged cliffs characterize the seacoast on the west side, where the mountains kneel into the Gulf of St. Lawrence, and gentler but still wildly beautiful shores define the eastern side.

Typical Acadian forest, a combination of hardwoods and conifers, carpets much of the region. Wild orchids bloom under the shade of thick spruce, balsam fir, and paper birch. The **Grand Anse River** gorge near MacKenzie Mountain is the Acadian forest's showpiece. Its terrain—with sugar maples, yellow birches, and rare alpine-arctic plants—has been designated an international biological preserve. The park is also a wildlife sanctuary for white-tailed deer, black bear, beaver, lynx, mink, red fox, snowshoe hare, and more than 200 bird species, including eagles and red-tailed hawks.

Hiking and Camping

The park offers 27 established hiking trails, ranging from simple strolls shorter than half a kilometer to challenging treks leading to campgrounds more than 20 km away. Many of the trails are level; a few climb up to awesome viewpoints. Some hug the rocky shoreline; others

CAPE BRETON HIGHLANDS NATIONAL PARK CAMPGROUNDS

Broad Cove Campground, tel. 285-2691, Ingonish, near ocean. Open mid-May to mid-October. Wheelchair accessible, swimming, hiking. Call for rates.

Marrach Group Campground, tel. 285-2691, Ingonish Beach. Open year-round. Hiking. Rates: $1.50 per person minimum.

Big Intervale Campground, tel. 224-2306, Cape North. Open mid-May to mid-October. Fishing, hiking. Call for rates.

MacIntosh Brook Campground, tel. 285-2691, Pleasant Bay. Open mid-May to mid-October. Call for rates.

Corney Brook Campground, tel. 285-2691, Corney Brook. Open mid-May to mid-October. Call for rates.

Chéticamp Campground, tel. 224-2310 or 285-2691, Chéticamp. Open year-round. Wheelchair accessible, fishing, hiking, playground. Call for rates.

Robert Brook Group Campground, tel. 285-2691, Chéticamp. Open mid-May to mid-Oct. Tents only, groups welcome, hiking, fishing. Rates: $1.50 per person minimum. Reservations required.

---

explore river valleys. No matter what your abilities may be, you'll be able to enjoy the park at your own speed.

On the light side, **La Prairie** trail is a 1.2-km riverside loop; the self-guiding **Le Buttereau** trail leads 1.9 km to wildflowers and good bird-watching opportunities. The **Bog** hike, only 0.6 km and wheelchair accessible, takes you to view the unusual insectivorous pitcher plants, as well as orchids, frogs, even moose.

For the more hearty, the seven-km **Skyline** loop climbs a headland, from which the lucky can spot pilot whales; along the way, look for bald eagles, deer, and bear. Serious backpackers can choose from the **Lake of Islands** (25.8 km round-trip) or **Fishing Cove** (16 km round-trip) trails. Lake of Islands leads to bogs, large barrens, and a wilderness campsite; Fishing Cove is a rugged journey to a campground and beach.

For details on hiking in the park, look for the book *Walking in the Highlands.* Topo maps are available at the park information centers near Chéticamp and at Ingonish Beach.

Campers can devote an entire week and never stay in the same campground twice. The park has about 360 **campsites** available on a first-come, first-served basis; costs range from $6 for a wilderness campsite to $10-16 for un-serviced to serviced sites.

CAPE NORTH AND INGONISH

Continuing Around the Cape
Within a few kilometers of the west entrance, the highway swoops up again, framed by the boiling gulf surf and **Cap Rouge,** the 421-meter-high inland headland. At Pleasant Bay, the park's northwestern corner, the highway turns inland and wraps upward to 455-meter-high **French Mountain.**

A level stretch barrels across a narrow ridge overlooking deeply scooped valleys. The road climbs up again, this time to **MacKenzie Mountain** at 372 meters, then switchbacks down a 10-12% grade. Another ascent, to **North Mountain,** formed more than a billion years ago, peaks at 445 meters on a three-km summit. The lookout opens up views of a deep gorge and the North Aspy River.

Cape North and Vicinity
The northernmost point on the Cabot Trail is Cape North. The 19-km road that connects Cape North and Capstick on St. Lawrence Bay rises and dips, affording dizzying ocean views and mountain scenery. En route, **Cabot's Landing Provincial Park,** the supposed landing site of English explorer John Cabot, offers a sandy beach on Aspy Bay (good for clam digging) and a picnic area, and marks the starting point for hikes up 442-meter-high Sugar Loaf Mountain. Whalewatching tours on the northernmost tip of the cape can be arranged at the town of Bay St. Lawrence, four km north.

If boat tours, swimming, whalewatching, and mountain climbing sound appealing, the privately operated **Meat Cove Campground,** in Meat Cove, tel. (902) 383-2379, is the place to experience the island's raw, northernmost wilderness. The campground, overlooking the ocean at road's end, has 12 unserviced campsites ($12 and up).

Open mid-May to late Oct., **The Markland Coastal Resort,** tel. 383-2092, is in Dingwall, five km off Cabot Trail. Amenities include gourmet dining, a pool, and a playground. Rates are $85-165.

Ingonish and Vicinity

From Cape North, the highway heads east to Neil's Harbour and then south past Black Brook Cove's white-sand beach. Clusters of seaports along North Bay are the first signs of civilization. Ingonish (pop. 600) was settled by the Portuguese in the early 1500s, then later by the French, who called it Port d'Orleans. They abandoned the once-vibrant seaport after the destruction of Louisbourg. Today Ingonish is a resort town in operation throughout the year and the eastern entry point for the national park.

One accommodation option is **Sea Breeze,** tel. 285-2879, P.O. Box 22, Ingonish, NS B0C 1K0. Open 15 May-15 Oct., it's eight km north of the entrance to Cape Breton Highlands National Park. Rates for the cabins, motel units, and cottages range $48-100.

The Cabot Trail has its devoted fans, and so does the **Keltic Lodge,** tel. (800) 565-0444 or (902) 285-2880, just off the scenic highway. Count on a visual feast. You'll enter the grounds on a posted lane at the village's Middle Head Peninsula. The lane meanders through thick stands of white birches and finishes at the lodge. The long, low, wood-sided lodge—painted bright white and topped with a bright red roof—is as picturesque as a lord's manor in the Highlands of Scotland.

Room choices are numerous. The main lodge has 32 rustic rooms off a comfortable lobby, furnished with overstuffed chairs and sofas arranged before a massive stone fireplace. Another 40 rooms are in the adjacent, newer White Birch Inn. In addition, nine cottages with suite-style layouts (nice for families) are scattered across the grounds. Rates are $224 to $239 d or t, meals included. The lodge is open June-Oct. during tourist season and Jan.-March for cross-country skiers.

Of the lodge's two dining rooms, the formal **Purple Thistle Dining Room** (tie and jacket required) has one of Nova Scotia's finest reputations, especially in seafood. Meals are five courses ($36) rather than à la carte, with an emphasis on lobster in varied creations and other seafood. If you're tooling along Cabot Trail and hope to stop here for dinner, reservations are very wise. The informal **Atlantic Restaurant** has lighter fare and is open mid-June to September.

The lodge also offers numerous recreation opportunities. Well-marked hiking trails meander through the adjacent national park woodlands and ribbon the coastal peninsula. An outdoor pool (a bit chilly), fishing, and tennis courts are also available. The **Highland Links** golf course, tel. 285-2600, part of the national park, lies adjacent. The course is open from late May to mid- to late Oct.; greens fee is under $24, and reservations are required.

South of Ingonish, the Cabot Trail descends hairpin turns. Stop at 366-meter-high Cape Smokey for a picnic or hiking along the clifftop, which has wonderful views. The steep and twisting road finishes in a coastal glide with views of the offshore Bird Islands. Lying off the northwest side of the Cape at the mouth of St. Ann's Bay, these two islands are the nesting site of a multitude of seabird species; boat tours are available out of Big Bras d'Or.

ST. ANN'S AND VICINITY

During the 1850s, some 900 of St. Ann's residents, dissatisfied with Cape Breton, sailed away to Australia and eventually settled in New Zealand, where their descendants today make up a good part of the Scottish population. Despite this loss of nearly half its population, St. Ann's is today the center of Cape Breton's Gaelic culture.

The only institution of its kind in North America, the **Nova Scotia Gaelic College of Celtic Arts and Crafts,** tel. (902) 295-3206, holds classes in Highland dancing, fiddling, piping, Gaelic language, weaving, and other subjects. The summer session attracts Gaelophiles from around the world. For four days in mid-August, students and other participants show off these skills at the Gaelic Mod, a grand Scottish cultural celebration held anually at the college. For more information, contact the college by mail at P.O. Box 9, Baddeck, NS B0E 1B0.

The **Great Hall of the Clans Museum,** tel. 295-3441, on the college campus, examines the course of Scottish culture and history, including the migrations that brought Highlanders to Cape Breton. Activities include weaving and instrument-making demonstrations, as well as music and dance performances. It's open July-Aug., daily 8:30 a.m.-5 p.m.; open in June and 1 Sept.-15 October, Mon.-Fri. 8:30 a.m.-5 p.m. Admission is $2, free for children under 12.

The **Lobster's Galley** at nearby South Haven, exit 11, tel. 295-3100, has waterfront views and pasta, salads, soups, and sandwiches for $6-15, plus excellent seafood dishes for a little more.

THE EAST

SYDNEY AND VICINITY

Nova Scotia's second-largest city and Cape Breton's largest, Sydney dominates the lowlands of the eastern island. In 1785, Loyalists from New York, and later Scottish Highlanders, settled what was then known as Spanish Bay and renamed it Sydney in honor of England's colonial secretary, Lord Sydney. For the next 35 years, the seaport was the capital of the colony of Cape Breton, until it was united with mainland Nova Scotia in 1820.

Sydney became known as Nova Scotia's Steel City in 1901. Boston entrepreneur Henry Melville Whitney established Dominion Coal and quickly enlarged the operation to include steel production. The Sydney area boomed, and the city ranked as Canada's third-largest steel producer through WW II. Hard times arrived, though, as oil began to displace coal as the industrial fuel of choice. Diminished demand and a half century of strikes closed the Dominion Mines in 1967. The federal government countered by forming the Cape Breton Development Corporation (DEVCO), a Crown corporation with three operating mines, and the province created Sydney Steel Corporation (SYSCO).

Sydney (pop. 29,444) rims the eastern side of Sydney Harbour. The TransCanada—which turns into Hwy. 125 at North Sydney—provides road access to the city. The highway curves south of the harbor and arrives in town with exits 6, 7, 8, and 9 leading to the main roads.

Sydney Harbour's configuration is similar to Halifax Harbour's, and as historic Halifax is concentrated on its own peninsula, so is Sydney's first-settled area. The tourist's Sydney, with the island's greatest concentration of hotels and motels, lies along the Esplanade at waterfront from the peninsula to the promenade's continuation as Kings Road. The shopping district on Charlotte St. is a block inland. Wentworth Park spreads inland off Kings Rd. and features walking trails and a lake salted with swans.

Nightlife in this steel town and seaport is noisy and steamy. Crafts shopping is among the best in the province—bootstrap economic development and re-education dovetails with the local passion for finely crafted, homemade wares. As for dining, locals like their meals plain, inexpensive, and centered on beef. But the influx of business travelers has encouraged local dining rooms to add more subtle culinary touches. Sydney's prime location puts visitors within convenient striking distance of sightseeing on much of the island.

Sights
St. Patrick's Church Museum, at 87 Esplanade, tel. (902) 562-8237, in Cape Breton's oldest Roman Catholic sanctuary, a Gothic-style former church built in 1828, showcases the city's history. Tours (for groups of four or more) of Sydney's historic north end can be arranged here. It's open mid-June to Labour Day, daily 9 a.m.-5 p.m.; admission is free.

Cossit House, 75 Charlotte St., tel. 539-7973, is almost as old as Sydney itself. The 1787 manse, home to Rev. Ranna Cossit, Sydney's first Anglican minister, has been restored to its original condition, and costumed guides give tours. It's open June to mid-Oct., Mon.-Sat. 9:30 a.m.-5:30 p.m., Sun. 1-5:30 p.m. Admission is free.

Rev. Ranna Cossit's Parsonage

The **Cape Breton Centre for Heritage and Science,** 225 George St., tel. 539-1572, offers displays on the social and natural history of eastern Cape Breton, art exhibits, and films. It's open daily 10 a.m.-4 p.m. June-Oct.; open the rest of the year Tues.-Fri. 10 a.m.-4 p.m., Sat. 1-4 p.m. Admission is free.

Accommodations

Keddy's Sydney Hotel at 600 Kings Rd., tel. (902) 539-1140, is part of waterfront hotel/motel row and has 187 rooms in the hotel and another 27 adjacent motel rooms. Rates range $40-80, and facilities include an indoor pool, sauna, whirlpool, dining room, and lounge.

Journey's End Motel at 368 Kings Rd., tel. 562-0200, overlooks the waterfront with 62 rooms ($55-75, with morning coffee and newspaper). **Best Western Cape Bretoner Motel,** 560 Kings Rd., tel. 539-8101, is set back from the busy road with 65 rooms (from $75), a dining room, and indoor pool. The **Rockinghorse Inn,**

tel. 539-2696, 259 Kings Rd., Sydney, NS B1S 1A7, is a heritage inn. Open year-round, it offers continental breakfast, wedding packages, and a library. Rates are $70-95.

Delta Mariner Hotel at 300 Esplanade, tel. 562-7500, is a well-designed, comfortable high-rise with 152 rooms ($76 and up), dining room, indoor pool, whirlpool, sauna, exercise room, and gift shop. **Cambridge Suites Hotel,** 380 Esplanade, tel. 562-6500, is another handsome high-rise with 150 basic to large suites ($79 and up with a light breakfast) and restaurant. On the roof level are a pool, sauna, exercise room, and sundeck.

Holiday Inn Sydney at 480 Kings Rd., tel. 539-6750, completes Sydney's high-rise hotel contingent with 167 spacious rooms ($99 and up) overlooking the harbor. It also offers a restaurant, lounge, indoor pool, whirlpool, sauna, and exercise equipment.

Food

Alexander's Steak and Seafood Restaurant, 480 Kings Rd., is Holiday Inn Sydney's culinary offering with basic beef and seafood in specials that change daily ($8-17). Dinner reservations are wise; call (902) 539-6750. A noon-2 p.m. buffet ($9) also lures crowds.

DesBarres Dining Room, at the Delta Mariner Hotel on the Esplanade, assigns menu creations to a talented chef who emphasizes steak and seafood variations ($10-15). Summer reservations are wise; call 562-7500.

Joe's Warehouse and Food Emporium, 424 Charlotte St., tel. 539-6686, began as a converted Canadian Tires warehouse. It's spacious enough to accommodate crowds who favor prime ribs or New York strip steak ($17-20) or the entree specials ($10-23); weekend reservations are wise.

Jaspers Family Restaurant at George and Dorchester streets, tel. 539-7109, is one of three local Jaspers restaurants. It's a trusty, reliable place with summer lobster in the shell ($13), seafood ($11), and steak ($14); open daily 24 hours.

Sobeys is the largest supermarket group; the chain's store on Prince St. is open Mon.-Wed. and Sat. 8 a.m.-6 p.m., Thurs.-Fri. to 9 p.m. Fast-food places proliferate at the malls on Prince and Welton streets.

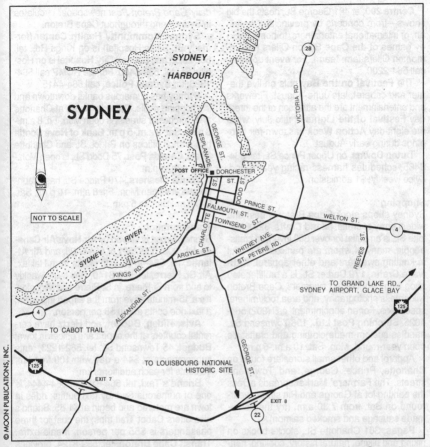

Entertainment and Events

The **Vogue Theatre** at 392 Charlotte St., tel. (902) 564-8221, has nightly movies, as does **Triple Cinemas** in the Kmart Shopping Plaza. **Centre 200,** 481 George St., tel. 539-1100, brings in concerts and large shows; check the billboard for current events. **Rotary** meets Tuesday and **Kiwanis** Thursday, both at Delta Mariner Hotel. You can watch big-screen sports television at **Steel City Beverage Room,** 264 Townsend St., tel. 539-6311 or 562-9174.

Smooth Herman's, tel. 539-0408, downstairs at Joe's Warehouse at 424 Charlotte St., has been around for years and lures a chummy bar crowd with nightly dancing, Mon.-Sat. to 3 a.m. Other nighttime action places are: **Bonnie Prince Beverage Room** at 50 Reeves St. near the Tartan Downs racetrack, with small bands and comedic antics; **Cutter's Lounge** downstairs at 458 Charlotte St., with the singles crowd, strobe lights, and chrome trappings; and **Old Sydney Pub** at 581 Grand Lake Rd. on Sydney's outskirts, with pub-style, relaxed ambience.

Hotel lounges cater to older, tamer crowds and tourists. Holiday Inn's **Alexander's Lounge** puts on Cape Breton Celtic shows, Mon.-Sat. to 1 a.m., as does Delta's **Pelican Lounge,** same evenings to midnight.

Centre 200, at 481 George St., hosts the big shows—from concerts by provincial, Canadian, or international entertainers, to home hockey games of the Cape Breton Oilers (an Edmonton Oilers farm team). For event updates, call 564-2200.

The **Festival on the Bay** puts on live theater and cabaret, late June-August. Fireworks and entertainment are the attraction of the three-day **Festival of the Lights** in mid-July, while the eight-day **Action Week** has town-fair trappings during early August.

Tartan Downs, on Upper Prince St., tel. 564-8465, schedules harness racing year-round, twice weekly; $1 admission.

Shopping

Sydney shops stock Cape Breton's best and widest array of crafts. **Island Crafts,** 329 Charlotte St., is an outlet for over 300 inventive craftspeople, many of whom are particularly skillful in knitting sweaters and other apparel. **Kittiwake Crafts,** 179 Cartier St., is a multifaceted shop with handcrafted sweaters, Cape Breton wilderness photography, and area rock/mineral specimens. For an appointment, call (902) 564-4025. **Stitching Post Ltd.,** 106 Townsend St., handles custom-made clothing and crafts; it's open year-round, Mon.-Sat. 10 a.m.-5 p.m.

Apparel and other small stores are found on Charlotte, Prince, George, and Townsend streets. The **Farmers' Market** spreads across the parking lot at George and Pitt streets year-round on Sat. from 7:30 a.m. (try the homemade sausage and smoked salmon).

Pages, 361 Charlotte St., stocks books on hiking and biking, natural history, cooking, heritage, and culture. **Quality Cameras,** George and Dorchester streets, tel. 562-3600, stocks film and equipment, and is equipped to handle minor camera repairs.

Information and Services

The **Cape Breton Tourist Association** is a five-minute drive from Sydney harborfront at 220 Keltic Drive, Sydney River, tel. (902) 539-9876 or (800) 565-9464 in Canada and the United States. It's open year-round, Mon.-Fri. 9 a.m.-5 p.m., July-Aug. to 9 p.m. **McConnell Memorial Library,** 50 Falmouth St., is open Tues.-Fri. 10 a.m.-9 p.m., Sat. to 5:30 p.m. The

daily *Cape Breton Post* newspaper circulates in Sydney and throughout Cape Breton.

Sydney Community Health Center (formerly St. Rita's Hospital) is on Kings Rd., tel. 562-2322; and **Sydney City Hospital** is on Hospital St., tel. 539-6400. For the **RCMP** call 564-1323; for **Sydney Police,** call 564-4415.

Sydney has numerous banks downtown and in shopping malls. **Canada Trust,** at Charlotte and Dorchester streets, is open Mon.-Fri. 8 a.m.-8 p.m., Sat. 9 a.m.-5 p.m. **Bank of Nova Scotia** has branch offices on Prince St. and Charlotte Street. **Canada Post,** 75 Dodd St., is open Mon.-Fri. 8 a.m.-5 p.m.

Vogue Cleaners, 470 Prince St., has a launderette; it's open Mon.-Fri. 8 a.m.-10 p.m., Sat. to 9 p.m., Sun. to 5 p.m.

Transportation

Sydney Airport is served by **Air Nova/Air Canada,** tel. (902) 539-7501 or 564-6498, and **Air Atlantic,** tel. 564-4545, with flights from Halifax. **Air St. Pierre,** tel. 562-3140, flies twice weekly to and from St-Pierre, in St-Pierre and Miquelon. It's a 15-minute drive from the airport into town; a taxi ride costs about $8 per person.

Avis, Tilden, Budget, and **Hertz** have car-rental counters at the airport and offices in town; **Budget,** 45 Townsend St., tel. 562-1223, rents subcompacts at $44 a day with 100 free km, 15 cents for each additional km.

Briand's Taxi, tel. 564-6161 or 564-4444, is one of numerous Sydney taxi outfits; rides in town are metered and begin at $1.85. Briand's also offers Cabot Trail trips; the cost for three passengers is $55 per person, meals extra. **Transit Cape Breton,** tel. 539-8124, provides public bus service in Sydney and area towns, Mon.-Sat. 7 a.m.-11 p.m. **Acadian Lines,** 99 Terminal Rd., tel. 564-5533, is open daily 6:30 a.m.-1 a.m. and has luggage-storage lockers; Sydney to Baddeck or Chéticamp costs $9 OW.

Sydney Harbour's three ports collectively ship two million metric tons annually. Sydney became a cruise-ship port of call in 1979, and Royal Viking, Cunard, Princess, and Seabourne ship lines include it on their eastern Canada cruise itineraries.

North Sydney

North Sydney, 25 km away, is the terminus for

the Marine Atlantic car/passenger ferries to Port aux Basques (year-round) and Argentia (mid-June to October only) in Newfoundland. Reservations are mandatory for both crossings. See the "Ferry Schedules" chart in the On the Road chapter for details. Write Marine Atlantic/Reservations, P.O. Box 250, North Sydney, NS B2A 3M3, or call (902) 794-5700 in Canada, (800) 341-7981 from the United States.

The **North Star Inn,** tel. 794-8581, 39 Forrest St., P.O. Box 157, North Sydney, NS B2A 3M3, is next to the ferry. It's open year-round, with a dining room, lounge, and whirlpool. Rates are $69-275. Or camp at **Arm of Gold Campground and Trailer Park** in Little Bras d'Or, tel. 736-6516. It's on Hwy. 105, three km from the ferry. Open mid-May to mid-Oct.; the rate is $9 minimum.

Glace Bay

Glace Bay, 21 km northeast of Sydney, is the former heart of Cape Breton's once-flourishing coal-mining industry. As early as the 1720s, the French exploited the area's extensive bituminous deposits, digging coal to serve the new capital of Louisbourg and initiating North America's first commercial coal-mining enterprise. Much of the reserves lie below the Atlantic, and the submarine seams have been worked as far as 15 km offshore. The industry supported a population of 28,000 in the 1960s, but Glace Bay has since shrunk to 19,500, which still makes it Cape Breton's fourth-largest community.

Today, the **Cape Breton Miners' Museum** is the main attraction for visitors. Retired miners guide you on an underground tour of a real mine, the Ocean Deeps Colliery, to show the rough working conditions under which workers manually extracted coal. The adjacent Miners' Village re-creates a miner's modest home, circa 1850-1900, and company store of the same period. A new attraction is a simulated, multimedia "trip" into the workings of a modern mine, using laser-disc projection and other special effects. On Tuesday evenings, the Men of the Deeps, a local singing group comprised of miners, gives concerts at the museum.

The Cape Breton Miners' Museum, tel. (902) 849-4522, is on Birkley St. at Quarry Point, 1.6 km from central Glace Bay via South Street. It's open early June to early September, daily 10 a.m.-6 p.m., till 7 p.m. on Tuesday; open the rest of the year weekdays 9 a.m.-4 p.m. Admission is $2.75 adults, $1.75 children, with an additional charge of $2.25 and $1.25, respectively, for the 20-minute mine tour.

Glace Bay's other claim to fame is that the "Wizard of Wireless," Guglielmo Marconi, sent the first west-to-east trans-Atlantic wireless message from here on 15 Dec. 1902. The **Marconi National Historic Site,** on Timmerman St. at Table Head, tel. 842-2530, explains Marconi's experiments and achievements and features a model of the original wireless radio station. It's open June to mid-Sept., daily 10 a.m.-6 p.m. Admission is free.

FORTRESS OF LOUISBOURG

After their defeat by the British at Port Royal in 1713, the French regrouped on Île Royale (Cape Breton Island), which they were allowed to keep under the terms of the Treaty of Utrecht. By 1720, their new capital, Louisbourg, was underway. It was planned not only as a fortified military center but also as their embodiment of a new Paris—France's governmental, commercial, and cultural center in the New World—situated on an uncomplicated small harbor fronting the Atlantic.

The dream might have worked. Louisbourg, with its transplanted French culture and social hierarchy, fed by trade from France, survived untouched by British reprisals for more than 20 years. Life in the French outpost went along placidly for the 2,000 transplanted French inhabitants, whose numbers swelled to 5,000 when ships from abroad were in port. But they lived with a sense of anxiety and expected England's invasion at any time.

In 1745, England struck for the first time, with horrendous force. The British Royal Navy blockaded the harbor. A massive volunteer militia led by a merchant from Maine pounded the seaport for seven weeks. Louisbourg fell, and the French were deported.

England controlled Louisbourg until 1748, when a treaty returned the fortress to France. Under French control, Louisbourg thrived again, but briefly. Led by James Wolfe, English forces

guarding the Fortress

NAN DROSDICK

attacked the port again in 1758 and Louisbourg fell for the final time.

"Louisbourg must be most effectively, and most entirely, demolished," Prime Minister William Pitt advised in London in 1760. Across the Atlantic, the British forces complied, blowing up every building, bastion, and wall. France's dream of a new Paris lay in ruins, never to rise again as a threat to the British. Some of the stones were used as ship ballast; some were used in buildings such as Government House in Halifax. Sydney's Anglican Church of St. George incorporated Louisbourg stone in its construction in 1785, as did Sydney's Roman Catholic Church of St. Patrick's in 1828.

The Fortress Grounds
For 200 years, the site was just weeds and piles of rubble. In the 1930s, private individuals established a small museum as a way to help preserve Louisbourg's legacy, but it wasn't until the 1960s, with federal government investment, that massive restoration efforts were undertaken. Today, at **Fortress of Louisbourg National Historic Site,** Parks Canada has reconstructed 50 of the original 80 buildings, right down to the last window, nail, and shingle, based on historical records. Two of the seven original bastions are in place. The site represents Canada's largest—and most magnificent, many people say—national historic park. The bulk of Louisbourg's $25 million reconstruction took place

between 1961 and 1984, and the 10-hectare site is now nearly complete.

Louisbourg reveals itself slowly. The seaport covers 10 hectares (25 acres), and you can spend the better part of a day exploring. From the visitor center, it's a brief bus ride across fields and marsh to the back side of the fortress. You walk from there. The reconstructed fortress and town open a window on New France; they are designed to reflect Louisbourg on a spring day in 1744, the year preceding England's first attack, when the seaport hummed with activity. The houses, fortifications, ramparts, and other structures—as authentically 18th-century French as anything you will find in France—were conceived as a statement of grandeur and power in the New World. Louisbourg's polarized social structure mirrored that of homeland France. The fancy houses lining cobbled lanes belonged to the elite, who ate sumptuous meals on fine china and drank the finest French wines. The simpler houses are the rustic cottages of the working class.

Well-informed guides and animators—portraying soldiers, merchants, workers, and craftspeople—are on hand to answer questions and demonstrate military exercises, blacksmithing, lace making, and other skills. L'Epée Royale and the Hotel de la Marine serve meals with an 18th-century flair, and hungry visitors can buy pastries at the Destouches House, and hearty, freshly baked soldiers' bread at the brick-oven bakery.

The 25 August **Feast of St. Louis** at Louisbourg attracts more than the usual number of sightseers. Celebrations finish with fireworks at 9 p.m.

Practicalities

Be prepared for walking, and bring a sweater or jacket in case of breezy or wet weather. Louisbourg's reconstructed buildings stretch from the bus stop to the harbor. Remaining ruins lying beyond the re-creation are marked by trails. You can wander on your own or join a tour: usually 10 a.m. and 2 p.m. for English tours and 1 p.m. for the French-language tour.

The Fortress of Louisbourg, on Hwy. 22, tel. (902) 733-2280, is open, fully staffed, and operates shuttle bus service July-Aug., daily 9 a.m.-6 p.m. In May, June, September, and October, it's open daily 9:30 a.m.-5:30 p.m. Admission is $6.50 adults, $3.25 ages 6-16, free for seniors and children under five.

Nearby accommodations include **Camilla Peck Tourist Home B&B,** 5353 Hwy. 22, Louisbourg, NS B0A 1M0, tel. 733-2549, an old-country working 100-acre farm on a hilltop. Rates are $32 s, $40 d; it's open June through October. **Louisbourg Motel,** tel. 733-2844, at 1225 Main St., Louisbourg, NS B0A 1M0, is wheelchair accessible. It's open year-round; rates are $43-55. The motel has dining rooms. Overlooking the harbor, **The Manse B&B,** tel. 733-2656, 7438 Main St., Louisbourg, NS B0A 1M0, is open 1 April-31 October. Rates include full breakfast: $32-40.

Mira Water Park and Campground, P.O. Box 63, Marion Bridge, NS B0A 1P0, tel. 564-1824, is eight km east of Marion Bridge on Hillside Road. It's open 24 May-5 Sept., with swimming and fishing. The rate is $11. **Louisbourg Motorhome Park,** P.O. Box 10, Louisbourg, NS B0A 1M0, is a campground on the harborfront, open 1 June-30 September. Sites are $9.

PRINCE
EDWARD
ISLAND

INTRODUCTION

Canada's smallest province, Prince Edward Island is about the size of the state of Delaware, twice the size of Luxembourg. Its shape could be likened to a giant, tattered butterfly, its wings outstretched and poised for flight at the southern, sheltered edge of the Gulf of St. Lawrence.

Prince Edward Island, or PEI, is beautifully manicured and predominantly rural. The fields of nodding wheat and neatly combed rows of potato plants that yield the island's agricultural mainstays spread across thousands of acres, interrupted by spanking-white farmhouses and tracts of woodland.

The last ice age is responsible for the ragged shape of the island, which in places seems only tenuously sutured together by slender isthmuses. The retreating ice sheets shoved several chunks of land together to form one landmass. The component parts are still clearly discernible: the island's central part is flanked, for example, with wing-shaped additions on both sides. The configuration is most noticeable at Summerside, which sits on a mere slip of a six-km-wide isthmus connecting the western and central sections. Nowadays, counties mark the province's three parts: Kings County on the east, Queens County in the center, and Prince County on the island's western side.

Being just 225 km from end to end (275 km by road), PEI may seem small enough to skim in a long day. But everything is spread out and the roads are narrow, undulating, and sometimes unpaved, forcing you to slow down and move at the island's more leisurely pace.

Over the years, PEI has acquired numerous nicknames. The province is known as the "Birthplace of Canada," a distinction earned in 1864 when representatives of England's colonies in eastern Canada convened for informal meetings in Charlottetown. Those meetings resulted in the creation of the Confederation of Canada three years later. The nationally esteemed painting that marked the event, "Fathers of Confederation," was painted by island artist Robert Harris.

In literary circles, Prince Edward Island is known as the pastoral "Avonlea" of island author Lucy Maud Montgomery's *Anne of Green Gables.* This juvenile novel and its sequels, set in the Cavendish area on PEI's gulf seacoast, draws many thousands of visitors from around the world to the area each year—visitors who read the books as children and fell in love with the stories and their setting.

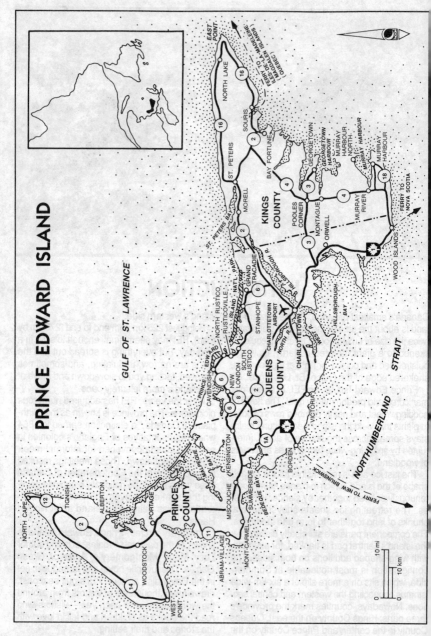

As for the rest of the Atlantic Canadians, they've dubbed PEI "Spud Island," a tribute of sorts to Canada's major producer of table and seed potatoes. Islanders themselves see their fertile province—about half of which is given over to farmland—as the "Garden of the Gulf" or the "Million Acre Farm."

All of which hardly hints at what it is that attracts nearly three-quarters of a million visitors a year to PEI. The province is a tranquil and harmonious reminder of what the world was like decades ago. Its long, untrafficked roads for biking, quiet woods and trails for hiking, scores of excellent beaches, and several splendid golf courses invite you to enjoy the outdoors. Island cuisine takes full advantage of local produce and the rich surrounding seas. Add summertime dinner theaters and plays, friendly people, shops with quality crafts, and a gentle, lovely landscape, and you'll understand what brings visitors back again and again.

THE LAND

At its highest, Prince Edward Island rises to a mere 152 meters, at Springton in northern Queens County. Its topography of predominately low, rolling countryside is a result—like the shape of the island—of the ice ages, when the islands were the highest level points on the rim of a plain that extended onto New Brunswick and Nova Scotia. As the ice sheet melted and retreated, it scooped out part of the plain and created the arc-shaped hollow that became Northumberland Strait. Then it gouged its fingers into the island edges and created fringing coastlines of bays, river estuaries, offshore islets, and dangling peninsulas.

The soil is another ice-age legacy—made up of benevolently light and loamy glacial debris, it's responsible for the province's notable success with agriculture. The soil's color is often a surprise to visitors. Its cinnamon-red hue is yet another ancient heritage, caused by iron-oxide compounds—rust—churned up by the ice sheets. (And the rust will stain clothing, so think twice before sitting on damp soil or red-tinged sand.) The burnished red hue also colors coastal headlands and sandstone cliffs.

Seacoasts and Ports

The northern coast, along the Gulf of St. Lawrence, is the tourist's PEI. Lucy Maud Montgomery described the foaming perfection to a friend in Scotland in 1906: "Some of our dips were taken in heavy surf. It was the cream of bathing to stand there and let a wave break up around one's neck in a glorious smother of white foam."

The gulf coast forms an almost even, curved line, and the sea sweeps in on a long roll through shallow waters, churning up silt along the way. The waves carry the silt to the shore, so much so that silt deposits clog harbors and rivermouths, which must be dredged continually to keep the ports navigable. The north-coast bays are protected by long sandspits and barrier islands.

The gulf coast's most famous stretch lies in Prince Edward Island National Park in northern Queens County. Red cliffs up to 30 meters high peer over the surf, and the sea washes up on pink- and white-sand beaches. Ribbons of wooden boardwalks, bike paths, hiking routes, and roads thread across the slender 40-km-long park.

Along this same stretch of coast, three bays—Tracadie (TRAK-a-dee), Rustico, and New London—are popular with tourists. To the west, Malpeque Bay nearly splits Prince County, and gives PEI's Malpeque oysters their name. Mollusk aquaculture began here decades ago. Today, oysters are farmed throughout the bay, helping make PEI Canada's number-one oyster-producing province.

PEI's Northumberland Strait coastline is distinctly different. Its jagged headlands are spliced with the majority of the island's 60 harbors. Charlottetown is situated on its own harbor at the confluence of the wide Hillsborough, North, and West rivers. It's the province's best-known port and a cruise ship port of call. Summerside, an hour northwest of Charlottetown, ranks as PEI's major produce-shipping port and is protected behind a peninsula. Other major ports include Georgetown—an hour east of Charlottetown and one of the province's oldest deep-water ports—and Souris, the fishing and ferry seaport, 45 minutes beyond Georgetown toward the island's eastern tip.

Green Spaces

PEI has 31 provincial parks, each unique and sometimes unusual. **Buffaloland Provincial Park,** for example, tucked away in a small forest at Milltown Cross in southern Kings County, supports a buffalo herd. Imported from western Canada, the bison roam the woods and emerge to feed at the road's edge during late afternoon.

Some parks commemorate historic events. The site of **Jacques Cartier Provincial Park** on Prince County's gulf coastline is said to have been the explorer's landfall in 1534. Western Malpeque Bay's coastal **Green Park** marks the shipbuilding realm of the James Yeo family, which reigned over the island's shipbuilding and politics during Canada's Great Age of Sail.

Other parks preserve idyllic landscapes. **Panmure Island Provincial Park** near Georgetown has its back to tranquil St. Mary's Bay and faces

the open gusty sea. The breezy **Cedar Dunes Provincial Park** at PEI's western tip invites walking along sand dunes and long, wide beaches.

Two provincial parks—**Brudenell,** at Roseneath in eastern PEI, and **Mill River,** at Woodstock in the west—have dual personalities, meshing privately operated resort hotels with provincially operated campgrounds; hotel guests and campers alike can take advantage of the parks' golf courses, tennis courts, canoes, stables, and riverfront beaches. In addition, the Mill River park boasts a full-facility recreational aquaplex and racquet club, a one-of-a-kind sports center in the province.

Camping sites, no matter the extras, are reasonably priced and range from $10 (bare-bones sites) to $17 (with electrical hookups). Campground facilities usually include sewerage hookups, a launderette, small general store, nature trails, kitchen shelters, free firewood, scheduled naturalist programs, and sometimes supervised swimming.

Provincial parks (as well as private campgrounds), with their respective addresses, phone numbers, seasons, and other details are listed in the provincial *Visitors Guide,* available from **Provincial Parks,** P.O. Box 2000, Charlottetown, PE C1A 7N8. Most parks are open from June into September or October, while the season at Brudenell and Mill River parks spans late May to early October. For reservations, call the respective park offices.

Development Issues

For land developers, Prince Edward Island is a delectable plum that's ripe for picking. The land lies mainly in farmlands and pleasant woodlands, and developers for years have eyed the province as a gold mine for luxury summer homes, hotels, and resorts. Environmentally conscious islanders have opposed absentee-landlord development and formed watchdog groups, such as **Friends of the Island,** and other environmental committees to keep an eye on development schemes.

Land-use conflicts have pitted farmers, fishermen, and environmentalists against powerful local business and tourism interests, as well as the federal government. The provincial government has walked the middle ground between the camps.

The Fixed Link

After more than a century of debate, a "fixed link" across the narrowest part of the Northumberland Strait—joining Cape Tormentine, New Brunswick, and Borden, PEI—is now under construction. PEI commercial interests favor the 14-km-long bridge, contending that it will move produce to market more efficiently than the current ferry system. Tourism interests want more tourists. The federal government wants to improve PEI's overall economy.

In opposition to the link, fishermen and environmental groups counter that the bridge supports across the strait will disturb inshore fishing grounds and also stall the spring ice thaw, delaying lobster molting, disrupting other marine species' life cycles, and possibly damaging the rich seabed. Environmental groups and other observers say that increased tourist saturation will stress the fragile ecology of the place and drastically alter the island's idyllic way of life. In "Fixed Link," Cavendish-area songwriter George Brothers observes:

> *On the one hand, there's a way of life.*
> *Some feel it will be lost.*
> *The other side wants progress.*
> *No matter what the cost.*

Nonetheless, 59% of the islanders voted in favor of the fixed link in a provincial plebiscite in 1988, and a majority continues to support it. The $620 million project, providing much-needed employment in an economically depressed region, is slated for completion in 1997.

CLIMATE

PEI basks in a typical maritime climate with one major exception: its growing season of 110-160 days is Atlantic Canada's longest. Moderated by open seas, frost-free days can extend from late April through mid-October.

Spring is short, lasting from May until mid-June. Summer is pleasant and warm and spans late June through early September. Summer temperatures peak July-August, with highs ranging 18-23° C; an unusually warm day can reach 35° C, while, at the other extreme, some summer days can be cool at just 5° C. Most islanders

rarely take the blankets off beds, even during summer.

The island is sun-washed and gleaming during summer. Showers come and go. When clouds move in and unite as a singular dull white sky, expect one to three days of showers. Annual precipitation amounts to 106 centimeters, half of that falling from May to October.

Autumn spans mid-September through October, and brings with it Atlantic Canada's brightest and most dramatic fall foliage. Colors peak from early to mid-October, finishing with a flourish as pre-winter breezes strengthen to full-blown winds that bring the leaves down late in the month.

The island gets more than its share of year-round breezes and winds. Summer breezes can be pleasantly warm, but the pace can occasionally pick up to outright gales, especially during late autumn.

The climate's fast-changing moods can make for dramatic photography. Storms create intensely contrasting sea and land colors; winds churn up the sea floor for waters as red as the soil, and puffy white clouds hurry across a lapis-blue sky. Summer showers enrich the farmlands with glistening freshness.

The island lures very few winter tourists. Winter temperatures can dip from -21 to 6° C after Christmas, and average -7° to 3° C.

FLORA AND FAUNA

In 1534, the explorer Jacques Cartier described the island as "wonderfully fair, filled with goodly meadows and trees." Cartier's goodly trees were typical Acadian forest, similar to the Great Lakes and St. Lawrence woodlands. Forest variety was plentiful and included spruce, birches, pines, elm, and the regal northern red oak, the provincial tree.

But centuries of downing trees for shipbuilding and clearing land for farms altered the landscape, leaving the island with the least amount of original wilderness of any Canadian province. In the 1950s, the provincial government began to reforest the island. The effort was led by J. Frank Gaudet, the first provincial forester, whose name now graces numerous provincial reforestation projects. For a close-up look at new projects underway, check out the provincial J. Frank Gaudet Tree Nursery, Upton Road at West Royalty, near Charlottetown, tel. (902) 368-4700. It's open June-Aug., Tues.-Fri. 10 a.m.-noon.

The province's six "demonstration woodlots," an outgrowth of the nursery, represent the provincial nursery's work in action. "Woodlots" as an image hardly describes the landscape to the uninitiated; rather, visualize plantations of mixed trees that welcome visitors with hiking trails beneath the leafy canopies.

Late spring and summer's warm temperatures urge columbines, bachelor buttons, pansies, lilacs, wild roses, and pink clover into blossom. The delicate lady's slipper is the provincial flower, most abundant in the shady woods in the Valleyfield area in Kings County. In summer, roadsides are splashed with the color of abundant wildflowers—the white umbels of Queen Anne's lace, yellow daisies, lupine, and the showy spikes of purple loosestrife, a pretty but aggressive and unwelcome pest.

Ruffled grouse, gray partridge, red fox, raccoon, and woodcock are spread throughout the province. Foxes are particularly important. The world's first successful captive breeding of silver foxes occurred in Prince County in the late 1800s.

Hundreds of varieties of birds inhabit PEI and some 303 species migrate through in spring and fall. The noisy blue jay, at home throughout the island, is the official provincial bird. The showiest species is the enormous, stately great blue heron, which summers on the island from May to early August. The rare piping plover may be seen (but not disturbed) on national park beaches. Arctic terns nest along Murray Harbour coastlines.

HISTORY

The First Visitors

The island's first visitors were the Micmac Indians, a branch of the eastern Algonquins. The island was their Abegweit ("Land Cradled on the Waves"), and they summered on the island for centuries. A Micmac legend relates that Glooscap, a god who roamed the earth as a giant man, fashioned the island out of clay in the shape of a crescent, set its trees and flowers in place, and transported it on his shoulders to its place at the gulf's edge.

Jacques Cartier bumped into the island on his first New World voyage, claimed it for France, and sailed off to explore the rest of the gulf and the St. Lawrence River. European settlers and subsequent turbulence followed. Queen Anne's War between England and France concluded with the Treaty of Utrecht, which awarded the island to the French. Port la Joye, established in 1719 where Charlottetown Harbour meets Hillsborough Bay, was the island's first settlement. It was the fortified military hub for farms across the island that contributed foodstuffs to the Fortress of Louisbourg on Cape Breton.

Settlement

In 1755, England deported the Acadians from Acadia (Prince Edward Island, Nova Scotia, and New Brunswick) and swept the area again for Acadians in 1758, after capturing Louisbourg. Port la Joye was renamed Fort Amherst, and the English Crown dispatched surveyor Samuel Holland to survey, parcel out, and name various places and sites on the newly acquired island.

One would think the most logical way to divide the island into counties would be along its own natural divisions. But for reasons known only to himself, Holland chose to ignore PEI's natural configuration. He drew county lines on perplexing slants and added some of the central island to the western county (Prince) and did a cut-and-paste job in the east as well.

Holland laid out Charlotte Town as the capital in 1763. The rest of the island was divided into 67 parcels and sold to absentee landlords at a lottery in England. On the island, tenant farmers worked the land and paid quitrents on leases controlled in England.

Prince Edward Island paid its own way as a self-sustaining outpost of the empire. The island became a separate colony independent of Nova Scotia in 1769, and quitrents paid for the maintenance of the colonial government.

Many Acadians managed to elude the net of deportation, and the province's contemporary Acadians are the descendants of those resourceful original settlers. Other immigrants followed, and Loyalists fleeing the American Revolution added an Anglo presence in the 1780s.

Scotch and Irish emigrants, displaced by land clearances, poverty, and religious persecution in the British Isles, began to arrive in the early 1800s.

Boom Decades

The thickly wooded island began to change. A road network was laid out by 1850. And by 1860, some 176 sawmills were transforming forests into lumber, greasing the island's economy and providing the raw materials for a thriving shipbuilding industry. The first census in 1798 had counted 4,371 islanders; by 1891, the number had grown to 109,000, close to the current population. Land ownership was a hotly contested, ongoing issue, and by the 1850s many islanders acquired title to their own land. By the time PEI joined the Confederation of Canada, half of the parcels were owned free and clear by the island's residents.

Confederation was another issue. In 1867, the island ducked the first opportunity to unite with the other eastern Canadian colonies (see "History" under "Charlottetown and Vicinity" later in this chapter), but joined in 1873, lured by the promise of federal railroad financing. Two years later, the Land Purchase Act settled the issue of land ownership, and the remaining landowners' parcels were sold to the farmers holding the leases on them.

The Twentieth Century

PEI flourished during the Great Age of Sail. Charlottetown, as the center of government and commerce, was enriched with splendid stone churches and public buildings. In the early 20th century, silver fox–breeding profits brought riches to western PEI. The lowly lobster, once used as fertilizer, caught the fancy of seafood gourmets and became the leading fisheries product by 1897.

In 1905, Ottawa turned down the provincial request for a tunnel to the mainland. But scheduled ferry service with the mainland started in 1916.

The island's good luck soured as WW I wound down. An epidemic nearly destroyed Malpeque Bay's fledgling oyster industry in 1917. The Great Depression took hold in the 1930s, and the population plummeted to 88,000 as islanders left for work elsewhere in Canada and the United States.

The provincial economy withered, and it was decades before it recovered. Scheduled icebreaker ferry service improved year-round transportation to the mainland in 1947. The Confederation centennial in 1964 prompted the federal government to mark the event by establishing the Confederation Centre of the Arts in Charlottetown, and the new complex became PEI's proud showplace for theater, art exhibits, and other presentations.

The province today maintains the tranquility associated with a rural countryside. The ravaged woodlands began to be restored by the provincial Forestry Act in 1949. Tourism developed in the 1960s as backcountry roads were paved, and the province added a second ferry service to the mainland. Higher education became more cohesive when Prince of Wales College and St. Dunstan's University were absorbed into the University of Prince Edward Island in the late 1960s.

GOVERNMENT AND ECONOMY

The province has a parliamentary government with a 32-seat provincial assembly for 16 electoral districts. In 1992, the Liberals won a landslide victory with 30 seats, while the minority Progressive Conservatives took the other two. The New Democratic Party has a foothold, albeit a slim one, in the province. PEI contributes four parliament members and four senators to the federal government.

Diminutive PEI supplies *half* of the world's supply of potatoes. Half of the crop is grown in Prince County, and the remainder is produced by farms scattered across the province. Local farmers travel abroad to 32 nations to advise their foreign counterparts on varieties and farming methods. The province also ranks first in Canadian oyster production, harvesting 10 million oysters annually and exporting most of them.

The island's beauty may be partially attributed to its agriculture, which accounts for 9.5% of the province's gross domestic product (GDP). The sector yields $120 million a year and employs 5,000 islanders on 2,800 farms, each of which averages 96 hectares. Grains, fruits, beef, pigs, sheep, and dairy products are other components of agricultural production.

Fishing is another strong income producer, reeling in $51.9 million annually. Some 4,900 fishermen on 1,500 vessels ply the sea for lobsters and cod, in addition to oysters. Island blue mussel cultivation is the province's newest aquaculture project—a highly successful venture that has produced mussels freer of salt and sand than their wild counterparts.

Farming and fishing remain crucial, but the economy is slowly changing. In the late 1960s, the request for a fixed link to the mainland collapsed and economic efforts were rechanneled to the Comprehensive Development Plan, aimed at bolstering education and industry. The optics and medical-component industries formed the gist of new light-industrial parks. Tourism became increasingly important and today earns $95 million annually, employing 2,500 islanders year-round and another 6,500 on a seasonal basis.

The province's GDP is about $2.25 billion. Inflation is just under four percent, lower than the national average. Unemployment measures 10-15%, due to the seasonal nature of fishing and farming. In 1991, personal per capita income was $18,500.

THE PEOPLE

Some 130,000 islanders are dispersed among almost 500 hamlets, villages, towns, and one city, Charlottetown, the provincial capital. Prince Edward Islanders are a special breed of Canadians, no matter their ethnic origin. An easygoing way of life places high on their list of priorities; people here tend to be relaxed, pleasant, and helpful, and are resistant to being hurried or hustled. They're courteous and they expect similar courtesies from their guests—aggressive mannerisms and loudness will get you nowhere.

The island has a youthful population: 40% of islanders are under 25 years old. Sixty percent of the people live in the countryside, while most of the others are concentrated in the urban centers of Charlottetown and Summerside.

With 22.4 people per square km, PEI has the highest population density of all the provinces. It's also said to be Canada's most ethnically homogeneous province. Anglos make up 80% of the population, of whom a third are Irish, and the remainder are Scottish descendants. Acadians represent 16% of the population, of whom five percent speak French. The Micmacs form four percent of the population. PEI still lures immigrants, mainly from Ontario, Nova Scotia, New Brunswick, and Alberta.

Islanders value their ethnic identities. Lineage details are abundant, carefully documented, and are available at the **Prince Edward Island Museum and Heritage Foundation,** 2 Kent St., Charlottetown, PE C1A 1M6, tel. (902) 892-9127.

Local Idioms

Stay tuned to the expressions islanders use to describe the island. For example, everyone who is not from the island they say is "from away." Prince County has numerous grandiose "fox houses" that were built with silver-fox fortunes decades ago, and if you hear an islander explain that a town has been "foxified," it means that it has a number of such lavish houses. On the roads, signs warn of "bad bumps," and some-

mending the nets

time advise drivers to "squeeze" left or right.

A route on foot through an interesting sightseeing place is called a "walk-about." A "run" is an entrance into a bay through flaking sand dunes. And a "feed" is the most lavish of dinners, usually a bountiful summertime lobster supper at one of the island's community supper halls.

Religion

Religious affiliations are important to islanders, who are overwhelmingly Christian. More than half are Roman Catholic, and the remainder belong to the Protestant sects, mainly Presbyterian and Anglican.

Crime

Islanders pride themselves on an almost crime-free environment. Part of the reason is the obvious fact that this *is* an island; what bank robber wants to wait around for the ferry to make his getaway? A crime of passion may happen every so often as in any place, but the most you can expect is minor theft. To eliminate temptation, lock your car, keep your luggage in the trunk, and take cameras and other valuables with you.

ARTS, CRAFTS, AND SHOPPING

Local artists capture the island in masterful watercolors, acrylics, oils, and sculpture. Local crafts include finely made quilts, knits and woolens, stained glass, jewelry, pewter, pottery, and handsome furniture. The "Anne" doll is the most popular souvenir, and it's produced in innumerable variations for as little as $20 to as much as $800.

An exquisite handmade quilt costs $400-800—seldom a bargain. But well-crafted quilts are sturdily constructed and will last a lifetime with good care. Sweaters ($75-275) are especially high quality. One of the best sources is **Great Northern Knitters,** tel. (902) 566-4922, with a factory outlet at West Royalty Industrial Park in Charlottetown. It's open year-round, weekdays 10 a.m.-5 p.m. The company owes its origin to the provincial Comprehensive Development Plan. Great Northern Knitters sells its line of warm, bulky sweaters in two Charlottetown shops and has another store in Nova Scotia, where the crew of the *Bluenose II* adopted

one of the styles for their official racing sweater.

Much of the creativity here springs from **Holland College of the Creative Arts,** the provincial applied-arts school. If you're interested in latest crafts trends, check out the college's gallery in Charlottetown.

The **P.E.I. Crafts Council** is another driving force. It counts about 100 provincial craftspeople among its esteemed ranks. **Island Crafts Shop** in Charlottetown functions as the council members' outlet; if you're interested in locating council crafts producers, ask for a membership list with shop or studio addresses and phone numbers.

Shopping Hours

In tourist areas, shops generally open daily between 8 and 10 a.m. and close between 8 and 10 p.m. Stores catering to islanders are normally open Mon.-Sat. from about 9 a.m. to 5 p.m.; most stores stay open until 8 or 9 p.m. on Friday nights. From late May to early September, provincial liquor stores at 16 locations are open Mon.-Fri. 10 a.m.-10 p.m.; most close Saturday at 6 p.m., while Charlottetown Mall and Oak Tree Place outlets are open until 10 p.m.

The provincial sales tax is 10%; clothing up to $100 is exempt. The federal GST adds seven percent, but is refundable (for purchases over $100) on application. (See "Money" in the On the Road chapter for details.)

ENTERTAINMENT AND EVENTS

Charlottetown Festival

The province enthusiastically promotes this event, and it's worth it; an island visit without seeing *Anne of Green Gables* is like bread without butter. The Anne musical is just one of a number of theatrical, cabaret, and musical productions staged concurrently mid-June to early September in the capital's sumptuous **Confederation Centre of the Arts** and smaller nearby theaters.

Other Events

Scores of local and regional events fill the province's festival calendar; the provincial *Visitors Guide* lists each and every event across the island, in chronological order. Some of the best are listed here.

On 1 July, **Canada Day** celebrations take place in Morell (Kings County) and Summerside (Queens County). At Montague, the **hot rod show** lures crowds for three days in early July. Mid-July brings the **Strawberry Festival** at Orwell Corner (a provincial historic site that marks the early settlement), Morell's five-day **Strawberry Festival,** and the Souris **Regatta,** a three-day event. Also in mid-July, Summerside's **Lobster Carnival** attracts hungry lobster fans to its week of festivities. Late July's **Islander Day** features sports competitions and sand-sculpture contests at P.E.I. National Park. The island's sentimental tribute to islanders who have left the island and returned for a visit is mid-August's **Old Home Week** in Charlottetown.

RECREATION

Lucy Maud Montgomery's sudsy, soft, and pervading image of the province as the politely genteel Avonlea is a bit deceiving. It's not all croquet and tea parties: the island abounds in opportunities for exciting sports and other outdoor activities.

Various packages are described under "Island Value Vacations" in the *Visitors Guide.* Sports like golf, fishing, biking, and camping can be booked before arrival and are often linked with accommodations with good value for the dollar. Other packages focus on dining, sightseeing, theater, or photography.

Getting Airborne
For a splurge, consider the thrill of ballooning. From high in the sky, with the island spread out beneath you, the plumped patchwork quilt of farms edged with fences and hedgerows is dazzling. **Pegasus Balloons** at the village of Rennies Road in northern Queens County, tel. (902) 964-3250, lifts off year-round, at sunrise or two or three hours before sunset (periods of calm winds). The cost is $125 per person, and you'll need to make advance reservations with several alternate dates.

Scenic Air Tours, at the Charlottetown airport, tel. 894-7205, delivers just what its name promises; rates start at $20 per person for a party of three.

Bicycling
The narrow roads that slice through the rolling countryside are sublime avenues for biking. The biking terrain is classified by the province as rolling, hilly, or level, though it's all pretty gentle. The highest peaks present no more than a four-degree incline. The greatest impediment is the wind, which can blow steadily at times. Apart from some stretches along the TransCanada Highway and some primary highways, road shoulders are narrow or nonexistent. Traffic is normally light, but bicycle helmets are recommended.

Most cycling rental shops are in Queens County. **MacQueen's Bike Shop,** 430 Queen St., Charlottetown, tel. (902) 368-2453, has one of the island's most complete selections and charges $10-20 day for standard and mountain bikes; they also have an outlet at Wood Islands ferry terminal. Others include **Shaw's Hotel Cycle Rental,** in Brackley Beach on the North Shore, tel. 672-2022; and **Cavendish Sunset Campground,** tel. 963-2440.

Cycle-touring packages are offered by **Singing Sands Sea Breeze Bicycle Expeditions,** tel. 357-2371; and **Freewheeling Island Adventure,** tel. 857-3600.

For On-Island Emergency Roadside Assistance for cyclists, call 368-2453.

Hiking
While there's nothing resembling remote wilderness on the island, the rolling countryside nevertheless lends itself to relaxed hiking on a variety of trails. Six self-guided trails lie within the provincial park system; the national park also has six marked trails. The province has been busy converting abandoned rail lines into hiking and bicycling trails; the network eventually will link the island end to end.

Horseback Riding
The island has horses, plenty of them, and none stouter than the working draft horses you'll see raking Irish moss on northern Prince County's seacoast. **Charlottetown Driving Club** on Kensington Rd. in Charlottetown, and **Summerside Raceway,** 477 Notre Dame St. in Summerside, have year-round harness racing.

A number of trail-riding outfits rent steeds for riding at $6-12 per person per hour. **Brudenell**

NAN DROSDICK

*Prince Edward Island
National Park*

Resort Trail Rides, tel. (902) 652-2396, at Rodd Brudenell River Resort in eastern Kings County, is one of the best. They can design a trail itinerary or overnight tour for you, June-September.

Golf

The season starts in late May when the ground dries out, and finishes in mid-October. Championship greens include those at Brudenell and Mill River provincial parks (in Kings and Prince counties, respectively) and the Linkletter course near Summerside.

GOLF PEI, P.O. Box 2653, Charlottetown, PE C1A 8C3, tel. (902) 368-4130, is an umbrella organization with 11 affiliated courses, all excellent (most are described in this chapter). Contact the organization for information and a listing of golf/accommodations packages.

Hunting and Inland Fishing

Hunters "from away" will need a $35 nonresident license and a provincial Firearm Safety Certificate, and bird hunters must buy a Canada Migratory Game Bird permit; for details, contact **Department of the Environment, Fish and Wildlife Branch,** tel. (902) 368-4684, or write to them at P.O. Box 2000, Charlottetown, PE C1A 7N8.

Open season on gray partridge, ruffled grouse, and migratory birds is early October to mid-December. **North Shore Outfitters,** 19 Keppoch Rd. at Southport in Queens County, tel. 963-3449 or 569-3423, charges $600 per person for a guided, three-day hunt with lodgings and meals.

Brook trout, found in virtually all streams, rivers, and ponds, are the most popular quarry of inland anglers; less common are rainbows, found mainly in the Dunk, Cardigan, and Sturgeon rivers and in Glenfinnan and O'Keefe lakes. Trout fishing requires a license; contact the Fish and Wildlife Branch in Charlottetown at the above address.

Sea Sports

Deep-sea fishing is popular here, with the primary game fish being the giant bluefin tuna, feisty enough to battle for 10 hours. Its season runs midsummer through October. Fishing charter companies are located mainly along the gulf seaports, with sizable concentrations at the Rustico ports and North Lake Harbour. Three-hour trips cost about $20 per person, with gear provided. Expect to pay about $300 for an eight-hour trip with four anglers. Charters are geared for groups of four to six anglers and depart between 8 and 10 a.m. No license is required. For details, contact the **Fish and Wildlife** branch office listed under "Hunting and Inland Fishing" above.

Windsurfing is best in northern Queens County on the gulf, where the winds are steadiest. **Beachcombing and sunbathing** are alternatives to getting out in the water. Beaches on the island are comprised of either white or red sand. If your beach of the day has red sand,

...ket—the iron-oxide stains ...eastern Kings County's ...d Murray Harbour coast- ...by the dozens; they like the ...thumberland Strait.

ACCOMMODATIONS AND FOOD

PEI offers more lodgings per square kilometer than any other Canadian province. You'll have a choice from among 2,000 bed-and-breakfasts, country inns, vacation farms, lodges, tourist homes, hotels, motels, resorts, houses, and apartments, not to mention campgrounds. The abundance can be baffling, but the *Visitors Guide* describes nearly all of them, arranged by sightseeing regions. Some lodgings are listed with a one- to five-star rating, but as the grading system is strictly voluntary, an absence of a rating carries little weight. Lodgings packages are another option, and the guide's "Island Value Vacations" lists a variety.

The **Bed and Breakfast and Country Inns Association of Prince Edward Island,** P.O. Box 2551, Charlottetown, PE C1A 8C2, produces a handy booklet, available at tourist information centers, which details some 80 or so member lodgings.

If you have questions about where to stay, call **Dial the Island** (the provincial information service) at (902) 368-5555, (800) 565-7421 in the Maritimes, or (800) 565-0267 from elsewhere in North America. **Murphy Tour Service Central Reservations,** tel. 892-0606, is another source; write to them at 64 Great George St., Charlottetown, PE C1A 4K3.

Another extremely useful reservations service is offered by **Paradise Island Reservations,** tel. (800) 265-6161, which can book all sorts of accommodations islandwide at no charge. Their switchboard is open 8 a.m.-midnight, Atlantic standard time.

Rates range from extraordinarily inexpensive to inordinately pricey. Overall, lodging costs are among Atlantic Canada's lowest. Generally, costs are highest in Charlottetown and Queen County's North Shore, both longtime tourist meccas. Best buys are in the hinterlands at either end of the province. Regardless, rates are

fair, with good value for the dollar; count on clean and tidy rooms, and courteous and helpful hospitality. Rates given in this chapter are in Canadian dollars, and do not include taxes.

Food and Drink

Island fare is *good.* Seafood lovers will be particularly enthralled. Where else in the world would McDonald's offer Lobster Burgers?

Summertime offers a feast of shellfish—Atlantic Canada's most abundant variety. If you're interested in Malpeque oysters on their own turf, the sweet mollusks are prepared islandwide in season. And the popularity of lobster as an entree has spawned a half dozen community halls (as big as German beer halls) known especially for boiled lobster and fixings.

Local produce and dairy products are delicious. Chefs make the most of island-grown succulent berries, locally produced maple syrup, and thick, sweet honey. **PEI Preserve Company** at New Glasgow near the gulf coast captures the height of the berry season in infinite varieties of bottled preserves, some spiked with brandy.

Restaurants run the gamut from purposely rustic or plain places furnished in early Formica, to haute-decor dining rooms with artfully created interior ambience. Plain or fancy, count on consistently good cooking—you can't go wrong. Charlottetown and Queens County's North Shore offer the most abundant dining choices. Options are sparse however on backcountry roads; it's wise to plan to arrive in towns at mealtimes when you're exploring the hinterlands. Acadian fare—found in abundance in southern Prince County's Mont-Carmel area—is excellent and reasonably priced.

If you're interested in bending an elbow with the locals, check out Canadian Legion halls and neighborhood taverns, where beer drinking is serious business. As for mixed drinks, a finely tuned martini is hard to find; basic scotch and water is a wiser choice. Restaurant wine lists are nothing to rave about, but a few places, such as the Inn at Bay Fortune's dining room at Bay Fortune, and Prince Edward Hotel's Lord Selkirk Room in Charlottetown, have worthy offerings.

INFORMATION AND SERVICES

Visitor Information

Politeness goes a long way. If you don't know something, ask around. Islanders go out of their way to be helpful.

The province's patient and thorough staff answers all kinds of questions at **Visitor Services**, tel. (902) 368-5555 in Charlottetown, (800) 565-7421 in the Maritimes, or (800) 565-0267 in North America; or write them at P.O. Box 940, Charlottetown, PE C1A 7M5. A copy of the excellent, detailed 160-page *Visitors Guide* is free, along with a highway map of the province.

The provincial **Tour the Island Visitor Information Centre** is at Oak Tree Place mall on University Ave., Charlottetown; open year-round. Branch offices across the island have varied seasons: at Borden, they're open mid-May to mid-Oct., daily 10 a.m.-6 p.m.; Wood Islands, mid-May to Sept., daily 9:30 a.m.-6 p.m.; Cavendish and Summerside, June to mid-Oct., daily 9 a.m.-6 p.m.; Portage and Souris, mid-June to early Sept., daily 10 a.m.-6 p.m.; and Pooles Corner, mid-June to early Oct., 9 a.m.-6 p.m. Hours are longer during peak tourist season from July to mid-August.

Publications

The daily *Guardian* ("Covers Prince Edward Island Like The Dew") is published in Charlottetown and circulates in Queens and Kings counties. The *Journal-Pioneer,* another daily, covers Prince County. The *Graphic* ("The Lively One") is a local newsweekly, while *La Voix Acadienne* is the Acadian newsweekly. A handy free tabloid, published monthly, is the *Buzz,* which lists entertainment and events, mainly in and around Charlottetown.

Though a bit cluttered with ads, a helpful 100-plus-page booklet available free at tourist info centers is *This Week on PEI,* which lists events, ferry schedules, accommodations, and the like, and gives a bit of background on places.

Health and Safety

No special inoculations or other health precautions are required to enter the province. Canadians are covered by national health care. For non-Canadians, a day's basic hospital costs (exclusive of doctor fees and treatment) are expensive: $740 at Charlottetown's Queen Elizabeth Hospital to $540 in Summerside. Smaller hospitals charge about $385 per day and are located in Alberton, O'Leary, Tyne Valley, Montague, and Souris.

Dentists can be found in Charlottetown, Summerside, Tignish, O'Leary, Wellington, Kensington, Hunter River, Crapaud, Cornwall, Parkdale, Southport, Morell, Montague, and Souris.

The **Royal Canadian Mounted Police** headquarters is at 450 University Ave., Charlottetown, tel. (902) 566-7100. It's open daily, 24 hours. For the RCMP highway patrol, call 566-7130.

Communications

The main **Canada Post** office is on Queen St., Charlottetown. Numerous retail post offices are scattered across the province; hours vary—some open at 7 a.m. and close at midnight.

PEI's telephone area code is **902,** the same as Nova Scotia's. **Island Tel** discounts long-distance calls 60% nightly from 11 p.m. to 8 a.m.; a 35% discount applies Mon.-Sat. 6-11 p.m. and Sun. 8 a.m.-11 p.m. Local tax is 10%, and a federal telecommunications tax adds another 11%.

Immigration

Visitors need an extension ($50 application fee) to stay on the island beyond 90 days. Before the time is up, contact the **Immigration Centre** in Charlottetown at 85 Fitzroy St., tel. (902) 566-7735; open Mon.-Fri. 8 a.m.-4 p.m.

Getting a temporary or permanent job is a drawn-out process and has to originate at the visitor's home base. The office answers questions and can provide the Canadian Consulate address nearest the visitor's origin to start the process.

WHAT TO TAKE

Clothing

Travel light; neither the airport nor the bus terminal has storage lockers. (Hotels and motels will usually handle short-term storage as favors to guests.)

The mark of the tourist in Charlottetown is attire that is too informal. You'll blend in comfortably with casual, upscale clothing. Bring along a sweater or jacket and raincoat and umbrella; seacoasts are breezy, and brief summertime showers come and go. Summertime is warm, and shorts, sandals, and light clothing are in order.

Money

If Prince Edward Island is your first stop, it helps to arrive with some Canadian currency for taxi rides and luggage tips. For the best exchange rates, convert foreign currency at the local banks, which are open Mon.-Wed. 10 a.m.-4 or 5 p.m., Thurs.-Fri. to 8 p.m. (a few banks are open Sat. 9 a.m.-3 p.m.). All major credit cards are accepted.

GETTING THERE

By Air

Most air service to the island is direct, but not nonstop, which means that the plane sets down someplace else before it arrives at the Charlottetown airport. International flights are routed through Halifax, Montreal, or Toronto. **Air Canada/Air Nova** connects Charlottetown with Toronto via Ottawa, and with Montreal, Boston, and Newark via Halifax. For reservations, call (902) 892-1007, or (800) 565-3940 from PEI. **Canadian Airlines International/Air Atlantic** flies about a dozen times daily to and from Halifax, a short 20-minute flight. For flight information, call 892-5358; reservations, 892-3581, or (800) 565-1800 from PEI. **Prince Edward Air,** tel. (800) 565-5359, has recently started up nonstop service between Halifax, Moncton, Charlottetown, and Summerside.

Advance airline reservations pay off. An economy Newark-Charlottetown ticket, for example, can cost about $700 RT, but Air Canada/Air Nova's **Seat Saver** promotion discounts that amount by 40-60%. Special fares such as this, however, have restrictions and are usually available for only a limited number of seats, so you need to book as far in advance as possible.

By Sea

If you arrive on a yacht, you can drop anchor for $10 a night at **Charlottetown Yacht Club,** Pownal St. Wharf, tel. (902) 892-9065; and at the

Silver Fox Yacht Club in Summerside. Charlottetown as a port of call ranks among Atlantic Canada's top cruise stops; among ship lines that drop anchor are: Crown Cruise Line, Crystal Cruises, Odessamerica Cruises, and Royal Viking Line.

Two ferry systems connect the island with the mainland, and another ferry links Québec's Îles-de-la-Madeleine (Magdalen Islands) in the gulf. Allow plenty of time going either direction; during the tourist season, the waiting lines for cars can be horrendously long—up to two or three hours. Tune in to local radio stations, such as 720 AM, which give regular status reports on crossing conditions and estimated waiting times. Schedules are posted at ferry terminals and roadside tourist centers.

Marine Atlantic, tel. 794-5700 in Canada, (800) 341-7981 from the U.S., links Borden, PEI (near Summerside), with Cape Tormentine, New Brunswick. (The fixed link will eventually span this route.) The year-round crossing takes 45 minutes, 60 minutes in winter, and round-trip passage (payable when leaving the island) costs $7.25 per adult, $3.75 for children aged 5-12 (under 5 years go for free), and $18 for a car. Bicycles are $3.50, motorcycles $9, and motor homes, campers, and cars with trailers are charged by length, $18-54. From late spring to late autumn, ferries each way depart every hour on the half hour; schedules are reduced the rest of the year.

Northumberland Ferries, tel. 566-3838, (800) 565-0201 in the Maritimes, sails between Wood Islands, PEI (an hour southeast of Charlottetown), and Caribou, Nova Scotia. The 75-minute crossing operates May to mid-December, with approximately 15 crossings daily during summer. Round-trip passage is $8.50 per adult, $4.10 for children aged 5-12 (under 5 free), and $27.25 per car. Bicycles are $4.75, motorcycles $13.50, and motor homes, campers, and cars with trailers are charged by length, $27.25-82.

CTMA Ferry, tel. 687-2181 or off-season at (418) 986-3278, connects Souris on the strait coast with Grindstone, Îles-de-la-Madeleine (Magdalen Islands), April through January. The 134-km crossing takes five hours. Round-trip passage is $36 per person, $53 for a car. For information on the Magdalens, contact Tourisme

Québec, P.O. Box 20000, Québec, G1K 7X2, tel. (800) 363-7777.

GETTING AROUND

The Road System

The island is webbed with highways and roads of all types. High-speed highways are numbered with single digits and include the TransCanada (Hwy. 1), which runs along the strait and connects the ferry terminals at Borden and Wood Islands; Hwy. 2 in Queens and Prince counties; and Hwys. 3 and 4 in Kings County, which slice through PEI's interior.

Primary and secondary highways are numbered with double and triple digits, respectively. Think of them as paved, two-lane rural routes, especially useful as driving entrees into the island's scenic countryside. At the bottom of the provincial road classification are paved, unpaved, and unnumbered local roads—the narrow driving lanes that angle across farmland fields and wander into remote places. They're gorgeous roads, most memorable when the surfaces are red clay. But they can be unexpectedly dangerous with steep, drop-off shoulders and surfaces that during rainstorms can become slippery as grease.

Seat belts are mandatory, as are safety restraints for child passengers; violations cost $25. Drinking while driving and "impaired driving" bring severe penalties.

Scenic Roads

Three established scenic drives grace Prince Edward Island: the 190-km-long **Blue Heron Drive** in Queens County, the 375-km **Kings Byway Drive** in Kings County, and the 288-km **Lady Slipper Drive** in Prince County.

Note that the circuits are named "drives." That's no exaggeration. PEI may be Canada's smallest province, but to circumnavigate the island's perimeter on the scenic routes takes more than 14 hours. The routes are well marked with symbols: a drawing of the island's blue heron for Blue Heron Drive; a crown of royal purple as the symbol for Kings Byway Drive; and the provincial orchidlike flower depicted in red for Lady Slipper Drive.

And if you think the foregoing coastal r are feasts for the eye, try the provincial **heritage roads**—stretches of pastoral roads untouched by commercialism or 20th-century changes. Marked with the silhouette of two trees on a maroon field, the roads run mainly across the island's interior. If you're a photographer or painter, bring appropriate gear. The old-time byways run through rolling countryside speckled with weathered barns and verdant farms.

Car Rentals, Taxis, and Public Transit

Major car-rental agencies have offices in Charlottetown and counters at the airport: **Budget Car and Truck Rentals,** tel. (902) 566-5525; **Hertz,** tel. 566-5566; **Airport Thrifty Car Rental,** tel. 566-1696. Local companies usually offer a more competitive rate than the large chains. For instance, **Discount Car Rentals** in Charlottetown, tel. 566-3213, charges about $30 per day with 200 km free and 14 cents per extra km. If requested, they'll pick you up at the airport.

Charlottetown **taxis** are plentiful; you'll pay about $3 to most anywhere in the city. Taxis cruise city streets or wait at the Prince Edward and Charlottetown hotels. **City Cab Taxi,** tel. 892-6567, offers 24-hour service. Outside of Charlottetown, a ride can be pricey: a run up to Cavendish costs $40 one-way; to Summerside, it's close to $60.

Public transit is limited. In Charlottetown, **Kiwanis Club** operates senior-citizen transit ($1) but anyone can hop on. Otherwise, **Island Transit** in Charlottetown operates province-wide bus service. Rail service was discontinued in 1990.

Tours

A number of operators around the island conduct local and regional tours. Many of the local tours are described in the text; below are a few of the larger outfits.

Abegweit Tours, tel. (902) 894-9966, conducts guided tours of Charlottetown ($6 adults, $1 child), the North Shore ($30/$15), South Shore ($28/$14), and other destinations, in red double-decker London buses that depart from Confederation Centre and the Charlottetown Hotel.

Scenic Air Tours, at the Charlottetown airport, tel. 894-7205, will take you up for a bird's-eye view of the island; rates start at $20 per person for a party of three.

Tours Acadie, P.O. Box 39, Mont-Carmel, PE C0B 2E0, tel. 854-2304 or (800) 567-3228, concentrates on the Acadian region of Prince County. **Birchvale Tours,** Wilmot Valley, Summerside RR 3, PE C1N 4J9, tel. 436-3803, arranges private tours of rural western and central PEI, including the Cavendish and Charlottetown areas.

BOB RACE

QUEENS COUNTY

Queens County is the definitive PEI, as you imagined the province would be. The region is temptingly photogenic, a meld of small seaports with brightly colored craft at anchor, and farmland settings with limpid ponds and weathered barns.

Rural roads are snugly narrow and punctuated every so often with smaller-than-small villages. Red-clay lanes depart the main paved roads and wrap up and across the undulating countryside like burnished red ribbons laced on verdant velvet. Barns crest the hilltops like lofty crowns, and boats with billowing sails skip across the bays that reach inland from the gulf coastline.

Visualize Queens County in two parts. The North Shore lies along the Gulf of St. Lawrence and has enjoyed decades of tourist renown. Here the sea is always at your shoulder, and the land is dotted with tiny villages. The South Shore rims Northumberland Strait's jagged seacoast, which holds seaports like Victoria and historic sites such as Orwell Village, the re-created settlement of PEI's early Scottish and Irish immigrants. This coast may be on the beaten tourist path someday. But for now, it's the lesser-known side of Queens County and only lightly explored by visitors. Queens County as a whole is divided in half by Hwy. 2, the expressway that slices across the island's midsection from Charlottetown to Summerside.

CHARLOTTETOWN AND VICINITY

As Atlantic Canada's smallest capital, Charlottetown (pop. 16,000)—the island's governmental, economical, cultural, and shopping center—makes no pretense of being a big city. Rather, this attractive town is walkable, comfortable, and friendly. Its major attractions include a beautiful harborside location, handsome public and residential architecture, sophisticated art and cultural happenings, and plentiful lodgings and appealing restaurants.

The city also makes a good sightseeing base. From centrally located Charlottetown to most any place on the island and back again is a feasible day's distance; for example, it's a quick 40 minutes by car northwest to Cavendish, and a mere two-hour drive to the island's most distant points, at the northeastern or northwestern tip.

HISTORY

After the fall of Louisbourg in the mid-1700s, the French abandoned their Prince Edward Island holdings at Port la Joye. The English renamed it Fort Amherst and fortified the site, then moved the settlement to the more defensible

inner peninsula tip within Hillsborough Bay. By 1758, they had established Charlotte Town, named for the consort of King George III. The town's grid was laid out in 1764 and was named the island's capital the next year. During the American Revolution, American privateers sacked the capital, then added insult to injury when they stole the island's government seal and kidnapped the colonial governor.

Charlottetown has always been the island's main market town; the land now occupied by Province House and Confederation Centre was once the colony's thriving marketplace. As in most early island towns, the majority of buildings

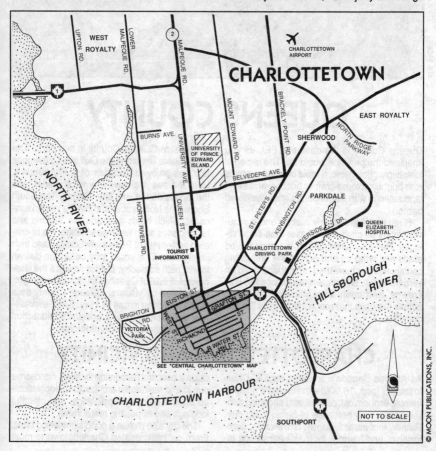

SEE "CENTRAL CHARLOTTETOWN" MAP

NOT TO SCALE

© MOON PUBLICATIONS, INC.

were constructed of wood rather than stone, and many were subsequently leveled by fire. The stone buildings, however, survived. One of these is the small, brick building at 104 Water St.—one of the capital's oldest buildings and now site of the Strawberry Patch restaurant and crafts shop.

Where Canada Began

In the fall of 1864, the colonial capital hosted the Charlottetown Conference, which led to establishment of the Dominion of Canada. The delegates who became Canada's founding Fathers of Confederation agreed that the city was the ideal, neutral site for the conference. Islanders were neither for nor against the idea of a dominion. But just in case the fledgling idea of forming a union did come to something, the islanders appointed several delegates to represent them.

The other delegates arrived by sea in groups from New Brunswick, Nova Scotia, and Upper and Lower Canada, now Québec and Ontario. Their respective ships docked at the harborfront, and one by one, the delegates walked the short blocks up Great George St. to the Colonial Building, as Province House was known then. The meeting led to the signing of the British North America Act in London in 1867 and the beginnings of modern Canada on 1 July of that year. The initial four provinces were Nova Scotia, New Brunswick, Québec, and Ontario. Prince Edward Island originally passed on membership and didn't join the Confederation until 1873.

Growth

Charlottetown's development paralleled the growth in profits from the Great Age of Sail. The building of St. Peter's Anglican Church at Rochford Square transformed a bog into one of the capital's finest areas in 1869. Beaconsfield, a tribute of Second Empire and Victorian gingerbread style at Kent and West streets, was designed by architect William Critchlow Harris for wealthy shipbuilder and merchant James Peake in 1877. The Kirk of St. James was architect James Stirling's tribute to early Gothic Revival. The brick Charlottetown City Hall, at Queen and Kent streets, was a local adaptation of Romanesque Revival.

GETTING ORIENTED

The city, small as it is, may be baffling for a new visitor due to the way historic and newer streets converge. The town began with a handful of harborfront blocks. The centuries have contributed a confusing jumble of other roads that feed into the historic area from all sorts of angles.

Newcomers tend to drive in circles for a while. When in doubt, head for the harbor, where all roads finish. It helps also to study a map before entering the traffic fray, which is especially stressful at commuting times (weekdays 7:30-8:30 a.m. and 4:30-5:30 p.m.).

The **TransCanada Highway** will take you right into the heart of town. It enters the city from the western part of the island, crosses the North River, turns south at the University of Prince Edward Island campus and becomes University Ave., then hits Grafton and turns east to head out of town across the Hillsborough River. For a more scenic access route, use treelined, residential **North River Road,** which also brings you directly downtown.

The commercial area is a small swatch of streets between Euston St. and the harborfront. **Old Charlottetown** (or Old Charlotte Town, depending on who's describing the area) has been restored with rejuvenated buildings and brick walkways, lit at night with gas lamps. **Peake's Wharf,** where the Fathers of Confederation arrived on the island, is now a tourist hub of sorts with restaurants and shops, and there's plentiful vacant land for more development.

The best residential areas, with large, stately houses (some designed by noted architect William Critchlow Harris), rim Victoria Park and North River Road. Working-class neighborhoods fan out farther north beyond Grafton St. and are marked with small, pastel-painted houses set close to the streets.

Central Charlottetown is pleasantly compact, attractive, and easily covered on foot. **Parking** can be difficult in the downtown area. Most downtown parking slots are metered (25 cents per half hour, free on Saturday). The streets behind Confederation Centre—Sydney, Dorchester, Richmond, etc.—offer unmetered parking. If all else fails, check out the parking garages; costs are comparable to metered parking. Inexpen-

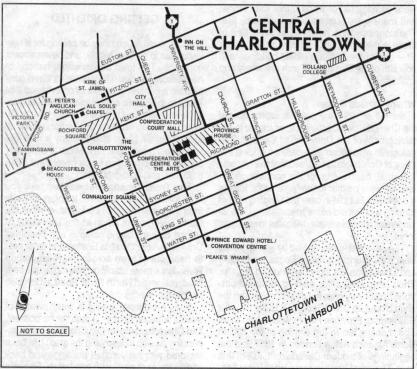

CENTRAL CHARLOTTETOWN

© MOON PUBLICATIONS, INC.

NOT TO SCALE

sive parking garages are at **Queen's Parkade** across from the City Hall on Queen St. and **Pownal Parkade** on Pownal Street. **Recreational vehicles** can park at waterfront and Great George Street.

Tours
Abegweit Tours, tel. (902) 894-9966, operates the red double-decker bus that lopes through Charlottetown on sightseeing tours ($6 for a 50-minute tour). The bus stops at Confederation Centre on Queen and Grafton streets, and runs mid-June through Sept., daily 10:30 a.m.-6:15 p.m. At harborfront, **Charlottetown Harbour Cruises** at Prince St. Wharf, tel. 368-2628, offers daily two-hour cruises at 2:30 p.m. ($11 adult) and 7:30 p.m. ($16), mid-June to early September.

Island Pride Tour Guide Service, tel. 675-3337, also conducts guided tours of Charlotte-

town, as well as other destinations around the island.

SIGHTS

The following sightseeing starts at City Hall and takes in about two dozen blocks.

City Hall
The red-brick city hall, at the corner of Kent and Queen streets, was built in 1888. Free summertime walking tours of the historic streets depart from here, July-Aug., weekdays 10 a.m.-5 p.m. Inside is the city's **visitor information office,** tel. (902) 566-5548.

All Souls' Chapel
A few blocks west of city hall, this remarkable chapel, tel. (902) 628-1376, aside **St. Peter's Anglican Church** on Rochford St. was a joint

Harris family creation. The architect William Harris styled it in island sandstone with a dark walnut interior. His brother Robert painted the murals and deftly mixed family members and friends among the religious figures. The chapel is open daily 8 a.m.-6 p.m.

Beaconsfield Historic House

This bright yellow, 25-room mansion at the corner of Kent and West streets, built in 1877 from a William Critchlow Harris design, has survived more than a century of varied use as a family home, a shelter "for friendless women," a YWCA, and a nurses' residence. The building was rescued in 1973 by the PEI Museum and Heritage Foundation, which turned it into foundation headquarters and a heritage museum.

A good bookstore is on the first level, and genealogical archives are kept across the hall and also upstairs. Outside, you can sit on the wide, front porch overlooking the harbor across the long lawn—it's a great place to have tea and scones. Beaconsfield, tel. (902) 368-6600, is open year-round; Tues.-Sun. 10 a.m.-5 p.m. in summer, shorter hours the rest of the year. Admission is $2.50, children under 12 free.

Victoria Park

Victoria Park, adjacent to Beaconsfield House, reigns as one of Charlottetown's prettiest settings, with 16 wooded and grassy hectares overlooking the bay at Battery Point. The greenery spreads out across the peninsula tip; to get there follow Kent St. as it turns into Park Roadway. The park's rolling terrain is the result of moraines, heaps of gravelly deposits left behind by ice-age glaciers.

Joggers like the park's winding paths, and birders find abundant yellow warblers, purple finches, and downy woodpeckers nesting in the maples, firs, oaks, pines, and birches. The white, palatial mansion overlooking the water is Fanningbank (Government House), the lieutenant governor's private residence—nice to look at, but it's closed to the public.

Province House National Historic Site

The nation of Canada began at Province House. The buff sandstone neoclassical edifice at the top of Great George St. was erected in 1847 to house the island's colonial legislature, and it

Province House

quickly became the center of public life on the island. It was the site of lavish balls and state functions, including the historic 1864 conference on federal union.

In the late 1970s, Parks Canada undertook restoration of the age-begrimed building, a five-year task completed in 1983. Layers of paint came off the front columns. The double-hung windows throughout were refitted with glass panes from an old greenhouse in New Brunswick. About 10% of the original furnishings remained in the building before restoration and were retained. Most of the rest were replaced by period antiques obtained in the other provinces and northeastern United States. A flowered rug was woven for Confederation Chamber, where the Fathers of Confederation convened. Every nook and corner was refurbished and polished until the interior gleamed.

Today, Province House National Historic Site, tel. (902) 566-7626, is one of Atlantic Canada's most significant public buildings. A Parks Canada staffer will put on a 15-minute slide show on request. The Fathers of Confederation Players, local actors and actresses in period garb, perform 15-minute "living history" tableaux at Province House in July and August.

The Provincial Legislature still convenes here; meetings are in session between mid-February and early May for five to 17 weeks, depending on how much provincial government haggling is underway. As a museum, the building is open July-Aug., daily 9 a.m.-8 p.m. with shorter hours the rest of the year. Admission is free; bilingual guides are available.

Confederation Centre of the Arts

Confederation Centre of the Arts, tel. (902) 628-1864, the other half of the complex shared by Province House, looms large at the corner of Grafton and Queen streets. The promenades, edged with places to sit, are great places for people-watching, and kids like to skateboard on the walkways.

The center opened in 1964 to mark the centennial of the Charlottetown Conference, as the confederation meeting became known in Canadian history. It's a great hulk of a place, compatible with its historic neighbor in its design and coloring.

The center houses four art galleries, a museum, the provincial library, and four theaters. Summertime's **Charlottetown Festival** lures locals and tourists to these theaters for dramatic and musical productions—most notably the popular *Anne of Green Gables* (which celebrated its 30th season in 1994). Reservations can be made by phone, tel. 566-1267 or (800) 565-0278. Performances are also offered at the **MacKenzie Theatre,** close by at University and Grafton; see "Theater" under "Entertainment and Events" below for details. In summer, free lunchtime performances are staged in the amphitheater between the art gallery and adjacent library.

The emphasis at the center is on the province—expect to see some of island artist Robert Harris's paintings, and one or two of Lucy Maud Montgomery's original manuscripts—but national arts exhibits also come through regularly. And regular gallery lectures explore the varied Canadian schools of art.

A gift shop stocks wares by the cream of PEI's artisans, and an informal courtyard restaurant serves sandwiches, salads, quiches, and

desserts. The art gallery and museum are open June-Sept., daily 10 a.m.-8 p.m., shorter hours Oct.-May. Admission is $3 adults, $2 children and seniors.

Outskirts

Farmers' Market is an island institution. The indoor market holds about 40 vendors selling everything from flowers and crafts to baked goods, produce, and fish. It's in a long, spacious building on Belvedere Ave. across from the university campus; open year-round, Saturday 9 a.m.-2 p.m., and also Wed. 10 a.m.-5 p.m. in July and August.

Holland College is a tidy teaching center, at Weymouth and Grafton, tel. (902) 566-9500. Arts and crafts are on exhibit in the gallery. It's open year-round, weekdays 8:30 a.m.-10 p.m., Sat.-Sun. 10 a.m.-6 p.m.; shorter summer hours.

Royalty Oaks Woodlot is a four-hectare spread of oaks in the suburb of East Royalty northeast of Charlottetown. The grove, spliced with a self-guided trail, represents PEI's choicest oaks, some soaring 20 meters high. The expanse is a show of brilliant color in fall—best in early October. To get there, follow St. Peters Rd. to Riverside Drive, and after passing the Kentucky Fried Chicken, take the first right onto North Ridge Parkway.

ACCOMMODATIONS

You'll find every kind of lodging, from plain budget places to sumptuous, expensive rooms in Charlottetown's 100-plus lodgings. Unless noted otherwise, prices given below are for a double room; seven percent GST and 10% provincial sales tax are not included. See the "Charlottetown Area Accommodations" chart for listings in addition to those described below.

Budget and Camping

The Canadian Hostelling Association's **hostel,** 153 Mt. Edward Rd. (near Belvedere Rd.), tel. (902) 894-9696, has 58 beds, showers, and a place for cooking in spartan quarters. It's open May-Oct.; $12.50 for CHA members, $16 for nonmembers.

The closest camping to Charlottetown is a convenient five-minute drive east across the

Hillsborough River at **Southport Trailer Park,** 20 Stratford Rd., Charlottetown, PE C1A 7B7, tel. 569-2287. The park, open mid-May to mid-Oct., has tent and full-hookup spaces, a laundromat, a kitchen shelter, and a waterside location looking across the harbor to Charlottetown; $17.50 per site. A motel ($65-70) and housekeeping cottages ($45-55) are also offered here.

Inns and B&Bs

MacKeen's Tourist Home, 176 King St., tel. (902) 892-6296, a beautifully restored old home, has a gem of a downtown location with two clean, plainly furnished guest rooms plus a suite that sleeps four to five guests ($35-45 with a light breakfast).

The elegant 1850s **Edwardian,** 50 Mt. Edward Rd. at Confederation St., tel. 368-1905, was the home of William Pope, one of PEI's Fathers of Confederation. The inn has one room plus a suite with jacuzzi within nonsmoking heritage quarters; $85-95 with a light breakfast.

Great George Inn, 68 Great George St., tel. 892-0606, is a few steps from Province House on a designated national historic street and has four nonsmoking guest rooms ($125 with a light breakfast) with kitchen access within historic quarters.

Dundee Arms Inn, 200 Pownal St., tel. 892-2496, around the corner from the Charlottetown Hotel, is a restored mansion awash with antiques. It offers eight gorgeously appointed, nonsmoking guest rooms ($95-105 with a light breakfast) and dining rooms.

Elmwood Heritage Inn, 121 North River Rd., tel. 368-3310, is a Harris house-cum-country inn and has three suites ($85-125 with a light breakfast) furnished with antiques and smoking limited to specific areas. Finding the inn can be a challenge—it's hidden by trees. Look for the red fire hydrant opposite the driveway or call first for directions.

MacInnis Bed and Breakfast, tel. 892-6725, 80 Euston St., Charlottetown, PE C1A 1W2, has four rooms (s and d) with TV, and does not allow pets or smoking. It's open year-round with rates of $32 s, $40 d. **Birch Hill Bed and Breakfast,** tel. 892-4353, 14 Birch Hill Dr., Charlottetown, PE CIA 6W5, has three large rooms and offers airport pick-up; rates are $35-40. **An Is-**land Rose Bed and Breakfast, tel. 569-5030, 285 Kinlock Rd., RR 1, PE C1A 7J6, has a view of the strait, three rooms, TV, and bikes. Adults are preferred; no smoking or pets. Rates are $45-55 per night.

Motels and Hotels

Inn on the Hill, 150 Euston St. at University Ave., tel. (902) 894-8572, is a handsome motel with 48 rooms ($90-110 for a double room, $129-151 for a suite) and a locally esteemed dining room, just three blocks from Province House.

Rodd Confederation Inn and Suites, on the TransCanada Hwy. where Hwys. 1 and 2 meet at West Royalty, tel. 892-2481, has 61 rooms ($68-94) along motel row, a restaurant, outdoor pool, and some nonsmoking rooms.

Best Western MacLauchlan's Motor Inn, 238 Grafton St., tel. 892-2461, is a three-block jaunt from Province House and has 123 hotel rooms ($101-150 for a room, $118-178 for a suite) fronting both sides of the street, connected beneath the road by a tunnel. Facilities include a restaurant, indoor pool, sauna, hot tub, and launderette. The ambience is friendly—it's a good place to meet other visitors.

Auberge Wandlyn Inn, also on the TransCanada Hwy. near the intersection of Hwys. 1 and 2, tel. 892-1201, has 73 rooms ($79-91) and an outdoor heated pool.

The Charlottetown—A Rodd Classic Hotel, Kent at Pownal streets downtown, tel. 894-7371 or (800) 565-RODD, P.O. Box 159, Charlottetown, PE C1A 7K4, is a red-brick Georgian gem with magnificent woodwork and furnishings made by island craftspeople. One of Canadian National Railroad's carriage-trade hotels, it's now part of the Rodd Hotels group and has 109 rooms ($99-139), a restaurant, whirlpool, indoor pool, and sauna.

Boxy **Prince Edward Hotel and Convention Centre,** 18 Queen St., Charlottetown, PE C1A 8B9, tel. 566-2222, overlooks the water from high-rise vistas with 211 rooms ($150-270), saunas, jacuzzis, a spa, restaurants, and a shopping arcade.

Islander Motor Lodge, tel. 892-1217, W.G. Barbour, 146-148 Pownal St., Charlottetown, PE C1A 3W6, offers dining, TV, a/c, and is located downtown. Rates are $58-98. **Queen's**

Arms Motor Lodge, tel. 368-1110, RR 7, West Royalty, TransCanada Hwy. at Lower Malpeque Road, has TV, a/c, a playground, an outdoor pool, and a restaurant. Rates are $50-98.

FOOD

In addition to the usual rash of burger and pizza fast fooderies, some of the island's best dining is found in Charlottetown. Islanders like to dine out, and the following list represents some of their favorites. Reservations are a wise precaution, especially during tourist season.

Local Treats and Specialties

Ice-cream fanciers whoop it up at **Cow's Homemade Ice Cream** across from Confederation Centre, where a dozen different flavors are scooped each day. The shop also stocks Cow's T-shirts ($20), the ones you'll see coming and going everywhere on the island. Health-food addicts go to the **Root Cellar** at 34 Queen St. for power drinks and sandwiches on whole-wheat bread.

Light Meals

For a selection of cozy restaurant-cafes, most with a streetside patio, stroll along Richmond St. between Queen and Great George. Known as **Victoria Row,** this pedestrian block of vintage buildings is usually buzzing with diners and shoppers ducking in and out of the adjacent crafts shops. In the evenings, musicians set up and entertain. Restaurants include: **Unicorn's,** 160 Richmond; **Black Forest Cafe and Bakery,** 146 Richmond, tel. (902) 628-2123, closed Sunday; **Kelly's Restaurant,** 134 Richmond; and the **Island Rock Cafe,** 132 Richmond, which presents live music in the evenings.

Kelly's, 52 Queen St., has a cozy setting within a former candy store and makes sandwiches and homemade desserts (try the house specialty—chocolate pecan pie) for lunch or dinner.

University Ave. has a number of spots for a light bite: The **Perfect Cup Cafe,** 42 University Ave., is the place for a cup of finely brewed coffee or steeped tea with biscuits, cinnamon rolls, homemade preserves, or a light lunch under $8. Breakfasts are hearty and well priced, with

an inexpensive special of eggs, toast, sausage, and hash browns. Open Mon.-Saturday. Next door, **Sam's Lunch Bar and Steak House,** 32 University Ave., tel. 628-1239, focuses on Lebanese and Canadian food, with breakfast, lunch, and dinner specials; open daily at 7 a.m. For more Lebanese food, try **Cedar's Eatery,** at 81 University, tel. 892-7377. **Cafe Soleil,** 52 University Ave., tel. 368-8098, is a bakery, cafe (good coffee-drink selection), and deli.

Strawberry Patch, 104 Water St., offers thick chowders, fresh salads, sandwiches on homemade whole-wheat bread, and thickly frosted carrot cake. The **Courtyard Restaurant** provides a culinary respite within the sunny dining room of the Confederation Centre of the Arts; entrees ($7-10) are geared to light fare—try crepes stuffed with crab and asparagus.

Off Broadway Cafe, 125 Sydney St., tel. 566-4620, is a local lunchtime favorite with poached seafood, lobster crepes, shrimp Provençal, and luscious desserts. Expect to pay $10-15 per person.

Dinner

Lobsterman's Landing, Prince St. Wharf at the foot of Prince St., tel. (902) 368-2888, combines a harbor view and open-air deck with delectable fresh seafoods ($8-20). **Peake's Quay Restaurant and Lounge,** 36 Lower Water St., tel. 368-1330, also boasts a harborside location, with informal indoor and outdoor dining and an enviable seafood selection ($9-18); try the scallops sauced with honey butter. **Doc's Corner Dining Room and Lounge,** 185 Kent St., tel. 566-1069, serves worthy mussel chowder, uncomplicated seafood, and steak dishes ($12-18) in quarters that in the 1850s housed a pharmacy and doctor's office. Doc's offers an outdoor patio and entertainment four nights a week.

Samuel's at the Inn on the Hill, 150 Euston St. at University Ave., whets the appetite with a creative menu of steamed island blue mussels, Malpeque oysters, some of the best beef in town, and rich chocolate desserts. Entrees range $11-22; reservations are required, call 894-8572. **Griffon Room** at the Dundee Arms Inn combines a well-appointed historic setting with elegantly conceived fine cuisine emphasizing red meats and seafood ($13-19). Reservations are required, tel. 892-2496. **Claddagh Room,** 131 Sydney St., tel. 892-9661, is authentically Irish, starting with owner Liam Dolan, from County Galway. Seafood is the specialty ($13-23); for lunch the Claddagh offers an all-you-can-eat mussel-and-chowder special for $7.95. Open weekdays for lunch and dinner, weekends dinner only. In the evenings, their **Olde Dublin Pub** has Irish entertainment.

Garden of the Gulf, 18 Queen St., tel. 566-2222, forms part of Prince Edward Hotel's lobby and serves buffets for breakfast, lunch, and dinner. Also at the hotel, **Lord Selkirk,** tel. 892-9052, has no equal for island ambience and cuisine. Entrees ($20-24) are unsurpassed in creativity and fine preparation—try chicken breast stuffed with duck sausage, awash in rich wine sauce ($20). Reservations are required.

Lucy Maud Dining Room, the dining room of the Culinary Institute of Canada, 305 Kent St., is open mid-Oct. to May, its student chefs serving six-course formal dinners ($30) three nights a week. Reservations are required; call 566-9550. **Confederation Dining Room** at the Charlottetown Hotel, tel. 894-7371, is a city landmark known for dependable fine dining ($17-22) and a lavish seafood buffet in summer.

Pat and Willy's is the unlikely name for the very popular Mexican/Italian/Canadian bar and grill upstairs at 119 Kent St., tel. 628-1333. Dinners run $6-15. For a variety of seafood and grill combinations, try the family-oriented **Town and Country,** 219 Queen St., tel. 892-2282, or the more formal **Stagecoach,** also on Queen.

Groceries

Sobey's Food Warehouse, 679 University Ave., is as large and well stocked as the name implies and has a deli with picnic ingredients. Another major and centrally located market is **Island Food Centre,** on Queen St. opposite the Confederation Centre of the Arts.

ENTERTAINMENT AND EVENTS

Movies

Charlottetown Mall Cinemas screens current films in five theaters. It's open nightly and for weekend matinees; for show times call (902) 892-0943. The **City Cinema,** 64 King St., tel.

368-3669, will appeal more to the art-house crowd. It presents two different films nightly—mostly a good selection of European and independent films. Matinees run at 1:30 p.m. on rainy weekends.

Theater

The **Confederation Centre of the Arts** is the performing-arts capital of the province and the site of the **Charlottetown Festival,** which runs from mid-June to early September. The festival is best known for the *Anne of Green Gables* musical; tickets cost $22-30. Also on the bill are repertory productions in the center's main theater and cabaret-style productions at the **MacKenzie Theatre,** the festival's second stage at University Ave. and Grafton Street. For tickets to either theater, call (902) 566-1267, or (800) 565-0278 within the Maritimes (May-Sept. only).

Each summer, the local Offstage Theatre troupe stages ***Annekenstein,*** an original farce they describe as "a loving lampoon of all things Anne"—just the antidote for all the L.M. Montgomery mania. Their venue is subject to change, so check local events listings or ask at the visitors information office.

Dinner-theater productions draw sizable crowds of islanders and tourists at the Prince Edward Hotel, tel. 566-2222, and at the Charlottetown Hotel, tel. 894-7371; cost is about $30 per person. The **Strathgartney Country Inn,** 20 minutes west of Charlottetown, tel. 675-4711, puts a twist on dinner-theater with its Murder Mystery Dinner, three nights a week; cost is about $25 per person.

Music and Nightlife

Charlottetown once rolled up the sidewalks at night, and it's still relatively sedate after dark. But in recent years, a rousing nightlife and pub scene has emerged, centered on drinking and dancing. Last call for drinks is at 1:30 a.m.; the doors lock at 2 a.m.

While night spots come and go, two mainstays are **Myron's Upstairs,** 151 Kent St., tel. 892-4375; and the **Tradewind Restaurant and Night Club,** 189 Kent St., tel. 894-4291, where you'll find music videos, beer-drinking ambience, a variety of happy-hour specials, and dancing on the stainless-steel floor. **JR's Place,** a large complex of restaurants and lounges at

Weymouth and King streets, is another favorite, with dancing and live country-western music.

The **Benevolent Irish Society Hall,** 582 River Rd., tel. 566-3273, hosts Friday-night *ceilidhs* (evenings of traditional Scottish and Irish dancing and music) in summer. The **Charlottetown Playhouse,** 91 University Ave., tel. 628-2267, puts on live blues Monday nights. **Apothecaries,** downstairs at 99 Grafton St., tel. 628-2359, has live music most nights, including "Jam Nite" on Thursdays. **Doc's Corner,** Kent and Prince, tel. 566-1069, features mostly rock and blues, with a bit of country, Wed.-Sat. nights.

On the entertainment spectrum's more sedate side, you'll find dim lights, comfortable surroundings, and a piano bar at **Gallow Lounge** at Inn on the Hill. And the comfortable **Province's Lounge,** decorated with the provinces' crests, holds down historic quarters at the Charlottetown Hotel. At **Sports Page,** 236 Kent St., tel. 368-3655, major sports events are shown on a big-screen TV and food is served until 1:30 a.m.

Events

Should you find yourself in town in the off-off-season, you might enjoy the hockey tournament and other winter sporting activities of the **Charlottetown Winter Carnival,** held in early February.

The summer season opens on **Victoria Day** in late May with a 21-gun salute at Victoria Park. During mid-July's **Charlottetown Race Week** keelboat and yacht races take place at the Charlottetown Yacht Club on Pownal St.; for details, call 894-3520. Also in mid-July is the island's **Rose Show,** with displays and a sale at Prince Edward Hotel.

The June-Sept. **Charlottetown Festival** presents musical theater and cabaret at the Confederation Centre and the nearby MacKenzie Theatre. For ticket information, call (902) 566-1267, (800) 565-0278 in the Maritimes, or write 145 Richmond St., Charlottetown, PE C1A 1J1.

Old Home Week in mid-August is the sentimental tribute to islanders who are now home "from away." The city unofficially shuts down for the festival's harness racing, horse and livestock shows, and the week-ending **Gold Cup and Saucer** parade through the streets of Char-

lottetown—said to be Atlantic Canada's biggest and best-attended parade.

The **Heritage Fall Festival** in September is a multicultural and artistic street fair featuring musical performances, children's activities, and international foods.

RECREATION

Outdoor Adventures

Underwater Services, 427 Mt. Edward Rd., rents scuba diving day-use equipment; a wetsuit is $15 per day, drysuit $30, air tanks $10. For details on dive sites, write to them at P.O. Box 1345, Charlottetown, PE C1A 7N1. **Island Rods and Flies** at 18 Birch Hill Drive in nearby Sherwood, tel. (902) 566-4157, stocks fly-fishing equipment and materials. They'll also work as fishing guides for $45 and up. You can rent equipment, canoes, and kayaks at **Sporting Intentions,** 570 N. River Rd. in nearby West Royalty, tel. 892-4713. **Bird's Eye Nature Store,** 177 Queen St., tel. 566-DUCK, sells birding supplies and appropriate gear.

Outside Expeditions, P.O. Box 2336, Charlottetown, PE C1A 8C1, tel./fax 892-5425, outfits half-day to five-day kayaking trips, including instruction and equipment. Prices start at $32 for a day-trip. **Paddle PEI,** 41 Allen St., Charlottetown, PE C1A 2V6, tel. 566-5673 or 652-2434, offers interesting guided kayak, canoe, and mountain-biking tours with an emphasis on the natural environment. Most of the tours are at Brudenell River Provincial Park.

MacQueen's Bike Shop, 430 Queen St., tel. 368-2453, provides complete bike and accessory rental and repairs, and can also arrange cycle-touring packages. **Smooth Cycle,** 25 Russet Dr., tel. 566-5530, also offers repair service.

Other Recreation

For harness racing, check out **Charlottetown Driving Park** at the Hillsboro Trotting Club on Kensington Rd., tel. (902) 892-6823. Races are run three days a week year-round. Admission is $2. Some hotels admit nonguests to fitness and pool facilities. **Prince Edward Hotel,** for example, charges $7.50 for a day-use pass.

SHOPPING

Island-made Wares

If you're an avid shopper with a penchant for crafts, head for the **Island Crafts Shop** at 156 Richmond St., tel. (902) 892-5152. It's the P.E.I. Crafts Council's retail outlet. A thorough browse among quilts, glassware, sculpture, clothing, knitted apparel, and jewelry ad infinitum will provide you an insight into what's available in the city and province. Craftspeople demonstrate their trades at the shop from time to time. The wares here tend to be one-of-a-kind. If you don't see exactly what you want, you could go directly to the maker; the membership list is available at the shop.

Down East Traditions, in the Prince Edward Hotel, 18 Queen St., tel. 566-1888, stocks locally produced arts and crafts, as well as quilting supplies. For more quilts, crochets, and embroidery, look into **Fancy Linens and Handcrafts,** 98 Kent St., tel. 566-3480.

The Two Sisters, 150 Richmond St., tel. 894-3407 (also at the Confederation Court Mall), is a Crafts Council member and stocks a luscious variety of island crafts. **Great Northern Merchants,** at 77 Water St. and at Charlottetown Mall, tel. 566-5969, stocks Great Northern Knitters' sweaters produced at the West Royalty Industrial Park plant. Knitted of oiled wool (oil makes the wool softer and warmer), the sweaters are mass produced, but each knitter works on the same sweater from start to finish—an arrangement that allows custom sizing as well as run-of-the-line production. The stores are open Mon.-Sat. 10 a.m.-5:30 p.m., and until 9 p.m. on Thurs. and Friday.

Ellen's Creek Gallery: You'll find a worthy collection of works by PEI artists at this fine arts gallery at 525 N. River Rd., tel. 368-3494. It's open year-round, Mon.-Thurs. 9 a.m.-5:30 p.m., Fri. 9 a.m.-9 p.m.

Sundries

The **Confederation Court Mall,** with some 90 shops—clothing, jewelry, gifts, 10 restaurants, etc.—takes up a city block in the heart of downtown. The **Charlottetown Mall** is just north of town, where the TransCanada hits University.

Department stores include **Eatons** at 167 Kent St., and **Zellers** at Charlottetown Mall, which stocks camping gear and also has a well-stocked deli and bakery. Both stores are open Mon.-Sat. 9 a.m.-5 p.m., Fri. to 9 p.m. For groceries, see "Food," above.

Bring enough film and supplies with you; special equipment and specific film speeds are hard to find. **PEI Photo Lab,** 55 Queen St., stocks the basics.

INFORMATION AND SERVICES

Visitor Information

The provincial **Tour the Island Visitor Information Centre** at the Oak Tree Mall on University Ave. next to Dairy Queen, tel. (902) 368-4444, answers questions and stocks literature about the province. It's open year-round, daily 8:30 a.m.-6 p.m., with longer hours from mid-June to August. Inside city hall, at the corner of Kent and Queen streets, is the **Charlottetown Visitor Information Office,** tel. 566-5548.

Library and Bookstores

The **public library,** tel. (902) 368-4642, is part of the Confederation Centre on Queen St., open Tues.-Thurs. 10 a.m.-9 p.m., Fri.-Sat. 10 a.m.-5 p.m., Sun. 1-5 p.m. September-May weekday hours are shorter.

Government Bookstore at 11 Kent St. near Beaconsfield House, tel. (902) 368-4000, is the best source for information on the island's environment, population, and economy; open weekdays 8 a.m.-4 p.m. For island literature and especially architecture and history coverage, check out the bookshop at **Beaconsfield House.** Gift boutiques and crafts shops also stock some island-related books.

The Bookman, 102A Kent St., tel. 892-8872, carries new, used, and rare books. Just around the corner at 169 Queen St. is the **Book Emporium,** tel. 628-2001, a general bookstore with a good PEI section.

Bookshops in the malls stock current books: **Coles** at Charlottetown Mall and Bookmark at Confederation Court Mall have the widest selections. If you like browsing for used books, shops along University Ave. near the campus cater to college students with similar tastes; **Washtub Used Furniture** at 245 University Ave. has one of the largest collections.

Health and Safety
Queen Elizabeth Hospital is on Riverside Drive, tel. (902) 566-6111. For **local police** call 368-2677; **ambulance,** 892-5311; **poison control,** 566-6250.

Banks and Post Office
Seven major banks handle money in the city, and most have branches in outlying towns. **Bank of Montreal** converts U.S. or British currency with no additional fee but does charge $9 minimum to handle other foreign currencies; its Confederation Court Mall office is open Mon.-Fri. 9 a.m.-5 p.m. while the Charlottetown Mall branch has longer hours, Thurs.-Fri. to 8 p.m., Sat. to 3 p.m.

    Canada Post at 135 Kent St., tel. (902) 566-7070, is open Mon.-Fri. 8 a.m.-5:15 p.m. with the philatelic bureau open daily 9 a.m.-4 p.m.

Laundries
Coin laundries are plentiful, and many also handle drop-off laundry; they're generally open daily 8 a.m.-11 p.m. Convenient to the city center are **CIC Laundromat,** Hillsborough at Grafton (Hwy. 1), open 7:30 a.m.-10 p.m., and **Downtown Convenience,** 54 Queen St., open daily.

TRANSPORTATION

Charlottetown Airport, tel. (902) 566-7997, lies four km from Charlottetown in the northern suburbs on Brackley Point Rd. at Sherwood. Though open daily 24 hours, it's a small airport sans banks, lockers, or a duty-free shop. For sightseeing and other information, use the free phone line to the tourist office. Between flights, the terminal is almost vacant, with no one at the car rental counters. Taxis wait outside during flight arrivals and charge about $6 for the 10-minute drive to town.

    Inner-city bus service is limited. Taxis wait at hotel and motel entrances and also cruise city streets—fare is under $5 for most destinations in town. For a quick ride to the beach, **Beach Shuttle,** tel. 566-3243, takes folks from points in Charlottetown to Cavendish ($8 OW, $12 RT), twice daily, June-September.

    Island Transit, 308 Queen St., tel. (902) 892-6167, operates scheduled service to Souris ($11 OW), June through mid-Oct., departing daily at 6 p.m.; to Tignish ($16 OW), year-round, departing Mon.-Tues., Thurs.-Sat. at 4 p.m.; and to New Glasgow, Nova Scotia (four hours, $21 OW), via the ferry from Wood Islands to Caribou, departing daily at 10 a.m. June to mid-October.

THE SOUTH SHORE

While the North Shore of Queen's County is the island's premier destination, the South Shore is closer to Charlottetown and possessed of its own charms.

    The **South Shore Tourist Information Centre** is located on the TransCanada (Hwy. 1) in Tryon, just over the Prince County line. **Provincial Visitor Information Centres** are located at the Borden and Wood Islands ferry terminals, and are open for ferry arrivals.

WEST OF CHARLOTTETOWN

A sense of city quickly fades as the Trans-Canada/Hwy. 1 peels out of Charlottetown and continues south and then southwest along

Northumberland Strait. This is farming country, richly productive in grains, potatoes, and orchard fruits. The TransCanada makes a direct route to the ferry terminal at Borden, the highway's island terminus, but numerous side roads invite exploring off the main highway.

Cornwall and Vicinity
Cornwall is one of the main service centers on the South Shore, with a concentration of restaurants, accommodations, and shopping.

    Obanlea Farm Tourist Home, on Hwy. 248 near North River on the city outskirts, tel. (902) 566-3067 (ask for directions), is surrounded by a pastoral landscape devoted to potato farming and cattle grazing; the farmhouse has three basic guest rooms ($25-30) and an apartment

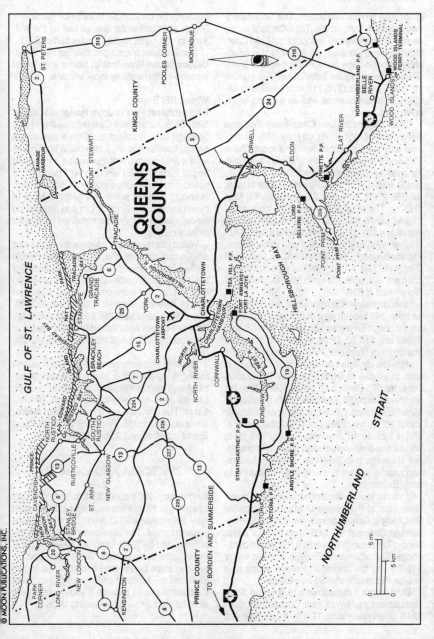

($35) with private entrances. The **Strathgart-ney Country Inn,** on the TransCanada at the hamlet of Strathgartney (midpoint between Charlottetown and Borden), tel. 675-4711, is an architectural heritage clone of Cavendish's pretty Green Gables House farmhouse. The historic inn has 10 rooms ($75-110 with breakfast) furnished with antiques as well as a dining room, open year-round.

Other options include **Chez-nous Bed and Breakfast,** tel. 566-2779, on Hwy. 248, 10 minutes west of Charlottetown. The rooms have TVs and refrigerators. Dining is also available. It's open June-Oct.; rates are $50-65, and breakfast is included. **Pye's Village Guest Home,** tel. 566-2026, P.O. Box 87, Cornwall, PE C0A 1H0, on TransCanada Hwy., is 10 km west of Charlottetown, with golfing and a beach nearby. Rates are $22-25; open mid-June to mid-September. With one apartment and three rooms, **Tighnabruaich,** tel. 566-5908, on Hwy. 248 (Ferry Rd.), is 10 km west of Charlottetown; cribs are available. It's open May-October. The nightly rate is $30.

Holiday Haven Campground, tel. 566-2421, on Hwy. 248 two km east of Cornwall, is located on 60 beautiful acres along the West River. Rates are $15.50-17.50. Amenities include a laundromat, fireplaces, showers, toilets, and a kitchen shelter; open June-October. Camping is also available at **Strathgartney Provincial Park,** tel. 675-3599, on the TransCanada at the village of Churchill. The park offers a spread of inland woodlands spliced by a river (with fishing) about 20 km southwest of Charlottetown. Facilities include 46 unserviced campsites ($13) and 12 two-way hookup sites ($16), hiking trails, hot showers, a launderette, kitchen shelters, and nearby campers' store; open mid-June to early September.

If you're tooling around hereabouts at mealtime, stop at the village of Meadow Bank for **McCrady's Green Acres** restaurant on Hwy. 19 near Cornwall, tel. 566-4938 (ask for directions). The search is worth it. Gourmet continental, Canadian, and English entrees range $10-20—try the shrimp in Pernod sauce or a choice PEI potato stuffed with lobster.

Dinnertime lures crowds to **Bonnie Brae Restaurant,** on Hwy. 1 near Cornwall, tel. 566-2241. Open year-round, 11 a.m.-9 p.m. daily, the restaurant is an islander favorite for Canadian, Swiss, and continental fare, as well as the mid-June to mid-Sept. nightly lobster buffet ($27).

Across the street from the Bonnie Brae, **Unique Island Woodcrafts** stocks a variety of wooden crafts made by local artisans.

Where PEI Began

Fort Amherst/Port la Joye National Historic Site, 35 minutes from Charlottetown on Hillsborough Bay, provides sublime views of the capital from its site on a peninsula tip. The island's first permanent European settlement began here in 1720 when three French ships sailed into Port la Joye (today's Charlottetown Harbour) carrying some 300 settlers. Most of them moved to the North Shore and established fishing villages, but the rest remained here at the military outpost.

Within just four years, adverse conditions had driven out most of the French. The British burned Port la Joye in 1745 and took control of the island. The French later returned to rebuild their capital, but were compelled to surrender Port la Joye to a superior British force in 1758. The British renamed the post Fort Amherst. After the British established the new capital at Charlottetown, Fort Amherst fell quickly into disrepair.

Nothing much remains of the fortifications today. A visitor center presents historical exhibits and displays explaining the history of the site. It's open mid-June to Labour Day, 10 a.m.-6 p.m. The grounds, which have picnic tables, are open year-round. The site is on Blockhouse Point Rd., off Hwy. 19; tel. (902) 675-2220.

VICTORIA AND VICINITY

Victoria (pop. 200), about 30 minutes from Charlottetown, or 15 minutes southeast of the Borden ferry terminal, marks Queens County's southwestern corner. The town owed its start to shipbuilding, and by 1870, Victoria ranked as one of the island's busiest ports. As the demand for wooden ships faded, the seaport turned to cattle shipping—herds of cattle were driven down the coastal slopes to water's edge, where they were hoisted on slings to waiting ships.

Today Victoria shows just a shadow of its former luster. The seaport slipped off the commercial circuit decades ago, and the settlement shrank to a handful of waterfront blocks. Happily, island craftspeople discovered the serene setting. It's still a quiet place where the fishing fleet puts out to sea early in the morning as the mist rises off the strait. But now the peaceful seaport also holds a modest arts colony.

If you're in town September through November, ask about the local legend: local folks say the image of a three-masted ghost ship, ablaze in the strait, can be seen when an autumn nor'wester blows in.

Entertainment

If an evening at the theater sounds good, try the **Victoria Playhouse** on Howard St., the repertory theater that showcases comedy and drama (adults $12, children under 12 $6), as well as concerts of jazz and folk music. It's open late June-early Sept., Tues.-Sunday. For reservations and dinner/theater packages, call (800) 925-2025 or (902) 566-1267 (June-Sept.).

Accommodations and Food

Victoria Village Inn on Howard St., tel. (902) 658-2288, is an 1870s heritage inn, awash with lustrous antiques in five guest rooms ($42-65, nonsmoking). Expect a healthful approach to cooking in the inn's dining room—no deep-fat frying or processed food and an emphasis on whole grains and freshest ingredients. Two or three entrees are offered daily ($15-23). The Inn is open May-October; call ahead for off-season dining.

Dunravin Lodge Cottage and Farm, tel. 658-2375, P.O. Box 40, Victoria, PE C0A 2G0, is located 1.2 km off the TransCanada Hwy. and overlooks Victoria village and the sea. Features include farm animals and children's activities for younger guests; babysitting is available. Leashed pets are okay. Open 18 June-25 Sept.; rates are $37-46. **Orient Hotel,** tel. 658-2503, is on Main Street. For reservations, write to P.O. Box 162, Charlottetown, PE C1A 7K4. The hotel has a tearoom, dining, bike storage, and a nearby beach. No pets or smoking allowed. The Orient is open May-Oct.; rates are $69-99.

For light fare, the **Landmark Cafe** at Howard and Main streets, tel. 658-2286, has homemade soup, pasta, salads, sandwiches, and desserts in a historic setting; open June-September. A crafts shop on the premises sells tinware, pottery, woodcrafts, and more.

Shopping

Island Chocolates on Main St., tel. (902) 658-2320, makes delectable candies of imported Belgian chocolate stuffed with fruit, cream, or nuts. Glass windows between the shop and production area encourage visitors to watch the process. It's open July-Aug., daily 9:30 a.m.-8:30 p.m., June and Sept. to 4:30 p.m. **Crafts at the Chocolate Factory** inside the shop (same hours) sells books, toys, and island-made arts and crafts including jewelry, pewter, pottery, Micmac baskets, knits, paintings, and sculptures. They'll also package the chocolates for presents or mailing.

Sea Shed Crafts at Main and Howard streets is another crafts source with similar stock plus tinware and silk-screen fabrics. It's open June-Aug., daily 10 a.m.-6 p.m., and in Sept. Wed.-Sun. 10 a.m.-6 p.m. Nearby, the **Studio Gallery** exhibits and sells local artists' works in photography, batik, etchings, and watercolors. It's also home base for Doreen Foster's etching studio. The gallery is open July-Aug., Tues.-Sun. 9 a.m.-5 p.m.

Borden Ferry Terminal

Back in the late 1700s, iceboats carrying mail and passengers crossed the strait when the island was icebound from December to early spring. The voyages were filled with hair-raising tales of survival, and the iceboats—rigged with fragile sails and runners—were often trapped in the strait's ice. Male passengers were sometimes put into harnesses to haul the boats over the uneven ice ridges.

By 1900, though, the province had turned to icebreaker boats that nosed through the winter ice. In 1916, the first car ferry sailed from Borden near Summerside, still the site of ferry service to Cape Tormentine, New Brunswick, and now also the site of one end of the fixed link being constructed to the mainland. An **information center** is located at the ferry terminal, and the **Gateway Tourist Information Centre** is four km east at Carleton Siding, open 8 a.m.-10 p.m.

Dutchess Gateway Bed and Breakfast, tel. 855-2765, 264 Carleton St., Borden, PE C0B 1X0, is close to the ferry, with dining nearby. Rates are $25-45. Non-smoking **Rest Awhile Inn,** tel. 855-2254, P.O. Box 133, Port Borden, PE C0B 1X0, is at 186 Howlan Ave.; open mid-May through September. Children-friendly, the inn features kitchens, a kennel, and nearby dining. The nightly rate is $35.

Ten minutes from Borden and Summerside in Central Bedeque (Prince County), **Pine-Lawn Bed and Breakfast,** tel. 887-2270, on Hwy. 112 off the TransCanada Hwy., is wheelchair accessible. A cot and crib are available, as well as a kitchen. No pets allowed. This bed and breakfast is open May -Oct.; rates are $25-30. Also in Bedeque, the **Mid Isle Motel,** tel. 887-2525, is on Hwy. 1A, 13 km west of Borden. Cots and cribs are available. The motel also offers TV, a coffee shop, and beach units. It's open June through mid-October; rates are $46-54.

EAST OF CHARLOTTETOWN

The TransCanada/Hwy. 1 departs Charlottetown and finishes at the Wood Islands ferry terminal. Turnoffs lead to several interesting places. Highway 2 runs northeast through Tracadie and continues all the way to Souris. In **York,** just off Hwy. 2 on Rte. 25, the **Potato Blossom Tea Room,** part of Jewell's Gardens and Pioneer Village, tel. (902) 368-7269, serves tasty island fare like potato pancakes, chowders, and fish cakes. It's open June-September.

Orwell

About a 25-minute drive east of Charlottetown, a marked road off the TransCanada leads to **Orwell Corner Historic Village,** the restored mid-19th-century farm village founded by early Scottish and Irish settlers. Buildings include the farmhouse, general store, dressmaker's shop, blacksmith's shop, church, and barns. The village is open mid-May to mid-October. During the prime summer season from late June to early Sept. it's open daily 9 a.m.-5 p.m. In early and late season, it's open Mon.-Fri. 10 a.m.-3 p.m. Admission is $3, children under 12 free.

For more information on tours, crafts demonstrations and events call (902) 651-2013.

Wednesday evenings from early July to late Sept., there's a *ceilidh,* featuring traditional music and song, with refreshments available. Adults $5, children under 12 free. In late August, **Scottish Festival and Highland Games** offers you the chance to sample the haggis and enjoy pipers, fiddlers, dancers, and traditional games. Adults $5, children under 12 $3.

For an overnight near Orwell, consider **MacLeod's Farm Cottages** on Hwy. 24 at Uigg, tel. 651-2303. In a farmland setting of grain fields and cattle pasture, MacLeod's offers a housekeeping unit in the main house ($40 d) and three outlying two-bedroom cottages ($60-70 d). It's open mid-May to mid-November.

Lord Selkirk Provincial Park

Tucked on the eastern shore of Orwell Bay, an inlet off the larger Hillsborough Bay, is beachfront Lord Selkirk Provincial Park, tel. (902) 659-2427 or 652-2356. The park, named for the Scottish leader of one of the early immigrant groups, is right off the TransCanada, a stone's throw west of Eldon. Here you'll find comfortable swimming in some of the island's warmest seas, and a beach perfect for clam digging. The park's 46 unserviced campsites ($13) and 26 two-way hookup sites ($16) are accompanied by a pool (extra charge), launderette, kitchen shelters, fireplaces, and a nearby campers' store.

A naturalist program runs throughout summer, and in early August, the park is the site of annual **Highland Games,** which include piping, dancing competitions, Scottish athletic competitions, and lobster suppers. The park is open late June-early September. For information write to P.O. Box 370, Montague, PE C0A 1R0.

Point Prim Lighthouse

Point Prim Lighthouse is at the end of Hwy. 209, which peels off the TransCanada and runs 10 km down the long, slender peninsula jutting into Hillsborough Bay. The unusual, 20-meter-tall tower, built in 1845, was designed by Isaac Smith, architect of Province House. It's Prince Edward Island's oldest lighthouse and Canada's only round, brick lighthouse tower. The view overlooking the strait from the octagonal lanternhouse at the top is gorgeous. It's open early

July-Aug., Mon.-Thurs. 10 a.m.-5 p.m., Fri.-Sun. 10 a.m.-7 p.m.; tel. (902) 659-2672.

The **Chowder House** at Point Prim, tel. 659-2023, serves fresh local clams and mussels, chowder, sandwiches, and homemade breads and pastries.

Area Crafts

Continuing on, the TransCanada curves down and around the strait toward the hamlet of **Flat River.** The studio of Roslynn and Robert Wilby at **Flat River Craftsmen,** tel. (902) 659-2530, is a showcase of earthenware, batik, clay jewelry, and sculpture; open year-round daily 9 a.m.-9 p.m. Hedwig Koleszar's studio at **Koleszar Pottery,** on Hwy. 204 near Belle River, tel. 659-2570, shines with silky-smooth porcelains in naturalist themes. Visitors are welcome to watch works in progress. It's open mid-May to mid-Nov., Mon.-Sat. 11 a.m.-3 p.m.

At the ferry terminal, **Wood Islands Handcraft Co-op Association,** tel. 962-3149 or 962-2253, has an outlet with weaving, pottery, knitted garments, furniture, and clocks; open June-Sept., daily 9 a.m.-5 p.m.

Wood Islands and Vicinity

Highway 1 (the TransCanada) ends at Wood Islands, terminus for the **Northumberland Ferry** to Caribou, Nova Scotia. A provincial visitor information center is located in the ferry terminal.

Meadow Lodge Motel, tel. (902) 962-2022, on the TransCanada two km west of the terminal, is a convenient accommodation if you're leaving the island early or arriving late. Rooms run $50-72 d. **Baba's House Guests,** tel. 962-2772, Belle River P.O., PE C0A 1B0, is on the TransCanada Hwy., six km from Wood Islands ferry. The inn has a peaceful view of the strait, TV, dining, and is nonsmoking. It's open 1 May through 15 October. Rates are $30-32.

A five-minute drive east from the ferry terminal, **Northumberland Provincial Park** on Hwy. 4, tel. 962-2163 or 652-2356 (winter), fronts the ocean, near enough to the terminal to see the ferries' comings and goings to Caribou, and remote enough for a reputation as a camping getaway. The park offers rental bikes, hayrides, a stream for fishing, an ocean beach with clam digging, and miniature golf. Facilities include 68 unserviced campsites ($13), 17 two-way hookup sites ($16), and nine three-way sites ($17), plus a launderette, kitchen shelters, a nearby campers' store, and hot showers. It's open mid-June to early September.

Onward

From Wood Islands, Hwy. 4 continues into Kings County, turning a sharp left inland to Murray River. Hwy. 18 sticks to the coast, wrapping around Murray Head before leading into the town of Murray Harbour and then into Murray River. Coverage of eastern PEI continues in the "Kings County" section below.

THE NORTH SHORE

Queens County's North Shore is a long swatch of PEI's loveliest seacoast. Visitors in the know and the discerning carriage trade have retreated here for decades. Outside of popular Cavendish, the rest of the North Shore is low-key and quiet.

"Utopian" Avonlea

The author Lucy Maud Montgomery penned northern Queens County's Cavendish into literary stardom. Montgomery as a young writer portrayed the village, and indeed the whole area, as an idyllic neverland called Avonlea, imbued with innocence and harmony.

As you drive the rambling red-clay lanes, and

walk the quiet woods, meadows, and gulf shore, you'll have to agree the lady did not overstate her case. The North Shore's most pastoral and historic places are preserved as part of **Prince Edward Island National Park.** And if you're in pursuit of the bucolic dream that Montgomery created, don't limit yourself to Cavendish. Queens County—especially the Gulf of St. Lawrence coastline—is virtually untouched by tacky, 20th-century commercialism.

Florid writing style notwithstanding, Montgomery created perfection on earth within the pages of her books, and through the decades more affection for a place has centered on Cavendish than perhaps anyplace else in North

America. Montgomery's Anne, the winsome, impressionable, and spunky heroine of *Anne of Green Gables,* has been loved by generation after generation of young readers around the world. And those children, as adults, are among the island's most numerous visitors.

Getting There

To get to the North Shore from Charlottetown, take Hwy. 2 northeast from the city and turn off on two-lane, backcountry Hwy. 6 to Grand Tracadie. Alternatively, follow Hwy. 2 to the northwest, veering right at Hwy. 13, which will take you right to Cavendish. Only Cavendish has commercial hype, and the rest of the region's villages are small to obscure and easy to miss.

THE EASTERN END

For lodgings, dining, shopping, and sightseeing, follow Hwy. 6 along the North Shore's eastern end. The sites listed below follow one after

Dalvay by the Sea

another, and the national park lies on the road's north side.

Grand Tracadie

Elegant, green-roofed **Dalvay by the Sea Hotel,** just off Hwy. 6 inside the park, tel. (902) 672-2048, appeals to guests who like an old-time money ambience. The rustic mansion was built in 1895 by millionaire American oil industrialist Alexander MacDonald, who used the lodging as a summer retreat. Today the hotel, its antiques, and its spacious grounds are painstakingly maintained by the national park staff. Its 26 rooms rent for $120-160 s, $150-270 d, $60-80 additional person, breakfast and dinner included. A cottage on the grounds is a honeymoon heaven. The hotel's dining room is locally renowned. Entrees ($15-30) feature formal Canadian cuisine and occasional French dishes. The emphasis is on freshest produce, seafood (try the poached salmon), and finest beef cuts; reservations are required. Other facilities at the hotel include a well-stocked gift shop, a nearby beach, a tennis court, bike rentals, a lake with canoes, and nature trails. Open mid-June to mid-September. The mailing address is P.O. Box 8, Little York, PE C0A 1P0.

Stanhope

Golfers like **Stanhope Golf and Country Club** off Hwy. 6 at the national park's edge, tel. (902) 672-2842. Its 5,206 meters overlook Covehead Bay. The club is open May-Oct.; greens fee is $17, and clubs can be rented. **Captain Dick's Lounge,** Hwy. 25, tel. 672-2235, offers about the only nightlife around, with live music (rock, dance) most nights at 9 p.m. Their restaurant is open Mon.-Sat. 4-9 p.m., Sun. noon-9 p.m.

One accommodations option is **Campbell's Tourist Home and Housekeeping Unit,** tel. 672-2421, Little York RR 1, PE C0A 1P0, on Hwys. 25 and 6. Cots and cribs are available, as well as dishwashers, microwaves, and laundry services. No pets are allowed. It's open year-round, and rates are $35-50. **Stanhope by the Sea,** tel. 672-2047, P.O. Box 9, Little York, PE C0A 1P0, Bay Shore Rd. (Hwy. 25), overlooks Covehead Bay and the national park. Bicycle and canoe rentals are available, and a beach is nearby. Open 22 June-6 September; rates are $70-95 including breakfast.

NAN DROSDICK

Brackley Beach

With its proximity to the national park, excellent beaches, golf, deep-sea fishing, and other attractions, Brackley Beach is a popular place and accommodations are plentiful.

Blue Waters Tourist Home, on Hwy. 15, tel. (902) 672-2720, is a large country home on spacious grounds overlooking Brackley. Rooms range $36-41 d. **Shaw's Hotel and Cottages,** on an unmarked lane off Hwy. 15, tel. 672-2022, overlooks the bay at the edge of the national park. This was the Shaw family's homestead in the 1860s and it's still in the family. The property has 22 rooms and suites ($170-190 d, with meals) in the main house; adjacent historic cottages ($185-225), built by the same island craftsmen who worked on Dalvay by the Sea; and newer upscale waterfront chalets ($180-237); open June-September. The ambience is informal and friendly—a nice place for meeting islanders and other visitors.

The main house's **dining room** is consistently good, especially at the Sunday buffet (under $30), which lures diners from Charlottetown. Entree choices ($20-30) are limited to two or three daily specials and include poached salmon and prime beef; reservations are required. The **Lobster Trap** is another dining option, a pub-style restaurant set off by itself on the grounds; the mood is informal as is the menu, with seafood platters, hamburgers, and French fries.

In the vicinity, the **Dunes Studio Gallery and Cafe,** on Hwy. 15, tel. 672-2586, is worth browsing for porcelains crafted by owner Peter Jansons; the shop is also an outlet for island craftspeople with a line of stoneware, framed photography, gold jewelry, pottery, watercolors, oils, and sculptures. The gallery is open May to mid-October. The cafe serves breakfast, lunch, and dinner (seafood, lamb, local produce) daily, and is open June-October.

Private campgrounds close by are **Dunwurkin by the Sea,** on Hwy. 6 between Brackley Beach and Oyster Bed Beach, tel. 672-3390 ($12.50-17.50); and **Vacationland Good Sam Park,** east of Hwy. 15, tel. 672-2317 ($15-17.50).

Recreation

North Shore Windsurfing and Bike Rentals, at Shaw's Hotel, tel. (902) 672-2022, is open to the public and rents water-sports equipment ($70 per day for a sailboard), canoes, and bikes; they advise novice windsurfers to stay on the tranquil, protected inner bays, rather than the windy, open gulf.

Families with young children might enjoy **Brackley Beach Entertainment Centre,** Hwy. 15, tel. 672-3333, with its 18-hole minigolf, waterslide, bumper boats, and other amusements.

Information and Services

For information about the area, stop at the **Beaches Association** office on Hwy. 15, tel. 672-3456, open mid-June to mid-Sept., daily 10 a.m.-6 p.m. **Banks** are scarce in the area—most everyone drives into Charlottetown. **Royal Bank** has offices in **Mount Stewart,** on Hwy. 2 east of Tracadie Bay, and **Hunter River,** five minutes from Brackley Beach at the intersection of Hwys. 2 and 13. They're open Mon.-Fri. 9:30 a.m.-4:30 p.m.

PRINCE EDWARD ISLAND NATIONAL PARK

Prince Edward Island National Park's sandy beaches, dunes, sandstone cliffs, marshes, and forestlands represent Prince Edward Island as it once was, unspoiled by the crush of 20th-century development.

The slender, 40-km-long coastal slice of natural perfection extends almost the full length of Queens County, and is bookended by two large bays. At the eastern end, Tracadie Bay spreads out like an oversize pond with shimmering waters. Forty km to the west, New London Bay forms almost a mirror image of the eastern end. In between, long barrier islands define Rustico and Covehead bays, and sand dunes webbed with marram grass, rushes, fragrant bayberry, and wild roses front the coastline.

Sunrise and sunset here are cast in glowing colors. All along the gulf at sunrise, the beaches have a sense of primeval peacefulness, their sands textured like herringbone by the overnight sea breezes.

Getting around is easy. Highway 6 lies on the park's inland side, connecting numerous park entrances, and the Gulf Shore Parkway runs along the coast nearly the park's entire

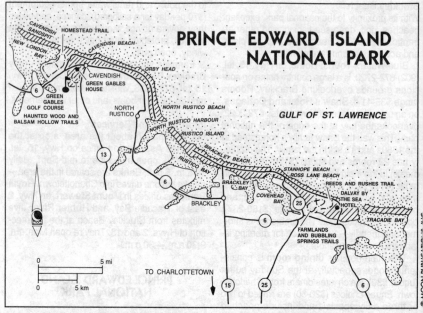

PRINCE EDWARD ISLAND NATIONAL PARK

GULF OF ST. LAWRENCE

TO CHARLOTTETOWN

length. You can drive through the park year-round. From late June to early Sept., the entrance fee is $5 a day per car, $10 for four days, or $20 annually.

Environmental Factors

The national park was established in 1937 to protect the fragile dunes along the Gulf of St. Lawrence, as well as cultural features such as the Green Gables House. Parks Canada walks a fine line, balancing environmental concerns with the responsibilities of hosting half a million park visitors a year. Boardwalks route visitors through dunes to the beaches and preserve the fragile landscape.

The park also preserves nesting habitat for some 25 pairs of endangered piping plovers—small, shy shorebirds that arrive in early April to breed in flat sandy areas near the high-tide line.

piping plover

Some beaches may be closed in spring and summer when the plovers are nesting; it's vital to the birds' survival that visitors stay clear of these areas.

Recreation

If you'd like to learn more about the park's ecology, join one of the **nature walks** led by Parks Canada rangers. The treks lead through white spruce stunted by winter storms and winds, to freshwater ponds, and into the habitats of such native animal species as red fox, northern phalarope, Swainson's thrush, and junco.

The unbroken stretches of sandy **beaches**—some white, others tinted pink by iron oxide—are among the best in the province. Half a dozen public beaches lie between Blooming Head and Orby Head, many backed by steep, red-sandstone cliffs. On warm summer days, droves of sunbathers laze on the shore and swim in the usually gentle surf. Stanhope, Ross Lane, Brackley, North Rustico, Cavendish, and Cavendish Campground beaches all have lifeguards on duty, and a variety of visitor facilities.

Bicyclists will appreciate the smooth, wide shoulders and light traffic along the Gulf Shore Parkway, which runs most of the length of the park.

Six established **hiking trails** range from the half-km, wheelchair-accessible Reeds and Rushes Trail beginning at the Dalvay Administration Building near Grand Tracadie, to the eight-km Homestead Trail beginning near the entrance to Cavendish Campground. The latter wends inland alongside freshwater ponds and through woods and marshes and is open to both hikers and bikers. Be wary of potentially hazardous cliff edges, and of the poison ivy and ticks that lurk in the ground cover.

Birdwatchers will be amply rewarded with sightings of some of the more than 100 species known to frequent the park. Brackley Marsh, Orby Head, and the Rustico Island Causeway are good places to start. The 18-hole **Green Gables Golf Course,** tel. (902) 963-2488, spread across 5,971 meters, is among Atlantic Canada's most popular golf greens.

During peak tourist season, sightseers create long waiting lines to enter **Green Gables House,** the farmhouse setting of *Anne of Green Gables.* Islanders describe Montgomery's fans as "pilgrims"; they flock to Montgomery's landmarks from as far away as Japan, where the Anne stories are extremely popular.

Campgrounds

The park's three campgrounds are distinctly different. **Stanhope Campground,** east of Brackley Beach, is closest to the seacoast and has 104 unserviced sites and 14 sites with three-way hookups. **Cavendish Campground,** closest to Cavendish and center of the park's naturalist programs, is most popular and has 226 unserviced sites and 78 three-way hookup sites. More remote **Rustico Island Campground** is situated on Rustico Island, the lengthy sandbar that lies across Rustico Bay's mouth. The campground's 148 unserviced sites are four km inland from the

sea in a wilderness setting that appeals to naturalists.

Campground facilities include campers' stores (in the campgrounds or nearby), kitchen shelters, launderettes, flush toilets, and (except Rustico Island) hot showers. The park staff is bilingual (English and French). Cavendish is open June to mid-Oct.; Stanhope, mid-June to early Sept.; Rustico Island, late June–early September.

Rates range from $12.50 to $19, on a first-come, first-served basis, except for the Brackley Group Tenting Area, tel. (902) 672-6350 (where reservations are required for groups). For more information write to District Superintendent, Parks Canada, 2 Palmers Lane, Charlottetown, PE C1A 5V6.

Other Lodgings in the Park

For a lodging variation, consider housekeeping cottages (open June to mid-Oct.) within the park. Near North Rustico, **Coast Line Cottages,** tel. (902) 963-2264 or 963-2398, are new and face the gulf. The four cottages ($70 d) are within walking distance to Doyle's Cove sandy beach. **Gulf View Cottages,** tel. 963-2052, is a larger complex offering a dozen two-bedroom cottages with front decks overlooking the gulf ($75-102 d).

Information

For park information, call (902) 963-2391 in summer, 672-6350 year-round. The **Cavendish Visitor Centre** is near the corner of Highways 6 and 13, in Cavendish, tel. 963-2391; the **Dalvay Administration Office** is across from the Dalvay by the Sea Hotel, on the Gulf Shore Parkway off Hwy. 6, tel. 672-6350; the **Brackley Visitor Centre** is at the intersection of Highways 6 and 15 in Brackley Beach, tel. 672-2259. For descriptions of hiking trails, organized activities, and other details, get a copy of the park's *Blue Heron,* a free booklet available at the offices above as well as at other tourist information offices. **Park Information Radio,** 1490 AM, broadcasts current park info and activities suggestions. Provincial roadside tourist centers have park updates. And **Environment Canada** is another source of information about the park; write to them at Canadian Parks Service, P.O. Box 487, Charlottetown, PE C1A 7L1.

AROUND RUSTICO BAY

A decade after the French began Port la Joye near Charlottetown, French settlers cut through the inland forest and settled Rustico Bay's coastline. England's Acadian Deportation in 1755 emptied the villages, but not for long. The Acadians returned, and the five revived Rusticos—Rusticoville, South Rustico, Anglo Rustico, North Rustico (pop. 635, the area's center), and North Rustico Harbour—still thrive and encircle Rustico Bay's western shore. Expect a composite of French Acadian and Anglo cultures on the gulf coast.

For entertainment in the Rustico Bay area, try to pin down the **Rustico Shindigs,** concerts of local Maritime music presented at different venues (the Farmers' Bank, Rustico Resort, Shaw's Hotel, Rustic Dreams, Marco Polo Land, and Mayfield Meadows) on a rotating basis. Admission is $1. Call any of the above venues (telephone numbers listed below) for details or pick up a schedule at a tourist info center.

South Rustico

For a look at old-time Acadian culture, check out the **Farmers' Bank Museum** on Hwy. 243 at the waterfront, tel. (902) 963-2505. Built in 1864 as Canada's first chartered people's bank, the building served as the early Acadian banking connection. Exhibits at this national historic site include heritage displays plus artifacts from the life of Rev. Georges-Antoine Belcourt, the founder. The museum is open late June to early Sept., Mon.-Sat. 9:30 a.m.-5 p.m., Sun. from 1 p.m. Admission is adults $1, children 50 cents.

Barachois Inn, Hwy. 243, South Rustico, tel. 963-2194, is a historic building overlooking Rustico Bay, and has six nonsmoking rooms ($95 with breakfast) brimming with antiques and paintings. It's open May-October.

Rustico Resort, at the intersection of Hwys. 6 and 242, tel. 963-2357, boasts golf greens known far beyond Atlantic Canada and described as "user-friendly" by *Golf Digest.* The golf course rents carts and clubs, and offers lessons from a pro. It's open May-Oct.; greens fee is $16. The resort's motel units are $84 d; housekeeping units $600-930 weekly (for two to eight people). There is also a dining room.

Cymbria Tent and Trailer Park, on Hwy. 242 off Hwy. 6, tel. 963-2458, is in a quiet location close to the beach; $13-16.

If you need a taxi, call **Cavendish Taxi and Tours,** tel. 963-2568; Cavendish to Dalvay by the Sea costs about $30 OW.

North Rustico and North Rustico Harbour

Half a dozen charter fishing operators tie up at North Rustico and North Rustico Harbour. The average rate is about $15 per person for a three-hour outing or $150 for a full day's charter, for cod, mackerel, flounder, and tuna. Most charters operate July to mid-Sept. or mid-October. The crew will outfit you in rain gear if needed, provide tackle and bait, and clean and fillet your catch. North Rustico operators include: **Court Brothers Deep-Sea Fishing,** tel. (902) 963-2322; **Aiden Doiron's Deep-Sea Fishing,** tel. 963-2442 or 963-2039; **Bob's Deep-Sea Fishing,** tel. 963-2666 or 963-2086. In Rustico Harbour, call **Capt. Vance Court** at 963-2322.

Andy's Surfside Inn, off Gulf Shore Parkway just 100 meters from the beach, P.O Box 5, Charlottetown, PE C1A 7K2, tel. 963-2405, $35 d, offers a laundromat, kitchens, TV, cribs, and bike rentals. **MacLure Bed and Breakfast,** on Rte. 6, tel. 963-2239, has three rooms for $30 d and offers meals on request for an extra charge. It's close to the Green Gables House, and the mailing address is Hunter River RR 2, PE C0A 1N0.

McMaster House Bed and Breakfast, tel. 963-3097, Hunter River RR 2, PE C0A 1N0, is on Hwy. 269 between Hwys. 6 and 13. The house is near dining and beaches in a tranquil setting. No smoking or children under 12 allowed. Open May-Sept.; rate is $30 including breakfast.

St. Lawrence Motel, tel. 963-2053, Hunter River RR 2, PE C0A 1N0, is on Gulf Shore Rd. in the national park between Cavendish and North Rustico. The motel overlooks the gulf and has suites, kitchens, and a recreation room. A national park beach is nearby. The St. Lawrence is open 24 May-10 Oct., and rates are $47-71. **Saint Nicholas Motel,** tel. 963-2898, Hunter River RR 3, PE C0A 1N0, is on Hwy. 6. The units have refrigerators, and dining is available nearby. Pets are not allowed. Open mid-May through mid-October; rates are $60-65.

The popular tour-bus stop **Fisherman's Wharf Lobster Suppers,** on Hwy. 6 at the seaport's wharf, tel. 963-2669, draws crowds for its abundant helpings. Dining options include a basic, fixed menu—$20 for a lobster or strip steak with buffet fixings, or $8-18 for broiled, boiled, poached, or fried seafood entrees—and all-you-can-eat deals on such piscatory palate-pleasers as steamed mussels and seafood chowder. The restaurant is open mid-May to October.

For picnic ingredients, stop at the **Island Food Centre** on Hwy. 6. It's open daily 8 a.m.-9 p.m. and has a well-stocked deli.

Oyster Bed Bridge

MacPherson's Farm Tourist Delight Bed and Breakfast, on Hwy. 251 near the intersection of Highways. 6 and 7, tel. (902) 631-0138, is in a secluded site on 105 acres and offers hiking, biking, fishing, and canoeing; $40 d. **Café St. Jean,** on Hwy. 6 about 10 minutes southeast of South Rustico, tel. 963-3133, serves French and Cajun cuisines ($14-25), and on some Sunday afternoons hosts free musical events (fiddling, step-dancing) on the lawn. The cafe is open June-September.

Stock-car racing fans head for the **Raceway Entertainment Park,** Hwy. 223 and Hwy. 6 intersection, tel. 964-3104. It's open mid-May to mid-September; admission $8-11.

Cheese Lady's Gouda Cheese in Winsloe North, tel. 368-1506, is owned by Dutch immigrants who make a variety of Gouda cheeses just like in the Netherlands. Visitors are welcome to watch the production process. It's open year-round, Mon.-Sat. 10 a.m.-6 p.m. To get there take Hwy. 223 east from Oyster Bed Bridge. The road soon bends southeast to Winsloe North.

CAVENDISH

Fame has transformed parts of this small town and vicinity into a tourist theme park, replete with typical commercial trappings such as roadside signs, amusement parks, and shopping malls. But the place is not as bad as it could be, compared, say, with some of the tackier, tourist-glutted seaside towns in the United States.

That said, Cavendish is still the county's (and the island's) main attraction. It's the icing on the cake that is Queens County, and its reputation attracts visitors by the hundreds of thousands. To dedicated readers of Lucy Maud Montgomery's sentimental books, the village's lure is emotional, like a shrine to a pilgrim. For others—those who don't know Anne of Green Gables from Anne Frank—plenty of other entertainment is available in the area.

For example, golfers tee off at Green Gables Golf Course alongside Green Gables House at the national park. Shoppers like the multitude of crafts shops with high-quality wares and the souvenirs galore. If you have sailing, windsurfing, or fishing in mind, you'll find water-sports outfitters with rental equipment along the North Shore coastline. Lodging options range from well-heeled carriage trade to bed-and-breakfasts to heritage country inns and contemporary motels in all price ranges.

Immigrants fleeing Scotland's poverty and religious persecution arrived at New London and Stanhope in the mid-1700s. By the 1790s, other Scots settled Cavendish—L.M. Montgomery's ancestors among them. The town was named for Field Marshall Lord Frederick Cavendish, patron landowner who acquired title in the 1760s.

The center of Cavendish now belongs to commercial interests, and the village's inhabitants live on the outskirts. Expect crowds. The provincial tourist office kept track of visitor numbers one recent summer, and to no one's surprise, they determined that over 400,000 visitors spent at least one day in Cavendish that season.

Sights

Green Gables House at the Hwys. 6 and 13 intersection within the park, tel. (902) 672-6350, reigns as the idyllic hub of a Montgomery sightseeing circuit. The restored 19th-century farmhouse, once home of Montgomery's elderly cousins and the setting also for the novel, is furnished simply and stolidly, just as it was described in *Anne of Green Gables*. Among other memorabilia in the pretty vintage setting are artifacts such as the author's archaic typewriter. On the grounds, the Balsam Hollow and Haunted Woods trails feature some of Montgomery's favorite woodland haunts, including Lover's

LUCY MAUD MONTGOMERY

Lucy Maud Montgomery was born at New London, Prince Edward Island, in 1874, a decade after the Charlottetown Conference. At the age of two, her mother died and her father moved to western Canada. Maud, as she preferred to be called, was left in the care of her maternal grandparents, who brought her to Cavendish.

Cavendish, in northern Queens County, was idyllic in those days, and Montgomery wrote fondly about the ornate Victorian sweetness of the setting of her early years. As a young woman, she studied first at the island's Prince of Wales College, later at Dalhousie University in Halifax. She then returned to the island as a teacher at Bideford, Lower Bedeque, Belmont, and Lot 15. In 1898, her grandfather's death brought her back to Cavendish to help her grandmother.

The idea for *Anne of Green Gables* dated to the second Cavendish stay, and the book was published in 1908. In 1911, Montgomery married the Rev. Ewen MacDonald at her Campbell relatives' Silver Bush homestead overlooking the Lake of Shining Waters. (The Campbell descendants still live in the pretty farmhouse and have turned their home into a museum.) The couple moved to Ontario, where Montgomery spent the rest of her life, returning to PEI only for short visits. Though she left, Maud never forgot Prince Edward Island. Those brief revisitations with her beloved island must have been painful; after one trip, she wistfully recalled in her journal:

"This evening I spent in Lover's Lane. How beautiful it was—green and alluring and beckoning! I had been tired and discouraged and sick at heart before I went to it—and it rested me and cheered me and stole away the heartsickness, giving peace and newness of life."

Montgomery died in 1942, and lay in state at the Green Gables House in the new national park before burial in the Cavendish Cemetery. As an author, she left 20 juvenile books and a myriad of other writings. Her works have been published worldwide, translated into 16 languages. In Japan, Montgomery's writings are required reading in the school system—which accounts for the island's many Japanese visitors.

Montgomery also inadvertently created an island phenomenon, giving PEI the persistent image as the utopian Avonlea, the name she had given the Cavendish area during her long years in publishing. Her heroine Anne is recreated in Charlottetown's annual summertime musical, and seems to be everywhere in PEI tourist advertising. The once rural Cavendish area has become a maze of theme parks, fast-food outlets, and souvenir shops in parts, and the village has repositioned itself as an official resort municipality to try to grapple with fame. Remarkably, obtrusive commercialism has made no inroads beyond the Cavendish area on Queens County's North Shore.

Montgomery wrote for children, and she viewed Cavendish and Prince Edward Island with all the clarity and innocence that a child possesses. Her books are as timeless today as they were decades ago. Some critics have described Montgomery's writings as mawkish. Contemporary scholars, however, have taken a new look at the author's works and have begun to discern a far more complex style. The academic community may debate her literary prowess, but no matter—the honest essence of Montgomery's writings have inspired decades of zealous pilgrims to pay their respects to her native Cavendish. To islanders, she is Lucy Maud, their literary genius, on a first-name basis.

BOB RACE

Lane. A tea room and gift shop are also on the premises.

The house is open daily, with bilingual guides on hand. If crowds bother you, plan to visit early in the morning. The site is open mid-May to Oct., daily 9 a.m.-5 p.m., July-Aug. to 8 p.m. Admission is free. Off-season tours are available; call 894-4246 to arrange.

Site of Lucy Maud Montgomery's Cavendish Home, Hwy. 6 near the United Church, tel. 963-2231, is the location of Montgomery's grandparents' homestead (now gone), where Lucy lived from 1876-1911 and wrote *Anne of Green Gables*. "I wrote it in the evenings after my regular day's work was done," she recalled, "wrote most of it at the window of the little gable room that had been mine for many years." The site includes the house's stone cellar set amid woods and gardens; the grounds also include a bookstore with books by and about Montgomery. It's open June-Aug., daily 9 a.m.-7 p.m.; Sept. to mid-Oct., daily 10 a.m.-5 p.m. Admission is $1. Montgomery is buried at the nearby United Church cemetery.

Accommodations

Kindred Spirits Country Inn and Cottages, on Hwy. 6, tel. (902) 963-2434, lies aside the national park's Green Gables House and golf course. It has 10 guest rooms ($65-95 with a light breakfast) in the main house and 13 outlying cottages ($110-140 for one to four guests); open mid-May to mid-October.

Silverwood Motel on Hwy. 6, tel. 963-2439, (800) 565-4753 in Canada (calls taken Feb.-Sept.), has 27 rooms and another 23 housekeeping units near the beach, arranged in one-to three-bedroom suites ($68-116). The motel is open mid-May to early Oct., and it has a pool, launderette, and dining room on site, and golf and tennis nearby.

Our Lady of the Way Tourist Lodge and Motel Units, tel. 963-2024 or 894-4489 (winter), Hunter River RR 2, PE C0A 1N0, is on Hwy. 13, 1.5 km south of Cavendish Beach. There are apartment and lodge units, a picnic area, and dining. Leashed pets are allowed. Rates are $35-60.

Fiddles 'N' Vittles Efficiency Units, tel. 963-3003 or 886-2928 (winter), Breadalbane RR 1, PE C0A 1E0, is located on Hwy. 6, two km west

LUCY MAUD MONTGOMERY'S CAVENDISH LANDMARKS

TO NORTH RUSTICO

TO NEW LONDON

CAVENDISH UNITED CHURCH

GREEN GABLES POST OFFICE

SITE OF MONTGOMERY'S CAVENDISH HOME

CEMETERY / MONTGOMERY'S GRAVE

TO HUNTER RIVER

FOOTPATH

GREEN GABLES HOUSE

HAUNTED WOODS

TEA ROOM

BALSAM HOLLOW

LOVERS' LANE

FOOTPATH

NOT TO SCALE

© MOON PUBLICATIONS, INC.

of the Cavendish entrance to the national park. The inn has a quiet country setting with a view of New London Bay, adjacent restaurant, and a pool. Rates are $69 d.

Cavendish Motel, tel. 963-2244, Green Gables P.O., PE C0A 1M0, is located at the intersection of Highways 6 and 13. The motel offers TV, barbecues, a dining room, and a playground. Pets are not allowed. Rates are $72-105.

Cavendish Beach Cottages on the national park's Gulf Shore Rd. within the park, tel. 963-2025, boasts 13 one- to three-bedroom housekeeping cottages with front decks ($95-125). The cottages are set back 200 meters from the beach, and are just a few steps from the park's jogging and hiking trails. They're open June to late Sept.; guests are exempt from the park's entrance fee.

Kirklawn Country Home, Hwy. 6, tel. 963-2439, in the 1840s homestead of one of Cavendish's founding families, appeals to couples or one or two families. The $165 per day rate for four guests ($6 each additional guest) rents the whole, fully equipped, five-bedroom house. It has an outdoor heated pool, and is set on a great spread of lawn. The house is available mid-May to early October.

Marco Polo Land on Hwy. 13 two km from Cavendish Beach, tel. 963-2352, is the island's definitive commercial campground, replete with resort trappings. Facilities include 475 sites (from unserviced at $17.50 to three-way hookups at $22), tennis courts, heated pools, a dining room, campers' store, and hot showers; open June to mid-September.

Cavendish Sunset Campground, tel. 963-2440, P.O. Box 217, PE C1A 7K4, on Hwy. 6, is opposite Cavendish Boardwalk and the entrance to the national park. Leashed pets are allowed and bike and movie rentals, laundromats, mini-golf, tennis, stores, and kitchen shelters are all offered. Dining is within walking distance. The campground is open mid-June to Labour Day. Rates are $17-20.

Food
Fiddles 'n Vittles, Hwy. 6 at the Bay View Motel, tel. (902) 963-3003, has pleased islanders for decades with bountiful seafood platters ($9-16). It's open June-early September. The **Lobster Factory,** in the Cranberry Village mall, Hwy. 6, tel. 963-3444, is a family restaurant serving chowder, shellfish, and other seafood.

Otherwise, Cavendish dining is relegated to burger, pizza, fried chicken, and other fast-food places. An alternative is to drive a few kilometers to one of the big lobster feeds put on in the area; see "Lobster Suppers" under "Vicinity of Cavendish," below.

For do-it-yourself meals, take your choice among the beach markets along major highways; shops at **Cavendish Beach Shopping Plaza** answer most needs. **Cavendish Board-**

walk mall is another source and also boasts **Cow's Prince Edward Island** homemade ice-cream shop. **Cavendish Shopping Centre** has a butcher shop and deli.

Entertainment and Recreation
Cruise along Hwy. 6 for Cavendish's noisy night scene, especially at **The Pier,** formerly Gilligan's Landing, with a weekend band, $3-5 admission. **Chevy's Rock 'n' Roll Forever Diner and Bar,** tel. (902) 963-2732, is entrenched in the area and also serves pizza, chicken, and sandwiches orchestrated to rock under the strobe lights.

For more pastoral pursuits, **Sunset Campground** on Hwy. 6 next to Cavendish Boardwalk, tel. 963-2440, rents standard and mountain bikes at $8-13 day, open mid-June to early Sept., daily 8 a.m.-10 p.m. For a round of golf at **Green Gables Golf Course** in the national park, expect to pay $17-19. It's open May-Oct.; reservations are wise during July and Aug., call 963-2488.

Rainbow Valley, Hwy. 6, is where islanders take their kids for tame entertainment ($9 adult, $8 children): water slides, rides, and picnic places. It's open June to early Sept., Mon.-Sat. 9 a.m.-8 p.m., Sun. noon-8 p.m.

Information and Services
The provincial **visitor information center** on Hwy. 13, tel. (902) 963-2639, is open June to mid-Oct., daily 9 a.m.-6 p.m., with extended hours in midsummer (till 9 p.m. in mid- to late June and till 10 p.m. July to mid-August).

Cavendish Taxi and Tours at Rusticoville, tel. 963-2568, operates a six-hour "Anne" shuttle tour ($15) of Montgomery landmarks; be at the tourist office at 10:30 a.m. and noontime for departures. The outfit also designs custom tours (from $30 an hour, four persons maximum).

VICINITY OF CAVENDISH

A web of hamlets encircles Cavendish. The rural scenery is lovely, and exploring the beaches and back roads should help you sharpen your appetite for a night at one of PEI's famed lobster-supper community halls, which are scattered hereabouts.

Lobster Suppers

The island's raison d'etre in summer is the abundant amount of lobster available here—more than in anyplace else in Atlantic Canada. Take your choice of chowing down ($20-25) at the trio below, open during the summer season Mon.-Sat. and sometimes Sun., 4-9 p.m; for details, call ahead. The price usually includes boiled lobster, chowder, salad, corn on the cob, vegetables, homemade bread and biscuits, and dessert. Some places serve buffet-style with unlimited fixings.

The crowds go to: **New London Lions Lobster Suppers** on Hwy. 6 at New London, tel. (902) 886-2599; **St. Ann's Church** on Hwy. 224 at St. Ann, tel. 964-2385; and **New Glasgow Lobster Suppers**, Hwy. 258 off Hwy. 13, New Glasgow, tel. 964-2870.

Stanley Bridge

For seaworthy sightseeing, check out the **P.E.I. Marine Aquarium** on Hwy. 6 west of Cavendish, tel. (902) 892-2203. The privately operated aquarium has native fish species in viewing tanks and exhibits on natural history and oyster cultivation; seals are kept outside in penned pools. The complex is open mid-June to mid-Sept., daily 9 a.m.-8 p.m. Adult admission is $4, children 6-14 $2.

In the vicinity, shoppers like the **Stanley Bridge Studios** on Hwy. 6, tel. 621-0314, where shelves and floor space overflow with woolen sweaters, quilts, apparel, stoneware, porcelain, jewelry, and Anne dolls. It's open June-Sept., daily 10 a.m.-5 p.m. **Old Stanley Schoolhouse** on Hwy. 224, tel. 886-2033, handles island-made quilts, weaving, pottery, pewter, folk art, and sweaters, open early June to mid-Sept., daily with similar hours.

The Smallmans, on Hwy. 254 three km south of Stanley Bridge, tel. 886-2846, offer three bed-and-breakfast rooms ($29-37 d) and one housekeeping unit ($75 for one to four people) in a scenic riverside setting, plus boating, swimming, and birdwatching.

St. Ann

The **Dyed in the Wool** shop on Hwy. 224 between New Glasgow and Stanley Bridge is Jill Allman's creation and melds crafts with wares woven from her own sheep's wool. The shop is open May to mid-Oct., daily 10 a.m. to dusk.

Blue Jay Cottages, off Hwy. 224 on New London Rd., tel. (902) 621-0709, has housekeeping units at $50-80.

New Glasgow

The island's finest berry and fruit crops fuel the wares of **P.E.I. Preserve Co.** on Highway 224, tel. 964-2524, where the proprietors stock a plethora of varied preserves (some spiked with liqueur). They also serve breakfast, lunch, and dinner in the sunny showroom furnished with wooden pews and tables. Hours are mid-May to mid-Oct., daily 9 a.m.-5 p.m., July-Aug. 8 a.m.-8 p.m.

New London

The **Lucy Maud Montgomery Birthplace,** at the junction of Hwys. 6 and 8, tel. (902) 886-2099, lies 10 minutes from Cavendish at what was once Clifton. The author was born in the unassuming farmhouse. Among the exhibits are her wedding dress, scrapbooks, and other personal items. The site is open daily June to mid-Oct., 10 a.m. to 5 p.m., July-Aug. 9 a.m.-7 p.m. Admission is $1 for adults, 50 cents for children 6-12.

Roberts' Tourist Home, on Hwy. 6, six km from Cavendish, tel. 886-2526, has two rooms at $20 per night. It's open June-September. If you're on the prowl for a place to eat close by, check out the **New London Wharf Restaurant,** on Hwy. 20, tel. 886-2422; the waterside dining room serves basic, hearty seafood ($7-25), open mid-June to September.

Questions on the area's highlights may be directed to **New London Tourist Centre** in the Lions' Building on Hwy. 6, tel. 886-2315. It's open June-Sept., daily 9 a.m.-8 p.m.

Long River

Kitchen Witch Tea Room and Eatery on Hwy. 234, tel. (902) 886-2294, occupies a two-room schoolhouse dating back to 1832. As the name implies, you can have your future read in your tea leaves if you like. The cozy restaurant is known for chowders, sandwiches, salads, and extraordinarily rich desserts. It's open mid-June to Sept. for breakfast, lunch, and dinner.

French River

Wild Goose Lodge off Hwy. 20 on the way to

Park Corner, tel. (902) 886-2177, is a gem of a contemporary-style lodge, gorgeously designed with suites ($95-105 for two or three bedrooms with kitchen facilities) that converge on a central lounge area; outside, there's a viewing deck that overlooks the countryside (and flocks of geese during autumn). The lodge is open May-November.

Park Corner
Anne of Green Gables Museum at Silver Bush on Hwy. 20, tel. (902) 886-2884, another Montgomery landmark and the ancestral home of the author's Campbell relatives, spreads out in a farmhouse setting in the pastoral rolling countryside. Montgomery described the house as "the big beautiful home that was the wonder castle of my dreams," and here she was married in 1911. The Lake of Shining Waters, described

in *Anne of Green Lakes,* lies across the road. The museum's exhibits include Montgomery's personal correspondence and first editions of her works. It's open June-Oct., daily 9 a.m.-6 p.m., July-Aug. until dark; adults $2.50, children under 16 are 75 cents.

The adjacent **Shining Waters Tea Room,** tel. 886-2003, serves island-style light fare, and the crafts shop sells Montgomery souvenirs as well as windchimes, quilts, and other crafts.

Onward
From Park Corner, Hwy. 20 leads west over the county line to Malpeque and Kensington, which are covered below in the "Prince County" section. Highway 6, running west from Cavendish through Stanley Bridge and New London, also continues to Kensington.

BOB RACE

PRINCE COUNTY

Along the southern portion of Prince County—the province's slender western part—the land is level, and the pastoral farmlands flow in gentle, serene sweeps to the strait coastline. Thick woodlands span the county's midsection, and you'll see fields of potatoes that blossom in July and green carpets of wheat nodding in the summer breezes. The northern tip is a remote and barren plain with a windswept coast, where farmers known as "mossers" use stout draft horses to reap Irish moss (a seaweed) from the surf.

Summerside, the province's second-largest town, boasts an ample supply of lodgings, restaurants, and nightlife. Just west of there is the province's largest Acadian area, the Région Évangéline ("Evangeline Region").

Count on high-quality crafts and wares at town boutiques and outlying shops throughout the region; the region's craftspeople are renowned for quilts, knitted apparel, Acadian shirts, and blankets.

The **climate** here is not so much moody as it is variable—be prepared to dress like an onion, ready to peel as you go from one area to another.

GETTING AROUND

Highway 2, PEI's main expressway, enters Prince County at the town of Kensington, glides past the seaport of Summerside on a narrow isthmus, and leads inland for 100 km to finish at the village of Tignish, near the island's northwestern tip.

This route is dubbed the Lady Slipper Drive, one of the provincial scenic sightseeing routes; it's signposted with a red symbol of the orchidlike flower. But the scenic route designation is somewhat misleading. The county's most idyllic scenery—and some of PEI's most spectacular sea views—lie well off this beaten path, at the sea's edges along Northumberland Strait and the Gulf of St. Lawrence.

Nonetheless, Highway 2 is useful as an access road through the region. Narrow roads amble along the coastline close to the sea. These byways—**highways 11, 12, and 14**—are also part of the Lady Slipper Drive scenic circuit, and though the route numbers change, the symbol will guide you to awesome coastal vistas. About 50 meandering side roads also turn off

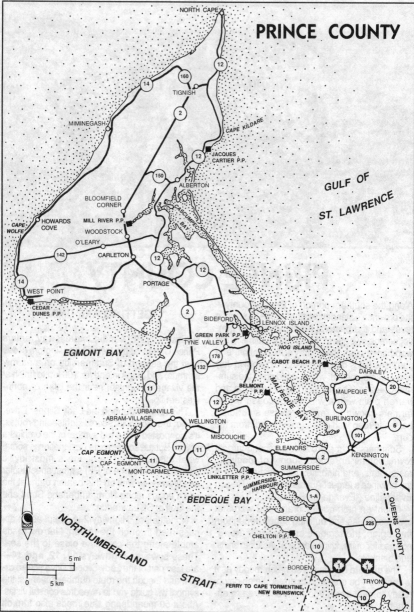

PRINCE COUNTY

GULF OF ST. LAWRENCE

NORTH CAPE

TIGNISH

MIMINEGASH

CAPE KILDARE

JACQUES CARTIER P.P.

BLOOMFIELD CORNER

ALBERTON

CAPE WOLFE

HOWARDS COVE

MILL RIVER P.P.

WOODSTOCK

O'LEARY

CARLETON

CASCUMPEC BAY

WEST POINT

CEDAR DUNES P.P.

PORTAGE

BIDEFORD

LENNOX ISLAND

GREEN PARK P.P.

TYNE VALLEY

HOG ISLAND

EGMONT BAY

CABOT BEACH P.P.

DARNLEY

BELMONT P.P.

MALPEQUE BAY

MALPEQUE

BURLINGTON

URBAINVILLE

ABRAM-VILLAGE

WELLINGTON

MISCOUCHE

ST. ELEANORS

KENSINGTON

CAP EGMONT

CAP-EGMONT

MONT-CARMEL

LINKLETTER P.P.

SUMMERSIDE

SUMMERSIDE HARBOUR

BEDEQUE BAY

BEDEQUE

CHELTON P.P.

QUEENS COUNTY

NORTHUMBERLAND

BORDEN

TRYON

STRAIT

FERRY TO CAPE TORMENTINE, NEW BRUNSWICK

© MOON PUBLICATIONS, INC.

0   5 mi
0   5 km

Highway 2 and connect with other secondary paved and clay roads. You may become temporarily lost on the roads, but not for long—the blue sea invariably looms around the next bend.

EASTERN PRINCE COUNTY

KENSINGTON AND VICINITY

Kensington lies at the intersection of six highways, including the trans-island Hwy. 2. It's a small place, but with a couple of interesting attractions nonetheless.

The **Veterans' Memorial Military Museum** on Hwy. 2 in the town's center traces islander military service from the Boer War to the Korean War, with uniforms, weapons, photographs, and other exhibits. It's open July to mid-Sept., Mon.-Sat. 10 a.m.-6 p.m.; free admission.

The early August **Step-dancing Festival/ P.E.I. Fiddlers in Concert,** held at the Community Gardens Arena Complex, makes for a fun weekend. Call (902) 836-3209 for details.

Green Valley Cottages and Bed & Breakfast is about five km north of town on Hwy. 102, surrounded by birch-studded farmland. Six cottages rent for $58-78 for up to four guests; two rooms in the main house run $42 d with light breakfast. The inn is open mid-May to Sept.; tel. 836-5667. Six-room **Victoria Inn,** tel. 836-3010, P.O. Box 717, Kensington, PE C0B 1M0, is located at 32 Victoria St. East, with nearby dining and beaches. The inn is open 1 June-15 September. Rates are $40-50. Open April - Nov., **Pickering's Guest Home,** tel. 836-3441, is located at 4 Russell St., off Hwy. 6, P.O. Box 71, Kensington, PE C0B 1M0. Some rooms have private kitchens, and the inn has dining. Nightly rate is $20.

The former Kensington train station houses the local **visitor information center.** Also at the depot, the **farmers' market** is a good place to come for fresh produce, baked goods, snacks, and crafts; it's open July-Sept., Sat. 10 a.m.-2 p.m. Rarely publicized but locally popular lobster suppers ($15) are the draw at the **Kensington Recreation Centre** at 21 School St., year-round, weekdays 11 a.m.-early evening.

Burlington
Woodleigh on Hwy. 234, tel. (902) 836-3401, is a sort of lilliputian Disneyland for Anglophiles. It was the creation of E.W. Johnstone, a retired WW I colonel, who made it his life's obsession to re-create on Prince Edward Island some two dozen British buildings with historical or literary significance—buildings that had impressed him during his service in Britain. His magnificently crafted, minutely detailed, scaled-down reproductions of British Isles landmarks include Dunvegan Castle, the Tower of London, St. Paul's Cathedral, Robbie Burns's cottage, Shakespeare's birthplace, and other sites, displayed on lovingly landscaped grounds. Johnstone was in his eighties and still at work on his chef d'oeuvre at the time of his death in 1984.

Woodleigh is open daily at 9 a.m. (variable closing times) late May to mid-October. Adult admission is $7.35, children 6-15 $4.10. In July and August, traditional Celtic and Acadian concerts are presented outdoors on the green.

SUMMERSIDE

Summerside (pop. 10,000) is PEI's major shipping port. It's got all of the bustle, yet none of the seaminess, usually associated with seaports. Here you'll find stately old homes with wide lawns, and quiet streets edged with verdant canopies. The town provides a plentiful mix of lodgings, dining places, and night spots—a rare combination on PEI outside of Charlottetown.

History
Summerside began in 1800 as Green's Shore, named after the tract's owner. By 1840, the settlement had an inn, the new name of Summerside, and a shipbuilding yard at the harbor. Its role as an important port began with rail service in the 1870s; potatoes from O'Leary were among the first exports. During WW II, a military installation was built on the outskirts of town and became a major contributor to the local economy. To everyone's chagrin, the base

closed in the late 1980s. A growing tourism industry is helping to fill the gap left by the closure.

Sights

The tourist's Summerside lies along Water St., Harbour Drive, and the first few blocks back from the harbor. This downtown area holds the port's most exemplary historic buildings, such as the Gothic-styled **Town Hall** at Fitzroy and Summer streets. Like Charlottetown, Summerside has revitalized parts of its harborfront, notably at Spinnakers' Landing, a complex of tourist shops and wharves begun several years ago when the military base was phased out. Most shops

stock a free pamphlet detailing a self-guided **walking tour.**

Taking its name from the Micmac Indian word for "hot spot," the modern **Eptek National Exhibition Centre and PEI Sports Hall of Fame,** at harborfront, tel. (902) 888-8373, has a spacious main gallery hosting national fine arts and historical exhibits. Memorabilia from the island's sporting history is housed in an adjacent hall. The center is open year-round, Tues.-Sun.; hours vary with the season. Admission is $2, children under 12 free.

Fox farming began on the island in 1894 and soon grew into big business, accounting for

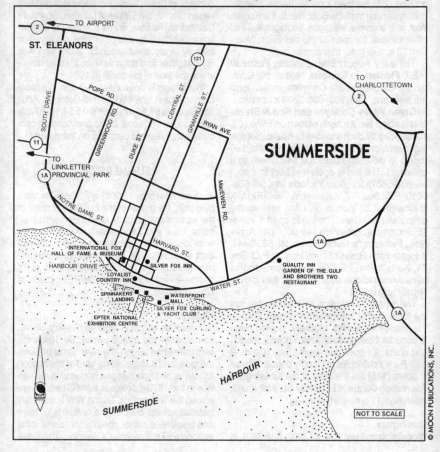

EASTERN PRINCE COUNTY 295

the Silver Fox

nearly one-fifth of the provincial economy within a couple of decades. In 1911, Frank Tuplin, one of the first to commercialize the industry, traded a breeding pair of silver foxes for a luxurious new home; by 1920, when the fashion for fur was in its heyday, a pair of prime silver foxes could fetch $35,000. The **International Fox Hall of Fame and Museum,** 286 Fitzroy St., tel. 436-2400, explains the region's heady fox boom and the methods of raising and pelting the animals. It's open May-Sept., Mon.-Sat. 8 a.m.-4 p.m.; adults $1, children under 12 free.

Accommodations
The closest campground to Summerside is **Linkletter Provincial Park,** about eight km west of town on Hwy. 11, tel. (902) 888-8366. The 72-acre campground, on a bayside beach, has 84 serviced and unserviced sites, $13-16. It's open mid-June to early September; the mailing address is Parks Division West, Woodstock, O'Leary RR3, PE C0B 1V0. **Rayner's Park,** tel. 436-4984, RR 2, Summerside, PE C1N 4J8, is on Hwy. 180 at Webber Cove in Lower New Annan. Leashed pets are okay. The park offers a laundromat, recreation hall, store, and washroom. Rates are $12-15.

Beladen Farm Tourist Home, tel. 436-6612, RR 2, Summerside, PE C1N 4J8, off Hwy. 2 on Dekker Rd., has a quiet country setting on a beef farm and offers TV and dining. The rate is $25. **Birchvale Farm Bed and Breakfast,** tel. 436-3803 or 888-7331, RR 4, Summerside, PE

C1N 4J9, is three km off Hwy. 1A on Hwy. 120, between 1A and 107 in Wilmot Valley. It's located on a farm and there is trout fishing nearby. No pets please. Rates are $26-30. **The Arbor Inn,** tel. 436-6847, 380 MacEwen Rd., Summerside, PE C1N 4X8, has suites, a jacuzzi room, and TV; playpens are available. Smoking is not allowed. Rates are $35-60. **Summerside Inn,** tel. 436-5208, 98 Summer St., Summerside, PE C1N 3J2, is close to downtown in a 100-year-old home with private baths. No smoking please. Rates are $40-55.

With dining nearby, **Baker's Lighthouse Motel,** tel. 436-2992, 802 Water St., Wilmot, PE C1N 4J6, is on Hwy. 11, two minutes east of Summerside. The units have refrigerators, and a laundromat is on site. Rates are $38-49. **Keddy's Linkletter Inn and Convention Centre,** tel. 436-2157, 311 Market St., Summerside, PE C1N 1K8, is centrally located, has TV, phones, kitchenettes, restaurant, a/c, and amenities for the physically challenged. Small pets are allowed. Rates are $65-135.

The **Mulberry Motel,** 6 Water St. East, tel. 436-2520, is a good budget-moderate choice that's centrally located. Motel rooms and housekeeping units run $38-50, while its housekeeping units at Shelton Beach are $50-55.

Travellers Inn on Hwy. 2 at St. Eleanors on Summerside's outskirts, tel. 436-9100 or (800) 361-7829, is one of the Auberge Wandlyn Inn properties and has better-than-average motel trappings with 24 rooms and 16 housekeeping units ($60-107 d), an indoor heated pool, hot tub, and pleasant atmosphere. The motel's **restaurant** serves basic beef and seafood dishes ($8-20).

Silver Fox Inn, 61 Granville St., tel. 436-4033, reigns locally as one of the seaport's "fox houses," built with a silver fox fortune and designed by architect William Critchlow Harris. The comfortable inn has six rooms furnished with antiques ($60-75 with a light breakfast).

Quality Inn Garden of the Gulf, 618 Water St. East, tel. 436-2295, has 84 rooms ($69-89) and a coffee shop. **Best Western Linkletter Inn,** 311 Market St., tel. 436-2157, is another motel variation with 108 rooms ($83-104) and a lounge, restaurant, and coffee shop.

The **Loyalist Country Inn** at 195 Harbour Drive, tel. 436-3333 or (800) 361-2668, faces Spinnakers' Landing. Part of the Rodd Hotel group, the inn has 42 spacious, sunny rooms ($69-104), a lounge, tennis court, and outside patio. Ten of the rooms have whirlpools. The inn's **Prince William Room** dining room offers specials like lobster crepes and poached salmon drenched with lobster sauce ($8-20); reservations are required.

Food

The Little Mermaid, on the waterfront at 240 Harbour Dr., tel. (902) 436-8722, proudly declares that it's operated by a fishing family. Seafood is the specialty. Prices on lobster, Malpeque oysters, and fish are reasonable, though most everything is fried. It's open for lunch and dinner April-October.

Brothers Two Restaurant on Water St. East, tel. 436-9654, is a local favorite for entrees ($8-17) such as hip of beef and sautéed scallops in white wine sauce. The restaurant has been a social hub for decades. The **Regent Restaurant,** ensconced within the former Regent Theatre at 12 Summer St., tel. 436-3200, is strong on basic red meats and seafood ($8-18).

Ming's on Water St. East, tel. 436-3838, sets an all-you-can-eat buffet; and Chinese is also the specialty at **King Wok,** on Water St. at Central, tel. 436-6333. The Silver Fox Curling and Yacht Club's **Beacon Lounge** at 110 Water St., tel. 436-2153, serves lunch 11:30 a.m.-2 p.m. and has good sea views.

For picnic fixings, check out **Best Buys** at 601

Water St. East; **Corner Grocery** at 399 Second St., open Mon.-Wed., Sat. 8 a.m.-6 p.m., Thurs.-Fri. to 9 p.m.; or **Green Gables Food Store** at 181 Granville St., open daily 6 a.m.-1 a.m. There's a large **IGA** grocery store on Harbour Dr., and **Lo-Food** is on Water St. downtown.

Entertainment

Capitol Twin Cinema at 9 Central Ave. has nightly movies; for the current flick list, call (902) 436-2614. **Starlight Drive In** on Water St. East shows current films, June to mid-Sept., Thurs.-Sunday.

Summerside has a fairly lively night scene. **Shaker's,** at 250 Water St., revels in rock 'n' roll and country music. The **Regent Lounge** at 12 Summer St. is the nightlife component of the restaurant of the same name, and has a disc jockey, strobes, videos, and an occasional live band. The **Legend Sport Bar** at the same address is quieter and its satellite-dish TV pulls in major televised sports events.

For a tamer evening drink, check out the **Green Lantern Pub** at Gentleman Jim, 480 Granville St., or the Loyalist Country Inn's **Crown and Anchor Tavern** at 195 Harbour Drive.

Acadians socialize at the **Club Social Français** at 222 First St.; it's a bar and lounge with entertainment, open Mon.-Sat. 11 a.m.-1 a.m., Sun. 4 p.m.-midnight.

The **College of Piping and Celtic Performing Arts,** 619 Water St. East, tel. 436-5377, affiliated with Scotland's College of Piping in Glasgow, presents a Highland summer concert series featuring pipers, stepdancers, fiddlers, and singers in its Ceilidh Cafe. The program, called "Come to the Ceilidh," takes place Thursday at 7 p.m. June-August. The college also offers short-term summer classes (about $20 hour) in Highland dancing, piping, and drumming. For details, call, or write to the Registrar at 619 Water St., Summerside, PE C1N 4H8.

A local thespian troupe known as **Feast Productions** stages comedy/musical spoofs hilarious enough to lure an audience from Charlottetown. The dinner theater shows ($27) are held at the Two Brothers Restaurant on Water St. East, late June to early Sept., Mon.-Sat. at 6:30 p.m. Dinner choices include salmon, chicken, or roast beef with fixings; reservations are required, call 436-7674.

In summer, **Spinnakers' Landing** at the waterfront puts on music and dance at its outdoor stage daily, and sponsors a harbor cruise; call 436-2246 for details.

Events
The two-day **Antiques & Crafts Sale** kicks off the summer season in late June at the Silver Fox Curling and Yacht Club. The **Lobster Carnival** in mid-July attracts islanders from across the province for a week of lobster suppers, livestock exhibitions, competitions, and entertainment, including a parade and a midway.

During mid-August, the yacht club hosts the **Players International Grand Prix Hydroplane Regatta** for two days, and the month finishes with the three-day **Atlantic Senior Open Golf Tournament** at the Summerside Golf and Country Club.

Recreation
Summerside Golf and Country Club off Hwy. 11 a few kilometers west at Linkletter, tel. (902) 436-2505, is among PEI's finest championship terrains with 18 holes across 5,705 meters overlooking the strait. Facilities include a clubhouse, a pro shop, and a lounge overlooking the 18th hole; call for reservations and tee-off times.

Summerside Raceway, at 477 Notre Dame St., tel. 436-7221, is a scaled-down version of Charlottetown Driving Park's harness-racing facilities—the races are just as intense but fewer in number. It's open May-Nov., with a race once a week over most of the season and nightly during the July Lobster Carnival. Admission is $1.

Linkletter Provincial Park offers sheltered **swimming;** free day use. **Travellers Inn** on Hwy. 2 has an indoor heated pool open 7 a.m.-10 p.m. ($5 for a day-use pass).

Shopping
At harborside Spinnakers' Landing, **Great Northern Merchants** serves as the Great Northern Knitters outlet with a line of bulky, warm sweaters. The store also stocks other provincial crafts and is open mid-June to Sept., Mon.-Sat. 9:30 a.m.-9:30 p.m., Sun. from 11 a.m. **Island Flower Farm Company Store,** tel. (902) 436-4104, occupies another shop in the complex and sells wreaths and flower arrangements made from island flowers.

Old Stanley Schoolhouse, a branch of JoAnne Schurman's well-known crafts shop at Stanley Bridge, stocks noteworthy quilts, pottery, pewter, sweaters, apparel, and folk art at the Loyalist Country Inn, 195 Harbour Drive. It's open daily 9:30 a.m.-6 p.m. **Eagle Feather Gallery,** on Hwy. 2 on Summerside's outskirts, tel. 436-5657, carries Micmac crafts—baskets, clay pottery, stone sculpture, paintings, dolls, and apparel—made at Lennox Island's Micmac reservation. Open mid-June to mid-Sept., 9:30 a.m.-5:30 p.m.

At **Village Craft House,** a five-minute drive from Summerside on Hwy. 1A at North Bedeque, tel. 887-2416, they make the fetching cloth Anne doll that's sold at the Confederation Centre of the Arts' gift shop in Charlottetown, and also stock exquisite handmade quilts. They're open May to mid-Oct., Mon.-Thurs. 10 a.m.-4:30 p.m. (Fri.-Sat. also in July and Aug.).

Zeller's department store is at the Waterfront Mall, and **Metropolitan Store** is in the Summerside Mall on Harbour Dr.; open Mon.-Wed. and Sat. 9:30 a.m.-6 p.m., Thurs.-Fri. to 9 p.m. **Sears Photography,** 243 Water St., tel. 436-6600, handles basic camera needs and stocks film and brand-name equipment.

For current books and island sightseeing plus historical coverage, look into **Coles The Book People** at 475 Granville St., tel. 888-2925.

The **Celtic Gift Shop,** at the College of Piping, 619 Water St. East, tel. 436-5377, stocks a wide selection of Celtic books and recordings, clan regalia, and island crafts. It's open June-September.

Information
The **Lady Slipper Visitor Information Centre,** on Hwy. 1A at Wilmot between Summerside and North Bedeque, tel. (902) 436-2511, answers questions and stocks free sightseeing literature on Summerside and the province. It's open early June to early Oct., 9 a.m.-6 p.m. (to 9 p.m. July-early Sept.).

Nautical maps ($12) are sold at the office of Lorne Driscoll at 355 Water St., tel. 436-2208; open Mon.-Fri. 9 a.m.-5 p.m. Land Registration Information System at 120 Water St. handles **topographical maps** and is open weekdays 8 a.m.-4 p.m.

The **Rotary Regional Library,** on Water St. near Spinnakers' Landing, is open weekdays 10 a.m.-5 p.m. The county's news is covered by the daily *Journal-Pioneer* and the weekly *La Voix Acadienne.*

Services

Prince County Hospital is at 259 Beattie Ave., tel. (902) 436-9131. The **RCMP** is at 337 Central St., tel. 436-9244.

Summerside serves as the county's financial center, with branches of **Bank of Nova Scotia, CIBC, National Bank of Canada, Royal Bank,** and **Toronto-Dominion Bank** centrally located and open Mon.-Wed. and Sat. 10 a.m.-4 p.m., Thurs.-Fri. to 6 p.m.

Bernard's Quick Mart, 126 Bayview Dr. off Hwy. 11, is one of several launderettes in town; open daily 7 a.m.-9 p.m.

Transportation

Prince Edward Air, tel. (800) 565-5359, flies between Summerside and Halifax. Summerside's airport, Slemon Park, is about 10 km north of town on Hwy. 2. **Courtesy Cab** at 15 Spring St., tel. (902) 436-4232, is one of several taxi outfits; expect to pay about $10 one-way for a taxi ride to or from the airport. **Silver Fox Curling and Yacht Club** has marina space for visiting boats and charges 50 cents per boat-foot; for details, call 436-2153.

AROUND MALPEQUE BAY

Sheltered from the open gulf by the long, narrow sandbar of Hog Island, the shallow waters of broad Malpeque Bay are tranquil and unpolluted. The bay's long, fretted coastline is deserted, nearly bereft of development apart from three small provincial parks. Conditions are perfect for the large oyster fishery that thrives here. Ten million Malpeque oysters—Canada's largest source of the shellfish—are harvested each year. The purity of the bay water in part accounts for the excellent flavor of the oysters, which has made them famed worldwide as a gustatory treat. You'll find them served in a variety of ways at restaurants in the region.

Cabot Beach Provincial Park

This provincial park, near the end of Hwy. 20, tel. (902) 836-5635 or 859-8790 (winter), occupies a gorgeous setting on a peninsula tip just inside Malpeque Bay. Facilities include 90 unserviced campsites ($12.50), 20 two-way hookup sites ($15.75), 20 three-way hookup sites ($16.25), a supervised ocean beach, launderette, kitchen shelters, and a nearby campers' store. The park is open mid-June to early September. Write for more information to Parks Division West, Woodstock, O'Leary RR3, PE C0B 1V0.

Cabot Reach on Hwy. 105 nearby, tel. 836-5597, is an unassuming roadside restaurant that gets ongoing rave reviews for Malpeque

oyster chowders and platters ($7-13); open June-September.

Malpeque

At turn-of-the-century **Malpeque Bed and Breakfast,** Hwy. 20, tel. (902) 836-5359, rates are a reasonable $40 d, or $45 d for the housekeeping cottage. **Malpeque Gardens** on Hwy. 20 began as an islander's gardening hobby and expanded to include numerous varieties of dahlia, begonia, and rose in gardens arranged among different *Anne of Green Gables* themes. The gardens are open late June to mid-Oct., daily 9 a.m.-5 p.m.; adults $4, children under 14 $2.

North Shore Pottery, Hwy. 20, tel. 836-4195, sells pottery, sculpture and decorative art pieces in "ironware," an island clay dug and named by potter-owner Friedrich Hermann for its distinctive black iron appearance. It's open mid-June to mid-Sept., daily 10 a.m.-6 p.m.

TYNE VALLEY

Quiet and bucolic, the crossroads hamlet of Tyne Valley (pop. 200), at the intersection of backcountry Highways 12, 178, and 167, lies two hours from Charlottetown, 45 minutes from Summerside, and uncountable kilometers from the rest of the modern world.

In the 1800s, Tyne Valley began as a Green Park suburb. Two generations of the Yeo family dominated the island's economy with their shipbuilding yards on Malpeque Bay, and the empire begun by James Yeo—the feisty, entrepreneurial English merchant who arrived in the 1830s—spawned the next generation's landed gentry.

The empire's riches are gone, but the lovely landscape remains, like a slice of Lucy Maud Montgomery's utopian Avonlea, transplanted from Cavendish to this corner of Prince County. To get there, follow Hwy. 12 around Malpeque Bay, or, from Hwy. 2, turn east on Hwy. 132 or 133. The paved and red-clay roads ripple across the farmlands like velvet ribbons on plump quilts.

The quiet village stirs to life once a year with the **Oyster Festival,** a multiday tribute to Malpeque oysters. Daytime oyster-farming exhibits and evening fried-oyster and boiled-lobster dinners are on the menu during early August.

Shopping

Tyne Valley is also known for handmade sweaters, and you'll find none better than Lesley Dubey's original Shoreline designs sold at **Tyne Valley Studio** on Hwy. 12, tel. (902) 831-2950 (open July-Aug., daily 9:30 a.m.-5 p.m.); and **Earlene's Knits,** also on Hwy. 12, tel. 831-3092 (open July-early Sept., daily 10 a.m.-7 p.m., after Labour Day to June, daily 11 a.m.-5 p.m.)

Accommodations

Doctor's Inn on Hwy. 167, Tyne Valley, tel. (902) 831-2164, belonged to the village doctor during the shipbuilding era, and the inn's luster still sparkles, polished by innkeepers Jean and Paul Offer. The Offers are also organic produce farmers, and during the mid-May to Sept. growing season, they conduct garden tours Tues.-Fri. at 1 p.m. Let them know you're coming 24 hours in advance.

The inn has a formal front entrance, but everyone arrives at the side kitchen door and enters the busy kitchen fray, as the Offers process, can, and preserve the backyard's produce. Beyond the door to the dining room, the inn's interior gleams with antiques. Dinner is served on request ($35 with wine) in the elegant, spacious dining room. Upstairs are two guest rooms ($40 with breakfast); reservations are wise.

Tyne Valley Inn on Hwy. 12, tel. 831-2042 or 831-2768, dates to the early 1900s and has six guest rooms ($50-75 with a light breakfast) and a dining room. It's open May-October.

VICINITY OF TYNE VALLEY

Port Hill

In Port Hill, three km east of Tyne Valley, **Yeo House** sits back on a sweep of verdant lawn. It's a gorgeous estate, fronted by a fence that rims the curving road. Inside, the rooms are furnished with period antiques. Up four flights of stairs, the cupola—from which James Yeo would survey his shipyard—overlooks the grounds and sparkling Malpeque Bay. The house is open mid-June to early Sept., daily 9 a.m.-5 p.m.; admission $2.50.

Behind the house, the **Green Park Shipbuilding Museum,** tel. (902) 831-2206, has exhibits explaining the history and methods of wooden shipbuilding, Prince Edward Island's main industry in the 19th century. The shipyard features a partially finished vessel cradled on a frame plus historic shipbuilding equipment.

Beautiful **Green Park Provincial Park** is within walking distance of Port Hill on an unmarked road that finishes at the Shipbuilding Museum. Malpeque Bay embraces the peninsula-bound park, and a three-km **hiking trail** brings you as deep into the bay as you can go without getting your feet soaking wet. (Wear sneakers anyway, and bring insect repellent; mosquitoes flourish in the marsh pools.) The trail starts among white birches, short and stunted due to the bay's winter winds and salt. Beyond there, the path wends through hardwood groves, brightened with ground cover of pink wild roses, bayberries, and goldenrod. Eventually, the trail gives way to marshes at the peninsula's tip. The small inland ponds at the bay's edge are all that remain of a local effort to start oyster aquaculture decades ago. Marsh hay and wild grasses bend with the sea winds. Minnows streak in tidal pools, and razor clams exude streams of continuous bubbles from their invisible burrows beneath the soggy sand.

A small **campground** fronts the bay beneath tree canopies on a sheltered coastal notch. It offers 18 unserviced and 19 two-way hookup sites ($13-17), with a launderette, kitchen shelters, hot showers, Frisbee golf, a river beach, and nature programs. It's open late June to early Sept.; for details, call (902) 831-2370.

Original Senator's House Inn, on Hwy. 12 in Port Hill, tel. 831-2071, was the home of second-generation Senator John Yeo, the provincial politician. The restored inn is among PEI's prized historic lodgings and features four rooms ($45-90 with a light breakfast) and a dining room, all glittering with polished antiques and open mid-June to mid-September.

Bideford

You'll find the modest **Ellerslie Shellfish Museum** at the end of a red-clay road off Hwy. 166 about 10 minutes from Tyne Valley, tel. 831-2934. Everything you could ever want to know about oysters and mussels is explained. A small aquarium contains mollusks, lobsters, snails, and inshore fish; outside, experimental farming methods are underway in the bay. Admission is $1.50 adults, 75 cents children under

12. The museum is open late June to early Sept., Sun.-Fri. 10 a.m.-4 p.m.

Lennox Island

A causeway off Hwy. 163 brings you to the **Lennox Island Micmac Nation,** a quiet community of 175 residents intent on cultivating oysters, spearing eels, trapping, and hunting, while pursuing recognition of their 18th-century treaties with England which entitled them to their land.

The province's Micmacs are said to have been the first Native Canadians converted to Christianity. The 1895 **St. Anne's Roman Catholic Church,** a sacred tribute to their patron saint, grips the island's coastline and faces the sea.

The nearby museum has paintings and artifacts; a crafts shop just north of the church markets Micmac baskets, silver jewelry, pottery, and other wares. The crafts shop is open year-round. The church and museum are open daily 1 July to 28 Aug.; the rest of the year call (902) 831-2653 for hours.

RÉGION ÉVANGÉLINE

The bilingual inhabitants of the Région Évangéline, the province's largest Acadian area, date their ancestry to France's earliest settlement efforts. The region offers French-flavored culture at more than a dozen villages spread between Hwy. 2 and the strait seacoast. Miscouche, the commercial center, is a 10-minute drive west of Summerside on Hwy. 2; 30 minutes from the seaport along the coastal Hwy. 11 is Mont-Carmel, the region's seaside social and tourist hub.

MISCOUCHE

As you approach from the east, the high double spires of St. John the Baptist Church announce from miles away that you've left Protestant, Anglo Prince Edward Island behind and are arriving in Catholic territory.

The village of 800 inhabitants at the intersection of Hwys. 2 and 12 began with French farmers from Port la Joye in the 1720s, augmented with Acadians who fled England's Acadian Deportation in 1755. The settlement commands a major historical niche among Atlantic

Canada's Acadian communities and was the site of the 1884 Acadian Convention, which adopted the French tricolor flag with the single gold star symbolizing Mary.

The **Musée Acadien de L'Î.P.É.** (Acadian Museum of P.E.I.) on Hwy. 2, tel. (902) 436-6237, is geared as a genealogical resource center and also has exhibits of early photographs, papers, and artifacts, and a book corner (mainly in French) with volumes about Acadian history and culture since 1720. Admission is $2.75 adults, children under six free. It's open year-round Mon.-Fri. 9:30 a.m.-5 p.m.; also open Sat. and Sun. 1-5 p.m. from mid-June to early September.

MONT-CARMEL

Two km south of Miscouche, the backcountry Hwy. 12 meets the coastal Hwy. 11 (Lady Slipper Drive), which lopes south and west across Acadian farmlands to this hamlet, best known for Le Village, a complex of lodgings with a restaurant. Mont-Carmel makes a handy sightseeing base for touring the Région Évangéline.

Sights

Facing the sea, **Le Village Pionnier Acadien** (Pioneer Acadian Village) on Hwy. 11, tel. (902) 854-2227 or (800) 567-3228, is a rustic re-creation of an early 19th-century Acadian settlement with a school, church, blacksmith shop, store, and houses. The complex also includes accommodations and fine dining and offers a variety of entertainment, including dinner theater (described below). It's open mid-June to mid-Sept., daily 9:30 a.m.-7 p.m.; adults $3, children 6-17 $1.50.

Our Lady of Mont-Carmel Acadian Church on Hwy. 11 reflects the cathedral style of France's Poitou region, where the French settlers originated. The cathedral is open Sunday during Mass. For permission to enter at other times, ask at the **Musée Religieux** (Religious Museum) across the road, tel. 854-2260; open July-Aug., daily 1-5 p.m.

Accommodations

Within the Acadian Village complex, the **Motel du Village,** tel. (902) 854-2227, offers good value with 20 rooms ranging $72-78 d, some with kitchenettes; open May-October. **Auberge du Village,** also tel. 854-2227, is the complex's upscale lodging. Its design is contemporary and many of its 30 rooms ($79-89) front the strait; open mid-May to mid-October.

Outside Acadian Village, privately operated **Cormiers' Cottages** on Hwy. 11, tel. 854-2262, overlooks the sea with a dozen two- and three-bedroom housekeeping cottages ($70-90 for four guests) and has a launderette and a grocery store on the grounds; open June-September.

Food

Le Village's **Étoile de Mer** restaurant, tel. (902) 854-2227, gets rave reviews for Acadian dishes ($5-12), especially the *rapûre*—luscious potato pie brimming with chicken chunks; open mid-May to early October. **La Cuisine à Mémé,** the complex's **dinner theater** with a comedy in French and English, includes a buffet and dessert ($26). It's open July-Aug., Tues.-Sat.; reservations are required.

The red, white, and blue Acadian flag is a symbol of pride in Acadian regions.

BOB RACE

Shopping

Artisanat du Village (Village Craft Shop), tel. (902) 854-3208, is an area outlet of locally created crafts and features quilts, hooked mats, and apparel; open mid-June to mid-Sept., daily 9 a.m.-7 p.m.

OTHER ACADIAN SETTLEMENTS

Cap-Egmont

Another Prince Edward Island oddity are the **Bottle Houses,** on Hwy. 11 overlooking the strait, tel. (902) 854-2987. They are the work of Edouard Arsenault who, in the 1970s, mortared together 25,000 glass bottles of all colors, shapes, and sizes to form three astonishing buildings—a chapel with altar and pews, a tavern, and a six-gabled house. The structures qualified for inclusion in *Ripley's Believe It or Not.* The admission of $3.25 adults, $1 children 6-16, allows you to roam the buildings and gardens. The site is open daily mid-June to late Sept., 10 a.m.-6 p.m.

Camping au clair d'la lune (Moonlight Camping), Hwy. 11, tel. 854-2746, provides a rare opportunity to camp in the Acadian area; the campground offers 50 unserviced campsites and another 50 three-way hookup sites ($10-12) with hot showers, a campers' store, launderette, and playground; open late May to mid-September.

Abram-Village

From Cap-Egmont, the scenic coastal Hwy. 11 wends north for 10 km and turns inland to this hamlet known for crafts. **Le Centre d'Artisanat** d'Abram Village (Abram's Village Handcraft Co-op), at the intersection of Hwys. 11 and 124, tel. (902) 854-2096, is the area's definitive crafts source. Here you'll find weavings, rugs, Acadian shirts, pottery, and dolls. It's open mid-June to mid-Sept., Mon.-Sat. 9 a.m.-6 p.m., Sun. 1-5 p.m.

Acadians festivals are centered here, too. During September's first weekend, Le Festival Acadien puts on dances, concerts, competitions, lobster suppers, and a fishing boat parade, combined with L'Exposition Agricole de Baie-Egmont et de Mont-Carmel, the area's agricultural fair.

Urbainville
PEI's famed potatoes are fashioned into potato chips at the Olde Barrel Potato Chip Co-operative on Hwy. 124; tours of the plant operate late June-Aug., Mon.-Fri. 10 a.m. For details, call (902) 854-3384.

WESTERN PRINCE COUNTY

Beyond Summerside and the Région Évangéline, Hwy. 2 cuts into the interior out of sight of the seas. Nonetheless, most backcountry roads off the main route eventually finish at the water. To the west, the Northumberland Strait is the pussycat of summer seas, and the warm surf laps peacefully along the southern and western coastlines. The Gulf of St. Lawrence, however, is more temperamental, with a welter of rolling waves breaking onto the north shore.

For sightseeing information, stop at the provincial visitor information center on Hwy. 2 at Portage near Carleton, tel. (902) 859-3215. Open late June-early Sept., daily 10 a.m.-7 p.m. And fill the tank before exploring the coastline beyond O'Leary, as gas stations are sparse.

MILL RIVER PROVINCIAL PARK

As you exit Hwy. 2 at Woodstock, you enter a wooded realm on a ribbon of a road into Mill River Provincial Park, tel. (902) 859-8786 or 859-8790 (winter). The park meshes lush landscapes with contemporary-style resort trappings and full recreation facilities, including the championship-quality Mill River Provincial Golf Course.

The park's riverfront campground has 18 unserviced and 54 two- and three-way hookup campsites ($13-17) as well as kitchen shelters, hot showers, a launderette, and nature programs. The park is open mid-June to early September. For more information write to Parks Division West, Woodstock, O'Leary RR 3, PE C0B 1V0.

The three-story Rodd Mill River Resort, tel. 859-3555, is a sleek, wood-sided hotel with 90 spacious rooms and suites ($95-110) and an indoor heated pool overlooking the woodlands. It's open May-Oct. for summer visitors and Dec.-March for winter cross-country skiers.

The resort's Hernewood Room, tel. 859-3555, boasts regionally renowned dining that draws an appreciative clientele from Summerside; expect a reasonably priced menu ($13-18) and seafood specialties with a fish-of-the-day emphasis on salmon, halibut, or lobster ($17); reservations are required during summer.

Recreation
Campers, resort guests, and day visitors all have access to the park's sports facilities. The eight tennis courts (lit for night games) beside the hotel are free (but hotel guests play first). At the campground, there's a marina with equipment for river exploring; canoes and boats rent for $4 an hour, $16 a day, and windsurfing boards are $9 per hour, $29 per half-day, or $46 per day.

The Rodd Mill River Aquaplex and Racquet Club, a one-of-a-kind recreational facility in the province, houses a pool, water slide, whirlpool, sauna, two squash courts, an exercise room with Nautilus equipment, a sun-deck, and changing rooms with lockers; open Mon.-Fri. 7 a.m.-10 p.m., Sat. from 8 a.m., Sun. 8 a.m.-9 p.m. A day-use pass costs $8 per person or $17 for a family; for details call (902) 859-3555.

The 18-hole Mill River Provincial Park Golf Course, tel. 859-2238 or 859-2448, presents golfers "one of the sternest tests," said Golf Illustrated. The greens span 5,944 meters, and are open mid-May to Oct.; during July and Aug., you'd be wise to make reservations 48 hours in advance. Greens fee is $16-20.

O'LEARY

On Prince Edward Island, O'Leary is synonymous with potatoes. Legend has it that the hamlet took its name from an Irish farmer who settled here in the 1830s. By 1872, rail service connected the hamlet with the rest of the island, and with that link in place, O'Leary was on its way to becoming Canada's largest potato producer.

O'Leary straddles backcountry Hwy. 142, a five-minute drive from Hwy. 2 and 50 minutes from Summerside. You might expect mountains of potatoes. Rather, O'Leary (pop. 900) is a tidy place, nestled in the midst of surprisingly attractive fields of low-growing potato plants. If you're in the area during the autumn harvest, you'll see the fields lit by tractor headlights, as the farmers work late at night to harvest the valuable crop before frost.

Prince Edward Island Potato Museum
The museum, at 22 Parkview Dr. (at Centennial Park, off Main St.), tel. (902) 859-2039, is a must stop for true spud fanatics. Interpretive exhibits combine local history with potato lore and agricultural methods. The museum is open mid-June to Aug., Mon.-Fri. 9 a.m.-4 p.m., Sat. 11 a.m.-4 p.m., Sun. 2-4 p.m. Admission is $2.50.

Practicalities
Expect plenty of potato recipe variations hereabouts. Potato burgers and potato "candy" bars are sold as snacks at the museum, and the **Railway Cafe** on Main St. at O'Leary's former rail depot gets rave reviews for its fluffy potato pancakes.

Shoppers like the crafts shops on nearby Hwy 2. For knitted apparel, quilts, and wooden objects, stop at the **Windmill Craft Co-op,** in red schoolhouse quarters at the crossroads hamlet of Woodstock; open July to early Sept., Mon.-Sat. 11 a.m.-5 p.m. **Natural Country Crafts** near Coleman on the highway has more of the same with an emphasis on sweaters, mittens, and baby clothing; to make sure someone is at the shop, call ahead at (902) 859-3603.

THE STRAIT COAST

Highway 14 (Lady Slipper Drive) exits the main highway at Carleton, doglegs west across the verdant farmlands, and heads to West Point at the island's western tip. From there, the scenic coastal route hugs the strait shore and brings some of the island's most magnificent sea views.

Potato fields peter out at the strait coastline, which is definitely off the beaten tourist route. The coast's long stretches of beach are interspersed with craggy red cliffs.

West Point
Cedar Dunes Provincial Park on Hwy. 14 fronts the strait at a windy beach backed by sand dunes. The small campground, tel. (902) 859-8785 or 859-8790 (winter), includes 20 unserviced campsites and another 22 two-way hookup sites ($13-16), a supervised beach, activities program, nature trail, kitchen shelters, a nearby campers' store, and hot showers. It's open late June to early September. For more information write to Parks Division West, Wood-

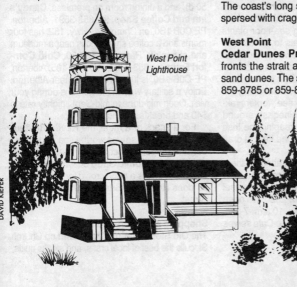

West Point
Lighthouse

DAVID KIEFER

stock, O'Leary RR3, Woodstock PE C0B 1V0.

Within the park is one-of-a-kind **West Point Lighthouse,** tel. 859-3605, a functioning Coast Guard lighthouse (in operation since 1875) that also serves as an inn. The access road runs through the park. Inside the lighthouse and the adjacent house are nine rooms ($70-110 d), a museum ($2 adults, free to overnight guests), and the former keeper's parlor, replete with historic artifacts. The museum and gift shop are open mid-May to late September. The dining room serves basic seafood and beef ($6-16) and overlooks the sea through wide windows. The **West Point Lighthouse Festival** in mid-July brings together a concert, children's activities, fishing-boat races, and a dance.

Four km north of the West Point Lighthouse, **Red Capes Inn,** tel. 859-3150, on Hwy. 14, West Cape, O'Leary RR 1, PE C0B 1V0, is near a restaurant and beaches and has a video room. The inn is open mid-May to mid-October. Rates are $37-59.

North of West Point

Beyond West Point, the scenic road cleaves to the coastline and heads north, first to **Cape Wolfe,** where British Gen. James Wolfe is said to have stepped ashore on the way to battle the French in 1759; and then to **Howards Cove,** fronted with precipitous cliffs of burnished red.

Storm winds whip the sea on this side of the island into a frenzy, churning sea-floor plants into a webbed fabric that floats to the surface and washes to shore. This seaweed, known as **Irish moss,** is used commercially as a stabilizer in ice cream and other foods. It is harvested from the sea by boat, and also from along the shore—after a storm you may see workers raking the surf's edge from Miminegash around North Cape to Cape Kildare, reaping the Irish moss and hauling it away with the help of draft horses.

In **Miminegash,** you can learn about all there is to know about Irish moss farming at the **Irish Moss Interpretive Centre,** housed in a vessel off Highway 152, tel. (902) 882-2920. It's open from late June to Sept., Mon.-Fri. 10 a.m.-7 p.m. Admission is $1. The Seaweed Pie Cafe serves light meals and has a gift shop.

ALBERTON

The seaport of Alberton (pop. 1,200) is the northern area's largest town. Named for Albert, the Prince of Wales, the town began in 1820 with 40 families who worked at the shipyards in nearby Northport. Deep-sea fishing aficionados will readily find charter boats here.

The **Alberton Museum** on Church St., tel. (902) 853-4048, ensconced within the old courthouse (a national historic site), exhibits the town's history with antiques, clothing, and farm tools, and chronicles the region's fox-farming past. It's open late June to early Sept., Mon.-Sat. 9:30 a.m.-5:30 p.m.; adults $2, students and seniors $1.

Accommodations and Food

For the flavor of an old-time house built with silver fox profits, try the **Poplar Lane Bed and Breakfast** on Poplar Lane off Main St., tel. (902) 853-3732. It's situated on grounds that were one of the island's first fox farms. Three guest rooms go for $35 a night with a light breakfast; open June to mid-September.

Travellers Inn Motel on Hwy. 12, P.O. Box 138, Alberton, PE C0B 1B0, tel. 853-2215, has 14 basic rooms and 10 housekeeping units ($40-50 d), and a dining room on premises. **Candy's Inn and Coffee Shop,** tel. 853-3591, Alberton, PE C0B 1B0, on Church St., Hwy. 152, has four rooms and a coffee shop, and is near a museum and shopping. Rates are $39.50. **Cold Comfort Farm,** tel. 853-2803, P.O. Box 105, Alberton, PE C0B 1B0, is just off Hwy. 12 near Alberton. Enjoy a solitary walk in the gardens during your visit. Open mid-June to mid-Sept., nightly rate is $40 and breakfast is included.

For a snack or a meal, the **Revilo Restaurant** on Main St. serves worthy seafood chowder and burgers concocted of scallops. **Candy's Inn and Coffee Shop** on Church St., tel. 853-3591, draws a noon crowd for sandwiches, as does **Holman's Snack Barn** at 100 Main Street.

Shopping and Recreation

The **Old Stone Station Craft Guild** on Church St. culls the best of local crafts, and stocks quilts, knitted apparel, and weavings; open July-Aug., Mon.-Sat. 10 a.m.-5 p.m.

Captain Craig Avery's vessel *Andrew's Mist,* tel. (902) 853-2307, takes anglers out to sea for deep-sea mackerel and cod fishing; adults $18, children under 12 $12 including bait and tackle. Trips depart from the wharf daily mid-June to September. Call for reservations.

TIGNISH AND VICINITY

Stories of legendary riches and the fur that created a haute-couture sensation almost a century ago embellish the lore of the remote northern peninsula. The world's first successful silver fox breeding began in the Tignish area in 1887. Charles Dalton—later knighted by the queen— was the innovator, and he joined with Robert Oulton from New Brunswick to breed the foxes. The pelts sold for thousands of dollars in fashion salons worldwide.

From 1890 to 1912, the Dalton and Oulton partnership kept a keen eye on the venture and the number of silver fox breeding pairs. As luck would have it, generosity was their downfall: their empire fell apart when one of the partners gave a pair of the breeding foxes to a relative. The cat—the fox, that is—was out of the bag. That single pair begat innumerable descendants that were sold worldwide, and breeding became an international business.

The area earned itself another major entry in national history when local fishermen organized Canada's first fishermen's union; the co-operative still processes and markets the bulk of the island's tuna. During summer, expect to see the "mossers"—Irish-moss harvesters clad in high rubber boots—in town.

Tignish (pop. 1,000) is simply laid out with Church St./Hwy. 2 as the main street. The town is 20 minutes from Alberton, a half hour from O'Leary, and 80 minutes from Summerside.

Sights
St. Simon and St. Jude Roman Catholic Church, tel. (902) 882-2488, is the town's stellar attraction, notably for its frescoes of the Apostles and its mighty pipe organ. The organ, built by Louis Mitchell of Montreal, features 1,118 pipes from six inches to 16 feet in length. It was installed in 1882, and until the 1950s, the organ was pumped by hand. The church is open daily, 8 a.m.-7 p.m.

The **Dalton Centre** on School St., tel. 882-2488, was fox baron Charles Dalton's gift to his hometown. Begun as a boys' school, the building is now a museum with a geneaology room and exhibits detailing local history. It's open mid-June to Aug., Mon.-Sat., 10 a.m.-5 p.m. Admission is $1.50.

Recreation
The town's port facilities are at the end of a clay lane at **Tignish Shore** on the gulf. **Mel's Deep-Sea Fishing,** tel. (902) 882-2983, operates three-hour deep-sea trips ($15) thrice daily; open early July-August.

Accommodations
Chaisson Homestead, tel. (902) 882-2566, 156 Chaisson Rd., Tignish, PE C0B 2B0, is located on a potato farm. Features include a beach, a restaurant, and nearby fishing. Open mid-April through Oct.; rates are $35-50. **Murphy's Tourist Home and Cottages,** tel. 882-2667, 325 Church St., Tignish, PE C0B 2B0, is on Hwy. 153. Pets are permitted. The home has cottages, dining, and a playground for younger guests; it's open 20 May-30 September. Rates are $25-45. **Island's End Inn,** tel. 882-3554, P.O. Box 88, Tignish, PE C0B 2B0, is on Hwy. 12 at Sea Cow Pond, six km north of Tignish. The inn overlooks the Gulf of St. Lawrence and has a nearby beach; open May-October. Rates are $45-60.

Food
Paul's Diner, 286 Philip St., tel. (902) 882-3287, lures locals with hamburgers, seafood platters, and homemade desserts. Quick-serve places are at **Tignish Legion Restaurant** on Phillips St., and **Village Café** at 284 Church Street.

Jacques Cartier Provincial Park
On Hwy. 12 southeast of Tignish on the gulf, tel. (902) 853-8632 or 859-8790 (winter), this provincial park occupies the site where the explorer Cartier is believed to have stepped ashore. The campground rims the gulf. It offers

a supervised ocean beach, 41 basic and serviced sites ($13-16), hot showers, a launderette, nearby campers' store, varied programs, and Frisbee golf. It's open late June to early September. For information write to Parks Division West, O'Leary RR 3, PE C0B 1V0.

North Cape

Some 20 minutes directly north of Tignish on Hwy. 12, the **Atlantic Wind Test Site** juts up from the windy plain with a federal project complex that tests and evaluates wind turbines. The visitor center, tel. (902) 882-2746, presents an audiovisual show; open July to late Aug., daily 10 a.m.-8 p.m; adults $2, students and seniors $1.

Dining is very fine at **Wind and Reef** on Hwy. 12 preceding the wind site, tel. 882-3535; the low profile roadside restaurant is among the island's best seafood places ($7-18 for a heaping platter) and overlooks the windy coastal setting; open June to mid-October.

KINGS COUNTY
INTRODUCTION

Kings County, at Prince Edward Island's eastern end, is cultivated in farms of corn, berries, grains, potatoes, and tobacco, and is rimmed on the north by forests and tracts of provincial woodlot plantations. The long northern coast is nearly straight and uninterrupted, except at large St. Peter's Bay and smaller Savage and North Lake harbors. The northern area is remote, lightly populated and developed, and, inland, thickly wooded. As any islander will tell you, the county's northern portion is "far out," i.e., far out of sight and out of mind from mainstream PEI and a world away from the tourist circuit.

The more heavily touristed eastern shore, by contrast, is tattered with little offshore islands and dozens of deeply indented bays and river estuaries. The region's southern climate is warm, humid, and almost tropical; islanders refer to this part of Kings County as PEI's "banana belt," and such crops as tobacco thrive here.

Sightseeing Highlights
Kings County is quiet compared to Queens

County. It has none of the hype of Cavendish, and its activities and sights are more limited. But the pastoral countryside is beautiful. If you're looking for sightseeing and recreation combined with naturalist attractions—coastal windswept peninsula beaches, sand dunes, and inland, an improbable herd of provincial bison—you'll find that and more in Kings County.

The region appeals to eclectic interests. Hikers like the provincial woodlot plantations with self-guided trails. Sightseers go for seal-watching cruises at seaports along the Northumberland Strait coastline. Anglers intent on catching trophy bluefin tuna head for the county's northeastern tip, where the strait meets the Gulf of St. Lawrence in a turbulent clash of seas. Golfers tee off at the championship Brudenell River Provincial Golf Course at Roseneath, or combine the game with scenery at Sea Cove Golf Course alongside Murray Harbour, where seals on offshore rocky islands share the day.

Gorgeous pastoral interior (especially in the southern area) notwithstanding, the sightseers' circuit lies along the county's sea-rimmed perimeter. This chapter divides the county into northern and southern halves, with Cardigan at roughly the midpoint.

HISTORY

Early Settlements

Unaware of the benevolent climate in the region's southern area, early French settlers from Port la Joye made their way up the Hillsborough River to the Souris area's inhospitable wilderness by 1724. Conditions were wretched. Plagues of field mice ravaged the fields and Souris village through the 1750s. Though the infestations eventually petered out, a reputation for rodents followed the seaport through the centuries, and gave the village its name; *souris* is French for "mouse."

Another early French settlement was centered at Trois Rivières, between what is now Montague and Georgetown. The French merchant John-Pierre de Roma saw the potential for an Acadian village with bridges, wharves, and houses. De Roma was able to realize his ambitious scheme, but a party of New England raiders leveled the place in 1745.

Growing Economy

Souris welcomed the Scots in 1772 and Irish immigrants in the early 1800s. The town soon emerged as an island shipbuilding center and re-

tained the role until the Great Age of Sail ended in the late 19th century. Simultaneously, canning as a method of preserving food developed as a seaport specialty, and for decades islanders stuffed lobster ad infinitum into cans for international export.

The seaport always held a prominent role in island life. Indeed, it was the port's reputation as an economic kingpin, as well as the Souris area's seacoast carved with attractive bays, that lured playwright Elmer Harris and his arts colony to Bay Fortune in the 1880s, and American actor Charles Flockton and a similar enclave to nearby Abell's Cove.

The naming of Georgetown was surveyor Samuel Holland's tribute to George III of England. The port boasted one of the island's most perfectly created deep-water harbors. Its early economy was built with British money, however, and when England's economy had a short-lived collapse, Georgetown lost its economic edge and never regained it. Georgetown slid into the shadows, replaced by Montague, first as a shipbuilding and shipping center and then as the area's principal market town.

TRANSPORTATION

From Charlottetown, getting into the county is efficiently quick. The provincial road system lies across the region's interior like a fork with the tines splayed out to the different parts.

Basin Head Fisheries Museum

BOB RACE

The TransCanada/Hwy. 1 leaves the capital heading east and connects with fast-moving Hwy. 3, the main access route into the county's interior, at Cherry Valley. From there, Hwy. 3 lopes across the countryside to Pooles Corner, the highway circuit hub, and on to Georgetown on the strait. Alternatively, stay on Hwy. 1 around the south coast to Wood Islands, where the coastal road becomes Hwy. 4, then Hwy. 18 to Murray Harbour, then Hwy. 17 to Montague, the southern area's main market town.

Highway 4's north-south route zips from Murray River to Souris, 81 km from the capital. Souris is also the departure point for the ferry to Québec's Îles-de-la-Madeleine. Narrower Hwy. 313 splays northwest off Hwy. 4 above Pooles Corner and routes traffic to St. Peters near the gulf coast. Highway 2 is the county's major access road to the north coast; it runs from Charlottetown to Souris, and intersects Hwy. 4 at St. Peters.

It's helpful to study a highway map before getting off the main roads onto the county's rambling network of paved and unpaved roads. The pace is slow on the scenic, backcountry roads that link the county's 100-plus, out-of-the-way hamlets.

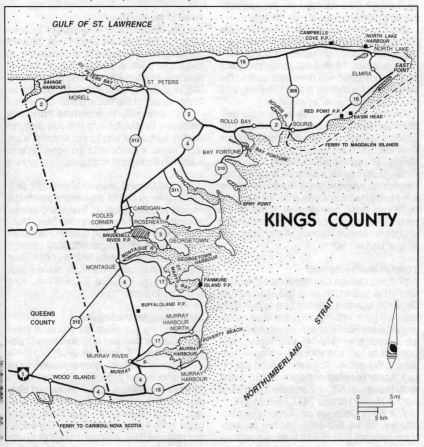

SOUTHERN KINGS COUNTY

AROUND MURRAY HARBOUR

Beyond Wood Islands, the 350-km-long Kings Byway Drive (signposted with the symbol of a purple crown) winds up the coast on its way north, changing route numbers innumerable times. The narrow seacoast road is scenic, with farmlands laid out on the intensely red earth on one side, and the sea and sapphire-blue sky on the other. On a clear day, you can see Nova Scotia's northern coast across the strait.

You'll pass through remote hamlets like Little Sands and White Sands, marked more by road signs than clusters of houses. At Murray Harbour's entrance, the road cuts across the tip of a peninsula studded with three lighthouses. The 35-km-long harborfront road on Highways 18 and 17 rims the harbor's perimeter.

Enormous numbers of seals live in this well-sheltered harbor, and they love to loll about on offshore islands. You can see some of them from the beach at Beach Point's Lighthouse, situated closest to the harbor entrance.

The Murray family settled the area, and has namesakes everywhere: the Murray River flows into Murray Harbour, whose entrance is marked by Murray Head; seal colonies cluster on the harbor's Murray Islands; and the three seaport villages are Murray Harbour, Murray River, and Murray Harbour North.

Town of Murray Harbour
Alpha and Omega Campground on Hwy. 18 east of the seaport, tel. (902) 962-2494 or (800) 561-2494, operates seal-watching cruises ($13; campers get a 10% discount) and has a campground aside Fox River with 30 unserviced and 12 serviced sites ($10-14), river fishing, rowboats, a beach, and showers. It's open mid-June to September. Alpha and Omega also offers **housekeeping cottages** at $55 d and **motel** rooms at $35 d. For more information write to Murray Harbour RR 1, PE C0A 1V0.

Fox River Cottages on Machon Point Rd. off Hwy. 18, tel. 962-2881, has two two-bedroom cottages ($62 d) with screened porches overlooking the Fox River; facilities include a canoe, a rowboat, and a laundry. It's open May-October. Also in the area, **Harbour Motel** on Mill Rd., tel. 962-3660, has seven basic rooms ($45-50) within walking distance of town.

In town, **Compass Rose Craft Studio** on Main St., tel. 962-3881, ranks high among islanders as a fine source for art and paintings, quilts, and antiques. Open June-Sept., Mon.-Sat. 10 a.m.-4 p.m., July-Aug. to 6 p.m.

Town of Murray River
The oval-shaped harbor is centered on the town of Murray River, southeastern Kings County's shopping hub. Restaurants are sparse hereabouts, so if you're passing through town at mealtime, check out **Terrace Heights** on Hwy. 348, tel. (902) 962-2465; they put on a hearty informal spread of seafood and beef ($10-19).

The four-day **Northumberland Provincial Fisheries Festival** during late July features country-fair hoopla with lobster suppers, a parade, races, a dance, and the opportunity to watch fish filleting and scallop shucking by local experts.

The **Old General Store** on Main St., tel. 962-2459, ranks as one of the island's best crafts sources and stocks folk art, linens, and domestic wares. It's open mid-June to mid-Sept., Mon.-Sat. varying hours. **Wood Islands Handcraft Co-op,** also on Main St., tel. 962-3539, trades in weavings, leather goods, knitted or crocheted apparel, and domestic wares, all island-made; open July-Aug., Mon.-Sat. 9 a.m.-6 p.m., June and Sept. to 5 p.m.

Sightseeing for the Naturalist
Seal-watching excursions are popular in these parts. **Garry's Seal and Bird Watching Cruises,** at the Hwy. 4 wharf, tel. (902) 962-2494 (reservations required), takes sightseers on its all-weather vessel through the Murray Islands for views of cormorants, terns, herons, and other seabirds. It then drops anchor at Reynolds Island, where the province's largest seal colony basks in the warm glow of the sun. The guided tour operates daily mid-April through Oct., with

up to five sailings July to mid-Sept.; adults $13.50, children under 12 $7.

Paddle PEI, tel. 566-5673, offers one- and two-day guided canoe and kayak trips that bring you close to seals, herons, and other bay wildlife. Trip dates are in July, Aug., and Sept., and cost about $75-175 per person.

If you like woodland walking, stretch your legs at **Murray River Pines,** a provincial woodlot near town. The site off Hwy. 4 is remote. Look for an abandoned mill, the former provincial Northumberland Mill and Museum, now closed; the woodlot is set inland behind the site. A 30-minute hike on the red-clay road leads to dense groves of red and white pines, abutted by stands of balsam, red maple, and red spruce.

The largest pines date to the 1870s, when England's Royal Navy cut down most of the forest for ship masts. Somehow these trees survived and have become havens for birds of all kinds, including blue herons, kingfishers, swallows, blue jays, and chickadees.

Alliston

Alliston is past Murray River on the way to Murray Harbour North. **Anchor of Hope Motel,** tel. 962-4101, Montague RR 4, PE C0A 1R0, is at the intersection of Hwys. 324 and 4, four km north of Murray River. The motel is near a store and a beach. There is also seal-watching nearby. Open mid-May to mid-Oct.; the rate is $40. Centrally located **Raven Inn,** tel. 962-4308, is on Greek River Rd., Murray River RR 1, PE C0A 1W0. Nature trails, cross-country skiing, and skating are nearby. Features include English breakfast, high tea, and a film library. The inn restricts smoking. Open year-round; the rate is $45.

Vicinity of Murray Harbour North

Kings Byway Drive winds out of Murray River and passes through this village marked only with road signs.

Lady Catherine's Bed and Breakfast, tel. 962-3426 or (800) 661-3426, Montague RR 4, PE C0A 1R0, is on Hwy. 17, 22 km southeast of Montague. Views are fantastic from the veranda, and recreation options include a nearby beach, golf, seal-watching tours, and bikes. Open year-round; rates are $40-48.

In the area, **Seal Cove Campground** off Hwy. 17, tel. (902) 962-2745 (reservations are wise), is a privately operated campground overlooking more offshore seal colonies. It has 17 unserviced and 50 serviced sites ($12-15), a bayside beach, launderette, and nine-hole golf course ($5 greens fee); open May to mid-October.

Poverty Beach, situated at the end of a spur off Hwy. 17 south of Murray Harbour North, is a long, narrow sandbar that separates the sea from the harbor. It's quiet, remote, and wrapped in a sense of primeval peacefulness. The peninsula is worth a trek, but think twice about swimming in the surf; powerful sea currents can be dangerous and no lifeguards are around to rescue floundering bathers.

Panmure Island, a similar remote and windswept wilderness, lies 15 minutes farther north off Hwy. 17. Take the Hwy. 347 spur as it rambles out the flag-shaped peninsula that wags between St. Marys Bay, Georgetown Harbour, and the sea.

A supervised beach fronts the strait, and a wisp of a road angles into the interior and emerges at waterfront with views of Georgetown across the harbor. Back on the mainland, **Panmure Island Provincial Park** shares the remote location just north of Gaspereaux on Hwy. 347, tel. 838-4719. A campground here has 22 unserviced sites and 16 two-way hookup sites ($13-16), supervised ocean swimming, a launderette, campers' canteen, fireplaces, and hot showers; open late June to early September. For more information write to Parks Division East, P.O. Box 370, Montague, PE C0A 1R0.

MONTAGUE AND VICINITY

Montague (pop. 1,400), Kings County's largest town, 45 minutes east of Charlottetown, has always been known for the Main Street bridge over the Montague River. In fact, the town began as Montague Bridge in 1825, when the bridge was made of logs, and the area had just four farms. Shipbuilding brought riches to the town, and many a schooner and other sailing craft was launched here on the broad river.

The town is uncomplicated, pretty, clean, and friendly. Everything important lies along Main St., which slices through town and proceeds up, over, and down the bridge. Montague secured its place as Kings County's main market center in the 1850s, and since the 1960s, the town has benefitted from the county's expanding dairy and tobacco production.

The **Garden of the Gulf Museum** at 2 Main St., tel. (902) 838-2467, is housed in an old post office overlooking Montague River at the bridge. The building is an impressive hulk of red sandstone with a steeply pitched roof, showing its French architectural influence. The collection includes exhibits on local history, including tidbits on de Roma's pioneer French settlement. The museum is open mid-June to mid-Sept., Mon.-Sat. 10 a.m.-5 p.m., Sun. 1-5 p.m. Admission is $2 for adults, children under 15 free.

Accommodations and Food

Manor House Bed and Breakfast at 65 Main St., tel. (902) 838-2224, has three nonsmoking rooms in a historic building furnished with antiques; $40 with breakfast. It's open June-September. **Countryman Bed and Breakfast** at 111 Chestnut St., tel. 838-3715, is another vintage charmer with four nonsmoking rooms, $42-55 with breakfast.

The purposely rustic, riverside **Lobster Shanty North Motel and Cottage** at 192 Main St. South (at town outskirts), tel. 838-2463 or 838-4689, has 11 motel rooms ($59 d) and one cottage ($59 d). The motel's river-view restaurant reigns as one of the island's best dining rooms and serves fried or broiled seafood, thick steaks, and roast beef ($9-18). Open May-Oct.; the mailing address is P.O. Box 158, Montague, PE C0A 1R0.

On the outskirts of Montague at Pooles Corner, the **Whim Inn** at the intersection of Hwys. 3 and 4, tel. 838-3838, is a basic motel in an area where large-scale lodgings are scarce. Facilities include 13 rooms ($55-60), eight housekeeping units ($65 d), and a dining room and lounge. **Boudreault's "White House" Tourist Home,** tel. 838-2560, Montague RR 2, PE C0A 1R0, is on Hwy. 17, one km east of Montague. Nearby attractions include golf, theaters, sealwatching, and dining. Open mid-June through mid-Oct.; rates are $35-40. **Parker's Bed and Breakfast,** tel. 838-3663, P.O. Box 398, Montague, PE C0A 1R0, is located at 90 Main St., south on Hwy. 4. Dining, seal-watching, and a museum are nearby. No pets or smoking allowed. Open 24 May through 31 Oct.; the rate is

$40. Open year-round, **The Sulky Inn,** tel. 838-4100, is at 4 Rink St., P.O. Box 286, Montague, PE C0A 1R0. The inn offers tennis, a curling rink, bowling, TV, mini-golf, a pool, dining, and cruises nearby. Pets are extra. The rate is $55.

For picnic fixings, the **Sobey's** supermarket on Main St. is open Mon.-Tues. 8 a.m.-6 p.m., Wed.-Sat. 8 a.m.-9 p.m.

Recreation

Town and County Aquatics Plus at Wood Island Hill Rd. near Hwy. 4, tel. (902) 838-3047, has squash courts, a pool, and exercise equipment ($7 s or $16 family for a 24-hour pass); open daily 6 a.m.-10 p.m. Call for directions.

Cruise Manada Seal-Watching Boat Tours, tel. 838-3444 (reservations are wise), leave from the town's marina on Hwy. 4, or from the Brudenell River resort wharf on Hwy. 3. Both two-hour cruises sail two to three times daily. An onboard narrator provides information on local history and natural wildlife such as harbor seals, great blue herons, gulls, and ospreys. The Montague-based tours operate mid-May to mid-Oct., while the Brudenell tours run July-Aug. only; tickets for either are adults $13.50, children under 12 $7. The outfit also handles river transport for the dinner theater at Georgetown.

Information and Services

The provincial **visitor information center** at Pooles Corner, tel. (902) 838-2972, answers travel questions and stocks island information; open mid-June to early Oct., daily 9 a.m.-9 p.m., after early Sept. to 6 p.m.

Kings County Memorial Hospital is at 409 McIntyre Ave., tel. 838-2152; find the **RCMP** at 38 Wood Island Hill Rd., tel. 838-2352.

CIBC bank, tel. 838-2134, is one of several town banks. It's open Mon.-Thurs. 9:30 a.m.-4:30 p.m., Fri. to 5 p.m. **Montague Taxi** is on 138 Sackville St., tel. 838-3000; rates are 70 cents per kilometer. **Ricky's Cycling Tours,** on the town outskirts on Hwy. 17, tel. 962-3085 (ask for directions), offers bike rentals and tours; open June-August.

Buffaloland Provincial Park

Six km south of Montague at the intersection of Highways 4 and 317, the 100-acre Buffaloland Provincial Park, tel. (902) 652-2356, may seem deserted at first glance. If you look closely, though, you'll spot bison and white-tailed deer roaming the woodlands.

The bison herd here began with 14 bison imported from Alberta in 1970, as part of a federal experiment to help preserve the almost-extinct species. There's still no population explosion, but the herd numbers 24 buffalo now. Between 3 and 5 p.m. the bison herd emerges to feed near the Hwy. 4 fence. The park is open daily year-round, free admission.

Heatherdale

For an overnight far from the madding crowd, consider **MacRae's Farm Bed and Breakfast,** at the intersection of Hwys. 206 and 316 south of Montague, tel. (902) 838-4783. The B&B has three rooms ($25) in the farmhouse of a dairy and cattle spread; open mid-June to September.

BRUDENELL RIVER PROVINCIAL PARK AND RESORT

This park-cum-resort occupies a gorgeous pastoral setting on the peninsula that juts out into Cardigan Bay between the Brudenell and Cardigan rivers. You enter the park from Hwy. 3 about

10 minutes beyond Pooles Corner, and the road winds through manicured grounds to the resort's main house and nearby chalets.

The Park

Facilities at the provincial park, tel. (902) 652-2756 or 652-2356 (winter), include 94 unserviced campsites ($13) and 16 two-way hookup sites ($16), hot showers, kitchen shelters, a launderette, interpretive programs, and a riverfront beach. The campground is open June through Sept.; reservations are accepted beginning 1 April. For more information write to Parks Division East, P.O. Box 370, Montague, PE C0A 1R0.

Golfers here enjoy the 18-hole **Brudenell River Provincial Golf Course,** tel. 652-2342, 652-2356 off-season. The course ranks among Atlantic Canada's superior golf greens and has been the site of four national and six CPGA tournaments; the season highlight is the three-day **CPGA Atlantic Class Golf Competition** in early Sept.; greens fee is $30 mid-June through Sept., $24 off-season. Reservations are wise.

Other sports choices include canoeing ($15 a day), windsurfing ($28 for a partial day), horseback riding ($14-20), tennis, and boat tours. All sports in the park are open to campers, resort

Buffaloland Provincial Park

guests, and day visitors alike. **Paddle PEI,** tel. 652-2434, conducts a variety of paddling and cycling trips at the park, and offers instruction in kayaking and windsurfing.

The Resort

Rodd Brudenell River Resort (part of the Rodd Hotel group), the park's resort component, tel. (902) 652-2332 or (800) 565-7633, has 50 rooms ($119-129 d) in the main lodge and 50 riverfront chalets ($85-105 d). It's open July to mid-October. The ambience is friendly and relaxed—a nice place to meet islanders and other visitors.

The resort's **Gordon Dining Room** is casually upscale and specializes in seafood entrees ($18-24); try the poached salmon awash in lemon sauce, and, for dessert, shortbread squares topped with lemon meringue or the homemade parfait.

The region's night scene, quiet though it is, is also centered at the resort. The **Nineteenth Hole** lounge is the golfers' domain by day, but at night, it's filled with recorded oldies and some rock; open nightly to midnight.

VICINITY OF BRUDENELL RIVER PARK

Georgetown

Once a major island shipbuilding center, this quiet port is now known for the **King's Playhouse** in the village's center on Hwy. 343. The local Homefree Productions repertory company stages drama and comedy shows ($10). Open late June-Aug.; for current plays and details on dinner theater packages, call (902) 652-2053. The two-day **Summer Days** festival features a parade, food vendors, boat races, and a harbor regatta during mid-July.

An enjoyable activity for a rainy day is to try your hand at the genteel art of brass rubbing. The **P.E.I. Brass Rubbing Centre,** at Georgetown's Holy Trinity Church, tel. 652-2511, has embossed brasses of medieval knights and ladies. You place a sheet of paper over the brass and rub it with a colored wax stick to produce a striking likeness. The rubbings make wonderful wall hangings. Cost is $5.50-15 per person, less for children 12 and under; all materials are supplied. The center is open late June to late Aug., Mon.-Fri. 10 a.m.-5 p.m., Sat. and Sun. 1-5 p.m. and upon request year-round. The Holy George English Tea Room serves tea with homemade bread and jam.

Cardigan

At this hamlet five minutes beyond the provincial park, the **lobster suppers** are not publicized, but they're well worth partaking in. You'll find them at the Olde Store, tel. (902) 583-2020, open June-October. Supper price is $16.

At the former railroad depot, **Cardigan Crafts Shop** is a reliable source of high-quality crafts including handmade textiles, stained glass, and warm sweaters. It's open mid-June to mid-Oct., Mon.-Sat. 10 a.m.-5:30 p.m., and also in July and August on Sun. 2-6 p.m. The shop also has a tea room.

For a river tour aboard a paddle steamer replica, check out **Great Eastern Riverboat Company** at the town wharf on Hwy. 321, tel. 892-6195; cruises ($12) on the wide Cardigan River to Cardigan Bay leave three times daily between July and mid-September.

NORTHERN KINGS COUNTY

From Cardigan Bay northeast to Souris, the Kings County coastline is deeply notched with a series of bays. The Kings Byway Drive is extremely circuitous hereabouts, taking long, lazy loops out along the intervening peninsulas. Along the route you'll find scattered backcountry hamlets, rivers, secluded coves, and empty beaches. If you're in a hurry, Hwy. 4 and then 2 will take you directly from Pooles Corner to Souris in just half an hour or so.

Little Pond

Highway 310 curves along Boughton Bay to Little Pond, where a surprising bit of civilization awaits. The **Ark Inn,** tel. (902) 583-2400, one of the island's most exquisite contemporary-style lodgings, lies off an unmarked road at Spry Point, the angled coastal hook that separates the bay from the sea. The inn's design incorporates one of the island's first architectural applications of environmentally sound solar light and heat. Visitors revel in its pristine elegance with seven rooms ($65-90)—two of which have whirlpools—and one suite ($100). Outside, seaside hiking trails lead to a white-sand beach.

The inn's two-level **dining room** has a sunny, greenhouse-style setting. The entrees ($14-22) are strong on natural foods with no preservatives; the prime roast beef served with Yorkshire pudding ($20) is an islander favorite.

Both the inn and the dining room are open mid-June to early September.

BAY FORTUNE AND VICINITY

Fortune River flows into Bay Fortune, whose name originated long before the fortunes of Broadway fueled the local retreats of producer David Belasco and playwright Elmer Harris.

In the late 1800s, Harris bought a chunk of land fronting the bay and set a sprawling summer house on a rise that peeled back from the sea. An entourage of thespians traveled with Harris, and for them the playwright designed the 19th-century version of a motel. The L-shaped addition, fronted with a porch, ended at the lighthouse-style tower, once Harris's study, and linked the "motel" with the main house.

The actress Colleen Dewhurst and actor George C. Scott later took over the place, and it has since been transformed into a highly esteemed country inn, the **Inn at Bay Fortune.** David Wilmer, the present innkeeper, bought the property from Dewhurst and extensively restored the interiors of the main house, tower, and adjacent wing rooms. The refurbished inn opened in the late 1980s, and is among the island's most celebrated lodgings. The 11 impeccably furnished suites with fireplaces are $110-160 d with full breakfast. The tower suite overlooking the sea is the prized place for an overnight, and the tower's top floor serves as a lounge with sea views.

A strong sense of conviviality pervades the inn's dining room, downstairs in the main house. Meals are served on the front enclosed porch during summer or inside with tables arranged before the fireplace when the weather is cooler. The creative menu features entrees ($17-20) emphasizing poultry (try the roasted duck cov-ered with a sauce of peach and raspberry vinegar preserves) and red meats, accompanied by an unusually full choice of wines. In 1993, *Where to Eat in Canada* proclaimed the cuisine "without question the best on the Island."

The inn is on Hwy. 310, tel. (902) 687-3745, and open June to mid-October.

Upriver is the hamlet of Dingwells Mills, where *Johnny Belinda,* one of Harris's most successful Broadway plays and later a movie, was set.

Fortune Bridge

Beyond the Bay Fortune hamlet, the scenic route parallels the Fortune River and crosses a bridge to riverside Fortune Bridge, once the site of Broadway producer David Belasco's summer home. The **Empty Nest** alongside Hwy. 310, tel. (902) 687-2387, fronts the river with two rooms ($25) in the house beneath tree canopies, open May-Oct.; ask for directions to the cliff where Belasco's sundial still stands.

Rollo Bay

The coastal circuit meets Hwy. 2 at Rollo Bay, where the **Rollo Bay Inn,** tel. (902) 687-3550, fronts the highway. The inn combines a re-created Georgian setting with 14 suites ($69-78 with breakfast) on spacious grounds and a restaurant serving basic island cuisine ($8-18).

Fiddlers from all over North America converge here for the **Rollo Bay Fiddle Festival** in mid-July. Events include open-air concerts and old-time dances. For details, call 687-2584.

SOURIS

Any islander will tell you that Souris is "far out," the end of the line on the beaten tourist track. The seaport (pop. l,400), notched on the strait seacoast 80 km east of Charlottetown and 44 km from Montague, garners unqualified raves for its setting. The port overlooks the sea from sloping headlands, bounded in part by grasslands that sweep down to the water and in other parts by steeply pitched red cliffs. On the port's southern boundary, the Souris River rushes toward the sea with a gush of red-colored water and pours into the blue strait, like a palette of blended watercolor pigments.

Souris is an active offshore-fishing port, a rarity on the island nowadays when mammoth trawlers flying international flags have almost depleted the once-abundant offshore fisheries' stock. And the seaport boasts more than its share of seafaring legends. On a misty night, you may see an apparition of a ship returning to port. Some folks swear the ship is the *Lydia*, built in a local shipyard and subsequently lost at sea on its first voyage in 1876. The valiant, drowned crew aboard the brigantine, the local legend claims, still attempt to return to home port.

Consider Souris as a sightseeing base. Souris to Grand Tracadie at the national park's eastern end is a mere two-hour drive, and Cavendish lies another half hour beyond there. The port's "far out" location translates as good value for the dollar in lodgings and dining. The restaurants are plainly furnished and specialize in seafood platters, ranked by islanders among the province's best and freshest.

Recreation and Events

For a coastal cruise to Basin Head, check out **Souris Light Cruises,** tel. (902) 687-2502. Daytime sailings feature coastal birdwatching, and sunset cruises are timed to take in the colorful twilight. Cruises (adults $20, children $10) depart the Souris town wharf, July to mid-Sept., daily. In June, the outfit offers eight-hour **lobster-fishing** expeditions. They supply lunch, gear, and instructions, and you'll take home a fresh lobster. Limited to two people, $75 each.

Summer starts with the **Canada Day** parade on 1 July. During late July, the **Celebration of the Sea** features a regatta, midway, and competitions for three days. **Eastern Kings Exhibition** has concerts, entertainment, and country fair trappings with cattle shows and judging during a late August weekend.

Accommodations and Food

Lighthouse and Beach Motel, across the Souris River at Souris West, tel. (902) 687-2339, P.O. Box 134, Souris, PE C0A 2B0, fronts the sea with 15 rooms ($39-80), a housekeeping suite with a whirlpool in the lighthouse keeper's former house ($150 d), and a white, sandy beach; open mid-June to mid-September.

Hilltop Motel, off Main St. near the ferry terminal in Souris, tel. 687-3315, fills the bill as a better-than-average motel with 12 rooms and 10 housekeeping units ($60-68 d) and a restaurant; open year-round. The mailing address is P.O. Box 742, Souris, PE C0A 2B0.

Matthew House Inn, at 15 Breakwater St. at harborfront near the ferry terminal, tel. 687-3461, P.O. Box 151, Souris, PE C0A 2BQ, is a restored Victorian house sparkling with antiques. It offers seven nonsmoking rooms with private bath ($85-140 with a light breakfast), laundry service, spa and exercise room, and bike rentals; open June-October.

Church Street Tourist Home, tel. 687-3065, 8 Church St., P.O. Box 381, Souris, PE C0A 2B0, is opposite the Ultramar service station. A kitchen and a phone are available, with dining, a beach, and the ferry nearby. Open May-Oct.; the nightly rate is $30.

Dining choices are limited, but the fare is worth savoring. The **Blue Fin Restaurant** at 10 Federal Ave., tel. 687-3271, has earned decades of plaudits for lavish, deep-fried seafood platters ($6-18). On Hwy. 2 across the river in Souris West, the **Platter House Seafood Restaurant,** tel. 687-2764, matches basic beef and seafood dishes ($8-15) with prime views of the sea and harbor through large windows; open May-October.

Shopping and Services

The **farmers' market** at the Silver Thread Club, at 75 Main St., lures local crowds for produce, fish, baked goods, and crafts, mid-May to mid-Sept. on Sat. noon-3 p.m. At centrally located Main Street Plaza, you'll find a grocery store and laundromat.

Souris Hospital is at 17 Knights Ave., tel. (902) 687-2467. **RCMP** is at 19 Church St., tel. 687-2027. **CIBC** on Main St. is one of several town banks; it's open Mon.-Thurs. 9:30 a.m.-4:30 p.m., Fri. to 5 p.m.

Magdalen Islands Ferry

A car/passenger ferry departs Souris Wed.-Mon. at 2 p.m., Tues. 2 a.m., for Cap-aux-Meules on Québec's Îles-de-la-Madeleine (Magdalen Islands). Ferries return Wed.-Mon. at 8 a.m., Tues. at 8 p.m. The 134-km crossing to the diminutive islands northeast of PEI takes five hours and costs $36 pp, $53 for a car round-trip. For more ferry details and reservations, call (418) 986-3278. For information on the Magdalens, contact Tourisme Québec, P.O. Box 20000, PQ G1K 7X2, tel. (800) 363-7777.

THE EASTERN CORNER

If you like photogenic landscapes, windy sea-coasts washed with tossing surf, and weath-ered seaports, consider northeastern Kings County for a revealing glimpse of this seafar-ing island as it once was. Beyond Souris, the strait seacoast stretches 25 km to windswept East Point, PEI's east tip. Between the two points lie the "walking" sand dunes and superb beach at Basin Head, as well as a pristine eco-logical spread and Red Point Provincial Park. On the equally remote gulf coast in this region, you'll find few tourists, a dozen tiny seaports, and a handful of lonesome lighthouses that stand as sentinels along the 75-km-long coastline, strewn with centuries of shipwrecks.

Townshend Woodlot

Townshend Woodlot is a 106-hectare spread that closely resembles the island's original Aca-dian forest. In 1970, the International Biological Program designated the setting as one of PEI's finest examples of old-growth hardwood groves. To get there, take Hwy. 16 north from Souris and turn inland at Hwy. 305 to the hamlet of Souris Line Road. The woodlot plantation lies off the road, is fairly well hidden, and obscurely marked—you may want to ask around for direc-tions in Souris; for details, call the provincial parks office in Charlottetown, (902) 892-7411.

Acquired by the province in 1978, the wood-lot lacks a clear hiking route, but it's easily walk-able on a level grade of sandy loam. The groves meld beech trees—a species that once domi-nated half the island's forests—with yellow birch, red maple, and sugar maple, whose dark brown trunks stretch up as high as 32 meters. Eastern chipmunks nest in underground tunnels here. And dwarf ginseng—rare on the island—and nodding trillium thrive.

Basin Head and Vicinity

Formed by the winds, most sand dunes grow and creep along, albeit at a snail's pace. Basin Head's dunes are known as "walking" dunes for their windblown mobility. The high silica con-tent of the sand here causes it to squeak audibly when crunched underfoot. Islanders poetically describe the phenomenon as "singing sands." The beaches at both Basin Head and adjacent Red Point Provincial Park are composed of singing sands. At Basin Head, the dunes are high and environmentally fragile; visitors should stay off the dunes and tread instead along the beach near the water's edge.

Behind the Basin Head dunes, **Basin Head Fisheries Museum,** off Hwy. 16, tel. (902) 357-2966, sits high on the headland overlooking an inlet. Here you'll find boats, nets, and a museum with expertly conceived exhibits detailing the historic inshore fishing industry. The museum is open Tues.-Sat. 9 a.m.-5 p.m. mid-June to early Sept., closed weekends after Labour Day; adults $3, children under 12 free.

Red Point Provincial Park, 13 km east of Souris off Hwy. 16, tel. 357-2463, has super-vised ocean swimming with a campground of 24 unserviced and 36 serviced campsites ($13-16), kitchen shelters, fireplaces, and hot show-ers. It's open mid-June to early September.

Beyond Basin Head, the landscape is pure drama. White, puffy clouds hurry across a Wedgwood-blue sky. At the northeastern tip, the strait and gulf meet in a lathered flush of cresting seas, sometimes colored blue and often tinged with red from oxide-colored silt.

Along the gulf, a score of lighthouses jut up from the coastline, silent witnesses to ships wrecked by the tumult of sea and wind. At the gulf's most easterly point stands the octagonal tower of **East Point Lighthouse** off Hwy. 16, tel. 687-2295, $2 admission. It's open June to early Oct., daily 10 a.m.-6 p.m., July-Aug. 9 a.m.-9 p.m.

South Lake

Highway 16 dutifully parallels the coastline, while the Hwy. 16A spur cuts off the main road. At the intersection, **South Sider Cookhouse and Wood Stove Bakery,** tel. (902) 357-2980, is a hospitable restaurant with hearty, inexpen-sive meals and a choice of desserts from the bakery.

Elmira

Elmira Railway Museum, inland on Hwy. 16A, tel. (902) 357-2481, was once the terminus of rail service to the area. The former depot serves as the unspoken testament to the island railroad's halcyon years with the province's only exhibits and documentation on rail service. It's open mid-June to early Sept., daily 9 a.m.-5 p.m.; adults $1.50, children under 12 free. Outside, you can hike into the interior along the abandoned railroad track.

North Lake and Vicinity

North Lake harbor is one of four departure points for deep-sea fishing; anglers try for trophy catches of bluefin tuna. Expect to pay $15-20 pp for a three- to four-hour trip, or $300 for an eight-hour charter with four fishermen aboard. Trips depart daily during the July to mid-Sept. season from North Lake, Naufrage, Launching, and Red Head harbors. **North Lake Tuna Charters** at North Lake harbor, with five tuna charter boats, is among the best; for details, call (902) 357-2055.

Bluefin Motel on Hwy. 16 at North Lake harbor's coast, tel. 357-2599, caters to fishermen with 11 basic rooms ($39-42) and a beach with clam digging; open mid-June to mid-October. For meals, try **Rod and Reel Restaurant** on Hwy. 16 at North Lake, tel. 357-2784. Its hearty seafood and hamburger platters ($6-15), have given it an untarnished reputation for satisfying demanding hungry fishermen; open mid-May to October.

Campbells Cove Provincial Park, on Hwy. 16 five km west of Elmira, tel. 357-2067, fronts the gulf with a beach, hot showers, kitchen shelters, and 36 serviced and unserviced sites ($13-16); open late June to early September. For more information write to Parks Division East, P.O. Box 370, Montague, PE C0A 1R0.

THE GULF SHORE

St. Peters

If you're in the area in early August, check out the port's five-day **Blueberry Festival,** an islander favorite with concerts, entertainment, blueberry dishes, lobster and beef barbecue, and pancake brunch at **St. Peters Park** on Hwy. 2, P.O. Box 51, St. Peters Bay, PE C0A 2A0.

Also at the park is a campground with a choice of 30 unserviced sites and 24 two-way hookup sites ($11-16); call ahead for reservations, tel. (902) 961-2786. The town operates the campground, which has a launderette, kitchen shelters, free firewood, two pools, mini-golf, and hot showers; open mid-June through September.

The Crab 'N' Apple Bed and Breakfast, tel. 961-3165, P.O. Box 9, St. Peters Bay, PE C0A 2A0, is on Hwy. 2, one km west from the junction of Hwys. 2 and 313. It has a view of the bay, nearby fishing and golf, and a laundromat. Open year-round; the rate is $35.

Morell

Berries are the focus at Morell, 40 minutes from Charlottetown. The St. Peters Bay seaport makes much of the harvest at mid-July's four-day **Strawberry Festival,** with a parade, strawberry desserts, and other community events.

A new 18-hole, par-72 golf course, the **Links at Crowbush Cove,** tel. (902) 961-3100 (reservations), lies five km north of Morell off Hwy. 2. **Kelly's Bed and Breakfast,** on Hwy. 2, tel. 961-2389, is conveniently close to the beach and the course. Its six rooms go for $30 d; open June-October.

The **Morell Canadian Legion,** Queen Elizabeth Dr., tel. 961-2110, puts on lobster suppers (under $19; salmon is an alternative choice); open June-early Sept., nightly 4:30-9 p.m.

NEWFOUNDLAND AND LABRADOR

INTRODUCTION

The province of Newfoundland (also known collectively as Newfoundland and Labrador), situated at North America's northeastern edge, is composed of two parts: the 110,681-square-km island of Newfoundland (nooh-fun-LAND), the world's 16th-largest island; and Labrador, which lies across the narrow Strait of Belle Isle from the island and forms the 295,039-square-km eastern flank of Canada's mainland.

The combined area is three times the size of New Brunswick, Nova Scotia, and Prince Edward Island put together, and more than twice the size of America's New England region. Cape Spear, the windy, boulder-bound promontory near the provincial capital of St. John's, is North America's most easterly point and lies closer to the British Isles than to central Canada.

Newfoundland's nearest neighbor is mainland Québec, which lies on Labrador's southern and western borders. The islands of St.-Pierre and Miquelon, France's last vestiges of colonialism in North America, lie 25 km off Newfoundland island's southern coast. Nova Scotia and the rest of Atlantic Canada lie southwest across Cabot Strait, the 125-km-wide channel between the Atlantic Ocean and the Gulf of St. Lawrence.

Access to the province is not difficult. Labrador's western area is connected to Québec with air, rail, and road links. Labrador's eastern area and the island of Newfoundland are linked by air to Halifax, Nova Scotia, Atlantic Canada's gateway. Newfoundland's capital of St. John's is also an international gateway, served by Air Canada's nonstop flights from London. By sea, two ferry routes connect Newfoundland island with North Sydney, Nova Scotia; one leaves from Channel-Port aux Basques at the southwestern tip, the other from Argentia on the Avalon Peninsula.

The province is a veritable ethnic stew, home to a number of different cultures. You'll hear a thick Irish brogue across the island's Avalon Peninsula. The King's English is savored in St. John's as an affectionate reminder of Newfoundland's historical link with the mother country, severed only as recently as 1949. An ancient French dialect is spoken on the western coast's Port au Port Peninsula.

In Labrador, the ethnic mix includes indigenous peoples (the Innu, Inuit, and Métis—the latter a blend of the indigenous people and the white settlers); the year-round and summertime Newfoundlanders; and French Canadians from Québec.

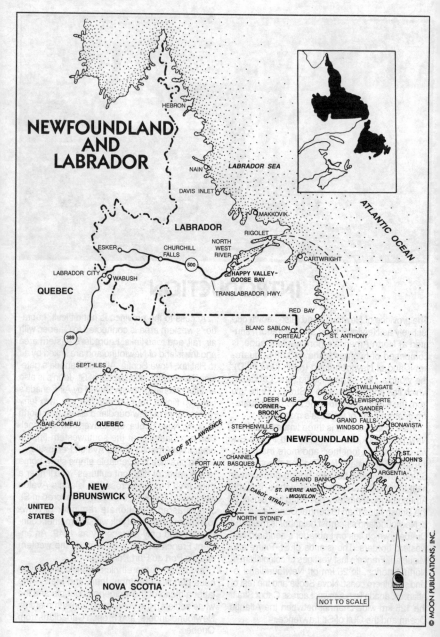

NEWFOUNDLAND AND LABRADOR

LABRADOR SEA

HEBRON

NAIN

DAVIS INLET

MAKKOVIK

LABRADOR

RIGOLET

ESKER   CHURCHILL   NORTH
         FALLS   WEST
                     RIVER

CARTWRIGHT

500

LABRADOR CITY

WABUSH

**HAPPY VALLEY-
GOOSE BAY**

QUEBEC

TRANSLABRADOR HWY.

389

RED BAY

BLANC SABLON

FORTEAU   ST. ANTHONY

SEPT-ILES

ATLANTIC OCEAN

TWILLINGATE
LEWISPORTE

DEER LAKE
**CORNER
BROOK**

GANDER

BAIE-COMEAU   QUEBEC

STEPHENVILLE

GRAND FALLS
WINDSOR

BONAVISTA

NEWFOUNDLAND

GULF OF ST. LAWRENCE

ST.
JOHN'S

CHANNEL-
PORT AUX BASQUES

ARGENTIA

GRAND BANK

**ST. PIERRE AND
MIQUELON**

NEW
BRUNSWICK

CABOT STRAIT

UNITED
STATES

1

NORTH SYDNEY

NOVA SCOTIA

NOT TO SCALE

© MOON PUBLICATIONS, INC.

SIGHTSEEING HIGHLIGHTS

The Great Outdoors

Seabirds by the thousands—Atlantic Canada's largest concentrations—nest on the Avalon Peninsula coastlines. Whales cruise offshore, lured by spawning, smeltlike capelin. Icebergs float south from the arctic in summer and bob off the island's seacoasts.

In Labrador, look up. The aurora borealis—the magnificent northern light show caused by charged particles in the upper atmosphere—provides a stellar attraction, illuminating the sky up to 243 nights a year. The northern lights appear to float lazily in the pale moonlight, and it's said they'll dance to your tune if you whistle.

Labrador's rare labradorite, or firestone, is a type of feldspar with iridescent peacock blue, green, gold, purple, or pink streaks. Found also in Finland and Madagascar, it's the best known and showiest of the province's 20 precious and semiprecious gems.

In summertime, wild berries of many varieties ripen in the province. Bakeapples, similar to Scandinavia's cloudberries, go into tasty desserts and preserves. Others include wild partridgeberries, squashberries, blueberries, blackberries, plum boys, bunchberries, dewberries, crackerberries, crowberries, strawberries, and black currants.

Apart from all that, many consider the fishing and hunting in Newfoundland and Labrador to be Atlantic Canada's best. Hikers will find both marked and roughly cut wilderness trails; and water-sports enthusiasts will find a number of activities to suit them, including canoeing, ocean kayaking, and scuba diving.

History and Tradition

The province's history is well documented in a trove of museums and attractions provincewide. St. John's traces its history to the 1500s, as does Trinity, the heritage village on Trinity Bay. South of St. John's, Ferryland began as Lord Baltimore's first New World settlement for English Roman Catholics.

Gander served as a military air base during WW II, and now keeps its heritage on display with a collection of notable aircraft. St. Anthony, on the tip of the island's Northern Peninsula,

owes its fame to Sir Wilfred Grenfell, the medical missionary who initiated medical care in the remote areas and encouraged crafts that are still produced and sold across the province.

Expect an astonishing variety of sweaters, jewelry embellished with Labradorite and other gems, hooked mats, pottery, dolls, weavings, apparel created in the finest fabrics, and carvings of moose or caribou antlers, whalebone, soapstone, and ivory.

The summertime festivals go on and on. Folk festivals are particularly notable, showcasing traditional music from new and established talents from the province, Canada, and abroad. Expect folk music in the local pubs, too, especially in St. John's, which has a rousing night scene. On the western coast of Newfoundland island, the Stephenville Theater Festival takes to the boards each July—its fame has spread far beyond the province. In Labrador's coastal villages, the annual Bakeapple Folk Festival in August is an unqualified must-see.

Other festivals mark special events. The province's plethora of crafts are shown and sold at provincial shows, such as mid-July's **Newfoundland and Labrador Craft Development Association Summer Craft Fair** in St. John's. And the **Royal St. John's Regatta** in early August is said to be North America's oldest organized sports event.

THE LAND

"The Galapagos of Geology"

"What the Galapagos are to biology, Gros Morne is to geology," declared Britain's Prince Edward when he formally opened Gros Morne National Park in 1973. UNESCO concurred, and one of the world's rarest windows on the ancient world's formation was designated a World Heritage Site in 1987.

Plate tectonics theory holds that the earth's crust is broken into many huge "plates" that float on the molten rock beneath them. The movement of the plates dictates the creation, position, and shape of the continents. According to this theory, long before Newfoundland was an island, it was a landlocked part of a great supercontinent formed during Precambrian times; the oldest rocks in both Newfoundland and Labrador are 3.8 billion years old. When the supercontinent broke apart, the land plates drifted and a rift formed. Water filled the rift during the Cambrian period, creating the Iapetus Ocean.

After another 50 million years, give or take, the land plates, which had previously moved apart, reversed direction and moved toward each other. As the land plates closed together, the continents converged with a profound smack. The plates were pushed together and up like a squeezed accordion. Pangaea, the second supercontinent, was the result, and Newfoundland, not yet an island, perched high and dry near the center. At that point, Newfoundland's only distinctive characteristic was a mountain rib (the budding Appalachian Mountains), formed from the earth's earlier faulting and upheavals. Later, the plates moved again, and Pangaea split apart. The Eurasian/African plate drifted east and southeast and settled in its present position as the continents of Europe, Asia, and Africa. The mountains of Great Britain and Scandinavia were formed from the mountain rib's northern end—the rib had severed at midpoint and half had traveled with the Eurasian/African plate.

The world as we know it began to settle into place. The Appalachian Mountains rimmed North America's eastern edge from Alabama in the southern U.S. to Nova Scotia's Cape Breton Highlands. Northeast of Nova Scotia, the mountain chain's low-lying peaks dipped beneath the Cabot Strait and reemerged on Newfoundland's western coast as the Long Range Mountains. Strewn among the mountains were a colossal geological heritage: remnants from the world's first supercontinent and parts of the Iapetus Ocean's sea floor. East of the mountains, the island's central plateau portion was made up of a great rectangular swatch of the crumpled, ancient seabed, 200-250 km in width and length.

A geological oddity was responsible for the island's southeastern portion; though most of the Eurasian/African landmass had wandered east and southeast, a chunk of the plate remained. It comprises the is-

The Lighthouse at Cape Spear overlooks the easternmost point of land in North America.

land's southeastern corner and the Avalon Peninsula.

Between then and now, the eons added a few more topographical touches. The retreating ice sheet uncovered the Labrador Trough, scooped out the Strait of Belle Isle, cut fjords into the coastlines, and scoured the interiors to create ponds, lakes, and the short Gander, Humber, and Exploits rivers. Subsequent erosion shaved the peaks of the Long Range Mountains.

The Contemporary Island

Newfoundland island rises from the sea as a massive, brooding countenance of rock. Numerous peninsulas radiate from its lofty central plateau into the sea to the northeast, ending in precipitous cliffs, massive headlands, and sandy or cobble beaches. Deep-water fjords, small coves, and great bays serrate the coastline. A 10-km-wide isthmus threads the main part of the island to the smaller Avalon Peninsula at Newfoundland's southeastern corner. The hilly interiors of both the main island and the peninsula are cloaked in dense woodlands and barrens laced with bogs, swamps, and muskegs.

The Atlantic Ocean embraces the northern, eastern, and southern coastlines, while the Gulf of St. Lawrence lies on the west. The narrow Strait of Belle Isle separates the island from Labrador to the north. The Grand Banks, once some of the world's richest fishing grounds, lie southeast, offshore at the continental shelf's edge.

Much of the island is exposed bedrock, mantled with a thin soil layer. The bedrock, consisting of sedimentary, volcanic, and granitic components, is littered in places with oddly placed boulders called erratics. Carried, then dropped, by retreating glaciers, the erratics are vestiges of the Ice Age. The Long Range Mountains, rimmed with a narrow coastal plain, dominate the western coastline. Agricultural regions and meadows are rare, but where they occur they are exceptionally lush. The island reaches its peak at 815-meter-high Lewis Hill, on the western coast near Corner Brook, the island's second-largest city.

BOB RACE

SUMMERTIME'S AMAZING ICEBERG PARADE

The spectacular icebergs that float past Labrador and Newfoundland every summer originate from southwestern Greenland's ice cap, where great chunks of ice calve off the coast and cascade into the bone-chilling Davis Strait. The young bergs eventually drift out to the Labrador Sea, where powerful currents route them south along the watery route known as Iceberg Alley.

The parade usually starts in March, peaks in June and July, and in rare cases continues into November. Iceberg-watching was spectacular in 1991. No one dares to predict the next exemplary year; icebergs have their own agenda.

Though no one actually counts icebergs, an educated guess has 10,000-30,000 of them migrating down from the north annually. Of those, about 1,400-2,000 make it all the way to the Gulf Stream's warm waters, where they finally melt away after a two- to four-year, 3,200-km journey.

No two bergs are exactly the same. Some appear distinctly white. Others may be turquoise, green, or blue. Sizes vary, too. A "growler" is the smallest, about the size of a dory, and weighs about 1,000 tons. A "bergy bit" weighs more, about 10,000 tons. A typical "small" iceberg looms 5-15 meters above water level and weighs about 100,000 tons. A "large" ice mass will be 51-75 meters high and weigh 100-300 million tons. Generally, you'll see the largest bergs—looking like magnificent castles embellished with towers and turrets—farther north; the ice mountains diminish in size as they float south and eventually melt. No matter what the size, what you see is just a fraction of the whole—some 90% of the iceberg's mass is hidden beneath the water.

Occasionally, a wandering berg may be trapped at land's edge or wedged within coves and slender bays. Should you be tempted to go in for a closer look, approach with caution. As it melts and its equilibrium readjusts, an iceberg may roll over. And melting bergs also often fracture, throwing ice chips and knife-sharp splinters in all directions.

Iceberg-watching

Iceberg-watching opportunities start along Labrador's coastline. Your best berg bet hereabouts is the view from one of the coastal ferries running between Newfoundland island and Happy Valley–Goose Bay.

Farther south on the coastline, sea currents diverge, and the parade separates. One route takes some of the smaller ice masses through the shallow, fast-flowing Strait of Belle Isle and into the Gulf of St. Lawrence. Here, **Roberts Boat Tours,** tel. (709) 931-2650, at Forteau on Labrador's strait seacoast, offers June-Sept. boat tours combining coastal iceberg-watching with jigging (hand-line fishing) for cod.

Another flock of bergs bypasses the strait and drifts toward Newfoundland's northern coast, where some loll aimlessly about the offshore islands. Concentrations are thickest at the seaport of **Twillingate** on Twillingate Island. The Long Point Lighthouse at the island's most northern point makes a good viewpoint. **Twillingate Island Boat Tours** at the Iceberg House, Hwy. 340, tel. 884-2317 or 884-2242, offers both iceberg-watching (best July-Aug.) and whalewatching tours with photo opportunities, from July to early September. **Fogo Island,** east of Twillingate, is another of the province's prime iceberg-watching locations.

Continuing south, the icebergs glide along the eastern coast of Newfoundland, propelled by the Labrador Current. Some wander close to shore and ditch among Terra Nova National Park's fjordlike bays. At the park's Newman Sound, **Ocean Watch Tours** operates federally approved ocean-exploration and research programs, and offers three-hour boat tours from late June to early September. Activities on the natural-history tours include seafloor dredging, plankton trawling, and coastline exploring combined with iceberg- and whalewatching. For details, call Ocean Watch at 677-2327, or write to them at Doryman Marine, Squid Tickle, Burnside, NF A0G 1K0.

St. John's counts iceberg-watching as a city attraction. Two of the best views are from the lofty Signal Hill promontory by the seaport's harbor entrance, and Cape Spear at the harbor's southeastern tip. (For information on boat tours from St. John's, see the "St. John's and Vicinity" section.)

Throughout the province, expect to pay $20-28 per person for a guided, two- to three-hour iceberg-watching boat tour.

Labrador

The province's mainland is known as the "The Big Land," a fitting handle for the triangle-shaped region that's three times as big as the island. The name Labrador comes from the Portuguese *terra del lavrador* (land of the farmer)—a name bestowed upon it most likely by an early Portugese fisherman or explorer traveling west from his home in the Azores.

Along the 7,886-km coastline of granite boulders, jagged fjords, coves, and harbors, a string of islands clutches at the Labrador Sea's chilly edge. Farther south, sandy beaches mix with headlands on the strait seacoast. The province's highest peak is 1,729-meter-high Mt. Caubvick, which overlooks the northern coast in the dark, ragged Torngat Mountains.

The interior's diverse terrain can be roughly divided into three regions. Across the triangle's broad southern plateau lie luxuriously thick woodlands ribboned with bogs. The midsection holds Labrador's slice of civilization, and is rimmed in part with the 160-km-long wall of the Mealy Mountains. The Labrador Trough—a region of swift rivers, waterfalls, rich iron-ore deposits, and, now, a mammoth hydroelectric plant—anchors the western midsection. The twisting, west-to-east TransLabrador Highway—in part a roughly cut forest-access road and, nearer to Labrador City, a gravel highway—connects western Labrador to the head of the 200-km-long Hamilton Inlet/Lake Melville fjord.

North of the midsection, Labrador's triangular tip narrows and ends in remote wilderness. The subarctic taiga, studded with a stunted coniferous forest, melds at timberline to the arctic tundra, which makes up the northernmost reaches of the province. Here lichens, sedges, and dwarf shrubs cross barren valleys, and steeply walled basins cut into angular mountains. From the northern shore, the Hudson Strait and the arctic's Baffin Island are north, and Greenland is northeast.

Parks

Virtually all of Newfoundland is pristine land, and the plethora of parks preserve the best of the best. The province claims two magnificent national parks, both on the island: Terra Nova, a scenic beauty with 400 square km of interior boreal forests, ponds, bogs, hills, and fjords; and stunning Gros Morne, an open book of primeval geological history with nine spectacular scenic areas.

The province also counts 76 provincial parks, the majority of them on the island. Most provincial parks offer such amenities as picnic tables and supervised beaches. Some parks have campgrounds, playgrounds, marked hiking trails, and scenic views. A few parks have visitor centers with interpretive programs. Six "wilderness and ecological reserves" feature seabirds by the thousands and extraordinary views, but for the most part no visitor facilities. Cape St. Mary's Ecological Reserve is the exception, with its summertime interpretive program.

Also see "Recreation" and specific regional listings, following, for more details on the province's parks.

CLIMATE

On a typical summer day, the weather's mood can swing from sultry to chilly. Brilliant sunshine one moment can turn into dark clouds the next, often bringing rain ranging from light sprinkles to drenching downpours. The island's eastern and southern seacoasts are frequently foggy due to the offshore melding of the warm Gulf Stream and cold Labrador current. Be prepared to dress like an onion, ready to peel, and keep a lightweight raincoat, umbrella, or hooded slicker handy.

Newfoundland Island

Overall, the island has a cool, moist maritime climate. Annual rainfall averages 105 cm. Summer high temperatures average 16° C, but hot spells (up to 24° C) are common, and the swimming season starts by late June. Summer's overnight lows range 9-12° C. The island's interior and low-lying coastal areas are the warmest and sunniest areas in summer.

Frost begins in early October on the southern coast, earlier farther north. Winter brings overnight lows down to -8° C and snowfall averaging 300 cm a year.

Expect year-round blustery winds along the Marine Drive and nearby Cape Spear on the east coast, and warmer and generally better weather year-round on the west coast. Finally, conditions are almost always severe at upper altitudes in the Long Range Mountains; the peaks are snow-covered year-round, and winds can blow to gale force.

Labrador

Labrador summers are short, generally cool, and usually brilliantly sunny except for periodic showers. The average summertime high temperature here is 18° C, but temperatures vary widely from one part of Labrador to another. In the western area, summer highs range 11-33° C. To the north, the subarctic region has cool and dry summers averaging 11° C during the day, though in the far north near Nain, pack ice and snow showers are common during July. Summer's fair weather notwithstanding, the temperature can drop rapidly after mid-August; bring gloves, rain gear, insulated underwear, lined rubber boots, and warm sweaters.

Frost starts during late August. Winter temperatures dip down to the -20s across Labrador and have plunged off the scale with a brutally cold -51° C in the western area.

Annual precipitation is 46 cm, half of which falls as snow between October and May. During January, an average 437 cm of snow falls across the central plateau.

Weather Information

Environment Canada Weather Service provides 24-hour weather forecasts and marine conditions for St. John's, tel. (709) 772-5534; stay on the line, and they'll answer questions about other areas of the province. For west-coast weather, call 695-2634 at Port aux Basques.

FLORA AND FAUNA

The forests of Newfoundland island are comprised mainly of black spruce and balsam fir, with occasional stands of larch, pin cherry, pine, paper birch, aspen, red maple, mountain maple, and alder. If you're hiking in alpine or coastal areas, you may encounter the formidable "tuckamore," a canopy-shaped thicket of stunted, hopelessly entwined fir and spruce. Walk around the thicket, not through it—the dense web mercilessly tears skin and clothing.

In Labrador, the southern forests are cloaked with 12- to 27-meter-high spruce, tamarack, juniper, and birch. Thirty-meter-high white spruce dominates the central area, while black spruce, a mere meter high, speckles the timberline area.

Wildflowers blossom profusely in summer; for an impressive sampler, check out Terra Nova National Park, home to 350 plant species. Across the island's marshes and bogs, expect to see white and yellow water lilies, rare orchid species, purple iris and goodwithy, and insectivorous plants such as the pitcher plant (the provincial flower). Daisies, blue harebells, yellow goldenrod, pink wild roses, and deep pink fireweed thrive in the woodlands. Bright yellow marsh marigolds are native to the western coast's Port au Peninsula.

Northern Labrador's tundra brightens with yellow poppies, heather buttercups, miniature purple rhododendrons, violets, and deep blue gentian, mixed among the white cotton grass. Bushy yellow moss campion thrives on the barrens' gravel surface, while farther south, daisylike arnica and purple saxifrage grow in rock niches.

No poison ivy, poison oak, or ragweed grows anywhere in the province. Mushrooms are everywhere, however; the chanterelles are culinary prizes, but the amanitas are deadly poisonous. Be safe and leave identification to the experts.

Birds

The province is alive with birds; the island counts 343 species, while Labrador has 90. Songbirds such as the black-capped chickadee are found in the island's interior. The sooty shearwater can be seen near Gander, and red-throated loons and great-horned and snowy owls inhabit the woodlands. The island's raptors include ospreys, gyrfalcons, and eastern North America's largest bald eagle population. The willow ptarmigan inhabits the Burin Peninsula; the rock ptarmigan is native to the Long Range Mountains. Labrador is home to ruffled and spruce grouse, ptarmigans, owls, woodpeckers, ravens, gyrfalcons, jays, chickadees, and nuthatches.

In summer, an estimated 11 million seabirds arrive and gather in 20 major colonies. These coastal colonies harbor 95% of North America's Atlantic puffins (the province's official bird), as well as countless common murres—Newfoundlanders call them "turres"—and gannets. Three of North America's six major gannet colonies can be found on Newfoundland's coastal cliffs.

If you're an avid birder, the ecological reserves will leave you breathless. The **Witless Bay Ecological Reserve,** offshore near St. John's, is the summer home of Atlantic puffins (North America's largest breeding colony), murres, Leach's storm petrels, gannets, cormorants, guillemots, and herring gulls. The **Cape St. Mary's Ecological Reserve,** North America's second-largest gannetry, is cloaked with 53,000 gannets, and augmented with common and thick-billed murres, black-legged kittiwakes (known locally as "tickleace"), black guillemots, great black-headed and herring gulls, and some razorbills.

The **Funk Island Ecological Reserve** lies 50 km offshore from Musgrave Harbour and is a favorite with the common murre. Off Labrador's coast, the **Gannet Islands Ecological Reserve** is equally remote and lies alongside the Marine Atlantic ferry route to Labrador; from the ferry you can catch awesome displays of 50,000 common murres, 35,000 puffins, and 8,000 other seabirds. North America's largest razorbill population nests at this site off the coast of Cartwright.

A checklist of provincial birds is available from the Department of Tourism and Culture, tel. (709) 729-2830 or (800) 563-6353 in Canada and the United States. Seabird-watching is best late May to mid-July, though seabirds cluster on the coastal cliffs through August and sometimes into mid-September.

Whales

Some 17 whale species can be seen off Newfoundland island's coastlines, and 10 species cruise Labrador's seacoast. The humpback, minke, fin, right, pothead, pilot, blue, sperm, and sei are most common; the beluga and narwhal are also occasionally seen. June and July are the prime whalewatching months. Most species, however, roam local waters longer, and the minke and pothead whalewatching season extends from May to October.

For the best whale shows, check out the island's Atlantic coastlines, from Fogo Island to St. Marys Bay. Pods of humpbacks frequent Bonavista and Trinity bays, especially off Trinity and Terra Nova National Park. Sperm and pothead whales are especially fond of the giant squid in Conception Bay near St. John's. An array of humpback, minke, and fin whales, bobbing amid tour boats, usually adds excitement to the seabird show at the Witless Bay Ecological Reserve.

On the western coast, fin, minke, humpback, and pilot whales are sighted offshore at Gros Morne National Park.

An "Impoverished" Animal Region

With only 14 indigenous mammals, the island is considered an impoverished animal region. Further, no skunks, snakes, or porcupines inhabit the area. Among the island's native animals are the hare, lynx, beaver, otter, muskrat, marten, mink, and fox. Labrador's northern tundra coastline is home to populations of red wolves, wolverines, porcupines, squirrels, weasels, and polar bears.

Some species have proliferated in amazing numbers. Moose number 175,000; bears 6,000-10,000. Caribou are even more numerous; 12 herds roam the island and are most plentiful in the Avalon Wilderness Reserve and across the Northern Peninsula. Four caribou herds inhabit Labrador, the most famous of which is the George River herd. Its 450,000 caribou migrate

BOB RACE

The puffin is Newfoundland's provincial bird.

eastward from Québec in late spring, to calve in the Torngat Mountains.

The Newfoundland Dog and Labrador Retriever

The large, long-haired Newfoundland dog is believed to have originated with the early Portuguese, who brought mountain sheepdogs across the Atlantic with them. Considered one of North America's finest show dogs, the Newfoundland is better known locally as a working dog. Its swimming prowess in rescuing shipwrecked fishermen and sailors from stormy seas has inspired local legends.

Contrary to the name, the Labrador retriever originated on the island of Newfoundland as a descendant of the Newfoundland dog. The retriever was known as the "lesser Newfoundland," "St. John's dog," or "St. John's water dog"—until its debut in London at the English Kennel Club in 1903.

HISTORY

Early Inhabitants

The province's earliest human history dates to between 8,000 and 10,000 years ago, when Maritime Archaic Indians followed the retreating Laurentide glacier into northern Labrador. By 7500 B.C., they were hunting seals and whales in the Labrador Straits. At L'Anse-Amour is a burial mound, discovered in 1973, dating from 6905 B.C. From here, the Indians migrated farther south to Newfoundland island. Another burial site at Port au Choix on the island dates to 4,300 years ago.

The Inuits arrived between 4,000 and 7,000 years ago. Descendants of the early Inuits still live in Labrador. Among the various Inuit groups, the Dorset Culture is among the most interesting to anthropologists. The Dorsets roamed as far south as Newfoundland island's Port au Choix on the Point Riche Peninsula 1,500-2,200 years ago, but they vanished between A.D. 1000 and 1200.

The Beothuk Indians, who adorned themselves with red ochre and lived on the island as early as A.D. 200, were extinct by 1823.

Earliest Explorers

As early as the fifth century, Brendan the Navigator, an Irish monk, sailed across the Atlantic in search of the "wonderful island of the saints." Some say he found it on Newfoundland; the *Navigatio Sancti Brendani Abbatis*, penned in the ninth century, described an island of steep cliffs, rocky inlets, fog, icebergs, and seabirds—all hallmarks of the island.

The Norsemen, or Vikings, from Greenland and Iceland sailed along Labrador's coast and up Hamilton Inlet. About A.D. 1000, they established a foothold at L'Anse aux Meadows. The site was North America's earliest European settlement, and has been designated a national park and a UNESCO World Heritage Site.

By the 1500s, European fishermen were familiar with the island and Labrador coastlines. Basques from Spain fished for cod off the Grand Banks—drying and salting the fish on the island's seacoasts—and hunted whales in the Strait of Belle Isle. From 1540 to 1610, five whaling stations employing 1,900 men served the area. The *San Juan,* one of the Basque whaling ships, sank at Red Bay; archaeological work dates the ship to 1565, and experts say the sunken ship, perfectly preserved by the cold sea, is North America's best-preserved shipwreck.

England's claim to the area dates to Giovanni Caboto (better known as John Cabot), the Venetian explorer-for-hire who sighted the "New Founde Lande" on a 1497 voyage. He had apparently learned about the island from Basque fishermen. Where Cabot actually stepped ashore is anyone's guess. The folks in St. John's say it was on their shores. Others in the province believe it was at Bonavista, which is where the 500th anniversary celebration of the landing is set for 1997.

French and English Claims

France's claim of sovereignty dates to the early 16th-century fishing fleets that dropped anchor from the Burin Peninsula to Channel-Port aux Basques. French explorer Jacques Cartier followed, skirting the coastlines of the island and Labrador on voyages between 1534 and 1542, and claiming for France all the land he saw. On the island, France claimed and defended the French Shore, from Cape Bonavista's tip to Cape Ray near Port aux Basques. The Peace of Paris in 1763 awarded fishing rights off the island to the French, but prohibited the western coast's permanent settlement. In 1783, the Treaty of Versailles limited France's fishing rights to solely the western coast.

Great Britain, for its part, was eager to establish trading centers in the New World. In 1558, private mercantile interests from England's West Country settled **Trinity,** the pretty, historic village on Trinity Bay. Trinity predates St. Augustine, Florida, which was settled by the Spaniards in 1564. The settlement emerged as a major trading and fishing center several decades later, and was also the site of England's first overseas court of justice, a vice-admiralty court established in 1615.

The fishing admirals evolved a system of raw justice. In lieu of a governor, the admirals of the season's first fishing ships ruled St. John's and each major bay. The nations jockeyed for dominance, but England eventually controlled the system. As a U.S. diplomat described the situation in the late 1700s, "Newfoundland has been considered, in all former times, as a great ship moored near the Grand Banks during the fishing season for the convenience of English fishermen."

Settlements: Legal and Illegal

The Crown granted Lord Baltimore the Avalon Peninsula for Roman Catholic settlement in 1623. But after enduring a harsh winter at Ferryland, Baltimore petitioned for another grant and moved the Catholics south to Maryland. With Baltimore out of the picture, Sir David Kirke, the British adventurer, received a grant for the island in 1637. Kirke, who had fled political upheaval in England, set himself up in Baltimore's baronial quarters at Ferryland, until the Dutch toppled the empire and dismantled the mansion in 1653.

Less pretentious outports such as Pouch Cove (carved on a cliff) began as illegal refuges for sailors and fishermen who had jumped ship and married local women. For them, any dent on the rocky shore would do. The settlements were discouraged, however, by British and French ships patrolling the coastlines. Any sign of life, like fireplace smoke issuing from a chimney, spelled eviction.

Early St. John's

St. John's evolved independently as a supply and fisheries center. Its mixed population of Spaniards, Portuguese, and French was hardly Anglo; consequently, the island's first officially chartered English colony was Cupids on Conception Bay, founded in 1610.

Still, St. John's was hard to ignore, and by 1675 a string of British forts guarded the harbor. England's most formidable foe was the French, entrenched since 1622 at Plaisance on Placentia Bay. After ongoing assaults, Plaisance slipped from French control with the Treaty of Utrecht in 1713. The British renamed the place Placentia and took over the fort.

England's New Colony

In 1711, a naval governor was appointed to strengthen England's control of the fishing-admiral system. Part-time government, administered by a summertime governor, followed in the late 1720s. Sporadic settlements took hold as immigrants, who had settled on the Avalon Peninsula, moved westward. Twillingate, begun by Breton fishermen about 1700, had 159 inhabitants by 1739. Bell Island, in Conception Bay, was settled by English and Irish immigrants in the 1740s.

The persistent French attacked St. John's from the Fortress of Louisbourg on Cape Breton, but the British finished off Louisbourg in 1758. A French contingent subsequently sailed across the Atlantic from Brest, and was defeated at the Battle of Signal Hill in 1762. That battle ended the Seven Years' War. The 1763 Treaty of Paris awarded the island and a mainland strip to England, while France acquired **St-Pierre and Miquelon,** small islands off Newfoundland's southern shore.

Navigator and explorer Capt. James Cook was dispatched in 1762 to survey England's new colonial acquisition. Cook's explorations probed Labrador's seacoast, and the Burin Peninsula and Corner Brook areas on the island. He also ventured inland—up the island's Humber River as far as Deer Lake. On the western coast, Anglo immigration soon followed to the Bay of Islands, Humber Arm coastline, and St. George's.

French Acadians from Nova Scotia, who had fled France's defeat at Louisbourg, settled on the Port au Port Peninsula in 1758. France wanted fishing rights on the island's western coast, and the Treaty of Versailles granted the request in 1783. England bitterly contested this claim through the late 1800s. In fact, when plans were made for the new railroad's terminus, England chose the more neutrally located Port aux Basques, rather than St. George's in the Acadian area, which the French claimed was within their jurisdiction. The sun was setting, however, on Atlantic Canada's French presence, and, in 1904, France relinquished the island's territorial fishing claims in a swap with England for Morocco.

The Beothuks' Demise

Across the island's central area, the arrival of Europeans foretold grave consequences for the Beothuks Indians, who had migrated from Labrador in A.D. 200 and spread across the Baie Verte Peninsula to Beachside, Twillingate, and the shores of the Exploits River and Red Indian Lake.

In 1769, a law prohibiting murder of the Beothuks was enacted, but the edict came too late. The Indians were almost extinct, and in 1819, a small group of Beothuks was ambushed by white men near Botwood. In the ensuing struggle, Demasduit, a 23-year-old squaw, was captured, and her husband and newborn infant were killed. She was taken to St. John's, where she died of tuberculosis in 1823, the last of her race.

Labrador Develops

Settlements spread to Labrador. The lure was trade, and by 1870, 500 schooners plied the coast. English law was administered first by a circuit court of justice, then with Labrador's first permanent court of justice at Rigolet, established in 1826. Trading posts started at North West River, Cartwright, and L'Anse au Clair, and English immigrants and Newfoundland *livyers* (permanent coastal residents) followed.

Remote Labrador also lured the do-gooders. German Moravian missionaries set up outposts at Nain, Hopedale, and other coastal sites in the 1700s. The area's famed medical missionary, Dr. Wilfred Grenfell of England, established a mission hospital at Battle Harbour in 1893—the first of many remote medical centers and nursing stations. Grenfell also encouraged Inuit crafts and trade and opened the first cooperative at Red Bay.

Fuller Government Evolves

Meanwhile, full-fledged dominion status came to the island. The former part-time governor was replaced by a full-time governor in 1811. The issue of land ownership was resolved, and settlers were allowed to own land by 1813. Newfoundland was granted self-government, and the first assembly was held in St. John's in 1855. Splendid official buildings went up: the Commissariat House, for Fort William's assistant commissary general; and the Government House—an expensive residential replica of the Admiralty House at Plymouth, England—for the governor.

Immigration fleshed out the island. A second wave of Acadians from Nova Scotia immigrated to the Port au Port Peninsula in the 1840s. Mass Irish immigration spread across the Avalon's Southern Shore, and by 1850 half of Newfoundland's inhabitants were Irish. Aside from the western coast's French ports, the island was decidedly pro-British, and when the question of Confederation arose in 1869, Newfoundlanders held a general election and voted resoundingly against it.

Communications and Industry

By 1844, steamer service linked St. John's with Halifax, and islandwide rail service started in the 1880s. The first trans-Atlantic telegraph cable to Europe was laid from **Heart's Content** on Trinity Bay in 1866; Guglielmo Marconi received the first trans-Atlantic wireless message from Signal Hill at St. John's in 1901.

Copper was first mined at Tilt Cove in 1864, and the discovery of iron ore on Bell Island led to over 70 years of prosperity, from 1893 to 1966. During that period, the Wabana Mines produced 30% of the iron ore smelted in Canada. Pulp and paper industries developed in the early 1900s at Grand Falls and Corner Brook. In Labrador, Garland Lethbridge of Paradise River developed a flash-freeze food-preservation method. Lethbridge shared the secret with Clarence Birdseye, an American who spent a year at Sandwich Bay in 1916. Birdseye subsequently sold the concept to General Foods for $22 million—without a cent to Lethbridge.

The Bad-luck Years

Bad luck struck Newfoundland in the early 1900s. In Labrador, the Spanish flu arrived

CROSSROADS OF THE WORLD

As the continent's closest gateway to Europe, Newfoundland played a significant role in the development of air travel across the Atlantic. Capt. John Alcock and Lt. A.W. Brown made the first successful trans-Atlantic flight in 1919, taking off from St. John's in a twin-engine biplane and landing tail-up in an Irish peat bog 16 hours later. Charles Lindbergh, the pioneer American pilot, flew over St. John's on a 33.5-hour nonstop New York-Paris solo flight in 1927, and in 1933 he touched down at Nain, Labrador, on another trans-Atlantic flight. American aviatrix Amelia Earhart chose Trepassey on the southern Avalon Peninsula as the departure point for her 1928 trans-Atlantic flight to Wales. On that flight, Earhart flew as a passenger. Her next flight, however, in 1932, won Earhart honors as the first woman to solo across the Atlantic. She left from Harbour Grace, near St. John's.

Wartime Aviation

By 1939, England was locked in mortal combat with Nazi Germany and needed aircraft and supplies. The British Air Ministry selected Gander (now nicknamed crossroads of the world), as a landing and refueling base on the trans-Atlantic supply route. Goose Bay Air Base, in Labrador, opened shortly thereafter; by 1940, the joint Canadian and U.S. air base had a staff of 5,000 military and 3,000 civilian personnel.

At the war's height, American-built aircraft destined for England touched down in Newfoundland and Labrador. About 500,000 U.S. pilots and crew members passed through major installations, such as Ft. Pepperrell, the military headquarters at St. John's, and bases at Goose, Gander, Torbay, Argentia, and Stephenville/Harmon.

Postwar Developments

Most military operations ceased in the 1960s, and U.S. Air Force involvement was taken over by the Canadian Ministry of Transport. The U.S. still has a small military presence at the Argentia, Gander, and Goose bases. The former Goose Air Base kept its military functions and has evolved as the Canadian Forces Base Goose Bay. It added a NATO Tactical Fighters Weapons Training Centre in the early 1990s, while the emergence of Happy Valley–Goose Bay as central Labrador's air gateway prompted the development of the commercial Goose Bay Airport. The former Gander base made the transition to a commercial airport. It offered polar flights to Europe and served as the gateway for political refugees from Cuba and the Iron Curtain nations, who touched down briefly before flying to other parts of Canada.

aboard a supply ship, and a third of the region's 1,200 Inuits perished. During WW I, cod and fur prices slumped, and the island's railroad went bankrupt. The Great Depression aggravated conditions, and in St. John's, a mob tried to lynch the prime minister. By 1933, Newfoundland was insolvent. England paid the debts (based on the personal credit of Sir Robert Bond, the St. John's millionaire who later became Newfoundland's prime minister), stripped Newfoundland of its dominion status, and returned it to the status of a crown colony, suspending the assembly and appointing a six-member commission to govern the island and Labrador.

The island, nevertheless, fared better during the Great Depression than the rest of Atlantic Canada. Zinc, lead, copper, silver, and gold were discovered at Buchans. The economy was aided coincidentally with the unprecedented economic boom that accompanied WW II. The location of Newfoundland and Labrador at North America's eastern edge was an enviable asset. Canadian, British, and U.S. military bases were built in rapid succession from Gander to Goose Bay. (See the special topic "Crossroads of the World.")

Nazi submarines plied the island's waters. In St. John's, Signal Hill was fortified against invasion, as was nearby Cape Spear. The Germans chose Bell Island in Conception Bay for an incursion attempt. They sank ships laden with iron ore and burned the piers. No place on the island or mainland was safe: a submarine sank the *Caribou,* a Nova Scotia ferry, off Port aux Basques; and in northern Labrador, the Germans actually landed and set up a weather station, probably the Nazis' only foothold in North America.

Confederation and Its Consequences

Wartime tolls notwithstanding, the economy had never been better. Buoyed by improved conditions, Newfoundlanders questioned the existing Crown commission-government arrangement. Confederation was rejected by the voters in 1946 and 1948. But when it appeared on the ballot again in 1949, a slender majority voted for union with Canada, and Newfoundland became the nation's 10th province.

A rite of passage can have pitfalls. Joey Smallwood, a schoolteacher and journalist from St. John's, carried the Liberal banner for Confederation and assumed government reign during the early Confederation years. Smallwood saw a profitable, efficient industrial society as the province's hope, and he advised Newfoundlanders to "Burn your boats." Under that strategy, the island's innumerable outports, many without municipal governments or services, were victims of the times.

A resettlement scheme began—still painfully remembered—under which many small outports were forcefully abandoned, with the inhabitants relocated to new or larger communities with services. Critics lambasted the displacement as a horrendous blow to the island's social texture. Other islanders saw a glimmer of hope and said that feudalism, the system that had prevailed since the fishing-admiral system, had finally ended.

The New Newfoundland

From this, a new Newfoundland emerged. Municipal government and town planning, both new concepts, began in the 1950s. Memorial University in St. John's, founded in 1925 as a college, was granted university status in 1949. Access to Labrador improved, as rail service and a road linked Labrador City with the province of Québec.

The provincial economy is now in flux. The seal industry, censured by animal activists, has been limited to the 30,000 seals legally culled by the Native people each spring. In 1977, the federal government sought to curb depletion of the Grand Banks fisheries by establishing a 320 km offshore fishing zone. That was admirable defensive thinking on the part of the Canadian government, but parts of the Grand Banks lie outside the designated zone, and these areas

still draw mammoth foreign trawlers that contribute to the depletion of the once-rich fisheries.

The codfish landings remained sparse, and in 1992, the Canadian government took drastic steps. Ottawa banned commercial salmon fishing in Newfoundland for five years and commercial cod fishing in the province's northeastern waters for two years. The moratorium put 19,000 fishermen and fish processors out of work for the first time in 500 years. The two-year codfishing ban expired in 1994, and fishermen prepared to go back to work. But to everyone's horror, not only had codfish populations off Newfoundland not recovered during the ban, they had actually diminished to almost nothing. The fishing ban was extended, and the future of this industry now looks exceedingly bleak.

Provincial economic expectations are now tied to the offshore petroleum and natural gas fields at the edge of the Grand Banks. The Hibernia oilfield—said to be the world's largest offshore oil reserve—along with the nearby Terra Nova and Whiterose sites are expected to yield 200,000 barrels of oil a day by 1996.

GOVERNMENT AND ECONOMY

The province's government is modeled on the British parliamentary system. The lieutenant-governor, appointed by the prime minister to a four-year term, heads the executive council and the legislative House of Assembly. The House of Assembly's 52 members are elected from the provincial districts. On the national level, the province sends seven members of parliament and six senators to Ottawa.

The Liberals narrowly lost the 1972 election. Since then, however, the party has continued to be a major political player. Other major parties include the Progressive Conservatives, the People's Party, the Independents, and the Conservatives. In Labrador, the New Liberal Party has had a considerable impact.

On the local level, the province has about 1,500 settlements, of which three—St. John's, Corner Brook, and Mount Pearl (a St. John's suburb)—are cities, 168 others are towns, and 140 are classified as communities. The remaining settlements are organized around local churches rather than municipal governments; in these hamlets, provincial taxes and services are lacking.

Economy

The gross provincial product was more than $10.3 billion in 1991. Manufacturing (at $660 million) and construction (at $760 million) were the top revenue earners. Electric power and water utilities brought in $439 million.

Mining placed fourth, earning $250 million. Most mining revenues come from western Labrador, where about 80% of Canada's iron ore is extracted. Other commercially mined minerals in the province include copper, lead, zinc, gold and silver, chromium, limestone, gypsum, aluminum silicate, and asbestos. Labrador also holds Canada's sole commercial deposit of pyrophyllite, which is used in the production of ceramics.

The fisheries, a chronic boom or bust industry, contribute $230 million annually to the provincial economy. Labrador produces half of Canada's commercial char. Pulp and paper factories earn $70 million, while agriculture earns $28 million in hay, root crops, vegetables, berries, and mink farming. A substantial crafts industry, with 2,000 artisans, earns $12-15 million annually.

PEOPLE

The province (pop. 568,474) is lightly settled, with a density of less than two people per square km. Cities, towns, and communities hold about 60% of the population; the remaining residents inhabit outports and remote areas.

On the island, many settlements lie along the coastline. About 40% of the population is found in St. John's and on the Avalon Peninsula. Labrador's 30,375 residents are concentrated east to west across the central plateau, while the seacoast is sparsely settled.

Early Ancestors

Most residents of the island trace their ancestry to the British Isles. The Irish are well represented—you'll find plenty of O'Rourkes, Murphys, and Mooneys at settlements from St. John's to Placentia Bay. Merchants from Scotland also

settled in St. John's, and were joined by Nova Scotian Scots who migrated from Cape Breton to the western coast. English descendants are spread throughout the province and trace their roots to the West Country—Devon, Dorset, Somerset, Hampshire—and the Channel Islands. The population of St. John's is a mix of English and Irish.

Among the minority ethnic groups here are the southwestern coast's small French population; the Micmac Indians of the Conne River Indian Reserve; and an American population that originated with a small number of military personnel who stayed on after being stationed here in WW II.

In Labrador, most of the inhabitants are "from away," meaning from other parts of Canada. Mixed among these are the Newfoundlanders who made their homes in Labrador long ago; some Newfoundlanders who summer there at the family fishing stations; and the indigenous Inuit, Innu, and Métis peoples, who live primarily at Davis Inlet, Sheshatsheits, the Lobstick Lake area, and along the northern coastline.

Religion

The island's Irish and French are Roman Catholics, while the English belong to the Anglican or United churches. Protestant evangelical denominations have strong followings and include the Salvation Army, Pentecostal, and Seventh-day Adventists. Labrador has a similar distribution, as well as Moravian, Church of the Nazarene, Plymouth Brethren, Baptist, and Methodist denominations. There's also a small Jewish population in St. John's.

Language

English—rich with clipped British accents and softly brushed Irish lilts—is the province's dominant language, spoken by more than 98% of the population. French is spoken on the southwestern coast, where Newfoundlanders are mainly bilingual (a mere 1.4% of the population speaks only French). Other languages occasionally heard among the population include Innu, Inuit, Chinese, German, and Spanish.

The English spoken in Newfoundland is a dialect unique to the province. It's so distinctive, it prompted Memorial University scholars to compile the province's own *Dictionary of New-*

foundland English, the definitive reference to the local language since 1982.

Every immigrant group to come along has contributed to Newfoundland English. For example, *droke,* a Celtic word, translates as a steep-sided valley cut with a stream. The Inuits contributed *komatik* (sled), among others. Many local words deal with dining. If you're invited to "have a scoff" or "boil up," be prepared to pull up a chair and share a meal; if it's a "mug up," you'll have tea or a snack.

Many words relate to fishing. A "tilt" translates as an open fishing shelter; a "hangashore" or "angishore" describes a man too lazy to fish; and "stages and flakes" are fish-drying racks set up on stilts. The 300,000-plus visitors who arrive in the province each year are known as "Mainlanders," who have "come-from-away"— "CFAs" for short.

Irish and Scottish musical traditions remain strong in Newfoundland.

KAREN McKINLEY

In a sense, Newfoundland has never quite fit the Canadian mold. Its culture has always been more entwined with the traditions of England and Ireland than the rest of Canada. This has occasionally led to tensions between citizens of the province and Canadians elsewhere in the country. In the 1940s, when Newfoundland was considering confederation with Canada, some ethnocentric Canadians used the word "Newfie" as a slur, belittling their culturally distinct Newfoundland cousins. To this day, the word amuses no one here.

Genealogy Resources
The best source for genealogical tracing is the **Provincial Archives of Newfoundland and Labrador** at Military and Bannerman roads in St. John's, tel. (709) 729-3065 (open Mon.-Fri. 9 a.m.-4:45 p.m.). Its free *Genealogical Package* describes the archives' holdings and how they can help trace family roots, and provides a list of private genealogists. For more information, contact the archives at the Colonial Building, Military Rd., St. John's, NF A1C 2C9.

Memorial University's **Centre for Newfoundland Studies,** tel. 737-7475, has directories of names and addresses dating to the 1800s, plus the nominal censuses for 1921, 1935, and 1945. The center is part of the university's main library on Elizabeth Ave.; open Mon.-Thurs. 8:30 a.m.-11 p.m., Fri. 8:30 a.m.-5:45 p.m., Sat. 10 a.m.-5:45 p.m., Sun. 1:30-9:45 p.m. (It closes an hour earlier during summer and is also closed between school semesters.)

In Labrador, *Them Days Magazines,* P.O. Box 939, Station B, Happy Valley–Goose Bay, Labrador, NF A0P 1E0, tel. 896-8531, publishes a quarterly magazine with features about the region's history and people. The company is also a source for historic diaries, letters, and other records. If you want to do a roots search, you'll need to know your family's name, regional relatives' names, and where family members lived. Be aware that *Them Days* is a publish-

Conduct and Customs
Historically at odds with the inhospitable land, treacherous seas, and capricious weather, Newfoundlanders have emerged from the centuries as passionate, resourceful survivors. Their long link with England has imbued them with a preference for formal courtesies. For example, they are soft-spoken and dislike loud talking or raucous laughter. Further, a Newfoundlander expects to finish a sentence without interruption. Like other Atlantic Canadians, you'll find the people here friendly, hospitable, patient, and sincere.

None of which precludes the passion with which they live. They're quick to joke and quicker to laugh. Further, Newfoundlanders are habitual iconoclasts, who lambast issues from religion to social conventions. They enjoy satire, and their political brickbats saturate the local newspapers. They're intuitively creative, and their music, crafts, and fine arts are among Canada's best.

ing company, not a genealogical society. But Labrador's early years are important to the staff members, and they'll help you as best they can. A subscription to the magazine costs $15 in Canada, $16 in the United States.

Crime

With no history of violent crime or multiracial upheavals, the province is among North America's safest places. It's so free of violent crime that the provincial police do not carry guns. Petty theft is more common; lock vehicle doors and keep valuables out of sight.

Don't ask for trouble, however, especially if you are a woman traveling alone. St. John's, as an international port, has a steamy bar scene rife with sailors. In the hinterlands, service stations are sparse, and the back roads are lightly traveled; bring a spare tire and make sure your vehicle is in good working condition.

CRAFTS

Newfoundland's exciting crafts scene owes its genesis to the province's demanding setting. Winters here are long and harsh, many areas are remote, and money is short during the fisheries' slack periods. Crafts, which can be produced in the home at any time of year, were taken advantage of early on to contribute a margin of comfort to the subsistence economy. The NONIA Handicrafts shop in St. John's, for example, is an outlet for the Newfoundland Outport Nursing and Industrial Association, an organization begun in 1924 to raise money for medical care in the remote outports.

Handmade crafts became an industry with clout in the 1970s, when the provincial government eyed them as a potential revenue earner. The **Newfoundland and Labrador Crafts Development Association** (NLCDA) was charged with developing the crafts industry, as well as running the Devon House gallery and retail shop in St. John's and thrice-yearly crafts shows. The association's $25 annual membership fee includes the NLCDA Newsletter, which reports on crafts developments. For details, write to the organization at 59 Duckworth St., St. John's, NF A1C 1E6. **Enterprise Newfoundland and Labrador** evolved next, with a mandate to work

behind the scenes, developing export markets and exhibiting the wares at national and international trade shows.

St. John's is the provincial crafts hub, but privately owned crafts shops flourish across the province. Every area has a crafts specialty. Tourist chalets on the TransCanada Highway are stuffed with bulky, warm fishermen's sweaters; knitted mittens and hats whose linings are "thrummed" with fleece; embroidered parkas trimmed with fox fur; and landscapes depicted on hooked mats and hangings. Gander is known for handwoven woolens; St. Alban's and the Conne River Indian Reserve feature carvings in bone, wood, rock, and moose or caribou antlers. The crafts shops of Labrador's northern Inuit settlements are centers for soapstone sculpture, caribou-leather moccasins, labradorite jewelry, and woven-grass baskets. Another irresistible buy is **Terra Footwear;** the deftly crafted suede hiking boots are manufactured in Harbour Grace and exported worldwide.

Crafts in St. John's

St. John's is the provincial crafts center. A number of apparel designers call St. John's home, and you'll find clothing in fluffy mohair, serviceable knits, sleek caribou, shiny fish skin, and lustrous leather. Among the best apparel designers here is **Woof Design,** tel. (709) 722-7555. Winner of the 1986 Newfoundland Export Award, the shop markets clothing in caribou-leather, tapestry, duffel, fine cotton, and mohair across Canada and the United States. The workroom and a retail outlet are located at 1 Prospect St.; open Mon.-Fri. 10 a.m.-5 p.m., Sat. 10 a.m.-3 p.m.

Cabot Institute, 50 Parade St., St. John's, NF A1C 4C7, tel. 753-2570, is the provincial applied-arts and technical college. It influences the local crafts scene with a textile-design program emphasizing batik, silkscreen, tie-dye, and fabric-printing techniques. Tours are available on request year-round, Mon.-Fri. 9 a.m.-4 p.m.

The capital has also emerged as the center for pyrophyllite etching, a new provincial craft. Similar to soapstone, the pale yellow or green pyrophyllite slabs are mined at nearby Manuels and are used in sculpture and scrimshaw plaques.

Typical Prices

When shopping around, expect superbly crafted wares at reasonable prices. A wool sweater, for example, will cost from $85 to $200, depending on the design's complexity; when it's washed, you'll smell the aroma of fresh lamb's wool. Yard goods are handwoven. Linen costs about $30 a meter, wool $50 a meter. The exquisitely crafted Grenfell-style coats have a hefty price tag, though, and you'll pay about $325 for a full-length coat or around $275 for a thigh-length model. Raw, gem-quality labradorite is $50 or more a pound.

For More Information

The provincial tourist office provides a good list of crafts shops and producers, as does the *Newfoundland and Labrador Travel Guide*. Enterprise Newfoundland and Labrador publishes a *Craft Directory* including a list of crafts stores and capsule biographies of some craftspeople; for a copy, call (709) 729-7000, or write the Cottage Industry Division, 136 Crosbie Rd., St. John's, NF A1B 3K3.

FINE ART

The fine-arts scene, again based in St. John's (with a smaller Corner Brook enclave), is similarly prolific, though provincewide you'll find far fewer art galleries than crafts shops.

Traditional oils, watercolors, and sculptures can be found, along with an artistic explosion of avant-garde work. Among the best-known artists are watercolorists Christopher and Mary Pratt and their daughter Barbara Pratt Wangersky; Pam Hall, who creates free-form stone, paper, canvas, plaster, and wood sculptures; Janice Udell, who paints exquisite watercolor sea- and landscapes; painter David Blackwood; and Diana Dabinett, another skilled painter who works in silk banners and framed pieces. For an overview of artistic activity in the capital, visit **Resource Centre for the Arts,** the **Eastern Edge Art Gallery,** or the provincially sponsored **Memorial University Art Gallery.**

Outdoor art abounds in the area. You'll find politically inspired murals along Water St. W in St. John's. At nearby Bell Island in Conception Bay, the Wabana Mines' demise inspired a stunning array of seven mur[...] time days. The murals w[...] of native artists headed [...] john, a wildlife artist no[...]

EVENTS AND ENTERTAINM[...]

Folk Festivals

Provincial folk festivals originated as family reunions decades ago and have grown to country-fair proportions—tempting enough to lure distant relatives from afar and visitors from all over the province. The festivals are consistently good summer entertainment. Local lodgings can be hard to get at festival time, so it's wise to make reservations early.

The **Burin Peninsula Festival of Folk Song and Dance** at Burin kicks off the season with authentic island songs, music, dance, and dance workshops in early July. The **Hangashore Folk Festival** at Corner Brook, and the **Exploits Valley Salmon Festival** at Grand Falls–Windsor, follow with more of the same in mid-July. The **New World Island Fish, Fun, and Folk Festival** at Twillingate, the **Southern Shore Folk Festival** at Ferryland, and the **Conception Bay Folk Festival** at Carbonear round out the month.

The festival season ends by mid-August. The **Newfoundland and Labrador Folk Festival,** held in early August in St. John's, ranks as the province's grandest folk hoopla and draws large crowds with its mix of folk ingredients and country-fair trappings. The **Heritage Folk Festival** at Glovertown features old-time Newfoundland music and recitations over three days in mid-August.

Other Festivals and Outdoor Entertainment

If you're interested in French-inspired airs and dance, check out **Une Journée dans le Passé,** in late July at Grand Terre (Mainland); and **La Longue Veillée,** in early August at the western coast's Cape St. George.

The smaller folk festivals are equally entertaining. In early July, Lewisporte, for example, puts on a lobster spread at the town's **Great Lobster Boil;** in mid-July, St. Anthony's **Cod Festival** features cod jigging, and North West River's **Beach Festival** lays out a Labradorian food spread. Equally bountiful feeds take place

Bakeapple Folk Festival, held in ...dor Straits communities in mid-Au-

...unt on summertime street entertainment, ...o. The **Buskers,** many of whom are Memorial University music students, perform at the drop of a hat in St. John's and other island towns. More events are described in the travel chapters below, but for a complete list of the sports events, country and town fairs, food festivals, regattas, and more folk festivals, see the provincial *Tourist Guide.*

Formal Entertainment
The formal performing arts are based in St. John's at the **Arts and Culture Centre,** the province's arts hub. The **Resource Centre for the Arts,** at the LSPU Hall (the former Long Shoremen's Protective Union hall on Duckworth St.), serves as an alternate venue, featuring avant-garde productions and a variety of comedy, drama, and musical entertainment. On an informal level, the biannual **Sound Symposium** takes over the capital for 11 days in early July with African rhythms and jazz, as well as new age, electronic, and traditional Newfoundland music.

Across the island, the **Stephenville Festival of the Arts** livens up the western coast with drama, music, and cabaret productions at Stephenville, July-early August.

Kissing the Cod
Newfoundlanders dote on the codfish, and locals invite visitors to pledge piscatory loyalty to King Cod in hilarious induction ceremonies regularly conducted on tour boats and in restaurants. To be "screeched-in" in proper style, a visitor dons fisherman's garb, downs several quick shots of Screech rum, kisses a cod, joins in singing a local ditty, poses for a photograph, and receives an official certificate. It's strictly tourist nonsense, but visitors love it.

Provincial Holidays
Newfoundland celebrates all of the national holidays, plus St. Patrick's Day, 17 March; St. George's Day, 24 April; Discovery Day, 24 June; Dominion (Memorial) Day, 1 July; and Orangemen's Day, 12 July. The holidays are observed on the nearest Monday in order to provide a long

weekend. St. John's also unofficially shuts down on St. John's Regatta Day, the first Wednesday in August, weather permitting.

RECREATION

Newfoundland, with its thousands of untouched acres of parks and wilderness, offers the perfect backdrop for the ultimate in outdoor recreation. The province boasts every option in Atlantic Canada's sports repertoire.

Consider the choices: scuba diving and kayaking in the Gulf of St. Lawrence or the Atlantic; golfing at the capital's Pippy Park, the Twin Rivers links at Terra Nova National Park's edge, or in Corner Brook; inland and coastal biking and hiking; big-game hunting; and angling for trophy-size fish.

On the island, canoeists explore whitewater and placid water alike on the Upper Humber, Main, and Gander rivers. The Avalon Peninsula attracts scuba divers, anglers, canoeists, hikers, and backpackers. The western coast caters to kayakers, the mountains to horseback riders, bikers, and climbers. Labrador attracts diehard anglers and hunters to backwoods sports camps, while naturalists take air tours along the seacoast in search of polar bears and caribou.

The Adventure-travel Experts
Whether you're an experienced adventure enthusiast, or a novice who wants to learn the ropes, numerous licensed adventure-travel companies and sports outfitters are available to help make the route smoother.

Gander River Tours, Dorman's Cove, Gander Bay, NF A0G 2G0, tel. (709) 256-3252, leads trips for experienced canoeists capable of dealing with the swift rapids on the 60-km Gander River system. A guided one- to three-day trip (from $165) includes everything: airport transfers if needed, equipment, meals, and overnight accommodations in cabins.

Between June and September, **Gros Morne Adventure Guides** leads geology and natural-history tours through the national park. The company is based on Main St. (near the Bank of Montreal) in Rocky Harbour. Kayaking is another of their specialties; a day with instructions and lunch costs $90, a two-hour paddle at sunset costs $35. For details, call (709) 458-2722 or 686-2241, or write to Sue Rendell, P.O. Box 101, Pasadena, NF A0L 1K0.

Corner Brook is the main "base camp" for recreation along the west coast. **Mi-Tour,** P.O. Box 839, Corner Brook, NF A2H 6H6, tel. 783-2455, offers a variety of trips, including guided backpacking or horseback riding through the lofty Long Range Mountains (from $200), and kayaking the turbulent Main and Humber rivers. The Humber, among the province's finest white-water rivers, foams with swift current from April to mid-July; from then until autumn, it turns into a tranquil, wetland plain supporting marsh flora and populations of beaver, moose, and caribou. The company rents canoes ($30 day) and also operates guided canoe trips ($125 day and up) for one and more days.

Notable Parks

Wildflowers brighten the landscape at **Cheeseman Natural Environment Park** near Port aux Basques, where pearly everlasting, violet bog aster, and yellow clintonia grow on the coastal barrens. At **Maberly Natural and Scenic Attraction Park** on Bonavista Peninsula's northern tip, birdwatchers can get an eyeful of flocks of seabirds nesting on offshore islands.

Black Bank Provincial Park, near Stephenville on Bay St. George, is an excellent place for swimming; it's got the island's warmest saltwater and a long, white sandy beach. **Northern Bay Sands Provincial Park,** on northern Conception Bay above Carbonear, also attracts sunbathers to its pleasant beach of fine, dark basaltic sand (which gets toasty warm when the sun's out).

Campers will find 2,300 campsites spread among 47 provincial parks. Most sites are unserviced ($7) and include a table, firepit with free wood, drinking water, cleared space or wooden platform for a tent, and pit toilets; partially serviced sites ($9) have showers. **Grand Codroy Outdoor Recreation Park,** beside the TransCanada near Port aux Basques, is the only fully serviced campground ($11) and has water, electricity, and sewer connections. Most commercial campgrounds have full facilities; for a full list, see the *Newfoundland and Labrador Travel Guide,* available from the Department of Tourism and Culture.

Cape Bonavista lighthouse

Terra Nova National Park is a scenic beauty with 400 square km of boreal forests, ponds, bogs, and hills embraced by a fjord-streaked coastline on the island's Eastport Peninsula. **Gros Morne National Park,** northwest of Deer Lake, melds geological history with nine spectacular scenic areas across 1,805 square km.

The park season opens between late May and late June, and continues until early September. For literature and details on the provincial parks, contact the **Provincial Park Division,** Department of Tourism and Culture, P.O. Box 8700, St. John's, NF A1B 4J6, or call (709) 729-5232 or (800) 563-6353. The provincial highway map lists the provincial parks and provides some details.

Seal-watching

Although 30,000 seals are legally culled each spring by the Newfoundlanders and aboriginal peoples, commercial seal hunting has been illegal for years. Seal-watching, instead of hunting, is now a popular pastime from March until May.

North Atlantic Seal Watch Expedition, 8 Virginia Place, St. John's, NF A1A 3G6, tel. (709) 754-5500, can take you for a close-up view aboard a ship, plane, or helicopter. It's not cheap, however. You'll pay $3500 and up for five days or more.

Fishing

The province's reputation for first-class fishing attracts anglers from across Canada, the U.S., and Europe. Inland waterways are choked with trout: speckled, rainbow, lake, brook, and brown. Atlantic salmon, some up to 18 kg, migrate on 200 rivers. In Labrador, a landlocked salmon (known locally as ouananiche) set the record at 10.29 kg in 1982. Lake trout and northern pike can tip the scales at up to 18 kg, and brook trout are trophy size. Wilderness fishing camps are abundant, and typically charge $250 and up per day, all inclusive with a guide.

Fishing seasons vary. Labrador's arctic char season spans mid-June to mid-September and peaks during August. In the Gros Morne area, brook trout are most plentiful June to mid-September, while the Atlantic salmon season spans mid-June to early September. Among the best salmon rivers are the island's Humber and Lomond rivers, along with Labrador's Eagle and Pinware rivers. You'll need a provincial fishing license ($50 for salmon and $5 for trout); in most cases, you'll also need an outfitter or a Newfoundlander relative with you as a guide. At the national parks, salmon fishing is restricted to fly-fishing on scheduled rivers; the required federal salmon permit costs $13 (a trout permit costs $4), and whatever you hook and keep has to be reported for statistical purposes.

The provincial waters are strictly monitored. For details, get in touch with the provincial tourist office for a copy of the federal Department of Fisheries and Oceans' free *Angler's Guide,* containing nonresident guide requirements, river statistics, and bag limits.

Hunting

Nonresident hunting is strictly regulated. You'll need an RCMP gun permit (available at a retail store or from an outfitter), and if you plan to light a fire to keep warm, you'll need a fire permit, available from the provincial Department of Forestry.

Licenses are available through outfitters. Requirements and prices vary. On the island, for example, one male caribou can be taken per license ($400 for a Canadian hunter, $600 for non-nationals). Bears and moose are two other popular big-game species. A small-game license for grouse, ptarmigan, and hare costs $25. Hunters favor the Long Range Mountains in fall for moose and black bear, and northern Labrador in spring for caribou.

The provincial tourist office has free copies of the *Newfoundland and Labrador Hunting Guide, Newfoundland and Labrador Hunting and Fishing Guide,* and the federal *Angler's Guide,* all of which detail regulations and list outfitters. Another contact is the **Wildlife Division,** Department of Environment and Lands, P.O. Box 8700, St. John's, NF A1B 4J6, tel. (709) 729-2815. The provincial *Travel Guide* lists a plethora of adventure-travel companies.

ACCOMMODATIONS

St. John's boasts the province's finest share of accommodations, with more than two dozen hotels, stunning historic inns and bed-and-breakfasts, functional motels, and smaller guesthouses and hospitality homes (variations on B&Bs). Outside the capital, motels lie along the TransCanada Hwy. at the major towns. Off the beaten track, accommodations are smaller and fewer.

All the major motel and hotel groups are represented: Best Western, Holiday Inn, and Journey's End, and in St. John's, the top-notch Canadian Pacific and Radisson. The locally owned Atlantic Inns of Newfoundland has lodgings at Corner Brook, Grand Falls–Windsor, and Gander; while Clayton Inns operates lodgings in Corner Brook, Gander, and St. John's.

Hostels are new on the scene. Private and provincial/national park campgrounds are plentiful.

Standards and Rates

Lodgings are licensed for minimum standards; the newer motels and hotels are equipped for wheelchair access. The star-grading system is new, and to date, only hotels, motels, and B&Bs have been reviewed. The grading is strictly voluntary, so an absence of stars has no weight. The provincial *Travel Guide* lists the approved lodgings by sightseeing regions. For reservations, phone or write the property directly; reservations are wise everywhere in July and August.

Rates (posted in each room) are set by the lodging owner; if the price you're charged and the posted rate differ, discuss it with the property owner or contact **Hospitality Newfoundland and Labrador,** tel. (709) 722-2000.

Most hotels, motels, and historic inns and bed and breakfasts accept major credit cards. Some smaller lodgings in the interior may want cash. All lodgings are taxed except trailer parks and hospitality homes with fewer than four rooms.

FOOD

Some visitors prefer basic, unadorned dining fare, and will find it in the standard steak, chops, seafood, and salads available at most restaurants across the province. Newfoundlanders, on the other hand, prefer their own culinary creations based on historical recipes and the ingredients available locally. If you're a culinary adventurer, you've arrived in the right province.

Many foods originated from the province's ties with England. Locals like gruel (oatmeal) for breakfast; tea biscuits (sweet cakes) with an afternoon snack; dumplings served with supper's stew; or hardtack, a dough mixture that when cooked with flaked, salted fish is known as "fish and brewis." For a special dessert, there's trifle, concocted of a cake layer, fresh summer berries, homemade vanilla custard, and a thorough dousing of sweet sherry, all topped with whipped cream.

Seafood is always on the menu, and if the menu says "fish," here that translates as cod. Local cooks use every part of the ubiquitous cod. All other fish species on the menu will be specifically named. Fillets (pronounce the "t" here) are broiled or dipped in batter or breaded and deep-fried. Cod tongues and cheeks are unusual taste sensations—the fish nuggets, encased in fish gelatin, are poached in a fish stock or fried, then served with lemon and tartar sauce.

Flounder, mackerel, shrimp, capelin, lobster, herring, and blue mussels frequently appear on menus. Wild game is abundant, and you'll

---

FAVORITE LOCAL FARE

seal flipper pie—nutritious, dark, gamy meat parboiled, baked in crust

jiggs dinner—boiled salted meat, cabbage, and vegetables in broth

crubeens—pigs' feet pickled in a brine

soused herring—herring pickled in a brine and bottled

fish 'n' brewis—salted cod, potatoes, hard biscuits cooked as a hash

pork scrunchions—diced pork fat used in fish 'n' brewis and other dishes

blood pudding—parboiled, fatty sausage fried for a main meal

figgy duff—boiled or baked dried-fruit dessert pudding

screech pie—rum-flavored chocolate pie baked in gingerbread crust

yum yums—sweet, shortbread cookies

thimbles—shortbread embellished with coconut and jam

---

find luscious pâtés and gourmet variations of smoked or roasted caribou, moose, partridge, duck, and rabbit on upscale restaurant menus. Moose meat is also available as fast-food mooseburgers served at some summer festivals and occasionally at hinterlands restaurants.

Available veggies consist of root vegetables such as parsnips, turnips and carrots, plus local (thanks to hydroponic nurseries) and imported tomatoes, lettuce, and green vegetables. Nutritious, reconstituted dried peas are used lavishly in soups.

With a fledgling tourism industry, Labrador has far fewer culinary dining opportunities. Deep-fried fish, fried or broiled steaks, and grilled hamburgers are the usual fare. Roast game and broiled Atlantic salmon and char are the real treats, and in Labrador City, French Canadian dishes such as *poutine* (French fries and cheese curds doused with gravy) are frequently on the menu. Credit cards are accepted for lodging and dining in the major towns; outlying settlements prefer cash.

Area Specialties

Some of the province's best meals are served at motel dining rooms along the TransCanada and other highways. Look for mooseburgers at Conception Bay and Northern Peninsula restaurants. Shrimp are Port au Choix's specialty, and the area's succulent scallops come from Port au Port Peninsula outports. Consider yourself lucky to sample the western coast's rhubarb—cooked in pies, served as a sauce, and bottled as a relish or jam. It's said to be Atlantic Canada's finest rhubarb variety. The province's many berry varieties ripen Aug.-Sept.; in season, they're good buys from roadside vendors.

bakeapples

Drink

Be on the lookout for iceberg cubes in your cocktails. In summer, icebergs float south from the arctic and a few ditch in coves and bays on the island's northern and eastern coastlines. Stranded at land's end, the bergs explode and splinter in pieces, and entrepreneurial iceberg vendors sell the remains to local restaurants. You'll know the real thing when you see it; iceberg pieces sizzle as they melt.

Rum ("dark and dirty," as locals describe it) is imported from Barbados; Screech, London Dock, and Old Sam brands are bottled in St. John's and sold locally. Gold Ribbon Deluxe and Kingsway rye whiskeys are locally bottled and sold everywhere. Newfoundlanders are avid beer drinkers and favor Labatts, potent Black Horse, Guinness Stout, Dominion, and India Pale Ale. No grapes are grown locally, but wine imports are plentiful from Chile, Australia, Europe, and the United States. Restaurants tend to charge hefty prices for wine, but don't count on bringing in your own bottle—it's considered improper everywhere.

Liquor outlets are owned by the province or privately operated as agency stores. Hours are Mon.-Sat. 9:30 a.m.-5:30 p.m.; some outlets stay open until 10 p.m. on Friday and Saturday nights. In bars, pubs, and taverns, alcohol is served Mon.-Sat. 9 a.m.-2 a.m., Sun. noon-midnight.

Dining Details

There's always a motel or hotel dining room open, but independent restaurants may close on Monday and sometimes Sunday. Service can be slow. If you've run out of patience and want to prod the waiter, a polite inquiry gets more response than a rude request. A tip is usually *not* included on the bill and 10-15% is customary. Most restaurants accept Visa (the favored plastic money) and other major credit cards.

INFORMATION AND SERVICES

Visitor Information

The **Department of Tourism and Culture,** P.O. Box 8730, St. John's, NF A1B 4K2, publishes the free *Newfoundland and Labrador Travel Guide.* This useful booklet details auto tours, attractions and activities, accommodations, events, and crafts stores arranged by regions on the island and in Labrador. Its free highway map includes provincial-park listings, local ferry phone numbers, and other travel information. Write for a copy, or call (709) 729-2830 in St. John's, (800) 563-6353 in North America (except the Yukon and Alaska), fax (709) 729-0057.

The provincial **visitor information centers** are open mid-May to September. Each center specializes in specific areas. The tourist centers in North Sydney, Nova Scotia (at the Marine Atlantic Ferry Terminal) and the island's Channel-Port aux Basques handle general provincial travel information for ferry passengers. The Clarenville center stocks information about the Bonavista and Burin peninsula areas; the Deer Lake office handles the Northern Peninsula and southern Labrador; Notre Dame Junction specializes in the central island; and Whitbourne stocks literature about St. John's and the Avalon Peninsula.

Many municipalities operate their own tourist centers. The centers are open year-round at St. John's, Corner Brook, Gander, and Grand

Falls–Windsor, while operations at Dunville, Glovertown, Goobies, Hawke's Bay, Marystown, Newville, Port au Port, St. Anthony, Stephenville, and Springdale are seasonal.

Destination Labrador, Labrador's tourism promotion and marketing organization, publishes the free *Labrador: Awaiting Your Heart and Soul,* with useful destination information. For a copy, call 944-7788 or (800) 563-6353 (ask to be transferred to the Labrador phone line), or write the tourism office at 118 Humphrey Rd., Bruno Plaza, Labrador City, Labrador, NF A2V 2J8.

Other Government Offices
The **immigration** process starts outside Canada, but federal immigration officers answer questions at the Employment and Immigration centers in St. John's, Clarenville, Harbour Grace, Marystown, and Placentia. To extend a visit, a non-Canadian requires an interview; for an appointment in St. John's, call (709) 772-5388 Mon.-Fri. 9 a.m.-4:30 p.m.

Canada Post, based in St. John's, has provincewide branch postal offices, open Mon.-Fri. 9 a.m.-5 p.m. Retail outlets augment the Canada Post and are open longer on weekdays and also on weekends.

Health and Safety
If allergies are a problem for you, breathe easily—there's no ragweed pollen in the province. No special health problems exist provincewide that require inoculations before arrival. If you're headed into the hinterlands during the summer, however, a thorough, heavy coating of insect repellent is in order to ward off the copious black flies and biting insects.

If you're not Canadian, make sure you have adequate medical insurance coverage. The basic day-rate costs $465 at the major hospitals in St. John's and Corner Brook; as an outpatient, you'll pay $58 per day.

Community and regional **hospitals** charge around $350 a day. On the island, they're found at Bell Island, Wesleyville, Buchans, Harbour Breton, Fogo Island, Gander, Twillingate, Rocky Harbour, Burgeo, Port Saunders, and Stephenville. In remote areas, a network of medical centers and nursing stations supplements the hospital system.

In Labrador, the main hospitals are in Labrador City, Churchill Falls, and Happy Valley–Goose Bay. The smaller International Grenfell Association medical stations, with headquarters at St. Anthony on the island, operate as a network at Paradise River, Nain, Makkovik, Hopedale, Black Tickle, Davis Inlet, Forteau, Postville, St. Lewis, North West River, and Cartwright.

In an emergency, contact one of the provincial **Royal Newfoundland Constabulary** detachments in St. John's, Gander, Corner Brook, Labrador City, and Churchill Falls, or the **RCMP,** which has major offices at St. John's, Corner Brook, and Happy Valley–Goose Bay, and detachments provincewide. St. John's also offers a **Poison Information Centre,** tel. (709) 722-1110.

Measurements and Money
Like everyone else in Canada, Newfoundlanders made the painful switch to the metric system in the 1970s, and they're still not entirely comfortable with it; you'll unofficially read and hear a mix of meters, feet, and so forth.

As in most places, the best currency-exchange rates are found at **banks.** Usual banking hours are Mon.-Wed. 10 a.m. to 3 or 4 p.m., Thurs.-Fri. 10 a.m.-5 p.m. Some are open Saturday morning. Major **credit cards** are accepted in the tourist areas. Farther afield, the lodgings want cash, but meals can usually be charged. No one wants personal checks.

Provincial and Federal Sales Taxes
The provincial sales tax (PST) is 12% on accommodations, meals, gasoline, and vehicle rentals. Some items are exempt: crafts made in the province, children's clothing and shoes, groceries, books without advertising, prescriptions, and items shipped out of the province within 30 days. The seven percent federal Goods and Services tax (GST) is levied on all purchases.

Tax refunds are feasible, but the process is lengthy. *Keep the original purchase receipts, and make copies.* For a PST refund, ask for a tax refund ($100 minimum purchases) application at any provincial visitor information center. After you've left the province, send the completed application and duplicate receipt copies to the **Tax Administration Branch,** Office of the Comptroller General, Department of Finance, P.O. Box 8720, St. John's, NF A1B 4K1.

The GST refund ($100 minimum purchases for goods used outside Canada) applies only to non-Canadians. Taxes on meals, camping/ trailer park fees, alcohol, tobacco, and gas are not refundable. Lodgings are exempt, so make sure the number of nights is marked on the receipt. The duty-free shops at St. John's International Airport, plus Argentia and Port aux Basques ferry terminals, have refund applications. For purchases under $500, fill it out on the spot and include the original receipts for a cash refund; over $500, you'll have to send the claim to **Revenue Canada, Customs and Excise,** Visitors' Rebate Program, Ottawa, ON K1A 1J5.

Communications and Time
The telephone area code for Newfoundland and Labrador is **709.** Newfoundland Telephone discounts rates 35% all day Sunday, as well as Mon.-Sat. after 6 p.m.; a 60% discount applies every day after midnight.

Time zones vary within the province. Newfoundland island and Labrador Straits communities are on **Newfoundland standard time,** a half hour ahead of the other Atlantic Canada provinces. The rest of Labrador sets the clock on **Atlantic standard time. Daylight saving time** starts the last Sunday in April and continues until the first Sunday in October.

Finally, if you're posting a letter to anyplace in Labrador, use the complete address: it's "Labrador, NF," rather than just "Labrador."

Publications
On the island, the *Evening Telegram* publishes provincial news daily from St. John's. Regional newspapers are published in Gander, Stephenville, Port aux Basques, Corner Brook, St. Anthony, and Grand Falls–Windsor. In Labrador, the weekly *Aurora* covers western Labrador news from Labrador City; the *Labradorian* and *Examiner* handle weekly central and coastal weekly news at Happy Valley–Goose Bay. Another dozen weekly and quarterly newspapers are published in the outlying areas.

Breakwater Books in St. John's ranks among the province's most esteemed sources for provincial books. *Newfoundland Lifestyle* is a glossy quarterly magazine published in St. John's with cultural coverage and insights into the province's lifestyle. *Newfoundland and Labrador Business Journal,* based in St. John's, covers provincial business developments monthly. *Them Days* magazine, a quarterly publication, covers Labrador's heritage and historical events from its base in Happy Valley–Goose Bay.

WHAT TO TAKE

For sightseeing, bring comfortable walking shoes, a lightweight raincoat and an umbrella, a warm jacket or sweater, and a hat or scarf if windblown hair or too much sun bothers you. In St. John's, dinner at a fine restaurant calls for a dress, stockings, and dress shoes for women, and a dress shirt, tie, and jacket for men. Out in the province, the dress code is more relaxed.

If the outdoors is on your agenda, be prepared to dress in layers with a cotton shirt, flannel shirt, sweater, and waterproof windbreaker. Also include woolen socks and hat; sneakers or boat shoes and rubber boots; sunglasses and suntan lotion; binoculars; and a slicker. Whalewatchers and ocean kayakers sometimes encounter rough water, so bring motion-sickness pills if you're subject to *mal-de-mer.*

Always include an effective insect repellent, preferably one containing DEET. Inland, pesky black flies are a problem, especially on windless days and at sunrise and sunset.

Photography Supplies
Bring what you need and include an extra camera in case your basic equipment breaks down miles from nowhere. Photography shops stock basic equipment and film, but are not geared for complex repairs. Include zoom lenses for distant landscapes, seascapes, and wildlife.

The weather changes quickly, so be prepared for varying light conditions; the best strategy is to bring a variety of film speeds in 24-exposure rather than 36-exposure rolls. On the island, the Grand Banks fog often shrouds the southern and eastern coastlines, so make the most of sunny days. The interior and western coast are sunnier. In Labrador, the coastal fog is less dense than on the island, and the interior has a sparkling blue summer sky.

GETTING THERE

By Air
Flights to Newfoundland island originate in Toronto and Halifax. A few trans-Atlantic flights arrive at St. John's and Gander. St. John's is a 90-minute flight from Halifax, two hours from Montréal, three hours from Toronto or Boston, four hours from New York/Newark, and five hours from London, England.

Air Canada flies nonstop from Toronto and London to St. John's, and **Air Nova**, Air Canada's affiliated carrier, flies from Newark to Halifax with ongoing service to Newfoundland's regional gateways at St. John's, Gander, Deer Lake, and Goose Bay, Labrador. Air Nova now flies out of Boston to Halifax and St. John's. **Air Atlantic,** Canadian Airlines International's partner, offers service from Halifax also, and serves the foregoing gateways plus Stephenville.

Labrador, on the other hand, has a divided orientation: Happy Valley–Goose Bay lies within the Atlantic Canada air network, while Labrador City and the Strait of Belle Isle settlements are served by flights from Québec. Central Labrador is served by **Air Nova** with flights from Halifax to Happy Valley–Goose Bay. In western Labrador, Wabush—three km from Labrador City—serves as the area's gateway with flights by **Air Atlantic** to and from Halifax and St. John's. **Air Alliance** and **Inter-Canadian** fly in from Québec. The strait settlements are served by **Air Canada/Air Nova** on direct flights from Montréal. Other Québec carriers come and go, so ask a travel agent about the current status.

By Land
The Iron Ore Company of Canada operates the **Québec North Shore and Labrador Railroad,** with twice-weekly service from Québec's Sept-Îles (accessible by air from Montreal or Québec City) on the northern St. Lawrence River to western Labrador's towns. The railroad's main job is hauling iron ore, but a separate passenger service operates also, and passengers ride along in comfort in a dome-topped passenger car equipped with lunch/snack facilities. For details and reservations, call (709) 994-8205.

Western Labrador towns may also be reached on Hwy. 389 from Québec's Baie Comeau. The 581-km drive takes about 10 hours on paved and unpaved surfaces through forest and tundra; for road conditions, contact the Québec Provincial Police at Baie Comeau, tel. (416) 296-2324.

By Sea
Marine Atlantic operates two ferry routes (reservations required) from North Sydney, Nova Scotia. One docks at Port aux Basques at the island's southwestern tip; the six-hour sailing is year-round. The other, to Argentia near St. John's, takes 12-14 hours and operates early June to late October. The crossing is occasionally rough, so bring along motion-sickness medication. For ferry reservations and information, call the shipline at (902) 794-5700 at North Sydney, (800) 341-7981 in the U.S., or write to them at P.O. Box 250 in North Sydney, NS B2A 3M3; or in care of the Terminal Supervisor, 121 Eden St., Bar Harbor, ME 04609, in the United States.

Cruise ships include St. John's as a port-of-call and occasionally also stop at Corner Brook, St. Anthony, Battle Harbour, Red Bay, Botwood, and Goose Bay. The cruise lines operating in the area include Seabourne Cruise Line, Odessa Cruise Line, Black Sea Shipping, and Royal Viking Line.

GETTING AROUND

By Air
Provincial Airlines, the provincial carrier, connects St. John's, St. Anthony, Deer Lake, and Goose Bay, as well as Québec's Blanc Sablon (the air gateway to Labrador's Strait of Belle Isle settlements) and France's St-Pierre and Miquelon. For details, call (800) 563-2800 within the province, (709) 576-1666 outside the province.

Labrador Airways, the region's airline, flies from Happy Valley–Goose Bay to remote settlements on the northern and southern coastline, plus St. Anthony on the island's Northern Peninsula tip. For details, call (800) 563-3042 within the province, (709) 896-3387 outside the province.

Air Nova, tel. (800) 4-CANADA in Canada, (800) 776-3000 in the U.S.; and **Air Atlantic,** (800) 426-7000, also crisscross the province.

SELECTED MARINE ATLANTIC FERRY SCHEDULES

For a complete list of all Marine Atlantic's rates and schedules in Atlantic Canada, contact Marine Atlantic Reservation Bureau, P.O. Box 250, North Sydney, NS B2A 3M3; tel. (902) 794-5700 in Canada, (800) 341-7981 in the U.S., fax (902) 564-7480. Rates are subject to change without notice.

NORTH SYDNEY, NOVA SCOTIA, TO/FROM PORT AUX BASQUES, NEWFOUNDLAND

Crossing time: Summer schedule—approximately 5 hours; rest of the year—6.5-7.5 hours.
Reservations: tel. (902) 794-5700 in Nova Scotia; tel. (709) 695-7081 in Newfoundland.
Fares: $17 adults, $12.75 seniors, $8.50 children, under 5 free.
Departures: Daily except holidays.

NORTH SYDNEY, NOVA SCOTIA, TO/FROM ARGENTIA, NEWFOUNDLAND

Crossing time: 18 hours.
Reservations: tel. (902) 794-5700 in Nova Scotia; tel. (709) 695-7081 in Newfoundland.
Fares: $47 adults, $35.25 seniors, $23.50 children, under 5 free.
Departures: From North Sydney, Tues. and Fri. at 7 a.m. and 4 p.m.; from Argentia, Wed. and Sat. at 9 a.m. (Newfoundland time).

LEWISPORTE, NEWFOUNDLAND, TO/FROM GOOSE BAY, LABRADOR

Crossing time: 35-38 hours.
Reservations: tel. (709) 535-6876 for Lewisporte; tel. (709) 896-0041 for Goose Bay.
Fares: $85 adults, $63.75 seniors, $42 children, under 5 free.
Departures: From Lewisporte, Tues. at 8 a.m. and Fri. at 6 p.m. (Newfoundland time); from Goose Bay, Sun. at 1:00 p.m. and Wed. at 11 p.m. (Atlantic time).

GOOSE BAY, LABRADOR, TO/FROM CARTWRIGHT, LABRADOR

Crossing time: 13 hours.
Reservations: tel. (709) 896-0041 in Labrador; (800) 341-7981 in the U.S.
Fares: $88.50 adult, $145 auto.
Departures: From Goose Bay, Wed. at 11:30 p.m. (Atlantic time); from Cartwright, Sat. at 6 p.m. (Atlantic time).

CARTWRIGHT, LABRADOR, TO/FROM LEWISPORTE, NEWFOUNDLAND

Crossing time: 24 hours.
Reservations: tel. (709) 535-6876, or (800) 341-7981 in the U.S. only.
Fares: $53 adults, $85 auto.
Departures: From Cartwright, Thurs. at 1:30 p.m. (Atlantic time); from Lewisport, Fri. at 6 p.m. (Newfoundland time).

By Land

One is never quite sure if the province's lack of consistent roads and sightseeing markers is a humorous intrigue to confuse visitors or a get-to-know-the-Newfoundlanders promotion sponsored by the tourist office. Regardless, you'll need logistical help getting around and sightseeing. Use a map to plot a day's itinerary before starting out, and be prepared to ask for directions along the way; Newfoundlanders are very helpful. If you arrive on the island with your own vehicle, you'll find service centers are often widely spaced. Make sure your vehicle is operating perfectly, and carry a spare tire, preferably new, with good tread.

On the island, the TransCanada Highway wraps around the island's perimeter in a 907-km horseshoe. The **Canadian National Roadcruiser Service,** a long-haul public bus system, follows the route and stops in towns and settlements; terminals are in St. John's, Gander, Grand Falls–Windsor, and Corner Brook. Numerous private bus companies link major towns with outlying areas. St. John's has public transit. There's no public transportation in Labrador.

The major car-rental firms are plentiful at the airports and main towns; Budget Rent A Car has 16 outlets across the province. In Labrador, some car-rental companies don't want their vehicles driven on the remote, mainly unserviced TransLabrador Highway. The road's status may change, so ask for an update if you're planning the trip.

You'll need to carry a valid driver's license, proof of registration, and insurance covering at least $200,000 of liability. Seatbelts for the driver and all passengers are mandatory. Drinking while driving and driving while intoxicated carry severe penalties. The **speed limit** is 90-100 kph on the TransCanada, 80 kph on other paved roads, and 60 kph on gravel roads. Single digits designate high-speed highways. Paved and gravel roads, optimistically known as highways, are numbered with triple digits. Beware of steep-shouldered roads.

In Labrador, the Happy Valley–Goose Bay area, western Labrador towns, and the strait settlements have road networks. Highway 500, the 526-km TransLabrador Highway, opened

fully in 1992 and links Happy Valley–Goose Bay with Churchill Falls, Wabush, and Labrador City, with side routes to Esker. Drive cautiously. It's easy to slide on the gravel roadbed, and the road is unserviced in the remote parts.

In you're interested in **biking,** the island's terrain calls for a mountain bike. Rentals are sparse outside of St. John's, so you may want to bring your own wheels.

By Sea
Marine Atlantic operates two spectacular, off-the-beaten-track sailings between Lewisporte on the island's northern coast and the Labrador coastline. Functionally, the two routes link the island with remote Labrador, but for adventure travelers, the sailing's bonus is an incredible array of whales, seals, seabirds, passing icebergs, and, if it's early or late in the season, some pack ice.

The shortest cruise is aboard the car ferry ($80 pp, $130 for the vehicle OW), and it's 35 hours OW from Lewisporte to Happy Valley–Goose Bay along Labrador's southern coast,

---

CAUTION: MOOSE ON THE LOOSE

Some Newfoundlanders won't drive between dusk and dawn on the island. The reason? Moose on the loose.

About 400 moose-and-car collisions occur annually, causing some $600,000 in damage. A moose collision is no mere fender-bender. These animals are big and heavy, and hitting one at speed will make a real mess of your car (it doesn't do the unfortunate moose much good, either). Consequences can be fatal to both parties. Vehicular collisions with the animals are rising, simply because there are both more vehicles and more moose on the island each year. Vehicle numbers are increasing by 30% every five years, and the dozen moose imported from Nova Scotia and New Brunswick in the late 1800s

have now multiplied to about 125,000.

Seventy percent of the year's collisions occur between May and October. Accidents occur mainly from 11 p.m.-4 a.m. (but that's no guarantee collisions won't happen at any hour). If you must drive after dark, use the high beams, scan the sides of the road, and proceed with caution.

Not to say that a moose makes a beeline for your speeding car. Moose, accompanied by swarms of biting insects, inhabit the remote interior. When the swarms thicken during the warm, moist summer, a severely bitten animal may stampede anywhere for relief. Some moose stray onto the TransCanada, perhaps attracted to the bright headlights, or enticed by roadside puddles, which provide drinking water and salt.

The province is aware of the situation and posts signs marked with the figure of a moose along the most dangerous stretches. Some 31 high-risk stretches lie along the TransCanada, especially from Terra Nova National Park to Gander and from Deer Lake to Corner Brook.

37 hours with coastal Cartwright as a port of call. From Lewisporte, the ferry departs twice weekly, mid-June to mid-September.

The second cruise is equally interesting and far more insightful, if you're interested in brief stops at the 48 ports of call along Labrador's entire coastline. The cruise has always been the sea link between Newfoundland and the Labrador coast for Newfoundland families who worked their summertime fishing stations. Not as many Newfoundlanders use the service since the codfishing ban. So while the ship still hauls supplies, there's room for adventure travelers and sightseers interested in the southern coastline's tiny outports and the northern coast's Inuit settlements.

Everything's included on the cruise, from the stateroom to meals, even selected port-of-call land tours. A standard stateroom holding four passengers costs $1500 pp RT, while a deluxe stateroom for two passengers is $3000 pp RT. Two ships sail the 15- to 17-day route and alternately depart Lewisporte every eight or nine days (depending on the weather), July-November.

If you're interested, the *Northern Ranger* has the tourist facilities, while the *Taverner* offers the basic services and the opportunity to rub elbows and sea legs, as it were, with the locals.

Both routes are solidly booked in advance, so make reservations three to six months ahead. For information, contact the Marine Atlantic phone numbers or addresses above. The Marine Atlantic provincial office handles the interprovincial sea network, and the shipline's Port aux Basques office handles the reservations; call (709) 695-4210 or 695-4211.

Otherwise, 13 seasonal and year-round, shorter-haul provincial ferry routes connect Newfoundland island to the offshore islands and remote coastal spans. Expect to pay $1.50 RT on short routes, while longer sailings are calculated by the nautical mile. Across the Strait of Belle Isle, frequent ferry service runs from St. Barbe on the Northern Peninsula to Blanc Sablon, Québec, from early May to early January. For details, call the **Northern Cruiser Ltd.**, tel. 722-4000, or the ferry terminal at 931-2309. Other ferry routes and phone numbers are listed on the provincial highway map, which is available at tourist offices.

Seasonal, privately operated boat service also connects Fortune on the Burin Peninsula with St-Pierre, the capital of St-Pierre and Miquelon, France's overseas archipelago province off Newfoundland's southern coast.

BOB RACE

NEWFOUNDLAND ISLAND

INTRODUCTION

Visualize the island of Newfoundland as not one, but two, similarly shaped islands: a mammoth main island, and a smaller one—the Avalon Peninsula—threaded to the main by a slender isthmus. The interiors of both sections rise in barren, lofty plateaus, while capes dotted with seaports angle out to the northeast and southwest.

Sightseeing Highlights
At 110,681 square km, Newfoundland is the world's 16th-largest island. If you're short on time, consider concentrating your itinerary on the smaller Avalon Peninsula, which offers more manageable sightseeing.

If you have two or three weeks, however, invest the time on the main island. Bluish green waters shimmer in limestone-cupped lakes at the **Blue Ponds Natural Environment,** a provincial park near Corner Brook. Majestic icebergs wander into fjords and coves on the eastern and northern coastlines. And all along the seacoasts, photogenic lighthouses perch atop precipitous cliffs overlooking the surf.

The ancient world heaved and formed richly diverse landscapes at **Gros Morne National Park.** A millennium ago, the Vikings arrived and established a coastal settlement (North America's first European settlement), now re-created at **L'Anse aux Meadows National Historic Park.** Before the Spaniards settled St. Augustine, Florida, the British created a mercantile center at **Trinity;** today it's a provincial heritage village, with brightly painted, saltbox-style houses lining its narrow lanes.

The appeal of raw wilderness aside, the main island caters to numerous other interests. Golfers like the 18-hole links at **Terra Nova National Park** and **Corner Brook.** Sightseers line up for boat tours led by knowledgeable skippers or academically trained guides, whose vessels nose among whales, seals, and icebergs. If you're interested in a quick trip to France, Fortune on the Burin Peninsula lies a two-hour boat ride from **St-Pierre,** the capital of France's archipelago province of St-Pierre and Miquelon.

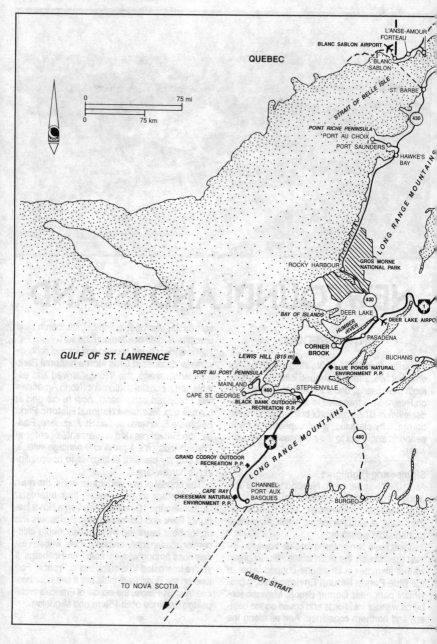

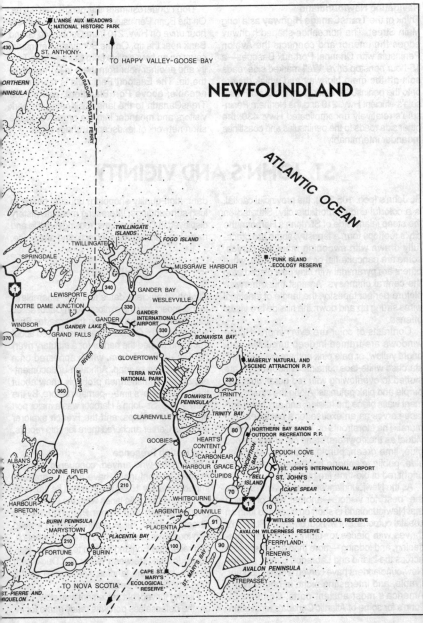

NEWFOUNDLAND

ATLANTIC OCEAN

L'ANSE AUX MEADOWS NATIONAL HISTORIC PARK

ST. ANTHONY

NORTHERN PENINSULA

TO HAPPY VALLEY-GOOSE BAY

LABRADOR COASTAL FERRY

430

TWILLINGATE ISLANDS

FOGO ISLAND

TWILLINGATE

SPRINGDALE

340

MUSGRAVE HARBOUR

FUNK ISLAND ECOLOGY RESERVE

LEWISPORTE

GANDER BAY

WESLEYVILLE

330

NOTRE DAME JUNCTION

GANDER

330

1

GANDER INTERNATIONAL AIRPORT

WINDSOR

370

GANDER LAKE

GRAND FALLS

GANDER RIVER

360

BONAVISTA BAY

GLOVERTOWN

MABERLY NATURAL AND SCENIC ATTRACTION P.P.

TERRA NOVA NATIONAL PARK

230

TRINITY

BONAVISTA PENINSULA

CLARENVILLE

TRINITY BAY

GOOBIES

80

HEART'S CONTENT

NORTHERN BAY SANDS OUTDOOR RECREATION P.P.

CARBONEAR

HARBOUR GRACE

POUCH COVE

ST. ALBAN'S

CONNE RIVER

210

CUPIDS

CONCEPTION BAY

BELL ISLAND

ST. JOHN'S INTERNATIONAL AIRPORT

WHITBOURNE

70

ST. JOHN'S

CAPE SPEAR

HARBOUR BRETON

BURIN PENINSULA

MARYSTOWN

210

ARGENTIA

DUNVILLE

91

PLACENTIA

PLACENTIA BAY

10

WITLESS BAY ECOLOGICAL RESERVE

AVALON WILDERNESS RESERVE

FERRYLAND

FORTUNE

100

90

RENEWS

BURIN

220

AVALON PENINSULA

ST-PIERRE AND MIQUELON

CAPE ST. MARY'S ECOLOGICAL RESERVE

ST. MARY'S BAY

TREPASSEY

TO NOVA SCOTIA

© MOON PUBLICATIONS, INC.

Navigating Newfoundland

Think of the **TransCanada Highway** as a long Main Street. The horseshoe-shaped highway edges the interior and connects the Avalon Peninsula with Channel-Port aux Basques—a 15-hour nonstop drive. Well-marked side roads split off the main highway and whisk drivers onto the peninsulas. Aside from the Burin Peninsula's efficient Hwy. 210 and the Northern Peninsula's relatively uncomplicated Hwy. 430, the other side roads to the peninsulas and coastlines meander interminably.

Don't underestimate the peninsulas' sizes. On the Burin Peninsula, for example, it's a three-hour drive on Hwy. 210 from Goobies to Grand Bank near the tip. On the Bonavista Peninsula, count on an hour's drive from Clarenville to Trinity and another hour from there to Bonavista at the tip. The Eastport Peninsula is more manageable; above Port Blandford, pull off the TransCanada to the lane designated for park visitors and meander into the preserve on the short network of landscaped, shady roads.

ST. JOHN'S AND VICINITY

St. John's (pop. 105,363), the provincial capital, is a colorful and comfortable city. Situated on the steep inland side of St. John's Harbour, the city's rooftops form a tapestry: some are gracefully drawn with swooping mansard curves, some are pancake-flat or starkly pitched, while others are pyramidal with clay pots placed atop the central chimneys. Against this otherwise picture-perfect tapestry, the tangle of electrical wires strung up and down the hillside is a visual offense.

Contrasts of color are everywhere. House windows are framed in deep turquoise, red, bright yellow, or pale pink and are covered with starched white-lace curtains. Windowboxes are stuffed to overflowing with red geraniums and purple and pink petunias. Along the streets, cement walls brace the hillside, and any blank surface serves as an excuse for a pastel-painted mural. The storefronts on Water Street, as individual as their owners, stand out in Wedgwood blue, lime green, purple, and rose. At streetside, public telephone booths are painted the bright red of old-time fire hydrants.

As the Newfoundlanders say, St. John's offers the "best" for visitors—another way of saying that Newfoundland is short on cities and long on coastal outports. But without question, St. John's thrives with places for dining, nightlife, sightseeing, and lodging—more than anywhere else across the island and Labrador. Simply put, the Newfoundlanders have carved a contemporary, livable, and interesting niche in one of North America's most ancient ports. Come to St. John's for some of Atlantic Canada's most abundant, high-quality shopping; unusual dining in lush surroundings; interesting maritime history displayed in fine museums; rousing nightlife and music; and an emerging, eclectic fine-arts scene.

HISTORY

St. John's officially dates to 1497, when Newfoundlanders say the explorer John Cabot sailed into the harbor and claimed the area for England. Portugal's Gaspar Côrte-Real arrived about 1500 and named the harbor (or a tributary river) the Rio de San Johem, which appeared on a 1519 Portuguese map. Although undocumented, European fishermen probably knew about the port in Cabot's time—perhaps before. By the early 1540s, St. John's Harbour was a major port on Old World maps, and the French explorer Jacques Cartier anchored there for ship repairs.

The British Presence

The British—who arrived, conquered, and remained for centuries—have had the greatest impact here. By 1528, the port had its first residence, and the main lanes were the Lower Path (Water Street) and Upper Path (Duckworth Street). In 1583, Sir Humphrey Gilbert arrived with four ships, disembarked on a harbor beach, and reiterated England's claim to the area. Harbourside Park, between Water and Duckworth streets, marks the landfall, known also as the King's or Gilbert's Beach.

Fishing thrived, but settlement was slow. Early on, the defenseless port was ready game for incursions by other European imperialists, and in 1665 the Dutch plundered the town. Nevertheless, by 1675, St. John's had a population of 185, as well as 155 cattle and 48 boats anchored at 23 piers. The English protected the harbor with Forts William, George, Castle, and Battery. They blocked the harbor's Narrows with chains and nets, and used lofty Signal Hill as a lookout to monitor friendly and hostile ships.

By 1696, the French emerged as England's persistent adversary. Based at Plaisance (Placentia), the French launched destructive attacks on St. John's in 1696, 1705, and 1709. Simultaneously, England developed Halifax, Nova Scotia, as a naval hub, and by 1762, dispatched a fleet that vanquished the French at the Battle of Signal Hill, North America's final land battle of the Seven Years' War.

Quid Non

Sir Humphrey Gilbert claimed the region for England in 1538.

The Early Port

St. John's was a seamy port through most of its early years. In a town bereft of permanent settlement and social constraints, 80 taverns and innumerable brothels flourished on Water Street, with a few stores on Duckworth Street and Buckleys Lane (George Street). The port's inhabitants were a motley mix of Spaniards, Portuguese, French, and British; as the latter gained dominance, Anglo immigration was encouraged.

Almost 4,000 settlers from England and Ireland arrived in the early 1800s, followed by another 10,000 Anglos in 1815. The new immigrants had fled the British Isles' poverty, but found the St. John's cupboard equally bare. They rioted en masse, and uncontrollable fires worsened conditions.

St. John's history has been punctuated with great fires. Those early conflagrations were fueled by various sources. Fish caught on the Grand Banks were often brought to port and laid out to dry on streetside fish flakes (wooden racks). During the great fires from 1816 to 1819,

sparks ignited the flakes' dry timbers and tree boughs, sending fires racing across the hillside. In 1846, the scene repeated itself, when sparks ignited barrels of seal and codfish oil.

Troubles and Triumphs

St. John's, like Halifax, was a British garrison town. With no foreseeable enemy, England withdrew the troops in 1870. The Royal Newfoundland Constabulary, modeled after England's occupying police force in Ireland, made its headquarters at Ft. Townshend in 1871.

In 1892, another huge fire destroyed the city from Water Street to the East End, leveling 1,572 houses and 150 stores and leaving 1,900 families homeless. St. John's rebuilt *again*. The stores, commercial buildings, and merchant mansions were re-created in Gothic Revival and Second Empire styles. The Anglican Cathedral of St. John the Baptist, on the site of the first 1720 church, was rebuilt within the Gothic stone walls.

The fire coincided with rail transportation's emergence, and St. John's was designated as the island's rail headquarters in 1892. The main Water St. rail station was styled with a flourish of Victorian gingerbread. In 1907, the fledgling Newfoundland Museum found a permanent home in the twin-towered brick building on Duckworth Street.

Inheritances and Additions

St. John's was beautiful at the turn of the century. From the British military occupation, the city inherited grandiose buildings. The Georgian-style Commissariat House on Kings Bridge Rd. was built in 1821; the stately, pillared Colonial Building on Military Rd. now houses the provincial archives. St. Thomas's Anglican Church, built first in 1699 as Fort William's garrison church, was torched by the French, then rebuilt in 1836. Prosperous citizens donated choice land for Bannerman and Bowring parks. Trolley cars tooled along the downtown streets and served as public transit until 1948. Atop Signal Hill, the city added Cabot Tower in 1947 as a tribute to both the 400th anniversary of Cabot's discovery and Queen Victoria's Diamond Jubilee.

World War II and After

St. John's thrived during World War II. Fort Pepperrell served as the operations headquarters for military bases across the island and Labrador. As defenses against German submarines that stalked the harbor entrance and local waters, Signal Hill and Cape Spear were fortified with anti-aircraft batteries, and nets were stretched across the Narrows' 174-meter-wide entrance. After the war, the U.S. Northeast Command, followed by NATO's 64th Air Division, occupied Fort Pepperrell until the base was deactivated in 1960.

Newfoundland joined the Confederation in 1949. An infusion of federal funding and 4,000 civil service posts buoyed the city's economy. In the 1960s, the city lost its commercial and residential cores as people and business fled to the suburbs, with their new malls, industrial parks, and housing. In 1966, downtown merchants and private parties galvanized interest in an almost abandoned downtown with the Downtown Development Corp., and in 1985, the federal government initiated the Main Street Program, Canada's first urban-rejuvenation project.

The Contemporary City

St. John's today is a handsomely historic and stylishly new city with a metropolitan-area population of 171,859. The town grew up from the harbor, and the harborfront is still the most colorful part—a promenade aside a long string of ships at anchor. Harbour Drive is lined with modern office buildings and Murray Premises—a group of warehouses built in 1846 that is now a national historic site holding a mall and museum complex. Water and Duckworth streets offer a colorful array of storefronts, while the steamy night scene continues until early morning at the bars, pubs, and clubs on pedestrian-friendly George Street. The city hall, built at a cost of $3.5 million, opened in 1970 on New Gower Street.

Overlooking the city from the top of the hill are C.A. Pippy Park, the 1,343-hectare gift of the town's famous millionaire merchant, and the Memorial University of Newfoundland. Nearby are the Arts and Cultural Centre and the Aquarena, the recreational mecca added to the city during the Canada Summer Olympic Games in 1977.

SIGHTS

Getting Oriented

The city's Old World street layout defies modern logic. The streets follow footpaths laid out by European fishermen and sailors centuries ago, when towns were not planned but simply evolved for everyone's convenience. Water Street (one of North America's oldest streets) and the other main streets rise parallel to the waterfront, and are intersected by roads meandering across the hillside. Historic stone staircases climb grades too steep for paved roads.

The following sights are listed starting at city hall near the harborfront and proceeding horizontally, wherever possible, across the hillside. Although locals lope up and down the hillside like agile mountain goats, beware of the steep inclines. Centuries ago, one pitched lane was known as Burst Heart Hill.

Be prepared to trek across the downtown area and drive everyplace else. Nobody covers St. John's in one day.

Near the Waterfront

The spacious wharf anchors half a dozen city blocks and provides a panorama of international ships and sightseeing boats. Depending on your orientation, the TransCanada Highway either starts in Newfoundland and ends in British Columbia, or vice versa. Outside **St. John's City Hall,** a large sign marked "0" km (on New Gower Street's northern side) initiates the national highway. Inside the building, displays of provincial fine arts adorn the lobbies; open Mon.-Fri. 9 a.m.-4:30 p.m., tel. (709) 576-8106.

The three-level **Newfoundland Museum at Murray Premises,** tel. 729-5044, fills a former fishery warehouse with exhibits depicting the province's maritime and military histories. The museum is located in the Murray Premises shopping complex, on Harbour Drive off the Bishop's Cove lane. It's open year-round, Mon.-Fri. 9 a.m.-4:45 p.m., Sat.-Sun. 10 a.m.-5:45 p.m.; free admission.

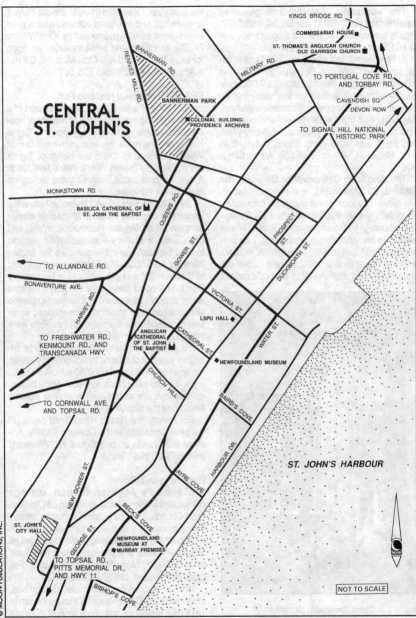

The splendidly restored and gleaming **Apothecary Hall,** 488 Water St., tel. 753-5877, recalls a pharmacy of 1895. It's open mid-June to mid-Sept., daily 10 a.m.-5 p.m.

At **Newfoundland Museum,** 285 Duckworth St. opposite Cathedral St., tel. 729-2329, the exhibits showcase Newfoundland's 9,000-year history with an emphasis on the aboriginal inhabitants, early European discoveries and settlements, and the 1800s' towns and outports. The museum is open year-round, Mon.-Wed. and Fri. 9 a.m.-4:45 p.m., Thurs. 9 a.m.-8:45 p.m., Sat.-Sun. 10 a.m.-5:45 p.m. Admission is free.

The **Anglican Cathedral of St. John the Baptist,** 22 Church Hill, is a national historic site revered by locals (and said to be haunted by a resident ghost). English architect Sir George Gilbert designed the impressive Gothic Revival edifice in Newfoundland bluestone. The cornerstone was laid in 1816, fire struck in 1846, and the Great Fire of 1892 almost gutted the church. Reconstruction within the walls started

Cabot Tower atop Signal Hill

NAN DROSDICK

the next year. Of special interest are the carved furnishings and sculpted arches, and a gold communion service presented by King William IV. The sanctuary and small museum are open for tours from May to mid-Oct., Mon.-Fri. 9 a.m.-4:30 p.m. For details, call 726-5677.

Signal Hill National Historic Park

In the 1700s, the peak here served as part of a British signaling system; news of friendly or hostile ships was flagged from Cape Spear to Signal Hill, where the message was conveyed to Fort William in town. In 1762, the Battle of Signal Hill marked the Seven Years' War's final North American land battle, with England victorious and France the loser.

The hilltop is pocked with historical remnants. England's Imperial Powder Magazine stored gunpowder during the Napoleonic Wars, and the Queen's Battery—an authentic outport tucked beneath the cliff—guarded the harbor Narrows from 1833. Public hangings were held at Gibbet Hill, the slope overlooking Deadman's Pond. The pond served as the port's reserve water supply in the event of a siege. Guglielmo Marconi received the first trans-Atlantic wireless message atop the peak, and exhibits within the Cabot Tower detail his work.

To get to the park, follow Duckworth St. across town until it turns into Signal Hill Road. It's open year-round, daily 8:30 a.m.-4:30 p.m., early June to early Sept. to 8 p.m. More historical displays are at the nearby **visitor center,** which has the same hours.

For hiking, the **North Head Trail** peels off the peak and leads to the Queen's Battery. Another trail wends across Signal Hill's leeward side to Quidi Vidi Village.

Returning to Town

St. Thomas's Anglican Church, at Kings Bridge and Military roads, is known as Old Garrison Church. The city's oldest surviving church building houses a cast-iron Hanoverian coat of arms over the door, attesting to the royal lineage. Sanctuary tours are available from late June to early Sept., Mon.-Sat. 2:30-4:30 p.m. For more information, call (709) 576-6632.

Now a national and provincial historic site, the three-story **Commissariat House** began in 1818 as a residence and office for Fort William's

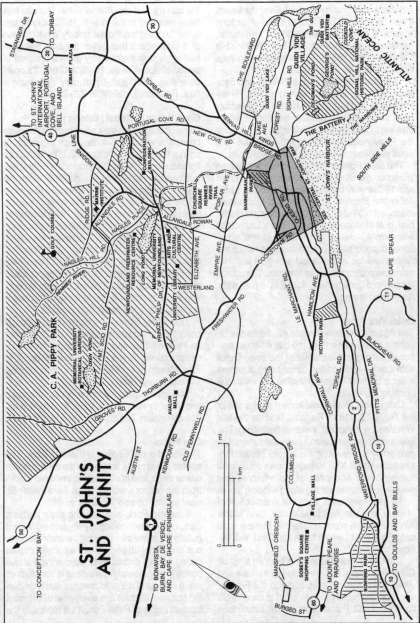

ST. JOHN'S AND VICINITY

© MOON PUBLICATIONS, INC.

assistant commissary general. Over the years, it was used as the St. Thomas's Church rectory, a nursing home, and a hospital. The interior, furnished with antiques, has been restored to the style of the 1830s. The house is open July-Aug., 10:30 a.m.-6 p.m. daily.

The **Colonial Building,** at Military and Bannerman roads, was the meeting place for Newfoundland and Labrador's House of Assembly from 1850 until 1959. The handsome white building of imported Irish limestone now houses the **Provincial Archives,** tel. 729-3065. It's open year-round, Mon.-Fri. 9 a.m.-4:45 p.m.

The early Roman Catholics aimed to make an impact on the St. John's skyline and did so in the mid-1800s with the **Basilica Cathedral of St. John the Baptist,** at Military and Monkstown roads, tel. 754-2170. The Romanesque cathedral, built of stone and shaped like a Latin cross with twin 43-meter-high towers, is now a national historic site. Guided tours point out the ornate ceilings embellished with gold leaf, numerous statues, and other features. The church is open mid-June to Aug., 9:30 a.m.-5 p.m. daily. Admission is free.

Quidi Vidi Area

The Atlantic's watery inroads permeate the St. John's area. Aside from the city's famed harbor, another sizable pocket of the sea—**Quidi Vidi Lake**—lies nearby. Its azure-blue waters meet a boulder-bound coastline, all within the bustling city limits.

Quidi Vidi Lake is best known as the site of the Royal St. John's Regatta, held on the first Wednesday in August, weather permitting. The lake's choppy water also lures windsurfers. Locals enjoy strolls along the grassy banks. Picturesque **Quidi Vidi Village** shows off colorful fishing boats anchored at the wharves and weathered houses strung along winding lanes.

To get there, start from the intersection of Military and Kings Bridge roads, then follow Kings Bridge a block up the hill. Make a right onto Forest Rd., which turns into Quidi Vidi Village Road.

The **Quidi Vidi Battery** sits high on a hill off Quidi Vidi Village Rd., overlooking the lake and village. The site owes its origin to the French, who built the battery in their effort to capture St. John's in 1762. France lost, and the British took

the battery and rebuilt it in 1780. The site has been restored to the War of 1812 glory years, when England fortified the battery in anticipation of a U.S. attack that never materialized. The battery is now manned by guides dressed in period uniforms of the Royal Artillery. It's open June-Aug., 10:30 a.m.-6 p.m. daily. Admission is free. For details, call (709) 729-2977.

Cape Spear National Historic Park

Cape Spear's eminently photogenic lighthouse crowns a windy, 75-meter-high promontory above the Atlantic Ocean. Built in 1836, the lighthouse ranks as the province's oldest extant beacon and was used until 1955, when the original lighting apparatus was moved to a more efficient building nearby. The keeper's living quarters have been restored. The visitor center displays antiques and maritime artifacts.

Outside the lighthouse, the precipitous slopes are sprinkled with World War II gun batteries. Hiking trails fan out from the peak. The 10-km trail to Maddox Cove starts here and winds south along the coast, through gullies, bakeapple bogs, and berry patches. If you're lucky, you'll see a family of shy foxes in the high grasses.

The cape, North America's most easterly point, lies six km southeast of St. John's Harbour as the crow flies and 11 km around Hwy. 11's coastal curve. To get there, follow Water St. to Pitts Memorial Parkway and turn left to Hwy. 11 (Blackhead Road).

The lighthouse and visitor center are open mid-June to early Sept., daily 10 a.m.-6 p.m.; free admission. The grounds are open 24 hours.

City Parks

The mood is Old English at **Victoria Park.** The spread offers paths and formal gardens beneath shade trees, and is situated a half-dozen blocks from the harbor's western end. Take Water St. west to find the park's entrance.

Bowring Park, arguably the city's prettiest park, has hosted visiting royalty and significant guests for many tree-planting ceremonies. Crocus and hyacinth beds make a colorful impact during spring, swans glide across the tranquil ponds in summer, and the setting is transformed into a canvas of dappled oranges and reds during autumn. Statues are everywhere, the most famous being of Peter Pan. It's a replica of the original in England's Kensington Gardens, and serves as a memorial to Sir Edgar Bowring's godchild, who died in an offshore shipwreck.

To get there, stay on Water St. until the road splits into Waterford Bridge and Topsail roads; continue on Waterford Bridge Rd. for three km to the park's entrance.

C.A. Pippy Park
Civilization ends and wilderness begins at this preserve, which covers 1,343 hectares of woodlands, grasslands, and rolling hills on the steep hilltop plateau. The park also features a botanical garden and a "fluvarium" (an exhibit that allows a close look at a stream's underwater inhabitants).

Developed along the rim of the hill, the park fronts Confederation Parkway/Prince Philip Drive and encompasses Memorial University's campus and the government Confederation Building complex. Barrens, marshes, woodlands, ponds, and streams make for a splendid landscape. Moose, muskrat, mink, snowshoe hare, meadow vole, and common shrew roam the hilly terrain, which is studded with balsam fir, spruce, and juniper. The green-winged teal, black and pintail duck, sora rail, American bittern, gyrfalcon, and pie-billed grebe are among the birds lured to Long Pond, the oval lake near the park's edge. Long Pond marks the start of the seven-km Rennies River Trail across the city's hillside to Quidi Vidi Lake.

Recreational facilities are spread across the park's developed edge. Off Ridge Rd., just above the hollow, there's an 18-hole golf course. The touted **Newfoundland Freshwater Resource Centre,** tel. (709) 754-FISH, is nearby. Park in the lot near the road and walk down the hillside to the handsome wooden building wrapped with an open porch. You'll enter on the second floor, a spacious room with ecological exhibits depicting Atlantic salmon and other fish species, marsh birds, and carnivorous plants. If you ask, you can see a natural-history audiovisual show. The **fluvarium,** the center's pièce de résistance, occupies the first floor. Nine windows pierce the walls and provide spectators a below-water-level look at the brook and brown trout, arctic char, and salmon in Nagle's Hill Brook. It's an innovative variation on the traditional aquarium.

The center is open Mon.-Sat. 10 a.m.-4:30 p.m., Sun. from noon; tours are scheduled Mon., Thurs., and Fri. at 11 a.m., 1 and 3 p.m. Admission is $3.

The **Memorial University Botanical Gardens** at Oxen Pond, the province's only botanical garden, covers 45 hectares off Mt. Scio Road. Garden environments include heather beds, a cottage garden, a rock garden, a boreal forest, and a bog, all resplendent with native flowers, shrubs, and trees. The gardens feature a medley of soft colors. Blue forget-me-not, white turtle-head and rhododendron, and pink Joe-pye-weed bloom among spiraea, northern wild raisin, dogwood, and high-bush cranberry. White birch, chokecherry, trembling aspen, ash, willow, and maple complete the botanical medley.

To get to the gardens, follow Allandale Rd. until it ends at Mt. Scio Road. Hours are May-Nov., Wed.-Sun. 10 a.m.-5:30 p.m. Garden tours are available June-July, and birdwatching walks are conducted June-September. Admission is free. For details, call 737-8590.

Academia
The nonsectarian, provincial **Memorial University of Newfoundland,** spread out on 82 acres in St. John's, trains physicians, nurses, and teachers, and also grants liberal arts degrees in English literature, economics, languages, and other majors. Other fields include the sciences with anthropology, engineering, biochemistry, and marine research—the latter offered at the Marine Science Research Laboratory on the Logy Bay campus. In addition, 40 off-campus colleges are located across the province. The university also functions as the keeper of provincial history and culture. Separate departments specializing in history include the **Centre for Newfoundland Studies** and the **Labrador Institute of Northern Studies.**

Other provincial colleges in St. John's include the **Newfoundland Institute of Fisheries and Marine Technology** for marine research and the **Cabot Institute,** emphasizing applied arts and technology.

Sightseeing Tours
McCarthy's Party has been on the sightseeing-tour scene for decades. From June to Aug., the

company offers daily 2.5-hour guided tours ($25) to Signal Hill, the cathedrals, and other major sites. For reservations, pickup anywhere in the city, and details, call (709) 781-2244.

City and Outport Adventure, tel. 747-TOUR, combines city and coastal sightseeing year-round in packages for three or four days. They also offer daily 2.5-hour tours (under $30) that can pick you up anywhere in St. John's.

Universal Helicopters Newfoundland Ltd., tel. 576-4611, whisks passengers aloft for aerial sightseeing from St. John's International Airport. Flights are offered year-round, but the weather is most cooperative April-October. Rates are $425 for a half hour (up to six passengers).

The city is also the base for numerous tour-company operations offering trips around the province. **Wildland Tours,** 124 Water St., St. John's, NF A1C 5J9, tel. 722-3335, operates naturalist trips led by academically trained guides and specializes in packages across the Avalon Peninsula, with a stop in historic St. John's. The eight-day "Newfoundland Adventure," offered mid-May to Aug., includes wildlife sightings at Witless Bay, Cape St. Mary's, Avalon Wilderness Reserve, and other places. The price is $1750 pp, all inclusive except for suppers.

ACCOMMODATIONS

St. John's boasts the province's most varied and impressive lodgings. The high-rise harbor-front properties are stunning and offer the city's best facilities . . . and highest prices. Costs are considerably less at the city's plentiful motels, historic inns, B&Bs, and heritage homes. Contact the hotels and motels in advance to inquire about any discounted weekend or unpublished rates. At the smaller inns and bed and breakfasts, ask about parking facilities; a few depend on metered street parking (free on weekends and Mon.-Fri. after 5 p.m.). Budget lodgings in town include one campground, a hostel, and seasonal campus housing.

Budget Overnights
Pippy Park Trailer Park, on Nagle's Place in C.A. Pippy Park, tel. (709) 737-3655, has 26 tent sites ($6), 26 unserviced sites ($11), 38 semiserviced sites ($13), and 94 fully equipped sites ($15). It's open May-Sept. on a first-come, first-served basis.

From mid-May to mid-Aug., **Memorial University of Newfoundland,** tel. 737-7590, offers rooms in the campus's student residence area for $16 a night or $90 a week for a single room; $25 a night or $140 a week for a double.

Catherine Booth House, 18 Springdale St., tel. 738-2804, is a conveniently located downtown hostel near Water Street. It's affiliated with the Salvation Army and offers 14 rooms for $30 s, $35 d, including a hot breakfast ($5 extra for supper).

Inns and B&Bs
Prescott Inn Bed and Breakfast, 17/19 Military Rd., tel. (709) 753-6036, has six rooms, most with fireplaces, for $62-76 including a full breakfast. The splendidly restored setting won the townhouse a Heritage House award. There's a spacious bathroom on each floor (one with a whirlpool), and a library with art and books about the province. The inn has a great location (with free, streetside parking) near historic St. Thomas's Anglican Church. No smoking.

Victoria Station Inn, downtown at 290 Duckworth St., tel. 722-1290, has similar heritage trappings, plus a notable restaurant offering alfresco dining in summer. The 10 antique-furnished suites with private baths go for $65-85. Some of the suites have fireplaces and jacuzzis. Parking is metered and on the street, aside from two first-come, first-served driveway spaces.

Compton House, 26 Waterford Bridge Rd., tel. 739-5789, once served as the mansion of C.A. Pippy, the merchant who donated St. John's local hilltop to the city for a park. The house has been grandly restored. Each of the four standard guest rooms has a private bath, and the two suites have a whirlpool in the bathroom. Parking is free, and the house is just a few minutes' walk to downtown. An overnight costs $69-99 during the week, $159 on the weekend, and includes a full breakfast. No smoking.

Motels and Hotels
Best Western Travellers Inn, 199 Kenmount Rd. near the hillside's Avalon Mall, tel. (709) 722-5540, has 91 rooms ($59-77), a restaurant, nightclub, and lounge. Parking is free. **Jour-**

ney's End Hotel, 2 Hill O'Chips, tel. 754-7788, offers similar trappings without the night scene. It has 164 rooms ($66 Fri.-Sun., $76 during the week, continental breakfast included), a well-known restaurant with a superb harbor view, and a prime downtown location (next to the Hotel Newfoundland).

Holiday Inn Government Centre, 180 Portugal Cove Rd., tel. 722-0506, is near Pippy Park, Memorial University, and the Confederation Building complex, and a quick five-minute drive from downtown. The popular motel has 188 rooms and suites (from $75). Amenities include dining rooms and a lounge, a shopping arcade with a launderette, a hairdresser and barber, a heated pool, and a golf driving range. Parking is free.

Radisson Plaza Hotel, 120 New Gower St., tel. 739-6404, is a stunning, avant-garde highrise that set the pace as Radisson's first Canadian hotel. It offers 285 rooms and suites (from $95); restaurants and a pub; fitness facilities including an indoor heated pool, exercise equipment, whirlpool, sauna, and squash courts; a shopping arcade; and free covered parking.

Hotel Newfoundland, at Cavendish Square near the Kings Bridge and Military roads' intersection, tel. 726-4980, has an auspicious location on the former site of Fort William. The first Hotel Newfoundland, one of Canadian National's deluxe properties, opened in 1925. After many years' service, it was demolished to make room for this handsome hotel. Opened in 1982, the property has 186 rooms ($125-160) and suites (up to $500), restaurants and a bar, a fitness center (with indoor pool, table tennis, squash courts, sauna, and whirlpool), shopping arcade with a hairdresser, and free parking.

FOOD

Dinner Dining

Ches's, 9 Freshwater Rd., tel. (709) 722-4083, is one of St. John's numerous fish and chips places and ranks among the best. Tender, deep-fried fillets and crisp French fries (from $5) are served in an atmosphere of formica and bright lights. Other Ches's shops are at 655 Topsail Rd. and 29-33 Commonwealth Avenue.

Seafood Galley, 25 Kenmount Rd., tel. 753-1255, eschews fancy trappings in a strip-mall setting just west of the Avalon Mall. The restaurant emphasizes good value for the seafood dining dollar with heaping platters to $16. For a sample, try the small fish and chips ($5), deep-fried in vegetable oil. The blackboard outside spells out the day's specials, which might include grilled or deep-fried fresh arctic char ($15), lobster/steak fillet ($16), Newfoundland dishes such as fish 'n' brewis with scrunchions ($6), or cod, cod tongues, fish fillets, and shellfish variations.

Matthew Restaurant at the Holiday Inn Government Centre, tel. 722-0506, has a fairly priced entree menu ($13-20); the table d'hôte ($18) features hearty spreads such as cod au gratin or roast caribou, chanterelle mushrooms, pasta, and berry parfait. The dining room boasts the town's best beef ($15-19) with prime rib, strip steak lavished in peppercorn sauce, broiled sirloin, and tenderloin medallions.

Woodstock Colonial Restaurant, tel. 722-6933, boasts a trove of exotic game selections—rabbit or seal-flipper pie ($17-18); stuffed, roasted partridge ($20)—as well as seafood or steak ($14-21). Reservations are required for the game dishes. The restaurant is a 25-minute drive on Topsail Rd./Hwy. 60 from St. John's to the town of Paradise; the brown building fronts the road.

Cellar Restaurant, tel. 579-8900 (reservations required), has cozy downstairs quarters on Baird's Cove, the short lane between Water St. and Harbour Dr., across from the former courthouse. This is the place for Newfoundland nouvelle continental ($14-24) and the house specialty: juicy, Cajun-style halibut or Atlantic salmon ($19), coated with a secret spice blend and seared in a hot cast-iron pan.

Newman's Fine Dining, the Radisson Plaza's gourmet restaurant, tel. 739-6404 (reservations required), melds French-inspired cuisine with Newfoundland basics for a tempting entree medley. For an appetizer, try the dark, gamy, and tender seal-flipper pie ($8) or rabbit terrine ($7). Entrees range from roasted wild rabbit ($23) and Caribou Terra Nova awash in port and partridgeberry sauce ($28), to pheasant breast served with bakeapples ($21). Uncomplicated seafood, lamb, poultry, veal, and beef

($16-24) are also on the menu. **Brazil Square,** the hotel's standard dining room, has a less costly menu ($9-18) but similarly exotic fare.

Cabot Club, tel. 726-4980 (reservations required), the Hotel Newfoundland's gourmet dining room, combines a superb view of the harbor's Narrows with an elegant menu ($18-25) featuring prime chateaubriand, steak Diane, or pepper steak prepared at table side, classic seafood dishes, and the five-course table d'hôte ($23). The **Outport,** the hotel's daytime dining room, lures locals with huge buffets served Mon.-Fri. at noon ($13); at Sun. brunch ($16); and Thurs. 5:30-8 p.m. (the keenly popular Newfoundland spread, $17).

Light Meals

Downtown, everyone meets at **Living Rooms Café** at Murray Premises for such delectables as French onion soup, stuffed crepes, salads, and desserts such as cheesecake or French truffle pie. It's open 11:30 a.m.-5 p.m. **Victoria Station,** 290 Duckworth St., offers similar fare. **Pasta Plus** at Haymarket Square, the restaurant/pub complex at 223-233 Duckworth St., features a bistro menu with homemade pastas and a gourmet-to-go counter.

Nautical Nellies, 201 Water St., has stouter fare such as Cornish beef pasty, fried cod or cod tongues, and steak and kidney pie ($7-9). The convenient fast-food place is **Ports of Food** at the Atlantic Place mall on Water Street. If afternoon tea sounds appetizing, take your place at the table with scones, crumpets, and small sandwiches at the **Court Garden,** Hotel Newfoundland, Mon.-Sat. 3-4:30 p.m.

Stores and Supermarkets

You'll find plenty of places to pick up do-it-yourself picnic ingredients. For some of the freshest produce, stop at **Lar's Fruit Mart,** 79 New Gower Street. **Auntie Crae's,** 8-10 Rowan St. at Churchill Square's Terrace in the Square, tel. (709) 754-0661, cooks homestyle fare and packages it to go. Its deli, bakery, and dining area are open Mon.-Thurs. and Sat. 8:30 a.m.-6 p.m., Fri. 8:30 a.m.-9 p.m., Sun. 10:30 a.m.-6 p.m.

For fancier deli, bakery, and takeout food, **Manna's European Bakery & Deli** fills the bill at 342 Freshwater Rd., tel. 739-6992. It's open Mon.-Sat. 9 a.m.-9 p.m., Sun. 10 a.m.-9 p.m.

Michel's Bakery, 799 Water St., tel. 579-0670, is another source for French breads and croissants, pâtés, homemade soups, and hot dishes. Michel's is open Mon.-Fri. 9 a.m.-7 p.m., Sat.-Sun. 10 a.m.-6 p.m.

For a tantalizing overview of Newfoundland cuisine, the centuries-old **Bidgood Supermarket,** tel. 368-3125, stocks every taste sensation known to the province, including seal, caribou, salted fish, salmon, and cod tongues and cheeks. It's open Mon.-Sat. 9 a.m.-6 p.m. Not much is prepackaged here, but the produce (especially western coast strawberries), berry preserves, shellfish, smoked or pickled fish, and sweet tea biscuits make delicious picnic additions. Bidgood's is in the town of Goulds, a 10-minute drive south of St. John's on Hwy. 10.

Health-food shops are scarce. **Mary Jane's,** 377 Duckworth St., stocks the city's most extensive line of vegetarian food, and offers a sandwich counter, bakery, and deli. Mary Jane's is open Mon.-Wed. and Sat. 9:30 a.m.-6 p.m., Thurs.-Fri. 9:30 a.m.-9 p.m., Sun. noon-6 p.m.

Sobey's, one of the largest supermarket chains, has branches at the Avalon Mall, another mall on Torbay Rd., and the Sobey's Square Shopping Centre at 760 Topsail Road. Hours are Mon.-Sat. 8 a.m.-10 p.m.

ENTERTAINMENT AND EVENTS

Cinemas

The Empire Theatres chain, tel. (709) 726-9555, operates **Avalon Mall Cinemas,** at Avalon Mall on Kenmount Rd., and **Topsail Cinemas,** at 760 Topsail Road. The two multiplex theaters offer nightly shows and weekend matinees ($4.25-7.50 admission).

The Night Scene

It's said St. John's has more pubs, taverns, and bars per capita than anyplace else in Atlantic Canada. The city's international port status is partly the reason. Even better, these watering holes serve double duty as venues for music of various styles, including traditional Newfoundland, folk, Irish, country-western, rock, and jazz.

The nightlife originated on George St.—once a derelict back street—and spread from there to other downtown-area bars and clubs. The weekend starts late Friday evening, picks up again on Saturday afternoon and lasts until 2 a.m., and, at some places, keeps up through Sunday.

Among George Street's abundance of pubs and eating establishments, **Trapper John's Museum and Pub,** 2 George St., tel. (709) 579-9630, ranks as a city entertainment mainstay, hosting notable provincial folk groups and bands, Sat.-Thursday. The patrons will gladly initiate visitors to Newfoundland with a screech-in ceremony for free. **Capricorns,** at 6 George St., tel. 579-0420, features weekend rock until 2 a.m. **Greensleeves Pub and Lounge,** 14 George St., tel. 579-1070, doubles as a weekend hub for rock music and Irish groups ($1 cover); on weeknights their satellite-dish TV is tuned to sports events.

Near harborfront, **Erin's Pub,** 184 Water St., tel. 722-1916, has Irish and local artists, Wed.-Sat. 9:30 p.m.-2 a.m. ($2 cover, Fri.-Sat.). **Nautical Nellies,** 201 Water St., offers more of the same, Fri.-Sun., $2-3 cover.

The nearby English-style pub **Duke of Duckworth,** 325 Duckworth St., features local bands Fri.-Sat., $1-4 admission. So does **Sundance Saloon** at 33A New Gower St., with Sat.-Sun. entertainment for a $4-8 cover. **Cornerstone Video Dance Bar,** 16 Queen's Rd., tel. 754-1410, is one of the town's few dance clubs ($2-3 cover). It features a live band on Sun. and videos Wed.-Saturday.

Farther up the hillside, **Bridgett's Pub,** 29 Cookstown Rd. (the short street between Freshwater and LeMarchant roads), tel. 753-9992 or 753-6432, draws crowds with Newfoundland music on Wed., and folk, rock, and some jazz Fri.-Sat. ($3-4 admission).

While you're in the neighborhood, check out **Port City Lounge,** 216 LeMarchant Rd., tel. 579-2001, for country-western and Newfoundland groups, Wed.-Sunday. Expect a $1 cover on Fri. and Sat. nights. For a change of pace, the **First City Night Club** at First City Motel, 479 Kenmount Rd., tel. 722-5400, presents the golden oldies, and hosts a live weekend band ($3.50 cover).

The hotel lounges share the weekend scene. Folk and Irish groups play at the **Narrows** lounge in the Hotel Newfoundland on Friday 5-8 p.m., and at the **Cat and Fiddle Pub** in the Radisson Plaza on weekends 2-11 p.m.

Performing Arts

The **Resource Center for the Arts,** LSPU Hall, 3 Victoria St., tel. (709) 753-4531, stages indoor productions ($5-9) during late July. The center also presents Lunchtime Theatre outdoors at the nearby park, weekdays 12:30-2 p.m. **Admiral's Feast,** Haymarket Square, 223 Duckworth St., puts on historical spoofs of the 1880s. Dinner ($35) is served from mid-May to Aug., Thurs.-Saturday. For details and reservations, call 739-6676.

St. John's Memorial Stadium, Lake Ave. near Quidi Vidi Lake, is the venue for most of the big concerts and theatrical productions that come to town. For upcoming events, ticket prices, and details, call 576-7657.

Festivals and Events

Everybody turns out for the **St. John's Day Celebrations,** a long-weekend's hoopla marking the city's birthday (24 June) with formal receptions, performing arts, and streets filled with vendors. The Newfoundland and Labrador Craft Development Association's three-day **Summer Craft Festival** is another popular event, showcasing provincewide crafts in early July.

The city shines as a music-festival venue. The biggest and best is early July's 11-day **Sound Symposium,** held in even-numbered years. Highlights include the noontime medley of harbor ship horns; citywide theater, workshops, and dance; and Newfoundland, folk, electronic, jazz, New Age, and African concerts.

Thousands of runners participate in early July's **H.G.R. Mews Memorial Road Race,** an eight-km sprint to the Quidi Vidi Boat House; and the **Miller Lite Road Race,** a 10-km run in mid-July.

The **Signal Hill Tattoo** is a tribute to the landmark Battle of Signal Hill that ended the war between the English and French in North America. The military event is staged dramatically with foot soldiers, artillery detachments, fife and drum bands, and more. It all takes place mid-July to late Aug., on Wed., Thurs., Sat., and Sunday. In late July, Prince Edward Plaza on George St. is the outdoor setting for the five-night **George Street Festival.**

In early August, the province's best performers take to the boards at the **Newfoundland and Labrador Folk Festival.** The festival also presents folk music, recitations, crafts shows, and festivities. Also in early Aug., the **Air Canada–St. John's Triathlon** ranks as the ultimate athletic feat, combining long-distance swimming and cycling with a marathon.

St. John's Annual Regatta Day, another city tradition, ranks as North America's oldest ongoing sporting event. It began in 1827 with fishermen at the helm; nowadays, the regatta combines experienced crews with sleek racing shells and 50,000 cheering spectators. It's held at Quidi Vidi Lake.

And there's no place better to celebrate New Year's Eve than at **First Light** along Harbour Dr. on the waterfront. Fireworks usher in the New Year, here at North America's most easterly edge.

RECREATION

Scuba
Situated on Atlantic Canada's oldest ship routes, the St. John's area is incredibly rich with shipwrecks. What's more, the waters here are as clear as the Caribbean—20- to 30-meter visibility is common—and reasonably warm from summer to autumn, though a wetsuit is advisable. **Oceanus Adventure,** tel. (709) 738-0007 or 738-1888, fax 738-2401, leads dive trips June-Oct., and favors nearby Conception Bay (other sites are available). Oceanus requires you to possess PADI or NAUI certification, plus a log-book record of recent dives. A day's dive, including transportation and all equipment, costs $75. Contact them at P.O. Box 13277, Station A, St. John's, NF A1B 4A5. **Sub Aqua Diving,** tel. 364-3483 or 579-9888, also leads dives.

Swimming
The **Aquarena** at Westerland Rd. and Prince Philip Parkway, tel. (709) 576-8626, has adult swims ($2.75) Mon.-Fri. 6:30 a.m.-10 p.m., Sat.-Sun. 8:30 a.m.-6 p.m. **Municipal pools** ($1) at Bowring, Victoria, and Bannerman parks are open July-Aug., 9 a.m.-7 p.m. daily.

Court Sports
The **YMCA/YWCA,** 34 New Cove Rd., tel. (709) 754-2960, has squash and racquetball courts, as well as exercise equipment and a sauna ($5 for a day-use pass valid anytime except week-

days 5-7 p.m.). The Y is open Mon.-Fri. 7 a.m.-11 p.m., Sat. 9 a.m.-9 p.m., Sun. 9 a.m.-5 p.m. **Riverdale Tennis Club,** Portugal Cove Rd., tel. 579-6600, and **Green Belt Tennis Club,** Lions Park Mayor Ave., tel. 722-3840, rent courts. Green Belt has indoor courts.

Golf
C.A. Pippy Park, tel. (709) 737-3655, features a golf course near the botanical gardens. **Bally Hally Golf and Country Club,** Logy Bay Rd., tel. 753-6090, is a private club with golf and curling facilities.

For hockey or ice skating, head to **St. John's Memorial Stadium** on King's Bridge Rd., tel. 576-7688.

SHOPPING

Crafts
Crafts shops downtown offer every conceivable craft available, and new developments continually increase the variety. One of the best places to start is **Devon House,** at 59 Duckworth St. near the Hotel Newfoundland, which is the Newfoundland and Labrador Crafts Development Association's gallery and retail crafts shop. It offers a sampling of traditional and contemporary wares; open Tues.-Fri. 10 a.m.-5 p.m., Sat. 10 a.m.-4 p.m.

For designer pieces, check out retail sales outlets in the artists' workroom/studios. **Bogside Weaving,** 209 New Gower St., tel. (709) 726-1401, is a prime source for woolen sweaters, jackets, and apparel for men and women. Though they're mainly exporters, Bogside also sells first- and second-quality apparel. Hours are Mon.-Fri. 10 a.m.-5:30 p.m. **Woof Design,** 1 Prospect St., tel. 722-7555, sells mohair, woolen, and caribou-leather apparel. It's open Mon.-Fri. 9 a.m.-5 p.m., Sat. 10 a.m.-3 p.m.

Other shops operate as cottage-industry outlets. **Nonia Handicrafts,** 286 Water St., is among the best crafts shops, carrying handwoven apparel, weavings, parkas, jewelry, hooked mats, domestic wares, and handmade toys. **Cod Jigger,** 250 Duckworth St., a similar cooperative, is another superb source for parkas, hooked mats, bone and talc carvings, quilts, knits, mittens and hats, crocheted items, and jewelry.

Some shops showcase the newest designs and first-quality wares of selected producers. **Newfoundland Weavery,** 177 Water St., tel. 753-0496, handles Bogside Weaving clothing, Placentia West Mat Makers's hooked mats, and other weavings, whalebone carvings, and jewelry from across the province. It's open Mon.-Sat. 10 a.m.-5:30 p.m., Thurs.-Fri. nights to 9:30 p.m., and Sun. 12:30-5 p.m.

Other shops sell a variety of wares: Grenfell parkas from St. Anthony, books about Newfoundland, local "Purity" candies, tinned biscuits or seafood, bottles of savory spice, pottery and porcelain, handmade copper and tin kettles, model ships, soapstone and stone carvings, fur pelts and rugs, apparel, folk art, and handwoven silk, wool, cotton, and linen. You can expect to find most of these goods at **Melendy's Kuffer Korner,** 336 Water St., and **Salt Box,** 194 Duckworth Street. Both are open Mon.-Sat. 10 a.m.-5:30 p.m.

Art Galleries

For an overview of Newfoundland's outstanding traditional and avant-garde fine arts, spend several hours at the **Memorial University Art Gallery,** tel. (709) 737-8209, which holds the city's most extensive exhibits. It's open Tues.-Sun. noon-5 p.m., and Fri. night 7-10 p.m., in the brown-brick Arts and Cultural Centre at Prince Philip Parkway and Allandale Road.

The **Resource Centre for the Arts,** 3 Victoria St., tel. 729-2179, is another notable gallery with regularly changing exhibits and periodic shows. It's open Tues.-Fri. 10 a.m.-5 p.m., Sat.-Sun. 2-5 p.m.

Top-notch private galleries are plentiful. **Christina Parker Fine Art Gallery,** 7 Plank Rd., tel. 753-0580 (ask for directions), showcases the avant-garde spectrum; open Mon.-Fri. 10 a.m.-6:30 p.m., Sat. 11 a.m.-5 p.m. For traditional art, check out the **Topsail Art Gallery,** tel. 834-3612; open Mon.-Fri. 10 a.m.-9 p.m., Sat. to 6 p.m., Sun. 1-6 p.m. **Emma Butler Gallery,** 111 George St., and **Pollyanna Art and Antiques Gallery,** 206 Duckworth St., both showcase lots of local art.

Stores and Malls

Among half a dozen suburban shopping malls, the largest are **Avalon Mall,** with a 100-plus shops on Kenmount Rd. near Confederation Parkway; **Village Shopping Centre,** with 80 stores at Columbus Drive and Topsail Rd.; and **Sobey's Square Shopping Centre,** with 40 stores at 760 Topsail Road. In general, mall hours are Mon.-Sat. 10 a.m.-10 p.m.

The better clothing shops are found at the Village Shopping Centre and at **Churchill Square,** a small complex on Elizabeth Ave. near the Arts and Cultural Centre. For photography equipment and film, try **Tooton's,** 307 Water St., tel. (709) 726-6050. Tooton's also has shops at the Avalon Mall, the Kmart Plaza at Torbay, and the Village Mall.

INFORMATION AND SERVICES

Visitor Information

The **City of St. John's Economic Development and Tourism Division** at city hall on New Gower St., tel. (709) 576-8106, fax 576-8246, answers questions and stocks free literature. The office is open year-round, Mon.-Fri. 9 a.m.-4:30 p.m. It has branch locations at the airport (also open year-round) and at the **Railcar Chalet** at harborfront (open June-Aug., 9 a.m.-7 p.m. daily). Its mailing address is P.O. Box 908, St. John's, NF A1C 5MC. Available literature includes various city maps and the following booklets: *A Step Back in Time,* describing self-guided walks through the city's five historic areas; *Walking Tour of Old St. John's,* which sums up most of the foregoing with written descriptions and a map; and *St. John's Tourist Information Guide,* with details on lodgings, dining and shopping places, and sightseeing highlights.

You'll find other free, privately published tourist literature at stores, hotels and motels, and restaurants. Among the most informative are *What's Happening,* with monthly updates and sightseeing feature coverage, and *Vacation Guide,* a softcover tourist guide crammed with details on sightseeing.

Maps, Bookshops, and Libraries

Peregrine Corp., 25 Stavanger Dr. off Torbay Rd., tel. (709) 726-0949, stocks topographical maps (from $9) for every part of the province; open Mon.-Fri. 9 a.m.-5 p.m.

Books about St. John's and the province are plentiful. The most esteemed source is **Dicks and Company,** tel. 579-3308, at ground level in downtown Scotia Centre on Water St. near the Ayre Cove lane; open Mon.-Sat. 8:30 a.m.-5:30 p.m. For secondhand and rare editions, check out **Afterwords Book Store,** 166 Water St., tel. 753-4690; open Mon.-Wed and Sat. 10 a.m.-5:30 p.m., Thurs.-Fri. until 9 p.m.

The largest library in town is Memorial University of Newfoundland's **Queen Elizabeth II Library,** tel. 737-7423; open Mon.-Sat. 8:30 a.m.-11 p.m., Sun. 1:30-11 p.m. To get there, turn into the campus at Westerland Rd. off Prince Philip Dr. and head for the massive building with windows tiered like steps.

At the smaller public libraries, decreased city funding limits the hours. City hall's **Gosling Library,** tel. 737-3114, is open Tues. 1-5:30 p.m. and 6:30-8:30 p.m., Wed.-Fri. 10 a.m.-12:30 p.m. and 1:30-5:30 p.m. At the Arts and Cultural Centre, the **A.C. Hunter Adult Library** is open Tues.-Thurs. 10 a.m.-9 p.m. and Fri.-Sat. 10 a.m.-5:30 p.m.

Newspapers

The *Evening Telegram* covers St. John's and provincial news daily, and the *Express* is the city's suburban weekly. The monthly *Newfoundland and Labrador Business Journal* covers provincial business developments.

Classes

Once a month, the **St. John's Folk Arts Council** sponsors folkdancing instructions followed by an evening of dance. For dates and the site, call (709) 576-8505. Memorial University of Newfoundland, tel. 737-7979, hosts an **Elderhostel** course for two weeks in July, with marine environment classes, whalewatching excursions, lodging, and meals for $355. For details and reservations call Elderhostel's national headquarters at (613) 530-2222 or write to them at 308 Wellington St., Kingston, ON K7K 7A7.

Health and Safety

Local hospitals include **Grace General Hospital,** 241 LeMarchant Rd., tel. 778-6222; **General**

HONORARY FOREIGN CONSULATES

Germany; 22 Poplar Ave.; tel. 753-7777

Great Britain; 113 Topsail Rd.; tel. 579-2002 or 579-0475

Iceland; 21 Military Rd.; tel. 754-2292

Portugal; 40 Mansfield Crescent; tel. 745-2271

Hospital, 300 Prince Philip Dr., tel 737-6300; and **St. Clare's Mercy Hospital,** 154 LeMarchant Rd., tel. 778-3111.

The **Royal Newfoundland Constabulary,** tel. 729-8000 or 911, handles local police matters; the **RCMP** is at 772-5400.

Banks and Postal Outlets

Seven major banks are located in metro St. John's. **Royal Bank,** tel. (709) 576-4222, has 10 locations in the city and suburbs. Most are open Mon.-Fri. 9:30 a.m.-5 p.m., while the office at 39 Commonwealth Ave. in adjacent Mt. Pearl stays open Thurs.-Fri. to 8 p.m., and offers Sat. hours 10 a.m.-3 p.m. There's a $1 service fee on each traveler's check transaction, but nothing extra to exchange U.S. or U.K. currencies.

The city has three main **Canada Post** offices. For buying stamps and mailing letters, the best bet is the office at 354 Water St., tel. 758-1003, open Mon.-Fri. 8 a.m.-5 p.m.; the philatelic window is open weekdays, 8 a.m.-noon and 1-4 p.m.

Retail postal outlets have longer hours. **Hunt's Ltd.,** tel. 753-7620, at the Churchill Square mall, is open Mon.-Wed. 9 a.m.-6 p.m., Thurs.-Fri. 9 a.m.-9 p.m., Sat. 9 a.m.-5:30 p.m.

GETTING THERE

By Air

Frequent nonstop and direct flights serve St. John's from provincial, regional, national, and international gateways. For an airline overview, see the "Getting There" and "Getting Around" sections in the Newfoundland and Labrador "Introduction."

It pays to buy a discounted fare. One of the best buys is the **Air Canada/Air Nova** advance-purchase fare with restrictions. For example, the regular economy RT fare from Boston to St. John's costs about US$944, while a 14-day advance purchase brings the fare down to about US$383. Fares are subject to change and currency fluctuations. For flight information or reservations, call **Air Canada/Air Nova** at (709) 726-7880 or (800) 563-5151 from Newfoundland, (800) 776-3000 from the U.S.; **Canadian International/Air Atlantic**, tel. 576-0274, (800) 426-7000 from the U.S. (or 722-0220 for flight information); or **Provincial Airlines**, tel. 576-1800.

St. John's International Airport, off Portugal Cove Rd., is a quick 15-minute drive from Water St. (about $12 by taxi). The airport is open 24 hours daily and has a duty-free shop. Budget, Thrifty, Tilden, and Avis have counters here and Hertz is nearby. The city's **Tourist Information Kiosk** at the airport, tel. (709) 772-0011, is open daily 9 a.m.-7 p.m.

By Sea

From early June through late October, **Marine Atlantic** offers twice-weekly ferry service from North Sydney, Nova Scotia, to Argentia on the Avalon Peninsula (a two-hour drive from St. John's). During late June and after September, the trip is an overnight sailing; cabins are all deluxe and outfitted with four beds. Otherwise, the ferry makes daytime crossings. Reservations are required on all crossings, and you should plan on being there an hour before departure. For details, call Marine Atlantic in North Sydney at (902) 794-5700, or (709) 227-2431 from Newfoundland, (800) 341-7981 from the United States. Also, see the "Ferry Schedules" chart in the On the Road chapter.

If you're arriving on your own yacht, you can tie up at **Royal Newfoundland Yacht Club**, Greenslades Rd. in Long Pond on Conception Bay, tel. (709) 834-5154. The club offers dock space for $25 a night, a dining room and bar, laundry, and showers. For details, write Royal Newfoundland Yacht Club, P.O. Box 869, Manuels, NF A1W 1N4. To arrange for customs clearance before arrival, call the **Canadian Customs** office at 772-5544.

GETTING AROUND

Driving and Buses

Locals complain that downtown parking space is scarce. Not so, the city says, countering that there are 1,500 parking slots at the Municipal Parking Garage on Water St., other downtown garages, and on the streets. Some 800 street spaces are metered for loonies (the $1 coin) and quarters; when the time is up, the cops are quick to ticket expired meters.

Expect the demand to outpace supply, however. It's just as easy to park uptown on an unmetered street and take a bus downtown. St. John's Transportation Commission's **Metrobus** operates public transit ($1.25 in exact change); for details, call (709) 722-9400.

CN Roadcruiser, tel. 737-5915, operates long-haul bus service along the TransCanada Hwy.'s length, with daily service from the former railroad terminal at Water St. near Patrick St.; open 7 a.m.-11 p.m. To Corner Brook, it's $65 OW, and to the ferry terminal at Port aux Basques, it's $80 OW. For more provincial lines, see the accompanying chart.

Taxis, Bikes, and Rental Cars

Taxis cruise downtown and also wait at the hotels and motels. **Dave Gulliver Cabs**, 5 Adelaide St., tel. (709) 722-0003, is among the largest outfits (from Water St., it's $12 to the airport or $6 to the Arts and Cultural Centre).

BUS COMPANIES

Various bus companies connect St. John's with the outlying areas.

To Bonavista	**Venture**	13 Queen St.	tel. 722-9999	$20 OW
To Burin	**Cheeseman's**	personal pickup	tel. 753-7022	$15 OW
To Carbonear	**Fleetline**	call for details	tel. 722-2608	$10 OW
To Placentia	**Newhook's**	13 Queen St./Avalon Mall	tel. 726-4876	$14 OW

Tips are optional but welcome. **Budgen's,** tel. 726-4400, has taxi stands all over the city.

Bike rental places are scarce. **Earle Industries,** 51 Old Pennywell Rd., tel. 576-1951, rents mountain bikes and all the equipment you'll need for a day ($25) or a week ($119). They also operate **Avalon Bicycle Tours** and have details about Avalon Peninsula trips. To get to the store, follow Empire Ave. until it turns into Old Pennywell Rd., then look for the Bay Bulls Trading Company building (the buff-colored brick one).

All the major car-rental companies, plus Discount, Sears, and Rent-a-Wreck have St. John's offices. **Budget,** 954 Topsail Rd., tel. 747-1234, has four locations. A small four-door Chevy Sprint with automatic transmission costs $189 a week with 1,400 free km, 20 cents for each additional km, and $10 a day for collision-damage insurance. Some credit-card companies offer automatic collision-damage insurance when you use their card for the rental. Note that this coverage is usually secondary to your personal auto-policy coverage. You might also be able to obtain a rental-car coverage rider from your insurance company for less money than the rental company's waiver charge.

THE AVALON PENINSULA

If sightseeing time is short and you must bypass the rest of Newfoundland, consider the Avalon Peninsula as a manageable stand-in. Life on the Avalon has a long history. The Basques and French fished the Southern Shore and Cape Shore seacoasts as early as the 1500s. The peninsula's name is attributed to Sir George Calvert (Lord Baltimore), who was evidently a passionate fan of the Arthurian legends. To him, the peninsula was akin to King Arthur's heavenly paradise, a haven for the beleaguered Roman Catholics from England. Or so he thought. Once settled at Ferryland in the early 1600s, Calvert's colony endured diminishing supplies and harsh winters. His wife, son, and the other colonists headed south to Maryland, and Calvert followed, leaving the plantation and the name of Avalon. Farther south on the peninsula, the *Mayflower* stopped at Renews during the Pilgrims' trans-Atlantic sailing from England to Massachusetts.

Remnants from the Past

Early French and British military incursions also molded the area. The HMS *Sapphire* sank during a 1696 naval battle, and lies off Bay Bulls. The same year, the French burned Carbonear, and they returned to torch the settlement again in 1705. The English settlers retreated to Carbonear Island, now a national historic site, for England's only early successful defense against the French in Newfoundland.

During WW II, German submarines saturated the offshore waters; sensitive harbors such as Bay Bulls were strung with nets to prohibit entry. At Bell Island's Lance Cove, German submarines aimed for a ship at anchor, missed, and badly damaged the pier.

The Avalon is still making history. In the 1960s, Parks Canada archaeologists initiated a project that stabilized the French and British fortification ruins at Castle Hill National Historic Park near Placentia. And another dig at Mistaken Point yielded one of Canada's most spectacular marine fossil finds in the 1980s.

Getting Around

You will be wise to tackle one peninsula at a time. For the Bay de Verde Peninsula, take the TransCanada/Hwy. 1 out of St. John's and turn north at Hwy. 70 to Carbonear, a two-hour drive from the city. From Carbonear, Victoria is a quick 10 minutes, and Heart's Content on Trinity Bay is another 15 minutes on Hwy. 74.

The Southern Shore is quicker to navigate, along faster-moving Hwy. 10, which rims the peninsula. Ferryland lies an hour from St. John's, and Mistaken Point Reserve is another two hours south. To reach Salmonier Nature Park, simply take the TransCanada Hwy., turn off on Hwy. 90, and you're there in an hour. The Cape Shore deserves a full day. The Cape Shore Loop, as it's known, peels off the TransCanada and rims the peninsula. It's paved alongside Placentia Bay, but gravel on the remainder of the route.

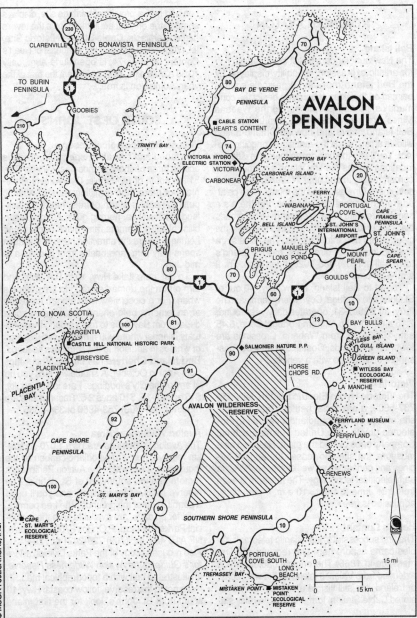

NORTHERN AVALON

Bell Island

The Newfoundlanders boast an incredible flair for artistic expression, an ability displayed by the **Bell Island murals.** Large-scale scenes painted on the sides of buildings depict the community's life and people during the Wabana Mines' ore-mining decades. John Littlejohn, a Bell Island native and now an Ontario-based wildlife artist, heads the ambitious, ongoing project. You'll find the half-dozen murals in different locations across the tiny island's northeastern corner, mainly in and near **Wabana,** the largest settlement. One assumes the murals were painted from historical photographs, yet there's a sense of real life to each painting—from a car's black luster to the animated figures and even the clear gleam of a miner's eyes. The murals are easy to locate; for directions, call the island's town hall at (709) 488-2025, open Mon.-Fri. 9 a.m.-4:30 p.m.

To get to Bell Island, follow Hwy. 40 out of St. John's to Portugal Cove's ferry terminal. The ferry, tel. 895-6931, operates daily year-round, 7:15 a.m.-11:10 p.m. from Portugal Cove, 6:45 a.m.-10:30 p.m. from Wabana. Crossings are fewer on weekends. Cost is 50 cents per passenger or $2.50 pp with a vehicle.

Victoria

The **Victoria Hydro Electric Station,** tel. (709) 737-5600, a provincial heritage site, was the site of one of Newfoundland's earliest hydroelectric plants. The United Towns Electrical Company once owned the plant. Restored as a museum, the site showcases the original turbines and generators as well as other exhibits on early electrical technology. The museum is open from late June to Sept., 10 a.m.-6 p.m. daily; admission is free.

Heart's Content

The first successful trans-Atlantic telegraph cables came ashore here and received the first message in 1866. The original cables, which extended from Valentia Island on the west coast of Ireland, are still visible at shoreline. The restored Cable Station, formerly a cable-relay station and now a provincial heritage site, displays some of the original equipment, plus the town's heritage artifacts. **Cable Station Historic Site,** tel. (709) 729-2460, one km northeast of Heart's Content on Hwy. 74, is open June-Aug., daily 10:30 a.m.-6 p.m., by appointment the rest of the year. Admission is free.

SOUTH OF ST. JOHN'S

Witless Bay Ecological Reserve

Newfoundland's seabird spectacle spreads across three offshore islands near Witless Bay, 31 km south of St. John's. Overwhelming displays of more than a million pairs of Atlantic puffins, Leach's storm petrels, murres, black-legged kittiwakes, herring gulls, Atlantic razorbills, black guillemots, and black-backed and herring gulls are the attraction here. The season spans May-Aug. and peaks from mid-June to mid-July.

To get there, take Hwy. 10 to Bay Bulls and turn off on the unmarked road to the outport's wharf. For a close view from a boat, make trip arrangements beforehand. Sightseeing boats depart from Bay Bulls to roam among the sanctuary islands, where you may also see icebergs or whales in addition to the countless seabirds. **Bird Island Charters** has daily 2.5-hour trips from April to October. A shuttle will pick you up at any of the city's lodgings. Fare is $25 adults, $15 ages 6-15, $10 ages 2-5. Reservations are required; call (709) 753-4850 or 334-2355.

Avalon Wilderness Area

The Avalon Wilderness Area is a 1,070-square-km reserve, home to woodland caribou by the thousands. It lies within the Avalon Peninsula's remote interior, southwest of St. John's. The reserve lacks visitor facilities, and you'll need a permit to enter the grounds. The free permits, valid for 90 days, are available from the provincial **Parks Division,** P.O. Box 8700, St. John's, NF A1B 4J6, tel. (709) 729-2421 or 729-2431. Also request a copy of the Parks Division's *Visitor's Guide to the Avalon Wilderness Reserve,* an illustrated text with a topographical map.

To get to the reserve, follow coastal Hwy. 10 south from St. John's, look for the first inland turn after La Manche Provincial Park, and follow Horse Chops Rd., a winding backcountry lane, into the reserve. Several rudimentary hunting lanes also enter the reserve from the west on Hwy. 90.

Ferryland

This east coast port is one of the province's earliest fishing villages, and the site of the colony founded by George Calvert in 1621. The colony was abandoned in 1629 and relocated to what would become Maryland. Calvert's mansion lies in ruin and is the site of an ongoing archaeological dig. The colony's history is depicted in exhibits at the **Ferryland Museum,** tel. (709) 432-2711. It's inside the courthouse, near the church on the main street; open mid-June to early Sept., Mon.-Sat. 10 a.m.-noon and 1-5 p.m., Sun. 1-5 p.m.

The two-day **Southern Shore Folk Festival,** held in Ferryland in late July, ranks among the province's most exuberant festivals of folk music, dance, crafts, and seafood. For more information, call 432-2820.

Mistaken Point

Now being considered for designation as a UNESCO World Heritage Site, the **Mistaken Point Ecological Reserve** lies alongside a remote coastline at the southern shore's tip. To explore the area, turn off Hwy. 10 at Portugal Cove South and follow the unmarked gravel road to Long Beach, where the reserve's gently rolling headland stretches to the sea. Bring a warm jacket to fend off the strong winds, and be ready for thick fogbanks from June to mid-July.

Hikers enjoy the trails that meander across the reserve, and photographers relish the offshore boulders and turbulent surf. The rocks at the ecological reserve, acclaimed as Canada's most important fossil site, contain impressions of 20 different species of multicelled marine creatures that lived 620 million years ago.

Look, but don't touch. Fossil poaching is prohibited and violators are severely prosecuted. For details and a copy of *Mistaken Point Ecological Reserve,* which describes the site and fossils, contact the provincial Natural Heritage Department, Parks Division, Department of Environment and Lands, P.O. Box 8700, St. John's, NF A1B 4J6, or call (709) 729-2421.

The Salmonier Area

Salmonier Nature Park, tel. (709) 229-7888, is easily accessible via a well-marked route on Hwy. 90, a 10-minute drive from the Trans-Canada Highway. A two-km boardwalk and wood-chip trail runs through a sample forest and across bogs, which back up to the Avalon Wilderness Reserve. Moose, caribou, lynx, bald eagles, snowy owls, polar bears, beavers, and other indigenous species are exhibited in enclosures. Facilities include trails, a visitor center, and shaded picnic tables. The park is open early June to early Sept., Thurs.-Mon. noon-7 p.m. Admission is free.

THE CAPE SHORE

Placentia

France chose the magnificent Jerseyside area overlooking Placentia Bay for its early island capital, Plaisance, and colonists and soldiers settled here in 1622. The early military fortification crowned a high hill overlooking the port at Jerseyside. The French launched assaults on St. John's from Le Gaillardin, the first small fort of 1692, and then from Fort Royal, the massive stone fortress built the following year.

England gained possession of the settlement in 1713 under the terms of the Treaty of Utrecht and renamed it Placentia. The hill on which the fortress stands became known as Castle Hill. Ruins of Fort Royal include a blockhouse, barracks, and guardrooms. Exhibits at the visitor center of **Castle Hill National Historic Park,** tel. (709) 227-2401, document French and English history at the site. Guided tours are offered in summer. Picnic tables are available and trails run along the peak's fortifications and the bay's stone beach. The park is open daily, 8:30 a.m.-8:30 p.m. in summer, 8:30 a.m.-4:30 p.m. the rest of the year. Admission is free.

Marine Atlantic operates a summer-only vehicle and passenger ferry between Argentia, just north of Placentia, and North Sydney, Nova Scotia. See the "Ferry Schedules" chart in the On the Road chapter. The **Harold Hotel,** on Main St. in Placentia, tel. 227-2107 or 227-2108, is just five km from the ferry terminal and makes a handy stopover. Rates are $48 s, $60 d. It's open year-round, and has a restaurant on the premises.

Cape St. Mary's Ecological Reserve

This spectacular seabird reserve lies at the Cape Shore's southern tip, 16 km up a gravel road off Hwy. 100. A 40-minute walk leads across the steeply banked headland to a seastack jammed with some 53,000 seabirds. The rocky pyramid seems to come alive with fluttering, soaring birds, whose noisy calls drift out to sea on the breezes. Expect to see northern gannets (one of North America's largest colonies), common and thick-billed murres, and black-legged kittiwakes, along with some razorbills, black guillemots, great black-backed gulls, and herring gulls.

The sanctuary's **visitor center** at the gravel road's end stocks informative literature and sponsors guided walks. It's open early June to early Sept., 10 a.m.-5 p.m. The well-marked seastack trail also starts from here. Stay on the trail and don't wander; the headland is edged by precipitous, 100-meter-high cliffs—a fall from them would be fatal.

EASTERN NEWFOUNDLAND

THE BURIN PENINSULA

The 200-km-long Burin Peninsula angles like a kicking boot off Newfoundland's southeastern coastline. Along the shore are a few scattered towns and villages, but the interior is a primeval, barren moonscape. Fishing has been the mainstay of the peninsula's communities since the 1500s.

Boat Harbour

A cottage industry here produces hand-hooked scenic mats made of reused fabric scraps. The mats and other homemade wares are sold at reasonable prices at the **Placentia West Craft Shop** on Hwy. 210, about one km south of the Boat Harbour intersection. The shop is open mid-May to mid-Sept., Mon.-Thurs. and Sat. 9 a.m.-5 p.m., Fri. 9 a.m.-7 p.m., Sun. 1-6 p.m.

Burin

Near the "heel" of the boot-shaped peninsula, Burin, settled in the early 1700s, lies in the lee of offshore islands. The islands generally protect the town from the open Atlantic, though they weren't enough to stop a destructive tidal wave in 1929. The islands also were a refuge for pirates, who could escape their pursuers among the dangerous channels. During his mapping expeditions of the Newfoundland coast in the 1760s, Capt. James Cook used Burin as a seasonal headquarters. A high hill above the town, where watch was kept for smugglers and illegal fishers, still bears his name—Cook's Lookout.

In early July, the **Burin Peninsula Festival of Folk Song and Dance** kicks off three days of Irish-inspired song and dance, children's games, seafood meals, and crafts shows and sales. The festival ranks among Newfoundland's most popular heritage events. Call (709) 891-1546 for more information.

Grand Bank

Grand Bank, on the toe of the Burin boot, is the best known of the peninsula's towns. Settled in the 1650s by the French and taken over by the British in the early 1700s, Grand Bank (pop. 3,500) has always been associated with the rich fishing grounds of the same name, the Grand Banks to the south and west of Newfoundland. The coastal waters still provide the town's livelihood. The Grand Bank Town Council, tel. (709) 832-1600, has outlined a Heritage Walk—which illustrates the town's cultural and architectural points of interest—as well as a pair of nature hikes.

You can't miss the **Southern Newfoundland Seamen's Museum**, on Marine Drive. Styled like an angular white sailing ship, the museum has exhibits on the Grand Banks fisheries and maritime history, with photographs, ship models, and other artifacts. It's open June-Aug., Mon.-Fri. 9 a.m.-4:15 p.m., Sat.-Sun. 10 a.m.-5:45 p.m.; shorter hours the rest of the year. Admission is free.

Fortune

The fishing village of Fortune, five minutes southwest of Grand Bank, is the terminus for the St-Pierre Ferry Service; see "Transportation and

Tours" in the St-Pierre and Miquelon section below for details. In Fortune, the **Fair Isle Motel,** Fortune Hwy., tel. (709) 832-1010, is two km from the ferry terminal and operates year-round. The 13 rooms run $59 s or d, and there's a restaurant on the premises.

ST-PIERRE AND MIQUELON

Centuries of fierce British and French battles ended in the mid-1700s with Britain's dominance firmly stamped across eastern Canada— *except* on St-Pierre and Miquelon, a trio of islands 25 km south of the Newfoundland mainland. In 1713, the Treaty of Utrecht awarded the islands to England. But France regained possession in the Treaty of Paris in 1763, and the islands have remained strongly French ever since.

During the Prohibition era in the U.S., St-Pierre served as a distribution center for bootleg alcohol that was stockpiled in warehouses by Canadian, American, and European rumrunners. An 80-boat fleet delivered cargoes of illicit liquor up and down the Eastern Seaboard from 1920 to 1933.

While French and Newfoundland inhabitants have coexisted peacefully and intermarried for centuries, the nations are periodically at political odds. In 1992, St-Pierre's confrontations with Canada made the headlines when scallop fishermen from Newfoundland were met by a French gunboat off the island. The fishermen had entered St-Pierre's 24-nautical-mile fishing zone, and the French vessel confronted and escorted the boats back to their home port. A political uproar ensued. Newfoundland contended that reciprocal fishing rights existed offshore, and that Newfoundland's fishing rights were ensured by existing Canadian-French agreements. High-level negotiations eventually smoothed out the problem.

France's Far-flung Archipelago Province
The province consists of three islands, with a combined land area of about 242 square km. Tiny St-Pierre (pop. 5,683) anchors the southeastern corner. The topography of this triangular island includes hills, bogs, and ponds in the north, lowlands in the south. The larger islands

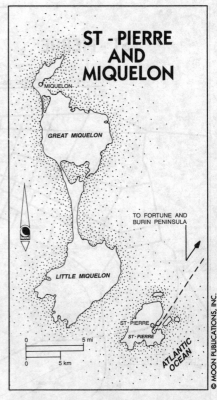

of Little Miquelon (pop. 709), sometimes called Langlade, and uninhabited Great Miquelon, joined by a sand-dune isthmus, lie to the west and north.

The capital, St-Pierre, on the island of the same name, is the most popular destination. It dates to the early 1600s, when French fishermen, mainly from Brittany, worked offshore. The port's mood and appearance are pervasively French, with bistros, cafes, bars, wrought-iron balconies, and an abundance of Gallic pride. St-Pierre borders a sheltered harbor filled with colorful fishing boats and backed by narrow lanes that radiate uphill from the harbor. The cemetery, two blocks inland from rue du 11 Novembre, has an interesting arrangement of aboveground graves, similar to those in New Orleans. The **St-Pierre Museum,** at 15 rue Doc-

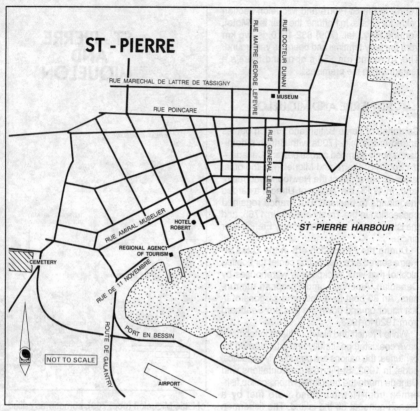

ST - PIERRE

RUE MARECHAL DE LATTRE DE TASSIGNY

RUE MAITRE GEORGE LEFEVRE

RUE DOCTEUR DUNAN

RUE POINCARE

■ MUSEUM

RUE GENERAL LECLERC

RUE AMIRAL MUSELIER

HOTEL ● ROBERT

REGIONAL AGENCY OF TOURISM ■

ST - PIERRE HARBOUR

CEMETERY

RUE DE 11 NOVEMBRE

PORT EN BESSIN

ROUTE DE GALANTRY

NOT TO SCALE

AIRPORT

© MOON PUBLICATIONS, INC.

teur Dunan, open by chance, documents the islands' history.

One of the islands' greatest attractions, of course, is the low duty rates on French wines and other goods. Visitors may bring back $100 worth of duty-free purchases after a 48-hour visit. You'll find shops with French wines and perfumes and half a dozen restaurants and brasseries.

Among the dozen small hotels, pensions, and bed-and-breakfasts, the largest lodging is the 54-room **l'Hôtel Robert** on rue du 11 Novembre near the harborfront, which hosted the American gangster Al Capone in the 1920s.

Transportation and Tours

St-Pierre Ferry Service, tel. (709) 738-1357, offers boats departing Fortune on the Burin Peninsula for St-Pierre, late June to early September. The crossing takes about two hours each way, and costs $50 RT. Reservations are required.

Plan to arrive a half-hour before departure and park in the lot ($6) near the Canadian customs building. To clear customs, Canadians and Americans need either a passport, a driver's license, or a Social Security card; visitors from Switzerland, the European Community nations, and Japan are required to have a passport. Travelers from everywhere else need a passport and a visa.

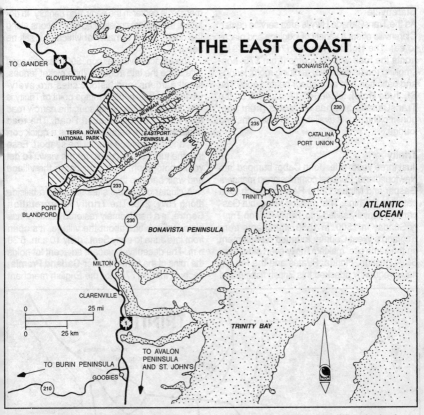

THE EAST COAST

TO GANDER

GLOVERTOWN

BONAVISTA

NEWMAN SOUND

230

235

TERRA NOVA NATIONAL PARK

EASTPORT PENINSULA

CATALINA PORT UNION

CLODE SOUND

233

230

TRINITY

PORT BLANDFORD

230

ATLANTIC OCEAN

BONAVISTA PENINSULA

MILTON

CLARENVILLE

0   25 mi

0   25 km

TRINITY BAY

TO AVALON PENINSULA AND ST. JOHN'S

TO BURIN PENINSULA

GOOBIES

210

If you're interested in a St-Pierre sojourn, it's easiest to go through **SPM Tours.** Its packages include bus shuttle from St. John's, the Fortune-St-Pierre ferry, and lodgings. Packages start at $176 for two nights, late June to early September. For details, call (709) 722-3892, or write to the company at 38 Gear St., St. John's, NF A1C 2J5.

Tour Explorateau offers 90-minute minibus tours of St-Pierre ($6). Tours depart the l'Hôtel Robert's parking lot near harborfront daily, from July to early September.

You'll need a local contact for other sightseeing and also for trips to the Miquelons; the best source is **l'Agence Régionale du Tourisme,** which can provide literature and a list of lodgings, restaurants, and other services. The of-

fice is at rue du 11 Novembre at harborfront; tel. (508) 41-22-22, fax 41-33-55.

Air St. Pierre, tel. (902) 873-3566, flies to the island year-round from Halifax, Nova Scotia. Flights are also available from St. John's and from Sydney, Nova Scotia.

THE BONAVISTA PENINSULA

The Bonavista Peninsula rises off the eastern coastline as a broad, bent finger covered with verdant woods, farmlands, and rolling hills. Paved Hwy. 230 runs along the peninsula's length, from the TransCanada to the town of Bonavista at the tip.

Clarenville

As the TransCanada Hwy.'s area service center, Clarenville offers a variety of lodgings and places to eat. The **Holiday Inn,** tel. (709) 466-7911, fronts the road with 64 rooms (from $75; non-smoking rooms available), a dining room, lounge and patio bar, and an outdoor heated pool. The **St. Jude Hotel,** tel. 466-1717, also lies on the TransCanada and has 65 rooms (from $86; nonsmoking rooms available), a restaurant, and lounge.

Trinity

Just three years after John Cabot bumped into Newfoundland, Portugal commissioned mariners Gaspar and Miguel Côrte-Real to search for a passage to China. That mission failed, but Gaspar accidentally sailed into Trinity Bay on Trinity Sunday in 1500. In 1558, merchants from England's West Country founded a settlement on the same site, making Trinity even older than St. Augustine, Florida. Pirates and the French navy frequently attacked this British fishing and mercantile center in the early 18th century. In defense, the settlers constructed fortifications along the coast, some remains of which can still be seen.

The attractive village (pop. 500) has changed little since the late 1800s. White picket fences, small gardens, and historic sites are everywhere. The best photo vantage point of Trinity is from the Hwy. 230 coastal spur, the narrow road also known as Courthouse Road. The road peels across the headlands, turns a quick corner, and suddenly overlooks the seaport. Ease into the turn so you can savor the view. To get your photograph, park your car in the village and walk back up the road.

A cluster of historic sites sits atop a hillside along Hwy. 230. The **Trinity Interpretation Centre,** in a handsomely restored building, has historical exhibits about the village. It's open from late June to early Sept., daily 10 a.m.-5:30 p.m. The deceptively vacant adjacent lot holds the ruins of the former **Lester-Garland Premises,** built in the 1770s for the English merchant

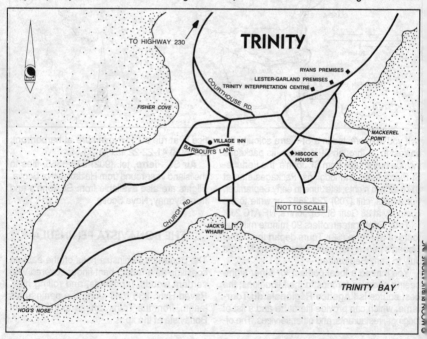

Francis Lester. Next to those ruins is the **Ryans Premises,** where a mercantile museum occupies the 19th-century residence and store.

For Trinity's other sites, drive into the village, park anywhere, and walk. Expect to wander; locals place more value on oral tradition than street signs. Emma Hiscock and her two daughters lived in the mustard-and-green **Hiscock House,** a block inland from the government wharf. They operated a forge, retail store, and telegraph office in the saltbox-style house in the 1800s. Costumed guides give free tours of the restored historic home. It's open June-Aug., daily 10:30 a.m.-6 p.m.; by appointment the rest of the year.

Village Inn on Barbour's Lane, tel. (709) 464-3269, offers 12 nonsmoking rooms (from $50; three rooms have private baths) in a heritage house with a long, open porch. Innkeeper/co-owner Christine Beamish runs the kitchen and lures gourmets from St. John's with sautéed cod tongues ($5) or capelin ($4) appetizers, and entrees such as fried cod ($11) and poached salmon ($16). Lodging and meal reservations are wise.

The other half of the inn's talented duo is Dr. Peter C. Beamish, who is also the director of Ceta-Research, an outfit devoted to the study of whales, dolphins, and porpoises. **Ocean Contact,** the company's seafaring component, takes sightseers along while conducting research out in the bay. The excursions ($38 for four-hour trips; longer packages available) depart daily mid-June to mid-Sept., weather permitting. For details or reservations, call 464-3700 or 464-3269, or write to Dr. Beamish at P.O. Box 10, Trinity, NF A0C 2S0.

Bonavista

Fifty kilometers from Trinity up Hwy. 230, Bonavista (pop. 4,600) began in the 1600s as a French fishing port, and later was taken over and fortified by the British.

The 1871 **Mockbeggar Property,** in the town center, has been a residence, carpenter's shop, and fish store. The house's last resident was F. Gordon Bradley, the province's first senator and a member of the federal cabinet in the 1950s. Bradley donated the property to the village. The **Bonavista Community Museum,** a kilometer away on Church St., tel. (709) 468-2880, houses genealogical records and exhibits on the area's history.

Some believe that the barren shoreline at **Cape Bonavista,** six km north of town, was the first landfall John Cabot spied in North America, on 24 June 1497. A major celebration is planned for the cape area in 1997, to mark the 500th anniversary of Cabot's discovery.

The photogenic 1843 **Cape Bonavista Lighthouse,** on Hwy. 230, tel. 729-2460, crowns a steep headland. The keeper's quarters inside the red- and white-striped tower have been restored. A climb up steep steps leads to the original catoptric light with Argand oil burners and reflectors. A more efficient but far less attractive metal tower, outfitted with an electric light, replaced the beacon in 1962. In July and Aug. the lighthouse is open daily 10:30 a.m.-6 p.m.; by appointment the rest of the year. Admission is free.

TERRA NOVA NATIONAL PARK

Above Port Blandford, the TransCanada Hwy. runs along Terra Nova National Park's western edge. Moose, black bear, beaver, rare pine martens, lynx, and bald eagles inhabit the hilly, inland boreal forest and wetlands of the 404-square-km preserve. Ocean currents push icebergs up to the rugged shoreline in summer, and from mid-May to mid-Aug., whales roam the deep-water fjords.

Water temperatures vary: the sea can be as warm as 20° C in the sheltered bays from late summer to early autumn, but temperatures never rise above a chilly -2° C in the fjord's depths.

More than a dozen trails thread through the reserve, providing some 100 km of hiking. Most are uncomplicated loop routes that meander easily for an hour's walk beneath tree canopies. The longest trek, the five-hour round-trip **Outport Trail,** connects the Newman Sound Campground with the fjord's southern coast. If icebergs or whales are offshore, you'll see them from the lookout tower on the sound.

Fishing is good in the park's many lakes and streams; game fish include brook trout, arctic char, and salmon. A national-park fishing permit is required for inland fishing, but not for saltwater angling for mackerel, cod, and other species.

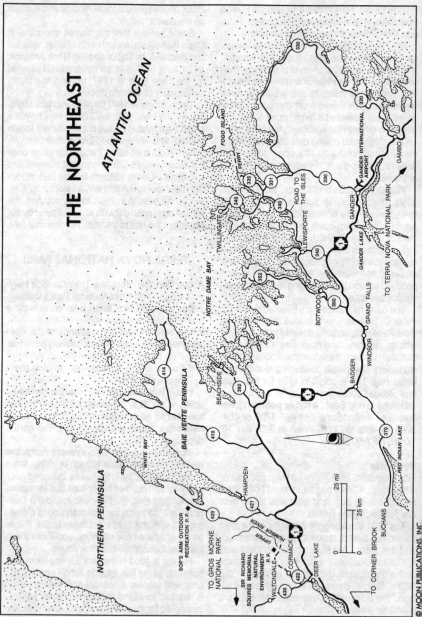

THE NORTHEAST

ATLANTIC OCEAN

© MOON PUBLICATIONS, INC.

Twin Rivers Golf Course lies at the park's southern entrance, where the 18 holes ($24-30 greens fee) overlook Clode Sound. The course is open late May-October. Reservations are required; call (709) 543-2626.

For informative boat trips, check out **Ocean Watch Tours,** tel. 677-2327, located at the wharf above the Newman Sound Campground. The three-hour morning trip ($26) noses among the fjord fingers looking for icebergs and whales, while the two afternoon trips ($22) are geared to sightseeing, and the shorter sunset tour ($18) explores an abandoned outport.

Terra Nova National Park is open year-round. Admission to the park during the summer is $4.25 per day, $9.50 for four days; admission is free from Labour Day weekend to Victoria Day weekend. Pets are allowed, but must be leashed.

Two **visitor centers**—one at Twin Rivers and another at Newman Sound—sell a topographical map of the park ($5) and stock books about the province's flora, fauna, and sightseeing. The centers are open late June to early Sept., daily 10 a.m.-8 p.m. For more information, contact the park at Glovertown, NF A0G 2L0, tel. 533-2801.

Accommodations and Camping

Terra Nova Lodge, the blue wooden building beside the golf course, offers comfortable, rustic accommodations with 76 rooms ($95), a dining room, exercise facilities, an outdoor heated pool, and walking trails overlooking Clode Sound. For reservations, call (709) 543-2525.

Wooded **Newman Sound Campground** has 400 semiserviced campsites ($10), as well as kitchen shelters and heated washrooms with hot showers. It's open year-round and staffed from late May to early Sept., when you'll find interpretive programs and rental bikes and canoes. A restaurant, campers' store, and launderette are nearby. Reservations are accepted.

DRIVING TIMES: NORTHEASTERN NEWFOUNDLAND ISLAND

From Terra Nova Nat'l Park to Gander: 40 minutes (57 km)
From Gander to Twillingate: almost two hours (102 km)
From Gander to Grand Falls–Windsor: over one hour (91 km)
From Grand Falls–Windsor to Deer Lake: over three hours (208 km)

GANDER TO TWILLINGATE

From the high central plateau, rolling hills descend gradually to the sea, where the northern coast is fringed with offshore islands. The TransCanada Hwy. cuts across the interior in a circuitous inland path, sometimes angling north to touch a deeply carved bay or reaching into the interior to amble amid the plateau's hills.

It's a six-hour drive across the island from Glovertown near Terra Nova National Park to Deer Lake, the gateway to western coast sightseeing highlights such as Gros Morne National Park. You can drive it in one day, but take more time if you can.

Gander

Adjoining the TransCanada Hwy., this airbase town proudly displays its memorials to aviation history. Gleaming, full-size models of WW II's Hudson, Voodoo, and Canso water bombers and a Beech-18 aircraft are positioned along the main street. At **Gander International Airport,** a massive mural inside the international lounge depicts more aviation history.

The **Silent Witness Memorial,** four km east of town off the TransCanada, marks the site of an aviation disaster. On a cold December day in 1985, the airport was a scheduled refueling stop for a DC-8 flight from the Middle East. The flight carried the U.S. 101st Airborne Division, better known as the "Screaming Eagles," who were returning home from a United Nations peacekeeping mission in the Sinai. The plane, with 248 soldiers and an eight-member crew, crashed shortly after takeoff between the Trans-Canada and Gander Lake.

The memorial park marks the crash site. As you drive through Gander on the TransCanada, look for the sign on the highway's southern side. An access road turns off the highway and peels down to the lake. A group of statues, of an American soldier and two children, backed by Canadian, U.S., and Newfoundland flags, overlooks the lake. The park spreads across the remote, rocky hillside, and flower bouquets lie here and there. The Screaming Eagles are still deeply mourned.

The spacious **Hotel Gander,** tel. (709) 256-3931, fronts the TransCanada, and offers 153 rooms and suites ($59-82), a dining room, lounge with entertainment, indoor pool, and exercise room. The **Holiday Inn,** 1 Caldwell St., tel. 256-3981, a few blocks from the highway, has 64 rooms (from $69), a dining room, outdoor heated pool, and launderette.

Twillingate

From Gander, Hwy. 330 heads north to **Gander Bay,** where Hwy. 331 curves farther northwest and lopes onto the northern archipelago as Hwy. 340, better known as the "Road to the Isles." A series of causeways connects roads across the islands. The narrow highway finishes at South and North Twillingate islands. The archipelago's most northwesterly point, the islands are washed by the Atlantic and shouldered by Notre Dame

Bay. The road crosses the southern island and eases into the tiny port at Twillingate Harbour.

Cross the causeway to Twillingate (pop. 1,400) on the northwestern island. Main Street runs alongside the harbor before it zips north and climbs to Long Point. If you're interested in local lore, stop at the **Twillingate Museum** on the western island, tel. (709) 884-5352. The gleaming, white-painted wooden building sits back from the road and is bordered by a white picket fence—altogether as proper as a former Anglican manse should be. The museum's exhibits include historic fishing gear, antique dolls, and several rare artifacts from the Maritime Archaic Indians. There are also details about local opera star Georgina Stirling, who took the stage name of Marie Toulinguet. She performed in Paris and Milan in the late 19th century, but her voice gave out prematurely, cutting short her concert career. She retired to Newfoundland to live out her days here in her hometown. Stirling now lies buried in St. Peter's Cemetery. The museum is open early June to mid-Sept., Mon.-Sat. 10 a.m.-9 p.m., Sun. from 2 p.m. Admission is 50 cents for adults, 25 cents for children.

Icebergs, which wander offshore and sometimes ditch at land's end in Notre Dame Bay, are one of Twillingate's main claims to fame. If you're interested in getting up close, stop at **Twillingate Island Boat Tours.** Their office, in the Iceberg House on the eastern harborfront, is open July to early September. For reservations, call 884-2317 or 884-2242. You may also see an offshore iceberg from Back Harbour, the semicircular bay a short walk behind the museum. Otherwise, head for Long Point, the high, rocky promontory that juts into the Atlantic Ocean aside Notre Dame Bay. Take Main Street north and follow the narrow road to **Long Point Lighthouse,** the local iceberg-vantage point. Bring rubber-soled shoes for scrambling across the boulders, and don't forget your camera—the beacon backed by the sea and sky makes a beautiful picture.

The **New World Island Fish, Fun, and Folk Festival** in late July is another reason to visit. The popular four-day festival features seafood, boat tours, music and dance, and fireworks at Twillingate and nearby outports. For details, call 884-2678.

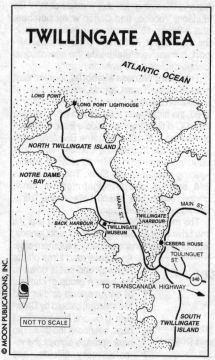

TWILLINGATE AREA

ATLANTIC OCEAN

LONG POINT
LONG POINT LIGHTHOUSE

NORTH TWILLINGATE ISLAND

NOTRE DAME BAY

MAIN ST.

MAIN ST.

BACK HARBOUR

TWILLINGATE HARBOUR

TWILLINGATE MUSEUM

ICEBERG HOUSE

TOULINGUET ST.

340

TO TRANSCANADA HIGHWAY

SOUTH TWILLINGATE ISLAND

NOT TO SCALE

© MOON PUBLICATIONS, INC.

GRAND FALLS–WINDSOR

Grand Falls and Windsor, as separate towns, predate the TransCanada Hwy. by decades. The two towns joined into a single municipality, an efficient political move but a logistical challenge for the visitor, who has to wander across the busy highway from place to place. Overpasses help, and the main difficulty is conceptual. Keep in mind that Windsor lies north of the TransCanada and Grand Falls south. Each town

has its own shopping area, and the Trans-Canada's shops makes a third.

Grand Falls offers the most sightseeing. Turn south off the highway to the **Mary March Regional Museum** on St. Catherine St., where exhibits about the area's Beothuk Indians, natural history, and geology fill the modern center; open year-round, Mon.-Fri. 9 a.m.-4:45 p.m. A re-created Indian village is situated in the woodlands behind the museum; open June-September.

The town is aptly named for its Grand Falls, a thunderous, whitewater gush from the Exploits River as it speeds alongside the town. To see the falls, take Scott Ave. off the TransCanada Hwy. or drive through town, turn west at the pulp and paper mill, and head north on a narrow, gravel lane. The river's famous for its Atlantic salmon. You can get a close look at them at the **Atlantic Salmon Interpretation Centre,** the wooden, A-frame building next to the river. The Environment Resources Management Association, a private conservation group, operates the center. Exhibits explain the salmon's life cycle and habitat. The center is open July-Sept., daily 9:30 a.m.-8:30 p.m. Outside, you can watch the migratory salmon through the fish-way's viewing windows.

During mid-July, the five-day **Exploits Valley Salmon Festival** takes over the whole area. Up to 10,000 spectators come for the province's only horse show, music (Irish, rhythm and blues, funk, and rock), and traditional Newfoundland food with an emphasis on salmon dinners.

Accommodations
Mount Peyton Hotel on the TransCanada Hwy., tel. (709) 489-4900, has 102 rooms from $70. The motel's dining room is locally known for fresh salmon, trout, crab, and lobster; locally grown broccoli, cauliflower, carrots, and turnips; and, for dessert, berries in all forms.

Carriage House Hospitality Home, tel. 489-7185, is located at 181 Grenfell Heights in the residential outskirts of Windsor. The nicely-appointed private home rents four spic-and-span guest rooms for $59 with full breakfast. Outside, there's a pool and stables.

WESTERN NEWFOUNDLAND

The TransCanada Hwy.'s route across the central island finishes at Deer Lake, the western coast gateway. Be prepared to make a directional decision here. At Deer Lake, backcountry Hwy. 430 heads northwest to world-class parks on the remote Northern Peninsula, while the TransCanada turns southwest to Corner Brook, Newfoundland's second-largest city, and Channel-Port aux Basques, terminus for the Nova Scotia ferry. The distance between these places is sizable.

Western Newfoundland may seem remote, but the area is surprisingly developed. Along the northwestern coast, Gros Morne National Park works nicely as a sightseeing base. Park campgrounds and community lodgings are plentiful. To the south, Corner Brook, the western coast business hub, offers city comforts.

CORNER BROOK

Known as the "Hub of the Province," Corner Brook is the western coast's commercial, educational, service, and governmental center. The area ranks as Newfoundland's second-largest city combining the city of Corner Brook (pop. 24,339) with outlying settlements on the Humber Arm (another 25,000).

Thirty-five km inland from the Gulf of St. Lawrence, Corner Brook lies picturesquely cupped in a 20-square-km valley bowl, rimmed by the deep-water Humber Arm—one of three fjords that branch off the Bay of Islands. Farther inland beyond Corner Brook, the Humber Arm narrows to meet the Humber River, one of the province's finest fishing rivers.

The auspicious peaks of the Long Range Mountains rise around the city. To the southwest lie the 815-meter-high **Lewis Hills,** the island's highest mountains. The 472-meter-high **Marble Mountain,** 10 minutes northeast, ranks as one of eastern Canada's finest ski mountains. And the barren orange-brown **Blow Me Down Mountain** is 35 minutes northwest on the gulf, commanding a stunning view of the Bay of Islands.

History
The area was known to early French fishermen and explorers, but it was England's Capt. James Cook who surveyed the bay and fjords in 1767 and named the Bay of Islands, River Hamberg (Humber), and Cook's Brook. Between 1779 and 1790, English Loyalist settlers founded Birchy Cove (Curling), Gillams, and Summerside. The area remained lightly settled through 1911, when a census counted 382 inhabitants.

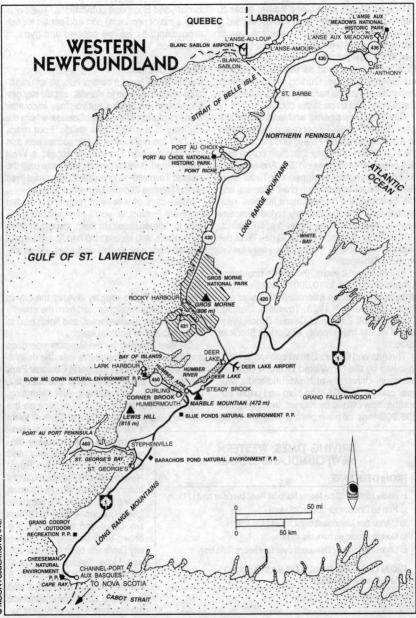

WESTERN
NEWFOUNDLAND

QUEBEC   LABRADOR

BLANC SABLON AIRPORT   L'ANSE-AU-LOUP
BLANC SABLON   L'ANSE-AMOUR
L'ANSE AUX MEADOWS NATIONAL HISTORIC PARK
L'ANSE AUX MEADOWS
436
ST. ANTHONY
430

STRAIT OF BELLE ISLE

ST. BARBE

NORTHERN PENINSULA

PORT AU CHOIX
PORT AU CHOIX NATIONAL HISTORIC PARK
POINT RICHE

430

LONG RANGE MOUNTAINS

ATLANTIC OCEAN

GULF OF ST. LAWRENCE

WHITE BAY

ROCKY HARBOUR

GROS MORNE NATIONAL PARK
▲ *GROS MORNE* (806 m)

420

431

DEER LAKE
DEER LAKE AIRPORT
HUMBER RIVER
DEER LAKE

BAY OF ISLANDS
LARK HARBOUR
BLOW ME DOWN NATURAL ENVIRONMENT P.P.
450
HUMBER ARM

1

STEADY BROOK

CURLING
CORNER BROOK
HUMBERMOUTH
MARBLE MOUNTAIN (472 m)
■ BLUE PONDS NATURAL ENVIRONMENT P.P.

GRAND FALLS-WINDSOR

▲ *LEWIS HILL* (815 m)

PORT AU PORT PENINSULA
460
STEPHENVILLE
ST. GEORGE'S BAY
ST. GEORGE'S

♦ BARACHOIS POND NATURAL ENVIRONMENT P.P.

LONG RANGE MOUNTAINS

1

0   50 mi
0   50 km

GRAND CODROY OUTDOOR RECREATION P.P. ■

CHEESEMAN NATURAL ENVIRONMENT P.P.
CAPE RAY
CHANNEL-PORT AUX BASQUES
TO NOVA SCOTIA

CABOT STRAIT

© MOON PUBLICATIONS, INC.

Corner Brook, as a place-name, dates to 1864, when Gay Silver from Halifax started a sawmill operation on what is now the Corner Brook Stream. Meanwhile, the area became part of the new railroad's network in 1898, and Humbermouth served as the line's regional maintenance center. Curling on the Humber Arm emerged as the transportation link between the railroad and ships at the docks.

Silver sold his sawmill and land to Christopher Fisher in 1881. Fisher resold the vast tract to the Newfoundland Power and Paper Company, a British company that then built a pulp and paper mill on the site in 1923. Andrew Cobb, a Halifax architect, designed the Tudor-style Glynmill Inn as construction crew quarters, and the Townsite, the management families' residential area. The handsomely styled company town is now a heritage conservation district. Corner Brook East and Corner Brook West developed haphazardly through the years for the workers' families.

In less than 10 years, the area's population jumped from 6,000 to 10,000. The British company sold the mill to International Power and Paper Company in 1928. Townsite, Curling, Corner Brook East, and Corner Brook West joined as the municipality of Corner Brook in 1956.

The Arts and Culture Centre opened in 1967, followed by the Sir Wilfred Grenfell College, Memorial University of Newfoundland's two-year college, in 1975. The pulp and paper operation, now owned by Kruger, Inc., produces 308,000 tons of newsprint a year for U.S., British, and European publications. The city is also a major provincial port and center for fish processing, as well as cement and gypsum production.

Getting Oriented

Corner Brook lacks a central hub, so an uninitiated visitor may tend to wander. Locals say getting around is a breeze, but you may encounter some confusion at the TransCanada, where the highway cuts a half-circle swath. Four roads peel off the highway in quick succession and lead into the city. The easiest access is West Valley Road. It leads directly into town past the historic Townsite—the prettiest residential area —and finishes at downtown West Street.

After days or weeks of roughing it on the Northern Peninsula, you'll find civilized comforts in Corner Brook. In town, expect to drive everywhere, and keep a map handy; sightseeing is scattered, and streets and sites are sometimes unmarked.

Sights

West Valley Road roughly divides the city in half. The following sights start from the street's southern side, proceed west, and finish next to the Humber Arm north of town.

On land donated by the Bowater operation and named for the chairman's wife, the delightful grassy and wooded **Margaret Bowater Park** is pierced by a fast-flowing river and waterfall. Locals enjoy the walking trails, river swimming, supervised outdoor pool, and picnics on the pitched hillside beside O'Connell Drive off West Valley Road. At the **Royal Newfoundland Constabulary Museum**, artifacts, uniforms, and photographs depict the Royal Newfoundland Constabulary's history in Corner Brook. It's open daily 8 a.m.-11 p.m. To get there, follow O'Connell Drive to University Drive and turn south; the brown-brick building on University Drive sits back from the corner. More history abounds at **Captain Cook's Monument.** A national historic site plaque and a sample chart commemorate the surveyor's Bay of Islands ex-

---

DRIVING TIMES: WESTERN NEWFOUNDLAND ISLAND

FROM DEER LAKE

to Rocky Harbour, Gros Morne National Park: over one hour (71 km)

to Port au Choix: four hours (233 km)

to L'Anse aux Meadows: eight hours (483 km)

to Corner Brook: 45 minutes (50 km)

to Channel-Port aux Basques: over four hours (268 km)

FROM CHANNEL-PORT AUX BASQUES TO L'ANSE AUX MEADOWS

13 hours (751 km)

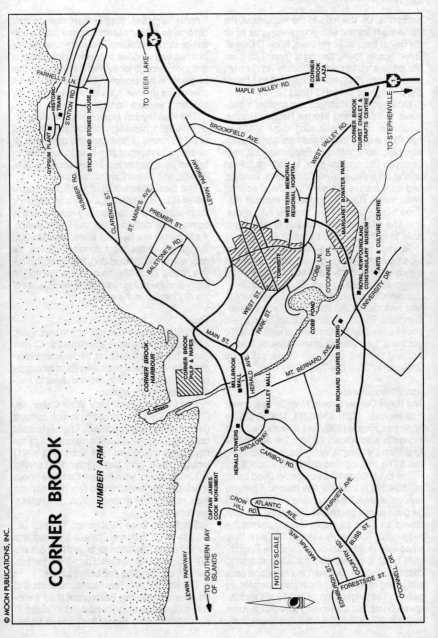

CORNER BROOK

HUMBER ARM

© MOON PUBLICATIONS, INC.

FARNELL'S LN.

HISTORIC TRAIN

STATION RD.

GYPSUM PLANT

HUMBER RD.

STICKS AND STONES HOUSE

CLARENCE ST.

ST. MARK'S AVE.

PREMIER ST.

BALSTONE'S RD.

TO DEER LAKE

MAPLE VALLEY RD.

BROOKFIELD AVE.

LEWIN PARKWAY

WEST VALLEY RD.

CORNER BROOK PLAZA

CORNER BROOK TOURIST CHALET & CRAFTS CENTRE

WESTERN MEMORIAL REGIONAL HOSPITAL

MARGARET BOWATER PARK

TO STEPHENVILLE

TOWNSITE

ROYAL NEWFOUNDLAND CONSTABULARY MUSEUM

ARTS & CULTURE CENTRE

COBB LN.

O'CONNELL DR.

UNIVERSITY DR.

WEST ST.

PARK ST.

COBB POND

MAIN ST.

CORNER BROOK PULP & PAPER

CORNER BROOK HARBOUR

MILLBROOK MALL

HERALD AVE.

VALLEY MALL

MT. BERNARD AVE.

SIR RICHARD SQUIRES BUILDING

HERALD TOWERS

BROADWAY

CARIBOU RD.

FAIRVIEW AVE.

CAPTAIN JAMES COOK MONUMENT

CROW HILL RD.

ATLANTIC AVE.

BLISS ST.

MAYFAIR AVE.

COUNTRY RD.

EDINBURGH ST.

FORESTSIDE ST.

O'CONNELL DR.

LEWIN PARKWAY

TO SOUTHERN BAY OF ISLANDS

NOT TO SCALE

plorations. On the road to the monument, the traveler is rewarded with glorious views as far as the Bay of Islands. To get there, follow O'Connell Drive across town, turn right (north) on Bliss St., make another right on Country Rd., turn left onto Atlantic Ave. with another left to Mayfair St., and right to Crow Hill Road.

One person's discards are another's treasures at **Sticks and Stones House.** The former owner of this unassuming house at 12 Farnell's Lane used infinite patience and all available resources, including Popsicle sticks, pebbles, can lids, and car grills, to create a folk-art setting on walls, shelves, cupboards, ceilings, and door frames. To get there, head east on West Valley Rd. until you reach Humber Rd., three blocks up from the Humber Arm shoreline. The house is open from July to early Sept., daily 11 a.m.-7 p.m. Admission is $2.

Railroad buffs will like the **Historic Train,** an old-time narrow-gauge railroad assemblage with a gleaming locomotive and box, baggage, day, dining, and sleeping cars. Once part of Newfoundland's railroad, the train has been beautifully restored by the Railway Society of Newfoundland. The locomotive and cars lie on an old track beside the gypsum plant at waterfront. To get there, take steep Farnell's Lane to Station Rd. and turn left. For a tour inside, call Philip Greenacre, (709) 634-7907.

Accommodations

The **Hotel Corner Brook,** Main St. near Lewin Parkway, tel. (709) 634-8211, has 50 plainly furnished rooms ($52) and a restaurant and lounge in a downtown setting. The **Journey's End Motel,** 41 Maple Valley Rd., tel. 639-1980, has 81 no-frills, comfortable rooms (under $60).

The lovely **Glynmill Inn,** on quiet Cobb Lane, tel. 634-5181, lies near the historic Townsite residential area. It's a charming inn banked with gardens of red geraniums. Rambling ivy, with leaves as large as maple leaves, covers the half-timber, Tudor-style exterior. The wide front steps lead to an open porch, and the English-style foyer is comfortably furnished with wing chairs and sofas. Between the reception desk and dining room there's a privately operated art gallery. The original inn of the 1920s had far fewer rooms, but a new wing brought the room count to 90 ($63-84). All the rooms are com-

fortably furnished, but the older ones feature old-time spaciousness and antique marble outfittings in the bathroom. The main-level restaurant has end windows overlooking the gardens, and room enough for the many tour groups that frequent the inn. However, the best restaurant is downstairs. It does full justice to tender, juicy beef from western Canada.

The **Holiday Inn Downtown,** 48 West St., tel. 634-5381, has a splendid location. The hotel with 103 rooms ($69) boasts the city's best facilities: a restaurant and lounge, an outdoor heated pool, barber and beauty shops, a launderette, and free underground parking.

The **Best Western Mamateek Inn,** Maple Valley Rd., tel. 639-8901, is arguably the city's most attractive contemporary lodging and is conveniently located beside the TransCanada. A *mamateek* is a Beothuk winter wigwam, and though this motel bears no resemblance, it's cozy with an accommodating, friendly staff. Fifty-five rooms ($69-83) fan out from the stylish lobby, and the dining room has splendid views of the city nestled in the valley.

Food

You'll find an adequate mix of fish, red meat, and provincial culinary specialties in Corner Brook, but locals favor beef, the rarer and thicker the better. Reservations are wise at all restaurants, especially during the mid-June to mid-September tourist season.

Don't miss Glynmill Inn's **Wine Cellar,** tel. (709) 634-5181, a cozy setting in high demand (reservations are required). The restaurant boasts a fine wine list and serves some of the city's best, unadorned beef. Entrees ($14-21) include grilled, juicy filet mignon ($21) served in 12-ounce cuts. Upstairs, the **Carriage Room** specializes in Newfoundland fare ($11-18) with fried, poached, or broiled salmon, cod, halibut, and lobster.

The **Seven Seas Restaurant,** 16 West St., tel. 634-6572, featuring Chinese fare, has also earned a fine reputation for table d'hôte dinners ($7-12) and the freshest, pan-fried halibut, salmon, cod tongues and boiled lobster.

The Holiday Inn's **Newfoundland Meat and Beverage Company Restaurant** does a succulent Steak Napoleon (tender sirloin awash in a mushroom wine sauce, $14) and its barbecued chicken and ribs dish ($11) is temptingly browned, crispy, and spicy. Overall, the entrees range $11-17. The buffet lunch (Mon.-Fri. noon-2 p.m., $9) includes soup, salad, hot dishes, and dessert. Sunday brunch ($10) is similarly bountiful.

The **Alpine Dining Room** at Best Western Mamateek Inn offers tempting table d'hôte meals. A typical array ranges from barbecued ribs ($15), seafood lasagna ($15), roasted prime ribs ($18), Atlantic seafood casserole ($16), and grilled New York sirloin ($16) to juicy T-bone steak ($18). The table d'hôte meals include the appetizer, entree, dessert, and coffee—a great buy. For dessert, the berry and cream pies are light and flaky, and the cheesecakes with berry toppings are creamy and smooth. You can't go wrong here.

For do-it-yourself meals and picnic fare, check out **Sobey's,** one of the town's largest supermarkets; it has a deli and bakery. Sobey's at the Valley Mall on Mt. Bernard Ave. is open Mon.-Tues. and Sat. 9 a.m.-6 p.m., Wed.-Fri. to 10 p.m. For fresh lobster, salmon, herring, and other fish, visit **Allen's Foodland,** 13 Killick Place in the city's West End. Hours are Mon.-Fri. 9 a.m.-9 p.m., Sat. to 5:30 p.m.

More For Less Food, 9 Herald Ave. near Canadian Tire, tel. 634-1452, sells natural foods in bulk as well as Newfoundland specialties, such as Mt. Scio savory spice and Purity candy. It's open Mon.-Sat. 9 a.m.-5:30 p.m., Wed.-Fri. until 9 p.m.

Entertainment and Events

The **Majestic Theatre** on Church St. shows two films nightly. Call (709) 634-6816 for the latest films. The **Millbrook's** two cinemas each have two shows nightly.

Once a week during July and Aug. 1-2 p.m., local musicians perform traditional Newfoundland music, show tunes, and contemporary rhythms at the Arts & Culture Centre's **Lunchtime Concerts,** University Drive next to the Newfoundland Constabulary, tel. 637-2580.

A rascal too lazy to fish or do anything else worthwhile is known as a hangashore or angishore. Corner Brook celebrates this penchant for the easygoing life at the three-day **Hangashore Folk Festival** in mid-July. You'll enjoy traditional Newfoundland music, dance, storytelling, and crafts, embellished with some newer island music at the Prince Edward Park, Hwy. 440, on the Humber Arm's northern side. **Corner Brook Day,** at the Margaret Bowater Park in mid-Aug., is devoted to competitions, game booths and stalls, picnics, and provincial music mixed among contemporary fare.

Recreation

The area's sports forte is **fishing,** and numerous outfitters are based in Corner Brook. **Wilderness Outfitters** handles custom fishing trips (from $110 per day) on the Humber River and western coast. Fish for salmon late June to early Sept. and for trout year-round. For details, call (709) 634-0582 or write to them at P.O. Box 775, Corner Brook, NF A2H 6G7.

Angus Wentzell's Hunting and Fishing Camps has camps at Angus Lake and Four Ponds in the area of the Main River, a Canadian heritage river. For $1500 per person, he'll fly you in on a floatplane and provide meals and fishing guides for a week of salmon fishing, July-August. You supply your sleeping bag and pay extra for the fishing license fee. Wentzell also arranges trips for hunting moose, caribou, and black bear. For details, call 634-2347 or write to him at P.O. Box 9, Corner Brook, NF A2H 6C3. For other outfitters in Corner Brook, see the tourist office's *Newfoundland and Labrador Hunting and Fishing Guide.*

Windsurfing and **canoeing** are other options. **Freedom Sports,** 89 West Valley Rd., tel. 634-0864, gives windsurfing instructions ($25 hour) and rents boards ($70). Novice boardsailors can take a lesson and then enjoy Stag Lake Provincial Park's tame waters. The Bay of Islands' outer bay is perfect for experienced windsurfers.

The **Mi-Tour** outfit at 7 Broadway, tel. 783-2455, rents canoes ($30 day) and arranges guided canoe trips (from $125 day); for more details on the company, call 783-2455, or write P.O. Box 839, Corner Brook, NF A2H 6H6.

The 18-hole, par-69 **Blomidon Golf and Country Club,** off West Valley Rd. beside the TransCanada Hwy., has a restaurant, pool, and scenic city views. Visitors are welcome. Open from June to mid-Oct., the greens fee is $25. For details and reservations, call 634-2523. At the **Arts and Culture Centre,** the heated, indoor pool ($3 admission) is open daily. For details, call 637-2546. **Margaret Bowater Park** has an outdoor, supervised pool; open July-late Aug., daily noon-6 p.m.

Shopping

Stores with a variety of wares line West St. and Broadway, the city's historic shopping district. General hours are Mon.-Sat. 9:30 a.m.-5 p.m., and Thurs.-Fri. until 9 p.m. Many shops have relocated to the shopping centers such as the **Millbrook Mall** on Main St.; **Valley Mall,** a large shopping center at 1 Mt. Bernard Ave.; and **Corner Brook Plaza,** situated behind McDonald's on the TransCanada.

Tooton's at Corner Brook Plaza and Nova Photo Express at Valley Mall, sell film and basic equipment, and can handle uncomplicated camera repairs.

For traditional, local crafts, head for the **Sora** shop, selling hand knits, quilts, jewelry, pottery, and pewter at the Corner Brook Plaza. The **Newfoundland Emporium** at 7 Broadway stocks the best in Newfoundland-only crafts (especially whalebone and soapstone carvings, sealskin products, and parkas from Labrador) and has a well-stocked book corner with provincial tomes. The **Corner Brook Tourist Chalet and Crafts Centre** on the TransCanada carries handmade sweaters ($65-165), locally made wares, Bogside Weaving merchandise from St. John's, and souvenirs. It's open Mon.-Fri. 8:30 a.m.-4:30 p.m. From June to early Sept. you can shop daily 8:30 a.m.-10 p.m.

Apparel is another provincial crafts specialty. If you've seen Grenfell Handicrafts' line, you may be interested in similar but different interpretations at the **Humber Handicrafts,** 139 Massey Drive, tel. (709) 634-6584. It's open daily 8:30 a.m.-5:30 p.m. Similarities between both places are strong. Both produce full-length coats, thigh-high parkas, waist-length jackets, and pullover cossacks in heavy "duffle" wool or "Canadian Mist," a synthetic-blend fabric. Both producers embellish the apparel with hand embroidery and trim the hoods and bottom-hem with fox fur. The Grenfell line is based on traditional loose-fitting Northern Peninsula and Labrador styles. Humber Handicrafts uses a slimmer cut. Prices are also similar; expect to pay $250 for a full-length woolen coat or $200 in Canadian Mist.

For local art, the **Ewing Gallery,** located in the Glynmill Inn's foyer, tel. 634-4577, showcases painting and original prints by western coast and provincial artists. It's open daily 11 a.m.-4 p.m. and 7-9 p.m. The **Franklyn Gallery,** 98 West. St., is another source.

Alteen's Jewellers, at 74 Broadway, tel. 639-9286, and at the Valley Mall, tel. 639-7362, features labradorite jewelry.

Information

The **Corner Brook Tourist Chalet** on the TransCanada Hwy. opposite Journey's End motel, tel. (709) 639-9792, stocks city and area literature and maps. The chalet is open Mon.-Fri. 8:30 a.m.-4:30 p.m., and from June to early Sept. until 10 p.m. The **Corner Brook Chamber of Commerce,** tel. 634-5831, shares the same building and hours.

The **city library,** in the Sir Richard Squires Building, the city's 10-floor high-rise on Mt. Bernard Ave., tel. 634-0013, is open Tues.-Thurs. 10 a.m.-8:45 p.m., Fri. to 5:45 p.m. New and used bookstores are sparse. **Coles The Book People,** tel. 634-4125, has a shop at the Valley Mall on Mt. Bernard Avenue.

The daily *Western Star* newspaper covers the western coast.

Everything you may want to know about Newfoundland's history, culture, flora, fauna, geology and fossils on the western coast, as well as landscape sketching, is offered in classes at the **Elderhostel.** Memorial University's Sir Wilfred Grenfell College sponsors the one-week classes ($376 pp) in July. For details, call the college's Department of Community Education at (709) 637-6200 or write to them at University Drive, Corner Brook, NF A2H 6P9.

Services

The **Western Memorial Regional Hospital,** tel. (709) 637-5000, is located on Brookfield Avenue. Other important emergency numbers include: **Royal Newfoundland Constabulary,** tel. 634-4222; **RCMP,** tel. 637-4400; and **Poison Control,** tel. 634-7121.

All the major **banks,** such as the CIBC, Royal Bank, and Banks of Montreal and Nova Scotia, have branch offices in the city. Services and hours are similar: for example, the **Bank of Nova Scotia** has offices at the Corner Brook

Plaza on the TransCanada and in town on Broadway and is open Mon.-Wed. 10 a.m.-3 p.m., Thurs.-Fri. to 5:30 p.m. There's no extra fee to change U.S. or U.K. currency or traveler's checks to Canadian dollars.

Canada Post is on Main St. near Park St., tel. 637-8800. Hours are Mon.-Fri. 8 a.m.-5:15 p.m. (philatelic window: 8:30-11:30 a.m. and 1-5:15 p.m.). Canada Post retail outlets are at the **Shoppers Drug Mart,** 93 West St. and, also, at the Millbrook Mall, Herald Ave., open Mon.-Sat. 9 a.m.-10 p.m., Sun. noon-9 p.m.; and **Allen's Foodland,** 13 Killick Place, open Mon.-Fri. 9 a.m.-9 p.m., Sat. to 5:30 p.m.

Canada Immigration at Herald Towers on Herald Ave., tel. 637-4200, is open by appointment.

You can stash your luggage ($1 a locker) at the **CN Roadcruiser Service** terminal on St. Mark's Ave., tel. 634-8244, open daily 10 a.m.-7 p.m. Launderettes are sparse. The **New-Lee Done Laundromat** has coin-operated laundry facilities at 15 Fairview Ave. and 25A Batstone's Rd., open daily 10 a.m.-10 p.m.

Transportation
Deer Lake Airport is the western coast's air hub and has service from across the province and from Halifax. Located 45 minutes northeast of Corner Brook, the small airport is open during flights and has **Budget, Thrifty,** and **Tilden** car rentals. **Air Nova,** Air Canada's affiliated carrier, flies in from Halifax and other provincial gateways. It pays to think ahead and buy a discounted Seat Saver round-trip fare. For example, a Halifax to Deer Lake discounted fare is $348, compared to the regular economy fare of $615, while St. John's to Deer Lake is discounted to $291 from $544. For details, call Air Canada at (800) 422-6232 (Canada), (800) 776-3000 (U.S.), or (709) 634-6682 (reservations and other information), or 634-2866 (departures/arrivals). The airport is also served by **Air Atlantic,** tel. 639-9981, and **Provincial Airlines,** tel. 635-8288.

Rental car counters are found at the airport. **Budget Rent A Car** charges $189 a week for a subcompact car (such as a two-door Sprint with automatic shift); the price includes 1,400 km free, 20 cents for each additional kilometer. An optional collision damage waiver costs $10 a day, while personal accident insurance is $2.50 a day. For details, call the Budget office at the airport at 635-3211; in Corner Brook, call the office in the Best Western Mamateek Inn at 639-9951.

The city has half a dozen cab companies whose cabs wait at lodgings, cruise business streets, and take calls. Taxi rides are metered and start at $2.15. **City Cabs,** 4 Caribou Rd., tel. 634-6565, is among the largest outfits.

The **CN Roadcruiser Service,** tel. 634-8244, operates frequent bus service along the Trans-Canada and charges $27 OW from Corner Brook to Port aux Basques and $65 OW to St. John's. The terminal is on St. Mark's Ave., with storage lockers ($1) available. The terminal is open daily 10 a.m.-7 p.m. For west coast bus travel, check out the **Viking Express,** tel. 634-4710. Buses depart from the Millbrook Mall and go north to Rocky Harbour ($11 OW) and St. Anthony ($41 OW) on Mon., Wed., and Fri. and return to Corner Brook on Sat., Tues., and Thursday.

If you're arriving on your own yacht, you can dock ($23 a night) at the **Bay of Islands Yacht Club,** tel. 785-7406. The yacht club, located at Allen's Cove Marina at Petries Point in the Curling area, is a 10-minute drive from downtown Corner Brook.

VICINITY OF CORNER BROOK

Lark Harbour
An hour's drive northwest of the city on Hwy. 450 leads you through a dozen or so Humber Arm fishing settlements to **Blow Me Down Provincial Park** on the Bay of Islands' southwestern corner. Incidentally, the park isn't extraordinarily windy, as the name might imply. Legend says a diminutive sea captain saw the mountain centuries ago and exclaimed, "Well, blow me down." The name stuck. Views of the bay, spread across 355 square km and speckled with islands, are worth the trip. You'll see the bay's fjord arms and the Lewis Hills, as well as bald eagles and ospreys gliding on the updrafts, and perhaps caribou and moose roaming the preserve's terrain. The remote setting has 28 campsites ($7), offering pit toilets, a comfort station, and hiking trails. Closer to the water, the nearby **Bottle Cove Provincial Park,** a day-

use preserve, has picnic tables and a trail to the cobble beach.

Steady Brook

Ten minutes northeast of Corner Brook, turn off the TransCanada Hwy. at the Steady Brook sign, and drive down Wilton St. to the dock on the Humber River. The river is best known for Atlantic salmon and trout fishing. If you're interested in a sightseeing approach, **Humber River Boat Tours,** tel. (709) 639-1538, operates two-hour cruises ($20), late May to early October. Reservations are wise.

Marble Mountain

On the TransCanada's inland side near Steady Brook, the **Marble Mountain Ski Area** hosts the Dec.-April ski crowd. The resort offers 26 runs (the longest at 3.2 km) and lifts that move 5,800 skiers an hour to the peak. The mountain gets 508 cm of snow annually; snowmaking equipment is used on 55% of the slopes. Cost is $19-26 for a day's lift ticket. For details, call (709) 634-2160 or 634-4563, or write Marble Mountain Ski Area, c/o Corner Brook Ski Club, P.O. Box 252, Steady Brook, NF A2H 2N2.

Hikes to the **Steady Brook Falls** attract the summer visitors. Follow the signs to the ski area and park in the back parking lot. A marked, 15-minute trail to the left (rocky in parts) leads up the mountain, with views of the waterfalls. From there, a three and a half-km one-way unmarked trail continues and brings you nearer to the peak. The views of the Humber Valley and Bay of Islands are splendid.

Blue Ponds Provincial Park

A half hour on the TransCanada southwest from Corner Brook, the park has two limestone lakes with crystalline, blue-green waters, hiking trails through the woodlands, and 61 unserviced ($7) campsites.

THE SOUTHWEST CORNER

Stephenville

The **Beavercraft,** 108 Main St., tel. (709) 643-4844, has been consistently voted as one of the island's best crafts shops, according to a reader survey by the *Newfoundland Herald,* a

shoppers' guide in St. John's. Beavercraft is best known for Winterhouses sweaters ($120-175), designed locally and produced by 60 cottage-industry knitters. Top shops in St. John's sell the sweaters.

The shop is also the source for "thrummed" mittens ($20-30) and caps. This revival of a traditional craft combines a knitted woolen facing backed with raw fleece. The shop shelves are stuffed with top-quality wares including Woof Design sweaters, Random Island Weaving cotton placemats, and handmade birch brooms. It's open Mon.-Sat. 9 a.m.-5:30 p.m., and Thurs.-Fri. until 9 p.m.

Barachois Pond Provincial Park

Hikers enjoy the park, one of the province's most popular preserves, for the 3.2-km trail through birch, spruce, and fir trees to Erin Mountain's barren summit. Be on the lookout for a rare Newfoundland pine marten along the way. The view at 305 meters overlooks the Port au Port Peninsula.

There's a commendable summertime interpretive program with guided walks and evening campfires, a lake for swimming and fishing, and 150 unserviced campsites ($7), some situated atop the mountain.

Channel-Port aux Basques

If you're waiting to board a ferry to Nova Scotia, it might be simplest to stay overnight in town. For details on the crossing, see "By Sea" under "Getting There" in this chapter's "Introduction."

The **Hotel Port aux Basques,** Grand Bay Rd., tel. (709) 695-2171, is two km from the ferry. It offers 50 rooms ($59) and a restaurant and lounge. The nearby **St. Christopher's Hotel** on Caribou Rd., tel. 695-7034, has 58 rooms ($68-75) and similar facilities.

If you're hauling a recreational vehicle, your choices are limited. You can overnight at one of the town's four lodgings, or you can pull into **Grand Codroy Provincial Park,** 30 minutes north of Channel-Port aux Basques on the TransCanada. Grand Codroy features 38 first-come, first-served, fully serviced sites ($11) with electricity and water.

For some sightseeing while in town, the **Port aux Basques Museum,** 118 Main St. opposite the town hall, tel. 695-7604, has some unusual artifacts: a 17th-century astrolabe retrieved from local waters; old-time navigational instruments and a diving suit; and remnants from the *Caribou,* the ferry torpedoed by a German submarine as it crossed the Cabot Strait during WW II. The museum is open late June-early Sept., daily 8:30 a.m.-8 p.m.; admission is $1 adults, 50 cents ages 6-15.

GROS MORNE NATIONAL PARK

UNESCO world heritage sites are scattered across the world. Egypt boasts the pyramids at Giza. France is known for Chartres Cathedral. Australia has the Great Barrier Reef. And now Newfoundland boasts Gros Morne National Park, a spectacular geological slice of the ancient world.

The Gros Morne preserve fronts the Gulf of St. Lawrence on a coastal plain rimmed with 72 km of coast edging sandy and cobblestoned beaches, seastacks, caves, forests, peat bogs, and breathtaking saltwater and freshwater fjords. The flattened Long Range Mountains, part of the ancient Appalachian Mountains, rise as an alpine plateau cloaked with black and white spruce, balsam fir, white birch, and stunted tuckamore thickets. Bare patches of peridotite, toxic to most plants, speckle the peaks, and at the highest elevations the vegetation gives way to lichen, moss, and dwarf willow and birch on the arctic tundra.

Innumerable moose, arctic hare, fox, weasel, lynx, and a few bears roam the park. Two herds of 600 woodland caribou inhabit the mountains and migrate to the coastal plain during winter. Bald eagles, ospreys, common and arctic terns, great black-backed gulls, and songbirds nest along the coast, while rock ptarmigans inhabit the mountain peaks. You might see willow ptarmigans on the lower slopes or, especially during the June to early July capelin run, a few pilot, minke, or humpback whales offshore.

The User-friendly Park
The park is remarkably user-friendly. Although the preserve spans 1,805 square km (more than half the size of Luxembourg), it's not so large that sightseeing is unmanageable. And while the majority of the park is mountainous wilder-

ness, a narrow coastal plain contains rare, ancient landscape, one of Gros Morne's most significant attractions.

Some 120 km of roads thread through this outdoor geological museum. No national park vehicle permit is needed. Almost 100 km of marked and unmarked hiking trails lead novice to expert trekkers into the park's nooks and crannies. Several privately operated boat tours probe the fjords, and if you're adventurous, private outfitters can make sea-kayaking arrangements. A provincial fishing license (available at any sports store) opens up angling for brook trout and arctic char on the fast-flowing streams and rivers. And if you'd like to know more about Gros Morne's natural history and geology, scheduled interpretive programs and evening campfires run from late June to early September.

Climate
The park enjoys a pleasant, cool climate, averaging 14 days of precipitation each month. At Rocky Harbour, a typical summer day is breezy with southwesterly winds. The temperature averages 15° C, while it's 2-4° C cooler and windier at higher elevations. For weather information, contact the **Newfoundland Weather Centre,** tel. (709) 256-6600.

Touching Base with the Ancient World
Wiltondale is Gros Morne's gateway, situated at the park's southeastern inland corner at the intersection of the two main roads, Highways 430 and 431. Geological sightseeing is distributed between two coastal areas: a **southern area**

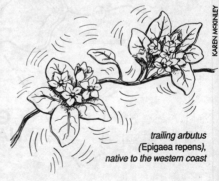

trailing arbutus
(Epigaea repens),
native to the western coast

KAREN McKINLEY

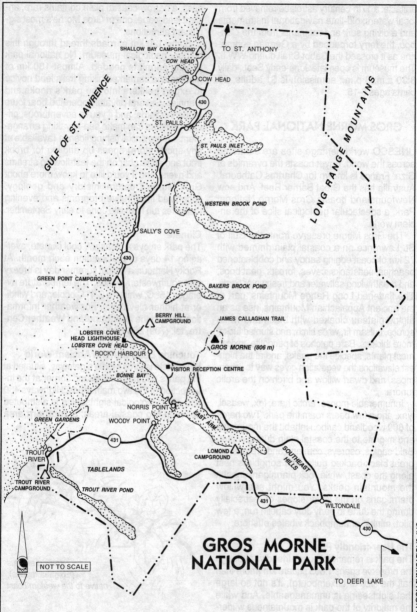

GROS MORNE
NATIONAL PARK

NOT TO SCALE

© MOON PUBLICATIONS, INC.

TO ST. ANTHONY

SHALLOW BAY CAMPGROUND
COW HEAD

COW HEAD

430

ST. PAULS

GULF OF ST. LAWRENCE

ST. PAULS INLET

WESTERN BROOK POND

SALLY'S COVE

430

GREEN POINT CAMPGROUND

BAKERS BROOK POND

BERRY HILL
CAMPGROUND

JAMES CALLAGHAN TRAIL

LOBSTER COVE
HEAD LIGHTHOUSE
LOBSTER COVE HEAD
ROCKY HARBOUR

GROS MORNE (806 m)

VISITOR RECEPTION CENTRE

LONG RANGE MOUNTAINS

BONNE BAY

NORRIS POINT
WOODY POINT

EAST ARM

GREEN GARDENS

431

LOMOND
CAMPGROUND

SOUTHEAST HILLS

TROUT
RIVER

TROUT RIVER
CAMPGROUND

TABLELANDS

TROUT RIVER POND

431

WILTONDALE

430

TO DEER LAKE

located between Wiltondale and the gulf coastline; and a **northern area** farther up the gulf coast. The park's prized geological tracts lie across the southern area. At Wiltondale, turn off Hwy. 431 for an hour's drive toward the gulf.

The spread known as the **Tablelands** is an odd sight compared to Newfoundland's rich verdant vegetation. It more resembles Hudson Bay's bleached, brown barrens. The 12- by 7-km chunk once lay beneath the ancient Iapetus Ocean as part of the earth's crust and upper mantle. Violent internal upheavals eventually thrust the unearthly landscape to the surface. The parched yellow and tan cliffs and boulders that result are formed of peridotite, an igneous rock found in the earth's mantle.

In contrast, the **Green Gardens** originated as lava from erupting volcanoes in the Iapetus Ocean. Look for a marked trailhead on Hwy. 431, halfway across the Tablelands road. A 10-km round-trip hiking trail starts out across Tablelands's crusty terrain and emerges on a high headland cloaked in rich green grasses overlooking the gulf. Below the headland, seastacks and caves rise from the beach floor beside cliffs pocked with pillow lava, the solidified remnants of molten rock from 100 km beneath the ancient sea floor.

Mountains and Fjords

The park's northern section is typical of the island's rocky seacoast and verdant hills and mountains, a distinct contrast to the southern area. To get there, retrace Hwy. 431 to Wiltondale and turn northwest on Highway 430, the main road.

Gros Morne Mountain, part of the Long Range Mountains but set by itself near the coastline, dominates this part of the park. You'll see the flattened peak as the highway threads through the park's interior, curves along the Southeast Hills, and dips down to sea level alongside the **East Arm,** one of the **Bonne Bay** fjord arms.

The James Callaghan Trail

For one of Atlantic Canada's more challenging mountain ascents, consider tackling Gros Morne's 16-km round-trip James Callaghan Trail. It's a colossal but rewarding experience. Tedious trudges up and down lead to an 806-meter-

high view of the park's forested flanks and slivered fjords. Look for the marked trailhead on Hwy. 430, some 30 minutes northwest of Wiltondale. Plan for a full day, and wear sturdy, high hiking boots. It's wise to bring a sweater, topographical map, compass, and drinking water.

The trail starts with about an hour's walk toward the mountain across a gently rising spruce and fir woodland, threaded with a dirt path and boardwalks. At Gros Morne's base, the route turns by several gullies, sometimes filled with snow-pocket remnants, and starts the ascent. Tightly packed boulders clog the upward route, and you'll scramble across the uneven surface and sometimes slip on gravel patches. The ascent takes about two hours, but it may seem longer, as you negotiate the boulder trail. The scree trail continues to rise, ascending through a haze of thick clouds banked on the steeply pitched trail gully.

Unexpectedly, the trail empties at a corner of the flattened peak. You'll tumble onto the peak, like a sailor with wobbly legs who's been at sea too long. You're hot, sweaty, exhausted, and disoriented. Throw yourself across the nearest flat surface. The bliss of solid, level ground is overwhelming. Moments pass as you reassemble your body parts.

The air is clear and exhilarating, but surprisingly chilly. You're aware of the clean, brisk wind. Wildlife is said to roam the plateau, but there's none in sight, only other mountain climbers clustered at the trail's entrance on the peak. Far below, climbers scramble fitfully up the rocky ascent. To the west rise the Long Range Mountains. Looking south, you'll see a sapphire fjord, laid like an angled ribbon across the green woodlands.

Exploring the peak takes minutes. The surface is mainly bare shale, limestone, and quartzite rock sprinkled with wild grass tufts. The sun feels deliciously warm, though the wind whistles across the stark terrain. Savor the peak's views. There are none on the wooded descent.

A few hikers backtrack and return on the boulder trail, but most climbers follow the cairns across the peak and go down Gros Morne's back side. It helps to make the descent in sight of another hiking party; rain sometimes washes out the trail, and if you go astray, you're lost together. Expect to descend hanging on tree branches, slipping across muddy patches, and following the trail like a bloodhound. The hours pass quickly, and the downward trail finishes tamely on the forest floor and feeds into a dirt path back to the trailhead.

Experienced climbers say the Gros Morne climb is not extraordinarily difficult. If you're a novice climber, however, you may want to retreat afterward to a soothing, hot bath in one of the area motels.

Fjords and Boat Tours

Like Scandinavia, the park is famous for fjords, fringed sea arms carved by the last ice sheet and shouldered by forests and cliffs. And like their Scandinavian counterparts, both the **Bonne Bay** and **St. Paul's Inlet** fjords open directly to the sea. The park's other fjords, however, are landlocked and known as "ponds." These ponds —**Trout River, Ten Mile, Bakers Brook,** and **Western Brook**—were carved by the ice sheets just like the other fjords. But in each case, when the enormous ice sheet melted out, the coastline —which had been compressed by the sheer weight of the glacier—rebounded like a sponge, rising above sea level and cutting the fjord off from the sea.

Daily boat tours lasting two to three hours ($15-25) explore some of the fjords from June to Sept., weather permitting.

More Unusual Formations

Unusual groups of faulted and folded rock layers lie along the coastline. For example, the **Lobster Cove Head,** a kilometer west of the village of Rocky Harbour, spreads out on rock layers. These layers formed as the North America plate slid beneath the eastern Eurasia/Africa plate 450-500 million years ago.

Check out the Lobster Cove Head lighthouse. The site is one of several places in the park offering guided walks, evening campfire programs, and weekend crafts demonstrations. Inside the lighthouse, exhibits depict local lore, geological facets, and ancient natural history. It's open June to early Oct., daily 9 a.m.-3 p.m., and from late June to early Sept., daily 10 a.m.-8 p.m.

More dramatically formed coastal rock lies farther north. **Green Point,** 10 minutes beyond Lobster Cove, presents a tilted, textured surface of ribbon limestone and shale embedded

---

FJORD CRUISES

To Bonne Bay: I'se da B'ye Tours; tel. 458-2730; departing from Norris Point boat ramp

To Western Brook Pond: Western Brook Pond; tel. 458-2730; departing from above Sally's Cove, Hwy. 430

To Trout River Pond: Tablelands Boat Tour; tel. 451-2101; departing from Trout River wharf

To St. Paul's Inlet: Seal Island Boat Tours; tel. 243-2471; departing from St. Paul's wharf

---

with fossils from the Cambrian and Ordovician periods. **Cow Head,** 40 minutes farther north, features a similar angled formation with limestone breccia (jumbled limestone chunks and fossils) spread across a small peninsula. The areas are richly textured. At Cow Head, the breccia looks like light-colored rock pillows scattered across a dark rock surface, while Green Point's surface is a rich green and textured like crushed velvet. The rock layers at both places originated during deep-water avalanches, as the Iapetus Ocean formed 460-550 million years ago.

Accommodations and Food

Almost 300 campsites (first-come, first-served) at five campgrounds lie within Gros Morne National Park. For details, call the **Visitor Reception Centre,** tel. (709) 458-2066.

Two campgrounds are open year-round and staffed from mid-June to mid-September. The **Berry Hill** site near Rocky Harbour has 156 sites ($12) and hot showers, toilets, fireplaces, and kitchen shelters in an inland wooded setting. The seaside **Green Point Campground** near a cobble beach has 18 campsites ($8), with fireplaces and kitchen shelters.

The remaining campgrounds ($8-9) are open from late June to early September. The **Trout River Campground,** situated near the Tablelands, Green Gardens, and the Trout River boat tour dock, boasts the park's most exotic setting. Facilities are limited to 33 campsites, pit toilets, and picnic tables. The **Lomond Campground** edges Bonne Bay's East Arm. Lomond offers 28 sites, limited facilities, and proximity to fishing streams. The **Shallow Bay Campground**, with 50 sites, fronts Shallow Bay at the park's northern edge.

Less intrepid visitors will find bed and breakfasts, housekeeping units, and motels at Rocky Harbour, the park's major service area, and also at Wiltondale, Woody Point, Norris Point, and Cow Head. In Rocky Harbour, the **Parsons Harbour View Cabins**, tel. 458-2544, charges $40-45 for its eight rooms or housekeeping units in the main house and adjacent motel. The sunny, small dining room is known for fried halibut and salmon, and flaky pies and tarts.

The **Ocean View Motel**, tel. 458-2730, offers 35 rooms (to $64) with a dining room and lounge, and beach access. It also operates the Bonne Bay and Western Brook Pond fjord boat tours. If you're looking for housekeeping units, check out the **Gros Morne Cabins**, tel. 458-2020, 458-2525, or 458-2369, featuring 22 one- and two-bedroom log chalets ($55-75) near the Endicott Cash and Carry store. The **Fisherman's Landing**, Main St. near the Ocean View Motel, is a good dining choice. It offers delectable fish dishes, such as a heaping platter of fried or broiled salmon, cod, or lobster (from $12), and a reputation for some of the best fried capelin, cod fishburgers, and bakeapple pies in the park.

In **Woody Point** on Hwy. 431 overlooking Bonne Bay's southern coastline, **Hostelling International** operates a 10-bed, dormitory-style hostel ($10) with kitchen facilities and hot showers, open May-Oct.; for details, call 453-2442 or 453-2470.

Information

Gros Morne National Park is open year-round. For details and literature, call (709) 458-2066, or write to the park at P.O. Box 130, Rocky Harbour, NF A0K 4N0. The **Visitor Reception Centre,** Hwy. 430 near Rocky Harbour, stocks literature, sells books about the park and Newfoundland, presents slide shows, and has changing exhibits on the park's geology, landscapes, and history. The center is open daily 9 a.m.-4 p.m., and from late June to early Sept. until 10 p.m.

The **Gros Morne Recreation Complex,** a few minutes north of Rocky Harbour on Hwy. 430, has an indoor heated pool and hot tub. It's

open late June to early Sept., daily 9 a.m.-9 p.m. A day-use pass is $3.

THE NORTHERN PENINSULA

Above Gros Morne, the Northern Peninsula sweeps northeast across mountainous, flat-topped barrens and ends in tundra strewn with glacial boulders. Highway 430 runs alongside the gulf on the coastal plain and extends the peninsula's full length, finishing at St. Anthony. For meals and lodgings, stop anywhere; one place is as good as the next. Make sure your car is in good operating condition, and watch the gas gauge. Gas stations are located at widely spaced settlements.

Port au Choix

The Maritime Archaic Indians and the later Dorset Inuits migrated from Labrador, roamed the Northern Peninsula, and then settled on this remote cape. In the 1960s, archaeological digs revealed Dorset dwellings in Phillips Garden and an incredible wealth of Indian cultural artifacts buried with almost 100 bodies at three nearby burial grounds. At the **Port au Choix National Historic Park,** tel. (709) 623-2608 or 623-2601, both cultures are represented by artifacts and exhibits at the visitor centre. It's open mid-June to early Sept., daily 9 a.m.-6 p.m. Admission is free. Outdoors, there are marked and unmarked coastal and hilltop hiking trails.

St. Barbe

The **Northern Cruiser Ltd.** has frequent ferry crossings to Blanc Sablon, Québec, early May to early January. The 90-minute crossing (bring a

---

DRIVING TIMES FROM ROCKY HARBOUR

To Port au Choix National Historic Park: three hours (172 km)

To St. Barbe ferry: four hours (247 km)

To St. Anthony: six hours (372 km)

To L'Anse aux Meadows National Historic Park: seven hours (412 km)

heavy sweater or jacket) costs $8 per person, $17 per vehicle. Vehicle reservations are accepted from mid-June to October. For details and reservations, call (709) 931-2309. Across the strait, you'll disembark and cross the border to Hwy. 510, an 80-km paved coastal road from Blanc Sablon to Pinware and on to Red Bay.

St. Anthony

In the late 1800s Dr. Wilfred Grenfell, a medical missionary from England, built the first hospital at St. Anthony in 1892. The village (pop. 3,200) still serves as the International Grenfell Association medical headquarters. Grenfell dedicated his life to building and raising funds for area hospitals, stores, schools, and orphanages. Grenfell helped foster financial independence for remote outports through profitable organizations, namely **Grenfell Handicrafts,** which still produces hand-embroidered cossacks, parkas, and jackets at the workroom/retail shop in the Brown Cottage near the hospital. This is the source for the fox-trimmed parkas and crafts sold islandwide. It's open Mon.-Fri. 9 a.m.-5:30 p.m.; from mid-June to early Sept., hours are extended to Sat. 9 a.m.-5:30 p.m., and Sun. 2-4 p.m.

In 1928, Grenfell was knighted for his efforts. He and his wife Anne Elizabeth are buried at Tea House Hill. Exhibits at the stately **Grenfell House Museum,** tel. (709) 454-3333, situated behind the Curtis Memorial Hospital in the village's western side, detail the work of Dr. Grenfell. The green-painted house is open mid-May through Sept., daily 10 a.m.-8 p.m. Admission is $1 adults, 50 cents ages 6-18. For more on Dr. Grenfell, see the "Introduction" to the Labrador section later in this chapter.

L'Anse aux Meadows

The island has no grapes, so this impressive Norse settlement couldn't have been the Norse "Vinland." It's believed the fossilized grapes found here originated farther south, perhaps from New Brunswick. Nonetheless, the current **L'Anse aux Meadows National Historic Site** was once a full-fledged Norse village serving as a sailing base for explorations throughout the area about A.D. 1000.

Long before archaeologists arrived, Newfoundlanders were aware of the odd-shaped, sod-covered ridges across the coastal plain. Newfoundland historian W.A. Munn speculated about the contents and origin decades ago. George Decker, from the Northern Peninsula, led Norwegian scholar-explorer Helge Ingstad and his wife, archaeologist Anne Stine Ingstad, to the area in the 1960s. The subsequent digs uncovered eight complexes of rudimentary houses, workshops with fireplaces, and a trove of artifacts, which verified the Norse presence. National recognition and site protection quickly followed in 1968. More digs by Parks Canada archaeologists led to the site's designation as a national historic park in 1977. UNESCO named the settlement a world heritage site the following year.

A gravel path and boardwalk across the grassy plain lead to re-created buildings overlooking Epaves Bay. You can see the artifacts, site models, and an audiovisual presentation at the Visitor reception Centre on Hwy. 436, a half hour's drive north of St. Anthony. The center's open mid-June to early Sept., daily 9 a.m.-8 p.m. The park grounds are open 24 hours. Admission is free.

For more information, write the Superintendent, L'Anse aux Meadows National Historic Park, P.O. Box 70, St. Lunaire-Griquet, NF A0K 2X0, or call (709) 623-2608 or 623-2601.

the remains of a Viking village at L'Anse aux Meadows

BOB RACE

BOB RACE

LABRADOR
INTRODUCTION

THE LAND AND PEOPLE

Spanning 295,707 square km, about three times the size of Newfoundland island, Labrador dominates Atlantic Canada. Known as "the Big Land," it covers more than twice the expanse of the Maritime Provinces. The region resembles an irregular wedge pointing toward the north pole, bordered on the east by the 8,000-km-long Labrador Sea, and on the west and south by the remote outskirts of Québec. Thorfinn Karlsefni, one of several Norse explorers who sailed the coastline around A.D. 1000, is said to have dubbed the region "Helluland" for the large flat rocks, and "Markland" for the woodlands. Jacques Cartier described the coastline as a "land of stone and rocks" during a 1534 voyage. The region once was Atlantic Canada's last frontier. But it's no longer isolated, having crossed the threshold from untamed wilderness into the modern world decades ago.

Spruce forests, interspersed with bogs and birch and tamarack stands, dominate the wilderness of southern Labrador. The Strait of Belle Isle, the narrow passage between Labrador and Newfoundland, features eight tiny ports within striking distance of Newfoundland's Great Northern Peninsula. This area was a Basque whaling center in the 1500s, and modern sightseers have rediscovered the strait and its archaeological treasures at Red Bay and L'Anse-Amour.

Highlights of the more remote southern coast include the 50-km Wunderstrands—a beach named by early Norse explorers—and the Gannet Islands Ecological Reserve. Both are located near Cartwright.

The watery complex of Lobstick Lake, Smallwood Reservoir, Michikamau Lake, and the Churchill River and its tributaries marks central Labrador. The Churchill flows out of the western saucer-shaped plateau and rushes eastward, widening into Lake Melville at Happy Valley–Goose Bay. The river meets the sea at Groswa-

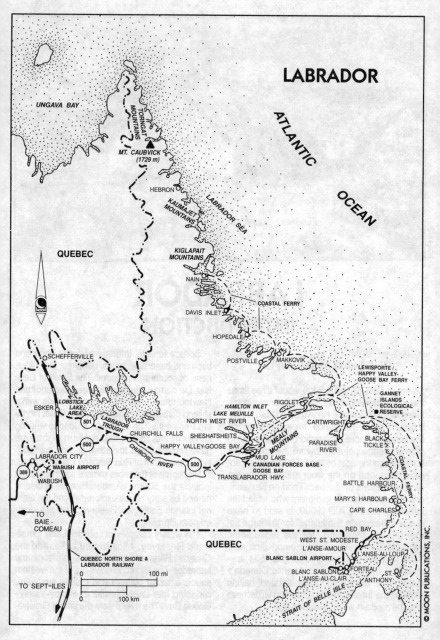

ter Bay. Happy Valley–Goose Bay, now Labrador's second-largest town, began with tents and tarpaulins as the Goose Bay airbase civilian settlement. One of North America's prime military installations in WW II, the airbase was once a berry farm at the head of Lake Melville.

In western Labrador, iron-ore mining developed in the late 1940s. Labrador City started as a mining town, and now serves as an economic and transportation center. It's Labrador's largest town (pop. 9,061). The air gateway to Labrador is based at adjacent Wabush. Northeast of Wabush, a massive hydroelectric plant, developed in the '60s, spawned another company town—Churchill Falls.

Heading north, the forests diminish in density and size until the treeline is reached. There barren, mountainous tundra continues north into a terrain of caribou moss (lichen), ferns, and stunted birch. Willows are brightened with summertime's tiny purple rhododendron, poppies, heather, buttercups, and violets.

The northern coast evokes images of another world. It's the Labrador as you may imagine: raw and majestic with the craggy Torngat, Kaumajet, and Kiglapait mountain ranges rising to the north. The region is sparsely populated with Inuits, who came off the ice to live in small, coastal settlements decades ago. Moravian mission sightseeing is a splendid bonus. You'll also find centuries-old German-style buildings at Nain, Makkovik, and at the national historic sites in Hopedale and Hebron.

Climate

Labrador's climate is subject to great extremes. Summers are short, cool to sometimes hot, and brilliantly sunny with periodic showers. Temperatures on July days average 21° C (and can rise to 38° C at Happy Valley–Goose Bay). Temperatures drop rapidly after mid-August; by November, daytime highs at Goose Bay fall to 0° C.

Winters are very cold and dry, with temperatures ranging from -20° C in the subarctic to -51° C in the western regions.

Summertime, then, is the optimal season for traveling in Labrador. From July to August, the mean temperature is 13° C, although the daytime high sometimes rises to 27° C. In Happy Valley–Goose Bay, July days average 21° C. August brings cooler temperatures. Rainfall av-

A vegetable garden thrives during North West River's brief growing season.

erages for the summer months vary: Eight cm in June, 10 cm in July, nine cm in August, and seven cm in September. Expect thunderstorms during July, and periodic fog on the coast. Summertime snow showers fall on the northern coast. Black flies and other biting insects are most numerous from July to early September.

Transportation in Labrador is conducted on a weather-permitting basis. Early-season ice packs and late-season storms can delay the ferries. The region's smaller aircraft need daylight and good visibility for flights. An absence of both may ground flights for days. Therefore, it's wise to add a few extra days at both ends of your itinerary and bring extra money, in case you're held up.

The Thinly Settled Region

Labrador (pop. 30,375) is sparsely settled. Approximately 850 Naskaupi and Montagnais Innu inhabit Davis Inlet and Sheshatsheits; 1,000 Inuits live in coastal settlements north of the

Hamilton Inlet; and 10,000 settlers—Europeans, Natives and others—populate the coastal and inland areas. Some 18,000 other inhabitants from Newfoundland and southern Canada are scattered in the larger regional towns and settlements.

Almost 70 small outports and settlements span the coastline's sheltered coves and harbors, while Labrador's larger commercial towns —Happy Valley–Goose Bay, Churchill Falls, Wabush (WAH-bush), and Labrador City—lie inland across the midsection.

HISTORY

Indigenous Peoples

Maritime Archaic Indians arrived in Labrador 7,500-9,000 years ago. They camped near the large rivers and hunted seals and walrus during the summer. Their domain included the strait coast. An archaeological dig at L'Anse-Amour uncovered a burial site (of a 12-year-old child) dating from 6905 B.C. The earliest Inuit presence in the region dates to 4,000 years ago.

Early Europeans

Basque whalers created the world's largest whaling port at Red Bay in the early 1500s and lived on nearby Saddle Island, where the whaling stations' red roof tiles still litter the beaches. Historians estimate that between 1550 and 1600, these whalers extracted some 500,000 gallons of oil annually from harpooned right and bowhead whales.

England's interest in Labrador began in the 16th century. Stories of the riches of the Orient fueled the search for a Northwest Passage, and the king sent John Davis to discover the route. The mission failed, but the navigator accidentally sailed into Davis Inlet on his second voyage in 1586 and returned to England with reports of seas teeming with cod, and black bears roaming the woodlands.

In 1668, King Charles II chartered the Hudson's Bay Company and charged the merchants

IN PURSUIT OF "THE BIG LAND"

"Labrador is part of Québec!" the French Canadians have asserted for centuries. "Never!" the British and the Newfoundlanders have traditionally countered.

Labrador is a choice piece of property, and Québec has been a longtime, avid suitor of North America's northeastern edge. Québec's interest in Labrador dates to 1744, decades before the British vanquished the French at the Fortress of Louisbourg in Nova Scotia and on Québec City's Plains of Abraham. At that time, the French cut a deal with the British: Québec got jurisdiction over Labrador, but the island of Newfoundland got fishing rights in Labrador's coastal waters.

The Treaty of Paris of 1763 went one step further, however, and awarded all of Labrador (undefined by a precise border) to Newfoundland. Newfoundland's claim gained more substance in 1825, when the British North America Act set Labrador's southern border with Québec at the 52nd parallel. Little by little, England whittled away Québec's share of Labrador.

Canadian Confederation

In the 1860s, Canadian nationalism emerged, as Nova Scotia, New Brunswick, and Québec banded together to form the Dominion of Canada. Prince Edward Island joined the Confederation a few years later. The dispute over Labrador, formerly between France and England, now involved the new Confederation of Canada.

From England's point of view, its colonial possession included the island of Newfoundland and mainland Labrador. Québec did not dispute England's sovereignty over Labrador. It did, however, continue to question the location of the border. Canada, ever aware that Québec was a founding Confederation member, backed the French Canadians' land claims.

By 1898, Québec pushed the Labrador border far eastward to what is now the Happy Valley– Goose Bay area at the head of the Hamilton Inlet. In 1900, Newfoundland acquired 50-year timber rights and licensed a Nova Scotian outfit to build two sawmills and a lumberjacks' camp at Mud Lake just north of Happy Valley–Goose Bay. Six years later, Québec challenged the legality of the sawmill's location and surveyed the area.

with developing Labrador trade. Captain James Cook surveyed the coastline a century later. After the mid-1700s, pioneer merchants built coastal trading posts and Anglo fishermen established the strait's largest fishing stations at Forteau.

The French staked claim to Labrador in 1702, granting to nobleman Courte Manche all the land from the Gulf of St. Lawrence to Hamilton Inlet. Trading posts followed at L'Anse-au-Clair, Forteau, West St. Modeste, and L'Anse-au-Loup on the strait. The merchant Louis Fornel solidified France's coastal control by garnering posts at Cape Charles, Davis Inlet, and Rigolet from 1743 to 1747.

Nonetheless, settlement was slow. Newfoundlanders and Anglo immigrants didn't settle L'Anse-au-Clair until 1825. The imprint of European architecture only reached the northern seacoast when the Moravians, an evangelical Protestant sect from Bohemia, established mission stations with prefabricated wooden buildings at Hopedale, Nain, Hebron, and other sites during the mid-18th and early 19th centuries.

The Grenfell Legend

Labrador's harsh living conditions and lack of medical care attracted Dr. Wilfred Grenfell, the British physician-missionary. Dr. Grenfell worked with the Royal National Mission for Deep Sea Fishermen on the North Sea. A visit in 1892 convinced him that serving the people of remote Labrador and northern Newfoundland was his calling. He established Labrador's first coastal hospital at Battle Harbour the next year. A hospital boat treated 15,000 patients along the coast in 1900. By 1907, he had opened treatment centers at Indian Harbour, Forteau, North West River, and seven other remote settlements.

Dr. Grenfell initiated a policy of free medical treatment, clothing, or food, in exchange for labor or goods. Funded by private contributions and the Newfoundland government, he opened cooperative stores, nursing homes, orphanages, mobile libraries, and lumber mills. He also initiated the Grenfell Handicrafts programs and home gardening projects. In 1912,

---

For Sale: Labrador

Labrador's precise border became a tedious issue for England. Newfoundland put Labrador up for sale. The land was first offered to Canada at $9 million in 1909. Canada ducked. Labrador went on the market again for $110 million in 1932. Again, Canada passed.

By 1927, the Mud Lake sawmill operation was bankrupt, and the border issue was still unresolved. It came before the Privy Council's Judicial Committee in London. In a sweeping decision, the committee set Labrador's western border far west of Mud Lake at the "height of the land," the watershed line separating the Atlantic Ocean from Ungava Bay. It now marks the boundary between Labrador and Québec Province. In the decision, Labrador acquired the wedge-shaped "Labrador Trough," a delta area potentially rich in iron ore deposits and hydroelectric power.

Québec's Clout Emerges

By the 1970s, Québec became a major player in Labrador's economy.

Ironically, Québec bought into Labrador's hydroelectric fortune during the reign of Newfoundland premier Joey Smallwood, who led the move to Con-

federation in the 1940s and advocated industrialization as an edge against the capricious fisheries. Based on his belief that hydroelectric power would bring in a modest financial return, Smallwood convinced the French Canadians to join in a development project. The potential wealth of the province's latent hydroelectric resources had been explored during the 1960s, and the Labrador Hydro Electric Company at Churchill Falls was formed by 1974.

As oil prices shot up in the mid-1970s, hydroelectric power became the cheaper energy alternative. Québec Province's Hydro-Québec, the project's largest shareholder, now earns $200 million annually, while Newfoundland, another company shareholder, earns $12 million. But the island receives none of the energy. In the late 1970s, Newfoundland considered a tunnel beneath the Strait of Belle Isle to transmit power. Costs, at $30-40 million, were considered prohibitive.

The western border remains fully unsurveyed, and Québec does not consider the issue settled. A fragile status quo exists between Newfoundland and Québec provinces.

he formed the International Grenfell Organization to consolidate the English, Canadian, and American branches that funded his work. The physician was subsequently knighted in 1928 and also awarded recognition by the Royal Scottish Geographical Society and other notable organizations.

Into the Twentieth Century

The economy slipped into a depression as codfish and fur prices dropped during WW I. The Moravian mission stores were absorbed by the Hudson's Bay Company, which eventually closed all hinterlands outlets except Rigolet, Cartwright, and North West River. An epidemic of Spanish flu—introduced from a supply ship—decimated a third of the indigenous population on the northern coast. The Inuit who survived resettled at Nain in 1918.

During WW II, Central Labrador thrived. The British Air Ministry selected the Goose Bay airbase site and built two airstrips with U.S. assistance. Before the war ended, 24,000 aircraft set down for refueling during the trans-Atlantic crossing. After the war, the U.S. used the base for its Northeast Air Command, followed by the Strategic Air Command in the 1950s. Currently, the Canadian Forces Base Goose Bay serves as central Labrador's commercial air gateway and as a low-level flight-training center for British, Dutch, and German air forces.

During the 1940s and '50s, tuberculosis was rampant among the Inuit. Medical authorities ordered almost one-fifth of the Inuit population into sanitoriums far from their northern domain. Never having been away from the North, the Inuit suffered a severe sense of disorientation. Eventually, the Inuit were moved away from their nomadic life in order to "benefit" from Canada's social welfare system of health care, education, and housing.

The Western Boom

Industrial western Labrador is booming. Labradorians knew of the area's iron-ore potential in the late 1800s, and ore deposits were discovered in 1936. The Iron Ore Company of Canada and Scully Mines, both near the twin towns of Labrador City and Wabush, now rank as the Canadian steel industry's largest supplier. The two produce six million metric tons of iron-ore concentrate and pellets a year. At Churchill Falls, the 5,428-megawatt hydroelectric plant ranks as one of the western hemisphere's largest single-site operations. The northern seacoast has shared western Labrador's industrial prominence since the discovery of uranium at Makkovik in 1973.

RECREATION

Many visitors to Labrador are anglers and hunters, who rank the sportfishing and trophy-size-wildlife hunting here among the world's best. The fishing is said to be Atlantic Canada's finest: it's not uncommon to land an ouananiche (landlocked salmon) weighing 11 kg. Brook trout here range 3-4 kg, lake trout to 18 kg, pike 9-14 kg, and arctic char 5-7 kg. Wild game found here includes caribou, moose, black bear, ruffled and spruce grouse, ptarmigan, ducks, lynx, and wolverines.

Naturalists and adventure travelers make up a new breed of visitors. Travelers interested in other cultures visit the indigenous peoples' settlements, while sports enthusiasts enjoy wilderness rafting, kayaking, canoeing, rock climbing, hiking, backpacking, and camping.

Outfitters

Many outfitters catering to sportfishers and hunters are based in Happy Valley–Goose Bay. An outfitter is a necessity on any nonresident's trip, according to the province.

Outfitters are licensed, and their wilderness lodgings are inspected by the province. An all-inclusive week's package has the highest price and usually includes license fees, lodgings, meals, a guide, and fly-in transportation from Goose Bay. You'll get the best buy if you bring along your pals to split the costs among a group of six or eight. If only one or two people make the trip, they generally have to pay a basic price *and* foot the fly-in cost of about $600 roundtrip for a float plane or $1700 roundtrip for a helicopter, from Goose Bay.

Allow enough lead time for arrangements, especially if you want to save some money and join a group. Contact the outfitter directly for details including the prime fishing season (fishing is best late spring to early fall, but big-game

FISHING AND HUNTING PACKAGES

Note: Add "Happy Valley–Goose Bay, Labrador, NF" before the postal code when writing to all addresses listed below. The area code for all telephone numbers listed is 709. Base prices listed exclude license fees or transportation from Goose Bay or both.

ONE-WEEK FISHING PACKAGES

Double Mer Fish Camp; P.O. Box 77, Stn. B, A0P 1E0; tel. 896-2635; $1600; big game also

Goose Bay Outfitters; P.O. Box 171, Stn. B, A0P 1E0; tel. 896-2423 in summer, 753-0550 in winter; $2100

Labrador Sportsfish; P.O. Box 411, A0P 1C0; tel. 896-3901 in summer, 781-2901 in winter; $2000; big game also

Last Frontier Lodges; P.O. Box 251, Stn. C, A0P 1C0; tel. 896-8511; call for prices

Minipi Camps; P.O. Box 340, Stn. B, A0P 1E0; tel. 896-2891 or 896-3024; call for prices

Mountain Outfitting; P.O. Box 7, Stn. B, A0P 1E0; tel. 896-2249; $1200

ONE-WEEK BIG-GAME HUNTING PACKAGES

Blizzard Corp.; P.O. Box 340, Stn. B, A0P 1E0; tel. 896-2891; call for prices

Hunt River Camps; P.O. Box 307, Stn. A, A0P 1S0; tel. 896-8049; $2000

---

seasons vary). The *Newfoundland and Labrador Hunting and Fishing Guide,* available from the provincial tourist office, lists outfitter packages and provincial regulations.

Tours

Air Northland, based at Goose Bay Airport, tel. (709) 896-8049, operates year-round sightseeing flights that will whisk you aloft for aerial views of Atlantic Canada's last frontier; $250 an hour for four passengers. The outfit also owns the 10-room **Border Beacon Lodge,** a renovated former radar station at Border Beacon about 100 km north of Goose Valley. A week's fishing or hunting with the company costs $1500-2000 pp including everything except licenses. For details, write to them at P.O. Box 307, Station A, Happy Valley–Goose Bay, Labrador, NF A0P 1S0.

Labrador Scenic, tel. 497-8326, specializes in tours to Labrador's central and northern wilderness areas, with an emphasis on the area's wildlife and the Innu and Inuit communities' history and culture. Expect to pay $200-300 a day for all-inclusive arrangements and travel by boat, air, or snowmobile. For details, write to the company at P.O. Box 233, North West River, Labrador, NF A0P 1M0.

Last Frontier Fishing Lodges, tel. 896-8511, handles primarily fishing packages, but they'll custom-design a whitewater-rafting trip for two or more rafters to the Parke Lake area about 50 km southeast of town.

Labrador Leisure Tours and Charters, an outfit based in Cartwright, tel. 938-7254 (after 6 p.m.), has six-hour sightseeing boat tours to the Gannet Islands Ecological Reserve. An incredible array of murres, Atlantic puffins, razorbills, and terns nest here July-September. The company charges $400 for up to 12 passengers; if you're watching travel costs, call ahead and try to find a place in a group that's already made reservations. For details, write P.O. Box 119, Cartwright, Labrador, NF A0K 1V0.

Nain, Labrador's most northerly town, is another good choice. The **Tasiujatsoak Wilderness Camp,** tel. 922-2201, caters to canoeists, hikers, rock hounds, photographers, campers, and naturalists interested in flora, fauna, seal- and whalewatching, and visits to Inuit settlements. For details, write P.O. Box 253, Nain, Labrador, NF A0P 1L0.

Nain is also one of dozens of ports of call on the **Marine Atlantic** coastal ferry cruises; for details, call 794-5700 or (800) 341-7981 (from the U.S.).

For other sports ideas and outfitters, see the provincial tourism guide. Finally, if you plan any kind of independent excursion or camping trip, register the itinerary with the RCMP; Labrador's wilderness is beautiful, but it's easy to become disoriented in it.

INFORMATION

The Newfoundland **Department of Tourism and Culture** publishes the free and helpful *Newfoundland and Labrador Travel Guide.* Write for a copy, or call (709) 729-2830 in St. John's, (800) 563-6353 in North America (except Yukon and Alaska), fax (709) 729-0057.

Destination Labrador, tel. 944-7788, (800) 563-6353 in North America (except Alaska and Yukon), fax 944-7787, handles Labrador as a whole. The helpful staff is based at 118 Humphrey Rd., Bruno Plaza, Labrador City, Labrador, NF A2V 2J8. The provincial tourist office in St. John's is another contact. It publishes *Labrador: Awaken Your Heart and Soul,* a free, four-color brochure with high-quality photography and varied maps. If you specify your particular interests and the areas you intend to explore, the tourist office will include appropriate additional literature.

For more specific area information, contact the area tourist offices directly. The **Labrador Straits Historical Development Corp.,** P.O. Box 81, Forteau, Labrador, NF A0K 2P0, tel. 931-8326, handles the Strait of Belle Isle settlements' information. For Labrador City, Wabush, and Churchill Falls information, contact the **Labrador West Tourism Corp.,** P.O. Box 1237, Wabush, Labrador, NF A0R 1B0, tel. 282-3337. The **Mokami Regional Development Association** at 365 Hamilton River Rd., tel. 896-3100, handles Happy Valley–Goose Bay area tourism.

TRANSPORTATION

By Air
Labrador City/Wabush is served by **Air Nova,** with connecting flights from St. John's. **Air Alliance** has flights from Montréal and Québec City. **Canadian Airlines International/Air Atlantic** flies from St. John's, Halifax, and Goose Bay, while **Air Canada/Air Alliance** flies in from Ottawa, Québec City, and Montréal. **Inter-Canadian** arrives from Montreal. Flights arrive

at the **Wabush Airport,** about seven km from Labrador City.

On the Strait of Belle Isle, the coastal settlements are served by flights from Blanc Sablon Airport, a few kilometers across the Québec border; the carriers include **Provincial Airlines,** from St. John's and Goose Bay, and **Air Nova** with connecting flights from Montréal/Sept-Îles and St. John's.

By Land
The 526 km TransLabrador Hwy. 500 crosses the region from Labrador City, Wabush, and Churchill Falls to Happy Valley–Goose Bay with a western Labrador extension (Hwy. 501) to Esker; for road conditions and weather updates, call the **Department of Works, Services, and Transportation** at (709) 635-2162. You'll find paved and unpaved roadways in the Strait of Belle Isle settlements, the Happy Valley–Goose Bay area, Sheshasheits, the North West River area, Wabush, and Labrador City. Beyond these, air travel—either on airlines or with bush pilots—is the main way to get around.

In western Labrador, the **Québec North Shore and Labrador Railway,** tel. 944-8205 or 944-2490, departs twice weekly from Labrador City to Sept-Îles. Tickets cost $46 pp OW and reservations are required. Québec Province's Hwy. 389 links Labrador City with Baie-Comeau, 581 km to the southwest on the north shore of the St. Lawrence River. For weather and driving conditions along this route, call the Québec Provincial Police at (418) 296-2324.

By Sea
A **cargo boat** service runs round-trip between Lewisporte and Nain. It takes a week in each direction as it stops at over 20 tiny communities along the way to load and unload goods. Passenger space on these boats is limited, and vehicles are not accepted. Call Marine Atlantic at (800) 563-6353 for information. Marine Atlantic also operates a **car ferry** from Lewisporte to Happy Valley–Goose Bay mid-June to mid-Sept.; see "Transportation" under "Happy Valley–Goose Bay" later in this chapter for details. Also see the "Ferry Schedules" chart in the Introduction chapter for information on additional routes in Labrador.

Several private tour-boat operators provide travelers with a leisurely atmosphere for sightseeing. **Labrador Adventure Tours,** of Happy Valley–Goose Bay, tel. 896-0936, takes passengers on a tour to Muskrat Falls or to the Mud Lake area. **Labrador Leisure Tours and Char-** **ters, Inc.,** P.O. Box 119, Cartwright, Labrador, NF A0K 1V0, tel. (709) 938-7254, offers tours to the Sandwich Bay area to cruise the Gannet Islands seabird reserve; the season lasts from 15 July to 15 September.

SOUTH AND CENTRAL LABRADOR

HAPPY VALLEY–GOOSE BAY

Happy Valley–Goose Bay (pop. 8,610) spreads across a sandy peninsula bordered by the Churchill River, Goose Bay, and Terrington Basin at the head of Lake Melville. The city is 210 km inland from the Labrador Sea, and serves as the region's administrative, service and transportation center. The town garnered this role thanks to both its prominence as a military airbase and the area's accessibility. The town is situated on a fog-free plateau allowing dependable air service, and its location at the head of Hamilton Inlet provides easy access for the Newfoundland coastal ferries.

Before the war, the area had a few small settlements, such as Kenemich, Mulligan, and Otter Creek. Robert Michelin, owner of "Uncle Bob's Berry Patch," sold the land for the airbase and later supplied cream, eggs, and salmon to the installation's messes. The town evolved as two distinct areas: Goose Bay, rimming the base; and adjacent Happy Valley, which became the base's residential and commercial sector. In 1961, the two areas joined as Happy Valley–Goose Bay and elected the first town council, which was Labrador's first municipal government.

The distinction between the two areas remains firm, so be prepared to consult a map as you wander around. Goose Bay connects to Happy Valley by the L-shaped Hamilton River Rd., the main drag. Loring Dr., the base's access road, feeds off Hamil- ton River Rd. and is another orientation point. You're never far from either road. Shops, restaurants, sightseeing, and lodging are sprinkled liberally on or near the two main streets.

North West River, an Anglo settlement named for the river, and adjacent **Sheshatsheits,** an Innu community, lie 32 km northeast and are considered the town's suburbs. Illustrious **Mud Lake,** site of the contentious lumber operation in the border dispute between Newfoundland and Québec, lies directly east across the Churchill River; to get there, follow Hamilton River Rd. east through Happy Valley to the river and ask around for a boat ($5-10) to take you across.

Sights

The white-wood **Labrador Heritage Museum** at the corner of Hamilton River Rd. and Halifax St., tel. (709) 896-2762, provides rare insights into Labrador's early years with photographs, manuscripts, books, artifacts, furs, native minerals, and other displays. It's open July-August, Mon.-Fri. 9 a.m.-5 p.m.; admission is $1. In the Northern Lights building at 170 Hamilton River Rd., the **Northern Lights Military Museum,** tel. 896-5939, offers exhibits pertaining to military history from WW I to the Vietnam War. Displays

caribou

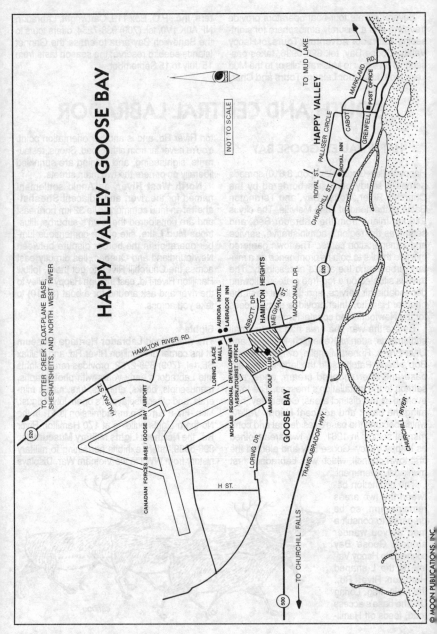

HAPPY VALLEY - GOOSE BAY

NOT TO SCALE

TO MUD LAKE

TO OTTER CREEK FLOAT-PLANE BASE,
SHESHATSHEITS, AND NORTH WEST RIVER

TO CHURCHILL FALLS

TO CHURCHILL FALLS

HAPPY VALLEY

MARKLAND RD.
POST OFFICE
GRENFELL
CABOT
PALLISER CIRCLE
Royal Inn
ROYAL ST.
CHURCHILL ST.

HAMILTON HEIGHTS
ABBOTT DR.
MACDONALD DR.
MEIGHAN ST.
HAMILTON

520

HAMILTON RIVER RD.
HALIFAX ST.
Aurora Hotel
Labrador Inn
Loring Place Mall
Mokami Regional Development Assn./Tourist Office
Amaruk Golf Club
LORING DR.

CANADIAN FORCES BASE / GOOSE BAY AIRPORT
H ST.

GOOSE BAY
TRANSLABRADOR HWY.

CHURCHILL RIVER

500

© MOON PUBLICATIONS, INC.

include uniforms, medals, documents, weapons, and photographs. Across the hall, the **Trappers Brook Animal Displays** exhibits stuffed native animals and birds—from beavers and bears to bald eagles. Both museums are open year-round, Mon.-Sat. 10 a.m.-4 p.m. Admission is free.

For informal sightseeing, check out **North West River** (pop. 515), a village on the river that was the center of the area until the 1940s. The settlement began as a French trading post in 1743, and the inhabitants are descendants of French, British, and Scottish settlers who arrived generations ago. To get there, follow Hamilton River Rd. north past the airbase until the road turns into Hwy. 520. Continue northeast for 30 minutes, cross the bridge into the settlement, and take a right on River Road to the **North West River Craft Shop**, near the International Grenfell Association hospital and the town hall. In the other direction, the road wraps around the coastline and leads to piers and pleasant views. If you'd like to meet some of the locals, arrive in late afternoon, when the Innu fishermen collect the day's catch from nets strung across the waterway.

Accommodations and Food

Bed and breakfasts offer the least expensive lodgings. The **Davis's Bed and Breakfast,** 14 Cabot St. in Happy Valley, tel. (709) 896-5077, has four nonsmoking rooms for $45, which includes a continental breakfast (a full breakfast costs $6 extra). Facilities include a dining room, laundry, and outside patio. The **79 MacDonald** at 79 MacDonald Dr. near the airport in Goose Bay, tel. 896-5031, has two nonsmoking rooms for $45 (with a full breakfast); open May to early September. **Blake's Bed and Breakfast,** at North West River, a 40-minute drive from Goose Bay, has four rooms with shared bath for $35-45 with breakfast; other meals on request. It's open year-round.

Happy Valley–Goose Bay has several motels. **Royal Inn,** 5 Royal Ave., Goose Bay, tel. 896-2456, has 18 rooms, efficiencies, and basic to deluxe housekeeping suites. Rates range $57-112; open year-round.

The town's two other motels are situated side by side on Hamilton River Rd. opposite Loring Dr., the airport's access road. The **Labrador Inn,** tel. 896-3351 or (800) 563-2763 in New-

foundland, has 74 basic to deluxe rooms ($62-96) and suites ($80-160). An airport shuttle is available. The inn has a coffee shop, and its **Torngat Lounge** offers occasional entertainment; open until 1 a.m. The **Naskaupi Dining Room** features pasta dishes and Mexican fare, New York sirloin, T-bone steaks, and pork chops all in the $9-15 range.

The **Aurora Hotel,** 382 Hamilton River Rd., tel. 896-3398 or (800) 563-3066, is smaller, with 37 rooms ($86-97), three suites ($133), and a reputation for some of the town's best dining at its **Gentleman Jim's Steak House.** When dining at Gentleman Jim's, try the moose or caribou burgers ($6) and charbroiled pork chops ($13) for lunch, and succulent prime ribs ($21) or other beef entrees for dinner. A pool table, dart boards, and bar are in the lounge, where the featured drink is Aurora Coffee ($7)—a potent brew of whiskey, liqueur, and espresso splashed with Bailey's Irish Cream and piled high with whipped cream. Guaranteed to thaw you out on brisk evenings.

Hungry locals who love beef head for **Tricia Dee's Steak and Rib Dining Room,** 96 Hamilton River Rd., tel. (709) 896-3545, where diners enjoy prime beef from western Canada and famous barbecued ribs ($10-18 for several ribs to a whole rack). All manner of steak cuts are also prepared anyway you'd like. For a homemade dessert, try the dark, rich black forest cake ($4) or fruit or cream pies.

Otherwise, fast food is the favored dining format. Try **Mary Brown's Fried Chicken** at Loring Place Mall, Loring Dr., and at 1 Churchill Street. Other quick-serve places have submarine sandwiches, pizzas, and hamburgers.

The **Terrington Co-op,** ensconced in a brown building on Abbott Dr. in Goose Bay's Hamilton Heights, is the town's largest grocery. It has a deli, canned goods, and fresh meat and produce; open Mon., Tues., and Sat. 9 a.m.-6 p.m., Wed.-Fri. until 9 p.m. **Pleasant Grocery,** 132 Hamilton River Rd. in Goose Bay, has longer hours (daily 10 a.m.-11 p.m.).

Golf

At the **Amaruk Golf Club,** alongside 327 Hamilton River Rd., tel. 896-2112 , the local golfers play the nine-hole green as soon as the snow's off the ground, usually mid-May or early June.

The greens fee is $15, and rental clubs ($5) and carts ($2) are available. Reservations are required.

Entertainment and Events

A current flick runs nightly at the **Arcturus Theatre** on 5th Ave., two blocks from Loring Drive. For show times, call (709) 896-5071.

Trapper's Cabin Bar and Grill, Aspen Rd. near Hamilton River Rd. and Loring Dr., tel. 896-9522, has a live band or other music Wed.-Sunday. Admission is $4. The **Sand Bar,** McKenzie Dr. near the Amaruk Golf Club, tel. 896-8839, features a local guitarist or other musician, Sun. 2-5 p.m.

In March, the town stages the **CFB Goose Bay Winter Carnival** with outdoor and indoor activities including snow-sculpting, ice-fishing, tobogganing, dances, and a parade.

The mid-July **North West River Beach Festival** is a big weekend bash with food, boat rides, square dances, crafts, and contemporary and traditional provincial and Native American music set on the beach at North West River. The first weekend in August, Happy Valley–Goose Bay hosts the three-day **Labrador Canoe Regatta** with voyageur canoe racing, music, and traditional food.

Shopping

Labrador Handicrafts, 367 Hamilton River Rd., stuffs shelves and racks with exquisitely crafted parkas, grass baskets and containers, hooked rugs, tea dolls, carvings, and jewelry. A large container holds raw labradorite sold by the piece. The shop is also the source for books about Labrador. It's open Mon.-Wed. and Sat. 9:30 a.m.-5:30 p.m., Thurs.-Fri. until 9 p.m.

Some of Labrador's most skilled craftspeople live and work in this area. As you're browsing through local shops, look for tanned slippers by Garmel Rich, Audrey Broomfield, and Naomi Jack; tea dolls by Angela Andrew; carved soapstone by Mike Massie; and labradorite jewelry in gold and silver settings designed by John Goudie.

For other wares, many shops are located on or near the main street. **Emrna Jane's,** 368 Hamilton River Rd. in the Glenn Plaza mall, and **Riff's Limited,** 2 Hillcrest Rd., stock apparel. **Lilek's Photo,** 106 Hamilton River Rd., tel. (709) 896-2641, has film and basic supplies.

Information

The tourist chalet operated by the **Mokami Regional Development Association** at 365 Hamilton River Rd., tel. (709) 896-3100, has a helpful staff and handles area tourism with literature and town maps. It's open mid-June to early Sept., daily 8:30 a.m.-8:30 p.m.; the rest of the year, Mon.-Fri. 8:30 a.m.-4:30 p.m. The Association's mailing address is P.O. Box 768, Station B, Happy Valley–Goose Bay, Labrador, NF A0P 1E0.

The town has emerged as a publishing hub. You'll find *Them Days Magazines,* Labrador's quarterly heritage magazine, at 3 Courte Manche St. in Happy Valley, tel. 896-8531. The *Labradorian* and the *Examiner,* both with weekly news coverage, are also based in town. No place in town stocks topographical maps, so bring what you need from St. John's.

Services

Melville Hospital (Grenfell Hospital, as it's locally known), tel. (709) 896-2417, is on Fifth Ave. near the airbase's Arcturus Theatre. The **RCMP** is at 149 Hamilton River Rd., tel. 896-3383.

Scotia Bank and **Royal Bank** have branches in town; Royal Bank has an office at 36 Grenfell St., Happy Valley, and the airport's Building 381 (the Canex Building) near the terminal. All are open Mon.-Fri. 9 a.m.-5 p.m.

Canada Post has branches on Hamilton River Rd. near the Aurora Hotel, tel. 896-2771, and on the base (catty-corner from the Arcturus Theatre), tel. 896-2261; they're open Mon.-Fri. 9 a.m.-5:15 p.m.

Sheppard's Laundry and Dry Cleaning at 17 Aspen Rd. has coin-operated washers and dryers; open Mon.-Fri. 9 a.m.-6 p.m., Sat. 10 a.m.-4 p.m. March's Laundry and Cleaners next to El Greco is another option.

Transportation

Air Canada's affiliated airline, **Air Nova,** tel. (800) 422-6232 in Canada, (800) 776-3000 in the U.S., has frequent nonstop service from Halifax and St. John's and direct flights from Newfoundland island's gateways, plus Moncton, New Brunswick, Montréal, Ottawa/Hull, and Toronto. **Air Atlantic,** tel. (800) 565-1800, also serves the town with flights from St. John's, Halifax, and Wabush.

Labrador Airways, tel. (709) 896-3387 outside the province, or (800) 563-3042 in Newfoundland and Labrador, serves as a regional carrier with air service to a dozen remote settlements on Labrador's coastline, as well as St. Anthony on northern Newfoundland island. **Provincial Airlines,** tel. 576-1666, (800) 563-2800 within Newfoundland and Labrador, has flights from St. John's and Blanc Sablon.

The **Goose Bay Airport** has an easy-in, easy-out terminal open 24 hours a day, with car rentals, coffee shop/lounge, and a gift shop. Taxis meet incoming flights.

The town is served by the **Marine Atlantic** coastal car ferry from Lewisporte, Newfoundland. The 35-hour sailing (37 hours when alternate sailings stop at coastal Cartwright) departs the island mid-June to mid-Sept., twice weekly. One-way fares are $85 adult, $42.50 ages 5-12, $140 for an overnight cabin with four beds, $140 for a car. For information, call Marine Atlantic at (902) 794-5700. Marine Atlantic's Port aux Basque office handles reservations for Newfoundland departures, tel. 695-4210 or 695-4211. In Happy Valley, call 896-0137 for arrivals and departures; tel. 896-0041 for reservations from Labrador. From the U.S., tel. (800) 341-7981.

Budget charges $53 a day with 100 km free for a Sprint, 15 cents for each additional km, and $10 for optional collision-damage insurance. They're based at Goose Bay Motors, 141 Hamilton River Rd., tel. 896-2972. Neither Budget nor Tilden allow their cars or vehicles on the TransLabrador Highway.

Local taxi rides are handled by **Deluxe Cabs,** tel. 896-2424, and **Airline Valley and Deluxe Taxi,** tel. 896-3311 or 896-3333. The latter outfit is based on Hamilton River Rd. near the Aurora Hotel; their cabs wait at the airport for incoming flights, and cruise in town. They charge by a fixed rate of $9 from the airbase to Happy Valley, $5 anywhere within either Goose Bay *or* Happy Valley, or $30 OW to North West River. A driver's tip is not expected.

The TransLabrador/Hwy. 500 links the town with Churchill Falls, Wabush, and Labrador City, with a seasonal extension (Hwy. 501) to Esker, western Labrador's rail hub. Between Happy Valley–Goose Bay and Churchill Falls, make sure your vehicle is in good condition, drive cautiously, and carry a spare tire. The narrow, 288-

km portion of the highway is unserviced to Churchill Falls. Plenty of pitfalls—steep shoulders and slippery stone surfaces, for example—line the route, so slow down to 40 kph. Beyond Churchill Falls, the highway's 238-km surface improves to a class-A gravel road.

WEST OF HAPPY VALLEY~ GOOSE BAY

Churchill Falls

Churchill Falls, located 200 km west of Happy Valley, is a relatively modern town with few attractions. The waters of the Churchill River drop more than 300 meters over a 32-km section—ideal for one of the world's largest hydroelectric generators. In an incredible feat of engineering, the water is diverted underground to the massive generators, which produce 5,225 megawatts of electricity. Organized tours of the facility can be arranged at the town office.

Labrador City/Wabush

West of Churchill Falls, the twin mining towns of Labrador City and Wabush—just 23 km from the Québec-Labrador border—process the diggings from North America's largest open-pit iron-ore mine. The towns, five km apart, are surrounded by rolling hills and abundant lakes. This area also attracts skiers to the **Smokey Mountain Alpine Ski Club,** tel. (709) 944-3505, open mid-Nov. to mid-May; and the **Menihek Nordic Ski Club,** tel. 944-6339 or 944-2154—a two-time host for World Cup events.

The **Two Seasons Inn,** Avalon Drive, tel. 944-2661, offers airport shuttle service, a restaurant, and all the amenities of a big-city hotel. Rates are $79 s, $84 d, and the inn is open year-round.

The **Wabush Hotel,** 9 Grenfell Drive, tel. 282-3221, also operates year-round, and features Chinese and Canadian dining, a barbershop, and convenience store. The 56 standard rooms go for $79 s, $84 d; suites run $98-106.

Labrador City has two nearby camping areas. **Duley Lake Provincial Park,** 10 km west of Labrador City, has a 100-site campground, a sandy swimming beach, and boating, fishing, and picnicking. **La Grande Hermine Park,** tel. 282-5369, is 33 km from the city, and offers 75 semiserviced sites at $10 per night. Facilities include a boat launch and pedalboat rentals.

THE STRAIT OF BELLE ISLE

Archaeologists have uncovered a Maritime Archaic Indian burial site at L'Anse-Amour, which contains artifacts dating back nearly 9,000 years. The aboriginal caribou hunters who lived here among retreating glaciers left only a few primitive campsites and ancient gravesites. It's not known whether they're related to the bands of Inuit or Beothuk who fished the Strait of Belle Isle up until a few centuries ago.

L'Anse-au-Loup, Capstan Island, Forteau, and West St. Modeste—just a quick ferry ride across the strait from St. Barbe on Newfoundland's Northern Peninsula—were once seasonally inhabited by Newfoundland fisherfolk.

L'Anse-au-Clair

Only five small lodgings lie along the entire coastal road, the largest of which is the **Northern Lights Inn,** tel. (709) 931-2332. It offers 28 rooms from $65, a dining room, crafts shop, and exercise room. Advance reservations are wise for the mid-August **Labrador Straits Bakeapple Folk Festival,** held here and in Forteau. The three-day festival includes traditional music, dance, storytelling, crafts, and meals. Call 931-2751 for details.

L'Anse-Amour

The **Labrador Straits Museum,** Hwy. 510 between Forteau and L'Anse-au-Loop, tel. (709) 927-5659, displays historical artifacts from the past 150 years of life on the Labrador coast, including an original *komatik* (sleigh) used decades ago. It's open July-Aug. daily, with varying hours keyed to the ferry schedule (usually 10

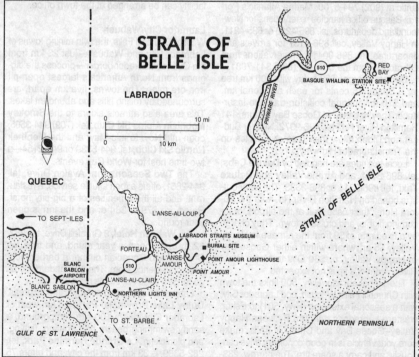

STRAIT OF BELLE ISLE

© MOON PUBLICATIONS, INC.

a.m.-6 p.m.). Admission is $1.50 adults, 75 cents children.

For some other interesting sites, turn off the main road after English Point and head toward the peninsula coastline. The Maritime Archaic Indians were the first known humans in the area. A cairn and national historic plaque mark the **Archaic Indian Burial Mound,** the New World's earliest known burial site. A 12-year-old Indian child was buried here about 6905 B.C.

Nearby is the **Point Amour Lighthouse.** The strait's rich sea has lured intrepid fishermen through the centuries: first the early Basques sailed galleons into Red Bay, then Newfoundlanders arrived in schooners to these shores. By 1857, shipwrecks littered the treacherous shoals, and the colonial government erected

this 33-meter-high beacon, Atlantic Canada's highest.

Red Bay

The road ends at this site, which each summer from 1540 to 1610 held five whaling stations manned by an estimated 1,900 Basques. Now a designated national historic site, you'll see Memorial University archaeologists scouring the rocky coastline for artifacts, and Parks Canada divers surfacing in the cold waters. Parks Canada discovered the *San Juan,* the oldest shipwreck north of the Caribbean, perfectly preserved here in the bone-chilling sea.

The **visitor center,** tel. (709) 920-2197, displays artifacts and shows an hour-long video explaining the *San Juan* discovery. The center is open from mid-June to Sept., daily 9 a.m.-5 p.m.

THE NORTH COAST

Labrador's cold, jagged coast has been a fishing settlement for centuries. The original inhabitants, the Inuit, have settled in Rigolet, Postville, Makkovik, and Nain. Though isolated, Lodge Bay—once a winter station for the fishermen of nearby Cape St. Charles—and Mary's Harbour have grown into small commercial centers. Nearby **Battle Harbour,** a fishing village since 1759 and one of the oldest European settlements on the Labrador coast, is being restored

to resemble its 1800s' condition.

The **Gannet Islands Ecological Reserve,** farther north, is a breeding colony for murres, puffins, and black-legged kittiwakes. North of Cartwright—a settlement named for 18th-century merchant-adventurer and coastal resident Capt. George Cartwright—lies the spot where Norse sailors first laid eyes on the coast.

The tradition of fishing and trapping is alive in **Rigolet,** a community between the Hamilton

Seaplanes are one of the most efficient ways to get around the remote Labrador wilderness.

NAN DROSDICK

Inlet and Groswater Bay. Few aspects of this town have changed over the last century, and the lifestyle of northern peoples here remains traditional.

Makkovik was first settled in the early 1900s by a Norwegian fur trader. In 1896 a Moravian Mission was built and used until the late 1940s. Villagers continue to fish and hunt and practice traditional customs. Several local shops sell Native crafts.

Heading north, at Kaipokok Bay you'll come to **Postville.** The settlement has been visited by indigenous people for fishing and hunting every spring for over 4,000 years. Farther north, **Hopedale** boasts the historic 1782 Hopedale Mission, the oldest wooden frame building east of Québec.

Nain is the northernmost municipality on the coast. Its population is just over 1,000. Prior to the cod-fishing moratorium, the fishing industry dominated. The fish plant once employed over 100 people. Electricity is provided by diesel generator; fuel and wood are used for domestic heat; local transportation is by boat in the summer and snowmobile in the winter. The only roads are within the town itself, which consists of a hotel, boardinghouses, stores, a post office, and a museum. Space is limited for the coastal boat trips to Nain, so book early. Beyond Nain, you must arrange boat transportation with local skippers.

RECOMMENDED READING

NEW BRUNSWICK

History and Culture

Belliveau, John Edward. *The Monctonians: Citizens, Saints and Scoundrels, Vol. 2.* Hantsport, NS: Lancelot Press, 1990. Moncton's history is as dishy as a soap opera.

Collie, Michael. *New Brunswick.* Toronto: Macmillan, 1974. Much has changed in the more than 20 years since this book was written, but much still rings true. Collie provides a poetic, highly personal, and often moving overview of the province, its history, and the psyche of its people.

De Mont, John. *Citizens Irving: K.C. Irving and His Legacy, The Story of Canada's Wealthiest Family.* Toronto: Doubleday Canada, Ltd., 1991. The Irving family is *very* private, and this unofficial biography is stuffed with well-documented unfavorable and favorable facts, legends, and speculation.

MacDonald, M.A. *Rebels and Loyalists: The Lives and Material Culture of New Brunswick's Early English-Speaking Settlers, 1758-1783.* Fredericton: New Ireland Press, 1990. MacDonald's slice of history is narrow, and his view is interestingly pervasive.

MacNutt, W.S. *New Brunswick: A History, 1784-1867.* Toronto: Macmillan of Canada, 1984. A penetrating overview of New Brunswick history, from the days of the founding Loyalists until Confederation—a time line of major and minor events.

Maxwell, L.M.B. *History of Central New Brunswick: An Outline of the History of Central New Brunswick to the Time of the Confederation.* Fredericton: York-Sunbury Historical Society. Black-and-white photographs and maps illustrate an academic, historical appraisal of the heart of the province.

Pincombe, C. Alexander, and Edward W. Larracey. *Resurgo: The History of Moncton.* Fredericton: Centennial Print and Litho Ltd., 1990. Moncton's official biography is short on scandal, long on personal and political tidbits, and altogether interesting from a historical point of view.

Wibur, Richard. *The Rise of French New Brunswick.* Halifax: Formac Publishing, 1989. Splendid academic treatise on early Acadians.

Wright, Esther Clark. *Loyalists of New Brunswick.* Yarmouth, NS: Sentinel Printing, 1985. More insights on the founding Loyalists.

Natural History

Folster, David. *Great Trees of New Brunswick.* Fredericton: Canadian Forestry Association of New Brunswick, 1987. An asset for every naturalist's bookshelf, the lavishly detailed coverage on provincial trees is a feast of information. Illustrated with color and black-and-white pictures.

Shaw, M. *Mount Carleton Wilderness: New Brunswick's Unknown North.* Fredericton: Fiddlehead Poetry Books and Goose Lane Editions, 1987. Marvelous descriptive and factual coverage with black-and-white photography of the highest mountain in the Maritimes.

Thurston, Harry. *Tidal Life: A Natural History of the Bay of Fundy.* Camden East, ON: Camden House Publishing, 1990. The lavishly illustrated contents describe natural habitats formed by the Fundy.

Recreation

Eiselt, Marianne, and H.A. Eiselt. *A Hiking Guide to New Brunswick.* Fredericton: Goose Lane Editions, 1991. Extensively detailed with abundant maps, the guide describes 107 hikes throughout the province.

Gillis, Stephen, and John Gillis. *No Faster Than A Walk: The Covered Bridges of New Brunswick.* Fredericton: Goose Lane Editions, 1988. An illustrated guide to the province's significant covered bridges.

Tracy, Nicholas, and Sarah Petite. *Cruising Guide to the Bay of Fundy and the Saint John River.* Fredericton: Goose Lane Editions, 1992. A useful guide to Fundy and Saint John sailing.

Wright, Harold E., and Rob Roy. *Saint John and the Fundy Region.* Saint John: Neptune Publishing Company Ltd., 1987. A sightseeing guide to the province's largest city, this handy compendium includes insights available only from a native. Also some Fundy sightseeing coverage.

NOVA SCOTIA

Culture

Field, Richard Henning. *Spirit of Nova Scotia.* Toronto: Dundurn Press, 1985. The Nova Scotians' historic use of textiles, sculpture, paintings, and decorated utilitarian objects is expertly explained by subject and splendidly illustrated with photographs.

*Morris, Julie. *Tracing Your Ancestors in Nova Scotia.* Halifax: Public Archives of Nova Scotia. This worthy pamphlet concisely explains how to search family roots with the use of the provincial archives in Halifax.

***Parsons, Catriona. *Gaidhlig Troimh Chomhradh (Gaelic Through Conversation).* South Gut St. Ann's: Gaelic College of Celtic Arts and Crafts. The college's mission is to keep the language alive, and it does so with this text and accompanying cassette tapes.

*Penney, Allen. *Houses of Nova Scotia: An Illustrated Guide to Architectural Style Recognition.* Halifax: Nova Scotia Museum and Formac Publishing, 1989. Penney, a professor of architecture, sums up provincial architectural styles and explains how to identify styles by dates, similarities, and differences.

History

*Crowell, Clement W. *Novascotiaman.* Halifax: Nova Scotia Museum, 1979. A sea captain's correspondence forms the basis for a retelling of the story of Nova Scotia's Great Age of Sail.

**Donovan, Kenneth, ed. *Cape Breton at 200.* Sydney: University College of Cape Breton Press, 1985. An essay collection recounting 200 years of social and economic highlights.

Johnston, A.J.B. *Louisbourg: The Phoenix Fortress.* Halifax: Nimbus Publishing, 1990. As the title states, Fortress of Louisbourg has risen in part again, and the text recounts the past and present with Chris Reardon's impressive glossy photographs.

Lyell, Charles. *Travels in North America in the Years 1841-2.* New York: Arno Press, 1978. The author included Nova Scotia in his 19th-century travel observations.

*Robertson, Marion. *Kings Bounty: A History of Early Shelburne, Nova Scotia.* Halifax: Nova Scotia Museum, 1983. Robertson recounts the early Loyalist years at Shelburne —the seaport that received the largest share of refugees fleeing the American Revolution.

**Tennyson, Brian, ed. *Impressions of Cape Breton.* Sydney: University College of Cape Breton Press. Cape Breton has impressed visitors since 1634, and the coverage compiles some of the visitors' more vivid impressions.

*Wallace, Arthur W. *An Album of Drawings of Early Buildings in Nova Scotia.* Halifax: Heritage Trust of Nova Scotia and Nova

Scotia Museum, 1976. A delightful pictorial insight into provincial architecture and the best known building.

Natural History and Geography

*Bates, Jennifer L.E. *Gold in Nova Scotia.* Halifax: Nova Scotia Department of Mines and Energy, 1987. Rare coverage of the province's gold abundance, augmented with photographs, maps, and figures.

*Dawson, Joan. *The Mapmaker's Eye: Nova Scotia Through Early Maps.* Halifax: Nova Scotia Museum, 1988. Nova Scotia evolved over the centuries, as did the art of mapping. This illustrated book is a cartographer's dream.

*Gilhen, John. *Amphibians and Reptiles of Nova Scotia.* Halifax: Nova Scotia Museum, 1984. Everything about the province's creepers and crawlers is included in this detailed text with photographs.

Hines, Sherman. *Nova Scotia.* Dartmouth: Stonehouse Publishing. The province's landscape has ignited the imagination of many photographers, one of whom is Nova Scotia's own Sherman Hines. Here his glossy plates show off the entire province.

*Johnson, Ralph S. *Forests of Nova Scotia: A History.* Halifax: Nova Scotia Department of Lands & Forests and Four East Publications, 1986. Veteran eastern-Canadian forester traces the life of provincial forests from the ice age to the environmental challenges of the present.

Lyell, Charles. *Geological Observations on the U.S., Canada, and Nova Scotia.* New York: Arno Press, 1978. During an early 1840s' visit, Lyell thought enough of Nova Scotia's unusual landscape and geology to give it equal space among the nations in this insightful account.

MacAskill, Wallace R. *MacAskill Seascapes and Sailing Ships.* Halifax: Nimbus Publishing. Cape Breton's famed photographer captures the misty moods of

fishermen, schooners, seaports, and seacoasts.

Natural History of Nova Scotia. Halifax: Departments of Education and Lands and Forests, two volumes. Everything on land or beneath the nearby seas is comprehensively detailed here with illustrations.

Nova Scotia Resource Atlas. Halifax: Nova Scotia Department of Development, 1986. An exhaustive compilation of facts about the land, resources, and people, augmented with oversize maps and detailed statistics.

*Tufts, Robie. *Birds of Nova Scotia.* Halifax: Nova Scotia Museum and Nimbus Publishing, 1986. Nova Scotia's definitive guide (with recent revisions by Ian McLaren) to each and every bird species, illustrated with magnificent color plates and line drawings.

Recreation

Bicycle Tours in Nova Scotia. Halifax: Bicycle Nova Scotia, 1982. Twenty pedal tours from Yarmouth to Cape Breton.

Canoe Routes of Nova Scotia. Halifax: Canoe Nova Scotia and Camping Association of Nova Scotia, 1983. A description of canoe routes for novice to expert paddlers.

Hiking Trails of Nova Scotia. Halifax: Canadian Hostelling Association, 1990. A guide to the province's better known hiking trails, accompanied by topographical data and maps.

Sources

Some of the above entries are marked with one or more asterisks and may be purchased or ordered through sources listed below. If the entry is unmarked, it may be purchased at commercial bookshops in Nova Scotia; outside the province, most bookstores can order requested books.

*The publications are listed in the *Publications Catalogue* and are available from the **Nova Scotia Government Bookstore,** One Government Place, 1700 Granville St.,

Halifax, tel. (902) 424-7580; write to them at P.O. Box 637, Halifax, NS B3J 2T3.

The books are among numerous Cape Breton titles published by the University College of Cape Breton Press, the **University College of Cape Breton, Glace Bay Hwy., Sydney, tel. (902) 539-5300, ext. 146; for details, write to P.O. Box 5300, Sydney, NS B1P 6L2.

***The text is one of a number of books and varied literature published by the **Gaelic College of Celtic Arts and Crafts,** South Gut St. Ann's, tel. (902) 295-3411; write them at P.O. Box 9, Baddeck, NS B0E 1B0.

PRINCE EDWARD ISLAND

Culture

Arsenault, Georges. *Les Acadiens de l'Ile, 1720-1980.* Ottawa: Lemeac, Inc., 1980. Insightful look in French at the province's Acadians by an islander who knows the culture and history from the inside.

Barrett, Wayne, and Anne MacKay. *Prince Edward Island—Red Soil, Blue Sea, Green Fields.* Halifax: Nimbus Publishing, 1988. Photography and text capture the province's beauty.

Bolger, F.W.P. *Spirit of Place: Lucy Maud Montgomery and Prince Edward Island.* Toronto: Oxford University Press, 1982. Among the best of the photography books depicting Montgomery's Island. Augmented with text, Bolger matches selected Montgomery quotes with glossy pictures by Wayne Barrett and Anne MacKay.

MacArthur, F.H. *Legends of PEI.* H. M. Simpson, 1978. More of the island's fanciful tales and often spooky legends.

Montgomery, Lucy Maud. *The Alpine Path.* Fitzhenry and Whiteside, Ltd., 1990. Some of Montgomery's most vivid descriptions of the island are found in this recounting of the author's life.

Montgomery, Lucy Maud. *Anne of Green Gables.* New York: Bantam Skylark, 1984. The juvenile story that started Montgomery's popularity as an author is as interesting today as when it was written.

Ramsay, Sterling. *Folklore PEI.* Square Deal Press, 1978. A rare look at provincial folklore.

Rubio, Mary, and Elizabeth Waterston, ed. *Selected Journals of Lucy Maud Montgomery.* Toronto: Oxford University Press, Vol. I, 1985, Vol. II, 1987. The editors have sifted through Montgomery's vast store of writing and selected some of the most interesting pieces.

Tuck, Robert C. *Gothic Dreams—The Life and Times of a Canadian Architect: William Critchlow Harris, 1854-1913.* Toronto: Dundurn Press, Ltd., 1978. A study of the life and work of the famous architect.

History

Bolger, F.W.P., ed. *Canada's Smallest Province: A History of P.E.I.* Charlottetown: PEI Centennial Commission, 1973. Bolger has selected some of the most interesting historical highlights of the island.

Bumstead, J.M. *Land, Settlement and Politics in 18th Century P.E.I.* McGill/Queen's University Press, 1987. The intellectual treatment will appeal to scholars.

Callbeck, Lorne C. *My Island, My People.* Charlottetown: P.E.I. Heritage Foundation, 1979. As the title implies, the author's roots go way back on the island, and the stories take in many major historical events.

De Jong, Nicholas J., and Marven E. Moore. *Launched from PEI—A Pictorial Review of Sail.* Charlottetown: P.E.I. Heritage Foundation, 1981. The illustrated book covers the province's Great Age of Sail.

Greenhill, Basil, and Ann Giffard. *Westcountrymen in PEI's Isle: A Fragment of the Great Migration.* Toronto: University of Toronto Press, 1975. Painstakingly researched and well written, the book looks into the island's share of the immigrant outpouring from across the Atlantic.

Smith, H.M. Scott. *Historic Churches of Prince Edward Island.* Erin, ON: Boston Mills Press, 1986. The story of the province's churches and their place in the island's history and architecture.

Tuck, Robert C. *Island Family Harris—Letters of an Immigrant Family in British North America: 1856-1866.* Ragweed Press, 1983. Read Tuck's book on architect Harris first, and if it whets your interest, follow it with Tuck's collection of the Harris family letters.

Natural History and Geology

Clark, A.H. *Three Centuries of the Island: A Historical Geography of Settlement and Agriculture in PEI.* Toronto: University of Toronto Press, 1959. The island's history is explored in a thorough geographical approach.

Cummins' Atlas of Prince Edward Island, 1928. Charlottetown: P.E.I. Historical Foundation, 1990. All the details are here, from maps and lists to history.

Gaudet, J.F. *Forestry Past and Present on PEI.* Charlottetown: PEI Department of Energy and Forestry, 1979. The province put Gaudet at the helm of its forestry department decades ago to assess the condition of the provincial woodlands. His book details what he found and the historical reasons for the forests' decline over centuries.

Meacham's Illustrated Historical Atlas of the Province of Prince Edward Island, 1880. Charlottetown: P.E.I. Historical Foundation, 1989. A helpful guide to tracing family roots.

NEWFOUNDLAND AND LABRADOR

General

Andrieux, J.P. *St. Pierre and Miquelon: A Fragment of France in North America.* Ottawa: O.T.C. Press, 1986. One of the most thorough books about France's overseas province, the small volume details sightseeing within a historical context, and is illustrated with historical photography.

Bursey, Brian C. *Exploring Labrador.* St. John's: Harry Cuff Publications, 1991. In this coffee-table edition, the author takes readers on a photographic journey to the region's settlements and remotest parts. The photographs are supplemented by an informative text.

Hansen, Ben. *St. John's, Newfoundland.* Dartmouth, NS: James-StoneHouse Publications Ltd., 1991. Hansen, an award-winning photographer from St. John's, captures the city in many delightful moods within a highly commendable, coffee-table compilation of color photography.

Norman, Howard. *The Bird Artist.* NY: Picador, 1995 (paperback). This tale of murder, passion and betrayal is set in the remote village of Witless Bay, Newfoundland. The book was a 1994 National Book Award finalist.

O'Flaherty, Patrick. *Come Near at Your Peril: A Visitor's Guide to the Island of Newfoundland.* St. John's: Breakwater, 1992. Often hilarious and always insightful, the author meanders across the island, explains the sights as no one but a Newfoundlander sees them, and reveals travel's potential tangles and torments.

Oppersdorff, Tony. *A Northern Odyssey.* Halifax, NS: Nimbus Publishing, 1991. A visual feast of Labrador's dramatic scenery.

Proulx, E. Annie. *The Shipping News.* New York: Touchstone (Simon & Schuster), 1993. Pulitzer Prize–winning story of a widowed journalist rebuilding his life on the Newfoundland coast.

Culture

Guy, Ray. *Ray Guy's Best*. St. John's: Breakwater, 1987. Every word from the local humorist's hilarious, often satirical, pen is worthwhile, and these short pieces—rueful insights on the province from oil expectations to fisheries woes—represent the local writer's finest columns.

Mannion, John J., ed. *Peopling of Newfoundland: Essays in Historical Geography*. St. John's: Memorial University of Newfoundland, 1990. Collected essays exploring the combination of history and geography that influenced the native peoples and settlers through the centuries.

Paddon, Harold G. *Green Woods and Blue Waters: Memories of Labrador*. St. John's: Breakwater. Life in Labrador is probed through Paddon's own settlement experiences and the yarns of fishermen and trappers.

Richardson, Boyce, ed. *Drumbeat: Anger and Renewal in Indian Country*. St. John's: Breakwater, 1992. Essays by prominent Innu leaders relate the often troubled, historic relationships with the federal and provincial governments and suggest solutions to the rising native anger.

Story, G.M., W.J. Kirwin, and J.D.A. Widdowson, eds. *Dictionary of Newfoundland English*. St. John's: Breakwater, 1990. The Newfoundlanders use their own version of the King's English—from "aaron's rod," a roseroot's local name, to "zosweet," a Beothuk word for the ptarmigan. This remarkably researched compilation translates words and adds historical, geographical, and cultural insights.

Zimmerly, David William. *Cain's Land Revisited: Cultural Changes in Central Labrador, 1775-1972*. St. John's: Memorial University of Newfoundland, 1975. Originally written as a doctoral dissertation, the incisive text is a rare look into the modern world's often-harsh effect on Labrador's peoples.

Geology and Natural History

Beamish, Peter. *Dances with Whales*. St. John's: Robinson-Blackmore Printing and Publishing Ltd., 1993. Dr. Beamish, who has researched Trinity Bay's whales for decades, explains the methodology involved in studying the various species' habits, peculiarities, and migrations.

*Burzynski, Michael, and Anne Marceau, eds. *Rocks Adrift: The Geology of Gros Morne National Park*. Ottawa: Environment Canada Parks Service, 1990. A handy paperback explaining the geological forces that created the national park's terrain; includes easy-to-read text, maps, and stunning photography.

History

Barkham, Selma. *The Basque Coast of Newfoundland*. St. John's: Great Northern Peninsula Development Corp., 1989. The author, an expert in early Basque history, presents rare, historic maps with a detailed text and takes the reader on a journey from the southwestern island to the Strait of Belle Isle.

Cardoulis, John N. *A Friendly Invasion: The American Military in Newfoundland and Labrador, 1940-1990*. St. John's: Breakwater, 1990. The author, formerly the American Legion Post commander at Fort Pepperrell, St. John's, vividly recalls the U.S. presence with personal recollections, historical data, and photography.

Neary, Peter, and Patrick O'Flaherty. *Part of the Main: An Illustrated History of Newfoundland and Labrador*. St. John's: Breakwater, 1983. The province's early years are clearly detailed and embellished with interesting graphics and black-and-white photography.

Rompkey, Ronald. *Grenfell of Labrador: A Biography*. Toronto: University of Toronto Press, 1991. Sir Wilfred Grenfell, the physician/missionary whose turn-of-the-century work left an indelible imprint on the province's remote areas, has had several biographers, but none as meticulous and incisive as Rompkey.

Sharp, J.J. *Discovery in the North Atlantic.* Halifax: Nimbus Publishing Ltd., 1991. An exciting, scholarly text with maps and reproduced drawings detailing Newfoundland's explorers from as early as the sixth century.

Tuck, James A., and Robert Grenier. *Red Bay, Labrador: World Whaling Capital, A.D. 1550-1660.* St. John's: Atlantic Archaeology, 1989. Recent archaeological discoveries form the gist for relating the early Basque whaling industry. Splendid color photography and black-and-white graphics.

Recreation

Burrows, Roger. *Birding in Atlantic Canada: Newfoundland.* St. John's: Jesperson Press Ltd., 1989. The cover of this definitive birding guide is graced with a puffin, the province's official bird. The book provides distribution information on the hundreds of native and migratory species in the region.

Gard, Peter, and Bridget Neame. *Trails of the Avalon: Hiking in Eastern Newfoundland.* Torbay, Newfoundland: Gallow Cove Publishing, 1989. Many of the Avalon's most interesting trails are detailed with text insights, photography, and directions.

Nicol, Keith. *Best Hiking Trails in Western Newfoundland.* Another fine hiking guide, this handy paperback includes trails from Port aux Basques to the Northern Peninsula, with maps and handsome color photography.

Walsh, David. *Intriguing Waters of Newfoundland.* St. John's: Jesperson Press, 1980. Details intriguing, shipwreck-littered scuba-diving sites and offers diving advice.

*The book is one of many titles about Canada available from **Canada Communications Group Publishing,** the federal publishing/distribution center; for details, call (819) 956-4802, fax (819) 994-1498, or write to them at the Publishing Division, Ottawa, K1A 0S9.

REGIONWIDE

Daigle, Jean, ed. *Acadians of the Maritimes.* Moncton: Centre d'Études Acadiennes, Université de Moncton, 1982. The history of the Acadians in Atlantic Canada is a tangled tale of upheaval and survival, cultural clashes and passions. Daigle's collection of Acadian literature is among the best on the bookshelves.

Dakers, Sonya. *Animal Rights Campaigns: Their Impact in Canada.* Ottawa: Science and Technology Division, revised 1991. The text deals clearly and comprehensively with the campaigns waged by animal activists and their effects on government policies. In Atlantic Canada, the animal-rights controversy centered on the harp seals, whose slaughter is now outlawed by the national government. *Harp Seals, Man and Ice* by D.E. Sergeant is a more specific review and tackles the harp-seal issue with a world overview.

Griffin, Diane. *Atlantic Wild Flowers.* Toronto: Oxford University Press, 1984. A glorious combination of text by Griffin and photography by Wayne Barrett and Anne MacKay—a must for every naturalist who revels in wildflowers.

Hardy, Anne. *Where to Eat in Canada.* Ottawa: Oberon Press, 1993. The author and her compatriot reviewers list the best dining across the nation, much of it in Atlantic Canada.

McCalla, Robert J. *The Maritime Provinces Atlas.* Halifax: Maritext, 1988. Everything you may want to know about the Maritime provinces' physical, economic, and human geography, depicted on maps and in tables and graphs.

Medjuck, Sheva. *Jews of Atlantic Canada.* St. John's: Breakwater, 1986. The Jews are among Atlantic Canada's smaller ethnic groups. The author traces their impact on, and roles in, the various communities across the region.

Sherwood, Roland H. *Maritime Mysteries: Haunting Tales from Atlantic Canada.* Hantsport, NS: Lancelot Press, 1991. No one takes ghosts, burning ships, and natural oddities lightly in Atlantic Canada. These mysteries are deftly handled in a collection of stories that are stranger than fiction.

*Available from the national **Canada Communications Group**; for details or a copy of the *Selected Titles,* a catalog that lists many technical books and research studies about Canada, call (819) 956-4802 or write to them at Publishing Division, Ottawa, Canada, K1A 0S9.

INDEX

Italicized page numbers indicate information found in
captions, charts, illustrations, maps, or special topics.

ABOUT THE AUTHORS

Nan Drosdick

Nan Drosdick was born and raised in New Jersey near New York City. She has worked exclusively in the travel industry as an editor, writer, graphic designer, author, television script writer, and photographer for magazines, newspapers, and book publishers for the past 25 years. She holds many distinguished awards, such as Israel's Benjamin of Tudela Award for travel writing excellence, and is a member of American Society of Journalists and Authors and Society of American Travel Writers. She thrives on travel, family, gourmet cooking, theater, the music of Getz and Stravinsky, Episcopalianism, and liberal causes.

Mark Morris

After years as an editor at Moon Publications, Mark Morris embarked on his own career in travel writing. His first book, *Ireland,* was jointly published in spring 1995 by Odyssey Publications and Passport Books. He then collaborated on *Oregon Coast Best Places* for Sasquatch Books, also published in 1995. But even after those experiences, writing a Moon Handbook proved to be the ultimate challenge.

Morris is currently the Lead Editor for electronic travel products at Microsoft Corporation, and he makes his home near Seattle, Washington.

ARIZONA TRAVELER'S HANDBOOK
by Bill Weir and Robert Blake, 500 pages, **$16.95**
"This is the best book ever published with practical travel information about the state." —*Arizona Republic*

ATLANTIC CANADA HANDBOOK
by Nan Drosdick and Mark Morris, 450 pages, **$17.95**
Like a corner of Europe, Canada's Atantic provincs harbor a multicultural melange where Irish brogue and Scottish kilts can be found along with historic French forts and deserted Viking villages. *Atlantic Canada Handbook* provides extensive coverage of this region, including New Brunswick, Nova Scotia, Newfoundland, and Prince Edward Island. While there are many guides to Canada, none offers the detailed regional coverage of this comprehensive handbook.

BIG ISLAND OF HAWAII HANDBOOK
by J.D. Bisignani, 347 pages, **$13.95**
"The best general guidebooks available." —*Hawaii Magazine*

BRITISH COLUMBIA HANDBOOK
by Jane King, 381 pages, **$15.95**
"Deftly balances the conventional and the unconventional, for both city lovers and nature lovers."
—*Reference and Research Book News*

CATALINA ISLAND HANDBOOK
by Chicki Mallan, 299 pages, **$10.95**
"*Catalina Handbook* should be aboard any vessel venturing to the fabled recreation spot." —*Sea Magazine*

COLORADO HANDBOOK
by Stephen Metzger, 418 pages, **$17.95**
"Hotel rooms in the Aspen area, in the height of winter sports season, for $20-$30? . . . who but a relentless researcher from Moon could find it?" —*The New York Daily News*

GEORGIA HANDBOOK
by Kap Stann, 350 pages, **$16.95**
". . . everything you need to know to enjoy a journey through Georgia." —*Southern Book Trade*

HAWAII HANDBOOK
by J.D. Bisignani, 1000 pages, **$19.95**
"No one since Michener has told us so much about our 50th state." —*Playboy*

HONOLULU-WAIKIKI HANDBOOK
by J.D. Bisignani, 365 pages, **$14.95**
"The best general guidebooks available." —*Hawaii Magazine*

IDAHO HANDBOOK by Bill Loftus, 310 pages, **$14.95**
"Well-organized, engagingly written, tightly edited, and chock-full of interesting facts about localities, backcountry destinations, traveler accommodations, and cultural and natural history."
—*Sierra Magazine*

KAUAI HANDBOOK by J.D. Bisignani, 228 pages, **$13.95**
"This slender guide is tightly crammed. . . . The information provided is staggering." —*Hawaii Magazine*

MAUI HANDBOOK by J.D. Bisignani, 370 pages, **$14.95**
"*Maui Handbook* should be in every couple's suitcase. It intelligently discusses Maui's history and culture, and you can trust the author's recommendations for best beaches, restaurants, and excursions." —*Bride's Magazine*

MONTANA HANDBOOK
by W.C. McRae and Judy Jewell, 400 pages, **$15.95**
"Well-organized, engagingly written, tightly edited, and chock-full of interesting facts about localities, backcountry destinations, traveler accommodations, and cultural and natural history."
—*Sierra Magazine*

NEVADA HANDBOOK by Deke Castleman, 450 pages, **$16.95**
"Veteran travel writer Deke Castleman says he covered more than 10,000 miles in his research for this book and it shows."
—*Nevada Magazine*

NEW MEXICO HANDBOOK
by Stephen Metzger, 329 pages, **$14.95**
"The best current guide and travel book to all of New Mexico"
—*New Mexico Book League*

NORTHERN CALIFORNIA HANDBOOK
by Kim Weir, 775 pages, **$19.95**
"That rarest of travel books–both a practical guide to the region and a map of its soul." —*San Francisco Chronicle*

OREGON HANDBOOK
by Stuart Warren and Ted Long Ishikawa, 450 pages, **$16.95**

TEXAS HANDBOOK by Joe Cummings, 484 pages, **$16.95**
"Reveals a Texas with a diversity of people and culture that is as breathtaking as that of the land itself."
—*Planet Newspaper,* Australia

"I've read a bunch of Texas guidebooks, and this is the best one."
–Joe Bob Briggs

TRAVEL MATTERS

Travel Matters is Moon Publications' free quarterly newsletter, loaded with specially commissioned travel articles and essays that tell it like it is. Recent issues have been devoted to Asia, Mexico, and North America, and every issue includes:

Feature Stories: Travel writing unlike what you'll find in your local newspaper. Andrew Coe on Mexican professional wrestling, Michael Buckley on the craze for wartime souvenirs in Vietnam, Kim Weir on the Nixon Museum in Yorba Linda.

Transportation: Tips on how to get around. Rick Steves on a new type of Eurail pass, Victor Chan on hiking in Tibet, Joe Cummings on how to be a Baja road warrior.

Health Matters: Articles on the most recent findings by Dr. Dirk Schroeder, author of *Staying Healthy in Asia, Africa, and Latin America.* Japanese encephalitis, malaria, the southwest U.S. "mystery disease" . . . forewarned is forearmed.

Book Reviews: Informed assessments of the latest travel titles and series. The Rough Guide to *World Music,* Let's Go vs. Berkeley, Dorling Kindersley vs. Knopf.

The Internet: News from the cutting edge. The Great Burma Debate in rec.travel.asia, hotlists of the best WWW sites, updates on Moon's massive "Road Trip USA" exhibit.

TRAVEL MATTERS **MOON** PUBLICATIONS *quarterly newsletter*

ISSUE 12   FOCUS ON U.S.A.   SPRING 1995

BLACKJACK, BLUES, AND BALES OF COTTON
Travels and Tangents in the New Mississippi Delta
by Jeff Perk

At night, the first you see of Tunica, Mississippi are the searchlights. Coming down Highway 61 from Memphis, or west on Route 304 from the Interstate, you see the swirling circles of light against low clouds, long white beams cutting through the humid night air, clearly visible even through the sputtering rain of bugs against your windshield. All around in the darkness is a rural landscape of farms, fields, and wood lots: the Mississippi Delta.

Technically speaking, the Delta begins around Cairo, Illinois, a full thousand river miles from the Gulf, but nobody pays attention to technicalities here. The Delta, as cotton historian David Cohn wrote, "begins in the lobby of the Peabody Hotel in Memphis and ends on Catfish Row in Vicksburg." The Delta is history and culture, as deep and fertile as the alluvial soil. The Delta is a century of King Cotton, from which a few reaped enormous wealth while everyone else was yoked with backbreaking labor. The Delta is field hands tilling and picking and praying and creating a musical tradition of hymns and hollers that begat blues, jazz, country, gospel and even, eventually, that hip-slinging white boy who rolled it all together, Elvis Aaron Presley. The Delta is the memory of slavery and secession and a chorus of ghosts as poignant and garrulous as they ever were alive, for here in the Delta, the dead aren't allowed to rest: Robert Johnson, Tennessee Williams, and old Sam Grant (General Ulysses S. to you) still exist in the present tense, as if they just stepped out for a drink or piss and might yet return. Past and present are swirled together like the bourbon and water in a frosty mint julep: you might be able to tell 'em apart to start, but after a few swigs, why try?

This, then, is the countryside through which you drive: old skeletons rattling around, fat brown moths staining your radiator, loose tufts of white cotton swirling beside the road in your wake, and, up ahead, dancing white beams of light. Lights that promise a dramatic change for the Delta, on par with Grant's armies, the Corps of Engineers, or the mechanized cotton harvester. Because behind those lights is money—lots of money, all just itching to build as much tackiness as traffic will bear.

Welcome to the new Delta: the land that gave us the blues now gives us blackjack, progressive slots, and lounge entertainers like Gary Puckett and Suzanne Somers. The land that exhausted the mule of many a poor sharecropper, that filled the inkwell of Faulkner's pen, now clamors to the sound of quarters dropping in slot trays and cards slapping felt. The change is dizzying: two-lane farm roads being turned into four-lane highways, mini-marts and motels and an endless parade of casino billboards sprouting like kudzu. Stand still and you're likely to be paved over.

Tunica County in the northwest corner of Mississippi is the scene of greatest transformation, but it isn't the only game along Old Man River. There are riverboat casinos up and down the Mississippi, from continued on page 3

There are also booklists, Letters to the Editor, and anything else we can find to interest our readers, as well as Moon's latest titles and ordering information for other travel products, including Periplus Travel Maps to Southeast Asia.

To receive a free subscription to *Travel Matters,*

call—(800) 345-5473

write—Moon Publications
P.O. Box 3040
Chico, CA 95927-3040,

e-mail—travel@moon.com

Please note: subscribers who live outside the United States will be charged $7.00 per year for shipping and handling.

MOON TRAVEL HANDBOOKS

NORTH AMERICA AND HAWAII

Alaska-Yukon Handbook (0161). $14.95
Alberta and the Northwest Territories Handbook (0676) . . . $17.95
Arizona Traveler's Handbook (0536) $16.95
Atlantic Canada Handbook (0072) $17.95
Big Island of Hawaii Handbook (0064) $13.95
British Columbia Handbook (0145). $15.95
Catalina Island Handbook (3751) $10.95
Colorado Handbook (0137). $17.95
Georgia Handbook (0609) $16.95
Hawaii Handbook (0005) $19.95
Honolulu-Waikiki Handbook (0587). $14.95
Idaho Handbook (0617). $14.95
Kauai Handbook (0013). $13.95
Maui Handbook (0579) $14.95
Montana Handbook (0544) $15.95
Nevada Handbook (0641). $16.95
New Mexico Handbook (0153). $14.95
Northern California Handbook (3840) $19.95
Oregon Handbook (0102). $16.95
Texas Handbook (0633). $16.95
Utah Handbook (0684) $16.95
Washington Handbook (0552). $15.95
Wyoming Handbook (3980) $14.95

ASIA AND THE PACIFIC

Bali Handbook (3379). $12.95
Bangkok Handbook (0595). $13.95
Fiji Islands Handbook (0382). $13.95
Hong Kong Handbook (0560) $15.95
Indonesia Handbook (0625) $25.00
Japan Handbook (3700). $22.50
Micronesia Handbook (3808) $11.95
Nepal Handbook (3646). $12.95
New Zealand Handbook (3883) $18.95
Outback Australia Handbook (3794) $15.95
Philippines Handbook (0048) $17.95
Southeast Asia Handbook (0021). $21.95

South Pacific Handbook (3999) $19.95
Tahiti-Polynesia Handbook (0374) $13.95
Thailand Handbook (3824) $16.95
Tibet Handbook (3905) $30.00
*Vietnam, Cambodia & Laos Handbook (0293) $18.95

MEXICO
Baja Handbook (0528). $15.95
Cabo Handbook (0285) $14.95
Cancún Handbook (0501). $13.95
Central Mexico Handbook (0234) $15.95
*Mexico Handbook (0315) $21.95
Northern Mexico Handbook (0226) $16.95
Pacific Mexico Handbook (0323) $16.95
Puerto Vallarta Handbook (0250) $14.95
Yucatán Peninsula Handbook (0242). $15.95

CENTRAL AMERICA AND THE CARIBBEAN
Belize Handbook (0307). $14.95
Caribbean Handbook (0277) $16.95
Costa Rica Handbook (0358). $18.95
Jamaica Handbook (0129) $14.95

INTERNATIONAL
Egypt Handbook (3891). $18.95
Moon Handbook (0668) $10.00
Moscow-St. Petersburg Handbook (3913). $13.95
Staying Healthy in Asia, Africa, and Latin America (0269) . . $11.95

* New title, please call for availability

PERIPLUS TRAVEL MAPS
All maps $7.95 each

Bali	Hong Kong	Penang
Bandung/W. Java	Jakarta	Phuket/S. Thailand
Bangkok/C. Thailand	Java	Sarawak
Batam/Bintan	Ko Samui/S. Thailand	Singapore
Cambodia	Kuala Lumpur	Vietnam
Chiangmai/N. Thailand	Lombok	Yogyakarta/C. Java

WHERE TO BUY MOON TRAVEL HANDBOOKS

BOOKSTORES AND LIBRARIES: Moon Travel Handbooks are sold worldwide. Please write to our sales manager for a list of wholesalers and distributors in your area.

TRAVELERS: We would like to have Moon Travel Handbooks available throughout the world. Please ask your bookstore to write or call us for ordering information. If your bookstore will not order our guides for you, please contact us for a free title listing.

> Moon Publications, Inc.
> P.O. Box 3040
> Chico, CA 95927-3040 U.S.A.
> Tel: (800) 345-5473
> Fax: (916) 345-6751
> E-mail: travel@moon.com

IMPORTANT ORDERING INFORMATION

PRICES: All prices are subject to change. We always ship the most current edition. We will let you know if there is a price increase on the book you order.

SHIPPING AND HANDLING OPTIONS: Domestic UPS or USPS first class (allow 10 working days for delivery): $3.50 for the first item, 50 cents for each additional item.

EXCEPTIONS:

Tibet Handbook and *Indonesia Handbook* shipping $4.50; $1.00 for each additional *Tibet Handbook* or *Indonesia Handbook*.

Moonbelt shipping is $1.50 for one, 50 cents for each additional belt.

Add $2.00 for same-day handling.

UPS 2nd Day Air or Printed Airmail requires a special quote.

International Surface Bookrate 8-12 weeks delivery: $3.00 for the first item, $1.00 for each additional item. Note: Moon Publications cannot guarantee international surface bookrate shipping. Moon recommends sending international orders via air mail, which requires a special quote.

FOREIGN ORDERS: Orders that originate outside the U.S.A. must be paid for with either an international money order or a check in U.S. currency drawn on a major U.S. bank based in the U.S.A.

TELEPHONE ORDERS: We accept Visa or MasterCard payments. Minimum order is US$15.00. Call in your order: (800) 345-5473, 8 a.m.-5 p.m. Pacific Standard Time.

ORDER FORM

Be sure to call (800) 345-5473 for current prices and editions or for the name of the bookstore
nearest you that carries Moon Travel Handbooks • 8 a.m.–5 p.m. PST.
(See important ordering information on preceding page.)

Name: _____ Date: _____

Street: _____

City: _____ Daytime Phone: _____

State or Country: _____ Zip Code: _____

QUANTITY	TITLE	PRICE

Taxable Total_____

Sales Tax (7.25%) for California Residents_____

Shipping & Handling_____

TOTAL_____

Ship: ☐ UPS (no P.O. Boxes)   ☐ 1st class   ☐ International surface mail

Ship to: ☐ address above   ☐ other _____

_____

Make checks payable to: **MOON PUBLICATIONS, INC**. P.O. Box 3040, Chico, CA 95927-3040
U.S.A. We accept Visa and MasterCard. **To Order**: Call in your Visa or MasterCard number, or send
a written order with your Visa or MasterCard number and expiration date clearly written.

Card Number: ☐ **Visa**   ☐ **MasterCard**

☐☐☐☐ ☐☐☐☐ ☐☐☐☐ ☐☐☐☐

Exact Name on Card: _____

Expiration date:_____

Signature:_____

F/95–AH

THE METRIC SYSTEM

1 inch = 2.54 centimeters (cm)
1 foot = .304 meters (m)
1 mile = 1.6093 kilometers (km)
1 km = .6124 miles
1 fathom = 1.8288 m
1 chain = 20.1168 m
1 furlong = 201.168 m
1 acre = .4047 hectares
1 sq km = 100 hectares
1 sq mile = 2.59 square km
1 ounce = 28.35 grams
1 pound = .4536 kilograms
1 short ton = .90718 metric ton
1 short ton = 2000 pounds
1 long ton = 1.016 metric tons
1 long ton = 2240 pounds
1 metric ton = 1000 kilograms
1 quart = .94635 liters
1 US gallon = 3.7854 liters
1 Imperial gallon = 4.5459 liters
1 nautical mile = 1.852 km

To compute celsius temperatures, subtract 32 from Fahrenheit and divide by 1.8. To go the other way, multiply celsius by 1.8 and add 32.

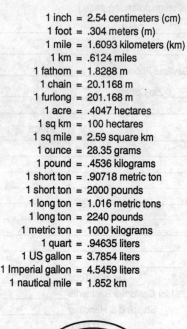

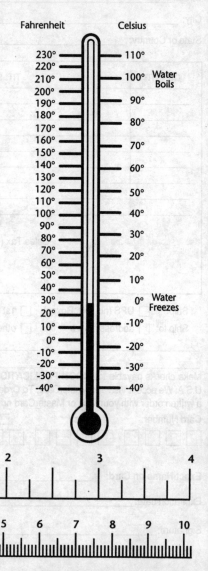